T0317663

Japanese Capital Markets
New Developments in Regulations and Institutions

EDITED BY

SHINJI TAKAGI

BLACKWELL
Oxford UK & Cambridge USA

Copyright © Basil Blackwell Ltd 1993

First published 1993

Blackwell Publishers
238 Main Street, Suite 501
Cambridge, Massachusetts 02142
USA

108 Cowley Road
Oxford OX4 1JF
UK

Library of Congress Cataloging-in-Publication Data

Japanese capital markets: new developments in regulations and
   institutions / edited by Shinji Takagi.
      p.   cm.
   Includes bibliographical references and index.
   ISBN 1–55786–255–9
   1. Capital market – Japan.   I. Takagi, Shinji, 1953–
HG5772.J365   1993
332.63′2′0952 – dc20   92–32848
                                                            CIP

British Library Cataloguing in Publication Data

A CIP catalogue record for this book is available from the British Library.

Typeset in 10 on 12 pt Times
by Best-set Typesetter Ltd., Hong Kong

This book is printed on acid-free paper

Contents

List of Figures

List of Tables

List of Contributors

Tomohiko Adachi is Senior Economist with Japan Securities Research Institute, Tokyo.

Jeffrey A. Frankel is Professor of Economics at the University of California at Berkeley.

Hideki Hanaeda is Professor of Economics at Seijo University, Tokyo.

James E. Hodder is Charles and Laura Albright Professor of Finance and Wisconsin Distinguished Professor of Business, School of Business, University of Wisconsin at Madison.

Hideki Kanda is Associate Professor in the Faculty of Law, University of Tokyo.

Kiyoshi Kato is Associate Professor in the Faculty of Business Administration, Nanzan University, Nagoya.

Richard C. Koo is Senior Economist at the Nomura Research Institute, Tokyo.

Motonari Kurasawa is Professor of Economics at Yokohama National University.

Junko Maru is Professor of Economics at Musashi University, Tokyo.

Colin McKenzie is Associate Professor in the Faculty of Economics, University of Osaka.

Ulrike Schaede is Visiting Assistant Professor, Walter A. Hass School of Business, University of California at Berkeley.

Megumi Suto is Associate Professor in the Department of Economics, Meikai University, Chiba.

Shinji Takagi is Senior Economist at the Institute of Fiscal and Monetary Policy of the Ministry of Finance, and Associate Professor in the Faculty of Economics, University of Osaka.

Toshiharu Takahashi was Associate Professor of Economics, Aoyama Gakuin University, Tokyo until his death in October 1992.

Fumihiko Tateno is Manager of the Funds and Foreign Exchange Division, Bank of Tokyo.

Adrian E. Tschoegl is Chief Economist of SBCI Securities (Asia), Ltd, Tokyo.

Shigeru Yamamoto is Senior Manager of the Securities Department, Industrial Bank of Japan, Tokyo.

List of Abbreviations

ACU	Asian Currency Unit
ADB	Asian Development Bank
APT	Arbitrage Pricing Theory
BA	Banker's acceptance
BB	Brokers' Broker (that is, *Nihon Sogo Shoken* – Japan Mutual Securities; and *Nihon Tento Shoken* – Japan OTC Securities)
BIS	Bank for International Settlements
BOJ	Bank of Japan
CAPM	Capital Asset Pricing Model
CB	Convertible bond
CBOE	Chicago Board Options Exchange
CD	Certificate of deposit
CP	Commercial paper
CRSP	Center for Research in Securities Prices
DCF	Discounted cash flow
DM	Deutsche mark
EC	European Community
EMS	European Monetary System
EPA	Economic Planning Agency (Japan)
FB	Financing bill
G-5	Group of Five (France, Germany, Japan, UK and US)
G-7	Group of Seven (France, Germany, Japan, UK, US, Italy and Canada)
G-10	Group of Ten (France, Germany, Japan, UK, US, Italy, Canada, Belgium, the Netherlands, Sweden, and Switzerland)
IBF	International Banking Facility
i.c.	Impact coefficient
IDM	Interdealer market
IMF	International Monetary Fund
IRR	Internal rate of return
IPO	Initial public offering

JASD	Japan Association of Securities Dealers
JASDAQ	Japan Association of Securities Dealers Automated Quotations
JOM	Japan Offshore Market
JSF	Japan Securities Finance Co.
JSRI	Japan Securities Research Institute
KSE	Kyoto Stock Exchange
LBO	Leveraged buy-out
LTD	Large-scale time deposit
MAFF	Ministry of Agriculture, Forestry and Fisheries (Japan)
mic	Market impact cost
MITI	Ministry of International Trade and Industry (Japan)
MMC	Money market certificate
MOC	Ministry of Construction (Japan)
MOF	Ministry of Finance (Japan)
NPV	Net present value
NSA	Nikkei stock average
NSE	Nagoya Stock Exchange
NTT	Nippon Telegraph and Telephone
NYSE	New York Stock Exchange
oed	Options expiration day
OLS	Ordinary least squares
OSE	Osaka Stock Exchange
OTC	Over-the-counter [stocks]
PER	Price–earnings ratio
S&P	Standard & Poor's
SCAP	Supreme Commander of Allied Powers
SEA	Securities and Exchange Act (US)
SEL	Securities and Exchange Law (Japan)
SII	Structural Impediments Initiative
SIMEX	Singapore International Monetary Exchange
SML	Securities Market Line
SQ	Special quotation
TB	Treasury bill
TDs	*Toroku* dealers
TIFFE	Tokyo International Financial Futures Exchange
TOPIX	Tokyo Stock Exchange Price Index
TTB	Telegraphic transfer buying
TTS	Telegraphic transfer selling
txc	Transactions cost

Introduction

Shinji Takagi

After years of rapid growth, the size of Japanese capital markets now ranks with that of US markets as the world's largest. At the end of 1990, for example, the total market value of stocks listed at the Tokyo Stock Exchange ($2,822 billion) exceeded that of the New York Stock Exchange ($2,692 billion). Japan's bond market is also large: the outstanding value of national government bonds, for example, was $1,211 billion (or 38.3 percent of GNP) at the end of 1990, compared with $3,365 billion (or 61.0 percent of GNP) in the United States. At the end of 1989, the outstanding value of personal financial assets in Japan ($6,294 billion or 226 percent of GNP) was more than one-half the amount in the United States ($11,193 billion or 213 percent of GNP).

Along with the increased size, the Japanese capital markets have also changed substantively in recent years. For example, there have developed new markets (such as the futures and options markets) as well as new phenomena to be explained (such as the emergence of so-called benchmark issues of government bonds). Cross-border capital transactions have largely been liberalized, allowing both Japanese and foreign participants greater access to each other's markets. At the same time, the increasing importance of the Japanese markets has prompted a number of academic studies on such issues as the cost of capital, corporate financing practices, the pricing of Japanese stocks, and stock trading rules.

In the light of these developments, the purpose of this volume is to survey recent institutional changes as well as the major results of recent academic analyses of capital and other related markets in Japan. The authors of the sixteen chapters in the volume are all recognized experts on the Japanese financial system with extensive experience in Japan, and were commissioned to write chapters on their respective fields of expertise. They include both academics and practitioners, with their collective knowledge covering a wide range of economics, finance, banking, and law. The good mix of Japanese and foreign authors should provide the reader with a more balanced perspective than would be possible with an exclusively Japanese or foreign authorship.

The chapters were explicitly written for general professional readership and not for a narrow academic audience. Each author was asked to

Table I.1   Types of domestic financial institutions in Japan (number of institutions in parentheses)

1.   Bank of Japan

2.   Banks (153)
    City banks (11)
    Regional banks (64)
    Regional banks II (68)
    Trust banks (7)
    Long-term credit banks (3)

3.   Financial institutions for small businesses
    Zenshinren Bank
    Shinkin banks (443)
    Shoko Chukin Bank
    Credit cooperatives (398)
    National Federation of Credit Cooperatives
    Labor credit associations (47)
    National Federation of Labor Credit Associations

4.   Financial institutions for agriculture, forestry and fishery
    Norin Chukin Bank
    Credit federations of agricultural cooperatives (47)
    National Mutual Insurance Federation of Agricultural Cooperatives
    Mutual insurance federation of agricultural cooperatives (48)
    Agricultural cooperatives (3,474)
    Credit federations of fishery cooperatives (35)
    Fishery cooperatives (1,666)

5.   Securities finance institutions
    Securities finance companies (3)
    Securities companies (210)

6.   Insurance companies
    Life insurance companies (27)
    Non-life insurance companies (25)

7.   Government financial institutions (11)

8.   Government
    Trust Fund Bureau of the Ministry of Finance
    Postal Savings System
    Postal Life Insurance and Postal Annuity

Source: Bank of Japan, *Economic Statistics Monthly*, March 1992

provide a fair amount of institutional detail, so that the chapter might serve as a comprehensive introduction to an aspect of Japanese capital markets. At the same time, the author was encouraged to provide new information obtained either from original research or from operational experience. As a result, the volume is rich in both institutional and analytical information that has not previously been made available in the English language. It is hoped that the reader will find the volume a useful guide to the institutions as well as the major analytical and policy issues of Japan's capital and other related markets.

This introduction will first provide brief background information on the major constituent institutions and markets in the Japanese financial system which are relevant to the topics discussed in the remainder of the volume. It will then summarize the content of each chapter in the briefest possible terms.

1 AN OVERVIEW OF THE JAPANESE FINANCIAL SYSTEM[1]

1.1 Institutions

Several thousand institutions of various sizes participate in the Japanese financial system (table I.1). At the head of the system is the Ministry of Finance, whose Banking and Securities Bureaux are the key regulatory bodies of a great majority of the constituent institutions. In the supervision of the financial system, the Ministry of Finance is supported by the Bank of Japan, the central bank, which is legally independent of the government. In Japan, the government also assumes a prominent role in direct financial intermediation through 11 government financial institutions, the Trust Fund Bureau of the Ministry of Finance, and the enormous Postal Savings System (under the Ministry of Posts and Telecommunications). In simple terms, the Trust Fund Bureau manages the funds deposited in the Postal Savings System, by purchasing government bonds or funding the lending activities of the eleven government financial institutions.[2]

In March 1992[3] the largest private financial institutions included eleven city banks, seven trust banks, and three long-term credit banks, which are all active in the international markets. City and regional banks constitute what are more generally known as ordinary banks under the Banking Law. The regulatory authorities, however, have treated city and regional banks somewhat differently in the past, by giving more favorable treatment to city banks in the establishment of nationwide or overseas branches. Regional banks are represented by two industry organizations; those belonging to the Second Organization of Regional Banks (68 in total) used to be now-defunct *sogo* (or mutual) banks, another category of financial institutions for small businesses.

In addition to these categories of banks, in March 1992 there were 443 *shinkin* banks, 398 credit cooperatives, 47 labor credit associations and over 5,000 agricultural and fishery cooperatives. These institutions are generally small, and their activities are often coordinated at the prefectural or national levels by their prefectural or national federations. At the national level, for example, the Zenshinren Bank (the Central Cooperative Bank for Shinkin Banks) represents *shinkin* banks, the National Federation of Credit Cooperatives is for credit cooperatives, the Norin Chukin Bank (the Central Cooperative Bank of Agriculture and Forestry) is for agricultural and fishery cooperatives, and so forth. The Shoko Chukin Bank (the Central Bank for Commerce and Industry) is a financial institution for cooperatives of small businesses, and is owned in part by the government and in part by small business organizations, including credit cooperatives. These institutions are large in size and prominent in the national market.

Functional separation has characterized the Japanese financial industry. For instance, there is a separation between long-term finance (trust and long-term credit banks) and short-term finance (ordinary banks), as well as between life insurance and non-life insurance. As a general rule, the trust business is exclusively reserved for trust banks, the life insurance business for life insurance companies, the casualty insurance business for non-life insurance companies, and so forth. The lending activities of financial institutions for small businesses are restricted to small firms as defined by the size of equity capital.

Most significant in this context is Article 65 of the Securities and Exchange Law (SEL), which separates the securities business from the banking business. As a result, large financial institutions have not been allowed to enter the securities business, except for government and other public-sector bonds. Moreover, the authorities have restricted entry by requiring a separate license for each of underwriting, distribution, broking, and dealing. Securities financing (for margin transactions) is provided by three specialized securities finance companies (see chapter 16). As will be discussed in chapter 4, the securities industry is characterized by an oligopolistic structure in which, of the 200 or so securities companies, the largest four dominate the market.

The system, based on the functional separation of various types of financial institutions, however, is in a state of transition. With the liberalization of interest rates and international transactions as well as with the advancement in financial technology, it is now widely recognized that the traditional system has outlived its usefulness. The Japanese authorities are in the process of reforming the financial system, and this reform, including the possible elimination of the separation between the securities business and the banking business, will be a topic for discussion in chapters 5 and 6.

1.2 Markets

Although it is somewhat arbitrary, a common practice in Japan has been to distinguish between money markets (in which the original maturities of instruments are shorter than one year) and capital markets (in which the original maturities are longer than one year). It is also common practice to make a further distinction between interbank markets (to which only financial institutions have access) and open markets (to which non-financial corporations have access) within the money markets. Major components of the money markets include the call and bill-discount markets, and the *gensaki* (bond repurchase) and commercial paper (CP) markets (table I.2). In addition, there are: small markets for banker's acceptances (BAs); markets for government financing bills (FBs) and Treasury bills (TBs);[4] a dollar call market; and an offshore market. The latter two can also be considered as part of the foreign exchange market. Recent developments in the money and foreign exchange markets will be discussed in chapters 13 and 14, respectively.

Major components of the capital markets can be divided into the bond and equity markets (table I.2). Of the bond markets, the government bond market is by far the largest, followed by the market for bank debentures. Bank debentures are bonds issued by six designated financial institutions: the three long-term credit banks (the Industrial Bank of Japan, the Long-term Credit Bank of Japan, and the Nippon Credit Bank), the Bank of Tokyo, the Norin Chukin Bank, and the Shoko Chukin Bank. In the domestic market, almost all industrial bonds are issued by electric power companies and Nippon Telegraph and Telephone (NTT) Company. In contrast, bond issues of other business corporations have been dominated by convertible bonds and bonds with warrants. These and other matters related to the debt financing of corporations will be the topic of chapter 3, while chapters 6 and 7 will discuss the bond market in general.

In recent years, the Japanese equity market has received substantial attention, in part owing to the spectacular increase in stock prices from the middle of the 1980s through late 1989, when the most widely used Nikkei Stock Average (NSA or Nikkei-225) increased by more than three times, from less than 12,000 to over 38,000 (figure I.1). Hotly debated both in the market and in the academic community at that time was the phenomenally high average price–earnings ratio (PER) of Japanese stocks, which was as high as 70 during parts of the period (figure I.2).

Table I.2 Outstanding balances in the major components of the money and capital markets (in hundreds of millions of yen)

At the end of:	1990	1991
Money markets		
(a) Interbank markets		
Call	239,866	353,169
Bills-discount	170,603	165,096
(b) Open markets		
Gensaki	66,114	60,453
Commercial paper	157,627	124,004
Government financing bills	255,050	209,870
Treasury bills	76,051	90,458
Capital markets		
Government bonds	1,564,267	1,611,173
Local government bonds	192,622	194,308
Government guaranteed bonds	196,814	198,500
Bank debentures	675,718	736,315
Industrial bonds	111,674	142,241
Convertible bonds	162,605	167,651
Bonds with warrants	14,678	18,459
Yen-denominated foreign bonds	57,549	61,859
Listed stocks	3,935,949	3,919,841
OTC stocks	119,722	130,019
Deposit markets		
Bank deposits	4,362,377	4,284,614
Certificates of deposits	182,477	168,642
Postal savings	1,336,980	1,524,145

Sources: Bank of Japan Tokyo Stock Exchange

Many theories have been advanced to explain the high PERs of Japanese stocks, including the distortions caused by unrealized capital gains on land, cross-holding of shares among affiliated Japanese corporations, and unique Japanese accounting practices. These issues will be discussed in chapters 1 and 3, and an econometric modeling of Japanese stock prices will be provided in chapter 11.

An important difference between the bond market and the equity market in Japan is that, while bonds are predominantly traded over the counter, stocks are almost exclusively traded at organized stock exchanges (table I.3). Given the increasing importance of the Japanese equity market, therefore, it is natural that a fair amount of interest has been shown

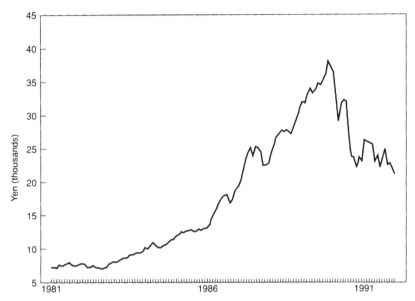

Figure I.1 Nikkei average stock prices (January 1981–February 1992)

Source: Bank of Japan

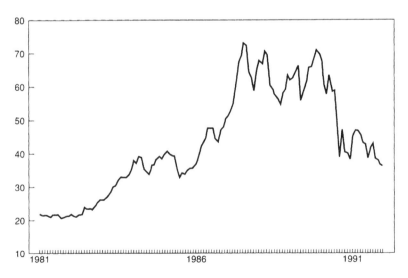

Figure I.2 Price–earnings ratio of TSE stocks (January 1981–February 1992; first section stocks only)

Source: Tokyo Stock Exchange

Table I.3 Trading value in the Japanese capital market (in hundreds of millions of yen)

During the year:	1990	1991
Bonds		
exchanges	63,392	35,369
over-the-counter	33,604,979	27,479,989
Stocks		
exchanges	231,837	134,160
over-the-counter	6,112	5,043

Sources: Tokyo Stock Exchange; Osaka Stock Exchange; Nagoya Stock Exchange; Japan Association of Securities Dealers; and Bank of Japan

in the trading rules, or the microstructure, of Japanese stock exchanges. There has also been active research on the pricing behavior of Japanese stocks. The pricing behavior associated with seasoned equity issues, the microstructure of Japanese stock exchanges, and the pricing anomalies of Japanese stocks will be discussed in chapters 8, 9 and 10, respectively.

In addition to the markets in traditional financial products, there are several derivatives markets in Japan, all recently established (table I.4). Within a relatively short period of time, the derivatives markets have grown to be a significant component of the Japanese financial market in terms of trading value. The value of trading in bond futures at the Tokyo Stock Exchange, for example, was over 30 times the value of spot trading at the exchange, and amounted to about one-half the total value of bond trading in the OTC market in 1990. Likewise, the value of trading in Nikkei-225 futures at the Osaka Stock Exchange in 1990 was about twice the value of spot trading at the Tokyo Stock Exchange and well exceeded the total value of spot trading at all the stock exchanges and the OTC market combined. Trading of stock index futures and options at the Tokyo, Osaka, and Nagoya Stock Exchanges will be the topic of chapter 12, and futures trading at the Tokyo International Financial Futures Exchange as well as currency options trading in the OTC market will be briefly discussed in chapter 14.

As an important development of recent years, the integration of Japanese financial markets with the major international markets should be mentioned. In this context, the single most important event was the revision, in December 1980, of the Foreign Exchange and Foreign Trade Control Law, which in principle liberalized all international capital transactions. Since the early 1980s, Japanese institutional investors, notably insurance companies and investment trusts (see chapter 15), have been

Table I.4 Major derivatives markets in Japan (date of establishment in parentheses)

Tokyo Stock Exchange
  10-year government bond futures (October 1985)
  20-year government bond futures (July 1988)
  20-year US Treasury bond futures (December 1989)
  10-year government bond future options (May 1990)
  TOPIX futures (September 1988)
  TOPIX options (October 1989)

Osaka Stock Exchange
  Nikkei-225 futures (September 1988)
  Nikkei-225 options (June 1989)

Nagoya Stock Exchange
  Option-25 options (October 1989)

Tokyo International Financial Futures Exchange
  Euroyen short-term interest rate futures (June 1989)
  Eurodollar short-term interest rate futures (June 1989)
  Yen/dollar currency futures (June 1989)

Over-the-counter market
  Currency options (spring 1984)

Sources: Tokyo Stock Exchange: Osaka Stock Exchange; Nagoya Stock Exchange; and chapter 14 of this volume

active purchasers of foreign securities. In addition, large Japanese business corporations have been raising a significant amount of capital in the Euro and other overseas markets. The value of cross-border securities transactions (in both directions) is now enormous, even compared with the value of real trade flows (table I.5). These and other issues related to the international aspects of Japanese capital markets, including the recent increase in foreign exchange transactions, will be discussed in chapters 1, 2, 3 and 14.

2 CHAPTER SUMMARIES

The sixteen chapters of the volume are grouped into six sections.

2.1 International Aspects of Japanese Capital Markets

Part I discusses the cost of capital in Japan and Japan's cross-border capital flows. In chapter 1, "The Japanese Financial System and the Cost

Table I.5   Cross-border securities investment (in millions of US dollars)

During the year:		1990	1991
Foreign investment in Japanese securities			
Stocks	purchases	124,849	139,060
	sales	−140,930	−93,791
	net	−16,081	45,270
Bonds	purchases	193,310	168,541
	sales	−175,871	−147,205
	net	17,439	21,336
Japanese investment in foreign securities			
Stocks	purchases	76,784	48,863
	sales	−70,528	−45,234
	net	6,256	3,629
Bonds	purchases	1,372,281	1,232,885
	sales	−1,343,320	−1,164,683
	net	28,961	68,202
Foreign bond issues in Japan		8,157	5,024
External bond issues by Japanese residents		39,423	65,749
Memorandum			
Japanese exports		280,374	306,597
Japan's current account surplus		35,761	72,598

Source: Bank of Japan

of Capital," Jeffrey A. Frankel surveys the literature on the cost of capital in Japan. Frankel argues that the cost of capital in Japan may well have been lower than in the United States in the 1970s and 1980s, at least for larger firms, reflecting lower real interest rates associated with the higher Japanese saving rate, the main bank system, and other unique institutional features of the financial system. However, recent financial liberalization measures in Japan have increased the importance of market finance and also facilitated arbitrage across different national markets. He concludes that these developments have virtually eliminated the difference in the cost of capital between Japan and the United States.

In chapter 2, "International Capital Flows and an Open Economy: the Japanese Experience," Richard C. Koo chronicles the events and the actions of policymakers and market participants associated with the rapid expansion of Japanese capital outflows during the decade of the 1980s. Following the revision of the Foreign Exchange and Foreign Trade Control Law in December 1980, Japanese institutional investors became and remained large net purchasers of foreign securities throughout much of the decade. Although the collapse of the bond and stock markets in late 1989 caused the Japanese investors to become net sellers of foreign securities in the early 1990s, Koo argues that the situation can reverse itself at any time. Because excessive capital outflows from Japan will have undesirable consequences for the exchange rate and the adjustment of external imbalances, he advocates that the authorities should dismantle outdated regulations in order to make Japan a more attractive place to invest.

2.2 The Framework of Capital Markets

Part II discusses the overall framework of Japanese capital markets in terms of corporate finance, industrial organization, and the regulatory system. In chapter 3, "Corporate Finance in Japan," James E. Hodder and Adrian E. Tschoegl analyze Japanese corporate financing and investment evaluation practices. They argue that government regulatory measures explain most of the differences in corporate finance practice between Japanese and US firms. With the relaxation of restrictions during the 1980s, however, Japanese corporate finance practices have been changing substantially. In particular, Hodder and Tschoegl note that Japanese firms have progressively shifted away from bank loans towards market funding sources, particularly in the offshore markets, and that the strength of main bank relationships has weakened in recent years.

In chapter 4, "The Securities Industry in Japan," Megumi Suto reviews the industrial organization of the Japanese securities industry in terms of market structure and corporate behavior. After presenting a brief historical overview, Suto mentions (a) a high level of market concentration, (b) a low degree of operational specialization, and (c) the formation of affiliated corporate groups as the key characteristics of the industry. Suto argues that the industrial organization as well as the underlying behavior of securities companies have largely been shaped by the protective regulatory attitude of the authorities, which has emphasized stability and investor protection over competition and operational efficiency. She predicts, however, that the prospective elimination of regulatory constraints is likely to result in greater competition and operational diversification in the future.

In chapter 5, "The Regulatory Environment for Japanese Capital Markets," Hideki Kanda discusses the structure, recent revisions, and proposed changes of the Securities and Exchange Law (SEL) as well as the unique characteristics of Japanese securities regulation. Kanda shows that political competition between the banking and securities industries, as well as between different government ministries, has often shaped much of the current regulatory structure. He describes the Japanese regulatory system as a system of *ex ante* monitoring, where all interested parties participate in the rulemaking processes, with the result that there is virtually no private litigation associated with the violation of the SEL. Although this system may have certain advantages over the US system of *ex post* monitoring, Kanda suggests the possibility that the internationalization of capital markets may change this distinguishing aspect of the Japanese regulatory environment in the future.

2.3   The Bond Market

Part III presents an overview of the structure of the Japanese bond market and an analysis of the secondary government bond market. In chapter 6, "The Japanese Bond Market," Shigeru Yamamoto presents a comprehensive overview of the primary and secondary bond markets in Japan, including the types of public and private bonds, the systems of issuing government and corporate bonds, and bond trading at securities exchanges and in the OTC market. As a further issue, Yamamoto discusses the recent and prospective changes in the fundamental structure of the Japanese bond market, such as globalization, securitization, and financial market reforms in different countries, and explains how the Japanese authorities are responding to those changes. In particular, he reviews the contents of the recently released recommendations of two government advisory bodies that cover how the definition of "securities" in the SEL can be broadened as well as how the barriers separating the banking and securities businesses might be removed.

In chapter 7, "The Secondary Government Bond Market in Japan," Toshiharu Takahashi reviews the institutional developments of the Japanese government bond market and discusses the phenomenon of benchmark issues in the secondary market. The government bond market is by far the most active bond market in Japan, accounting for almost 80 percent of total bond trading. Within the government bond market, moreover, as much as 80 or 90 percent of trading is further concentrated in a single benchmark issue. Takahashi argues that, prior to September 1983, benchmark issues represented a transaction rule in the interdealer market by which the transactions costs associated with search and negotiation would be reduced. In the latter half of the 1980s, when an increasing number of banks were authorized to conduct dealing in government bonds, however, he argues that the role of benchmark issues expanded to include that of reducing the settlement cost of speculative bond trading.

2.4 The Equity Market

Part IV deals with the primary and secondary equity markets, the pricing anomalies of Japanese stocks, and the modeling of Japanese stock price indexes. In chapter 8, "Seasoned Equity Issues in Japan," Hideki Hanaeda discusses the choice faced by Japanese corporations between public offering and rights offering of seasoned equity issues. In recent years, a majority of Japanese corporations have preferred public offering as a form of equity financing, although rights offering is generally thought to be cheaper. Hanaeda argues that, given the need to limit the increase of outstanding stocks by public offering at a higher market price, ownership distribution and access to financial services are two key factors accounting for the preference of Japanese corporations for public offering. Indeed, he shows that rights offering firms tend to have a more concentrated distribution of ownership and are thus concerned about the dilution of equity ownership which would result from public offering; and that rights offering firms tend to have less need for capital-market financing and thus rarely need the financial services of underwriters. Regardless of which method of equity financing is used, however, there is little evidence to suggest that investors who subscribe to new issues receive more than average risk-adjusted normal returns.

In chapter 9, "The Organization and Microstructure of the Secondary Stock Market in Japan," Shinji Takagi traces some of the recent institutional changes in the secondary stock market and discusses the intra-daily pricing of stocks at the Tokyo Stock Exchange. The Japanese stock market, including the OTC market, is an auction market where trading is conducted according to competitive auction rules. Takagi shows that, while there is a presumption that price movements in such a market tend to be volatile and unidirectional, successive price changes of actively traded stocks at the Tokyo Stock Exchange are in fact small and negatively correlated, in a manner similar to the successive price changes of stocks in a specialist-dealer market. The negative serial correlation of successive price changes may reflect the presence of market-making activity, where member firms and other market participants are simultaneously placing both buy and sell orders against the random arrival of market orders. He concludes that, at least for blue-chip stocks, the competitive auction rules seem to be providing adequate liquidity: the spread is small and trading intensity is high.

In chapter 10, "Stock Return Regularities on the Tokyo Stock Exchange," Kiyoshi Kato summarizes the calendar anomalies of Japanese stock returns, and discusses the profitability of trading strategies based on those anomalies. For example, Kato presents evidence that (a) January and June returns from small firms are significantly higher; (b) depending on company size, returns are variable throughout the month; and (c) Monday and Tuesday returns are more likely to be negative. He also shows that the over-reaction effect, in which stocks with abnormally high positive (negative) returns during a given period have abnormally high negative (positive) returns during a subsequent period, disappeared in the 1980s. Although trading strategies based on these anomalies earned an annual return of as much as 49 percent during 1974–87, however, the strategies may not be workable in practice because they involve purchases of small company stocks with small numbers of outstanding shares and limited liquidity.

In chapter 11, "Modeling the Behavior of Japanese Stock Indexes," Adrian E. Tschoegl argues that over 90 percent of the changes in the five major stock-price indices in recent years could be explained by a simple econometric model made up of industrial production, the money supply, the long-term prime rate, and the dollar exchange rate, and that the behavior of the indices was no less explicable by fundamentals than that of foreign stock-price indices in New York, London, Frankfurt, and Paris. The discrepancy between the index and the level predicted by the model, however, contains useful information about the market's future direction. According to Tschoegl, the deviation between market and model represents the influence of psychology relative to economic fundamentals, and the greater the deviation, the less likely it is that the deviation will increase. Based on this model, he accounts for the large swings in stock market prices in recent years, including the boom of 1986–9, the crash of October 1987, and the bear market of 1990–1.

2.5   Futures, Money, and Foreign Exchange Markets

Part V discusses the three important markets which are closely connected with the capital markets. In chapter 12, "Stock Futures and Options Markets in Japan," Tomohiko Adachi and Motonari Kurasawa discuss the stock derivatives markets in Japan. After outlining the institutional features of the markets for stock-index futures and options, Adachi and Kurasawa discuss the conceptual problems associated with the Nikkei-225, which is by far the dominant index used in futures and options transactions in Japan. Because the Nikkei-225 is a price-weighted index, a given percentage change in the price of high-valued stocks with low capitalization and liquidity has a greater influence on the index than that of low-priced stocks with high capitalization and liquidity. As a result, they argue that the Nikkei-225 is potentially vulnerable to index manipulation. Moreover, the Nikkei-225 shows an abnormal movement during the closing minutes of trading on options expiration days, primarily reflecting the sharp price movement of high-valued stocks with low capitalization and liquidity. There also seem to be inexplicable profit opportunities from certain types of arbitrage activities.

In chapter 13, "The Money Markets in Japan," Colin McKenzie reviews recent liberalization measures in Japan's money markets and analyzes their effect on the pattern of causality among interest rates and on the bid–ask spreads in the *gensaki* market for certificates of deposit, using data from the period of 1985–91. McKenzie finds that there was no consistent pattern of feedback relationships among interest rates in recent years and that the variation in spreads in the *gensaki* market could not be well explained by two deregulatory measures associated with the inter-bank markets. It is thus not possible to identify the impact of particular deregulatory changes on the operation of the money markets. He suggests the possibility that the liberalization of the money markets in Japan may well have been completed for all practical purposes by the year 1985 and that the recent deregulatory measures had only a marginal impact.

In chapter 14, "The Foreign Exchange Market in Japan," Fumihiko Tateno presents an overview of Japan's foreign exchange transactions, which are almost entirely concentrated in Tokyo. As an important feature of the Tokyo market, direct market participants are limited to authorized foreign exchange banks, foreign exchange brokers, and the monetary authorities; securities and insurance companies are excluded from direct participation. After tracing some of the major institutional developments in recent years, he discusses current market practices and related markets. Tateno argues that, while the Tokyo market has become similar to other major international markets in terms of trading practices, important issues remain concerning the wisdom of maintaining specific trading hours, the appropriateness of foreign exchange position controls by the bank regulators, and market practices on newly emerging products.

2.6   Investment Trusts and Securities Financing

Part VI discusses two aspects of Japanese capital markets for which little information has been available in English. In chapter 15, "The Structure and Performance of Investment Trusts in Japan," Junko Maru discusses the Japanese system of investment trusts, which are diversified funds operated by investment companies similar to mutual funds in the United States. Japanese investment trusts are all contractual-type, where the funds take the form of trust agreements between investors and trustees who invest in securities to earn returns on their behalf. She argues that the contractual form of Japanese investment trusts may in part explain their poor risk-adjusted returns, because the contractual-type funds with the repurchase obligation must be redeemed on demand, such that they must hold a significant amount of liquid assets with low rates of return.

In addition, government regulations restrict the activities of investment trusts, preventing the funds from taking the most efficient investment strategy.

In chapter 16, "Securities Financing in Japan," Ulrike Schaede discusses the Japanese system of margin transactions, which account for a much smaller portion (15 to 16 percent) of total trading than in the United States. In margin transactions, customers either purchase securities with money borrowed from a broker or sell securities that are borrowed from a broker. An important aspect of the Japanese system of margin transactions is the role of three securities finance companies that lend either money or securities to brokers and investors. There is a close connection between the securities finance companies, the stock exchanges, and the regulatory authorities, in that the securities finance companies often act as the policy instruments of the Ministry of Finance. She argues that various government regulations (such as on short sales) help maintain the viability of the securities finance companies, and that the authorities are likely to preserve and possibly expand their roles in the overall regulatory framework in coming years.

3   ADDITIONAL COMMENTS AND ACKNOWLEDGEMENTS

In the preparation of this volume, considerable effort was made to ensure that the content is both accurate and current. In order to check accuracy, each chapter was reviewed in draft form by the editor and one or two referees. Thanks to a grant received from the Suntory Foundation, moreover, eight of the contributors held a mini-conference in Tokyo in October 1991 to provide comments on each other's contributions. Each author, however, assumes sole responsibility for the opinions and interpretations expressed, as well as for any errors which may remain.

In general, information in the volume is current as of the time of writing in late 1991 or early 1992. Owing to the publication lag, however, most statistical data are current through 1989 or 1990, depending on the speed with which a particular set of data becomes available in published form.

Finally, the editor gratefully acknowledges the financial support of the Suntory Foundation, which facilitated some of the research reported in the volume as well as the editorial assistance of Jessica Goodfellow. Most importantly, he thanks the authors for their excellent contributions.

This volume is dedicated to the memory of Toshiharu Takahashi, whose untimely death in October 1992 brought much sorrow to his colleagues and friends.

NOTES

1 A comprehensive survey of the Japanese financial system is provided by Suzuki (1987). For a summary and analyses of major institutional developments in the money, bond and equity markets through the latter part of the 1980s, see Takagi (1988, 1989).
2 For an outline of the system of government financial institutions in Japan, see Takagi (1990).
3 In Japan, the fiscal year runs from April to March (for example, fiscal 1991 begins on April 1, 1991 and ends on March 31, 1992). The financial year of many Japanese corporations often coincides with the government fiscal year.
4 Financing bills are issued to finance seasonal shortfalls in government revenue, while Treasury bills are ordinary government bonds with an original maturity of less than a year.

REFERENCES

Bank of Japan, *Economic Statistics Monthly*, monthly issues.
Suzuki, Yoshio (ed.) 1987: *The Japanese Financial System*. Oxford: Clarendon Press.
Takagi, Shinji (1988): Recent developments in Japan's bond and money markets. *Journal of the Japanese and International Economies*, 2, March, 63–91.
Takagi, Shinji (1989): The Japanese equity market: past and present. *Journal of Banking and Finance*, 13, September, 537–70.
Takagi, Shinji (1990): Outline of public finance in Japan. In Dick K. Nanto (ed.), *Japan's Economic Challenge*, Washington, D.C.: US Government Printing Office, 27–45.
Tokyo Stock Exchange, *Monthly Statistic Report*, monthly issues.

Part I

International Aspects of
Japanese Capital Markets

1

The Japanese Financial System and the Cost of Capital

Jeffrey A. Frankel

This chapter examines a number of important interrelated questions concerning the structure of Japanese financial markets and the behavior of observed financial prices in the 1980s. The first questions, of particular concern to American businessmen, are:

(a) Was *the cost of capital to Japanese firms* lower than the cost of capital to US and other firms, thereby providing an explanation for the higher rate of investment in Japan?[1] And if so, why? The cost of capital is usually represented as a weighted average of the cost of borrowing (measured, for example, by the real interest rate) and the cost of equity financing (inferred, for example, from the ratio of required corporate earnings to the price of equity). This standard way of viewing the cost-of-capital question is incomplete.[2] But, for the moment, it does serve to introduce the next two Japanese financial prices whose behavior has been puzzling.

(b) Was *the Japanese interest rate* lower than in the US and other industrialized countries, in real terms? If so, why?

(c) Why were *Japanese equity prices* so high relative, for example, to earnings? Why did they rise so much in the 1980s? One of a number of possible contributing explanations for high price–earnings ratios is (b) above, a low interest rate (used to discount expected future earnings, or dividends into current equity prices). Another is a high

Parts of the paper draw on parts of two earlier papers: "Japanese finance: a survey," in *Japan: has the door opened wider?*, ed. Paul Krugman, Chicago: University of Chicago Press, 1991; and "The Japanese cost of finance: a survey," *Financial Management*, Spring 1991. I should like to acknowledge financial support from the Center for Pacific Basin Monetary and Economic Studies at the Federal Reserve Bank of San Francisco, and the Japan–United States Friendship Commission, an agency of the US Government.

I gratefully acknowledge advice and suggestions from David Meerschwam, and comments on earlier drafts from: James Ang, Alan Auerbach, Sudipto Bhattacharya, Robert Dekle, Ken Froot, Michael Kinsley, Ryutaro Komiya, Paul Krugman, Hiro Lee, Yuzuru Ozeki, Ulrike Schaede, Hiroshi Shibuya, and Shinji Takagi. I thank Ken French, James Poterba, and David Hale for data. I should also like to thank Shang-jin Wei for research assistance. A disclaimer that the survey is not completely exhaustive applies, in particular, with respect to writings that appear only in Japanese.

expected real growth rate in the economy (raising expected future earnings relative to observed current earnings). Because corporations hold land, yet another contributing factor to high equity prices is high Japanese land prices.

(d) Why were *Japanese land prices* so high relative, for example, to rents? Why did they rise so much in the 1980s? The two contributing explanations given for high equity prices apply equally here: a low interest rate (used to discount expected future rents into current land prices) and a high expected economic growth rate (raising expected future rents relative to observed current rents).

No single paper can hope to answer all these questions. Much is written every year on the subject of Japanese financial markets. The institutional details, as well as the market prices themselves, change rapidly, by virtue of domestic financial deregulation and innovation, international financial liberalization, and tax reform. This chapter seeks to survey work on these issues, including a variety of recent contributions to the study of one or other of the financial market issues enumerated above, sufficiently briefly to see how the different questions fit together. It does not purport to be an exhaustive literature survey, however.

There is a fundamental thread that winds through the issues, and it is worth spelling it out here. The chapter subscribes to the common view that a low real discount rate and a high expected growth rate are two major factors explaining high price–earnings ratios in the stock market and high price–rental ratios in the land market in Japan in the 1980s. A major apparent puzzle that remains is to explain why price–earnings and price–rental ratios were not just as high (or even higher) in the 1960s and 1970s, when Japanese real interest rates were just as low (or even lower) and Japanese growth rates were just as high (or – until 1973 – even higher). The difficulty, in other words, is to explain why price–earnings and price–rental ratios increased so much in the 1980s.

The proposed answer is that in previous decades, and especially prior to 1973, institutional aspects of the Japanese financial system, such as those discussed in Meerschwam (1989), rendered the observed interest rate largely irrelevant for the pricing of assets such as equities and land. This answer implies that anyone able to borrow from a bank or government agency, at artificially low interest rates, for the purpose of acquiring land or corporate equity, could have made "excess" profits; but not just anyone was able to do so. Such sources of funds were not available to the man-in-the-street, or even to the corporation-in-the-street. To those favored corporations who did have access to such funds, such as members of the industrial groupings known as *keiretsu*, the number of profitable investment projects typically exceeded the supply of funds available.

The international financial liberalization that has taken place in Japan over the last ten years has been important for many reasons, not least because it forced the pace of domestic financial liberalization. The structural changes of the 1980s included both the accumulation of a vast pool of savings – particularly in the hands of institutional investors – and the development of active bond and equity markets in which these funds could be invested. The increase in the pool of funds available for arbitrage purposes helps to explain the price increases in the equity and land markets in the 1980s.

Another major effect of Japanese financial liberalization in the 1980s may have been to bring the level of "the" cost of funds in Japan up to the level of the world real interest rate, as is often suggested.[3] This chapter updates the analysis for the events of 1990, and finds that the cost of capital now appears to be approximately as high in Japan as in the United States, as the result of increases in interest rates and an accompanying decline in the Japanese stock market.

The chapter begins with the issue of access to cheap borrowing; it shifts to a consideration of the equity markets (including such issues as dividend-payout rates, PERs, and corporate taxation); it considers domestic and international determinants of the real interest rate; and it concludes with a discussion of internal financing. Measurement and accounting problems occur from the beginning and will be discussed as we proceed. But throughout, the chapter attempts to concentrate on those trends in financial prices that are so strong that one cannot easily attribute them entirely to measurement problems.

1 THE STANDARD WEIGHTED-AVERAGE MEASURE OF THE COST OF CAPITAL

The claim that the cost of capital was lower in Japan, perhaps giving Japanese firms an "unfair" advantage, was brought by some American businessmen in the early 1980s. Some of the original statements focused only on differences in interest rates. Later versions were more complete.[4]

A traditional measure of the cost of capital is a weighted average of the cost of borrowing and the cost of equity:

$$r_c = wr_d + (1 - w)r_e, \qquad (1.1)$$

where r_d is the cost of debt, r_e is the cost of equity, and w is the relative weight of debt in total financing. Under this definition, the claim can be broken down into some combination of the following three possibilities: (a) the cost of borrowing was lower in Japan; (b) the cost of equity was lower in Japan; or (c) the weight on debt-financing (versus equity-financing) was higher in Japan. All three statements contain some truth.[5]

1.1 Real Interest Rates

Nominal interest rates in Japan have been below those in the United States during most of the postwar period, and continuously from 1977 to 1989. Japanese inflation has also been relatively low since 1977; and it is of course the real interest rate, not the nominal rate, that matters for investment. But calculations suggest that Japanese real interest rates were below US real rates virtually continuously from 1967 to 1988.

Bernheim and Shoven (1987) estimated that the Japanese real interest rate on average lay below the US real rate during the period 1971–82, although the difference was fairly small for the long-term rates, which presumably are the ones that matter for investment.[6] Lawler, Loopesko and Dudey (1988: 26) showed real interest rates on Japanese one-year government bonds that were below US yields during virtually the entire 1965–88 period. Friend and Tokutsu (1987) found that the real cost of debt, weighted between short term and long term, was 1.7 percent lower in Japan than in the US on average over the period 1970–84.[7]

It should be noted that some of these calculations may understate the Japanese real interest rate in the 1960s and 1970s. The actual inflation rates that are used overstate expected inflation rates, and the government bond rates that are used were too low to be willingly absorbed by private investors. Also, for the case of borrowing from banks, firms were required to maintain "compensating balances," which did not pay interest. But for the 1980s one can use interest rates that do not have such problems.

In the period 1982–4, the US long-term real interest rate rose substantially above that in Japan and other G-7 countries. The increase in the US real interest differential from 1981 to mid-1984 is often credited with much of the explanation for the contemporaneous appreciation of the dollar. The differential in real interest rates is widely considered to have been the result of a US fiscal expansion, coming at the same time as fiscal contraction in Japan and some major European countries.[8] Bernheim and Shoven (1987) put the US–Japan long-term real interest differential, on average for the period 1983–5, at 2.0.

The US–Japan real interest differential was smaller after the midpoint of the 1980s[9] than it had been in the first half of the decade. This differential, even though small, was still present, however, in 1989. In early 1989, the long-term real interest differential was over one point, and the short-term differential was larger, as is illustrated in figures 1.1 and 1.2, respectively. We postpone until section 4 the question of how such a differential could have persisted despite the apparent international inte-

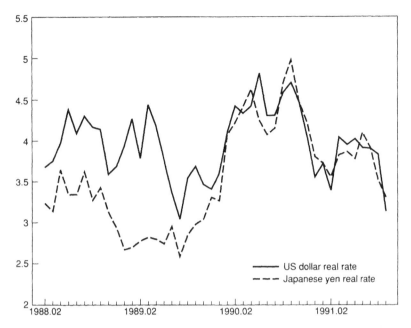

Figure 1.1a Ten-year real interest rates (February 1988–September 1991)

Source: *Currency Forecasters' Digest*

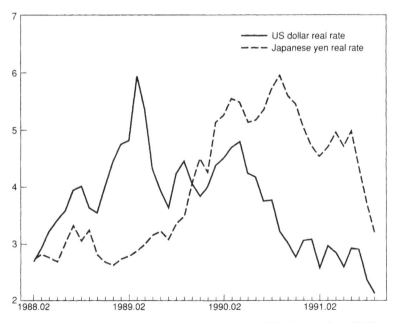

Figure 1.1b One-year real interest rates (February 1988–September 1991)

Source: *Currency Forecasters' Digest*

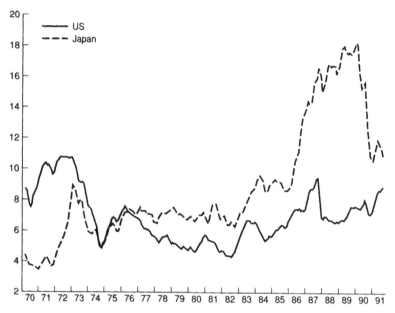

Figure 1.2   P/E multiples in Japan and the US: ratio of price to cash earnings

Source: David Hale, Kemper Financial Services

gration of financial markets. As discussed below, further narrowing of the real interest differential took place in the second half of 1989. (The long-term nominal interest rates in the graphs are ten-year government bond yields. Expected inflation is measured by a survey of forecasters conducted by *Currency Forecasters' Digest*.[10])

The standard capitalization formula for the equity price–dividend ratio and the price–rental ratio is

$$\frac{1}{r - g,} \tag{1.2}$$

where *r* is the real interest rate used to discount expected future dividends or rents to the present, and *g* is the expected growth rate of dividends or rents, as the case may be. The formula is also sometimes used to think about the price–earnings ratio for equities. (For the formula to be correct, "earnings" should really be defined as net profits after new investment. See note 15.)

Sometimes the best we can do to get an idea of the expected growth rate of dividends or rents is to assume that it is equal to the expected growth rate of the economy. If $r - g$ were a number like 0.02 in the world economy at large, then the Japanese interest rate need only be lower by 0.01 – or the growth rate higher by 0.01, for that matter – to explain a doubling of the price–earnings ratio. French and Poterba (1989: 19) point out that a lower real rate of interest in Japan could explain the high level of Japanese stock prices *on average* during their sample period (the 1970s and 1980s), though it cannot explain the *increase* during the last three years, 1986–8.

Because the real interest differential is thought to be small (with the exception of the early 1980s), those who argue that the cost of capital is low in Japan and that this has presented a problem for the "competitiveness" of US industry ever since 1973 (such as Hatsopoulos, Krugman and Summers 1988; and Poterba 1991) tend not to emphasize the real interest rate. They choose, rather, to emphasize the cost of equity financing and the relative weight of debt versus equity in corporate financing. (We return to the role of the real interest rate later, however.)

1.2   Leverage (Debt–Equity Ratios)

In the past, Japanese corporations have had a much higher ratio of debt to equity than have US corporations; that is, they have been much more highly leveraged. (In terms of equation (1.1), the debt–equity ratio is $w/(1 - w)$.) In the period 1970–2, for example, debt–equity ratios in Japan were four times as high as in the United States. This commonly observed characteristic of the Japanese system is one major reason why calculations often show a lower overall cost of capital in Japan than in the United States; equity-financing is known to be more expensive than debt-financing in any market, presumably because portfolio investors demand a higher expected return on equity to compensate them for higher risk. It must be noted from the outset that the apparent conclusion that a given firm can lower its cost of capital by increasing the weight of debt is illusory. It would only hold if both the cost of equity and the cost of debt could be assumed to be independent of leverage. To the contrary, both would in fact be expected to rise: the former as the firm's levered beta rises, and the latter as its credit rating falls (McCauley and Zimmer 1989: 24).

How have Japanese firms been able to rely so heavily on debt? As a number of authors have pointed out, a particular debt–equity ratio that would be very risky for a US firm would be less risky for a Japanese firm. There are several reasons for this:

(a)   Much of the borrowing, particularly for members of a *keiretsu*, was from the firm's main bank. A main bank would not cut off lending in time of financial difficulty; on the contrary, it would do all it could to see the company through. Hoshi, Kashyap, and Scharfstein (1990) examined a sample of 125 Japanese firms that ran into financial trouble over the period 1978–85. They found that those who had a main bank – and especially those who were members of a *keiretsu* – were buffered from their financial distress and enjoyed subsequent recovery of earnings as compared to other firms.[11]

(b) Until recently, all loans had to be collateralized. This certainly reduced the risk from the viewpoint of the bank; and this in turn helps to explain the reduced danger, from the viewpoint of the corporation, that bank lending (as well as the ability to sell bonds) would dry up in time of difficulty.

(c) Such government policies allowing the formation of cartels in

Table 1.1 Price–earnings ratios, dividend–price ratios (in percent), and debt–equity ratios, Japan and the United States, 1970–88

Year	P–E		D–P		D–E	
	Japan	US	Japan	US	Japan	US
1970	9.0	18.6	3.9	3.3	1.63	0.54
1971	13.5	18.7	3.9	2.9	2.13	0.50
1972	23.3	19.3	2.4	2.5	2.23	0.48
1973	13.9	12.3	2.1	3.4	1.38	0.69
1974	16.5	7.9	2.7	5.0	1.44	1.04
1975	25.2	11.8	2.5	2.8	2.13	0.78
1976	22.0	11.2	2.1	3.7	1.88	0.72
1977	19.3	9.1	2.0	5.0	1.82	0.85
1978	21.5	8.2	1.7	5.2	1.62	0.91
1979	16.6	7.5	1.8	5.3	1.78	0.83
1980	17.9	9.6	1.6	4.4	1.59	0.64
1981	24.9	8.2	1.5	5.3	1.64	0.76
1982	23.7	11.9	1.4	4.6	1.44	0.70
1983	29.4	12.6	1.2	3.7	1.03	0.62
1984	26.3	10.4	1.2	4.1	0.93	0.74
1985	29.4	15.4	1.2	3.4	0.71	0.66
1986	58.6	18.7	0.8	3.0	0.45	0.65
1987	50.4	14.1	0.8	3.2	0.43	0.71
1988	54.3	12.9	0.6	3.0	0.36[a]	0.71[a]

Entries reflect values on last trading day of each year.

The debt–equity ratio is defined as the book value of debt divided by the market value of equity. The debt–equity ratios for the US are from the Federal Reserve Board. The debt–equity ratios for Japan for 1970–5 are from Ando and Auerbach (1990). Ratios for 1976–87 are based on the data for "All Industries" from Daiwa Securities.

[a] French and Poterba's calculations (1989, 1990).

Source: French and Poterba (1989)

event of recession reduced the risk of financial difficulty or bank-ruptcy.[12]

(d) The practice of paying workers a substantial fraction of their com-pensation in the form of twice-yearly bonuses that vary with the success of the company acts as a sort of profit-sharing mechanism, and again reduces the risk of bankruptcy.

Abegglen and Stalk (1985: 165) offer an accounting reason why a given corporate balance sheet that might spell excessive risk in the United States would be less worrisome in Japan: a typical Japanese firm does not consolidate the financial assets held by its subsidiaries into its own balance sheet – although a corresponding US firm might do so – and carries land and securities on its books at original cost. They think that such a firm is in a stronger financial position than its balance sheet suggests. Some of these accounting questions are discussed under the heading of price–earnings ratios below.

In any case, it is important to note that the seemingly robust view that "Japanese firms are much more highly leveraged" now appears to be a thing of the past. The debt–equity ratio fell throughout most of the 1970s and 1980s, and by 1986 had, by one measure, fallen *below* the level in the United States, as shown in the last two columns of table 1.1.[13] This reversal was due only in part to the increase in corporate leverage in the 1980s that generated so much alarm in the United States. It was due primarily to the decline in Japan, which was in turn due, at least in an arithmetic sense, to the soaring value of Japanese equities in the late 1980s and to decreased reliance on the main bank system, as well as to the reduced need for external financing of any sort after 1973. Each of these factors will be discussed below.

2 EQUITY CAPITAL

2.1 The Rate of Return on Equity: Stock Prices and Dividends

The third of the standard components of the overall cost of capital, after leverage and the cost of debt, is the cost of equity financing, r_e in the standard equation (1.1). It is the most ambiguous of the components to measure. One approach has been to use the realized market rate of return on equity, that is, the dividend–price ratio plus the rate of increase of equity prices. Baldwin (1986) and Kester and Luehrman (1989) were unable to reject the hypothesis that the level of expected returns on equities for any given level of risk was similar in the two countries. Ando and Auerbach (1988a) found, for the period 1966–81, that returns were actually considerably *higher* in Japan. (In addition to their calculation of the average rates of return, they also looked at earnings–price ratios, discussed below.)

Subsequently, on a much larger sample of firms than that used in their earlier study, but with a similar methodology and time period, Ando and Auerbach (1988b) found that the overall rate of return on capital was substantially lower in Japan than in the United States after all. They found that the before-tax returns were 6.5 percent in Japan, versus 12.3 percent in the United States. After-tax returns were 2.5 percent versus 5.6 percent. (The time period was 1967–83.)

Stockholders' realized rate of return on equity is a very noisy indicator of their *ex ante* expectations. As McCauley and Zimmer (1989: 9) and Poterba (1991: 24) pointed out, an increase in the discount rate, by causing an immediate fall in stock prices, would even show up perversely in the short run as a lower rate of return rather than a higher one. Friend and Tokutsu (1987: 317) remarked that, while realized market rates of return on equity were higher in Japan (over the period 1962–84) than in the United States, a reverse answer results if the dividend–price ratio is added to the rate of growth of dividends per share, rather than to the rate of growth of prices. Looking at the problem from the viewpoint of the market investor, rather than the firm, might give the wrong answer if the stockholders' return to capital measured over a finite sample differs from what managers perceive as their required rate of return. Hatsopoulos and Brooks (1987) and Hodder (1988b, 1991) dissented from the Baldwin and Ando–Auerbach approaches on these grounds.[14]

In the absence of a speculative bubble, stock prices can be thought of either as the present discounted value of expected future dividends, or the present discounted value of expected future free cash flow, where the latter is often proxied by earnings. (Free cash flow is defined as profit after tax, minus changes in working capital, minus other capital spending, plus depreciation.[15]) We consider the subject of dividends first, and turn to earnings in the next subsection.

There has been little upward trend in Japanese dividends per share over the last 20 years.[16] This makes it especially difficult to explain the high level of Japanese stock prices, if one follows the common approach of choosing the formula for the present discounted value of future formula and estimating expected dividends from actual realized. On the other hand, the observed high level of prices relative to dividends would be perfectly understandable if the increase in dividends were thought still to lie in the future.

If dividends are treated as expected to grow at a constant rate g_d from now on, then the current dividend–price ratio should equal $r_e - g_d$, where r_e is the required rate of return on equity capital (which may be higher than the real interest rate because of a risk premium). As of 1988, the dividend price ratio was only 0.006 in Japan, compared to 0.030 in the United States (third and fourth columns of table 1.1). If r_e is assumed to be the same in the two countries, then the 1988 levels of stock prices make sense if, and only if, the dividends were expected to grow at a rate 2.4 percent faster in Japan than in the United States.

Why should Japanese dividends grow rapidly in the future, given that they have not done so in the past? We have no good theory of how shareholders wish to receive the return on their equity investment, that is, in the form of dividends or capital gains, or of how managers choose to pay dividends. In a sufficiently abstract (Modigliani–Miller) world the payout rate is indeterminate. On the one hand, tax considerations point to postponing the payment of dividends. On the other hand, the hypothesis that managers sometimes use funds for purposes other than maximizing shareholder welfare points to shareholders insisting on early payment of dividends.

Corporations do determine dividends, one way or another. One hypothesis is that some shareholders like to receive quarterly checks for liquidity reasons. They could instead sell some stock to generate cash, but they would incur transactions costs by doing so.

The payout rate, that is, the ratio of dividends to earnings, has been declining gradually in Japan since the early 1960s, and is lower than in the United States. (The dividend payout rate can be computed from table 1.1 by taking the product of the PER and the dividend–price ratio.) Over the period 1980–8, it averaged 0.357 for Japan and 0.469 for the United States. This difference would be larger if Japanese earnings were adjusted upward for the factors described in the next section.[17]

The ratio of retirees to people of working age is close to a minimum in Japan now, and will soon begin to rise until, by 2020, it will be the highest of the major industrialized countries. It is plausible that wealthy Japanese retirees in the future will wish to receive high dividend payments on their holdings. Thus it is not entirely implausible for the expected future growth rate of dividends in Japan to be almost as high as the rate of return on capital, or for it to be 2.4 percent higher than the growth rate in the United States, notwithstanding the dividend record of the past 20 years.

Another – consistent – explanation of why Japanese dividends might rise in the future, even though they have been low in the past, is that Japanese corporations have over the postwar period had many profitable investment opportunities; but until the late 1980s they have not had sufficiently free access to securities markets to drive their cost of capital into equality with the rate of return on these investments. For this reason, they have chosen to finance investment out of retained earnings. Even in the United States, a rapidly growing company may pay no dividends at all, for example, but rather it will reinvest all its earnings into highly profitable projects. Japan has been going through a collective life-cycle similar to such a company. At some point in the future, the extra growth opportunities of Japanese corporations will disappear, and they will be free to begin paying out a higher level of dividends.

Such considerations suggest that looking at the past history of dividends may not be very useful. An alternative approach is to look at the amount of *earnings* the firm is required to generate per unit of equity, that is, the inverse of the price–earnings ratio. If one is trying to determine whether the Japanese stock market is overvalued, looking at earnings or cash flow has the advantage that they may be tied more directly to the productive capacity of the economy, as compared to dividends.

2.2 Price–Earnings Ratios

The price–earnings ratio (like the price–dividend ratio) has been observed to be higher in Japan than in the United States ever since the early 1970s. Because this difference could be explained by a lower discount rate in Japan, it is often the basis of arguments that the cost of equity capital is lower in Japan. But the difference could also have other explanations, such as a higher expected growth rate in Japan. If a high growth rate were the complete explanation, one would not want to attribute the high PERs to a low discount rate. More broadly, one would not necessarily want to attribute the superior performance of Japanese industry to a low cost of capital. We now turn to the subject of the high and (in the 1980s) increasing PERs in Japan, an important question in its own right.

Some authors, such as Ando and Auerbach, have looked at the price–earnings ratio because they are interested in the cost-of-capital question, and they consider PER to be inversely related to the required rate of return r_e. Others, such as French and Poterba (1989) and Lawler, Loopesko and Dudey (1988) are interested in the price–earnings ratio for its own sake. As shown in the first two columns of table 1.1, the reported price–earnings ratio for Japanese firms has been higher than that in the United States ever since 1972, and reached 58.6 – three times as high as the US level – in 1986. In the stock market crash of October 1987, decline in Japan was smaller and shorter-lived, with the result that by the end of 1988 Japan's reported PER was more than four times that in United States and the rest of the world. (See figure 1.2, which is based on data from David Hale of Kemper Financial Services. Some updated figures for December 1990 are reported in the last part of this section.)

Such an apparent discrepancy would be difficult to explain. If earnings were expected to grow at rate g_e, then the price–earnings ratio should equal $r_e - g_e$. The end-1988 differential between reported price–earnings ratios in the United States and Japan was 0.06 (= 0.078 − 0.018). The real growth rate of the Japanese economy had averaged 1.56 percent faster than the US economy over 1980–8; there was no particular reason to expect the real growth rate of the economy to increase in the future, or to expect the growth rate of earnings or cash flow to be higher than the growth rate of GNP. Thus the required rate of return on capital r_e would have to have been more than four percentage points lower than in the United States to explain the difference in reported price–earnings ratios. Such a finding would support the cost-of-capital-advantage school, but seems too large to be plausible.

Hatsopoulos and Poterba (1991: 11–12) point out that stockholders' required rate of return on equity will differ from the price–earnings ratio to the extent that some part of earnings is reinvested by managers rather than paid out, and is reinvested at a rate of return that differs from the stockholders' required return. They acknowledge that the price–earnings ratio will accurately reflect the required return in the special case where the return on reinvested earnings is the same as the stockholder return. But they focus on an example where the stockholders cannot prevent managers from undertaking projects that are not profitable at current required returns. This case, which implies that the price–earnings ratio understates the true required rate of return, would appear to be more applicable to the United States than to Japan, if the literature on information and incentive problems described in section 4 of this paper is to be believed. It would appear to follow that the US–Japanese difference in required rates of return on equity is even larger than price–earnings ratios imply.[18]

French and Poterba (1989), Ando and Auerbach (1988a, 1988b, 1990), Lawler, Loopesko and Dudey (1988), and Hatsopoulos and Poterba (1991) all emphasize the importance of correcting earnings for a number of measurement problems. Ando and Auerbach (1988a,b) focused on three distortions related to inflation: depreciation accounting, inventory accounting, and accounting for nominal liabilities. They found that correcting for these distortions increased estimated earnings, and therefore reduced the price–earnings ratio for virtually all the Japanese firms in their sample, while it had no systematic effect for the US firms.[19] The principal apparent source of the effect was that the Japanese firms relied more on debt than on equity (see above), so the fact that inflation reduced the real value of their outstanding liabilities was more important for them. Apparently the fact that the inflation rate was lower in Japan had less of an effect than the higher debt–equity ratio. If reliance on debt is indeed the source of the effect, then the fact that the debt–equity ratio in Japan appeared to have fallen below that in the United States by 1986 (and that inflation fell in both countries in the 1980s) suggests that inflation accounting may no longer be as important for the price–earnings comparison.

French and Poterba (1989) had other corrections to make to reported earnings and therefore to price–earnings ratios. First, earnings reported by US corporations include the profits of subsidiaries, while those reported by Japanese firms do not (only actual dividends received from subsidiaries), so their earnings look smaller. A calculation to convert PERs to what they would have been if there were no cross-holding of corporate equity (which requires adjusting both earnings, by removing intercorporate dividends, and share prices) reduced the Japanese PER. In 1988 the adjustment was big enough to reduce it 33 percent, from 54 to 36. This corresponds well to a finding of Ando and Auerbach (1990) that an adjustment to firms' accounting earnings for cross-holdings raises the Japanese cost of capital by about 1 percentage point. In March 1990, however, a similar calculation by Zielinski and Holloway (1991: 135) reduces PERs only 8 percent, from 48 to 44. Suzuki (1991: 12) says that the reduction should be 20 percent.

Second, reported Japanese earnings also look smaller because they deduct (both on the firms' tax returns and on their financial statements) generous allowances for special reserves for such possible future contingencies as product returns, repairs, and retirement benefits. But this effect was relatively small.

Third, Japanese firms often take greater depreciation allowances. This factor, like the previous two, works to reduce reported earnings. (Unlike US firms, when a Japanese firm claims a high depreciation allowance for tax purposes, it must do the same on its income statement.) French and Poterba (1989) considered two different ways of correcting for the difference in depreciation accounting. The effect of all three corrections together was to reduce the 1988 PER in Japan from 54.3 to either 23.2 or 32.1, depending on which depreciation correction was used. Lawler, Loopesko and Dudey (1988: 24) made their own adjustments for depreciation and consolidation of earnings, which produced a very similar result. The analogous downward adjustment in US price–earnings ratios was much smaller. Overall, these accounting differences in earnings explained about half the difference between Japanese and US ratios.[20] This still left Japanese equities about twice as high as US equities at the end of 1988. Or, if our interest is in the cost-of-capital question rather than in the was-Japan's-market-too-high question, the correction still left 1988 Japanese price–earnings ratios at about half US levels.

Once we get the corrected Japanese price–earnings ratio up to the neighborhood of 0.04, it becomes slightly easier to explain the differential *vis-à-vis* the United States (which was at 0.09 when similarly adjusted by

Table 1.2 Adjusted price–earnings ratios, Japan, 1975–88

Year	Unadjusted P–E	Cross-holding Factor	Interim P–E	Reserves factors	Depreciation adjustment Method 1 Factor	Method 1 P–E	Method 2 Factor	Method 2 P–E
1975	25.2	0.784	19.8	0.98	0.599	11.5	0.905	17.2
1976	22.0	0.824	18.1	0.97	0.655	11.6	0.920	16.1
1977	19.3	0.797	15.4	0.97	0.684	10.2	0.926	13.7
1978	21.5	0.792	17.0	0.97	0.704	11.7	0.931	15.3
1979	16.6	0.778	12.9	0.97	0.717	9.0	0.935	11.7
1980	17.9	0.770	13.8	0.97	0.755	10.1	0.947	12.6
1981	24.9	0.764	19.0	0.97	0.702	13.0	0.932	17.1
1982	23.7	0.769	18.2	0.97	0.700	12.4	0.931	16.3
1983	29.4	0.795	23.4	0.97	0.692	15.8	0.936	21.1
1984	26.3	0.734	19.3	0.97	0.711	13.3	0.943	17.5
1985	29.4	0.694	20.4	0.97	0.668	13.3	0.924	18.2
1986	58.6	0.695	40.7	0.98	0.624	24.8	0.908	35.7
1987	50.4	0.665	33.5	0.97	0.660	21.5	0.920	29.8
1988	54.3	0.669	36.3	0.97[a]	0.660[a]	23.2	0.920[a]	32.1

The unadjusted P–E ratio corresponds to the NRI 350 index.

[a] Estimates using 1987 data.

Source: French and Poterba (1989)

French and Poterba). If, for example, the expected rate of growth of earnings g_e in Japan were 2.5 percent faster than in the US and the required rate of return were 2.5 percent lower, that would explain the differential. But if it is true that the required rate of return was lower by, say, 2.5 percent, what could have been the source of this difference?

There is one potential explanation, but it seems implausible: that the "equity premium" (defined as the expected rate of return on equity minus the interest rate) was smaller for Japan. This would in theory require the Japanese stock market to have been less risky than the American stock market. Ueda (1990: 362–4) argues that the risk premium in the Japanese stock market declined sharply between 1982 and 1988, but finds little evidence of a corresponding decline in riskiness. Lawler, Loopesko and Dudey (1988: 26–7) conclude that uncertainty in the two stock markets was roughly similar in the late 1980s (despite some possible differences in the past), whether estimated from the standard deviations of monthly changes or from the expected volatilities implicit in stock-index options. Thus there is little evidence of the smaller uncertainty in the Japanese market that would normally be required to justify a smaller risk premium.[21]

We consider in turn three other serious possibilities to explain the apparently lower required rate of return on equity capital in Japan: more favorable tax treatment; a lower real interest rate; and internal financing that is cheaper than the market interest rate. We shall see that the third explanation seems especially appropriate for the period before liberalization, and the second explanation for the period since liberalization. But there is also a fourth possibility to consider: that the increase in stock prices in the late 1980s was a speculative bubble.

2.3   Corporate Taxation

Corporate taxation is one respect in which the effective cost of capital facing the firm can differ from the observed rate of return on investment: it is of course the *after*-tax cost of capital that should matter for investment decisions. It would presumably be more convenient for any American businessman who wished to claim that Japanese industry had an "unfair advantage" in the form of a low cost of capital, if the source of the advantage was more-favorable tax treatment by the Japanese government.

In the past, the corporate income tax rate in Japan has been much *higher* than in the United States, especially after the more-favorable US tax treatment of business adopted in 1981; or even than in other countries, such as the United Kingdom which cut its corporate tax rate in 1984.[22] In 1985 the Japanese government raised 5.9 percent of its tax revenue from corporations, as compared to only 2.1 percent in the United States.[23] This has made it difficult to claim a tax advantage for Japanese industry. (We treat separately the possibility that favorable treatment of *saving* in the Japanese tax system has been one of the causes of high household saving in Japan. This effect, if it existed, would operate via a low real interest rate.)

Indeed, when Ando and Auerbach (1988a) computed after-tax price–earnings ratios and after-tax return-to-capital rates, they found that "it is Japanese, not American, firms that are taxed more heavily on their real incomes." They registered two possible qualifications. First, one would prefer to look at the marginal effective tax rates that are relevant to the firm's decision whether to invest, rather than the average tax rate. They noted that such measures were unavailable for Japan. Second, their calculations apply to the unlevered firm; but a corporation derives tax advantages from borrowing since interest payments are tax-deductible and one might expect these advantages to be larger for Japanese firms (both because until recently they have had higher debt–equity ratios and because the corporate tax rate that they are deducting against was higher). But Ando and Auerbach computed an upper bound on this tax advantage, and claimed that it was very small. Thus they felt able to "rule out" the claim that the corporate tax system gave Japanese firms a cost-of-capital advantage. Noguchi (1985), taking into account the advantages of borrowing, also concluded that the tax burden was higher on Japanese, not US, corporations.

Other authors have ascribed more importance to the tax advantages of borrowing in Japan. Hatsopoulos and Brooks (1987), for example, emphasized that the definition of tax-deductible borrowing is more permissive in the Japanese tax code than in the American.

Bernheim and Shoven (1987) disputed the prevailing approach in public finance of presupposing that the (pre-tax) real interest rate must be constant across countries, in light of the observed failure of this condition. They first computed the after-tax cost of capital under the 1980 tax codes, using the actual interest rates and inflation rates that held on average for the 1970s (which entails assuming a US–Japan real interest differential of 1.5 percent). They found a smaller tax wedge on capital in Japan than the United States, with the result that the after-tax cost of capital in Japan was negative.[24] They attributed this result to the greater importance of interest payments in Japan.

Bernheim and Shoven then repeated the computations for 1985 tax codes, using the actual interest and inflation rates for the early 1980s. Despite the adoption of accelerated depreciation allowances in the US tax code in 1981, the estimated US cost of capital rose substantially in the 1980s, as a result particularly of the much higher real interest rate (5.0 percent, as compared to 2.0 percent in the 1970s). The real interest rate was higher in Japan as well, but there remained a substantial difference in the after-tax costs of capital in 1985 (5.5 for the US versus 2.8 for Japan).

The central message of Bernheim and Shoven is that variation in real interest rates tends to dwarf variation in corporate tax laws as determinants of the cost of capital. They subsume in this message the changes in the 1986 tax reform (including the removal of the investment tax credit that had been increased in 1981), which was under debate at the time that they were writing. Fukao (1988: 339–41) found a less-favorable tax wedge (less negative) for Japan than the United States during the period 1981–4, but found that the combination of the 1986 US tax reform and lower inflation rates brought the post-1986 tax wedge in the United States very close to that in Japan.

In December 1988 the Japanese Diet approved a tax reform which had long been sought by the ruling Liberal Democratic Party. Among other things, the reform cut the Japanese corporate tax rate from 42 percent[25] to 37.5 percent (with the full cut not effective until 1990). This left the tax rate only slightly higher than the current rates in the United States (34 percent) and the United Kingdom (35 percent). When state and local taxes on corporations are added in, the Japanese rate is about 50 percent and the US rate about 40 percent (these figures are taken from Shoven 1989). One of several motives for the Japanese tax reform is that the Ministry of Finance fears that, in the absence of international harmonization of corporate tax rates, business would increasingly be able to find ways to arbitrage across tax jurisdictions.

Shoven (1989) updated his calculations of the effective tax rates on corporate investment. He found that the effective tax rate on investments in Japan was up sharply to 32 percent in 1988 (as compared to 5 percent in 1980). Part of the reason was the tax reform: in Shoven's calculations – unlike those of Ando and Auerbach – the high *average* corporate tax rate in Japan worked to reduce the effective *marginal* tax rate on new investment, because it increased the value to the corporation of borrowing to finance the investment and deducting the interest payments from its taxable income. He thus estimated that the reduction in the average corporate tax rate in itself raised the effective tax rate 9 percentage points.

The major reason for the increase in the marginal effective tax rate on investment was not the tax reform, however, but rather the sharp decline in expected inflation relative to the 1970s. This decline was estimated to have raised the effective tax rate by 23 percentage points. The fall in the inflation rate in Japan (from 9 percent in the 1970s to 1 percent) means that the favorable distortion caused by the tax-deductibility of nominal interest payments was reduced. This left the effective Japanese tax rate still somewhat below the US rate, which was at 41 percent in 1988 (up from 29 percent before the Tax Reform Act of 1986).

It is possible that the moderate tax advantage that remained in Shoven's figures did not adequately take into account the downward trend in the Japanese reliance on debt,[26] and that by now little is left of the Japanese tax advantage. Ando and Auerbach (1988a, 1988b) dismissed altogether the importance of taxes in this context. Takenaka (1986) concluded that the impact of the investment tax credit on Japanese investment is negligible. Bernheim and Shoven (1987) concluded that "under prevailing tax systems, differences in the cost of capital between countries are largely attributable to differences in domestic credit market conditions, rather than to taxes."

Since these papers were written, the difference in tax treatment between the two countries has, if anything, narrowed further. The Japanese tax reforms that took effect in April 1988 and April 1989 raised the tax rate on Japanese saving in a number of ways.[27] Iwata and Yoshida (1987) calculated that the abolition of the pro-saving bias in the (then-proposed) reforms would increase the total tax wedge in Japan, and thereby narrow the differential in the corporate cost of capital *vis-à-vis* the United States, despite the accompanying reductions in Japanese corporate taxes. (They, unlike Shoven, found that the latter work to reduce the after-tax cost of capital in Japan.)

If the public finance experts think that taxes are of, at best, second-order importance in comparing the cost of capital between the US and Japan – or that the difference has, if anything, gone *against* Japanese corporations – why should an international economist disagree?

2.4 Total Stock Market Capitalization and the Late 1980s Run-up

The empirical fact that dominates the study of Japan's stock market is the tremendous run-up in prices in the 1980s. We have already discussed the level of stock prices when they are compared to dividends and when they are compared to earnings. The same trend is evident when comparing total capitalization (price times number of shares) in Japan to capitalization in the United States.

Total stock market capitalization in Japan had by 1989 surpassed the US: 44 percent of the world vs 29 percent, in the conventional statistics. Hale (1989) opined that the dramatic reversal of the rankings of US and Japanese capitalization over the course of the 1980s represented the financial market's negative judgment on Reaganomics, as compared to policymaking by bureaucrats in the Japanese Ministry of Finance. On the other hand, when Murphy (1989) observed the same reversal, he worried that Japan's policymakers were not ready to accept the responsibility of greater weight in the world system.

Market values need to be adjusted for the double-counting that results from intercorporate share ownership. Nearly two-thirds of corporate equity in Japan is held by other corporations. When French and Poterba (1989) adjusted the Japanese market for cross-holdings, they found that it was still smaller than in the US: 33 percent of the world capitalization as against 36 percent for the US. When McDonald (1989) adjusted for cross-holdings (or *mochiai* in Japanese[28]), as of early 1989, he found that the Japanese market was indeed larger than the US market: 39 percent as compared with 33 percent. But the ranking again reversed with the fall of Japanese stock prices in 1990.[29]

In any case, the growth of the Japanese market in the 1980s (a 68-fold increase over 1970) is astounding by any test. French and Poterba (1989) observed that the magnitude of the 1986–8 run-up in the stock market was equally impressive when measured relative to GNP. Their computed ratio of adjusted equity to GNP fluctuated between 0.14 and 0.33 during the period 1970–85, and then rose sharply to 0.68 by 1988. Meanwhile, the US ratio, though more than twice as high as the Japanese ratio in the early 1970s, was only 0.49 in 1988.

The only ratio where French and Poterba did not find potentially explosive behavior was the ratio of equity prices to the replacement cost of capital, that is, Tobin's Q. They did find that the Q ratio in Japan increased about 35 percent from 1973 to 1987, to 0.67 or 0.77, depending on the method of calculating net equity outstanding. (Horiuchi 1990: 19, reports that typical Japanese computations of Q are in a lower range of 0.5 to 0.7, for the period 1974–86.) But the United States ratio, at 0.71, was in about the same range. Similarly, estimates of Japan's Q in Hoshi and Kashyap (1990), though slightly above 1, show no sharp increase in the late 1980s.

That the replacement cost of capital in Japan increased almost as much as stock market prices, French and Poterba attributed to the fact that land prices had almost doubled since 1983, and to the fact that companies hold a lot of land. Firms usually carry land holdings on their books, not at current market price, but at the price of acquisition (which, in the case of land held since the nineteenth century, is essentially zero). French and Poterba thus tentatively concluded that the puzzle as to why equity prices rose so much in the 1980s may be the same as the puzzle why land prices rose so much in the 1980s. Ando and Auerbach (1990) reached a similar conclusion: that even a conservative calculation to adjust corporate earnings for land appreciation can fully account for the apparent differential in rate of return *vis-à-vis* the United States, while admitting that this answer only pushes the question of the source of the 1980s run-up from the stock market onto the land market.[30]

2.5   Land Prices

The soaring price of land in Japan in the 1980s was a major phenomenon in its own right. In 1986 the price of land in Tokyo (for residential use) was 150 times the price in New York, 16 times the price in London, 35 times that in Paris, and 11 times that in Munich.[31] The unit cost of land for the country overall was about 40 times as high as in the United States.[32] Thus the value of all the land in Japan is several times as great as the value of all the land in the (much larger) United States.[33] A favorite "factoid," which is apparently true, is that the grounds of the Imperial Palace in Tokyo, when evaluated at the land prices of the surrounding area, is worth more than all the land in the State of California.[34]

The price of land, analogously to the price of equity, should equal the present discounted value of future rents (in the absence of a speculative bubble). If rents are expected to grow at rate g_r, then the price–rental ratio should be given by

$$P_{land}/\text{rent} = \frac{1}{r - g_r}$$

Thus the same possible explanations arise for high land prices as arise for high equity prices: a low discount rate r or a high growth rate g_r. Noguchi (1987, as described by Ito 1989) observed that the price–rental ratio was much higher in Tokyo than in other major world cities,[35] and concluded that about half the Japanese land price was a speculative bubble, that the demand for land was based on a self-confirming expectation of future capital gains. But Ito (1989) disagreed, arguing that Noguchi omitted the possibility that expectations of rising land prices could have been correctly based on fundamentals, because the relative price of land will increase in a growing economy where the supply of land is fixed by geographical and other factors.

There are a number of special institutional features that affect the Japanese land market, such as building height restrictions and sunshine laws, special protection for rice paddies, and a level of taxation of capital gains at the time of sale that is much greater than annual property taxes.[36] Some of these features can be viewed as contributing to the inelasticity of the supply of land.

In terms of the above equation, a high value for g_r could explain the high price–rental ratio. Ito showed in an overlapping generations model, where land is a substitutable factor of production, that if land is in fixed supply, its relative price will increase at a rate essentially given by the real growth rate of the economy. Sachs and Boone (1988) argued similarly. Boone (1989a) concluded that one can explain the difference between Japanese and US land values by fundamentals, if the Japanese GNP is expected to grow at roughly 2 percent a year faster than US GNP.

The institutional factors listed above are often cited as causes of the high cost of land in Japan. They were one component of the Structural Impediments Initiative (SII), which was launched by the US government in 1989, on the theory that the high cost of land was in turn a cause of low consumption and low imports in Japan. The land-taxation factor, in particular, entered prominently into the June 1990 report on SII by the two governments.

In the absence of macroeconomic differences such as interest rates and expectations, however, these institutional factors could not in themselves explain the high price of land. In the first place, Boone (1989b) studied data across regions of Japan and found that factors such as excess concentration in the Tokyo region, agricultural protection, and tax policies did a poor job of predicting variation in land costs.[37] In the second place, even if these institutional factors could explain the high cost of land in Japan overall, they could not serve as an explanation for the high price–rental *ratio*. As Boone (1989b: 14) noted, these factors would predict that not only land prices in Tokyo, but *rents* as well, should far exceed those in other world capitals, and this was not the case.

The expected-growth argument favored by both Boone and Ito tells us why land price–rental ratios in Japan were high as of 1989. But it does not tell us why they should have *increased* so much over the last 18 years. According to the theory, the price and rent should both rise proportionately with economic growth. Instead, while land and housing prices sky-rocketed, the rental rate remained approximately constant in real terms. As a result, the price–rental ratio for housing increased by 67 percent between 1970 and 1987. The price of land alone went up even more than the price of housing over this same period. The price–rental ratio for land increased by 14 percent between 1975 and 1986, 27 percent in the three big cities (see Iwata and Yoshida 1988: 510).

Ito's theory may, however, give us a reason why land price–rental ratios in Japan should be *higher than in the United States*, even disregarding any difference in the real growth rates of the economies. Ito shows that if the supply of available land increases at the growth rate of the economy, then the relative price of land will be constant. In terms of the equation, if the supply of land is more elastic in the United States than in Japan, then g_r will be lower and therefore P_{land}/rent will be lower in the United States.

2.6   Speculative Bubbles

There is always the possibility of a speculative bubble in the 1980s to explain the price of land, the price of equity, or both. In surveys of institutional investors conducted by Shiller, Kon-ya and Tsutsui (1991b) in mid-1989, late 1989, and early 1990, many respondents chose the statement, "Stock prices in Japan, when compared with measures of true fundamental value or sensible investment value, are too high." (In August 1991, when Iraq invaded Kuwait and the Japanese market fell precipitously, the percentage of respondents finding the market "too low" rose sharply, and the percentage finding it "too high" fell.[38])

It is sometimes argued that special institutional features of the Japanese stock market, such as the dominance of trading by the big four security firms and administrative guidance by the Ministry of Finance,[39] keep prices artificially high. It has been argued, for example, that such features might explain why the Japanese market "was not allowed" to fall as far in the crash of October 1987 as other countries' markets.[40] From a 1989 survey of 139 Japanese institutional investors, Shiller, Kon-ya and Tsutsui (1991a: 12–13) report that 68 percent agreed with the statement: "The Ministry of Finance will take steps to assure that stock prices in Japan will not lose too much of their value in another crash," while only 12 percent disagreed.[41]

What means does the Japanese government have to control the stock market (aside from monetary policy)? Hardouvelis and Peristiani (1989: 19) found that "Margin requirements in Japan have proved to be an effective tool of controlling wild gyrations in stock prices." Hardouvelis and Peristiani (1990: 27) also found that "margin policy in Japan has been useful even during the 1980s, a period when Japanese capital markets were increasingly deregulated."

Financial economists have not yet been able to construct good models of what gets speculative bubbles started, or what causes them to collapse. We do not even have much idea whether bubbles are more or less likely in perfectly competitive "efficient" markets than in markets where trading is characterized by turnover taxes, larger transactions costs, oligopolistic market-makers, and government intervention (all characteristics which are attributed to Japanese stock markets).[42]

In 1990 the Japanese stock market lost almost half its value. On first consideration, this plunge could be interpreted as clear evidence that the run-up of prices in the late 1980s was indeed a speculative bubble. Unfortunately for this view, the macroeconomic fundamentals changed dramatically at the same time. A new Bank of Japan governor, less enthusiastic than some others in the Japanese government about buying dollars to support the US currency and more intent on fighting inflation, began to tighten Japanese monetary policy in mid-1989, raising real interest rates to a sharply higher level in 1990. Notice from figure 1.1a that the long-term real interest differential *vis-à-vis* the United States vanished at the end of 1989, and from figure 1.1b that the short-term real interest differential actually reversed sign. The Japanese stock market fell sharply at the beginning of 1990, presumably as a result of the increase in interest rates, and fell again in August, presumably as a result of the beginning of the Kuwait crisis. Before we attribute the 1980s ascent in Japan's equity (and land) prices to a speculative bubble, we should pursue the possibility that the cycle can be explained by interest rates.[43]

We can try some simple calculations to see if the changes in macroeconomic fundamentals can explain the decline of the Japanese stock-market between late 1989 and the end of 1990. The calculations use monthly survey data collected from a sample of banks and multinational corporations by *Currency Forecaster's Digest* of White Plains, New York.

Table 1.3 estimates that the Japanese ten-year real interest rate was 2.6 percent in September 1989, and the ten-year expected rate of economic growth 3.7 percent (both about the same as for late 1988). One is tempted to take the difference $r - g$ as an estimate of $r_e - g_e$ and see if it equals the ratio of earnings to prices. But the difference, -1.1, is less

Table 1.3 Can macroeconomic fundamentals explain the 1990 P–E decline? (Figures in percent)

	September 1989	December 1990	July 1991
Japan[a]			
Interest rate (10-year)	4.86	5.60	6.71
Expected inflation rate (CPI, 1989–98)	2.25	2.70	2.70
Real interest rate r	2.61	3.90	4.01
Expected real growth rate (1989–98) g	3.75	4.05	3.95
r − g	−1.14	−0.15	0.06
United States[b]			
Interest rate (10-year)	8.15	7.97	8.28
Expected inflation rate (CPI, 1989–98)	4.75	4.40	4.35
Real interest rate r	3.40	3.57	3.93
Expected real growth rate (1989–98) g	2.70	2.45	2.35
r − g	0.70	1.12	1.58
			Change 1989–90
Differential $(r − g)_{US} − (r − g)_J$	1.84	1.27	−0.57
Japan E–P (unadjusted)[c]	1.60	2.47	+0.87
US E–P (unadjusted)[d]	6.47	6.73	+0.26
Differential $(E–P)_{US} − (E–P)_J$	4.87	4.26	−0.61

Sources:
[a] From *Currency Forecasters' Digest*
[b] From *Currency Forecasters' Digest*
[c] From *Nikkei* data bank
[d] From *Economic Indicators*, Council of Economic Advisers

than zero, and would thus apparently be capable of explaining any price–earnings ratio, no matter how high.[44] Clearly, the real interest rate must underestimate the required rate of return on capital – presumably due to a risk premium of the sort discussed above in the section on price–earnings ratios – or else the GNP growth rate must overestimate the rate of growth of earnings.[45]

The comparable calculations for the United States show that the differential between the real interest rate and the expected growth rate was 0.7 percent in September 1989 (down 1 percent from late 1988). French and Poterba's figures, after adjustment of earnings, show that the US PER exceeded the Japanese PER by about 0.054 in late 1988. Price–earnings ratios were almost the same at the end of 1989 as they were at the end of

1988. Thus at the end of the 1980s there was an apparent "overvaluation" of the Japanese stock and land markets that could be attributed either to (a) a speculative bubble, or (b) a higher equity risk premium for the United States than for Japan, or some other source of bias in $r - g$ (as an estimate of the difference between the relevant discount and growth rates) that is greater for the United States.

Let us consider the second hypothesis, and assume that the difference in risk premiums (or other source of bias) between the two countries remained the same at the end of 1990 as in late 1989: about 3 percent if unadjusted earnings figures are used. Is the 1990 increase in Japanese real interest rates capable of explaining the collapse of the Japanese market? As of December 1990, the real interest rate in Japan was up by 1.3 points. As a result, the difference between the US and Japanese estimates of $r - g$ was down by 0.6 points from September 1989. Over the same period, the difference in (unadjusted) PERs fell by 0.6 points. Thus the increase in real interest rates in Japan can explain most of the decline in the stock market in 1990 *vis-à-vis* the United States, and there is not necessarily a need for recourse to the hypothesis of a burst speculative bubble. Suzuki (1991: 10–11) comes to the same conclusion.

It should be noted, however, that it is the intrinsic nature of such calculations that nearly inconsequential changes in the computed macroeconomic fundamentals are apparently capable of "explaining" large changes in the stock market.[46] Perhaps the appropriately balanced judgment would admit that there may have been a bit of bubble component in the late 1980s, but would point out that the decline was deliberately triggered by the authorities raising interest rates, in order to head off a still-larger bubble.

What are the implications of the 1990 developments for the cost-of-capital question? The difference in real interest rates between the United States and Japan has disappeared completely. There is probably now relatively little left also of the difference in PERs once the accounting adjustments are made to Japanese earnings.[47] Some may continue to believe that the standard weighted average of debt and equity is not relevant for Japan because many corporations still get much of their financing from main banks. This point is developed in the last part of this chapter. Even in the case of bank borrowing, however, there is reason to think that the era of cheap finance is over. Japanese banking was itself the industry hardest hit in the 1990 stock market collapse, and is now under pressure to restrict lending in order to meet stringent new international standards for capital adequacy.[48]

In short, though by most measures the cost of finance in the 1980s was lower in Japan than in the United States, this appears no longer to be the case. Whether this is cause for rejoicing among American businessmen is another question. Given the high degree of international integration that has taken place over the last ten years, fluctuations in saving are reflected in capital flows between Japan and the rest of the world as easily as in domestic investment. In other words, corporate borrowers in Japan are not the only ones to feel the effect of a decreased availability of Japanese savings; borrowers in the United States and elsewhere in the 1990s will feel it as well.

3   DETERMINANTS OF THE REAL INTEREST RATE

If one thinks of the real interest rate as equilibrating the various sources and uses of funds, then a low real interest rate in the 1970s and 1980s would be explained by some combination of four factors: a high corporate saving rate net of investment; a high public saving rate; a high household saving rate; and a high availability of savings from abroad. Each factor probably has played a role at one time or another in Japan.

We know that the government was a source of cheap capital for many firms in the 1950s and 1960s, but that it went sharply into deficit and became a big *user* of funds after 1973. The Ministry of Finance took pains to cut the government budget deficit in the early 1980s, but the deficit has nevertheless been relatively high throughout the post-1973 period, and thus cannot explain a low real interest rate during this period.

The corporate sector was in deficit in the postwar period until the first oil shock. We know that the corporate deficit has been sharply lower since then,[49] as the result of a fall-off in the previously high level of investment, which helps explain the cheap capital after 1973. But the high Japanese private saving rate is the factor most often cited as applying throughout the period.

3.1   Household Saving Rate

The Japanese household saving rate is among the highest of industrialized countries: saving (expressed net of depreciation) averaged 16.0 percent of disposable income over the period 1980–9. By comparison, net saving in the United States averaged only 6.0 percent of disposable income over the same period.[50] The question of why the saving rate is so high in Japan is another major topic in itself. We briefly run through some of the arguments that have been suggested. (Horioka, 1990, offers what is probably the most up-to-date and comprehensive of a number of surveys.)

Hayashi (1986, 1989) claims that much of the apparent differential in personal saving rates between Japan and the United States can be explained by four accounting differences.[51] But even after adjustment, a substantial differential remains. In fact Dekle (1990) argues that the large capital gains on land (for the period 1956–87) should be included in an appropriate measure of Japanese saving, and that doing so *raises* the household saving rate, to 38 percent of disposable income in Japan compared to 13 percent in the United States. Dekle and Summers (1991) argue further that Hayashi's adjustments are exaggerated, particularly his estimates of Japanese replacement cost depreciation. They present new estimates, based on household balance sheet data rather than on the usual national income accounts, that show a large gap remaining: the estimated saving rate averaged between 15 and 30 percentage points higher in Japan than in the United States in the early 1980s.

At least six reasons for the high Japanese saving rate have been given, by Hayashi, Horioka, and others.

3.1.1 High growth rate

The older dissaving generation is always outweighed by the younger saving generation (as in the life-cycle hypothesis of Franco Modigliani).

3.1.2 Demographics

Currently Japan has one of the longest life expectancies and smallest ratio of aged to working-age population: 15 percent, compared with 20 percent in the US and 23 percent over all the OECD countries. Horioka (1986) has estimated that the age ratio can explain a difference in saving rates of 11.5 percent.

Over the next 30 years, Japan will change from the country with the highest ratio of working-age population to elderly of the G-5 countries, 5.9 in 1985, to the lowest, 2.3 in 2020 (Shoven 1989). A simulation by Auerbach, Kotlikoff, Hagemann and Nicolletti (1989: 117), based on the rapid aging of the Japanese population, predicts that the national saving rate in Japan will decline over the period 1990 to 2028 from 22 percent (close to Germany's) to a minimum of 1 percent, falling below the US national saving rate in the year 2020.[52] On the other hand, Shibuya (1990: 42) argues that the effect of aging on the Japanese saving rate will be limited (less than 3 percentage points), because it will be accompanied by a longer retirement span, necessitating increased saving by the working-age population in accordance with the life-cycle model.

Another possible explanation for the high saving rate in Japan – not one of the six explanations that appear on standard lists – is that it is the only non-nuclear country of the G-10.[53] Slemrod (1988) points out that a higher perceived threat of nuclear annihilation should reduce people's saving rate by reducing their expected horizons, and offers supporting evidence from a cross-section of 20 countries. Survey results show that Americans report a higher perceived likelihood of world war than do the Japanese, and indeed report the highest of all 20 countries. (Not taken into account is any tendency for the Japanese to rate their odds of nuclear annihilation, conditional on world war breaking out, as lower than Americans.)

3.1.3   An underdeveloped social security system

Here there are conflicting effects on the saving rate. On the one hand low social security benefits encourage workers to save more, but on the other, it encourages them to retire early. Horioka argues that they approximately cancel out. Yamada (1990), however, finds in simultaneous-equations estimation that the benefits effect outweighs the early-retirement effect.

3.1.4   The bonus system of employee compensation

The lump-sum payments at the end of each half-year might act as forced saving. This would require a sort of "calendar illusion." Ishikawa and Ueda (1984) find that the bonus system does indeed have an effect on saving, though they estimate it to be at most 3 percentage points.

3.1.5   The high price of land and housing

Even before price increases in the late 1980s, housing prices in Japan were almost twice as high as those in the United States. They are 2.5–2.7 times higher if differences in floorspace are taken into account.[54] As a result, housing constitutes 65 percent of saving in Japan as compared to 31 percent in the United States.[55]

Horioka (1985, 1988) explains that, while opinion surveys in the United States report old age as the most important motive for saving, surveys in Japan place saving to buy a house as more important (together with education and marriage). Horioka (1986) estimates that high land prices explain a difference in saving rates of 5.0 percent. Hale (1987: 27) believes that "Any set of structural reforms which reduce the price of housing while increasing the tax incentive to own it could have a more dramatic effect on savings and consumption than many policies seemingly targeted on savings behavior itself."[56]

The implications of expensive housing, by itself, for the saving rate are not as clear as often asserted. Sachs and Boone (1988) construct a model to answer the question of what would happen to savings if land prices fell in response, for example, to the sorts of measures often urged on Japan by Americans: the ending of prohibitions on rice imports and the liberalization of land-use restrictions. Their model predicts that saving would *rise* rather than fall, due to the fall in wealth. Similarly, Shibuya (1988) estimates that the wealth effect would nearly eliminate any positive effects of land prices on saving; and Yoshikawa and Ohtake (1989) show that the estimated positive effect of higher land prices on saving by future home-buyers may be more than offset by estimated reductions in saving on the part of those who completely abandon plans to buy a home.

A positive effect on saving does follow from the unavailability of consumer credit. Hayashi, Ito, and Slemrod (1988) report that the Japanese have to accumulate up to 40 percent of the purchase price as a down payment.[57] Also, mortgage interest is not tax-deductible as it is in the United States.

The Japanese appear to have a greater cultural bias against personal indebtedness than do Americans; rather than using credit cards to postpone payment for purchases, for example, the Japanese are fond of magnetic cards that allow them to *prepay*, and then deduct purchases as they are made. Arguing against the idea that the Japanese are culturally predisposed to save more is the fact that the high saving rates are only a phenomenon of the postwar era (according to Hale 1987: 26; and Balassa and Noland 1988: 81).

Also sometimes listed as reasons for high saving rates in Japan are obstacles to consumption, such as the inefficient retailing system, the lack of space in living quarters for consumer durables, and the lack of leisure time in the work-schedule (see, for example, Balassa and Noland 1988: 94). But economic theory is dubious as to the implications for the savings rate of institutional impediments that apply to future consumption as much as to current consumption. Wealth is only of use to the household to the extent that it is consumed sooner or later.

Balassa and Noland (1988: 92) argue that a special combination of high housing prices and the strategic bequest motive on the part of the elderly are the best explanations of high saving. Dekle (1989a) also focuses on the behavior of the Japanese elderly, finding that they are not dissaving as they should; Dekle (1989b) shows that the reason could be a combination of a strong bequest motive and a constraint against borrowing on home equity.

3.1.6 Tax incentives

In the past, the tax system has deliberately increased the after-tax return to households in a number of ways. Capital gains from sales of equities were excluded from personal income taxes (avoiding what Hatsopoulos 1991: 12, called the double-taxation of retained earnings that penalizes

US investment). Also, the Japanese could escape paying taxes on much of their savings by taking advantage of such exemptions as deposits in the *maruyu* system and the postal savings system. A family of four could legally hold $455,000 in tax-free assets (Shoven 1989). Furthermore, many households held more tax-free accounts than the number to which they were legally entitled; the total number of accounts in the postal savings system was twice the population (Rosenbluth 1989: 180).

The 1987 tax reform, effective April 1988, abolished tax-exempt savings accounts. But it retained two pro-saving features of the tax system. First, when a saver does pay tax on interest earnings or dividends, they are taxed separately from their income tax and at a rate lower than the top marginal rate. Second, although the December 1988 tax reform, effective April 1989, instated the taxation of capital gains on sales of securities, the tax rate is still below that of the United States (especially since the 1986 US tax reform) and other major countries. The saver gets the option of 1 percent of the value of the transaction or 20 percent of the capital gain.[58]

Although one of the reasons behind the Japanese tax reform supposedly was foreign pressure (*gaiatsu*) to make the Japanese system less pro-saving, and therefore more like the US system, the effect of this decrease in the after-tax return on the supply of saving and therefore on the real interest rate is not clear. In theory, the substitution effect and income effect go in opposite directions. Saxonhouse (1982) believes that the Japanese are, in fact, target-savers: because their goal is to save enough to buy a home, a decrease in the after-tax rate of return means that they now need to save *more*, not less, to achieve the same goal. In empirical studies, a positive effect of the after-tax return on the saving rate has been difficult to find. (For Japan, see Makin 1985; and Hayashi 1986. Iwata, Suzuki, and Yoshida 1988: 129–31, however, broke down the tax rate and other variables by income class, and did in this way find evidence of an effect on saving.) A simulation analysis in Hayashi, Ito and Slemrod (1988) concluded that the Japanese saving rate would go down by a few percentage points if Japan were to abolish the *maruyu*, but this was not a statistical test. Results in Shibuya (1990) predicted that there would be no long-run effect.

There was apparently no sign of a significant decrease in the household saving rate in Japan in the aftermath of the April 1988 abolishment of the *maruyu*. It should be noted that the second tax reform also instituted a sales tax – indeed, this was its politically most controversial feature – which could in theory have either a positive or negative effect on the saving/consumption decision, depending particularly on whether households believe that the government will raise the sales tax rate in the future.

3.2 International Capital Mobility

Even if a tax reform or a land-use reform were to reduce the Japanese level of household saving toward that in Western countries, there is a serious further question as to whether such a change would lower the Japanese real interest rate or the cost of capital to firms. If capital is perfectly mobile internationally, it is argued, then a decline in national saving should not put any upward pressure on the rate of return within Japan. Rather, it should be entirely offset by increased borrowing from abroad (and decreased lending) at an unchanged rate of return. However, it is fairly clear that such a decrease in saving *would* reduce the Japanese current account surplus – and all the more so if capital is highly mobile – which is what many Americans want.

Feldstein and Horioka (1980) initiated what has proven to be a long-lasting debate by observing that changes in countries' rates of national saving in fact had large effects on their rates of investment, and by interpreting the finding as evidence of low capital mobility. The paper was subjected to many econometric attacks, but the basic results seem to hold up. The "saving-retention" coefficient did finally begin to decline in the 1980s, however, according to the latest studies (Feldstein and Bacchetta 1989; and Frankel 1991b; the latter paper contains 65 references on the subject, many of them demonstrations that one can have a high correlation between saving and investment despite perfect capital mobility).

It is possible to test the international equalization of rates of return more directly. Many studies have documented the failure of real interest rates to be equalized across countries,[59] which seems to confirm the Feldstein–Horioka results. We saw in section 1 that the Japanese real interest rate was below the US rate throughout the 1980s. But the Japanese government announced the removal of controls on international capital movements in 1979–80, and further liberalization measures in 1983–4, partly in response to pressure from the US Treasury.[60] It is often argued that if capital markets are open, international arbitrage should eliminate real interest differentials. Is it possible that the announced Japanese liberalization has failed to be genuine or complete?

A number of studies have shown, using data on *covered* interest differentials, that the 1979–80 and 1983–4 liberalizations did indeed have the effects advertised.[61] By now, covered interest parity holds as well for Japan (*vis-à-vis* the Eurodollar market) as it does for such major countries as Canada, Germany, and the United Kingdom: the differential between the dollar interest rate and the interest rate on domestic currency is equal to the discount on the dollar in the forward exchange market. This finding suggests that Japan is highly integrated into world financial markets with respect to the movement of capital across national boundaries.

The finding still leaves open the possibility of differences associated with the *currency* in which an asset is denominated, as opposed to the *political jurisdiction* in which it is issued. For example, investors' expectations that the dollar may in the future depreciate against the yen in nominal terms almost certainly explain why the yen interest rate was less than the dollar interest rate in the 1980s.[62] Similarly, expectations that the dollar may depreciate against the yen in *real* terms may explain why the yen *real* interest rate was less than the dollar real interest rate. In that case, the original Feldstein–Horioka view is correct: real interest rates are not necessarily equalized internationally and changes in saving (even if truly exogenous) need not be offset by borrowing from abroad and thus may be heavily reflected as changes in investment. And yet the explanation may be the imperfect international integration of goods markets that allows failures of purchasing power parity, rather than imperfect international integration of financial markets. If there is no way of arbitraging directly among countries' goods or among their plant and equipment, and if plant and equipment are imperfect substitutes for bonds *within* each country, then perfect international arbitrage among countries' bonds is not sufficient to equalize real rates of return among countries' plant and equipment.

It is quite likely that, by the 1980s, investors had come to hold an expectation of future yen appreciation. The issue is discussed elsewhere.[63] One piece of evidence is survey data on investors' forecasts.[64] By 1989, however, expectations of future yen appreciation, according to surveys, had disappeared.

We have argued that, even if Japanese corporations are now no more highly levered than American corporations, and even if international arbitrage now equates the Japanese and foreign nominal interest rates (when expressed in a common currency), the Japanese real interest rate could still lie below the foreign rate. A real interest differential in the 1980s – whatever its source – could in turn help explain high average price–earnings ratios in the Japanese stock market, high price–rental ratios in the Japanese land market, and a lower cost of capital to some Japanese firms.[65]

The argument about the low real interest rate might seem to apply to the past in Japan as much as, or more than, to the 1980s. Similarly, the argument that the expected rate of real economic growth in Japan is high applies to the past as much as, or more than, to the 1980s. How can one explain that price–earnings ratios and price–rental ratios were not also high in the past, that is, that they rose sharply in the 1980s? We address this question in the course of the next part of the chapter.

4 INTERNAL CORPORATE FINANCING AND MAIN BANKS VS THE MARKET

The standard formula for the price–earnings ratio and the price–rental ratio, $1/(r - g)$, assumes that r, the real interest rate (or a required rate of return equal to the real interest rate marked up by a risk premium), is relevant for discounting expected future returns. This assumption is appropriate for economies where corporate finance is oriented around a unified central market, that is, a common pool of funds into which most savers deposit and from which most investors draw.[66] This description applies relatively well to the United States, and it applies increasingly to Japan today. But it did not apply very well to Japan in the 1970s, and still less so in the 1960s, as Meerschwam (1989) explains at greater length. In the terms used by Zysman (1983), Japan has a "credit-based" financial system such as Germany and France have, rather than a "capital market-based" financial system such as the United States and the United Kingdom have.[67]

The existence of lending by government agencies to favored firms in favored industries at subsidized rates, and the artificial "repression" of other interest rates through regulation and administrative guidance, have always been major ways that Japanese corporations have been thought to have an "unfair" cost-of-capital advantage in the past. Of 12 government financial institutions – which as recently as 1980 supplied 17 percent of funds for investment in plant and equipment – the Japan Development Bank and the Small Business Finance Corporation were particularly notable in channeling subsidized investment funds to selected industries (Lee 1988: 25–36). The general low-interest rate policy of the government before 1973 was explicit.[68]

Equally familiar is the claim that large corporations or *keiretsu* take profits from one activity and cross-subsidize investment in another.[69] But it has seldom been clear why Japanese industry should want to do this. If the investment is expected to be profitable in the long run, than it should be undertaken in a market-oriented financial system such as the United States, with the investment funded by borrowing in the market, if necessary, as readily as under the Japanese system.

4.1 How the Japanese System has Avoided Information and Incentive Problems

Recent theoretical developments have helped us understand better how the cost of internal finance can be less than the cost of external finance.[70] One route is asymmetric information between the firm's managers and the typical stockholder or bondholder in the market regarding the rate of return on an investment. Another route is incentive or "agency" problems.

"Internal finance" in the United States means the corporation's financing of an investment out of retained earnings (or out of depreciation charges), as opposed to financing at market rates by borrowing from a bank or issuing securities.[71] Retained earnings are also important in Japan: important to understanding why the cost of capital remained low in the 1970s. When the Japanese economic growth rate fell off with the oil shock of 1973, the number of profitable investment projects fell relative to the supply of funds available. (In the national savings identity, the offset to the increase in the saving–investment balance of the corporate sector was primarily a large increase in the government budget deficit in the 1970s, followed by a large increase in the current account surplus in the 1980s.) In other words, since 1973 firms have been able to finance investments out of retained earnings to a much greater extent than previously.[72] Retained earnings can be a cheaper source of financing than issuing corporate debt or equity, because they are not penalized by problems of incomplete information or incentive incompatibility.

It can be argued that, in Japan, borrowing by a firm from its main bank under a long-term relationship avoids incentive and information problems as effectively as does internal finance. The reasoning is that the main bank, like a large shareholder – which, in fact, it often is – can keep close tabs on what goes on inside the firm, thus largely obviating the information and incentive problems.[73] Japanese financial institutions (including not just banks, but also life insurance companies and other institutional investors), unlike their US counterparts, are allowed to take large debt *and* equity positions in the same firm. Prowse (1989) argues that this difference constitutes in itself a way that the Japanese system is better able to circumvent agency problems.[74]

Hodder (1988a) concludes that the advantages of "lender monitoring" are key, and that they may explain why studies like Ando and Auerbach (1988b) find that the cost of capital is lower in Japan than in the United States. His argument is that the advantages of lender monitoring may show up in part as low reported price–earnings ratios because banks receive payments for their services in the form of "compensating balances" and transactions fees, which come out of reported corporate earnings, rather than in the form of interest payments.[75]

Aoki (1990: 17–18) describes an equilibrium whereby a main bank preserves its reputation as a reliable monitor of firms by voluntarily forgoing the priority of its claims in the process of reorganization or liquidation of a troubled client firm. Aoki (1991: 34) suggests that this equilibrium is delicate, and is only preserved by (implicit) Ministry of Finance regulation that keeps the list of eligible banks from changing.

Empirical evidence in support of the proposition that internal and main-bank finance are cheaper than external or market finance is offered by some recent microeconomic studies of the determinants of firm investment. It often appears that variables such as cash flow do a better job econometrically of explaining business fixed investment than theoretically preferable variables such as the real interest rate and Tobin's Q (at least when each factor was considered on its own).[76] The new theories of information and incentive problems, however, now provide the desired rigorous theoretical basis for including cash flow. Fazzari, Hubbard, and Petersen (1988) have recently estimated regression equations for investment on a cross-section of US firms. They distinguish firms that pay low dividends, which they assume are liquidity-constrained, from others. They show that cash flow is a more important determinant of investment in the former group, which they interpret as evidence in favor of the internal-finance hypothesis. (Tobin's Q, the ratio of the market price of equity to replacement cost, is also included as an explanatory variable, to capture expectations of the return to investment.) One can interpret such findings as analogous to the Feldstein–Horioka result: just as a high correlation of national saving and investment across countries suggests that there may exist some barriers that separate individual countries from the worldwide capital market, so high correlation of corporate saving and investment across firms suggests that there may exist barriers that separate individual firms from the nationwide capital market.

Hoshi, Kashyap and Sharfstein (1989) apply a similar methodology to Japan, where the segregation of firms can be more definitively accomplished. They break down a sample into two groups. One consists of 121 "affiliated" firms: those with ties to large banks (typically a main bank) that are part of its *keiretsu*. The other consists of 25 "independent" firms, without close links to any particular bank. They find that among the independent firms, cash flow positively affects investment (and Tobin's Q does not), while among the affiliated firms cash flow has no significant effect (while Q does have an effect).[77] The conclusion is that the first group faces a barrier between the cost of financing investment out of retained earnings and the cost of borrowing, like American firms do, while the latter can borrow from their affiliated banks as easily as financing out of retained earnings. The authors conclude that one possible implication is that "the institutional arrangements in Japan may offer Japanese firms an important competitive advantage."

4.2 The Loosening of the System and the Shift Toward Market Finance

The hypothesis that internal and indirect finance (especially from the main bank) is cheaper than direct or market finance can thus support the claim that the true cost of capital to Japanese corporations (at least to those that are members of *keiretsu*) has been low in the past. But established banking relationships have begun to break down in Japan and the market has begun to take their place, as corporations begin to use banks less and bond markets more, a process that accelerated in the 1980s as the result of international liberalization as well as domestic deregulation.[78] In the 1970s, the non-financial corporate sector issued stock and marketable debt securities on a scale that averaged only 13 percent of total outside financing including borrowings from banks; in 1987 that ratio increased to 30 percent, as many firms found they could raise funds more easily or more cheaply on the open market (Bisignano 1990: 41 and table 10).

But if the relevant cost of issuing debt was higher in the more market-oriented 1980s than it had been in the past era of cheap bank finance, this raises some difficult questions. The first question, which we now consider, is how one explains the fact that price--earnings and price--rental ratios were lower in previous decades than in the late 1980s.[79] The second, why firms would voluntarily abandon advantageous banking arrangements, is addressed subsequently.

We must ask who would have had the opportunity to arbitrage between the low "cost of capital" and the high expected future return to holding land or equities. For those who had the opportunity to buy land, plant, and equipment, or equity, the *opportunity cost* of funds was high, a figure closer to the observed rate of return on equity than to the observed interest rate or the still lower cost of internal finance.[80] The individual small investor did not have such opportunities; he was given little alternative to depositing his savings in a low-interest-rate account.[81] The same was to a certain extent true of institutional investors such as pension funds and insurance companies, and in any case the pool of available savings in such institutions was far smaller than in the 1980s. A corporation favored with access to cheap loans from the government or from its main bank was not generally free to use those funds to "speculate" in land or in the shares of other corporations. Nor was the firm allowed to buy back its own shares, when it should have had plenty of profitable new projects in which to invest.[82] Thus the arbitrage between the interest rate and real assets that we take for granted in a market-oriented system was not entirely relevant in the earlier period.

As noted, firms have begun to rely less on banks for their financing and more on marketplace borrowing, due in large part to deregulation and internationalization. The most important liberalizations include:

(a) the removal of ceilings on interest rates after 1978 (in response to growing reluctance on the part of banks to absorb growing quantities of government debt at artificially low interest rates);

(b)   the switch to a presumption that firms were allowed to sell bonds to foreign residents (as part of the Foreign Exchange Law Reform) in 1980;

(c)   the legalization of warrant bonds in 1981;

(d)   the legalization of non-collateralized bonds for sufficiently safe corporations beginning in 1983;

(e)   the liberalization of issues of Euroyen bonds as part of the yen/dollar negotiations between the Ministry of Finance and the US Treasury in 1984.

More recent measures taken pursuant to the Yen/Dollar Agreement include:

(f)   establishment of new short-term financial markets (in yen-denominated banker's acceptances, June 1985,[83] short-term bonds, November 1986, and commercial paper, November 1987);

(g)   further liberalization regarding the Euromarket (such as allowing foreign companies to lead-manage Eurobond issues in December 1986, and introducing rating systems for Eurobonds in 1987);

(h)   establishment of an offshore market in Japan (December 1986);

(i)   the admission of major American securities companies to the Tokyo Stock Exchange (approximately 22 by the end of 1987);

(j)   inclusion of foreign firms in the syndicate through which the Japanese government sells its bonds and in the trust business (nine banks authorized after October 1985);

(k)   in addition, the Ministry of Finance liberalized restrictions on what share of their portfolios Japanese insurance companies and trust banks could hold in the form of foreign securities (in 1986 and 1987).[84]

Note that even for those steps that represent domestic innovation or deregulation as opposed to international liberalization, foreigners have been an important driving force. There has been both direct political pressure on the Japanese government from foreign governments and competitive pressures on Japanese financial institutions from the activities of foreign rivals.[85]

By 1989 Japanese bond issues in the Euroyen market, which had been growing rapidly for ten years, reached 40 percent of total public corporate issues.[86] Often the Eurobonds issued by Japanese corporations, particularly convertible and warrant issues, were ultimately acquired by *Japanese* residents. Hale (1990: 5) estimates that 60–70 percent of Japanese corporate bonds issued in the Euromarket in 1989 were bought by Japanese investors. In this way internationalization facilitates an end-run around remaining domestic Japanese rigidities, and makes Japanese finance more competitive, even when neither the borrower nor the lender is foreign. The transactions costs that remain in Japanese financial markets are large enough to be exploited by major corporations that take money raised at a low interest rate offshore and invest it in other financial instruments, an example of earning profits by *zaiteku* or financial engineering.[87]

In a follow-up to their first paper, Hoshi, Kashyap and Sharfstein (1990b) address the gradual weakening of the links between banks and affiliated firms that has been taking place in Japan. Choosing 1983 as the first year in which the effects of deregulation were fully felt, they begin with their sample of firms that had close banking ties during the period 1977–82, and divide it into a subsample that shifted emphasis thereafter from bank borrowing to direct market finance, and a subsample that continued to rely primarily on their banks. They find that the former group developed a strong sensitivity of investment to cash flow after 1983, while the latter group did not. This constitutes further evidence that bank borrowing in Japan obviates some of the usual costs of external financing.

4.3   Is the Shift to Market Finance Good or Bad?

Some have surmised that if public policy and the main bank system have kept the cost of capital artificially low in Japan in the past, the deregulation and internationalization of Japanese financial markets must now have eliminated that advantage. Even if we could be confident that that Japanese cost of capital has been raised in this manner, that would still leave open the question of whether or not the traditional system produced a greater level of economic efficiency for the economy overall. On the one hand, any way of obviating information or incentive problems must represent a gain; on the other, the exclusion of certain firms and certain industries from the privileges of cheaper financing is only beneficial if there exists some decision-making mechanism superior to the market to decide who is worthy of inclusion and who is not, a debatable proposition.

It is also possible that the previous system of denying Japanese savers, banks, and taxpayers an opportunity to earn an equilibrium rate of return on their savings, even if inefficient in the economists' sense that it failed to maximize intertemporal welfare, nevertheless produced an (artificially) high level of investment. Zielinski and Holloway (1991: 152) speak of "chronic overinvestment in plant and equipment" resulting from cheap capital, at the expense of that Japanese public. Such a proposition would be consistent with the legendary Japanese corporate emphasis on maximizing market share at the short-run expense of current profits.[88] Blinder (1991) also argues that Japanese corporations maximize growth rather than profits, and includes among the implications the proposition that Japanese firms act *as if* they have a lower cost of capital than American firms. Horiuchi (1990: 26) attributes a corporate emphasis on growth rather than shareholder profits to managers maximizing their own personal objectives, protected from the sort of merger-and-acquisition activity that disciplines managers under the US system.

An alternative line of argument is that it is the US system that is inefficient, in which case it would appear that American pressure on Japan to speed financial liberalization constitutes an effort to "drag the Japanese down to the US level." Hatsopoulos, Krugman and Summers (1988) argue that the US market system gives rise to an inefficiently low level of investment because of excessive concern with short-term profits and capital gains, at the expense of longer-term investment opportunities. McKinnon and Robinson (1989) argue that excessively short investment horizons in the United States (in contrast to Japan) are attributable to high interest rates, which are in turn attributable to the risk of dollar depreciation against the yen under the floating exchange rate system.[89]

In any case, a puzzle remains. If the effective cost of capital under the traditional system is less than the market interest rate under the new system, why are Japanese firms voluntarily giving up their advantageous main-banking relationships for the difficulties of the marketplace? Hodder (1988a) concludes that if firms are leaving their main bank relationships, it must be because it is advantageous to do so, though he also concludes that it must have been advantageous for them to enter into these relationships in the first place.

Hoshi, Kashyap and Sharfstein (1990a) suggest a possible explanation of the paradox: there are hidden costs to the system of bank monitoring; and a cheaper way of overcoming the information and incentive obstacles to borrowing – which is available only to older, well-established, successful firms – is to take advantage of the firm's reputation by issuing highly rated bonds. It is noteworthy that agencies that rate the creditworthiness of corporations (the analogues of Moody's or Standard and Poor's) did not develop in Japan until recently. One might interpret the finding of Ando and Auerbach (1990) that the required rate of return in Japan declines with the size of the corporation as evidence that larger companies are indeed better able to develop reputations and thereby overcome obstacles to borrowing.

There are alternatives to the hypothesis that the corporate migration away from reliance on banking relationships is the manifestation of newly exploitable reputations. It is possible that the trend is not even desirable from the viewpoint of the well-established firms. One approach would be to model cooperation between a firm and its main bank as an equilibrium which is only sustainable in a repeated game if the relevant discount rate is sufficiently low. There is a temptation in each period for defection from the relationship: when the corporation is experiencing bad times, the bank will be tempted to defect, and when the corporation is experiencing good times it will itself be tempted to defect. Only if the discount rate is low will the prospective future benefits of continuing the relationship (the avoidance of information problems via monitoring) be sufficiently important to sustain the cooperation. It could then be argued that, because the interest rate has in the past been lower in Japan than in the United States, it has been easier to sustain such cooperative relationships. But now that the relevant interest rate in Japan has risen to the world level, it is harder to sustain such cooperation, and long-term banking relationships are coming apart.

It may not be possible for trust and long-term relationships to survive in an environment where newcomers deal only in explicit contracts. Rajan (1991) develops a model with precisely this property. In this model, the private information that a bank obtains with regard to a firm's sequence of investment projects gives the bank some monopoly power, which it is able to exploit by extracting rents from the firm in the terms of short-term loans. When an arms-length bond market is then introduced, some firms will switch their financing to it (notwithstanding the problem that investors lack information about the firm) in order to escape the bank's clutches. Even though such firms find it in their private interest to switch, the result may be a net loss in efficiency for the economy, due to the loss of banks' monitoring role. It is likely that some firms will gain from a switch to a market system while others will lose.

Meerschwam (1990: 6–7) acknowledges the possibility that "insiders," those corporations with access to preferentially priced funds, may in the past have had an advantage over "outsiders," and that this advantage was lost when the latter gained access to the escape route of borrowing abroad. If the outsiders had previously been subsidizing the insiders, their escape from the closed system may have driven up the cost of capital for the former.[90]

5   CONCLUSIONS

The overall conclusions that emerge from the literature may be summarized as follows:

(a)   The cost of capital was lower in Japan than in the United States in the 1970s and 1980s.

(b)   Two aspects of this difference were lower real interest rates and low required returns on equity.

(c)   Low real interest rates and high expected growth rates can go far toward explaining the high *levels* of equity and land prices (relative to earnings and rents, respectively), but not the great *increases* of the 1980s.

(d) The high Japanese saving rate was responsible for the low real interest rates and low required returns on equity; Japanese tax policy plays no clear role.

(e) The main bank system has effectively reduced the cost of capital for affiliated corporations below what they would have had to pay bond holders to compensate them for problems of incentive and information regarding investment projects.

Further conclusions of this paper are as follows:

(f) It was possible for the real interest rate in Japan in the 1980s to be below that in the United States, despite international arbitrage.

(g) The main relevant effect of the internationalization in Japan may have been to accelerate the process whereby corporate finance becomes market-oriented, so that:

(h) affiliated firms are losing the special privilege of borrowing at a cheaper rate; while:

(i) unaffiliated firms and others that may have been exploited by their banks are now able to borrow more cheaply than before, at the going market interest rate.

(j) The increased availability of funds that can be used for asset-market arbitrage allowed the great run-up in equity prices and land prices in the 1980s.

Finally, the events of 1990 suggest some additional conclusions:

(k) Increases in interest rates and declines in the stock market in Japan in 1990 have left the cost of capital there approximately as high as in the United States.

(l) Given the earlier international financial liberalization and integration, the post-1990 increase in the cost of capital in Japan may hurt borrowers in the US and elsewhere almost as much as Japanese corporate borrowers.

NOTES

1 Early claims that Japanese firms had a cost-of-capital advantage over American competitors include Hatsopoulos (1983) and Semiconductor Industry Association (1980). Poterba (1991) offers a concise summary.
2 For example, Meerschwam (1989, 1990) and Hodder (1988b, 1991).
3 For example, by Balassa and Noland (1988: 113).
4 For example, Hatsopoulos and Brooks (1986, 1987) and, especially, Hatsopoulos, Krugman and Summers (1988). Lippens (1991) argues that a wide

variety of estimates from different studies support the claim that US industry labors under a higher cost of capital than Japanese industry.

5 The three-way breakdown was calculated by Friend and Tokutsu (1987), among others.

6 Their figures were 0.2, 0.3, or 0.9, depending on whether expected inflation is estimated, respectively, by the inflation rate over the preceding year, the average *ex post* rate, or a simple ARIMA model.

7 Kester and Luehrman (1989) find no systematic difference.

8 The US net national saving rate – the amount of private saving, net of depreciation, left after financing the government budget deficit – declined from 5.9 percent of GNP in 1980 to 2.6 percent in 1989. In Japan the net national saving rate rose from 18.3 percent in 1980 to 19.7 percent in 1989 (the statistics are from the *OECD National Accounts*). One of many possible references on the capital inflow that resulted from the shift in the US monetary/fiscal mix in the 1980s is Frankel (1988a). References on the forces behind the inflow from Japan in particular are given in Frankel (1988b).

9 A value is given of 0.58 according to French and Poterba (1989: 40) (average of first quarters of 1986, 1987 and 1988); they use long-term government bond yields, minus previous year's inflation rate.

10 *Currency Forecasters' Digest*, ed. Alan Teck (White Plains, N.Y.). I obtained this data by subscription to the Institute for International Economics.

11 Other references include Abegglen and Stalk (1985); Bisignano (1990: 38); Borio (1990: 26–31); Crum and Meerschwam (1986); Frost (1987: 41); Gerlach (1989: 153–4); McCauley and Zimmer (1989: 21); Meerschwam (1989); and Nakatani (1984).

12 Caves and Uekusa (1976: 480) suggest that highly leveraged firms are more likely to collude, as a way to reduce risk. On the so-called recession cartels, see Yamamura (1982) and Meerschwam (1989: 17).

13 The debt–equity ratio actually fell to half the US level in an estimate for 1988 (according to French and Poterba 1989: 8 and table 4; and Bisignano 1990: chart 3). Others' figures show the Japanese ratio still above the US level (for example, Frost 1987: 41; and McCauley and Zimmer 1989: 13). Borio (1990: 8–11) also shows the Japanese debt–asset ratio still above the US level as of 1987, even for the measure that uses market values (which shows greater convergence).

14 We save until later the argument that firms may have access to some funds that are cheaper than the expected rate of return on capital (that internal financing is cheaper than *either* the cost of debt or the cost of equity).

15 How does the use of price–earnings ratios bias the calculation, relative to a more correct calculation that would use free cash flow, which subtracts off investment, in place of earnings? More of earnings are thought to go to net investment in Japan than in the United States, in line with its higher growth rate. The implication is that the true equity cost of capital r_e was even lower in Japan than would appear from our attempt in the next section to apply the capitalization formula to the price–earnings ratio.

16 Minimum dividend-payout rates were established in the early 1970s (Meerschwam 1989).

17 For example, Zielinski and Holloway (1991: 167).

18 This is the same direction of bias suggested in note 15.

19 When Ando and Auerbach applied a corresponding correction for their measure of total return to capital, on the other hand, they found that the median rate for Japan fell more than that for the US.

20 When Aron (1989) converted the Japanese price–earnings ratio to US accounting practices, and adjusted for cross-holding, he lowered it from a reported 49.6 in 1989 to 19.1 (compared to 13.5 in the United States).

21 A possibility that does not appear to have been considered is that Japanese investors are less risk-averse than American investors, and Japanese stocks – for whatever reason – are held primarily by Japanese investors. This hypothesis has the virtue that, in commonly specified intertemporal utility functions, the parameter determining risk-aversion is the same as the parameter determining the rate of time preference; the claim that Japanese are less impatient than Americans sounds more familiar than the hypothesis that they are less risk-averse.

22 Hale (1987: 1).

23 Shoven (1989). See also Noguchi (1985).

24 Consistent with the findings of Shoven and Tachibanaki (1988). Kikutani and Tachibanaki (1990: 287–8) fine-tune the earlier calculations (particularly with regard to depreciation); they conclude that the 1980 marginal tax rate on capital in Japan was again lower than in the United States, primarily due to the tax-advantage of debt. They also find that the Japanese marginal tax rate was as low in 1961 as in 1980.

25 The tax rate on undistributed profits during the period 1984 to 1987 was 43.3 percent (Homma, Maeda and Hashimoto 1986: 14; and Homma 1987: 21). However, it had been lower in the 1950s and 1960s, ranging from 35 percent to 40 percent (Homma et al. 1984: 124, table 2.39; and Shoven and Tachibanaki 1988: table 3.6).

26 Recall the figures from French and Poterba that by 1988 the debt–equity ratio in Japan had fallen below that in the United States. Noguchi (1985: 9, 18) listed the fall in the debt–equity ratio as one of several reasons why the tax burden on Japanese investment increased in the late 1970s and early 1980s (though, like Ando and Auerbach, Noguchi thought that the Japanese burden had been higher than the US burden all along). The most important of the reasons (as with Shoven) was the fall in the inflation rate.

27 The previously existing pro-saving bias in the Japanese tax system, compared to the American system, constituted part of the difference in "tax wedges" computed by Bernheim and Shoven (1987). It is discussed below, under the topic of determinants of the real interest rate in Japan.

28 Gerlach (1989: 156–62).

29 The observed re-reversal of size, even when no account is taken of cross-holdings, came in March 1990. See for example, Zielinski and Holloway (1991: 5).

30 Ueda (1990: 357) found that the market value of corporate shares after 1983 surpassed the officially reported value of corporate assets including land. But in the final version of his paper he does not rule out the possibility that land

prices were a major factor in the rise in stock prices, in light of claims that the official land prices greatly understate true land values.

31   Iwata and Yoshida (1988: 509).

32   Ito (1989). In 1987 the average price of usable land in Japan was 90 times that in the US, according to Boone (1989b).

33   In 1984, the value of land in Japan was 3.17 times GNP, while in the US it was only 0.80 times GNP (Sachs and Boone 1988).

34   For example, Sachs and Boone (1988) or Boone (1989a).

35   About five times higher than London. Boone (1989b: 47) estimated that the price of land in Tokyo was 150 times that in New York, despite little difference in rental rates on apartments and buildings.

36   On the last point, see K. Takagi (1989).

37   Rose (1990: 13, 33) claimed support for a model of land values across 27 cities (with significant coefficients on population and income), but only when Tokyo was excluded from the sample as an "outlier."

38   Interestingly, *American* respondents at all survey dates are far more pessimistic about the Japanese market than Japanese respondents. Shiller, Kon-ya and Tsutsui (1991b) interpret this finding as support for the claim of French and Poterba (1990) – based on the observation that investors in each country each hold most of their portfolios in their own country's assets – that investors in each country expect the rate of return on their own stock market to be higher than on the other's.

39   The Ministry of Finance began to look after the stability of the Japanese stock market after a crash in 1965. S. Takagi (1989) discussed the history and institutional features of the market.

40   Lawler, Loopesko, and Dudey (1988: 31–3); Murphy (1989); and Zielinski and Holloway (1991: 71–4).

41   The Japanese respondents attribute their October 1987 crash to contemporaneous US developments. But, like American respondents, they rate news of price movements themselves as a more important influence on their behavior than news regarding fundamentals.

42   Aggarwal, Rao, and Hiraki (1990) found evidence in the Tokyo Stock Exchange that stocks with low PERs had higher returns than stocks with high PERs (as others have found in the United States).

43   In the March 1990 version of their 1989 paper, French and Poterba had the misfortune to write, "Real interest rates increased by approximately 1.0 percent in January 1990. If the argument that movements of this magnitude were central in pushing up share prices [after 1985] is correct, prices should have fallen more sharply in the 1990 episode than they have at this writing" (29). The present section of the paper updates this premature computation.

44   This situation is not uncommon among countries (Abel, Mankiw, Summers, and Zeckhauser 1989: 3).

45   As noted earlier, the capitalization formula does not strictly apply to PERs, because the portion of earnings that are reinvested are not available as returns to the stockholder. (This just makes the gap between the discount rate–growth rate differential and the PER that much harder to explain.) One would be on firmer theoretical foundations to match up the calculations

reported in this section to observations on the price–dividend ratio, for the case of stocks, or the price–rental ratio, for the case of land. Unfortunately, reliable recent data for land are not available.

46 For example, the small further rise in the US discount rate between December 1990 and July 1991, also shown in table 1.3, is sufficient to wipe out half the 1989–90 change.

47 Hatsopoulos and Poterba (1991: table 6) report adjusted PERs up through 1990 (while adjusting accounting earnings in a way that they now regard as better than the adjustments made in French and Poterba 1989). They conclude that the adjusted PER, even after the 1990 crash, is still higher in Japan than in the United States. But the difference is much smaller than it was during the period 1983–9.

48 In 1988 Japan agreed with other major countries, through the Bank for International Settlements in Basel, to raise the minimum capital–asset ratios of its international banks to 8 percent by 1993 (the same as other countries' international banks). Japanese banks were initially able to attain this ratio easily by issuing large amounts of equity on the booming stock market. But the 1990 stock market plunge put many of the banks back below the 8 percent capital–asset ratio (Hale 1990; and Zielinski and Holloway 1991: 179–88).

49 Indeed, Balassa and Noland (1988: 84) reported that the Japanese corporate sector was in surplus in the years 1974–7, although others showed only a declining deficit (where both financial and non-financial corporations were included; Lincoln 1988: table 3.2, 76–7).

50 Major European countries lie between these two extremes. (The statistics are from the *OECD Economic Outlook*, July 1991, 3.)

51 According to Blades (1988: 18–19), adjusting for consumer durables in 1986 raises the US household gross saving ratio from 11.5 percent to 22.1 percent, while only raising the Japanese ratio from 21.2 percent to 25.8 percent. When the saving ratios are averaged over 1970–86, adjusting raises the US ratio to 23.6 percent and the Japanese ratio to 26.1 percent. See also Balassa and Noland (1988: 80–96). Takayama et al. (1988) go so far as to say, on the basis of several accounting corrections, that the Japanese saving rate is not high at all.

52 Emmott (1989: 25–90 and 249–53) foresees that the demographic trends will lead not only to a decline in Japanese saving rates but also to a decline in foreign fear of Japanese financial power.

53 To be precise, it is the only major industrialized country that (in pretense at least) does not officially allow nuclear weapons on its territory.

54 Horioka (1988: 218).

55 Frankel (1988b: fn. 33).

56 Similarly, Maki (1989) concludes that to reduce the saving rate and thereby the trade surplus, among "the urgent policies in Japan is to depress land price increases, especially in urban areas."

57 Horioka (1988: 219), on the other hand, reports that although Japanese families *plan* down payment ratios of 45 to 55 percent, *actual* down payments are as low as 20 percent. He argues (229) that an increase in the availability

of mortgage credit would not decrease total saving, but would only result in a combination of lower prepurchase saving (to make the down payment) and higher postpurchase saving (to pay off the loan).

58   Ministry of Finance (1988); Shoven (1989); and Zielinski and Holloway (1991: 31).

59   Glick (1987) and Glick and Hutchison (1990) examine real interest differentials among Japan and other Pacific countries in particular.

60   The story of the US Treasury campaign for the liberalization of Japanese financial markets, which began in October 1983, is told in Frankel (1984).

61   Otani and Tiwari (1981); Frankel (1984, 1988a, 1988b); Eken (1984); and Ito (1986).

62   The interest differential could in theory be explained by either of two terms (after the possibility of a covered interest differential, or political premium, has been eliminated), both associated with the currency: expected depreciation or an exchange risk premium. The possible exchange risk premium between the dollar and yen is examined by Fukao and Okuba (1984); Fukao (1987); Frankel and Froot (1987); Ito (1988); and Frankel (1988b).

63   The section on long-term real appreciation of the yen in Frankel (1991a) attributes the 1950–89 trend (which averaged in excess of 3.5 percent per year) to a steady increase in the Japanese price of non-traded goods relative to traded goods.

64   Survey data on the yen are used in Frankel and Froot (1987); Ito (1990); and Froot and Ito (1989).

65   One must note, however, that if "the" real interest rate were lower in Japan than the United States only because of an expected rate of real appreciation of the yen in terms of a basket of goods that includes non-traded goods, it can only explain high equity prices or a low cost of capital *within the non-traded goods sector*, or for the average across the entire economy. It cannot explain a low cost of capital for Japanese firms producing *traded* goods, which are the ones from whom American businessmen fear competition.

66   Note that this does not preclude some firms having projects with rates of return greater than the market rate or internal funding sources at costs less than the market rate; it requires only that the market rate be the marginal cost of funds for most firms.

67   Other cross-country studies of corporate finance structure include Mayer (1988); and Bisignano (1990).

68   For example, Tamura (1987).

69   Abegglen and Stalk (1985); and Hodder and Tschoegl (1985).

70   For example, Bernanke and Gertler (1989) in the macroeconomic literature; and Myers and Majluf (1984), and Jensen and Meckling (1976) in the finance literature. The first two focus on information costs, the last on incentive problems. For a concise statement of this literature, see Hubbard (1990).

71   More net financing of investment comes from retained earnings in the United States (and the United Kingdom) than in Japan and other countries with bank-oriented financial systems. Mayer (1988) argues that the absence of long-term banking relationships in the former countries is a handicap that forces corporations to rely on retained earnings.

72 Aoki (1984: 195, 219; 1989: 99–138) examines the increased reliance on internal finance in the 1970s. He argues that firms could have advantageously cut dividend payout rates in the 1960s and obtained more of their financing internally, but were kept from doing so by powerful banks who encouraged their clients to overborrow.

73 For example, Crum and Meerschwan (1986); Hamada and Horiuchi (1987); Hodder (1988a,b); and Hoshi, Kashyap, and Sharfstein (1990a,b).

74 Horiuchi, Packer and Fukuda (1990) test the alternative hypothesis proposed by some that the key element of the main bank relationship is risk-sharing (for example, Nakatani 1984, who finds that the profit rates and growth rates for group-affiliated firms are less variable than for independent firms), as opposed to minimizing information problems. They find no evidence to support the alternative.

75 On the general point that the apparent cost of borrowing is understated in Japan by the requirement of compensating balances, see, for example, Bronte (1982: 17).

76 For example, Jorgenson (1971); and Meyer and Kuh (1957).

77 Hayashi and Inoue (1990) find that Q is significantly related to firm growth, and that much, though not all, of the power of cash flow to explain investment in a cross-section of Japanese firms disappears when correcting for the endogeneity of cash flow. They do not segregate affiliated and non-affiliated firms.

78 Crum and Meerschwam (1986) and Meerschwam (1989), for example, discuss the decline of "relationship banking," and its replacement by the market. See also Kyuno (1989: 5).

79 Despite the diminished importance of subsidized government lending and the main bank system, the era of cheaper capital through internal finance was prolonged past 1973 in Japan by the greater availability of retained earnings when the number of profitable investment projects that needed to be financed diminished after the oil shock. The share of funds coming from internal finance narrowly defined (retained earnings and depreciation charges), as opposed to external finance (securities issues and borrowings), rose from 32.9 percent in the period 1970–4 to 46.3 percent in the period 1975–8, and stayed in that neighborhood subsequently (1979–85; see Tamura 1987: 3). It is the changes of the 1980s that need explaining, not the changes after 1973.

80 When markets in government bonds and other instruments did begin to develop, especially in the 1970s, the observed interest rate was presumably somewhere between the low cost of internal and subsidized finance and the high rate of return to physical investment.

81 As noted in Meerschwam (1989), only pre-existing shareholders received advantageous new-share subscription rights.

82 The commercial code still prohibits companies from buying back their own shares (Hatsopoulos and Brooks 1987: 12; and Zielinski and Holloway 1991: 106, 226).

83 Volume in the yen-denominated BA market soon began to decline, however, in favor of other instruments, and it died out completely in November 1989 (*Nihon Keizai Shimbun*, Dec. 14, 1989).

84   Lincoln (1988: 130–210); Shinkai (1988); Hoshi, Kashyap, and Sharfstein (1990a); Crum and Meerschwam (1986); Feldman (1986); Frankel (1984); Sakakibara and Kondoh (1984); Suzuki (1987); Ido (1989); and Bisignano (1990: 41–5), among many other sources.
85   Rosenbluth (1989) examines the various political and market forces that brought about Japanese financial liberalization.
86   Bisignano (1990: 42 and table 8).
87   Emmott (1989: 108–12) suggests that only government regulation kept Japanese corporations until the 1980s dependent on bank borrowing, and that all parties in Japan are now benefitting from the changes. Deregulation of domestic securities markets and, especially, the opportunity to issue securities abroad have recently allowed corporations to obtain cheaper funds in the Euromarket (see also Rosenbluth 1989: 137–166). The shift has also benefited Japan's securities firms. Even Japan's banks are compensated for the loss of domestic loan business by the opportunity to underwrite corporate securities abroad, a business from which they are still excluded at home under Article 65 (the equivalent of the American Glass–Steagall Act, which was written into Japan's financial system during the postwar occupation).
88   For example, Abegglen and Stalk (1985); Crum and Meerschwam (1986); and Meerschwam (1989).
89   Stein (1989) offers a theory with more rigorous foundations.
90   To validate this hypothesis, one would like evidence that banks and other financial institutions are supplying less credit to their previously privileged domestic clients (or offering less-favorable terms), and instead taking advantage of the higher interest rates in the United States by lending abroad.

REFERENCES

Abegglen, James and Stalk, George, Jr 1985: *Kaisha: the Japanese corporation.* New York: Basic Books.
Abel, A., Mankiw, N.G., Summers, L. and Zeckhauser, R. 1989: Assessing dynamic efficiency: theory and evidence. *Economic Studies*, 56(1), 1–26.
Aggarwal, Raj, Rao, Ramesh and Hiraki, Takato 1990: Regularities in security returns on the Tokyo Stock Exchange: P/E, size, and seasonal influences. *Journal of Financial Research*, 13, Fall.
Ando, Albert and Auerbach, Alan 1988a: The corporate cost of capital in the US and Japan: a comparison, NBER Working Paper no. 1762. In J. Shoven (ed.), *Government Policy Towards Industry in the United States and Japan*, New York: Cambridge University Press, 21–49.
Ando, Albert and Auerbach, Alan 1988b: The cost of capital in the US and Japan: a comparison, NBER Working Paper no. 2286. *Journal of the Japanese and International Economies*, 2(2), 134–58.
Ando, Albert and Auerbach, Alan 1990: The cost of capital in Japan: recent evidence and further results, NBER Working Paper no. 3371. *Journal of the Japanese and International Economies*, 3(4), 323–50.

Aoki, Masahiko 1984: Shareholders' non-unanimity on investment financing: banks vs. individual investors. In M. Aoki (ed.), *The Economic Analysis of the Japanese Firm*, Amsterdam: North-Holland, 193–224.

Aoki, Masahiko 1989: *Information, Incentives and Bargaining in the Japanese Economy*. Cambridge: Cambridge University Press.

Aoki, Masahiko 1990: Toward an economic model of the Japanese firm. *Journal of Economic Literature*, 28 (March) 1–27.

Aoki, Masahiko 1991: The Japanese firm as a system: survey and research agenda. Harvard–Stanford Workshop on Economic Policy, Kennedy School of Government, November.

Aron, Paul 1989: Japanese P/E multiples: the tradition continues. *Japanese Research Report*, no. 35, Daiwa Securities America, Inc., October 23.

Auerbach, A., Kotlikoff, L., Hagemann, R. and Nicoletti, G. 1989: The economic dynamics of an ageing population: the case of four OECD countries, NBER Working Paper no. 2797. *OECD Economic Studies*, 12 (Spring) 97–130.

Balassa, Bela and Noland, Marcus 1988: *Japan in the World Economy*. Washington, D.C.: Institute for International Economics.

Baldwin, Carliss 1986: The capital factor: competing or capital in a global environment. In Michael Porter (ed.), *Competition in Global Industries*, Boston, Mass.: Harvard Business School Press, 185–223.

Bernanke, Ben and Gertler, Mark 1989: Agency costs, net worth and business fluctuations. *American Economic Review*, 79, 14–31.

Bernheim, Douglas and Shoven, John 1987: Taxation and the cost of capital: an international comparison. In C.E. Walker and M.A. Bloomfield (eds), *The Consumption Tax: a better alternative?*, Cambridge, Mass.: Ballinger, 61–85.

Bisignano, Joseph 1990: Structures of financial intermediation, corporate finance, and central banking. Basel: Bank for International Settlements, Dec.

Blades, Derek 1988: Household saving ratios for Japan and other OECD countries. In *Global Role of the Japanese Economy with Affluent Savings and Accumulated Wealth*. Papers and proceedings of the Fifth EPA International symposium, Tokyo, Oct. 13–14.

Blinder, Alan 1991: Profit maximization and international competition. In R. O'Brien (ed.), *Finance and the International Economy*, The AMEX Bank Review Prize Essays, Oxford: Oxford University Press.

Boone, Peter 1989a: High land values in Japan: is the archipelago worth eleven trillion dollars? Harvard University, Nov.

Boone, Peter 1989b: Perspectives on the high price of Japanese land. Harvard University, June; and EPA Discussion Paper no. 45.

Borio, C.E.V. 1990: Leverage and financing of non-financial companies: an international perspective. *BIS Economic Papers* 27, Basel: Bank for International Settlements.

Bronte, Stephen 1982: *Japanese Finance: markets and institutions*. London: Euromoney Publications.

Caves, Richard and Uekusa, Masu 1976: Industrial organization. In Hugh Patrick and Henry Rosovsky (eds), *Asia's New Giant*, Washington, D.C.: Brookings Institution, 459–523.

Crum, M. Colyer and Meerschwam, David 1986: From relationship to price banking: the loss of regulatory control. In T. McCraw (ed.), *America vs. Japan*, Boston, Mass.: Harvard Business School Press.

Dekle, Robert and Summers, Lawrence 1991: Japan's high saving rate reaffirmed, NBER Working Paper no. 3690, April. *Bank of Japan Monetary and Economic Studies*, 9(2), 63–78.

Eken, Sena 1984: Integration of domestic and international financial markets: the bequests of the Japanese elderly. *Economic Letters*, 29, 129–33.

Dekle, Robert 1990: Alternative estimates of Japanese saving and comparisons with the US: can the capital gains to land be included in "Saving"? Bank of Japan and Boston University, December.

Dekle, Robert and Summers, Lawrence 1991: Japan's high saving rate reaffirmed, NBER Working Paper no. 3690, April. *Bank of Japan Monetary and Economic Studies*, 9(2), 63–78.

Eken, Sena 1984: Integration of domestic and international financial markets: the Japanese experience. *International Monetary Fund Staff Papers*, no. 31, 499–548.

Emmott, Bill 1989: *The Sun Also Sets: the limits of Japan's economic power*. New York: Times Books.

Fazzari, Steven, Hubbard, R. Glen and Petersen, Bruce 1988: Investment and finance reconsidered. *Brookings Papers on Economic Activity*, 1, 141–96.

Feldman, Robert 1986: *Japanese Financial Markets: deficits, dilemmas, and deregulation*. Cambridge, Mass.: MIT Press.

Feldstein, M. and Bacchetta, P. 1989: National savings and international investment. Forthcoming in D. Bernheim and J. Shoven (eds), *National Saving and Economic Performance*, Chicago: University of Chicago Press.

Feldstein, M. and Horioka, C. 1980: Domestic saving and international capital flows. *Economic Journal*, 90, 314–29.

Frankel, Jeffrey 1984: The Yen/Dollar Agreement: liberalizing Japanese capital markets. *Policy Analyses in International Economics*, no. 9, Institute for International Economics, Washington, D.C.

Frankel, Jeffrey 1988a: International capital flows and domestic economic policies. In M. Feldstein (ed.), *The United States in the World Economy*, Chicago: University of Chicago Press.

Frankel, Jeffrey 1988b: US borrowing from Japan. KSG Working Paper 174D, Harvard University. In G. Luciani (ed.), *Structural Change in the American Financial System*, Rome: Fondazione Adriano Olivetti, 1989; excerpts (translated into Japanese) in *Kinyu Journal*, July 1988 and February 1989. To be reprinted in D. Das (ed.), *International Finance*, London: Rontledge.

Frankel, Jeffrey 1991a: Japanese finance: a survey. In Paul Krugman (ed.), *Trade with Japan: has the door opened wider?*, Chicago: University of Chicago Press; revised version in *Financial Management*, Spring 1991.

Frankel, Jeffrey 1991b: Quantifying international capital mobility in the 1980s, NBER Working Paper no. 2856. In D. Bernheim and J. Shoven (eds), *National Saving and Economic Performance*, Chicago: University of Chicago Press.

Frankel, Jeffrey and Froot, Kenneth 1987: Short-term and long-term expectations of the yen/dollar exchange rates: evidence from survey data. NBER Working

Paper no. 2216, and *Journal of the Japanese and International Economies*, 1, 249–74.

French, Kenneth and Poterba, James 1989: Are Japanese stock prices too high? ["preliminary" version]. CRSP Seminar on the Analysis of Security Prices, University of Chicago, April; revised version, MIT Economics Working Paper no. 547, Feb. 1990; and NBER Working Paper no. 3290, March 1990. Forthcoming as Were Japanese stock prices too high? *Journal of Financial Economics*, 1991.

French, Kenneth and Poterba, James 1990: Japanese and US cross-border common stock investments. *Journal of the Japanese and International Economies*, 4, 476–93.

Friend, Irwin, and Tokutsu, Ichiro 1987: The cost of capital to corporations in Japan and the USA. *Journal of Banking and Finance*, 11, 313–27.

Froot, Kenneth and Ito, Takatoshi 1989: On the consistency of short-run and long-run exchange rate expectations. NBER Working Paper no. 2577; and *Journal of International Money and Finance*, 8(4), 487–510.

Frost, Ellen 1987: *For Richer, For Poorer*. Council on Foreign Relations, New York.

Fukao, Mitsuhiro 1987: A risk premium model of the yen–dollar and DM–dollar exchange rates. *OECD Economic Studies*, 9, autumn, 79–104.

Fukao, Mitsuhiro 1988: Balance of payments imbalances and long-term capital movements: review and prospects. In Masaru Yoshitomi (ed.), *Correcting External Imbalances*, Tokyo: Economic Planning Agency.

Fukao, Mitsuhiro and Okubo, T. 1984: International linkage of interest rates: the case of Japan and the United States. *International Economic Review*, 25, February.

Gerlach, Michael 1989: *Keiretsu* organization in the Japanese economy: analysis and trade implications. In Chalmers Johnson, Laura d'Andrea Tyson and John Zysman (eds), *Politics and Productivity: the real story of why Japan works*, Cambridge, Mass.: Ballinger.

Glick, Reuven 1987: Interest rate linkages in the Pacific Basin. *Federal Reserve Bank of San Francisco Economic Review*, no. 3, 31–42.

Glick, Reuven and Hutchison, Michael 1990: Financial liberalization in the Pacific Basin: implications for real interest rate linkages. *Journal of the Japanese and International Economies*, 4, 36–48.

Hale, David 1987: Tax reform in the US and Japan: the movement towards international tax convergence. US–Japan Consultative Group on International Monetary Affairs, San Diego, February.

Hale, David 1989: The Japanese Ministry of Finance and dollar diplomacy during the late 1980s: or, how the University of Tokyo Law School saved the United States from the University of Chicago Economics Department. Chicago: Kemper Financial Services.

Hale, David 1990: Economic consequences of the Tokyo stock market crash. US–Japan Consultative Group on International Monetary Affairs, Washington, D.C., July 23.

Hamada, Koichi and Horiuchi, Akiyoshi 1987: The political economy of the financial market. In Kozo Yamamura and Yasukichi Yasuba (eds), *The Poli-*

tical Economy of Japan, vol. 1: *The Domestic Transformation*, Stanford, Cali.: Stanford University Press, 223–60.

Hardouvelis, Gikas and Peristiani, Steve 1989: Do margin requirements matter? Evidence from the Japanese stock market. Federal Reserve Bank of New York, October.

Hardouvelis, Gikas and Peristiani, Steve 1990: Margin requirements, speculative trading and stock price fluctuations: the case of Japan. Federal Reserve Bank of New York Research Paper no. 90-06, July; revised, Jan. 1991.

Hatsopoulos, George 1983: High cost of capital: handicap of American industry. Study sponsored by the American Business Conference and Thermo Electron Corp., April.

Hatsopolous, George 1991: The cost of capital: reflections of a CEO. *Business Economics*, 26(2), 7–14.

Hatsopoulos, George and Brooks, Stephen 1986: The gap in the cost of capital: causes, effects, and remedies. In Ralph Landau and Dale Jorgenson (eds), *Technology and Economic Policy*, Cambridge, Mass.: Ballinger, 221–80.

Hatsopoulos, George and Brooks, Stephen 1987: The cost of capital in the United States and Japan. International Conference on the Cost of Capital, Kennedy School of Government, Harvard University.

Hatsopoulos, George, Krugman, Paul and Summers, Larry 1988: US competitiveness: beyond the trade deficit. *Science*, July 15, 299–307.

Hatsopoulos, George and Poterba, James 1991: Rates of return on Japanese and US nonfinancial companies: new evidence on international cost of capital differences. Harvard/Stanford Workshop on Economic Policy, Kennedy School of Government, November.

Hayashi, Fumio 1986: Why is Japan's saving rate so apparently high? *NBER Macroeconomics Annual 1986*, vol. 1, Cambridge, Mass.: MIT Press, 147–234.

Hayashi, Fumio 1989: Is Japan's saving rate high? *Federal Reserve Bank of Minneapolis Quarterly Review*, Spring, 3–9.

Hayashi, Fumio 1990: Taxes and corporate investment in Japanese manufacturing, NBER Working Paper no. 1753. In Charles Hulten (ed.), *Productivity Growth in Japan and the United States*, NBER Studies in Income and Wealth, vol. 53, Chicago: University of Chicago Press, 295–316.

Hayashi, Fumio and Inoue, Tohru 1990: The relationship of firm growth and Q with multiple capital goods: theory and evidence from panel data on Japanese firms. Institute for Empirical Macroeconomics Discussion Paper 13, Federal Reserve Bank of Minneapolis; and NBER Working Paper no. 3326, April.

Hayashi, Fumio, Ito, Takatoshi and Slemrod, Joel 1988: Housing finance imperfections, taxation, and private saving: a comparative analysis of the US and Japan. *Journal of the Japanese and International Economies*, 2(3), 215–38.

Hodder, James 1988a: Capital structure and cost of capital in the US and Japan. Stanford University, July.

Hodder, James 1988b: Corporate capital structure in the United States and Japan: financial intermediation and implication of financial deregulation. In J. Shoven (ed.), *Government Policy Towards Industry in the USA and Japan*, Cambridge: Cambridge University Press, 241–63.

Hodder, James 1991: Is the cost of capital lower in Japan? *Journal of the Japanese and International Economies*, 5(1), 86–100.

Hodder, James and Tschoegl, A. 1985: Some aspects of Japanese corporate finance. *Journal of Financial and Quantitative Analysis*, 20(2), 173–90.

Homma, Masaki 1987: An overview of tax reform in the US and Japan. US–Japan Core Group, San Diego, Feb.

Homma, M., Atoda, N., Hayashi, F. and Hata, K. 1984: *Setsubi Toshi to Kigyo Zeisei* [Investment and Corporate Tax Structure], Tokyo: Economic Planning Agency.

Homma, M., Maeda, T. and Hashimoto, K. 1986: The Japanese tax system. *Brookings Discussion Papers in Economics*, June.

Horioka, Charles 1985: The importance of saving for education in Japan. *Kyoto University Economic Review*, 55(1), 41–78.

Horioka, Charles 1986: Why is Japan's private savings rate so high? *Finance and Development*, Dec.

Horioka, Charles 1988: Saving for housing purchase in Japan. In *Global Role of the Japanese Economy with Affluent Savings and Accumulated Wealth*. Papers and proceedings of the Fifth EPA International Symposium, Tokyo, Oct. 13–14; and *Journal of the Japanese and International Economies*, 2(3).

Horioka, Charles 1990: Why is Japan's household saving rate so high? A literature survey. *Journal of the Japanese and International Economies*, 4(1), 49–92.

Horiuchi, Akiyoshi 1990: Some aspects of the capital market mechanism in Japan. Hawaii Conference on International Financial Markets, Center for Japan–US Business and Economics Studies, New York University.

Horiuchi, Akiyoshi, Packer, Frank and Fukuda, Shin'ichi 1990: What role has the "main bank" played in Japan? *Journal of the Japanese and International Economies*, 2(2), 159–80.

Hoshi, Takeo and Kashyap, Anil 1990: Evidence on Q and investment for Japanese firms. *Journal of the Japanese and International Economies*, 4(4), 371–400.

Hoshi, Takeo, Kashyap, Anil and Sharfstein, David 1988: Corporate structure, liquidity, and investment: evidence from Japanese panel data. Sloan Working Paper no. 2071–88, September; reprinted in *Quarterly Journal of Economics*, 1990.

Hoshi, Takeo, Kashyap, Anil and Sharfstein, David 1990a: Bank monitoring and investment: evidence from the changing structure of Japanese corporate banking relationship. NBER Working Paper no. 3079. In R.G. Hubbard (ed.), *Asymmetric Information, Corporate Finance, and Investment*, Chicago: University of Chicago Press, 1990.

Hoshi, Takeo, Kashyap, Anil and Sharfstein, David 1990b: The role of banks in reducing the costs of financial distress in Japan. NBER Working Paper no. 3435; *Journal of Financial Economics*, Sept.

Hubbard, R. Glen 1990: Introduction. In R.G. Hubbard (ed.), *Asymmetric Information, Corporate Finance, and Investment*, Chicago: University of Chicago Press, 1–14.

Ido, Kiyoto 1989: Internationalization and implementation of the new foreign exchange control law. *FAIR Fact Series: Japan's Financial Markets*, vol. 19.

Ishikawa, Tsuneo and Ueda, Kazuo 1984: The bonus payment system and Japanese personal savings. In M. Aoki (ed.), *The Economic Analysis of the Japanese Firm*, Amsterdam: Elsevier Science Publishers, 133–92.

Ito, Takatoshi 1986: Capital controls and covered interest parity. NBER Working Paper no. 1187; and *Economic Studies Quarterly*, 37, 223–41.

Ito, Takatoshi 1988: Use of (time-domain) vector autoregressions to test uncovered interest parity. *Review of Economics and Statistics*, 70, 296–305.

Ito, Takatoshi 1989: Japan's structural adjustment: the land/housing problem and external balance. International Monetary Fund (revised Feb., NBER Summer Institute).

Ito, Takatoshi 1990: Foreign exchange rate expectations: micro survey data. *American Economic Review*, 80(3), 434–49.

Iwata, Kazumasa, Suzuki, Ikuo and Yoshida, Atsushi 1988: Capital costs of housing investment in Japan. Discussion Paper no. 44, Economic Planning Agency, Tokyo, Dec.

Iwata, Kazumasa and Yoshida, Atsushi 1987: Capital cost of business investment in Japan and the United States under tax reform. International Conference on the Cost of Capital, Kennedy School of Government, Harvard University.

Iwata, Kazumasa and Yoshida, Atsushi 1988: Housing, land and taxation system in Japan. In *Global and Domestic Policy Implications of Correcting External Imbalances*. Papers and proceedings of the Fourth EPA International Symposium, Economic Planning Agency, Japan.

Iwata, Kazumasa and Yoshida, Atsushi 1990: Capital cost of business investment in Japan and the United States under tax reform: the case of an open economy. *Japan and the World Economy*, 2.

Jensen, Michael and Meckling, William 1976: Theory of the firm: managerial behavior, agency costs and ownership structure. *Journal of Financial Economics*, 1, 305–60.

Jorgenson, Dale 1971: Econometric studies of investment behavior: a review. *Journal of Economic Literature*, 9, 1111–47.

Kester, W.C. and Luehrman, T. 1989: Real interest rates and the cost of capital: a comparison of the United States and Japan. *Japan and the World Economy*, 1, 199–232.

Kikutani, Tatsuya and Tachibanaki, Toshiaki 1990: Taxation of income from capital in Japan: historical perspectives and policy simulations. In Charles Hulten (ed.), *Productivity Growth in Japan and the United States*, NBER Studies in Income and Wealth, vol. 53, Chicago: University of Chicago Press, 267–93.

Kyuno, Masao 1989: A glimpse of the financial revolution in Japan. *Journal of International Economic Studies*, 3, 1–24.

Lawler, Patrick, Loopesko, Bonnie and Dudey, Marc 1988: An analysis of some aspects of the Japanese stock market. Nov. 10 ["not to circulate or be quoted without permission of authors"].

Lee, Hiro 1988: *Imperfect Competition, Industrial Policy, and Japanese International Competitiveness*, Ph.D. dissertation, University of California, Berkeley, September.

Lincoln, Edward 1988: *Japan: facing economic maturity*. Brookings Institution, Washington, D.C.

Lippens, Robert 1991: The cost of capital: a summary of results for the US and Japan in the 1980s. *Business Economics*, 26(2), 19–25.

Maki, Atsushi 1989: Savings and portfolio behavior of Japanese households: effects of purchasing housing and preparation for retirement. *Japan and the World Economy*, 1(2), 145–62.

Makin, John 1985: Saving rates in Japan and the United States: the roles of tax policy and other factors. Paper prepared for Savings Forum, Philadelphia, May.

Mayer, Colin 1988: New issues in corporate finance. *European Economic Review*, 32(5), 1167–89.

McCauley, Robert and Zimmer, Stephen 1989: Explaining differences in the cost of capital. *Federal Reserve Bank of New York Quarterly Review*, Summer, 7–28.

McDonald, Jack 1989: The *Mochiai* effect: Japanese corporate cross-holdings. *Journal of Portfolio Management*, 16(1), 90–5.

McKinnon, Ronald and Robinson, David 1989: Dollar devaluation, interest rate volatility, and the duration of investment. CEPR Conference on Economic Growth and the Commercialization of New Technologies, Stanford, Cali., September 11–12.

Meerschwam, David 1989: The Japanese financial system and the cost of capital. National Bureau of Economic Research. In Paul Krugman (ed.), *The US and Japan in the '90s*, Chicago: University of Chicago Press.

Meerschwam, David 1990: The United States and Japan's dangerous liaison and the irrelevance of the cost of capital. Harvard Business School.

Meyer, John and Kuh, Ed 1957: *The investment decision*. Cambridge, Mass.: Harvard University Press.

Ministry of Finance 1988: Main points of tax reform. Dec. 24, Tokyo.

Murphy, R. Taggart 1989: Power without purpose: the crisis of Japan's global financial dominance. *Harvard Business Review*, March–April, 71–83.

Myers, Stewart and Majluf, N. 1984: Corporate financing and investment decisions when firms have information that investors do not have. *Journal of Financial Economics*, 13, 187–221.

Nakatani, Iwao 1984: The economic role of financial corporate grouping. In M. Aoki (ed.), *The Economic Analysis of the Japanese Firm*, Amsterdam: Elsevier Science Publishers.

Noguchi, Yukio 1985: Tax structure and saving–investment balance. US–Japan Consultative Group on International Monetary Affairs, Hakone, Japan, March.

Noguchi, Yukio 1987: Land price swollen by bubbles (in Japanese). *Toyo Keizai*, 77, November, 38–45.

Otani, Ichiro 1983: Exchange rate instability and capital controls: the Japanese experience, 1978–81. In D. Bigman and T. Taya (eds), *Exchange Rate and Trade Instability: causes, consequences and remedies*, Cambridge, Mass.: Ballinger.

Otani, Ichiro and Tiwari, Siddath 1981: Capital controls and interest rate parity:

the Japanese experience, 1978–81. *International Monetary Fund Staff Papers*, 28(4), 793–815.

Poterba, James 1991: Comparing the cost of capital in the United States and Japan: a survey of methods. *Federal Researve Bank of New York Quarterly Review* 15, no. 3–4, 20–32.

Prowse, Stephen David 1989: Firm financial behavior in the US and Japan: the role of agency relationships. NBER, August 11.

Rajan, Raghuram 1991: Insiders and outsiders: the choice between relationship and arms length debt. Unpublished, Sloan School, MIT, Jan.

Rose, Louis 1990: Land values and housing rents in urban Japan. Working Paper no. 90-27, Economics Department, University of Hawaii, August.

Rosenbluth, Frances McCall 1989: *Financial Politics in Contemporary Japan*. Ithaca: Cornell University Press.

Sachs, Jeffrey and Boone, Peter 1988: Japanese structural adjustment and the balance of payments. NBER Working Paper no. 2614, June; and *Journal of the Japanese and International Economies*, 3, 286–327.

Sakakibara, Eisuke and Kondoh, Akira 1984: *Study on the Internationalization of Tokyo's Money Markets*, Tokyo: Japan Center for International Finance, Study Series no. 1, June.

Saxonhouse, Gary 1982: Japanese saving behavior: a household balance sheet approach. University of Michigan, Ann Arbor, Mich., November.

Semiconductor Industry Association 1980: US and Japanese semiconductor industries: a financial comparison. Report prepared by Chase Financial Policy, June.

Shibuya, Hiroshi 1988: Japan's household savings: a life-cycle model with implicit annuity contract and rational expectations. International Monetary Fund, Feb.

Shibuya, Hiroshi 1990: An extended life-cycle model of saving with endogenous retirement and bequest: Japan's aggregate household saving. Institute for Monetary and Economic Studies, Bank of Japan, May.

Shiller, Robert, Kon-ya, Fumiko and Tsutsui, Yoshiro 1991a: Investor behavior in the October 1987 stock market crash: the case of Japan. *Journal of the Japanese and International Economies*, 5(1), 1–13.

Shiller, Robert, Kon-ya, Fumiko and Tsutsui, Yoshiro 1991b: Speculative behavior in the stock markets: evidence from the United States and Japan. NBER Working Paper no. 3613, Feb.

Shinkai, Yoichi 1988: The internationalization of finance in Japan. In T. Inoguchi and D.I. Okimoto (eds), *The Political Economy of Japan*, vol. 2: *The Changing International Context*, Stanford, Cali.: Stanford University Press, 249–71.

Shoven, John 1989: The Japanese tax reform and the effective rate of tax on Japanese corporate investments, NBER Working Paper no. 2791. In L. Summers (ed.), *Tax Policy and the Economy*, Cambridge, Mass.: MIT Press.

Shoven, John and Tachibanaki, Toshiaki 1988: The taxation of income from capital in Japan. Center for Economic Policy Research Publication no. 60. In J. Shoven (ed.), *Government Policy towards Industry in the United States and Japan*, Cambridge: Cambridge University Press.

Slemrod, Joel 1988: Fear of nuclear war and intercountry differences in the rate of saving. NBER Working Paper no. 2801, December.

Stein, Jeremy 1989: Efficient capital markets, inefficient firms: a model of myopic corporate behavior. *Quarterly Journal of Economics*, 104, 655–69.

Suzuki, Yoshio 1987: *The Japanese Financial System*. Oxford: Clarendon Press.

Suzuki, Yoshio 1991: Japan in the world economic scene. Nomura Research Institute, June.

Takagi, Keizo 1989: The rise in land prices in Japan: the determination mechanism and the effect of the taxation system. *Monetary and Economic Studies*, 7, 2, August.

Takagi, Shinji 1988: Recent developments in Japan's bond and money markets. *Journal of the Japanese and International Economies*, 2(1), 63–91.

Takagi, Shinji 1989: The Japanese equity market: past and present. *Journal of Banking and Finance*, 13, 537–70.

Takayama, Noriyuki et al. 1988: Household asset holdings, and the saving rate in Japan. In *Global Role of the Japanese Economy with Affluent Savings and Accumulated Wealth*. Papers and proceedings of the Fifth EPA International Symposium, Tokyo, Oct. 13–14.

Takenaka, Heizo 1986: Economic incentives for industrial investment: Japanese experience. Institute for Fiscal and Monetary Policy, Ministry of Finance, Japan, February.

Tamura, Tatsuro 1987: Changes in corporate fund-raising and management, part 2. *Japan's Financial Markets*, 29, Foundation for Advanced Information and Research, Japan.

Ueda, Kazuo 1990: Are Japanese stock prices too high? *Journal of the Japanese and International Economies*, 3(4), 351–70.

Yamada, Tesuji 1990: The effects of Japanese social security retirement benefits on personal saving and elderly labor force behavior. *Japan and the World Economy*, 2(4), 327–63.

Yamamura, Kozo 1982: Success that soured: administrative guidance and cartels in Japan. In K. Yamamura (ed.), *Policy and Trade Issues of the Japanese Economy*, Seattle: University of Washington Press, 77–112.

Yoshikawa, Hiroshi and Ohtake, Fumio 1989: An analysis of female labor supply, housing demand and the saving rate in Japan. *European Economic Review*, 33(5), 997–1023.

Zielinski, Robert and Holloway, Nigel 1991: *Unequal Equities: power and risk in Japan's stock market*. Tokyo and New York: Kodansha International.

Zysman, John 1983: *Governments, Markets and Growth*, Ithaca, N.Y.: Cornell University Press.

2

International Capital Flows and an Open Economy: the Japanese Experience

Richard C. Koo

1 INTRODUCTION

One of the most significant financial phenomena of the 1980s must have been the massive increase in outflows of Japanese capital. From 1980 to 1989 the cumulative deficit on Japan's long-term capital account reached $642 billion, far above the cumulative current account surplus for the same period of $415 billion. Few corners of the world were spared this Japanese onslaught, which went after everything from bonds, equities and golf courses to office buildings. In many financial capitals of the world it was said that the Japanese had replaced the Arabs of the 1970s and early 1980s.

It became apparent that the outflows exerted tremendous downward pressure on the exchange rate. Except for a few years following the Plaza Accord of September 1985, the weakness of the yen was a constant concern within policy, business and academic circles. This weakness, in turn, caused trade imbalances to widen and trade friction to worsen.

In the 1990s, however, something else started to happen, and the Japanese have now become net sellers in a number of key foreign markets for the first time in recent history. Japanese money, which added so much upward momentum to markets ranging from US Treasury long bonds to real estate in Sydney, Australia, is heading back home.

The purpose of this chapter is to explain what went on during this period, its economic significance, and its policy implications. It is a first-hand account of what happened, from the viewpoint of a market participant. As such, it is hoped that the following pages will provide those outside the market – who may only have access to published statistics and occasional interviews with participants – with some sense of what government and private-sector investors were doing during this period. The emphasis is on portfolio flows rather than on direct investment.

Section 2 guides the reader through some of the regulatory changes in the early 1980s that led Japanese investors to seek foreign assets so aggressively. Section 3 discusses the mechanics of the rush to invest overseas in the first half of the decade and the implications for the exchange rate. Sections 4 and 5 look at the sudden fall in the value of the dollar after the Plaza Accord of 1985 and the efforts made in Japan and the US to prevent Japanese investors offloading their dollar assets. Sections 6 and 7 examine the environment for investment overseas once the dollar had reached its nadir and settled in a narrower trading range against the yen.

Section 8 is devoted to an examination of the turmoil in Japanese financial markets that began in 1990, and the implications for cross-border capital flows. It shows how the situation that emerged in that year was the exact opposite of the one that occurred just two or three years earlier. Section 9 examines the structural causes of capital flows. It suggests the possibility of "overfinancing" in the world of free capital movements across national borders, and the policy implications for Japanese and US authorities.

This chapter is based on information from sources that the author believes to be reliable, but this cannot be guaranteed. This note of caution needs to be sounded because of the nature of administrative guidance in Japan, where unwritten instructions are as potent and as frequent as written ones. It is based on what market participants, including policymakers, believed to be the case at the time.

2 A NEW INVESTMENT ENVIRONMENT

2.1 The Beginning

Japanese investment activity abroad was in principle prohibited until December 1980. Prior to that date, insurance companies and securities investment trusts, the two groups that could invest abroad, had to obtain permission from the Ministry of Finance before moving funds overseas. Since this procedure limited mobility, very little investment actually took place before December 1980.

Toward the end of the 1970s, however, investment opportunities in Japan began to shrink rapidly compared with the capital-hungry days of the 1950s and 1960s. This is because the two oil crises in the 1970s convinced many Japanese corporations that the days of double-digit GNP growth were over, and that they had to correct their overdependence on debt in preparation for a more moderate growth period ahead.

As a result, many major corporations that were borrowing money heavily in the 1950s and 1960s began paying back some of their loans, starting in the late 1970s. As competition for the domestic lending market intensified, more and more high-cost lenders such as life insurance companies had to relinquish their market shares to low-cost lenders such as banks. They had to endure very low rates of return from those corporate clients they were able to hold on to.

Pressure built up, therefore, for these institutional investors to be able to invest abroad. The second oil crisis that began in 1979 also demonstrated the vulnerability of the Japanese economy and markets to developments abroad, and added to the arguments in favor of international diversification of portfolios. Some insurance companies even cited the frequency of earthquakes in Japan as a reason to place investments abroad, arguing that nearly one-tenth of all the world's recorded earthquakes take place around Japan.

In fact, however, life and casualty companies have never been liable to pay for damage in the event of a major earthquake. Only specialized earthquake insurance companies cover these risks, and this group has always invested a large portion of its assets abroad.

In December 1980 the Ministry of Finance finally agreed to liberalize foreign security investments with the revised Foreign Exchange and Trade Control Law. Although the investments were allowed in principle, the MOF kept very many restrictions in place in view of the investors' severe lack of experience of investing abroad, and relaxed them only gradually over time. The restrictions included: limitations on the type of foreign assets that could be purchased; the share of foreign assets as a percentage of total assets; and foreign investment as a percentage of new investments made each month.

2.2   The Investment Environment Abroad

While Japan was liberalizing cross-border capital flows, similar developments were also taking place abroad. In the US, for example, the Monetary Control Act of October 1979 liberalized interest rates. This, together with the tight monetary policy that followed, resulted in sky-high interest rates and made US assets look extremely attractive. In the UK, capital controls were also relaxed in 1979. Just around the turn of the decade, therefore, three international financial centers lowered barriers against each other more or less coincidentally.

Changes in the regulatory environment did not stop at the beginning of 1980. In 1984 Mr Sprinkel, the former Under-secretary of the Treasury, visited Japan. He asked financial institutions and securities houses for their cooperation in financing the US deficits. At the same time, the US Treasury also issued bonds specifically designed for foreigners. Because of Mr Sprinkel's sales pitch, those bonds were called Sprinkel bonds in Japan. In July 1984 the US also abolished withholding tax on interest income for non-residents.

The resultant increase in the movement of capital across national borders defied all earlier forecasts and pushed the world's financial markets into totally uncharted waters. This was most apparent in the foreign exchange markets, where, in spite of a flood of forecasts for a lower dollar from very many economists throughout the first half of the 1980s, the dollar kept on strengthening. Indeed, if one takes the entire decade of the eighties, the dollar was weak in only three out of ten years, that is, the three years immediately after the Plaza Accord. In the remaining seven years, the dollar moved very erratically, causing severe imbalances in trade flows.

This is not to deny that there were no occasions before the 1980s when capital flows determined exchange rates. For example, during the sterling crisis in the 1960s and the US dollar crisis in the 1970s, capital movements frequently had a major impact on exchange rates. But those flows were typically of the short-term, hot-money variety, and were reversed as soon as the expected movements in the exchange rate took place. What distinguished the 1980s from the 1970s is that the flows were long-term, lasting for years and seldom reversing direction. The reasons for this are not hard to find.

2.3   Domestic and International Capital Flows

Capital flows, to be sure, take place domestically as well. In the US, for example, when oil is hot, money tends to flow from New York to Texas. In Japan, when the city of Sendai was considered to be a possible candidate for taking on some of the capital city functions of Tokyo, money flowed out of Tokyo and Osaka to the Sendai real-estate market. But such flows tend to stop after a few weeks or months when asset prices in the new locations appreciate to a point where the return on additional investment is no higher than it is at home.

Since Sendai and Tokyo, or Houston and New York, have been in the same monetary zone for hundreds of years, most of the obvious opportunities to pick up additional yields have been fully explored and exploited by investors. Thus, unless there are some new technological developments or new infrastructure developments that suddenly make one area much more attractive than others, domestic capital flows tend to be fairly limited in scope and duration.

Across national borders, however, most capital markets remained remarkably well insulated and isolated from each other for *hundreds of years* until the early 1980s, thanks to regulatory restrictions and communication/transaction difficulties. So the kind of arbitrage flows that have happened domestically every day for the last few centuries seldom took place across national borders.

With the rapid developments in communications technology, the international opportunities suddenly made available to national investors appeared to be almost infinite when the regulatory barriers were lifted in the late 1970s and early 1980s. This was particularly true for Japanese investors, many of whom had been enduring very low rates of return at home for some time.

Since the Tokyo capital market had been isolated from those in Sydney, London and New York for hundreds of years, the capital flows that started effectively in December 1980 could not overnight equalize the marginal rates of return between Tokyo and foreign markets. Indeed, the process of equalizing the marginal rates of return in these markets is still going on today, a full ten years after it started.

As was indicated at the beginning in reference to the long-term capital account deficit, the resultant flood of portfolio investments overwhelmed trade-related foreign exchange transactions and became the main determinant of exchange rates. Indeed, because of the magnitude of the flows involved, the dynamics operating in the foreign exchange market have shifted from equalizing trade balances between countries to equalizing the marginal rates of return on investment across countries. The world was to discover what "open economy" really meant when not only the goods market, but also the capital markets, were integrated across national borders.

2.4 The Investors

The first groups allowed to engage in foreign investment activities were individuals, non-financial corporations, banks, insurance companies, and securities investment trusts. This left pension trusts and many smaller financial institutions, as well as public-sector investors, still unable to invest abroad.

For the individuals and non-financial corporations, no explicit limitations remained on what they could do with their funds abroad. To buy and sell foreign securities, however, the Ministry of Finance stipulated that the transactions had to be dealt with through securities houses located in Japan. This was done in part because of the government's desire to collect as much accurate data as possible on the international transactions of its residents. By collecting reports from securities houses located at home, the Ministry of Finance is able to track the activities of individual investors and non-financial corporations.

The activities of financial institutions are divided into two groups: those that are allowed to deal with foreign institutions directly, and those which must go through securities houses at home. Most major insurance companies, banks and securities houses are allowed to deal directly abroad. As of March 1991 there were 334 financial institutions in this

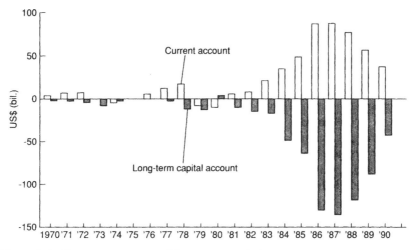

Figure 2.1 Japanese current and long-term capital accounts

Source: Japanese Ministry of Finance

category. In return for the privilege, these institutions are required to report fully their foreign activities and holdings to the authorities.

Smaller, less-experienced financial institutions are required to carry out their transactions through resident securities houses when dealing in foreign securities, just like individuals and non-financial corporations. In putting together Japan's international accounts, therefore, the Ministry of Finance combines individual reports from the 334 financial institutions that are allowed to deal directly abroad with the reports from the resident securities houses that cover the transactions of all other investors.

For insurance companies, the limit on their foreign holdings was set initially at 10 percent of total assets. There was also a so-called flow limit, which stated that not more than 20 percent of new money could be invested in foreign securities each month.

For securities investment trusts, the general rule stated that 30 percent of total assets could be in the form of foreign assets, but the Ministry of Finance also approved the percentage of foreign securities on a fund-by-fund basis. Some funds, such as the *Nai-Gai-Sai* Fund (which literally means Domestic–Foreign Bond Fund) could hold as much as 50 percent of total assets in the form of foreign assets.

After these groups, other institutional investor groups were gradually allowed to enter foreign markets. In 1981 pension trusts were allowed to invest abroad. Since, at that time, they and life insurance companies were the only groups allowed to manage pension money in Japan, the limit on foreign holdings by pension trusts was made roughly similar to that for life insurance companies.

In 1983 the Postal Life Insurance was allowed to invest abroad. This group, which is a part of the Ministry of Post and Telecommunications, offers life insurance through post offices located throughout Japan. As such, it was the first government agency to be allowed to invest in foreign securities. The initial limit on this group's holdings of foreign securities was set at 10 percent of total assets. In view of its public-sector status, however, investments were limited to bonds only, with a strong preference for those issued by public-sector entities.

In 1985 credit cooperatives and credit associations were allowed to invest abroad. For the former, the limit was set at 20 percent of total assets. Yearly purchases of foreign securities were also limited to 10 percent of total security holdings. For the latter, the limits were much lower because of their small size.

3   BEFORE THE PLAZA ACCORD

3.1   The Rush

In the period between December 1980 and the Plaza Accord of September 1985, the popularity of foreign security investments grew exponentially. So popular were these securities that by 1984 both life and casualty insurance companies had largely reached their limits on foreign security holdings. The reasons for this popularity were many.

First, starting with an almost exclusively domestic portfolio, the urgency for international diversification, which could potentially increase returns while simultaneously reducing risks, was considered great.

Second, rates available abroad were much higher than those at home. Long bond rates in the US were well over 10 percent for most of the early 1980s, and other markets, such as the UK, Canada, and Australia, were also offering attractive rates relative to those available at home.

Third, Japanese regulations on many institutional investors such as life insurance companies stipulated that only interest and dividend income could be used for paying out dividends to policyholders. This regulation was designed to discourage the pursuit of capital gains and speculative behavior in general. Foreign bonds offering significantly higher interest income, therefore, attracted many Japanese investors.

Fourth, exchange rate risk, which should have dampened the enthusiasm for foreign securities investment by inserting an additional risk element, worked in reverse during this period. This is because the flood of funds flowing out of Japan continued to keep the yen weak and made foreign securities even more attractive. A vicious circle of sorts was very much in existence as far as exchange rate risk was concerned. The situation lasted right up to the Plaza Accord of September 1985.

Fifth, institutional investors such as insurance companies have always been high-cost lenders relative to commercial banks. When the capital requirements of Japanese corporations began to slow down in the late 1970s and early 1980s, these groups were squeezed out of the domestic lending market. As a result, they began to seek opportunities elsewhere.

Banks, on the other hand, were constrained by the foreign exchange exposure requirements imposed on them by the monetary authorities. Since these requirements also covered their holdings of foreign securities, their foreign security activities had to be funded almost entirely by foreign currency liabilities. Even though banks have become very active players in the foreign securities market, their aim is essentially yield-curve play, with the occasional pursuit of capital gains.

3.2   Strong Dollar or Weak Yen?

During the first half of the 1980s, the reasons for the continued weakness of the yen were debated in many academic and policymaking circles. The weakness was particularly puzzling because Japan's current account surplus was expanding rapidly during this period. The expanding trade surplus and the resultant increase in trade friction were also becoming major policy issues on both sides of the Pacific Ocean.

It was not a straightforward debate, however, because there were disagreements between economists as to whether it was the yen that was weak or the dollar that was strong. The first group argued that the archaic Japanese financial system, with its multitude of controls and regulations, made the Japanese financial markets unattractive places to invest. Many people abroad, including Prime Minister Thatcher of the UK, even suggested that the Japanese authorities might have been deliberately keeping the yen weak in order to win export markets abroad. This group proposed, therefore, that deregulation of Japanese financial markets would help attract foreign funds to Japan and strengthen the yen.

Based on this argument, the so-called Yen–Dollar Committee was set up by the US Treasury Department and the Japanese Ministry of Finance. The US position, based on many complaints from non-Japanese investors that there was no easy place to invest funds in yen, was to create Japanese markets attractive enough for foreigners to place their funds.

Later in the negotiations, in addition to the concern over the weak yen and the corresponding loss of export competitiveness of US manufacturers, the US side began to express concern about the strength of Japanese financial institutions, especially banks. It was argued that because regulated interest rates on bank deposits in Japan were set so far below market rates, the banks were effectively given subsidies to expand their activities abroad, and that these low cost funds allowed Japanese banks to offer paper-thin spreads and take business away from American and European banks. For these two reasons, the US pushed hard for financial deregulation and the creation of attractive markets for investment in Japan. The new yen-based Bankers Acceptance Market was created along these lines.

In retrospect, the US position was only partially correct, and the Bankers Acceptance Market died quite soon after its creation, mostly because of the lack of interest on the part of the private sector. Certain tax difficulties also speeded its demise. More importantly, the difference in the magnitudes of capital flows on the inflow and outflow sides meant that a slight increase in the attractiveness of the Japanese markets could have done little to stem the tide of funds flowing out of Japan.

The pressure created by the US to deregulate Japanese financial markets, however, also made it very difficult for the Japanese authorities to invoke their traditional weapon of moral suasion to restrain Japanese investors from buying assets abroad. The authorities were afraid of doing anything that would suggest that Japan was deviating from its chosen path of financial deregulation. This strengthened the hand of those institutional investors who were demanding additional deregulation of foreign security investments. The net result was an even greater outflow of capital from Japan and a weaker yen.

3.3   The Threat of Protectionism

It was not until 1985, when the protectionist threat had reached an explosive state in the US, that the Japanese authorities were willing to break the taboo by starting to drop serious hints about the possibility of re-imposing capital controls. In early September 1985 Prime Minister Nakasone suggested that such controls might be needed to strengthen the yen in order to avert a major trade war with Japan's main partners.

Not everyone agreed that the problem was that the yen was too weak, however. Indeed, there was no shortage of economists arguing that it was the dollar that was too strong, especially in view of the fact that European currencies were also falling at the same time as the yen *vis-à-vis* the dollar. This group argued that the huge budget deficit in the US had been pushing up US interest rates and attracting funds from abroad, keeping the dollar strong. This argument, which makes the exchange rate endogenous to the system, also suggests that any attempt to correct the value of the exchange rate would fail if it did not first correct the fundamental cause: the budget deficit.

This group had quite a few followers on both sides of the Pacific Ocean, especially among academics. The Japanese policymakers also liked the idea because it absolved them of any wrongdoing, and it linked trade friction to the supposed source of all evil, the US budget deficit. For the Republican administration in the White House, however, this argument was of little relevance because what was needed in 1985 was a quick fix to deflect the overwhelming protectionist sentiment engulfing the US Congress. By then, the containment of the federal budget deficit had eluded them for many years, and no one in the administration had any illusions about achieving such a containment in the near future.

In February 1985 there was a switch of personalities at the US Treasury, namely the departure of Donald Regan and the appointment of James Baker as the new Secretary of the Treasury. Don Regan, a former top executive of Merrill Lynch and a staunch believer in free markets, had never been enthusiastic about foreign exchange intervention. As a result, the US Treasury, which has a mandate to intervene in the foreign exchange market, did so only very infrequently and only when so-called disorderly conditions were observed in the market. The disorderly conditions were defined to include situations such as exceptionally wide spreads between the bid and the offer rates, gapping in quoted rates, and traders so scared that they refused to answer their telephones. James Baker, on the other hand, had had plenty of dealings with Congress as Chief of Staff of the White House, and knew how serious the protectionist threat had become on Capitol Hill. He knew something had to be done quickly before protectionism took over everything.

4   A RAPIDLY STRENGTHENING YEN

4.1   The Plaza Accord and the Central Bank Terror

On September 23, 1985, the Plaza Accord was announced by the G-5 countries to correct the overvaluation of the dollar. The massive intervention that followed finally pushed down the dollar, and started its long and tenuous decline.

The Plaza Accord, however, had three conceptual risks. First, if the theory that it was the US budget deficit that was pushing US rates up and keeping the dollar strong was correct, no amount of intervention would work, since the real cause of the dollar's strength was left intact.

Second, there were worries that if the correction of the dollar really took place, billions of dollars of assets that foreigners already held in the US were likely to be liquidated, for no financial textbook suggests holding onto assets denominated in a falling currency. Thus, there was a real risk that a dollar fall would turn into a dollar collapse, with foreigners dumping their holdings of US securities, resulting in skyrocketing US interest rates.

Third, there was concern that a weak dollar would ignite inflation in the US. The chairman of the Federal Reserve System at that time, Mr Volcker, indicated in the July 1985 testimony to Congress that a fall of the dollar beyond the initial 10 percentage points would have inflationary repercussions.

In retrospect, none of these concerns materialized. First, the G-5 effort worked in part because it managed to terrorize the market. The initial bout of intervention was able to push the dollar down from ¥240 to ¥220. The dollar, however, stopped falling at that level. Many market participants argued that nothing had really changed, and that intervention would have only a temporary impact. Indeed, many argued that at ¥220 the dollar was a bargain.

The Bank of Japan, sensing that the G-5 message had been ignored, started the "terror" by jacking up short-term interest rates by well over 100 basis points overnight on October 24. Furthermore, the timing of this rate increase was extremely critical because it took place only three days after the opening of the new bond futures market in Japan. The preparations for the new market had taken many years, and its launch was viewed as a major landmark in Japan's financial history. Hundreds of investors were invited to participate in the opening.

The total collapse of this market and its subsequent closure after only three days of existence imparted an unmistakable sense that the Bank of Japan would do *anything* to push the yen higher. Even though the bond futures market itself was reopened after a few days, no one had any illusions about the BOJ's intentions any longer.

4.2   Currency Hedges Come into Play

With weak economic indicators coming from the US, especially in the area of trade performance, Japanese institutional investors began to place hedges on their dollar portfolios. Since placing hedges in this context meant selling dollars forward, the selling pressure pushed the dollar down even more. The falling dollar prompted even more investors to place hedges, and the dollar weakened further. Thus, a new vicious (or virtuous, depending on one's point of view) circle emerged that was the exact reverse of the one operating in the early 1980s.

There is no reliable data on exactly what proportion of portfolios of institutional investors are hedged at any one time. There is, however, a reasonable proxy for this in the form of the foreign currency positions of banks in Japan. When placing hedges by selling dollars forward, someone, by definition, must be on the other side of the transaction. In this case, the other parties were mostly banks. The banks, in turn, had to get dollars from somewhere to sell to the institutional investors. Since dollars are not available in Japan, they had to get them from abroad, mostly from the Euromarket. This inflow of dollars from abroad shows up as foreign currency liabilities of banks in Japan.

Hedging is, of course, not the only use of these funds. Indeed, some of these funds were used outright to buy foreign securities, while others were sold in the foreign exchange market and converted into yen for other uses by Japanese residents. The point here is that since long-term capital account data do not distinguish between those purchases financed with yen funds and those financed with borrowings from abroad, in order to see the net yen-based outflows from Japan one must remove from the long-term capital account those activities that are financed with inflows of dollars from abroad.

Statistics show that from December 1985 to December 1990 Japanese banks took on $216 billion in foreign currency liabilities from abroad. The fact that there had been little or no trend in Japanese banks' foreign currency liabilities prior to December 1985 suggests that people's views toward the dollar must have changed quite dramatically just around that time.

Many people have wondered why the Japanese deficit on the long-term capital account picked up sharply in 1986 just when the yen was appreciating most rapidly. If the Japanese were buying that much more abroad, one would have expected the yen to be weaker. Because of this, some observers have even concluded that balance-of-payments statistics are no longer useful in understanding exchange rates.

There are two parts to the story. First, the reason the long-term capital account deficit increased in 1986 is that interest rates were coming down rapidly in the US and elsewhere, and many investors seeking capital gains, especially banks, were capitalizing on that situation by buying long bonds in the US.

The reason for the yen's strength during this period was that investors were also busy placing hedges on their dollar investments, both new and old. Furthermore, as noted earlier, banks are not allowed to buy foreign securities unhedged. As a result, their purchases of long bonds in the US, which show up as purchases of securities in the long-term capital account, were actually financed with borrowings of short-term dollars abroad.

Between December 1985 and December 1987, when the decline of the dollar was most rapid, banks in Japan took on an average of $6 billion per month in new foreign currency liabilities from abroad. To see exactly how much of the long-term capital outflow was actually yen-based, therefore,

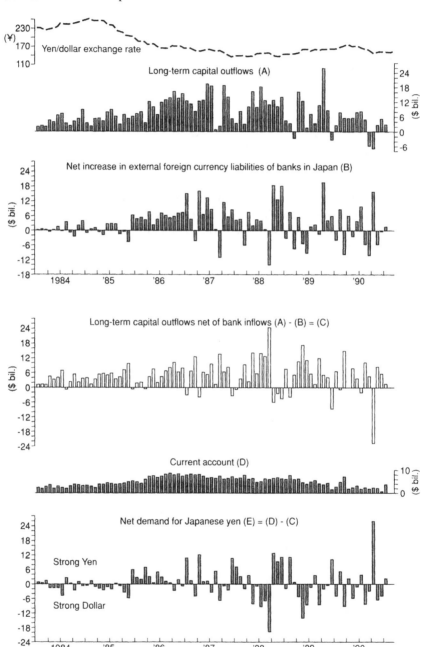

Figure 2.2 Exchange rate and capital flows

Sources: Japanese Ministry of Finance and the Bank of Japan

one must subtract the increase in foreign currency liabilities of banks in Japan from the long-term capital account deficit.

The result, which is shown in figure 2.2C, indicates that in the first half of 1986, when the appreciation of the yen was most rapid, the yen-based outflow from Japan was close to zero and was actually negative in four out of six months. When this "adjusted long-term capital outflow" (that is, long-term capital outflows minus the increase in foreign currency liabilities of banks in Japan) is compared with the current account, it is possible to establish some idea of the balance of demand in the foreign exchange market from the trade and capital flows.

The result is shown in figure 2.2E. This suggests that if the amount is above zero, the current account is dominating the adjusted long-term capital account, that is, the yen should be stronger, and vice versa. One can indeed see that in most months of 1986 the current account did overwhelm the (adjusted) long-term capital account, and the yen appreciated. The trend continued into 1987.

This analysis of course assumes that all outflows from Japan are to the dollar area, and that there are only two currencies, the dollar and the yen. Also, since 1987 onwards there have been certain fiscal year-end peculiarities to the statistics, especially those for the foreign currency liabilities of banks in Japan. These are especially noticeable for September, but some are apparent during March as well.

In spite of these limitations, a simple regression of the results of figure 2.2E and the actual exchange rate shows a reasonable fit, as shown in figure 2.3. This suggests that balance-of-payments statistics are not that useless after all. When proper adjustments are made for currency hedging activities, the movements in trade and capital flow numbers do show correlation with exchange rate movements.

5 PREVENTING A ROUT

5.1 Keeping Japanese Investors in Dollars

The first problem concerning the Plaza Accord – that such intervention activities alone should not have worked – did not arise, because investors were largely terrorized into hedging their dollar portfolios. This resulted in the vicious circle of an ever-declining dollar. The second problem, of preventing Japanese investors from pulling out of the dollar and causing dollar interest rates to skyrocket, was a little more complicated.

It should be noted that, contrary to popular belief abroad at the time, Japanese investors had been sensitive to foreign exchange risk when investing abroad since the beginning of the 1980s. Before December

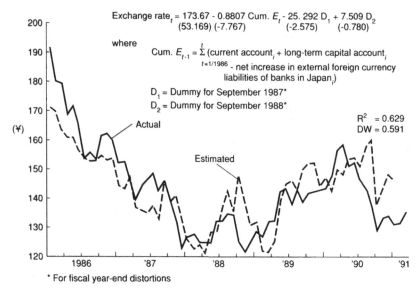

Figure 2.3   An exchange rate estimation*

* For fiscal year-end distortions.

Sources: Japanese Ministry of Finance and the Bank of Japan

1985, however, their approach to hedging was somewhat different. First, the main reason for buying foreign assets was to seek assets with characteristics different from those of the yen. As such, Japanese investors bought paper almost exclusively from the US, UK, Australian, and Canadian markets for most of the 1980s. This is because most of these economies are rich in the natural resources that Japan lacks. After the experience of two oil crises, most Japanese investors are keenly aware of the fact that Japanese markets and the Japanese yen are vulnerable to oil and other commodity price fluctuations. In this sense, foreign securities investment itself was viewed as a hedge against disturbances in markets for natural resources.

While buying foreign bonds, therefore, many Japanese investors were also adding to their portfolios those assets that tend to move in the opposite direction to the US, UK, Australian, and Canadian markets. These included mostly domestic demand-related assets such as equities of Japanese real estate and construction companies. Their reasoning was that when oil prices are high, the US, UK, Australian, and Canadian parts of their portfolios should do well. When oil prices are low, interest rates should also be low at home, and domestic construction should do well.

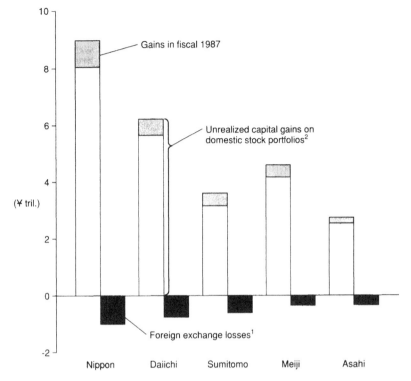

Figure 2.4   Foreign exchange losses of the five largest life insurance companies

[1]   Cumulative real and valuation losses on foreign securities from fiscal 1985 to fiscal 1987.
[2]   As of the end of March 1988.

Sources: *Nikkei Newsletter* on bond and money, *Kinyu-Zaisei-Jijo*, various issues

Indeed, in 1986 the price of oil collapsed to less than $10 a barrel at one point, and the Bank of Japan behaved aggressively in easing monetary policy. The result was a boom in domestic demand-related stocks, which skyrocketed in value. For major life insurance companies, for example, the increase in the value of unrealized capital gains on their domestic stock portfolios in fiscal 1987 was almost as large as their entire foreign exchange-related losses from fiscal 1985 to fiscal 1988. This is shown in figure 2.4. The same international diversification strategy also worked in fiscal 1989, ending in March 1990. But this time, many investors were saved by having good performances in their foreign security portfolios when the weak yen and high interest rates at home pushed the domestic stock market sharply lower.

The second way in which the risk was "covered" by Japanese investors

Figure 2.5 Changes in yen and dollar values of 30-year US Treasury bonds (March 31, 1985 = 100)

Source: Nomura Capital

was by favoring long bonds when buying dollar-denominated paper. Investors reasoned that if and when the dollar came down, it would be accompanied by falling dollar interest rates. They argued that as long as they were at the long end of the market, such a decline in interest rates should produce substantial capital gains on the bonds to offset foreign exchange losses.

To a remarkable degree, this strategy worked right up until March 25, 1987, a full year and a half after the Plaza Accord. From 1985 to that critical date, the increase in the value of the long bond due to falling US interest rates held down the loss in foreign exchange to only about 10 percent of the face value, even though during the same period the dollar fell by nearly 40 percent. This is shown in figure 2.5. Thus, up until March 25, 1987, Japanese investors incurred large losses with foreign exchange, but the losses were tolerable in view of the stronger stock market in Japan and long bond prices in the US.

During this period, the Ministry of Finance and the Bank of Japan were also busy trying to stop investors unloading their dollar portfolios. They had two concerns. First, the rapid appreciation of the yen prompted Japanese manufacturers to scream for help. After all, Japan had been very much an export-driven economy during the previous 40 years, and losing this important source of demand was considered unthinkable in most parts of the country, including the government bureaucracies. It was feared that the unloading of dollar assets by Japanese investors would turn the orderly decline of the dollar into a fully fledged collapse, robbing Japanese corporations of precious time to adjust to the reality of the new exchange rate; such a decline of the dollar could push Japan into a major depression. Second, they were concerned that, given the large dependence of US markets on Japanese capital, if the Japanese really "pulled the plug", as it was called in those days, the US economy could collapse under the weight of skyrocketing interest rates. That, in turn, could push the rest of the world economy and financial markets into a terrible tailspin.

Although both concerns were real throughout the post-Plaza Accord period, the concern for the domestic exporters was probably more important in the late 1985–6 period, while the concern for the US and the global economy was probably more important in the 1987–8 period. This shift simply reflects the fact that by the middle of 1987 the Japanese economy was already beginning to show signs of strength, so much so that by September of that year the Bank of Japan was actively considering raising interest rates. The concern for the US and for the global economy continued, however, especially after Black Monday in October 1987.

5.2 More Deregulation

In addition to concern over the weak domestic economy, the need to keep Japanese investors from selling their dollar holdings prompted the Bank of Japan to lower its discount rate five times in just over a year, pushing it down to 2.5 percent by February 1987. The Ministry of Finance did its part by relaxing limits on foreign security holdings aggressively, starting in April 1986. In April the limit that restricted foreign assets to 10 percent of total assets for insurance companies and pension trusts was raised to a whopping 25 percent. The limit that restricted purchases of foreign assets in each month to 20 percent of new investments was also raised to 40 percent.

Although these changes were generous, many institutional investors had actually long since gone over their 10 percent limit by using a loophole in the original regulations. The trick took the form of purchases of so-called *sushi* bonds and foreign currency bank deposits.

Sushi bonds are foreign-currency-denominated bonds issued by Japanese corporations. Since the original regulations limited Japanese insurance companies, to purchases of "foreign bonds" rather than "foreign-currency-denominated bonds", such bonds were issued to take advantage of the regulations. Since the issuers knew that all insurance companies were up against their limits and therefore constituted captive buyers, the return on *sushis* was frequently below-market. Since only the Japanese would eat them, these bonds were called *sushi* bonds. Some bonds offering significantly below-market rates were also called *rotten sushis* or even *natto* bonds. The term *natto* refers to a very healthy Japanese dish made of fermented soy beans, which many non-Japanese find totally unfit for human consumption.

Foreign currency deposits were also outside the original regulations. These high-yielding instruments sometimes accounted for over 90 percent of so-called cash holdings of insurance companies. In addition to the US dollar, Australian and Canadian dollar deposits were common, thanks to the high interest rates they offered. The MOF was concerned about this loophole too, so the new regulations with their 25 percent limit actually included all foreign and foreign-currency-denominated assets. Ultimately, then, the raising of the limit was not as generous as it first appeared.

The raising of the limit in April 1986, however, failed to offer any help in keeping the dollar from falling further. Hard pressed to do something about the rapidly appreciating yen in order to win time for manufacturers in Japan, the MOF raised the limits again in August, only four months after the April change. This time, the limit was raised to 30 percent, and all flow limits on monthly purchases were abolished.

Many smaller financial institutions were also allowed to invest in foreign securities for the first time during this period, and the limit for Postal Life Insurance was raised from 10 to 20 percent in early 1987. Even Postal Savings, whose funds had largely been taken over by the Trust Fund Bureau of the Ministry of Finance, were given funds to invest themselves, possibly in foreign securities.

In addition to deregulation, moral suasion was also used extensively during this period. The MOF told Japanese investors how much good the US had done for Japan after the war, and how important it was for Japan to stay with the dollar to prevent the total collapse of the world financial system. For many senior managers of financial institutions in Japan who lived through those postwar years, this was a hard argument to ignore. Although many young Japanese fund managers were not around when the US was rebuilding Japan after the war, many have heard stories from their parents, and felt obligated to stay with the dollar as well. Some of them actually indicated that they were paying back their parents' debt.

5.3　The Louvre Accord and its Collapse

In spite of these desperate efforts on the part of the MOF, purchases by investors remained moderate. And most of the purchases that did take place were hedged on the currency side, as noted earlier. The dollar had already fallen to the ¥150 range by August 1986. The ministry,

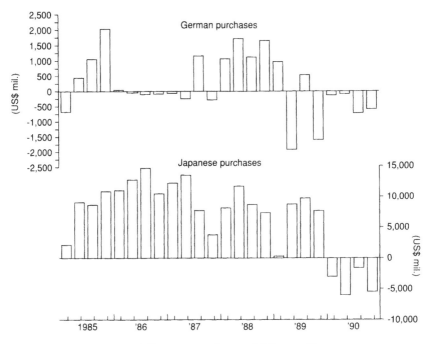

Figure 2.6   Japanese and German purchases of US securities

Sources: MOF and Bundesbank

however, was at least able to keep Japanese investors from turning net sellers in the US, which was an achievement in itself. In contrast, German investors had been unloading their dollar securities since the beginning of 1986. This contrast is shown in figure 2.6.

The Minister of Finance at that time, Mr Miyazawa, flew to Washington in late October 1986 to conclude the first "Baker–Miyazawa" Agreement. The point of the exercise was to prompt the Americans to say that the dollar has fallen far enough, in exchange for a Japanese pledge to expand domestic demand and imports.

Although the agreement worked to calm the foreign exchange market briefly, the Japanese government's subsequent announcement in December of economic forecasts for the following fiscal year contained little in the way of additional measures to increase domestic demand. Feeling betrayed, the US began to express displeasure with the stance taken by the Japanese, and the dollar started to fall again. Alarmed by the renewed weakness of the dollar, Miyazawa flew to Washington again in January to conclude "Baker–Miyazawa Agreement II," and this was followed by the G-7 agreement in the Louvre, Paris, in late February, where all the members of the G-7 agreed that the dollar had fallen far enough.

The announcement of the Louvre Accord was welcomed with a great sense of relief in Japan, and seeing that ¥150 was indeed the floor for the dollar, many investors expressed interest in returning to the US market again. Indeed, the early part of March saw very active buying by Japanese investors in the US market.

All this changed on March 25, 1987. On that day the dollar fell below ¥150, the supposed floor for the US currency under the just-signed Louvre Accord. Although short-term fluctuations are no cause for alarm as long as the authorities implement measures to correct the situation immediately, the initial response from the central banks to the incident was far from convincing. Worst of all, it took place only five days before the all-important fiscal year-end in Japan.

The net result was massive panic selling of dollar securities by Japanese investors, who believed that the Louvre Accord, signed only four weeks previously, had already fallen apart. For the first time since the Plaza Accord, therefore, the worst-case scenario had raised its ugly head. Those Japanese investors who patiently endured the dollar's decline in the hope that everything was under control realized how wrong they had been. The dollar was indeed a hopeless case.

According to foreign securities traders at the time, billions and billions of dollars-worth of US paper was sold every day up to the fiscal year-end, and even beyond. By the time the central banks realized what had happened it was already too late. The dollar had already fallen to ¥145 by the end of the month, and US long rates had begun their upward spiral. Indeed, Japanese investors were moving funds out of US Treasury bonds and, not finding a convenient place to park them, placing them in the Japanese government bond market.

As a result, while US long rates were skyrocketing, Japanese long bond rates were falling like a stone, both starting on March 25. Up to that time, long rates in Japan were stuck at around 4.5 percent, and, in spite of repeated attempts by various market participants, it had not been possible to go below that figure for nearly a year.

The fall of the dollar that started on March 25 changed all that. As the dollar continued to fall well into April and early May, eventually reaching ¥137 by early May, long rates in Japan continued to fall, with an all-time low of 2.55 percent by early May. That rate was almost the same as the Bank of Japan's discount rate at the time. Long rates in the US continued their climb from 7.5 percent all the way up to 9 percent during the same period. Thus, from March 25 to the middle of May, there was a classic foreign bail-out situation. Many American investors, who had also grown extremely sensitive to the movements of Japanese investors, prob-

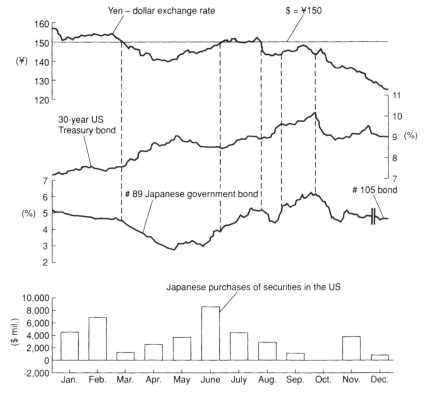

Figure 2.7   Capital flows, exchange rate and long-term interest rates in 1987

Sources: Japanese Ministry of Finance and Nomura Capital

ably added to the collapse of the bond market in the US by joining the bandwagon. These movements are shown in figure 2.7.

Initially, the US authorities were not aware of the panic that was taking place in Japan, and most observers on Wall Street or in Washington tried to explain the rising long rates in the US by citing an emergence of domestic inflationary expectations. Once the real cause became known, however, the Federal Reserve acted swiftly by raising short-term interest rates to defend the dollar. The Fed even considered a hike in the discount rate in May to defend the currency.

In Japan, the Ministry of Finance was trying to recover from its loss of credibility with investors who believed in Baker–Miyazawa I, Baker–Miyazawa II and the Louvre Accord. However, it was no longer possible for the ministry to dissaude Japanese institutional investors from selling dollar securities.

Realizing their limitations, the MOF in May changed its focus of attention to banks. What the MOF did was to ask for every conceivable kind of data on banks' foreign exchange dealings. The reporting requirements, which included such sensitive data as each day's maximum and minimum positions, was so onerous that the Tokyo foreign exchange market was almost brought to a standstill. Although it was only an increase in reporting requirements, banks rightly sensed that the reports could be used to pin the blame for the decline of the dollar on them. They feared that they could be made a target of the anger of Japanese workers and corporations suffering under the strong yen. Although this additional reporting requirement was against the spirit of financial liberalization that had been agreed within the context of the Yen–Dollar Talks, there were no complaints from the US side. This was in spite of a host of complaints lodged against the ministry by the foreign banks operating in Tokyo, whose main line of business had frequently been foreign exchange trading. The US had a far bigger problem on its hands with its long rates skyrocketing.

With such efforts on both sides of the Pacific, the dollar began to show some strength toward the end of May, and by early July it recovered to the ¥150 level. The recovery of the dollar also coincided with an increase in Japanese long bond yields and a decline in their US counterparts. It should also be noted that in spite of massive selling in late March, Japanese investors never really became *net* sellers in the US during the spring and early summer months. Compared with net purchases of $4.6 billion in January and $6.7 billion in February, however, the March figure was $1.0 billion, in April $2.1 billion and in May $3.3 billion. Thus, Japanese investors tried to stay in the market the best they could, but the net purchase figures fell sharply, adding to the strains on the US side.

These figures are shown in table 2.1, which indicates the geographic distribution of Japanese purchases abroad. The table includes all securities. The entry for Luxembourg is thought to comprise mostly Eurodollar securities, including Euroequity warrants and convertible bonds issued by Japanese corporations. For more recent years, large amounts of Euroyen securities issued by Japanese corporations abroad are also included here. As far as capital flows are concerned, therefore, the entry for Luxembourg is largely neutral since the securities are issued by Japanese corporations and purchased by Japanese investors.

Not everything was back to pre-March 25 days, however. One major impact of the debacle that followed March 25 was the loss of one of the most potent forms of hedges employed by Japanese investors against foreign exchange risk. As indicated earlier, many Japanese investors preferred long bonds in the US, believing that the fall of the dollar would be associated with a fall in US interest rates. By holding on to long bonds, they were hoping to offset foreign exchange losses with the appreciation in bond prices that came from lower interest rates.

Although the rationale worked remarkably well until March 25, 1987, as indicated earlier, their panic selling of dollar bonds in response to the collapse of the US currency below ¥150 also resulted in a sharp fall in bond prices. This meant that these investors were hit from both sides at the same time, and their losses mounted quickly. This double blow invited further panic selling, pushing down the dollar and long bonds even further. In yen terms, in the short period between March 25 and early May their portfolios, consisting mostly of long dollar bonds, lost nearly 20 percent of their value. This is in sharp contrast to a less than ten percent decline in the yen value of these securities during the whole period of the dollar's fall from September 1985 to March 1987. Figure 2.4 illustrates the point.

6   THE DAM GIVES WAY

6.1   The End of Japanese Buy-and-Hold

Because of the massive losses, it was no longer possible for the Ministry of Finance to stop investors selling their dollar securities. The era of Japanese investors buying and holding their dollar securities was over. From this period onward, therefore, the Japanese were forced to de-emphasize long-term buy-and-hold strategies and concentrate their efforts on the pursuit of short-term trading for capital gains, especially with regard to dollar securities.

For example, starting with the May 1987 auction of bonds for the US Treasury quarterly refunding, the widely reported "Japanese participation" figures lost all their meaning. Before the May 1987 auction, most figures relating to "Japanese participation" literally meant Japanese investors buying and holding those bonds they purchased in the auction. Thus, when it was reported in the press that the Japanese took 25 percent of the auction, a large portion of the purchases actually made it to Japanese shores.

After March 25, however, it was possible for Japanese investors to be selling the amount they hoped to obtain in the auction days or weeks before it actually took place, in order to make room for the new securities. They could also choose to sell in the futures market to hedge their risks prior to their participation in the auctions. Indeed, one of the changes that the MOF allowed after the March 25 episode was to allow Japanese investors to participate in foreign futures and options markets to hedge

Table 2.1 Net purchases of foreign securities by country (US$ million)

	Total	US	UK	Germany	Netherlands	France	Luxembourg	Switzerland	Australia	Canada	Others
4/77–3/78	942	581	195	26	6	−2	116	−1	−0	6	15
4/78–3/79	9,728	8,416	809	92	52	15	210	−1	12	48	76
4/79–3/80	11,684	8,676	1,386	218	−34	−6	191	3	58	1,215	−23
4/80–3/81	19,672	13,371	1,375	229	91	46	844	36	65	3,465	132
4/81–3/82	7,856	2,056	1,816	451	107	−41	2,263	16	201	886	102
4/82–3/83	5,772	359	1,837	−100	−98	144	1,298	44	1,826	43	419
4/83–3/84	14,492	5,608	2,424	169	34	22	3,378	358	931	1,173	395
4/84–3/85	30,611	12,618	4,127	7	39	33	7,842	903	1,891	2,279	873
4/85–3/86	66,237	40,142	5,494	801	−16	39	13,492	353	296	1,818	2,818
4/86–3/87	111,188	50,718	14,521	4,321	93	726	27,158	263	86	5,518	4,786
4/87–3/88	74,908	33,296	6,717	4,931	646	800	22,037	303	2,060	165	3,951
4/88–3/89	90,199	28,373	10,881	5,574	653	816	33,782	891	588	3,775	4,870
4/89–3/90	105,798	23,224	5,875	5,967	340	4,090	47,257	1,340	1,983	2,499	13,217
CY 1985	55,406	31,271	6,192	433	−50	38	11,666	529	962	2,247	1,645
CY 1986	101,027	49,587	12,789	3,203	78	423	24,309	95	−296	6,642	4,196
1987 Jan.	10,800	4,581	1,251	407	−6	14	3,136	18	−4	1,010	393
Feb.	11,184	6,727	694	484	37	52	1,821	60	146	729	435
Mar.	6,334	967	1,062	643	14	256	2,148	54	254	333	601
Apr.	9,473	2,085	933	2,237	73	401	2,819	29	462	72	362
May	7,440	3,308	787	105	241	71	2,018	56	185	44	625
June	13,934	8,169	1,033	1,180	118	31	3,095	17	160	−242	375
July	10,401	4,092	1,328	581	40	72	3,195	22	288	−35	819
Aug.	6,667	2,828	235	−115	24	35	2,637	16	266	−46	788
Sept.	3,543	838	466	225	−1	38	1,980	16	14	348	−382
Oct.	5,157	−39	464	−183	136	55	3,299	3	157	253	1,011
Nov.	3,716	3,471	−120	−110	−35	23	−66	15	369	254	−83
Dec.	1,963	365	546	183	−103	0	1,106	78	115	−216	−111

CY 1987	90,610	37,392	8,678	5,635	537	1,048	27,187	383	2,413	2,503	4,834
1988 Jan.	1,505	1,008	528	229	−6	10	18	20	80	−136	−247
Feb.	10,784	7,074	212	391	24	−10	2,760	33	0	1	300
Mar.	317	95	304	209	135	73	−824	−2	−36	−132	493
Apr.	7,400	2,549	651	1,175	32	75	2,431	22	248	183	33
May	11,684	6,892	735	840	112	129	1,785	61	102	734	295
June	7,713	2,359	1,055	854	113	125	2,351	43	−187	362	639
July	14,964	5,558	2,808	429	64	108	4,212	311	295	198	980
Aug.	8,946	4,239	915	−17	51	357	2,430	78	409	−218	703
Sept.	3,669	−990	737	229	10	−276	2,869	55	541	163	331
Oct.	7,524	2,460	555	461	100	5	2,390	92	274	249	939
Nov.	7,649	3,757	850	351	50	−38	2,198	44	−166	81	523
Dec.	6,752	1,213	1,350	883	75	5	2,828	147	246	−121	128
CY 1988	88,908	36,215	10,699	6,035	758	561	25,449	902	1,806	1,364	5,117
1989 Jan.	4,521	621	1,251	416	20	13	347	86	1,053	271	443
Feb.	11,883	5,473	−210	340	49	308	5,905	48	−726	165	531
Mar.	−2,506	−5,758	184	−387	−23	5	4,036	−96	−1,501	1,708	−675
Apr.	13,095	5,220	1,855	19	−167	180	6,651	66	−576	−1,868	1,714
May	8,378	2,412	1,382	435	101	208	1,036	0	2,085	−22	740
June	9,926	1,153	826	39	−39	465	5,612	136	1,084	−385	1,036
July	10,140	1,466	−197	622	219	613	4,836	120	988	731	742
Aug.	11,159	5,548	1,908	470	319	911	1,769	156	−1,790	509	1,358
Sept.	9,522	2,681	1,081	−30	−158	294	4,754	169	−250	787	194
Oct.	17,163	7,560	374	721	−136	747	4,724	133	524	1,003	1,511
Nov.	11,566	2,214	1,345	310	99	119	3,997	277	181	1,099	1,925
Dec.	8,824	−2,084	1,344	1,576	−32	−6	4,412	151	467	762	2,233
CY 1989	113,670	26,508	11,143	4,531	254	3,858	48,078	1,248	1,538	4,760	11,753

Table 2.1 Continued

	Total	US	UK	Germany	Netherlands	France	Luxembourg	Switzerland	Australia	Canada	Others
1990 Jan.	1,862	-1,882	-641	1,588	-36	776	-108	18	-310	1,496	960
Feb.	6,167	3,160	-1,700	1,124	-25	-383	4,115	-31	151	-181	-64
Mar.	-2,004	-4,224	-1,702	-907	195	166	5,459	145	-571	-1,432	868
Apr.	569	-5,002	1,363	-871	-2	1,422	2,486	54	241	303	576
May	5,597	649	1,006	-755	187	946	1,599	147	587	101	1,131
June	5,758	-1,612	-641	322	-17	594	3,101	105	513	277	1,856
July	9,927	3,336	485	205	76	777	2,329	59	-251	1,055	2,259
Aug.	5,478	22	1,825	-924	123	-426	2,102	318	0	179	1,656
Sept.	-1,216	-4,970	1,359	-1,366	-333	-1	3,531	109	-597	-603	1,519
Oct.	-2,530	-4,385	-823	129	-126	229	1,708	330	-537	-572	1,078
Nov.	1,718	-426	772	-963	25	615	863	329	-869	293	882
Dec.	8,128	-777	653	399	125	846	5,239	310	508	-56	
CY 1990	39,455	-16,111	1,955	-2,019	192	5,559	32,424	1,892	-1,135	860	15,838
4/77–12/90	582,517	214,273	63,455	18,862	1,971	11,682	182,826	6,268	9,592	23,867	45,705

Source:　Ministry of Finance

their portfolios. Since that May 1987 auction, therefore, frequently reported "Japanese participation" figures have only meant "participation by US subsidiaries of Japanese-named securities houses run mostly by the local staff for the local market."

6.2 Toward Black Monday

In spite of the Fed's action to defend the dollar and the MOF's gruesome reporting requirements to keep Japanese banks from selling dollars, the June US trade deficit reported in August was so bad (the figure has since been revised downward) that the dollar began its tumble from the ¥150 level again. The Japanese investors who returned to the market in the May, June and July period began in August to reduce their purchases in the US, adding to upward pressure on US interest rates again.

At home, the sharp increase in the yield on long bonds, back to 4 percent from the record low yield of 2.55 percent, resulted in the so-called "Tateho shock." This incident involved a medium-sized chemical company named Tateho, which was caught on the wrong side in its bond futures speculation. The Tateho collapse suddenly made people aware of the size of the risk involved in trading activities, since it was said at the time that there were many more Tatehos around.

The event resulted in even higher interest rates at home and made US assets relatively less attractive. Even the Federal Reserve's decision to raise its discount rate on September 4, 1987, to maintain interest rate differentials in favor of the dollar, could do little to calm the market. At the same time, the Bank of Japan began to contemplate monetary tightening in view of the fact that the Japanese economy had weathered the *endaka* or strong-yen shock, and monetary conditions were deemed too loose to stop upward price pressures developing. By this time, the money supply was growing rapidly and, based on historical experience, the BOJ began to worry that inflation could not be too far away. Indeed, toward the end of September the BOJ allowed short-term rates to rise sharply to nearly 5 percent, as the first step toward ending the easy monetary policy. Some BOJ officials were openly dropping hints that a hike in the discount rate could come in late October or November.

Significantly higher rates at both the short and long ends at home meant much less incentive for investors to look abroad, and Japanese purchases abroad continued to fall sharply into September and October. This coincided with much higher bond yields in the US as market participants there realized that Japanese rates were going up fast and Japanese investors were holding back their purchases in the US.

It was in this highly vulnerable state that the Germans, too, started openly raising rates. At that time, the German discount rate was also very low, at 3.0 percent. Citing domestic economic strength and the possible rekindling of inflation, the Bundesbank began edging rates up in late September.

All this suggested to the market that the G-7 coordination efforts, where surplus countries were expected to keep rates low to stimulate domestic demand and deficit countries were expected to keep rates high to constrain domestic demand, were failing. It suggested that the monetary authorities in surplus countries were only looking at their own narrow national interests. These concerns became real when, in the second week of October, the then US Treasury secretary James Baker openly criticized the German action in raising rates, and suggested that the G-7 process was collapsing.

Since the solidarity of the G-7 countries was critical in preventing confidence in international financial markets crumbling, its demise suggested that the safeguards in place, such as the moral suasion by the Ministry of Finance to stop the Japanese pulling out of the US market, had disappeared. These fears, together with the fact that the Japanese were actually reducing their purchases in the US, pushed long bond yields in the US all the way back to nearly 11 percent. The move triggered arbitrage activities between the stock and bond markets, causing a massive collapse of the New York stock market, now known as Black Monday.

Given the complexity of computer-driven index trading that was already in wide use at the time, the full picture of the exact mechanism of that event may never be known. But it is probably safe to say that the decline in Japanese buying which started with the bad trade figure released in August probably had a lot to do with bringing US long rates up to the critical point.

In terms of actual selling by the Japanese in the US market, the Ministry of Finance figures show that in October 1987 the Japanese did become net sellers for the first time in recent memory. But the amount involved was only $39 million. Thus, it is hard to argue that Japanese *selling* had much to do with Black Monday. The lack of Japanese *buying*, however, probably had plenty to do with Black Monday.

The only other country where the Japanese were net sellers in October 1987 was Germany, to the tune of $189 million. For all foreign markets combined, the Japanese were still net buyers to the extent of $5.2 billion in that month. It is interesting to note that during the same month foreigners sold over $12 billion in Japan, or 315 times the amount that the Japanese sold in the US.

6.3   Reporting the Losses

From October to December 1987, Japanese interest abroad was very low as the dollar continued to fall from ¥140 toward the ¥120s. Most investors in Japan, like those abroad, stayed home to watch what would happen to the global economy in the aftermath of the worldwide stock market crash. Also, the embarrassing losses of some investors in their foreign portfolios were making headline news in Japanese newspapers at the time.

Because of the sharp appreciation of the yen since the Plaza Accord, the Ministry of Finance had to arrange some mechanism to smooth out the reporting of the foreign exchange losses that Japanese investors were incurring. Such measures were considered appropriate in view of the fact that some of these losses had been incurred as a result of MOF requests not to sell foreign securities, especially dollar securities. It was feared that forcing investors to report losses promptly could cause panic selling and exacerbate the collapse of the dollar.

As a result, it was decided in 1986 that investors should be allowed three years, to the end of fiscal 1988, to bring the book value of their foreign security holdings back to the market value. Investors could choose in which currencies they would recognize losses for each of those three years. For example, some investors could choose to recognize their losses in Australian dollar-denominated securities in the first year, in Canadian dollar and German mark-denominated securities in the following year, and in US dollar-denominated securities in the final year. In this way, only cumulative income statements over the three-year period made any sense.

Exactly how much was lost by Japanese investors holding foreign securities in the post-Plaza period is not at all easy to determine. This is because some of these losses were exaggerated by the conservative accounting system widely used in Japan. In particular, "the lower of the acquisition cost or the market value" rule means that while all losses, realized or unrealized, are recognized, only some of the unrealized capital gains are recognized. In particular, unrealized capital gains are recognized only for listed securities and only to the extent that there are losses on the foreign exchange side. Book entries in Japan, therefore, can only go down, never up. As a result, there were often substantial unrealized capital gains hidden in some of the loss figures reported.

There is an additional twist in the accounting system where unlisted foreign-currency-denominated securities are concerned. Because of the difficulty in marking these securities to market, the law stipulates that institutions need not change their book entries and recognize losses unless the exchange rate moves more than 15 percent against the book value.

The reason this 15 percent rule attained such importance in the market is that US Treasury bonds are considered unlisted securities under the strict definition of listed securities, because there is no exchange that actually lists US Treasury papers. Even though these papers are the most widely traded financial instruments in the world, with prices readily available almost anywhere, for accounting purposes they are considered unlisted papers. Since US Treasuries accounted for a huge portion of Japanese investor holdings, whether the 15 percent rule applied or not became a major source of concern among market participants all around the world. It was feared that if the rule were triggered by exchange rate movements, the Japanese could dump their holdings before the fiscal year-end in March. The situation made many market participants around the world very nervous from the middle of February to the end of March in the years 1987 to 1989.

To make matters worse, there were additional complications regarding the treatment of US Treasuries. They arose because a number of major financial institutions, mostly those with headquarters in Osaka, such as Sumitomo Life, argued to the tax authorities years ago that US Treasuries should be treated as listed securities, given their exceptionally liquid nature. These investors had an incentive to use this argument because, for tax purposes, listed securities allow them to claim more losses to reduce their tax liabilities than do unlisted securities. In order to claim losses on unlisted securities, investors have to wait until the exchange rate has moved at least 15 percent against the investment. No such minima are set for listed securities. The Osaka tax bureau agreed with the arguments and allowed those investors headquartered in Osaka to treat US Treasuries as listed securities. Those with headquarters in Tokyo, however, had to treat such securities as unlisted. These differences made the reading of income statements even more difficult, given the large share of US Treasury papers in investors' portfolios.

6.4   The Japanese Marshall Plan

With the above in mind, the top five life insurance companies alone, which accounted for about 23 percent of all Japanese foreign securities purchases by 1988, had lost $25.3 billion by the end of March of that year. The total losses incurred by the entire Japanese investment community in the two and a half years after the Plaza Accord probably reached many times this amount.

Some have called this the Japanese Marshall Plan for the US. And it is not without foundation, in that the US provided $2 billion to rebuild Japan after the war, and another $2.4 billion during the Korean War, making a total of $4.4 billion from 1945 to 1953. With the US consumer price index increasing by 490 percent during the last four decades, the above outlay in real terms in 1988 would have been worth about $22 billion, an amount smaller than the total foreign exchange losses endured by the top Japanese life insurance companies between 1985 and March 1988. Most of those losses were absorbed by realizing some of the previously unrealized capital gains that investors had in their domestic equity portfolios.

6.5 The Dollar Hits the Bottom

Around Christmas 1987, the G-7 countries met again to proclaim the "Christmas Agreement," which was based mainly on the short-lived Louvre Accord, indicating that the dollar had fallen far enough. By then the market had lost confidence in the G-7 process and had largely ignored the agreement by pushing the dollar even lower. Just before the year-end, the then French Finance Minister stated that the G-7 had in store for the market a new strategy, but his warning shots were also ignored.

On January 4, 1988, the first business day of the new year, the dollar hit its all-time low of ¥120.25. It was at that moment, however, that the G-7 central banks came in with massive intervention to push the dollar higher, propeling it back up to ¥125 in no time. The fact that the central banks were willing to create a disorderly market in order to push the dollar higher took participants by surprise, since most of them had believed up to then that the central banks may have come in to stop the dollar falling, but never to actually push it higher. Many who thought that shorting the dollar was a safe bet and believed that the worst that could happen to them was the dollar not falling, were very badly burnt on this occassion. The message was well taken, and the dollar began its slow recovery.

Among economists, however, the doom-and-gloom scenario for the dollar remained popular, with many expressing the view that the US currency would eventually fall to ¥100 or even ¥80. In this climate, and after suffering astronomical losses and public embarrassment, most fund managers were too scared to try the dollar again in the near future.

Indeed, in 1987 there were many rumors of Japanese investors moving funds away from the US and into Continental European markets. Although the actual amounts involved were small, the talk was serious enough for policymakers and market participants to take notice. Most Japanese investors considered Continental European assets to have characteristics too similar to yen assets to warrant the additional efforts needed to study the markets and invest in them. The fact that they were looking into these markets after March 1987 suggested that people really were losing confidence in the dollar and that they may have been ready to pull out of the US market.

Although many investors had the option of bringing funds back to Japan, and many did so, as mentioned earlier, in many institutions funds were allocated first to such categories as domestic stocks, domestic bonds, domestic loans and foreign securities. Because different departments were made responsible for each of the markets, the funds allocated to foreign securities often stayed there until the next major review. It is likely that it was just such funds that flowed into European markets from the US in the 1987–8 period.

In terms of numbers, purchases in the US fell from $49.6 billion in 1986 to $37.4 billion in 1987. At the same time, purchases in Germany increased from $3.2 billion in 1986 to $5.6 billion in 1987.

Just as Japanese investors were getting ready to move into Continental European markets in early 1988, however, the US trade performance began to show a marked improvement, providing support for the dollar. At the same time, the issue of withholding tax surfaced in Germany, causing a massive outflow of funds away from that country. As a result, the deutsche mark began falling sharply in 1988, hurting the Japanese who moved funds there and forcing them to redirect their investment efforts once more.

For most of 1988 the dollar and the yen stayed together, although at one point the dollar reached as high as ¥137, while the mark and other EMS currencies remained very weak. The relative strength of the yen in that year was mostly because the majority of Japanese investors had had their fingers burnt too badly in the US to try again in that market so soon. Germans and other Europeans who fled the US market as early as 1986 were both willing and able to return there once US indicators (in this case the trade figures) began to show signs of improvement.

7   A NEW LEASE OF LIFE FOR THE DOLLAR

7.1   Securities Investment Trusts and Portfolio Insurance

One group that did show interest in the dollar market in 1988 was securities investment trusts. They were moving back to the US armed with the new funds set up from May to invest in US Treasuries. The new feature of the funds was the incorporation of the latest computer-driven portfolio insurance programs, which were believed at that time to reduce foreign exchange risk significantly. Since the funds had just been formed, they were also not constrained by what had happened to the dollar prior to that date.

Starting with an exchange rate of around ¥125, in a matter of weeks the funds were able to attract nearly $8 billion, mostly from individuals and smaller institutions. Their subsequent buying of dollars pushed the dollar from the ¥120s to the ¥130s during the summer months, where it reached at one point ¥137. The dollar lost steam again, however, when the new funds had exhausted their buying, and fell once again to the ¥120s in October, also due in part to the portfolio insurance being used. Indeed, the problem was that all four big securities houses offered very similar funds, with very similar portfolio insurance programs. This meant that the entire $8 billion tended to move together. With most other investors staying on the sidelines, their purchases frequently pushed the dollar up, and their selling pushed the dollar down.

In the late September–early October period, the dollar was easing gradually, but when it broke through ¥130 (which happened to be an important trigger for the computer-driven portfolio insurance), all four funds issued sell orders for dollars within a very short timespan, causing a sharp fall from ¥130 to about ¥127. This sudden fall induced panic among other investors, who thought that the dollar was already out of the danger zone. Their rush to increase hedges on their dollar portfolios pushed the dollar even lower, where it eventually reached the ¥120 level again.

This taught securities investment trusts an important lesson: that it is dangerous to follow the advice of the computer when all the other participants in the market have similar programs. Furthermore, other players in the market quickly learned the characteristics of the programs and began to exploit them. They did this deliberately by momentarily pushing exchange rates in thin markets, such as Wellington, New Zealand, so that the buy or sell orders from these funds would be triggered. Because the funds were approved by the Ministry of Finance based on this portfolio insurance feature, it was not possible for their managers to ignore the computer-driven instructions completely. In the end, many fund managers decided to get around the problem by rearranging their trading so that at the end of each week, for example, the portfolio would at least be consistent with the direction given by the computer.

In the meantime, fund managers faced with an order from the computer to sell $100 million may have bought $200 million first and then sold $300 million later. This sort of smokescreen tactic was especially important in the Tokyo market, where too many people are looking over each other's shoulders to see how many dollars or yen they have left to sell.

7.2   New Interest in the Dollar

In addition to the new funds from the securities investment trusts, toward the end of 1988, many other Japanese investors were also becoming interested in the US market. They were seeing the improvements in US trade performance that were contrary to the "twin deficit" argument to which so many economists subscribed back in the early 1980s. Recall that, based on this argument, the US current account deficit should not get better unless the budget deficit problem was also corrected. The fact that the US economy was expanding strongly with a declining external deficit encouraged many fund managers who were looking into the dollar markets. Their (correct) reasoning was that since economists had failed to anticipate the improvements in the US trade balance, there was a possibility that they would also be wrong in their exchange rate forecasts. The senior management of these funds, however, needed a little more time to recover from the wounds incurred over the two-and-a-half year decline of the dollar following the Plaza Accord. As a result, no major actions were taken until April 1989, the beginning of fiscal 1989.

Once the new fiscal year started, however, foreign securities and dollar securities in particular came under especially heavy demand, and the dollar began to climb sharply. Sensing the new trend, Nomura Securities, the largest securities house in Japan, also started a massive campaign to promote foreign securities from the beginning of the new fiscal year, and this move was soon followed by other securities houses.

Realizing that the situation had changed, the Federal Reserve Bank of New York began "reverse intervention" on March 30, selling dollars for yen for the first time since the dollar-selling intervention that immediately followed the Plaza Accord. This intervention, which took place at around ¥133, was joined by the Bank of Canada, followed a few days later by the Bank of Japan. The coordinated action did manage to keep the dollar in a relatively narrow range for about a month.

This period just happened to coincide with a worsening of the trade relationship between Japan and the US, and Congress was eagerly awaiting the administration's decision on applying the punitive measures now available under the "Super 301" provision of the new Omnibus Trade Act. Sensing that the weak yen could only strengthen the protectionist argument in the US Congress, the administration was trying hard to stop the yen falling.

The momentum was unstoppable, however, and in May, in spite of massive intervention by the central banks, the dollar broke through, reaching as high as ¥152 by early June. This time not only securities investment trusts but all investors were involved. Furthermore, in addition to more purchases, many investors were beginning to remove the hedges they had earlier placed on their portfolios. The new buying and the removal of old hedges both worked to push the dollar higher, and made the job of central banks trying to contain the dollar's appreciation a very difficult one.

7.3 The Return to the Pre-Plaza Dilemma

Indeed, in some very important ways, the world returned to its pre-Plaza state, the major differences being that the dollar started from a very low level and US indicators, such as the trade deficit, began to improve rapidly. With no major changes in investment opportunities in Japan since the early 1980s and most assets such as land and equities priced very high, the change in the dollar's direction and the improving US trade outlook made US assets almost irresistible to Japanese investors.

The policymakers, on the other hand, were put in a very difficult position. This is because, even though the external imbalances were on the way to correction, Japan was still a country with a huge surplus, and had to keep its currency high and domestic demand strong in order to make sure the reduction in its external surplus continued. The reverse applied to the US.

The reason for the difficulty was that, once confidence returned to the dollar, investors would rush to buy the currency while it was still cheap. But their purchases would push the dollar higher and defeat the improving trend in the trade balance. In terms of policy response, the weakening yen meant that Japan had to raise its interest rates to defend the currency. But such a policy runs the risk of weakening domestic demand in the surplus country.

In the case of Japan, where lay-offs are uncommon, a fall in domestic demand as a result of higher interest rates can easily translate into an export drive. Such a drive can then effectively defeat any benefit from a stronger yen brought about by higher interest rates. Based on this argument, the Ministry of Finance and MITI raised strong objections to higher rates in Japan. The Bank of Japan, on the other hand, appeared to be concerned that without higher rates to defend the yen, the currency could fall further and increase the export competitiveness of Japanese manufacturers. They feared that such a development could only worsen protectionist threats abroad. Both arguments had their merits, and one could not tell in advance which would eventually prevail.

The reverse problem arose in the US between the Federal Reserve, on the one hand, and the Treasury, on the other. After the foreign exchange intervention effort to contain the dollar had failed in May, the administration appeared to lean toward the thought that the only instrument left to keep the dollar low and stable was to bring down interest rates.

The Fed, on the other hand, was concerned that the Treasury would use the exchange rate as a means to press for monetary easing from the central bank. After all, the US was still a deficit country, and a premature reduction in rates could rekindle domestic demand and increase imports, thus defeating the benefit of a low and stable dollar that lower interest rates would bring.

What this debate in Japan and the US shows is that when the currency of a deficit country is rising, monetary policy actions to contain the rise have the highly undesirable side-effects of pushing domestic demand in both the surplus and deficit countries in the unwanted direction. And it was this debate over undesirable side-effects that made the G-7 coordination process appear to falter from about May 1989. The G-7 countries were working together as closely as ever. The problem was that there were no clear-cut monetary policy remedies to the problem at hand.

In retrospect, from a policy perspective, a falling dollar was easier to respond to then than a rising dollar. When the dollar was falling, and when market participants feared its possible collapse, policy responses were all very straightforward. Japan, the surplus country, would simply lower interest rates to both reduce the relative attractiveness of the yen while encouraging domestic demand and imports. The US, the deficit country, would raise interest rates to maintain the relative attractiveness of the dollar while constraining domestic demand to reduce imports and increase exports.

The world was extremely lucky, however, because just around that time the US economy started to lose steam. This allowed Mr Greenspan, the chairman of the Federal Reserve, to lower rates without worrying about a massive explosion in US domestic demand. Similarly, the Japanese economy was near the end of its second year of expansion and was close to overheating by the middle of 1989. This allowed the BOJ to increase rates without worrying too much about the immediate collapse of Japanese domestic demand. Furthermore, some of the undesirable side effects of low rates, such as skyrocketing asset prices, were rapidly becoming major social issues. The Bank of Japan, therefore, raised its discount rate in May, both to defend the yen and to correct the extremely loose monetary policy that had been in operation since February 1987. What would have happened had the Japanese economy remained weak and the US economy remained strong when the dollar began strengthening does not bear thinking about.

7.4 The European Revival

In the meantime, the Tiananmen Square incident in China in June 1989 and the Recruit scandal at home at about the same time, affecting some of the most powerful politicians in Japan, took the strength out of the yen well into the second half of 1989. In the Recruit scandal, it was eventually found that a number of senior members of the Takeshita government had accepted preflotation shares from a company called Recruit Cosmos, in return for granting the company the right to publish a careers/job-opportunity publication. Up to that point, such information was handled almost exclusively by the government's employment office. The weakness of the yen, together with the continued strength of the economy, prompted the BOJ to raise its discount rate once more in October.

When the Berlin Wall came down on November 9, a totally new investment horizon was introduced and even more money left Japan, making the yen the weakest currency among all the industrialized nations. The talk of EC '92, together with all the excitement that the fall of the Berlin Wall brought to the market, suddenly transformed the image of Europe from that of a place rich in cultural achievements but behind in state-of-the-art technology to something much younger, much bolder and much more forward-looking than most other parts of the world.

The 1990s, which many in Japan thought would be an Asian decade, suddenly appeared instead to be a European decade. The contrast between a Europe bursting with energy and idealism and an Asia mired in scandals (Japan) and repression (China) became almost too stark to ignore. Even the seemingly unstoppable economy of South Korea began to lose some of its luster, if only temporarily. At the same time, the taken-for-granted political stability of Taiwan came into question, with increased demands for democracy and self-determination. From "Japan *über Alles*" in the late 1980s, suddenly the talk was of Japanese pessimism or, as the title of the book by Bill Emmott of the London *Economist* suggests, "*The Sun Also Sets.*"

The rush by Japanese investors for European paper reached such a point that it was said there was more liquidity for Deutsche Bank stocks in Tokyo than there was in Frankfurt. It is probable, however, that most Japanese investment in Europe after the fall of the Berlin Wall went into deutsche mark bank deposits. This is because there were also concerns that the Bundesbank would continue to seek tight monetary policy to keep inflation rates under control during the reunification of East and West Germany. The prospect made both bond and equity investment in Europe less attractive.

8   THE END OF AN ERA

8.1   The Great Contraction

In view of the continued weakness of the yen, when at the beginning of 1990 the BOJ began to hint that the third discount rate hike on Christmas

Day, 1989, would not be the last one, the Tokyo bond market collapsed, with the yield skyrocketing from just below 6 percent to over 7 percent. This was soon followed by the massive collapse of the stock market from its all-time high of ¥38,915 on the Nikkei on the last day of 1989. Although the stock market kept going up during the second half of 1989, in spite of three discount rate hikes by the BOJ, the prospect of a fourth hike and the collapse of the long bond market were just too much for the stock market to ignore.

Furthermore, by late 1989 the social outcry over the land issue had reached an explosive state, and the monetary authorities and financial circles in general were considered responsible for the land price appreciation. Although the real reason for this appreciation had always been the ill-conceived building regulations that limited the supply of floor space (the most powerful substitute for land), the social atmosphere was such that a convenient scapegoat was much in demand.

The BOJ, together with the Ministry of Finance, were therefore forced to bring down land prices single-handedly by means of monetary policy. In December 1989, the newly appointed governor of the Bank of Japan, Mr Mieno, explicitly mentioned the correction of outrageous land prices in Japan as one of the goals of his administration. This added to fears that the central bank could go beyond traditional macroeconomic considerations in tightening its monetary policy. Since that would entail the creation of an acute cash squeeze to force land speculators into distress selling, many feared that the BOJ would not stop tightening the screw until bankruptcies and foreclosures had become commonplace.

The collapse of the bond and stock markets at home changed the entire foundation of Japanese investments abroad, for investors now had to take profits wherever they could abroad in order to make up for their huge losses at home. After all, that was what international diversificiation was all about. Since all this coincided with and, in some sense, was triggered by the weak yen, foreign markets, especially those in the US and Germany, were attractive places to take profits. Literally from the first business week of the 1990s, therefore, Japanese investors began to sell abroad.

The collapse of the Tokyo stock market also meant that one of the key hedging instruments for foreign securities investment was lost. This is because, in encountering foreign exchange risk, many investors relied on the cushion provided by the huge unrealized capital gains in their domestic equity portfolios. As noted earlier, this cushion allowed major Japanese insurance companies to absorb $25.3 billion in foreign exchange losses in their US dollar portfolios during the 1985–7 period. The collapse of the Tokyo market meant that this critical cushion was lost, and any foreign exchange or capital losses incurred abroad would hit their bottom lines directly. This fact forced them to look into exchange rate and other risks far more carefully than they had done in the 1980s.

8.2   BIS Capital Adequacy Requirements and Capital Flows

To make matters worse, the collapse of the stock market hit Japanese banks' capital bases directly. This is because the new capital adequacy requirements drawn up for the Bank for International Settlements (BIS) by the monetary authorities of the major industrialized countries in the late 1980s required that by 1993 banks active in international markets should have capital equivalent to at least 8 percent of their total assets. Because much Japanese capital was in the form of unrealized capital gains on domestic stock portfolios, the BIS allowed 45 percent of the unrealized gains to be included when calculating a bank's capital.

When the Tokyo stock market was rising strongly in the 1980s, the BIS requirements were a non-issue, and Japanese banks continued on their relentless asset-expansion path. Since the beginning of 1990, however, the collapse of the stock market has meant that there is now a strong likelihood that these banks may not be able to meet the 8 percent requirement. Although the requirement itself is to be met in 1993, most rating agencies are already using or referring to BIS standards as a basis for making credit judgments on banks. Since the cost of raising funds has been made dependent on a bank's position relative to the BIS regulations, no bank has been able to ignore the requirements since the late 1980s. This has been especially true in the highly competitive interbank market, where banks with poor ratings are routinely forced to pay a much higher spread in order to attract funds.

The stock market crash had two effects. First, banks in Japan suddenly became very cautious and ended their aggressive approach aimed at winning clients at home and abroad. For institutional investors who had long been considered high-cost lenders, this was their first opportunity in nearly a decade to re-enter the Japanese domestic lending market. With Japanese interest rates now quite high, their allocation of funds changed dramatically from foreign securities and domestic equities to domestic loans.

The second impact was created by banks rushing to obtain subordinated loans to strengthen their capital bases. As the loans were priced over the long-term prime rate, which reached as high as 8.9 percent in September 1990, insurance companies, the major suppliers, found them very attractive. Even though these loans were called "subordinated," few in Japan thought major banks such as Sumitomo or Mitsubishi would ever go under. As such, the loans were just as good as lending to triple-A names, but with a very attactive price for the lenders.

At the same time, the deposit interest rate deregulation, that started with the Yen–Dollar Talks mentioned earlier, entered its final stages, with banks finally allowed to offer attractive savings instruments *vis-à-vis* insurance companies. Indeed, it was the uneven pace of financial deregulation that brought such a large volume of funds to insurance companies and away from banks, starting around 1985. The insurance companies were allowed to offer attractive savings vehicles ahead of banks, and managed to attract funds that usually headed toward bank savings.

As a result, for the first time in many years, institutional investors such as life insurance companies began feeling a cash shortage. In order to make room for banks' subordinated loans, therefore, they had to sell their foreign and domestic bond holdings, resulting in even higher interest rates, especially at home. The higher bond yields brought about by insurance companies selling their domestic bond holdings pushed the stock market even lower, and increased the need for Japanese banks to issue even more subordinated loans. Saddam Hussein's adventure into Kuwait also added to upward pressure on interest rates by pushing the price of oil higher and rekindling fears of inflation around the world. This made the vicious circle even worse. Most of the nearly $10 billion of net selling of foreign securities that took place in September–October 1990 was a result of this spiral. The vicious circle lasted well into late 1990.

It should also be noted that banks are not allowed to buy foreign securities unhedged because of the foreign exchange exposure requirements imposed on them by the monetary authorities. Since institutional investors such as insurance companies are allowed to buy foreign securities with their yen funds, the shift of funds away from institutional investors to banks means the total amount of yen funds available for foreign securities investment has been shrinking. Of this shrinking pool of funds, more and more of it has been going into domestic lending, including to banks in the form of subordinated loans. Thus, much of the mechanism which led to the astronomical increase in Japanese purchases of foreign securities in the 1980s began working in reverse in the 1990s.

8.3   Stubbornly High US Long Rates

Luckily, by 1990 the US current account deficit had fallen by $68 billion from its peak in 1987, due mostly to the lower value of the dollar achieved via the Plaza Accord. This reduction in the need for funds from abroad allowed US markets to withstand Japanese selling and stopped them falling into the kind of difficulties experienced in 1987.

The Japanese withdrawal from the market did keep US long rates higher than usual, despite the very weak US economy that has been a feature since the second half of 1990. This is not hard to understand in view of the fact that the Japanese preferred the long end of US Treasuries all along and frequently constituted nearly one-third of total buying at that end of the market. The departure of this group from the market must be considered a major structural change.

The net selling by the Japanese investors in the US market in 1990 was $16 billion for all securities. Since in the previous year net purchases of $26 billion for all securities were recorded, the total shift in demand was $42 billion. A large portion of this $42 billion shift is likely to have been concentrated in the long bond market in view of its liquidity. It is not surprising, therefore, that the yield remained high at that end of the market in spite of the weak economy.

It should be mentioned that the situation could have been far worse during the first half of 1990. This is because some of the panic in Tokyo was caused by mistaken reports in a major Japanese newspaper that the US actually wanted a strong dollar. The *Nikkei* newspaper quoted the then Vice-chairman Johnson of the Federal Reserve as stating that the dollar had fallen far enough. The comment, however, was actually made in a conference with Tietmeyer of the German Bundesbank concerning the rapidly appreciating deutsche mark, not the rapidly falling yen. In a panic-stricken Tokyo market, however, this implied that the BOJ would have to tighten controls further to defend the yen, causing even more damage to domestic markets in the process.

Operating in their defensive mode, the next instinctive move of most Japanese investors was to determine where to take profits abroad to make up for expected losses at home. It was said that as much as $20 billion was lined up during the second quarter of 1990 for liquidation abroad in order to take profits should the Tokyo market fall much further.

Fortunately, the US side realized the danger and Treasury officials testified in Congress that the US actually wanted a strong yen and not a strong dollar. The testimony helped to reverse the direction of the yen, which at one point reached ¥160, and helped the Tokyo stock market to regain stability in no small way.

8.4 Changed Relationship between the Exchange Rate and Capital Flows

The episode of 1990 also suggests that the relationship between the exchange rate and capital flows was reversed compared with the 1980s. In the 1980s, a strong dollar generally meant more Japanese buying, and many in Wall Street argued for a strong dollar, believing that it would be good for the US market (and for their bonuses).

In the 1990s, a strong dollar is actually detrimental to lower US interest rates. This is because, in the face of weak domestic equity and bond markets, a strong dollar means more BOJ tightening to defend the yen, further erosion of the Tokyo markets and an increased need for Japanese investors to take profits abroad.

The key here is, of course, the Tokyo stock market. When it was strong, as in the 1980s, a strong dollar encouraged people to go abroad thinking that if something should go wrong, they could always tap some of the unrealized capital gains in their domestic equity portfolios to absorb losses. When the Tokyo market is weak, as it has been so far in the 1990s, a strong dollar only encourages Japanese investors to take profits abroad to make up for losses at home.

9 "OVERFINANCING"

9.1 The Concept of "Overfinancing"

The experiences of the 1980s and 1990s suggest that undesirable movements in exchange rates not only threaten world trade with protectionism, but also jeopardize financial markets and the growth of the world economy. In particular, the problems that monetary authorities encountered in keeping the dollar low and stable made so many other aspects of their economic policies more difficult.

The dollar was rising in the first half of the 1980s and again in 1989, because more funds from abroad were trying to enter the US than the US actually needed from abroad to finance its current account deficit. This condition, where too much money tries to go into a deficit country *ex ante* and pushes up its exchange rate *ex post*, causing a further deterioration in its external balance, was a new phenomenon of the 1980s brought about by long and sustained cross-border capital flows. These in turn were made possible by the deregulation of capital movements across national borders. Since there is no phrase appropriate to designate this condition in the economics literature, it is simply called here "overfinancing" of the current account deficit.

The state of overfinancing can be said to exist when, *ex ante*, the money that is trying to enter a deficit country is larger than that country's need to finance its current account deficit. Since, *ex post*, only the amount equal to the current account deficit of the country can actually lay a claim on that country's assets, the adjustment is made in the exchange rate. Thus, in the state of overfinancing, the currency of the deficit country should be appreciating.

This is not all bad, of course. The overfinancing condition should improve the terms of trade of the deficit country and increase its domestic demand as interest rates are lowered and asset prices are raised by a process of that much more foreign buying in the country. The free movement of capital across national borders has also increased the efficiency of capital use all around the world. Those investments that were yielding only a 2 percent return in a surplus country may now be earning 10 percent in a deficit country. Such a development no doubt contributed to the long economic expansions seen in many countries in the 1980s, in spite of repeated forecasts of economic downturns from business-cycle-minded economists.

The problem, however, is that on the trade front an overfinancing situation puts manufacturers in the deficit countries in an extremely difficult position. As the usual relief that comes from exchange rate adjustment never materializes, exporters and import-competing industries in deficit countries are placed at an increasing disadvantage relative to foreign producers. It was common to hear in the US around 1985 that "industries which would have disappeared in 30 years' time have disappeared in three years." And the ensuing popularity of protectionism in the US came mighty close to undermining the entire free-trade system of the world.

The real challenge posed by the free movement of capital across national borders, therefore, is how to contain its undesirable trade consequences, while retaining its positive contribution through increased efficiency of capital. Three remedies have been put forth so far.

9.2   Remedies for Overfinancing

The first remedy is the monetary policy remedy mentioned earlier, that is, to raise rates in the surplus country and lower rates in the deficit country to discourage funds flow. But, as noted earlier, this entails some highly undesirable side-effects, namely, that interest-sensitive domestic demand will move in the opposite direction to that desired by the policymakers. When the economy of the surplus country is weak and that of the deficit country strong, this monetary policy option is simply unusable.

The second remedy is simply to reintroduce the capital controls, effectively bringing the world back to the 1970s. In the short run, this may work. If the MOF telephones institutional investors and tells them not to sell or buy certain securities, for example, chances are high that the investors will listen for a while. They do not want to be named publicly as the culprits in bringing about situations considered undesirable by the authorities. This cannot last for long, however, if the investment opportunities so missed are considered too great. For example, when life insurance companies were up against the 10 percent limit on their foreign holdings, many simply lent money to friendly corporations and asked them to buy foreign securities on their behalf. In this way, the insurance company's accounts will only show yen loans to domestic corporations, although the money is actually going elsewhere. Thus, even though the second option should correct the overfinancing problem in theory, without a massive investment in policing the flows the chances are high that regulatory constraints alone will not be effective.

In addition to the problem of enforcement, reintroducing capital controls means much-reduced efficiency of capital around the globe and much-reduced growth potential for the world economy. Thus, for both efficiency and enforcement reasons, this option is not a viable one, except in short-run emergency situations.

9.3   The Real Solution

The last, and the only real, solution to the problem of overfinancing is to get to the heart of the issue: the lack of investment opportunities in the surplus countries. From this perspective, if Japan had everything in the way of social infrastructure and was enjoying a living standard that was the envy of the world, nothing more could be done. Indeed, when the UK and the US were major capital exporters, people in these countries enjoyed the highest living standards in the world. For investors there, rates of return were frequently higher abroad, where living standards were lower and where the given technological knowhow associated with the investments could still do a lot more good.

In the case of Japan, however, nothing could be further from the truth. Starting from the infamous "rabbit hutch" housing conditions, the long working hours, lack of roads, airports and sewerage systems, and crowded trains all suggest that there is very much room for improvement. Indeed, many Japanese fund managers buying foreign securities have all felt a huge contradiction: "Why should we be lending money to those people who live far better than we do, in the US, Australia, or Canada? This money should be spent improving conditions for people who live right here in Japan."

The problem, however, is that there really are no attractive investment opportunities at home because of the hundreds and thousands of regulations that make the return on necessary investments highly unattractive. For example, the office vacancy rate in Tokyo is said to be around 0.3 percent. In such a tight market and with rising rents, one would expect to see much more construction going on to meet the demand. Unfortunately, the rate of return on rental buildings in the city of Tokyo is only around 1.8 to 3.0 percent. This low return is a result of the severe limit on the height of buildings, very high land prices, the enormous time needed to get permission and land cleared to build major structures, and the limit on the rents people can afford to pay. It is not uncommon to wait for years, if not decades, to get major construction projects going in Japan. The trouble and cost involved are just too much for most investors to bear, especially when similar structures can be built in Los Angeles or New York in just two or three years.

It should be noted that, although earthquakes are common in Japan, technology was developed many decades ago to build even skyscrapers that are earthquake-proof. Only a handful of true skyscrapers have actually been built, however, because of zoning and other restrictions.

The tragedy of the 1980s, if one existed, was that the Japanese were hamstrung by their own outdated and ill-conceived regulations, which forced investment funds out of Japan, causing the yen to weaken, the trade surplus to expand and "Japan-bashing" to worsen. Unfortunately, most policymakers and practitioners in the private sector in the 1980s received their economics training in the 1970s. And what was taught in the 1970s and earlier never prepared them for the world of overfinancing that was brought about by long and sustained capital movements across national borders.

When these phenomena appeared in the early 1980s, therefore, most had no idea of how to handle them; hence the debate on whether it was the dollar that was strong or the yen that was weak. Everyone worried about how to finance the expanding US current account deficit when the real problem for most of the 1980s was that there was just too much financing. Except for the critical post-Plaza adjustment period of about three years, therefore, the real problem was how to keep too much foreign – especially Japanese – money from trying to enter the US. It was only toward the end of the 1980s that policymakers, especially in the US, began to contemplate the possibility that they had been worrying about the wrong problem all along.

9.4   The US–Japan Structural Impediments Initiative

The redepreciation of the yen that started in 1989, together with the lack of significant improvement in US–Japan trade – in spite of the halving of the value of the dollar against the yen – finally prompted the US to think seriously about the structural issues involved. The fact that US–EC trade improved so much in favor of the US during the same period made it even more necessary to look at the structural issues in Japan. This concern resulted in the US–Japan Structural Impediments Initiative (SII).

Although the final document of the SII included everything from purely macrocyclical measures such as ¥430 trillion of public works expenditure to purely trade-related issues such as revamping anti-monopoly laws in Japan, the real thrust of the agreement was to make more Japanese money stay at home. It proposed, for example, a major overhaul of outdated Japanese tax regulations on land, as well as deregulation of land use.

In this sense, the SII was the first major departure from the original and mostly incorrect worries of the 1980s about how to bring Japanese money to the US. It was also the first economic policy initiative in the world that took full account of the new reality brought about by the free movement of capital across national borders. After a full decade of trial and error, therefore, policymakers finally began to address the core problem: the lack of investment opportunities in Japan.

There were many in Japan who resented being told by the Americans when to open and close large stores and how to tax land. They argued that such intrusions constituted foreign meddling in the internal affairs of Japan. What they failed to realize was the fact that once capital flows are freed, changes in what were formerly considered purely domestic matters can have a devastating impact on the exchange rate and trade flows by affecting the magnitude and direction of capital flows.

For example, it is probably safe to say that if the mayor of Tokyo, Mr Suzuki, decided to raise the height limit on buildings in the city tomorrow, that alone would do more to push the yen higher and keep it there than any change in monetary policy could hope to achieve. This is because significant relaxation of this limit would allow builders to put up more buildings in the city which has the world's greatest shortage of office and residential space. For it does not take a genius to find that the Tokyo market, with its 0.3 percent vacancy rate, offers a better investment climate than New York with its 15 percent vacancy rate. The money that used to flow out of Japan and weaken the yen would then stay home to finance the construction. This would mean strong domestic demand and a strong yen at the same time, and should go a long way toward addressing the trade imbalance issues. The bigger housing and office spaces so constructed would also help increase the Japanese appetite for all sorts of goods, including imports.

In the pre-1980 world, foreigners could not have cared less about how high the buildings in Tokyo were allowed to go because, in the absence of non-trade-related capital flows, exchange rates tended to move in such a direction to balance trade. In the post-1980 world, however, the overwhelming dynamics operating in the foreign exchange market have been to equate the marginal rates of return on investment across countries instead of trade flows across countries. As a result, issues affecting domestic investment opportunities can no longer be separated from trade issues. This scheme is shown in figure 2.8.

The SII started out on a very positive note, receiving widespread

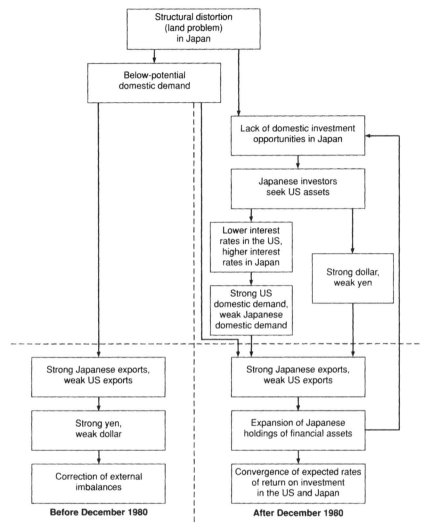

Figure 2.8 Net economics of deregulated international capital flows

Source: Nomura Research Institute

support from the Japanese public. As it was the final attempt by the Republican administration to head off anti-Japanese protectionism in Congress, the Japanese government also realized that there was no time to waste. The final agreement on the SII was signed in June 1990.

Just as the Japanese public and political leaders were about to embark on a major restructuring of the Japanese economy, Saddam Hussein came along in August 1990 and attracted all the attention of the US and Japanese public to him. Subsequent concerns over oil supplies and the debate over Japanese contributions to the US-led multinational effort in the Middle East took most of the momentum out of the SII discussions.

9.5 Japan as a Capital Exporter or Merchandise Importer?

The reforms suggested in the SII, if implemented, will increase demand for capital in Japan and reduce funds availability elsewhere. Some may argue that such a policy is detrimental in a world with a supposed savings shortage. But it will increase Japanese domestic demand and strengthen the yen at the same time, and this should go a long way toward correcting Japan's external imbalances. Since Japan has been running a current account surplus with most countries in the world, the SII will benefit a large number of countries, including the US, which will be able to reduce their much-detested deficit with Japan. The reduction in their deficits will allow the countries concerned to offer more help, compared to previously to those in need of capital. Such a development will also reduce trade friction and invigorate a business atmosphere that has been poisoned by it.

It should also be noted in this regard that the Japanese government is not in a position to enjoy the country's current account surplus. Japan's surplus is with the private sector, not with the government. Latin America, which has been in dire financial straits since the early 1980s, has never received much help from Tokyo, and there is no reason to think that the situation for the Eastern European countries will be any different.

What the US and many other countries need is the opportunity to reduce their deficits with Japan, not find ways to maintain these deficits. In the long run, therefore, the SII approach is far more sustainable politically and economically than any effort to increase Japanese "capital exports."

10 CONCLUSION

The relaxation of capital controls in key financial centers all around the world in the 1979–80 period opened up huge investment opportunities for Japanese investors for the first time in history. This brought Japanese capital to the global market in quantities unforeseen by most policy-makers and market participants at the beginning of the 1980s.

Even though Japan lagged far behind others in the area of social infrastructure investment, many investors felt they had no other choice but to seek investment opportunities abroad because of outdated and ill-conceived regulations reducing rates of return on needed investments at home. The huge outflows of capital from Japan overwhelmed trade flows and produced a weak yen, and this in turn exacerbated Japan's trade surplus and worsened trade friction or "Japan-bashing."

Not understanding what was really going on, policymakers and market participants in the 1980s worried constantly about the need to find sufficient financing for the US external debt. It took policymakers nearly ten years to realize that the real problem during most of the 1980s, except the three years immediately following the Plaza Accord, was just the opposite: too much money was moving toward the US, not too little. This situation, called here overfinancing, required adjustments in structural policies because monetary policy remedies would have had too many undesirable side effects.

This realization finally took the form of the SII, signed in June 1990. The SII basically said that Japanese money should be spent actually in Japan, by removing the host of regulatory and tax obstacles in the way of necessary domestic investment. Instead of worrying about financing the US current account deficit, therefore, the policy thrust now is to make Japan an attractive place in which to invest.

From May 1989 the strong economy, the weak yen and sky-high land prices prompted the Bank of Japan to tighten monetary policy sharply, resulting in a collapse of the bond and stock markets. The collapse at home prompted Japanese investors to take profits abroad, turning them into net sellers in some key markets for the first time in recent history.

The BIS capital adequacy requirements for banks, deposit interest rate deregulation, high domestic interest rates and the weak yen all made investors extremely cautious about investments abroad. The policy-led credit crunch, therefore, ended the outflow of funds from Japan that characterized so much of the 1980s.

The real cause of Japan's external imbalances and poor living conditions at home remains unresolved. The fall in investments abroad seen since the beginning of 1990 could reverse itself when the policy-led tight money conditions in Japan are relaxed.

The lesson of the 1980s is that once free movement of capital is allowed across national borders, many formerly purely domestic matters, such as sunshine laws and limits on the height of buildings in the city of Tokyo, are no longer domestic matters because they can affect capital flows, which in turn affect exchange rates and trade flows. The definition of an open economy will have to be modified, depending on whether the economy's capital market is open or not.

In an open economy with a closed capital market, therefore, changes in the domestic investment environment will have only an indirect impact on exchange rates and trade flows. In an open economy with an open capital market, however, changes in the domestic investment environment can have a direct and sometimes major impact on the exchange rate and trade flows.

Policy actions to address this new reality are already in place in the form of the SII, but a lot more needs to be done. It is hoped that the lesson of the 1980s has been correctly learned, and that constructive measures can be put in place without delay. If the free movement of capital across national borders and all its implications finally prompts the Japanese government to address the domestic distortions such as the land problem that they have ignored in the postwar years, Japanese capital will have served its most useful purpose in the world: making Japan a better place to live in for the benefit of all.

The reforms suggested in the SII, if implemented, will increase demand for capital in Japan and reduce funds availability elsewhere. But this will increase Japanese domestic demand and strengthen the yen at the same time, and should go a long way toward correcting Japan's external imbalances. An increase in exports to Japan also means opportunities for exporting countries to reduce their much-dreaded deficits with Japan. This means growth opportunities for all countries with goods to sell to Japan, which may include those in Eastern Europe. In the long run, this approach is far more sustainable politically and economically than any effort to increase Japanese "capital exports."

It should also be remembered that, during the critical exchange rate adjustment period from 1985 to 1988, Japanese investors did make the impossible possible by staying with the dollar most of the way, in spite of mounting losses. Their sacrifices, which some have called the Japanese Marshall Plan, allowed the dollar to drop without bringing down the US financial markets and the economy with them. Just as the Japanese used the original Marshall Plan effectively as a foundation to produce one of the mightiest economies in the world, it is hoped that the US will also make the best use of the opportunities provided to meet the challenge of reindustrialization.

Restructuring the Japanese economy so that it is a good place to live as well as a good place to work is going to be a major undertaking. This is especially true after nearly 40 years of neglect of some of the key policies issues, such as land, that are needed to improve living conditions. Reindustrializing the US economy after the inflationary neglect of the 1970s and the strong-dollar days of the 1980s will be no easier. It is encouraging to note, however, that these two largest economies in the world are on the right track. After years of trial and error, the world is finally learning to live with, and to make the best use of, free movements of capital across national borders.

REFERENCES

Bank of Japan, *Economics Statistics Monthly*, monthly issues.

Bordo, M.D. and Schwarz A.J. 1990: What has foreign exchange market intervention since the Plaza Agreement accomplished? NBER Working Paper no. 3562.

Dominguez, K.M. 1989: Market response to coordinated central bank intervention. NBER Working Paper no. 3162.

Frankel, J.A. 1984: The Yen/Dollar Agreement: liberalizing Japanese capital markets. *Policy Analyses in International Economics* no. 9, Institute of International Economics, Washington, D.C.

Fukao, M. 1990: Liberalization of Japan's foreign exchange controls and structural changes in the balance of payments. *Bank of Japan Monetary and Economic Studies*, 8, 101–65.

Ito, T. 1986: Capital controls and covered interest parity between the yen and the dollar. *Economics Studies Quarterly*, 37, 233–41.

Ito, T. 1990: Foreign exchange rate expectations: micro survey data. *American Economic Review*, 80, 434–49.

Koo, R.C. 1985–91a: Capital flows. *Nomura Investment Review*, Nomura Research Institute (monthly).

Koo, R.C. 1985–91b: *Japan and International Capital Flows*, Nomura Research Institute (annual).

Koo, R.C. 1987: Foreign securities investment by Japanese investors. *Zaikai Kansoku*, Nomura Research Institute, May, 80–95.

Koo, R.C. 1988a: How the Japanese will spend their $80 billion. *Euromoney*, September, 394–400.

Koo, R.C. 1988b: The international role of Japanese capital in 1988. *Nikkei Financial 88*, 60–70.

Koo, R.C. 1988c: Japanese investment in dollar securities after the Plaza Accord. *US Foreign Debt*, hearing before the Joint Economic Committee, Congress of the United States, September 13, 1988, 72–93.

Koo, R.C. 1988d: Tokyo's Rx for the US. *Financial World*, December 13, 22–4.

Koo, R.C. 1990: The weak yen – the flip side of the coin. *Tokyo Business Today*, June, 8–10.

Koo, R.C. 1991: The Plaza Accord and its geopolitical implications. In G. Kozmetsky and R. Smilor (eds), *Globalism Crosses National Boundaries*, IC² Institute, University of Texas at Austin.

Lewis, K.K. 1990: Occasional interventions to target rates with a foreign exchange application. NBER Working Paper no. 3398.

McKenzie, C.R. 1985: Liberalization of the Japanese capital market and the determination of the yen/dollar rate. *Pacific Economic Paper* no. 130, Australia–Japan Research Centre.

Ministry of Finance, International Finance Bureau, *Annual Report*, annual issues.

Otani, I. and Tiwari S. 1981: Capital controls and interest rate parity: the Japanese experience. *IMF Staff Papers*, 28, 793–815.

Part II

The Framework of Capital Markets

3

Corporate Finance in Japan

James E. Hodder and Adrian E. Tschoegl

1 AN OVERVIEW OF JAPANESE FINANCIAL STRUCTURE

Over the last decade, the success of Japanese firms in international competition has drawn considerable attention to financial practices in Japan as a possible source of competitive advantage. This chapter focuses on Japanese corporate financing and investment evaluation practices. Japanese practices appear strikingly different in comparison with practices at typical US firms. Our intention is to provide both information on the nature of those differences and a framework for understanding why they exist.

Some aspects of Japanese corporate finance have changed dramatically over the last few years. Most of these changes are the result of changes in the structure of Japanese financial markets, which in turn can be traced to regulatory changes. Indeed, the ongoing "liberalization" of Japanese financial markets provides both opportunities and risks. In such a dynamic environment, a framework for understanding corporate financing and investment practices becomes extremely important.

A useful starting point for our discussion is a comparison of aggregate balance sheets for the corporate manufacturing sectors in the US and Japan. Table 3.1 displays these balance sheets for the years 1980 and 1990. This data provides a broad overview on the financial structure of Japanese corporations plus an indication that substantial changes have been taking place in recent years.

A frequently mentioned characteristic of Japanese firms is a low ratio of shareholders' equity to total assets. This characterization is strongly supported by the 1980 figures in table 3.1, where the equity–asset percentage for US firms (49.5 percent) is almost 2.5 times the figure for Japan (20.6 percent). A low equity–asset ratio is equivalent to a high

We would like to thank Professors Shinji Takagi and Hideki Hanaeda for helpful comments on an earlier draft. Rolf Winzeler provided useful information on institutional details. Nevertheless, all errors and opinions remain our own.

Table 3.1 Aggregate balance sheet for manufacturing corporations in Japan and the United States (percentage)

| | Japan | | United States | |
	1980	1990	1980	1990
Assets				
Cash and marketable securities	13.1	16.7	5.3	4.4
Receivables	26.6	24.3	17.0	13.9
Inventories	17.9	12.0	19.8	14.3
Fixed Assets	34.5	38.2	55.1	64.0
Other Assets	7.9	8.8	2.8	3.4
Total Assets	100.0	100.0	100.0	100.0
Liabilities				
Trade payables	26.7	20.1	9.9	7.9
Short-term debt	16.8	13.5	5.0	6.3
Long-term debt	15.8	11.6	16.7	23.9
Other liabilities	20.1	22.8	18.8	21.8
Total liabilities	79.4	68.0	50.5	59.8
Shareholders' equity	20.6	32.0	49.5	40.2
Total liabilities and shareholders' equity	100.0	100.0	100.0	100.0

Some columns do not add perfectly, due to rounding.

US data are for December 31 of the calendar year indicated. Japanese data are as of March 31, which corresponds to the fiscal year-end for most Japanese corporations.

Sources: Bank of Japan, *Economic Statistics Annual*; US Department of Commerce, *Quarterly Financial Report for Manufacturing, Mining and Trade Corporations*

degree of financial leverage, with the 1980 Japanese equity–asset ratio of 20.6 percent implying a debt–equity ratio of almost 4 to 1. Note, however, that financial leverage has changed dramatically for firms in both the US and Japan over the last decade.

In the US, there has been a notable decline in shareholders' equity as a percentage of total assets (leverage has increased), largely due to the wave of leveraged buy-outs (LBOs), mergers and share repurchases. In contrast, the equity–asset ratio for Japanese manufacturers has grown substantially between 1980 and 1990, that is, leverage has decreased. Indeed, that ratio has steadily increased from 17.2 percent at the end of December 1976. In other words, Japanese manufacturers have almost doubled their aggregate equity–asset ratio since 1976.

The above comments are based on reported book values for shareholders' equity. Frequently, book values dramatically understate the true equity values for Japanese firms because of "hidden" assets. There are also differences between US and Japanese accounting practices. In terms of hidden assets, land as well as shareholdings in other firms are carried at acquisition cost rather than current market value; and for many Japanese firms, the difference is enormous. Several studies have attempted to adjust for such hidden assets and accounting differences or, alternatively, have simply calculated debt–equity ratios using market values for a firm's equity.[1] Overall, such studies suggest that Japanese firms have been substantially less levered than indicated by book value ratios. Furthermore, the studies confirm that leverage has been declining dramatically.

Returning to table 3.1, we can observe another prominent characteristic of Japanese balance sheets, the relatively heavy reliance on financing via short-term debt and trade payables. Over time, the percentage of short-term debt has declined but still exceeds the long-term debt percentage. Furthermore, short-term debt plus trade payables is almost three times the long-term debt position for Japanese manufacturers in 1990. The situation for US manufacturers is basically the reverse, with much greater reliance on long-term debt and a relatively modest dependence on trade payables. In other words, Japanese firms have not only tended to borrow more but have also relied much more heavily on short-term funding sources than their US counterparts.

With regard to asset composition, both countries have seen a dramatic decline in inventories as a fraction of total assets. This trend has been consistent throughout the 1980s and presumably results from the aggressive pursuit of streamlined production processes and "just-in-time" inventory practices. Both economies now use substantially less working capital relative to production or sales than they did a decade ago.

Given the heavy use of trade credit, the relatively large receivables position of Japanese firms is no surprise. We can, however, note percentage declines for both payables and receivables at Japanese firms. This supports the perception of a lessening dependence on trade credit by Japanese firms; however, their trade credit positions are still very large by US standards. This may reflect the slower progress in deregulation of short-term capital markets in Japan compared with the long-term markets.

Table 3.1 also indicates increasing liquidity in the form of cash and marketable securities for Japanese manufacturers. Furthermore, the Japanese positions are enormous by US standards – the 1990 Japanese figure is 3.8 times that for the US firms. Historically, a substantial portion of cash positions at Japanese firms represented compensating balances on commercial loans. However, the use of compensating balances has decreased during the 1980s as Japanese lenders have moved toward market-

Table 3.2 Net sources of funds for non-financial corporations, 1985–9 averages (percentage)

	Japan	US
Internal funds (depreciation and retained earnings)	53.4	85.7
Equity issues	4.5	−23.2
Bonds	5.9	21.6
Commercial paper	2.3	2.0
Loans (incl. foreign)	33.8	13.9

Sources: Bank of Japan, *Economic Statistics Annual*; Bank of Japan, *Comparative Economic and Financial Statistics: Japan and Other Major Countries*; Board of Governors, Federal Reserve System, *Flow of Funds Accounts*

rate loans and fee-based services. Consequently, the effective increase in liquidity at Japanese firms during the 1980s was even greater than indicated by the figures in table 3.1.

Much of this liquidity increase occurred relatively suddenly during the second half of the 1980s in parallel with expansion of the money supply, lower interest rates, rising land prices, and other aspects of the "bubble economy" in Japan. As an illustration, consider liquidity relative to sales (measured by cash + deposits + marketable securities/sales) as reported by the Bank of Japan for a set of "Principal Enterprises" – roughly 600 large non-financial firms. That liquidity ratio was quite stable during fiscal years 1980–5, ranging between 1.09 and 1.18 months of sales. In fiscal 1986, it suddenly jumped to 1.49 months and subsequently rose to a peak of over two months by fiscal 1989. That ratio has since fallen to 1.5 months as firms have drawn down "excess" cash reserves; and it may well return to a level at or below that which prevailed in the early 1980s.

It is also instructive to examine aggregate figures on funding sources for US and Japanese firms. Table 3.2 presents comparative data on such sources for the non-financial sector in each country during the last half of the 1980s. The first thing to note is that Japanese firms have relied much less on internal funding sources (depreciation and retained earnings) than have their US counterparts. This has caused Japanese firms to depend more on external financing, the bulk of which has come in the form of loans. As we shall see shortly, this dependence on loans (primarily from private financial institutions) is actually less today than it was several years ago.

Equity issues for Japanese firms have risen from 2.8 percent of total funding in 1985 to 7.8 percent in 1989. This increase is obscured by the five-year average in table 3.2. Nevertheless, equity issues remain a rather modest percentage of total funding for the bulk of Japanese firms. It is worth emphasizing that these are aggregate figures; and some firms (particularly large firms with superior market access) have obtained a substantially larger fraction of their funding in recent years from equity issues. Parenthetically, the large negative figure for the US is due to leveraged acquisitions and mergers plus corporate share repurchases, which together have resulted in substantial net retirements of corporate equity since 1983. For a more historical perspective, net equity issues by US firms in the 1970s averaged 4.1 percent – very similar to the recent Japanese average.

Despite a dramatic growth in bond issuance by Japanese corporations, bond issues have played a modest role as a percentage of total funding; and their role is substantially smaller than in US firms. Overall, table 3.2 indicates that Japanese firms have not only depended more on external funding than their US counterparts but have also depended more on loans from financial intermediaries rather than on market-based financing (equity, bond, and commercial paper issues). Again, these are aggregate figures which represent a blending of large and small firms.

In Japan, the bulk of market-based financing is undertaken by the large firms, for whom it represents a substantially higher percentage of total funding than suggested by aggregate figures for the entire non-financial corporate sector. Bank of Japan figures for principal enterprises also indicate that these firms have been utilizing a greater fraction of internal funding than the non-financial corporate average. Consequently, these large firms in recent years have become much less dependent on commercial loans than their smaller counterparts.

To allow for a longer time perspective, table 3.3 provides five-year

Table 3.3 Net sources of funds for Japanese non-financial corporations: five-year averages (percentage)

	1970–4	*1975–9*	*1980–4*	*1985–9*
Internal funds (depreciation and retained earnings)	43.2	51.9	55.8	53.4
Equity issues	3.3	3.3	3.5	4.5
Bonds	1.7	2.5	1.4	5.9
Commercial paper				2.3
Loans (incl. foreign)	51.7	42.3	39.3	33.8

Sources: Bank of Japan, *Economic Statistics Annual*; Bank of Japan, *Comparative Economic and Financial Statistics: Japan and Other Major Countries*

averages on funding sources for Japanese non-financial corporations dating back to 1970. Although the pattern varies, internal and external sources have each funded roughly half the asset acquisitions of these firms over the last two decades. Furthermore, a portion of those new assets simply offset the effect of depreciation on the existing asset base. In other words, *net* asset growth is funded by retained earnings plus external funding. Clearly, heavy dependence on external funding is not a new phenomenon for Japanese firms.

Table 3.3 also suggests that market-based financing did not increase substantially as a percentage of total funding until the last half of the 1980s. Until then, market-based sources accounted for only 5–6 percent of total funding. During the early 1970s, loans represented a staggering 91 percent of external funding. Even during the last half of the 1980s, loans still accounted for 72 percent of external funds. From an asset growth perspective, external funding can be critical. During the 1970–4 period, for example, external sources provided funds equivalent to 85 percent of asset growth. Moreover, loans themselves funded some 77 percent of that asset growth. Such figures leave little doubt about the tremendous importance of commercial lending for the past growth of Japanese industry.

2   BORROWING PATTERNS AND PRACTICES

During the mid-1970s there was a shift towards greater internal funding. This shift is generally attributed to slower aggregate growth by Japanese firms, allowing them to fund more of that growth via retained earnings. Asset growth did indeed slow dramatically. Total assets for Japanese manufacturers grew at an annual average of 17.7 percent during the 1960s and the first half of the 1970s. However, that growth rate slowed to only 7.4 percent on average during the remainder of the 1970s and 1980s. Under these circumstances, depreciation became a greater fraction of net funding and basically accounts for the upward shift of internal funding in table 3.3.

Although loans continued to fund a very large fraction of asset growth after the mid-1970s, the dramatic slowing of that growth meant a weakened demand for commercial loans. This general trend toward lessened dependence on the banking sector gained further momentum during the 1985–9 period as market-based funding began to play a larger role in Japanese corporate finance. Table 3.4 provides annual figures on funding sources for this period and separates bond issues into domestic and external (overseas) components.

In this table, a pattern of rapidly increasing equity and external bond financing is quite apparent. Interestingly, the domestic bond component

Table 3.4 Net sources of funds for Japanese non-financial corporations (percentage)

	1985	1986	1987	1988	1989
Internal funds (depreciation and retained earnings)	58.4	59.1	54.7	50.9	44.1
Equity issues	2.8	2.7	4.4	4.7	7.8
Domestic bonds	1.0	1.9	2.5	1.5	1.1
External bonds	3.3	3.2	4.0	3.9	7.3
Commercial paper			1.8	6.9	2.9
Loans (incl. foreign)	34.5	33.1	32.6	32.2	36.9

Sources: Bank of Japan, *Economic Statistics Annual*; Bank of Japan, *Comparative Economic and Financial Statistics: Japan and Other Major Countries*

has remained very small. We also see the advent of the Japanese commercial paper (CP) market in late 1987, and its explosive growth during 1988. Although the CP market continued to grow in 1989 at a 41 percent annual rate, this rate was substantially less than the market's 447 percent growth in 1988. Clearly, creation of a Japanese commercial paper market filled a significant need.

Overall, market sources provided slightly over one-third of external funds for Japanese non-financial firms in both 1988 and 1989. If we focus on large firms, which have much better access to market-based financing, the figures are even more dramatic. In fiscal year 1989, the 638 principal enterprises surveyed by the Bank of Japan obtained over two-thirds of their net external funding from market sources.

Japanese firms' historical dependence on loans for external funding has been largely a regulatory phenomenon. During much of the 1970s, government restrictions on corporate borrowing and equity offerings abroad were severe. With limited exceptions, Japanese firms were restricted to domestic funding sources. At the same time, the banks tightly controlled access to the Japanese corporate bond market and imposed cumbersome and relatively expensive issuance procedures. The commercial paper market did not exist (until 1987), and equity issues were not generally attractive for a variety of reasons which we shall discuss later. To complete the picture, foreign bank branches in Japan were (and remain) a very small factor in commercial lending. At the end of 1990, such branches accounted for less than 3 percent of total bank lending in Japan.[2]

As the government relaxed restrictions during the 1980s on offshore funding, bond floatation, commercial paper issuance, and so on, Japanese firms progressively shifted towards market funding sources. However, during their rapid growth phase (roughly 1950–74) Japanese firms had virtually no alternative but commercial loans to satisfy their enormous appetite for external funding. This rapid growth era also saw occasions of credit tightness. Consequently, a firm's relationship with key lenders was extraordinarily important. In the face of such pressures, most large Japanese firms entered into a "main bank" relationship with one of the major banks.[3] Typically, the main bank supplied a substantial fraction (for example, 25 percent) of the firm's borrowing requirements and also acted as agent and advisor on other loans.

The precise nature of the main bank relationship has varied across firms and banks, as well as over time. The relative indebtedness of the client firm has been an important determinant of that relationship. For cash-rich companies, the main bank has exercised little control and acted more like a financial adviser. In contrast, heavy borrowers have been monitored via extensive formal and informal contacts with the bank at a variety of levels. In such situations, the bank has access to a wide range of privileged information and exercises considerable influence over the client firm – potentially including veto power over major capital expenditures. At financially troubled firms, key executives have frequently been replaced by bank personnel – giving the bank effective control over that firm's operations.[4]

Historically, the main bank's power derived from several sources. In addition to providing a substantial fraction of a client firm's loans, the main bank's favorable recommendation was critical for that firm obtaining loans from other Japanese lenders. Typically, a large fraction of a corporation's loans were short-term and had to be "rolled over" frequently.[5] Again, the main bank's favorable recommendation was critical. Typically, a firm's main bank acts as trustee on secured bond issues; and until March 1979, Japanese firms were precluded from issuing unsecured bonds. The vast majority of bank lending has also been collateralized, and banks have had strong powers to seize collateral if there has been a threat of default. The main bank also typically owns shares in client firms. However, this does not seem to be the major source of influence, since the bank is limited by law to holding no more than 5 percent of a firm's outstanding shares; prior to 1977, the percentage was 10 percent.

A firm's main bank has also had major obligations regarding the interests of other lenders. Because of its superior information, other banks have accepted the main bank's recommendation regarding loans to a client firm with little question, and have even viewed that recommendation as a quasi-guarantee. In turn, the main bank is expected to monitor its client firms and take action as necessary to prevent losses for itself and other lenders. In cases of client bankruptcy, main banks have absorbed the losses of other lenders and, in return, have had first call on the collateral backing the loans. In such cases, the main bank has consolidated the claims of a large class of creditors, reducing the risk of opportunistic behavior by some of those creditors.

A spectacular and widely cited example of such actions was the 1977 failure of Ataka and Company in which the two main banks (Sumitomo and Kyowa) apparently compensated other lenders and lost ¥106 billion and ¥46 billion, respectively.[6] More recently (in 1991), Sumitomo assumed the debts of the bankrupt Itoman Corporation. Currently, the Azabu Tatemono and Dai-Ichi Real Estate groups have put themselves under the control of Mitsui Trust and Banking. Also, the Long-term Credit Bank has assumed management leadership of EIE International and is currently directing the firm's restructuring. By contrast, when Aoyama Building Development went bankrupt in January 1991 with total debts of ¥110 billion, no banks were involved, since the primary creditor was a non-bank. In two other recent bankruptcies (Nanatomi: January 1991, ¥286 billion; and Maruko: August 1991, ¥278 billion) the banks withdrew their support.

These last two cases illustrate the importance of understanding that the main bank's "obligation" does not reside in some legal document, but rather depends on acceptable business practice within the Japanese banking community. What is acceptable may depend strongly on the particular situation. Consequently, there are bankruptcies in which other lenders incur losses despite the apparent existence of a main bank relationship. There can also be degrees of acceptability, and perceptions can vary across lenders. However, main bank behavior which was generally perceived as unacceptable would seriously undermine that bank's ability to conduct business in the future – and hence its future profitability. Consequently, the main bank's obligation to other lenders may be somewhat vague and distinctly case-specific; nevertheless, it is still a serious business obligation with a powerful enforcement mechanism.

As Japanese firms (on average) have become relatively less dependent on external funds and market financing alternatives have improved during recent years, the strength of many main bank relationships appears to have waned. Nevertheless, there remain many highly levered firms for whom the main bank's support is critical. Also, the long tradition of a main bank relationship carries considerable weight with most Japanese firms. There may be a sense of obligation due to past support or sensitivity to the possibility that bank support might be necessary at some future date. Also, the role of Japanese banks in providing financial information and advice is very significant. Consequently, for a variety of reasons, bank relations are still important; however, their intensity seems to have declined roughly in parallel with the need for bank support.

3 FINANCIAL LIBERALIZATION AND DEBT-ISSUING PRACTICES

It is clear that the ongoing financial liberalization in Japan is having important effects on corporate financing patterns. In some respects, financial liberalization has been taking place since the 1960s; however, the process accelerated dramatically in the 1980s. The revised Foreign Exchange and Foreign Trade Control Law in December 1980 removed major impediments to offshore financing by Japanese firms and improved access by foreigners to Japanese financial markets. Beginning around 1984, the liberalization process accelerated with a number of regulatory changes which were at least partially in response to external pressure for greater openness of Japanese financial markets. Since then a stream of regulatory changes have eliminated a variety of interest rate restrictions, allowed trading in new types of securities (such as futures, options, and swaps), relaxed controls on both domestic and foreign financial institutions, and generally promoted freer and more flexible financial markets. However, some regulations and practices which cause distortions and result in unusual financing patterns still remain.

Not infrequently, the elimination of one restrictive regulation results in a "regulatory arbitrage" opportunity with market participants using their increased freedom to exploit (circumvent) profitably another, still-existing regulation. This continues until the consequent pressure on the second restriction forces its elimination or modification. This may induce an arbitrage opportunity regarding a third regulation, and so on. Consequently, the liberalization process tends to produce windows of opportunity permitting firms to earn additional profits (or to reduce financing costs) by exploiting regulatory differences.

The *sushi* bond provides a classic example of such regulatory arbitrage. The *sushi* bond was a foreign currency bond (for example, the Eurodollar) issued offshore by Japanese industrial corporations and purchased by Japanese insurance companies at higher prices (lower interest rates) than other potential buyers were prepared to pay. The differentiating characteristic of a *sushi* bond was that Japanese firms were on both sides of the transaction. The motivation for *sushi* bonds was a Ministry of Finance (MOF) regulation which limited the foreign currency investments of insurance companies to 10 percent of total assets; however, foreign currency issues by Japanese firms were not subject to that restriction. Consequently, such issues commanded a premium from Japanese insurance companies desiring to increase their foreign currency positions beyond the 10 percent limit.

When Japanese firms became able to issue foreign currency bonds offshore and swap (after April 1984) the proceeds into yen, they discovered that this was less costly (for example, 50 basis points less) than a comparable domestic yen borrowing. Apparently some borrowers simply re-lent the proceeds of their *sushi* bond issues at an arbitrage profit. The resulting surge in *sushi* bond issues caused MOF to relax (in March 1986) the restriction on insurance companies' foreign currency assets. As a consequence, Japanese insurance companies were no longer prepared to accept the lower yields on *sushi* bonds, and issuance of such bonds ceased almost immediately.

The story of *sushi* bonds is but one example of how regulatory patterns have driven the bond issue practices of Japanese firms. As we shall see shortly, there have been several dramatic shifts in funding patterns which can be traced to regulatory changes. It is also important to understand that the government's own financing needs have been an important influence on market regulations as well as the general character of the domestic bond market. Indeed, that market has been dominated by government issues since the mid-1970s with corporate issues representing a relatively small fraction of the total market. For example, during the 1986–90 period, straight corporate debt issues accounted for just 3 percent of total bond issues in Japan. If convertible and warrant bonds are included, the figure rises – but only to 17 percent.

Table 3.5 provides additional data on domestic bond issues by Japanese firms during 1975–90. The vast majority of straight debt consists of issues by electric power companies plus Nippon Telegraph and Telephone (NTT). In recent years, other Japanese corporations have essentially forsaken the domestic straight debt market in favor of other funding sources, including offshore bond issues. This striking aversion to domestic issues has produced enormous pressure for regulatory and procedural changes. Currently, the whole matter of bond issuance procedures, legal requirements and fees is under review; and substantial changes are likely.

To a large extent, the underlying problems for domestic corporate bond issues have to do with who determines issue terms and collateral requirements. It was only after 1979 that Japanese firms were allowed to issue unsecured bonds for the first time since the 1930s. Initially, only two firms were eligible to make unsecured issues. This situation continued until January 1983, when the restrictions on convertible bonds were further relaxed so that some 30 firms became eligible to issue such bonds without collateral. Subsequently, restrictions for both convertibles and straight bonds were relaxed in stages until several hundred firms were eligible for unsecured issues as of November 1988.

The official logic for a collateral requirement has been the protection of investors. However, this restriction has also made bond issuance in Japan relatively unattractive. Not only did corporate issuers have to pay management fees and underwriting commissions, but they also had to

Table 3.5 Domestic public bond issues by Japanese firms (billion yen)

Year	Straight bonds Electric	NTT	Other	Convertible bonds	Warrant bonds	Total
1975	580	88	885	408		1,961
1976	815	165	411	59		1,450
1977	849	175	326	120		1,470
1978	821	210	509	293		1,833
1979	1,004	105	242	371		1,722
1980	864	130	185	104		1,283
1981	901	130	358	364	20	1,773
1982	841	120	306	448	44	1,759
1983	439	105	209	827	10	1,590
1984	727	185	85	1,209	13	2,219
1985	538	235	112	1,904	10	2,799
1986	490	300	186	2,744	116	3,836
1987	530	385	28	5,257	33	6,233
1988	688	150	72	6,640	0	7,550
1989	520	60	4	6,867	385	7,836
1990	1,678	150	6	2,727	925	5,486
1983–90 Totals	5,610	1,570	702	28,175	1,492	37,549

Source: *Tokyo Stock Exchange Fact Book*

compensate a trustee for a variety of services which substantially increased issue costs. Firms also had to obtain approval on the terms and timing of issues from a committee dominated by a group of large banks (referred to as "commissioned banks"). This procedure is cumbersome and lacks flexibility regarding issue terms.

This bond issuing procedure endowed the Japanese banks with considerable control over industrial firms' access to debt markets. Under the main bank lending system, such control was important for dealing with highly levered clients. In recent years, financially healthy firms have naturally tended to view this process as (at best) an expensive nuisance. Consequently, offshore issues have been attractive as a way around cumbersome and expensive procedures in the domestic market. Indeed, an MOF estimate suggests that bond flotation offshore as of 1990 was still roughly 50 basis points less expensive.[7] Earlier, the gap was presumably at least as large.

Table 3.6 illustrates the rapid growth in offshore bond issues by Japanese firms over the last decade-and-a-half. Offshore corporate issues did occur during the 1960s; however, MOF prohibited such issues for

Table 3.6 Offshore bond issues by Japanese firms (billion yen)[a]

Year	Straight bonds	Convertible bonds	Warrant bonds	Total
1975	310	105		415
1976	294	210		504
1977	252	197		449
1978	224	338		562
1979	266	617		883
1980	219	514		733
1981	141	811		952
1982	568	677	101	1,346
1983	1,214	1,075	128	2,417
1984	625	1,322	446	2,393
1985	1,675	1,029	679	3,383
1986	1,437	426	2,007	3,870
1987	1,252	986	3,173	5,411
1988	774	918	3,682	5,374
1989	873	1,677	9,281	11,831
1990	1,678	901	2,906	5,485
1983–90 Totals	9,528	8,334	22,302	40,164

[a] Includes private placements.

Source: *Tokyo Stock Exchange Fact Book*

most of the early 1970s due to balance of payments considerations. The prohibition was lifted (in two stages) during 1974; however, offshore issues still required MOF approval. It was not until the early 1980s, when Japanese participation no longer required MOF permission (at least in principle), that the offshore market really began to take off. The ability to use swaps and undertake Euroyen issues after April 1984 further increased the attractiveness of offshore financing. From tables 3.5 and 3.6 we can see that total corporate issues during the 1983–90 period were greater in the offshore market than domestically. The fact that a very large fraction of offshore issues wound up in Japanese investors' portfolios provides a strong indication that the domestic market was inefficient.

In the domestic market, convertibles have dominated straight issues since 1983. This is particularly true if we focus on firms other than NTT and the electric power companies, which have issued primarily straight bonds.[8] There seem to be several reasons for this. First, collateral requirements have been relaxed more rapidly on convertibles – resulting in lower effective issue costs for more firms. Second, issuing terms on straight corporate debt have been tied to government bond yields in ways which made many corporate issues relatively unattractive for initial purchasers. In contrast, terms on convertibles were more easily adjusted to make them attractive for purchasers. Third, the lower coupon rate on a convertible coupled with the generally low dividend yield on shares (after conversion) implies a lower cash flow drain relative to issuing straight debt.

In addition, a fourth reason may rest in limitations on the total amount of bonds a firm can issue. Historically, a firm could not issue bonds in excess of its (paid in) capital plus reserves. The June 1990 revision to the Commercial Code (effective 1 April 1991) roughly doubled the limit; but even this relaxed constraint can be binding for a rapidly growing firm needing external funds.[9] Possibly anticipating the need for an equity issue in the near future, many firms in Japan appear to have used convertibles as an indirect means of equity issuance. Thus, a convertible issue provided immediate funding but, as it was converted into shares, enhanced a firm's ability to issue additional bonds in the future. We shall return later to the question of why direct equity issues were unattractive as a funding mechanism. However, there were apparently several reasons why convertibles were more attractive than straight debt issues in the domestic market.

In the offshore market, too, convertible and warrant bonds have generally dominated straight issues. Note, however, the dramatic shift from convertibles to warrant bond issues in 1986. This switch to warrant bonds is apparently due to a combination of two factors. First of all, most offshore issues were not denominated in yen. See table 3.7, where the category "other" includes yen issues plus those in several additional currencies. Some foreign currency issues have been used to hedge firms' exchange rate exposure from operations or other financial positions. The remaining foreign currency issues were typically swapped to create yen-denominated liabilities. Convertibles are not well-suited for either hedging or swapping. Convertibles are less effective hedges because the outstanding amount (size of the hedge) changes with conversions, which may occur rather quickly. For the same reason (that is, principal and interest flows change randomly), convertibles are not suitable for swap transactions.

Prior to the end of 1985, firms seeking a swap transaction or a foreign currency hedge tended to utilize straight debt.[10] Warrant bonds can also be effectively used for swapping and hedging because the dates and amounts of principal and interest payments are known.[11] Some firms did issue warrant bonds in the offshore market during the early 1980s; however, these bonds met with a less than overwhelming reception. Then,

Table 3.7 Currency of offshore bond issues by Japanese firms (million US dollar equivalent)

Year	Dollars	D mark	Sw. franc	Other[a]
1975	810	344	413	21
1976	1,169	349	581	
1977	1,321	245	485	
1978	544	1,101	1,130	
1979	720	730	2,714	36
1980	990	535	1,943	197
1981	2,410	120	1,831	388
1982	2,234	241	3,631	197
1983	3,976	491	6,544	224
1984	8,633	504	5,602	355
1985	11,626	759	6,079	2,249
1986	16,340	983	7,890	3,754
1987	26,529	781	8,994	5,887
1988	33,590	1,503	9,785	2,286
1989	71,900	3,626	13,610	4,398

[a] The category "other" includes issues in a variety of currencies as well as Euroyen.

Source: Ministry of Finance, *Yearbook of International Finance Bureau, 1990*

in November 1985, the Japanese security firms lifted a "self-imposed" restriction on domestic trading of warrants which had been detached ("stripped") from the bonds with which they were issued. This opened the door for retail sales of detached warrants, which turned out to be enormously popular with Japanese investors. Trading warrants was also for a time very profitable for foreign and domestic securities firms in London and Japan.

During the 1986–9 period, Japanese share prices were generally very strong, and warrant bonds issues were deemed very attractive. The value of attached warrants resulted in bond coupon rates substantially below those for comparable straight debt. In some cases, the coupon rate was reduced so much that the apparent interest rate, after swapping back into yen, was negative. Certainly, including the warrant value in the calculation would remove the apparent negative *ex ante* cost. However, the 1990 decline in the Japanese stock market has resulted in warrants on recent issues (such as 1989) which are substantially "out of the money." If these warrants expire worthless, the issuing firms will indeed have obtained a windfall on their bond issues.[12] Instead of rejoicing, however, these firms

Table 3.8   Offshore bond issues by Japanese firms during fiscal year 1989 (billion yen equivalent)

Currency	Straight bonds	Convertible bonds	Warrant bonds	Total
Dollar	542	98	7,550	8,190
D mark	17	73	398	488
Sw. franc	101	1,568	290	1,959
Euroyen	155			155
Other[a]	305		32	337
Total	1,120	1,739	8,270	11,129

[a]   Other includes issues denominated in European Currency Units (ECU) as well as Canadian dollars, French francs, and Dutch guilders.

Source: Bond Underwriters' Association of Japan, *Bond Market in Japan 1990*

are allegedly distressed and concerned that losses suffered by purchasers of their securities will adversely affect the viability of future issues.

Another interesting aspect of the offshore bond market is the currency distribution of different bond issue types. Table 3.8 provides data on 1989 issues by currency. Over 90 percent of the warrant bonds were denominated in US dollars. In contrast, over 90 percent of the convertible issues were in Swiss francs. This apparently has to do with a preference by individual Swiss investors for convertibles.[13] The swap markets are generally deepest for dollar transactions; consequently, dollar issues make particular sense where the intention is a swap into yen. Straight debt issues were spread somewhat more evenly across currencies, with the other currencies category including several ECU issues as well as issues in Canadian dollars and French francs. It is reasonable to conjecture that selection of these currencies was based on hedging considerations.

The typical maturity for recent warrant bond issues has been four years. Maturities less than four years are unattractive because they would be subject to a 20 percent withholding tax on coupon payments. On the other hand, longer maturities would increase the value of the warrants and lower total interest costs (over a longer span of time). Longer maturities also reduce the frequency of issues by a given firm and, consequently, its total issuing costs. Nevertheless, the general pattern has been that firms issue for the minimum maturity which avoids withholding taxes. Out of the almost 400 offshore warrant bond issues during 1989 and 1990 listed in *Annual Securities Statistics*, only five had initial maturities of greater than five years and roughly 80 percent had maturities of four years.[14] One explanation is that firms may be limiting warrant maturities in the hopes of increasing their equity base more rapidly.

Overall, the main story for corporate bond issues during the last decade has been the shift to issuing overseas. This is clearly due to reduced regulatory constraints on access to offshore markets where there is greater flexibility and lower costs. The rise of the offshore primary market has, however, seriously undermined the domestic primary market. Consequently, efforts are currently underway to reform domestic bond issuance procedures and make them more competitive with offshore markets. This will presumably require more flexibility with regard to pricing and issue terms as well as largely eliminating the additional costs imposed by the commissioned bank system. Otherwise the dominance of the offshore markets is likely to continue.

Let us turn briefly to a discussion of the commercial paper (CP) market. As mentioned earlier, the CP market came into existence in late (November) 1987 and grew extremely rapidly. Within two years, the outstanding amount of commercial paper exceeded that for straight corporate bonds. To a large extent, this rapid growth evidences an enormous pent-up demand for an efficient short-term funding source other than bank loans. Previously, firms could borrow via bond repurchase agreements (*gensaki*) or in offshore markets; however, these alternatives typically entailed added costs or complexities (such as legal requirements) which made them less attractive. As an indication of this, borrowing by non-financial corporations in the *gensaki* market dropped drastically after the Japanese CP market came into existence.

The rapid growth of the Japanese CP market also appears to have been fueled by arbitrage situations where top-rated industrial firms were able to profit from issuing commercial paper and placing the proceeds in large-scale time deposits (LTDs) at Japanese banks.[15] This is another example of the financial arbitrage opportunities which have appeared at times during the course of financial liberalization. It should also be mentioned that the commercial paper market has represented both a funding mechanism and an investment vehicle for industrial corporations. At the end of March 1990, industrial (non-financial) firms owned some 27 percent of the over ¥13 trillion outstanding.

4 EQUITY FINANCING, OWNERSHIP STRUCTURE, AND DIVIDENDS

An often-mentioned and important characteristic of Japanese equity markets is the widespread cross-holding of listed shares by other corporations.

Table 3.9   Share ownership of Japanese firms by type of investor, March 1990

Investor category[a]	Percentage of listed shares	Percentage of market value
Government	0.7	0.3
Banks	22.1	21.3
Investment trusts	3.7	3.7
Annuity trusts	0.9	0.9
Securities firms	2.0	2.0
Life insurance companies	13.1	11.8
Non-life ins. companies	4.1	3.9
Other financial institutions	2.1	1.9
Business corporations	24.8	29.5
Individuals and others	22.6	20.5
Foreigners	3.9	4.2

[a] Coverage includes all domestic firms listed on any Japanese stock exchange.

Source: *Tokyo Stock Exchange Factbook*, 1991

Table 3.9 provides aggregate percentage holdings by investor category for all firms listed on any of Japan's eight stock exchanges. There are slightly over 2,000 listed domestic firms in Japan, including almost all large firms. Notable exceptions are the large life insurance firms which are mutual companies and hence not listed.[16] Despite not being listed, the life insurance companies are a significant factor in the cross-holding story. Investment trusts listed in table 3.9 are analogous to mutual funds in the US, and the category "business corporations" should be interpreted as non-financial corporations (not necessarily listed on an exchange).

Banks, insurance companies (both life and non-life), plus business corporations controlled 64.1 percent of listed shares (representing 66.5 percent of market value) as of March 1990. This group of owners is sometimes referred to as "stable shareholders," on the presumption that their ownership positions are motivated by business relationships and will be held indefinitely. It is standard practice in Japan for a firm to own shares in its important customers and suppliers. For listed subsidiaries (which are relatively common), the fractional ownership by the parent firm may be substantial (for example, 60 percent). More typical is the non-subsidiary situation where fractional shareholdings are frequently only a few percent. However, in the aggregate these small holdings may sum to a large fraction of the firm's outstanding shares. Indeed, banks and insurance companies, whose individual holdings are legally limited to a relatively small fraction of any single firm's shares, collectively hold almost 40 percent of listed shares.[17]

Traditionally, cross-holdings are intended to promote a strong business relationship between firms rather than to profit from anticipated share price appreciation. This relationship motivation generally applies to holdings by banks and insurance companies as well as those by non-financial firms. The main bank relationship is a classic example, with the bank typically holding around 5 percent of a client's shares, in addition to being its key lender. Often, the main bank also provides a variety of other banking services for a client firm. Other banks who are substantial lenders to that firm would hold smaller share positions.[18] In a similar manner, insurance firms maintain share positions to promote lending and pension fund management as well as insurance business.

The stereotype is that stable shareholdings are not sold, since to do so signals the demise of the underlying relationship. Indeed, stable shareholders are frequently expected to maintain their percentage ownership by acquiring the appropriate fraction of new issues. This characterization has considerable validity; however, it is also simplistic, particularly when applied to broad aggregates. For example, the banking sector became relatively active traders during the later 1980s, peaking at 20 percent of total trading value in the Japanese market during 1989. This contrasts with roughly 3 percent in the early 1980s and figures of around 1 or 2 percent during the mid-1970s.

It is likely that the additional bank trading activity came from two sources. The largest portion presumably came from trading by trust accounts (particularly, *tokkin* funds), which were allegedly used as an investment vehicle by industrial firms "playing the market" during the later 1980s. The other possibility is sale-and-repurchase operations for the bank's own account, in which the same ownership position is maintained but the book value of that position is increased and accounting income generated.

Among the other major shareholders, insurance companies continued to engage in relatively little trading for their own account – on average, slightly less than 1 percent of total trading value throughout the 1980s. In the past, business corporations were more active traders than either banks or insurance companies. For example, trades by business corporations accounted for slightly over 7 percent of total volume during the 1975–83 period. Trading by this group also increased during the later 1980s and represented 11.5 percent of average total trading value during the 1986–89 period. Again, these figures may include sale-and-repurchase transactions where firms maintained ownership positions in others while dressing up their own balance sheets and income statements.

Even in the peak trading year of 1989, business corporations plus banks and insurance companies accounted for slightly under one-third of total trading although they controlled roughly two-thirds of total share value. If we go back a decade to 1979, this group still owned 60 percent of market value but accounted for only 12.5 percent of trading volume. It is possible that stable shareholdings are not as stable as in the past. On the other hand, most shares held by this group may indeed represent stable shareholdings, with their increased trading in recent years attributable to trading "additional" share positions (above and beyond their stable shareholdings). In this vein, it has been suggested that an important reason for firms trading via trust accounts was their consequent ability to trade anonymously in shares of corporations for which they were also stable shareholders.

The extensive cross-holding of shares identified above essentially precludes hostile takeovers.[19] Such takeovers have occurred, but they are rare events. More typical is the friendly takeover arranged by the main bank to strengthen a financially ailing client. Insulation from the threat of hostile takeovers is widely viewed in the US as allowing Japanese managers to have a long-term perspective on investment decisions. This view has merit, but it should not be overdone. Recall the relatively high leverage, heavy short-term debt positions, and extraordinary dependence on bank lending which has characterized the financial structure of most Japanese firms for much of the last two decades. Japanese managers may not have needed to worry about corporate raiders buying up their shares, but they had to pay careful attention to how their plans and performance were viewed by the firm's main bank.

Cross-holding is also viewed as contributing an upward bias to reported price–earnings (P/E) ratios for Japanese firms. The reasoning is that unrealized capital gains on stable shareholdings increase the shareholding firm's own stock price but not its reported earnings.[20] For many Japanese firms, such unrealized gains appear substantial – despite the major drop in share prices during 1990. When coupled with the typically small dividend yield in Japan, the effect of stable shareholding on reported income appears substantially smaller than its impact on the owner's share price. Sometimes the earnings to price ratio (inverse of P/E) is used as a (very) rough indicator of a firm's cost of equity capital. Given the problems induced by cross-holding, this sort of estimate for a Japanese firm should be treated with considerable caution.

Cross-holding also creates measurement problems for portfolio investment managers. First, it dramatically inflates the reported size of the stock market relative to the underlying aggregate value of non-financial assets (such as plant and equipment) owned by listed firms. Estimates suggest that the reported aggregate value of Japanese shares may be as much as double that of the underlying assets.[21] Since aggregate values for different countries' stock markets are used to determine portfolio weights in some global investment strategies, this issue has substantial implications for portfolio managers. There is also a misweighting problem for reported returns on stock market indexes such as TOPIX and related problems for statistical estimates, such as the "beta" of a firm's stock, which are based on reported returns.[22]

As mentioned above, dividend yields on Japanese stocks are extremely low. This situation results from the traditional practice of setting the dividend rate at 10 percent of par value. For most Japanese firms this entails a five yen per share dividend on a (typical) 50 yen par value. Five yen per share is actually a minimum requirement for listing on the First Section of the Tokyo Stock Exchange (TSE). Also, failure to maintain the payment of dividends at that rate can result in delisting. Consequently, five yen per share has a relatively serious regulatory implication; and a firm's failure to pay at least that rate is a very negative signal about its financial health.

For the 1,165 firms listed on the First Section of the TSE in 1990, the average dividend paid was actually ¥8.04 per share.[23] On the other hand, the average price of those shares during December 1990 was ¥1246. The result is a tiny dividend yield: 0.6 percent per annum using the December price figure. This yield percentage is actually up from 0.4 percent at the beginning of 1990, when market share prices were much higher.

For a historical perspective, the dividend rate in 1970 was an average of ¥6.55 per share. However, share prices were much lower; and the resulting weighted average yield was 4.3 percent. Dividend yields were even more substantial in the 1950s and 1960s. However, as stock prices climbed during the 1970s and 1980s, dividends per share did not keep up – although they have increased somewhat. The net result has been an average dividend yield which has declined rather consistently over the last two decades and has been less than 1 percent since 1985. It should be emphasized, however, that the dividend payout rate as a percentage of after-tax profits has been substantial. For all listed Japanese non-financial firms, that payout rate averaged 36 percent from 1986–90.

We now turn to another interesting aspect of the Japanese equity markets: new issue practices. Prior to 1970, virtually all equity fund raising was via rights issues at par. Given the (virtually required) dividend payment at 10 percent of par value, this was a relatively expensive form of funding from a cash flow perspective. Since the early 1950s, share price appreciation has caused market prices almost without exception to exceed par value. During the 1970s, public share issues at prevailing market prices became popular. Issuing at market prices was attractive because it

Table 3.10 Increases in outstanding shares, listed Japanese firms (million shares)

Year	Rights	Public	Private	Conversions[a]	Warrants	Gratis	Total
1980	1,761	1,619	311	2,209		3,264	9,206
1981	5,624	2,361	100	2,536		3,486	14,228
1982	1,932	1,760	112	1,103	11	4,242	9,503
1983	1,005	514	589	2,006	118	3,740	8,465
1984	1,170	779	320	2,836	208	3,621	9,516
1985	910	591	118	3,515	447	3,786	10,064
1986	371	347	78	2,831	876	3,334	9,066
1987	548	718	314	4,754	2,266	3,278	12,412
1988	849	1,286	170	4,623	2,123	3,945	13,153
1989	803	3,559	94	5,523	2,448	5,550	18,418
1990	759	1,284	253	1,859	579	4,432	14,650

[a] Conversions includes those for convertible bonds plus a minor amount of preferred shares.

Source: Tokyo Stock Exchange, *Annual Securities Statistics*, 1990

allowed a firm to raise more capital than with a par value issue having the same expected dividend payout.

By 1980, public share issues provided 84 percent of the funds raised from new equity issues by listed firms. However, public issues in that year accounted for only 18 percent of the total number of new shares issued by the same firms (see table 3.10). In fact, gratis issues (essentially stock dividends) were the largest source of new shares in 1980, followed by convertible bond (CB) conversions and rights issues. The basic pattern of market equity issues accounting for a large fraction of equity funds raised but a small fraction of new shares has continued.

Part of the reason for this pattern is that gratis issues have been widely used as a mechanism for increasing dividends. Conveniently, such issues also serve to dilute potential control implications of public issues. As we saw earlier, convertible bond and warrant bond issues have been a major funding mechanism since the early 1980s (see tables 3.5 and 3.6). A substantial portion of those CBs have been converted, accounting for 26 percent of new shares from 1981 to 1990. Exercised warrants also became a significant contributor to share increases in the later 1980s, accounting for 15 percent of new shares during the 1987–89 period.

As previously discussed, convertible and warrant bond issues have been advantageous relative to straight bond issues because of less-restrictive and expensive issuing regulations. They have also had advantages as equity issuance mechanisms relative to public equity offerings.

Perhaps most importantly, the underwriting commission has apparently been lower on convertible and warrant bonds relative to equity issues, particularly in the offshore market.

In addition, there has been pressure in the past for firms making public equity offerings to return to shareholders a portion of the premium between the issue price and the share's par value.[24] This was not attractive to issuing firms; however, the procedures for implementing this policy were somewhat vague and discretionary. In practice, it does not appear to have been rigorously enforced. Nevertheless, convertibles and warrants were viewed as even less subject to this policy – particularly if they were offshore issues. The overall effect has been a marked tendency for indirect equity issues via warrants and convertibles.

5 INVESTMENT EVALUATION PRACTICES

Discounted cash flow (DCF) techniques such as net present value (NPV) and internal rate of return (IRR) are not widely used within Japanese firms. In some cases, these techniques are utilized. For example, finding the "all-in cost" of a swapped foreign currency bond is an IRR calculation. However, such usage seems to be relatively rare and largely reserved for specialized evaluations conducted within the finance department. A more typical approach is to include an imputed interest charge in an investment's projected cash flows. This "interest" charge is based on the amount of funds the firm has invested and effectively incorporates the "time value of money" into an investment project's evaluation.

To illustrate the idea of imputing interest, consider a hypothetical example taken from Hodder (1986). The proposed investment involves ¥1 billion and is expected to generate ¥200 million annually for ten years. Interest will be charged to the project at a rate of 10 percent on the outstanding investment balance, which for profitable projects will decline over time. Calculations in table 3.11 indicate that the investment will pay for itself (residual investment goes to zero) in slightly over seven years. In the jargon of DCF procedures, this approach would be described as a discounted payback calculation using a 10 percent discount rate.

There are numerous variations on the above theme, and many Japanese firms use even simpler procedures where they calculate the return for a "typical" year. To illustrate, consider year one in the example of table 3.11. After the interest charge, the project earns ¥100 million during that year on a ¥1 billion investment; that is, a 10 percent return (after interest charges). The reciprocal of this return can also be used as an estimate of project payback – in this case, ten years. Again, there are

Table 3.11 Investment project cash flows with imputed interest charges (million yen)

Year	Project cash flows	Imputed interest	Adjusted cash flows	Residual investment
0	−1,000			1,000
1	200	100	100	900
2	200	90	110	790
3	200	79	121	669
4	200	67	133	536
5	200	54	146	390
6	200	39	161	229
7	200	23	177	52
8	200	5	195	0
9	200	0	200	0
10	200	0	200	0

many variations on the way in which different firms make these one-year return or payback calculations.

The one-year return calculation is relatively crude compared with the more detailed calculation in table 3.11. In our example, the return clearly depends strongly on which year is chosen as typical (for example, for year 6, the return is 41 percent). Nevertheless, managers with considerable experience using such a procedure can get a sense of the proposed project's anticipated profitability. If one were choosing between differing swap structures, such a crude procedure would be disastrous. However, many R&D, manufacturing, and marketing investments are characterized by cash flow estimates which are vague and highly uncertain. Under such circumstances, focusing discussion on the underlying cash flow assumptions may be far more productive than refining the return calculation. This indeed seems to be the emphasis in investment evaluation at most Japanese firms.

Discussions in Japanese firms regarding sales forecasts, production cost projections, possible competitor responses, government actions, and so on, involve managers from a range of functional areas (such as marketing, manufacturing, and accounting). For major investments, competitor actions are a major concern, with this aspect of the analysis having a defensive flavor. For example, someone might ask: "What happens if we do not invest in developing this new technology, but our competitors do?" More generally, there is recognition that the status quo is subject to change. The emphasis in Japan is on verbal discussions rather than on building computer models to analyze these issues. Meaningful participation in such discussions by a wide range of Japanese managers essentially requires analytical calculations to be relatively simple and clearly understood by all.

In part, this preference for simple calculations has to do with the fact that very few Japanese managers have attended a business school or been otherwise formally introduced to discounted cash flow techniques. Consequently, they are not comfortable with such procedures. However, even in the US many (if not most) manufacturing, R&D, and marketing managers are not all that comfortable with DCF procedures. Even for someone with considerable experience, such procedures can be tricky and may sometimes obscure what is driving a project's value. Consequently, there is often an inherent trade-off between the use of sophisticated analytical techniques and the participation level of individuals from diverse backgrounds. Japanese firms have clearly opted for increased participation, except in situations where analytical precision is critical.

It is also important to emphasize that the calculated payback or return estimate described above may carry relatively little weight in the decision of whether or not to invest in a particular project. Consequently, an investment project which appears marginal (or worse) financially may be undertaken because it protects the firm's competitive position or promotes some other fundamental objective. One could rightly argue that a correctly performed financial evaluation would reveal that such a project is not financially marginal. However, that sort of evaluation might require formally modeling complex dynamic strategies or operating options associated with the project. Typically, management would not even consider attempting such a complex financial evaluation because few managers would understand its details and be able to discuss it effectively. Thus, it is appropriate that the emphasis on using simple (even crude) techniques be coupled with a healthy skepticism about their accuracy and that limited weight be placed on their results.

In recent years there has been considerable debate regarding a possible cost of capital advantage for Japanese firms relative to their US competitors.[25] At first glance, a lower cost of capital might be viewed as the reason for a 10 percent implicit interest rate in the above example, as compared with substantially higher discount rates of 15 percent to 20 percent (or more) typically used by US firms. However, the difference between typical US discount rates and Japanese implicit interest charges is primarily due to a differing treatment of risk. US discount rates are generally risk-adjusted (larger for riskier investments), whereas the Japanese implicit interest charges are not adjusted for risk. Japanese managers do consider risk but in a qualitative manner rather than attempting quantitative adjustments to their financial calculations. The Japanese approach avoids the potential problem of discount rates which over-adjust for risk and may, consequently, explain a large part of Japanese firms' greater willingness to undertake seemingly risky projects.[26]

The key to a cost-of-capital advantage for Japanese firms appears to be the main bank system. Cost differences have occurred across markets, giving rise to the arbitrage opportunities discussed earlier. Typically, however, these situations have involved lower costs offshore relative to costs in the Japanese market. Furthermore, the differentials (for example, 50 basis points) have been too small to influence materially the relatively imprecise financial evaluation procedures commonly used for physical investment decisions (such as in new plant and equipment).

At least in the past, however, the main bank system seems to have allowed rapidly growing clients to source large amounts of capital at costs substantially below what would have prevailed in "arms-length" markets. This clearly had a substantial influence on investment decisions. The open question is whether the main bank system can still provide such an advantage. As many Japanese firms have become financially stronger and regulatory restrictions have eased, firms have been shifting their fundraising from intermediaries and towards securities markets. One can infer from this that at least some Japanese firms are finding security issues cheaper and/or less burdensome than borrowing via loans – that is to say, they are no longer deriving a substantial cost advantage from the main bank relationship.

Newer or smaller firms may still derive an important advantage from the main bank system, for example, when funding rapid growth via heavy borrowing under main bank auspices. However, financial liberalization tends to undermine the main bank system because firms have greater access to market debt (bonds and commercial paper) as well as borrowing from foreign financial institutions. This makes it potentially much more difficult to monitor and control client behavior. Consequently, the key to an effective main bank system under these circumstances seems to be an enforceable agreement or mechanism which restricts the access of heavy borrowers to alternative debt sources. If this condition can be satisfied, the main bank system should continue to be viable and advantageous for firms which need strong bank support.

6 CONCLUDING COMMENTS

Corporate financial patterns and practices in Japan appear quite different, particularly in comparison with those in the United States. In large part, these differences are due to differing institutional and regulatory structures. Frequently, a strange financing pattern turns out to be the rational economic response to a constraining regulation. The key to understanding such patterns is identifying the underlying structure of constraints. This is not always easy because regulations may be obscure, and regulatory agencies can act behind the scenes to influence behavior strongly without actually issuing regulations.

This does not mean that all financial behavior in Japan is a highly sophisticated response to obscure constraints. Until recently, Japanese financial markets had for decades been largely isolated. Market participants understood their environment but had little knowledge or experience of the financial technologies developed abroad. One does not come to understand, for example, option pricing overnight. Consequently, observing mispriced warrants in the retail market or some similar phenomenon should not be surprising.

Traditionally, much of corporate finance in Japan revolved around the main bank relationship. This is changing for many firms. Indeed, financial liberalization has created serious difficulties for the main bank system. Nevertheless, that system seems likely to adapt and continue to provide valuable support for rapidly growing firms. Exactly how this will come about is not yet clear; however, there are substantial incentives for preserving the system's advantages. Consequently, we should expect the main bank system to evolve rather than disappear.

More generally, the effects of financial liberalization over roughly the last decade have been enormous. The process of change will continue, both because of continuing liberalization and because some financial patterns (such as aggregate leverage) change sluggishly. Increasing financial sophistication and a consequent ability to exploit opportunities arising from regulatory changes will also continue to alter corporate financial practices for some time to come. It is reasonable to expect that the role of offshore financing will not decline. Untangling the web of domestic regulations, traditional practices, and conflicting interests of various financial constituencies will take time. During that period, offshore financing will probably grow substantially; and we shall continue to observe arbitrage situations bringing about market efficiency.

NOTES

1 See, for example, Aoki (1984), Kester (1986), or French and Poterba (1991).
2 See Tschoegl (1988) for a more detailed discussion of foreign banks in Japan.
3 Sometimes, there was more than a single main bank. Typically, however, one of these banks played a more prominent role with the other(s) being more secondary. Various aspects of the main bank system have been discussed by a number of authors including Aoki (1984, 1988), Hodder (1988), Hodder and Tschoegl (1985), Horiuchi et al. (1988), Hoshi et al. (1990), and Sheard (1989).

4   A widely cited and classic example of such bank intervention is described in Pascale and Rohlen (1983). That article provides a variety of details on Sumitomo Bank's rescue of Toyo Kogyo (now Mazda) during the mid-1970s.

5   Although this practice has been changing, only slightly over one-half of commercial bank loans had maturities greater than one year as of March 1990. In theory, the Japanese banking orientation toward loans which were, at least technically, short-term resulted from a desire to match maturities of assets (loans) and liabilities (deposits). Since the vast majority of deposits were short-term, the notion was that loans should also be short-term. Such loans could be rolled over to provide longer-term funding; however, this was at the lender's discretion. Whatever its benefits with regard to maturity matching, the emphasis on short-term loans resulted in a powerful control mechanism over borrowers who needed such loans rolled over.

6   Prindl (1981) contains an account of this episode from the perspective of a US banker resident in Japan at the time.

7   To quote the *OECD Economic Surveys: Japan* (OECD 1989–90: 100): "A rough estimation based on market conditions in February 1990 indicates that the costs of issuing convertible bonds amounting to $100 million by Japanese companies was 1.38 percent in the Euro market, compared with 1.92 percent in the domestic market (source: Ministry of Finance)."

8   The general preference of these utilities for straight debt issues seems largely due to the regulatory structure on setting utility rates for consumers and how financing costs influence those rates.

9   At the same time a provisional law on corporate bond issuance restrictions was also revised. Bonds with warrants were included among the types of bonds subject to the (relaxed) limit, in addition to secured corporate bonds, convertibles and corporate bonds issued abroad (Bond Underwriters' Association of Japan 1991).

10 Parenthetically, offshore straight bonds did not suffer the problem of having their coupon rates tied to yields on Japanese government bonds. This was another advantage to going offshore, particularly for a straight debt issue.

11 In some cases, warrant bonds have provisions which allow the bond to be used as part payment of the warrant exercise price. Under such circumstances, the principal and interest payments would again become uncertain. However, this problem can easily be eliminated by not including such an exchange provision.

12 The vast majority of these bonds were issued with relatively short maturities (for example, four years). Given the 40 percent decline in the TOPIX index during 1990, there is a substantial probability that a number of the warrants will indeed expire worthless.

13 Issues in the Swiss market tend to be of relatively small size and are converted to equity fairly rapidly, market conditions permitting. Swiss retail investors reportedly like the protection of the bond while awaiting the opportunity to convert (see Bond Underwriters' Association of Japan 1990: 20).

14 The maturity pattern for offshore convertibles is similar. However, maturities for domestic convertibles are typically longer. Since 1985, there have been

numerous domestic issues with 15-year maturities; and the majority of domestic issues have had maturities of at least nine years.

15 Apparently similar arbitrage transactions involved redepositing the proceeds of short-term bank loans into the deregulated LTDs or alternatively placing the proceeds in CDs. See, for example, the discussion of "financial round-tripping" and the enormous flows of corporate funds into deposits with liberalized interest rates during 1988 and 1989 in the July 6, 1990 "Market Analysis" from the Japanese Economic Research group at Salomon Brothers.

16 In contrast, the non-life (casualty) insurance firms are almost all stock companies.

17 The relevant statute is article 11 of the Antitrust Law. In general, banks are limited to 5 percent of a firm's shares. Trust banks may hold shares in excess of 5 percent when they are acting as nominees. All banks may exceed the limitation when they acquire shares in the course of taking over collateral or take payment for a loan in the form of shares. Insurance companies are permitted to hold up to 10 percent of a firm's outstanding shares.

18 Somewhat symmetrically, non-financial firms also hold a large fraction of bank and (listed) insurance company shares. The National Federation of Stock Exchanges' (1990) *Kabushiki Bunpu Jokyo Chosa* (Stock Distribution Situation Survey) indicates that, as of March 1990, non-financial corporations held 41 percent of the shares of listed firms in the finance and insurance industry.

19 In fact, there was a round of share exchanges between Japanese firms in the early 1970s which were apparently designed to protect them from foreign takeover following the (partial) opening of the Japanese stock market to foreign investment. Private placements of equities or convertible bonds have also been used to counter takeover threats. See, for example, the discussion in Viner (1987), as well as Isaacs and Ejiri (1990), of the 1985 confrontation between Minebea, Sankyo Seiki, and Trafalgar Holdings.

20 Unrealized gains on real-estate holdings have a similar effect. Such holdings are very substantial for some Japanese firms. Indeed, purchasing shares in a Japanese firm is sometimes viewed as purchasing a portfolio of real-estate, shares in other firms, and operating assets. The effect of cross-holding price–earnings ratios became most apparent in the second half of the 1980s when the Bank of Japan's monetary policy fostered the "bubble economy" with its dramatic land and stock price increases. In the 1960s, 1970s and early 1980s the effect of cross-holding on PERs was far less apparent.

21 See French and Poterba (1991). The first analysis of this problem seems to be McDonald (1989).

22 Fedenia, Hodder and Triantis (1991) explore these issues in some detail.

23 This figure, as well as the others on dividends quoted below, are from the *Tokyo Stock Exchange Fact Book*.

24 See for example, Japan Securities Research Institute (1984) for a description of the guidelines on returning this premium.

25 See Hodder (1991), as well as references cited there, regarding this debate.

26 Several authors, including Kaplan (1986) and Hodder and Riggs (1985), have suggested that US firms frequently use discount rates which are too large.

REFERENCES

Aoki, M. 1984: Aspects of the Japanese firm. In M. Aoki (ed.), *The Economic Analysis of the Japanese Firm*, Amsterdam: North-Holland, ch. 1.

Aoki, M. 1988: *Information, Incentives, and Bargaining in the Japanese Economy.* New York: Cambridge University Press.

Bank of Japan, *Comparative Economic and Financial Statistics: Japan and other major countries*, various issues.

Bank of Japan, *Economic Statistics Annual*, various issues.

Board of Governors of the Federal Reserve System, *Flow of Funds Accounts*, various issues.

Bond Underwriters' Association of Japan, *Bond Market in Japan*, various issues.

Fedenia, M., Hodder, J.E. and Triantis, A.J. 1991: Cross-holding and market return measures. Working Paper, Graduate School of Business, University of Wisconsin – Madison, June.

French, K.R. and Poterba, J.M. 1991: Were Japanese stock prices too high? *Journal of Financial Economics*, 29(2), 337–63.

Hodder, J.E. 1986: Evaluation of manufacturing investments: a comparison of US and Japanese practices. *Financial Management*, Spring, 17–24; reprinted in S. H. Archer and H. S. Kerr (eds), *Readings and Cases in Corporate Finance*, New York: McGraw-Hill, 1988.

Hodder, J.E. 1988: Corporate capital structure in the United States and Japan: financial intermediation and implications of financial deregulation. In J. B. Shoven (ed.), *Government Policy Towards Industry in the United States and Japan*, New York: Cambridge University Press.

Hodder, J.E. 1991: Is the cost of capital lower in Japan? *Journal of the Japanese and International Economies*, March, 86–100.

Hodder, J.E. and Riggs, H.E. 1985: Pitfalls in evaluating risky projects. *Harvard Business Review*, January–February, 128–35; reprinted in *Managing Projects and Programs*, Cambridge, Mass.: Harvard Business School Press, 1989.

Hodder, J.E. and Tschoegl, A.E. 1985: Some aspects of Japanese corporate finance. *Journal of Financial and Quantitative Analysis*, 20(2), 173–91.

Horiuchi, A., Packer, F. and Fukuda, S. 1988: What role has the "main bank" played in Japan? *Journal of the Japanese and International Economies*, 2, 159–80.

Hoshi, T., Kashyap, A. and Scharfstein, D. 1990: The role of banks in reducing the costs of financial distress in Japan. *Journal of Financial Economics*, 27, 67–88.

Isaacs, J. and Ejiri, T. 1990: *Japanese Securities Market*. London: Euromoney Publications.

Japan Securities Research Institute, *Securities Market in Japan*, various issues.

Kaplan, R. S. 1986: Must CIM be justified by faith alone? *Harvard Business Review*, March–April, 87–95.

Kester, W.C. 1986: Capital and ownership structure: a comparison of United States and Japanese manufacturing corporations. *Financial Management*, Spring, 5–16.

McDonald, J. 1989: The *Mochiai* effect: Japanese corporate cross-holdings. *Journal of Portfolio Management*, Fall, 90–4.

Ministry of Finance 1990: *Yearbook of International Finance Bureau*. Tokyo: Ministry of Finance.

National Federation of Stock Exchanges 1990: *Kabushiki Bunpu Jokyo Chosa* (Stock Distribution Situation Survey). Tokyo: National Federation of Stock Exchanges.

Organization for Economic Cooperation and Development 1989–90: *OECD Economic Surveys: Japan*. Paris: OECD

Pascale, R.T. and Rohlen, T.P. 1983: The Mazda turnaround. *Journal of Japanese Studies*, 9(2), 219–63.

Prindl, A.R. 1981: *Japanese Finance: a guide to banking in Japan*. New York: John Wiley.

Salomon Brothers 1990: Japanese Economic Research, Market analysis. July 6.

Sheard, P. 1989: The main bank system and corporate monitoring and control in Japan. *Journal of Economic Behavior and Organization*, 11, 399–422.

Tokyo Stock Exchange, *Annual Securities Statistics*, various issues.

Tokyo Stock Exchange, *Tokyo Stock Exchange Fact Book*, various issues.

Tschoegl, A.E. 1988: Foreign banks in Japan. *Bank of Japan Monetary and Economic Studies*, 6(1), 93–118.

US Department of Commerce, *Quarterly Financial Report for Manufacturing, Mining and Trade Corporations*, various issues.

Viner, A. 1987: *Inside Japan's Financial Markets*. London: *The Economist* Publications.

4

The Securities Industry in Japan

Megumi Suto

1 INTRODUCTION

This chapter reviews the industrial organization of the Japanese securities industry. In particular, it discusses some distinctive features of the industry's market structure as well as the behavior of securities companies. It also touches upon some current issues with which the industry is now confronted after the unprecedented prosperity it experienced in the 1980s.

Section 2 provides a brief historical sketch of the postwar development of the securities industry in Japan. Section 3 discusses the market structure of the industry as well as some of the notable structural changes of recent years. Section 4 analyzes the unique behavior of Japanese securities companies. Section 5 discusses some of the current issues which face the Japanese securities industry at the beginning of the 1990s. Finally, section 6 presents a proposal for the restructuring of the securities industry.

2 AN HISTORICAL OVERVIEW OF THE SECURITIES INDUSTRY

In postwar Japan, the securities industry has experienced drastic organizational changes along with the growth and development of the securities market. The postwar period up to the beginning of the 1990s can be divided into four distinct phases of industrial development.

2.1 Growth of the Securities Market after the Second World War

After the Second World War, stock exchanges were reopened under a new system in 1949. Underlying that new system was the Securities and Exchange Law of 1948, which was based on such US federal laws as the

Shinji Takagi, Hideki Hanaeda, Toshiharu Takahashi and Colin McKenzie provided comments on an earlier draft.

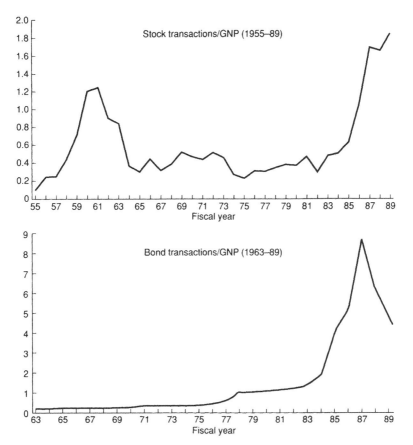

Figure 4.1 Growth of the securities market in Japan

Sources: Tokyo Stock Exchange, *Tokei Geppo* (Statistical Monthly), various issues; Economic Planning Agency of Japan, *National Income Statistics*, annual issues

Securities Act of 1933, the Securities and Exchange Act of 1934, and the Banking Act of 1933. The institutional framework of the postwar financial system was largely established in the first half of the 1950s.

However, the securities market did not function well until the latter half of the 1950s. Although stock trading temporarily boomed with the release of privately held stocks resulting from the dissolution of *Zaibatsu* corporate groups, the growth of stock investments was limited by the low level of household assets and income. Moreover, the central government refrained from issuing government bonds under the balanced budget principle, and placed strict controls on the flotation of corporate bonds in order to protect the banking sector.

Table 4.1   Sales of newly issued securities, 1956–88

	Corporate bonds purchased by financial intermediaries (%)	Stocks publicly sold at current prices (%)
1956–60	80.1	7.6
1961–65	81.7	3.1
1966–70	78.9	7.8
1971–75	66.5	41.2
1976–80	61.8	68.6
1981–85	63.6	73.5
1986–88	32.0	74.3

Source: Government and Corporate Bonds Underwriting Association, *Koshasai Geppo* (Monthly Report) and *Koshasai Nenpo* (Annual Report); Tokyo Stock Exchange, *Tokei Geppo* (Statistical Monthly)

In the latter half of the 1950s, the stock market grew rapidly along with the recovery of the real economy. The increase in personal savings and the resulting accumulation of personal assets brought about a rapid expansion of securities investments by individuals. The volume of stock transactions rose from 10 percent of GNP in 1955 to 131.3 percent in 1961, and the securities industry enjoyed a high level of prosperity for the first time since the war (figure 4.1).

At the beginning of the 1960s, the share of equity finance in the total volume of funds raised by the corporate sector was no less than those in other industrial countries.[1] Until the beginning of the 1970s, however, more than 90 percent of new stocks were rationed to stockholders, and more than 80 percent of corporate bonds were purchased by financial intermediaries by rationing or allocation (table 4.1). Thus, the apparent growth of the primary market did not mean that the market mechanism was functioning in the allocation of funds.

Under these circumstances, the key factors that determined the competitive position of securities companies during this period were the "marketing power" and the "sales network" of individual firms in providing investment trusts and brokerage services in stocks and bank debentures to a large number of small investors. In response to the emerging demand for retail services, the securities companies expanded their sales networks by increasing the number of branch offices and sales staff. Initially the Big Four (Nomura, Nikko, Yamaichi, and Daiwa) had an advantage over the smaller local firms because they had already set up nationwide branch networks as specialists in government and corporate

Table 4.2 Size of securities companies, 1949–63

| | Number of sales offices per firm | | | Total | Number of securities |
	Big Four	*Semi-majors*[a]	*Others*	*number*	*companies*
1949	36.8	8.4	1.5	1,889	1,152
1958	89.5	22.5	2.4	1,984	527
1960	108.5	33.3	2.8	2,537	518
1963	113.3	40.5	3.0	2,922	559

[a] There were ten semi-majors.

Source: Ministry of Finance, *Shokenkyoku Nenpo* (Annual Report of the Securities Bureau)

bonds before the war. Moreover, the larger firms actively made efforts to expand their branch networks in response to the growing securities investments by individuals (table 4.2). They also had the advantage of being permitted to operate investment trusts and to manage the securities deposited by their customers.[2]

In sum, not only were the major securities companies in a favored position to capture the expanding demand of individual investors for retail services, but also they could strategically utilize the existing trading system for their own advantage. As a result, the oligopoly market structure of the postwar securities industry, with high market concentration of the Big Four, was established during this period. The share of the Big Four in the total volume of stock transactions rose from 33.2 percent in 1953 to 64.9 percent in 1960; the Big Four's share in the outstanding balance of investment trusts during this period was over 90 percent (table 4.3).

2.2 The Stock Market Crisis and the Reorganization of the Industry

The prosperity of the securities market came to an end in the early 1960s, causing serious difficulties to the management of securities companies that had pursued aggressive marketing strategies. At around the same time, the Bank of Japan responded to a deterioration in the balance of payments by tightening monetary conditions. The result was the stock market crash of 1965, also known as the Securities Market Crisis (or *Shoken Kyoko* in Japanese).

In April 1962 bond transactions virtually ceased; in February 1965 new equity issues completely ceased. In June and July 1965 the Bank of Japan provided financial support to the failing Yamaich and Oi securities com-

Table 4.3   The market share of the Big Four, 1953–63 (%)

	Stock transactions	*Outstanding balance of investment trusts*
1953	33.2	95.9
1955	49.7	95.1
1958	62.5	93.2
1960	64.9	85.4
1963	55.2	n.a.

Source: Same as for table 4.2

panies. In October the Securities and Exchange Law was fundamentally revised, resulting in the first institutional reform of the industry since the war.

The focus of the 1965 reform was to correct the anomalies in existing securities regulations and the trading system. These were manifested as a conflict of interests between investors and securities companies. From the point of view of investor protection and fairness of transactions, the government chose to strengthen their regulations on the behavior of securities companies as well as of the exchanges. The authorities recognized the need to rationalize and stabilize the management of securities companies so as to maintain order in securities transactions and to protect investors from unfair trading. The guiding principle of securities industry regulations was thus changed from the ideal of US securities legislations based on free entry and screening by competition.

The 1965 reform (a) introduced a licensing system for securities operations; (b) reinforced the supervision and administrative guidance of the Ministry of Finance; and (c) classified the responsibilities of the sales personnel employed by securities companies.

Under the new licensing system, separate licenses for brokerage, dealing, underwriting and distribution are granted on the basis of equity capital and other managerial criteria. A firm can be permitted to engage in all four areas of securities operations if it has equity capital of 1 billion yen. Only firms with equity capital of 3 billion yen can become lead underwriters, thus becoming integrated firms, called *Sogo-Shoken* in Japanese.

Mergers, ownership transfers, liquidation of business, change of company name, establishment and relocation of branch offices, and financial position came under the supervision and guidance of the Ministry of Finance. The behavior of securities companies has since been significantly affected by the arbitrary guidelines of the Ministry of Finance. In addi-

Table 4.4 The income structure of securities companies, 1968–78 (%)

	Commission and fees received			Gains on trading	Margin interests
	Brokerage	*Underwriting*	*Distribution*	*trading*	*interests*
1968	56.7	4.2	8.4	3.2	27.5
1970	53.5	4.7	7.9	2.8	31.1
1972	54.3	5.1	8.3	14.8	17.5
1974	47.5	7.1	13.0	0.4	32.0
1976	48.1	7.1	12.8	9.8	22.2
1978	49.2	9.1	12.9	11.1	17.7

Source: Ministry of Finance, *Shokenkyoku Nenpo* (Annual Report of the Securities Bureau), annual issues

tion, the newly introduced registration system for sales staff not only classified their responsibilities but also stipulated a code of conduct for each area of responsibility.

After the introduction of the new regulatory system, the number of securities companies decreased drastically from the peak of 564 in 1962 to 255 at the end of 1968. The number of branch offices also declined from 2853 to 1825 during the same period. In subsequent years, however, the number of firms has remained fairly stable under the licensing system, and the number of branch offices has been allowed to increase in a controlled manner by the Ministry of Finance.

2.3   Provision of New Securities Services in the 1970s

For several years following the crash the securities market experienced a gradual recovery, and entered a new stage of development in the early 1970s. During this period, two notable changes took place: namely, new demands for securities services and an increasing concentration of securities transactions in Tokyo.

First, in the primary market, an increasing amount of stocks and convertible bonds were issued at market prices under the support of the regulatory authorities. At the same time, the government began to issue a large number of long-term bonds in 1975 to meet the shortfall in revenue associated with the first oil crisis. As a result, there emerged a new demand for underwriting services in corporate bonds; so securities companies began to devote more resources to bond operations. The share of brokerage revenue in the total income of securities companies began to decline from the middle of the 1970s (table 4.4). Competition in securities underwriting and bonds trading became fierce among integrated com-

Table 4.5 Transaction matrix of securities companies in terms of market share (1972–7)

1972 \ 1977	Share in commissions and fees (%)						Number of firms (1972)
	0.05	0.05–0.1	0.1–0.2	0.2–0.5	0.5–5	>5	
<0.05	78 (0.940)	5 (0.060)					83
0.05–0.1	15 (0.385)	22 (0.564)	2 (0.051)				39
0.1–0.2		18 (0.409)	26 (0.591)				44
0.2–0.5			10 (0.270)	27 (0.730)			37
0.5–5				4 (0.211)	15 (0.789)		19
>5						4 (1.000)	4
Number of firms (1977)	93	45	38	31	15	4	226

For each element, the upper figure is the number of firms that moved from the row entries (1972) to the column entries (1977); and the lower figure (in parentheses) is its ratio to the total number of firms in the relevant share group in 1972.

Source: Suto (1987: 81 and table 3.3)

panies. The Big Four, which maintained customer relationships with large business firms, were in an advantageous position to become lead underwriters and to extend the scope of their activities in order to meet the diversified needs of their customers.

Second, with the development of telecommunication and information networks in the 1970s, economic activities in Japan became increasingly concentrated in Tokyo, resulting in a corresponding concentration of securities business in Tokyo. The gap between the Tokyo Stock Exchange and the regional exchanges widened sharply in terms of market depth, breadth and resilience.

In consequence, during the 1970s regional differences and variations in company size widened ever more rapidly. The transition matrix in table 4.5 indicates that, in terms of commissions and fee revenues, the oligopolistic tendency of the industry increased from 1972 to 1977.

2.4   Expansion of the Securities Market in the 1980s

Throughout the 1980s, and especially during the second half of the decade, the securities industry experienced an extraordinary growth of activities and profits, as indicated by table 4.6. The growth of the Japanese securities industry in the 1980s was remarkable not only in relation to the growth of manufacturing industries in Japan but also in comparison to the US securities industry. In the terms of revenues, the relative share of the securities industry in the economy increased after the middle of the 1980s, overtaking the US securities industry in 1986 in terms of GNP share (table 4.7). The profit rate (pre-tax rate of return to equity capital) of the Japanese securities industry continued to rise throughout the period, while that of the US securities industry declined.

The unprecedented growth of the Japanese securities industry during the 1980s occurred in the context of financial liberalization and rapid expansion of the securities market, supported by a high exchange rate of the yen and low interest rates. It was during this period that the large integrated companies actively pursued diversification of their domestic and overseas operations. Prompted by the liberalization of international capital flows, more and more Japanese corporations increased the share of funds procured in the overseas markets as a way of avoiding domestic regulations; at its peak in 1985 this share was over 40 percent of total fund procurement (table 4.8). As a result, securities companies faced new competition in the overseas markets from commercial banks, which were allowed to do some securities business in the domestic market.

In the domestic market, the Ministry of Finance gradually relaxed the legal separation between securities companies and banks. For example, banks were permitted to sell long-term public bonds over the counter for

Table 4.6 Growth of securities business, 1970–90 (in hundreds of millions of yen; 1970 = 100)

Year[b]	Received commissions and fees		of which: (Brokerage)		(Underwriting)		(Distribution)		Transaction volume[a]	
1970	2,646	(100)	1,926	(100)	171	(100)	285	(100)	414,854	(100)
1971	2,806	(106)	2,029	(105)	208	(122)	327	(115)	464,715	(112)
1972	4,064	(154)	3,131	(163)	296	(173)	481	(169)	712,511	(172)
1973	5,185	(196)	3,763	(195)	550	(322)	663	(233)	845,712	(204)
1974	3,711	(140)	2,440	(127)	368	(215)	671	(235)	750,109	(181)
1975	4,257	(161)	2,695	(140)	477	(279)	828	(291)	892,086	(215)
1976	5,760	(218)	3,875	(201)	569	(333)	1,033	(362)	1,191,592	(287)
1977	6,441	(243)	4,118	(214)	649	(380)	1,330	(467)	1,615,076	(389)
1978	8,255	(312)	5,426	(282)	1,008	(589)	1,423	(499)	2,683,818	(647)
1979	8,830	(334)	6,181	(321)	844	(494)	1,375	(482)	3,055,308	(736)
1980	8,741	(330)	6,202	(322)	907	(530)	1,181	(414)	3,527,629	(850)
1981	10,442	(395)	7,765	(403)	1,032	(604)	1,135	(398)	4,094,512	(987)
1982	8,487	(321)	5,255	(273)	1,262	(738)	1,340	(470)	4,133,975	(996)
1983	12,432	(470)	9,011	(468)	928	(543)	1,613	(566)	6,263,819	(1,510)
1984	15,227	(575)	10,429	(541)	1,241	(726)	1,782	(625)	7,451,016	(1,796)
1985	19,404	(733)	13,991	(726)	1,537	(899)	2,509	(880)	14,905,179	(3,593)
1986	30,552	(1,155)	23,840	(1,238)	1,456	(851)	3,819	(1,340)	24,614,948	(5,933)
1987	41,102	(1,553)	31,157	(1,618)	2,368	(1,385)	5,613	(1,969)	40,823,863	(9,841)
1988	38,430	(1,452)	27,436	(1,425)	3,932	(2,299)	4,526	(1,588)	33,598,410	(8,099)
1989	45,085	(1,704)	31,143	(1,617)	5,188	(3,034)	5,454	(1,914)	28,155,163	(6,787)
1990	26,402	(998)	18,692	(971)	1,624	(950)	3,117	(1,093)	23,302,625	(5,617)

[a] The volume of transactions includes all securities transactions by domestic companies.
[b] Fiscal year; in 1990, the year-end was changed from September to March.

Source: Ministry of Finance, *Annual Report of Securities Bureau*, annual issues

Table 4.7 Pre-tax profit rates to equity capital of Japanese and US securities companies

	Ratio of total revenue to GNP	*Pre-tax profit rates to equity capital (%)*
Japan		
1980	0.495	20
1981	0.546	23
1982	0.465	12
1983	0.503	27
1984	0.711	30
1985	0.872	40
1986	1.222	53
1987	1.489	52
1988	1.309	32
1989	1.487	29
USA		
1980	0.587	50
1981	0.649	49
1982	0.745	41
1983	0.868	37
1984	0.828	13
1985	0.962	29
1986	1.181	28
1987	1.123	5
1988	1.062	10
1989	1.138	7

Source: Ministry of Finance, *Annual Report of the Securities Bureau*, annual issues; Economic Planning Agency of Japan, *National Income Statistics*, annual issues; Securities Industry Association, *SIA Trends*, May 1990; Council of Economic Advisors, *Economic Report of the President, 1990*

the first time in April 1983, and to deal in public bonds in July 1984. The range of public bonds authorized for bank transactions was expanded in the late 1980s to include such derivatives as futures and options. At the same time, the government authorized securities companies to go into gray areas such as the marketing of gold bullion, transactions in certificates of deposits (CDs) and commercial paper (CP) issued in overseas markets, and transactions in the domestic CDs, yen-dominated bankers' acceptances (BAs), and so on. The resulting conflict of interests between different types of financial institution was made clear when the extraordinary expansion of the securities market came to an end in late 1980s

Table 4.8   Procurement of funds by Japanese corporations in domestic and overseas markets

Year	Total (hundreds of millions of yen)	Composition of funds procured (%)				Ratio of funds procured overseas (%)				
		Stocks	Corporate bonds	Convertible bonds	Bonds with warrants	Total	Stocks	Corporate bonds	Convertible bonds	Bonds with warrants
1970	13,841	47.8	43.9	8.3	–	1.3	0.3	–	14.1	–
1975	26,342	35.1	45.5	19.5	–	18.8	2.3	24.5	35.5	–
1980	30,443	41.6	38.3	20.1	–	26.0	8.6	14.4	84.2	–
1981	50,138	41.5	26.3	30.9	1.3	28.0	13.8	3.7	66.1	68.9
1982	39,645	27.2	43.6	26.4	2.8	36.2	5.8	39.4	60.0	58.3
1983	45,387	20.4	26.9	45.2	7.5	44.0	8.4	33.1	58.0	95.0
1984	59,939	14.4	30.9	47.4	7.3	47.5	5.7	61.2	43.2	99.3
1985	64,995	10.2	36.7	39.0	14.2	50.2	1.6	60.4	37.4	94.0
1986	93,019	6.8	28.2	42.5	22.5	44.3	0.1	62.6	12.3	95.0
1987	134,325	15.8	12.9	45.6	25.6	40.0	1.8	47.4	17.6	100.0
1988	192,137	23.8	8.3	42.0	25.9	36.0	0.4	52.9	13.2	100.0
1989	283,085	27.9	6.5	33.1	32.4	40.5	4.2	60.5	18.5	90.0
1990	94,668	7.0	46.1	15.1	31.9	57.4	0	52.7	36.1	79.8

Source: Government and Corporate Bonds Underwriting Association, *Koshasai Nenkan* (Annual Report), 1989

and major scandals involving the Big Four broke out in the summer of 1991.[3] There is no doubt that fundamental changes in the postwar regulatory framework of the securities market and industry will be forthcoming in the near future (see section 5).

3 THE MARKET STRUCTURE OF THE SECURITIES INDUSTRY

The market structure of the Japanese securities industry has three distinguishing features: a high level of market concentration; a low degree of operational specialization; and the existence of several affiliate groups among securities companies.

3.1 A High Level of Market Concentration

The number of domestic securities companies has continued to decrease since the licensing system was introduced in 1968 (table 4.9). Among some 200 firms, securities operations in four major areas (brokerage, dealing, underwriting, and distribution) have been highly concentrated in a small number of integrated companies, especially the Big Four.

In fiscal 1990, the share of the Big Four was 39.1 percent in stock transactions, 72.1 percent in bond transactions, 64.3 percent in underwriting of stocks, 74.1 percent in underwriting of bonds, and almost 66 percent of pre-tax profits (table 4.10). The Big Four are even more dominant in some of the new fields of operations, such as international services and transactions of stock derivatives (table 4.11). Among the Big Four, Nomura has dominated the other three in almost all fields of securities operations, so that the Japanese securities industry in fact has a pyramid structure with Nomura at the top.

3.2 A Low Degree of Operational Specialization

As a second feature, the Japanese securities industry lacks the diversity of companies that characterizes the US industry. In Japan, there is only a handful of specialized companies, including investment trust companies, investment advisory companies, and interdealer broker companies. For the most part, there are only two types of securities companies in Japan, namely integrated companies (which provide complete services on a nationwide basis) and smaller companies (which specialize in stock brokerage for individual investors). Integrated companies are capable of providing services in all areas of business that are legally permitted for securities companies. There are no companies specializing in investment banking or

Table 4.9   Number of firms and branch offices

	Big Four	Other integrated companies	Others	Total
Number of firms				
1970	4	–	–	248
1975	4	7	225	236
1980	4	8	217	229
1985	4	16	192	212
1986	4	21	186	211
1987	4	24	183	211
1988	4	30	176	210
1990	4	38	168	210
Number of branch offices per firm				
1970	86	–	–	1,823
1975	88	52	5	1,887
1980	94	52	6	2,044
1985	103	48	5	2,301
1986	108	42	5	2,363
1987	114	41	5	2,492
1988	122	40	6	2,632
1990	134	37	6	3,133

Source: As for table 4.6

wholesale business because of the historically limited scope of the primary market. The kind of interfirm differences between integrated and other companies in the scale and scope of activities also exist between the Big Four and the other integrated companies. The differences between the two groups is remarkable, even in terms of the level and volatility of profit rates: the Big Four have enjoyed a conspicuously higher rate and stability (table 4.12).

The securities companies can thus be classified into three major groups: the Big Four; a handful of other integrated companies; and a large number of small firms that are highly specialized in stock brokerage. In this sense, the Japanese securities industry consists of three tiers in terms of operational specialization. This structure became firmly established in the latter part of the 1960s with the introduction of the licensing system, which made minimum capital requirements mandatory for the management of securities companies in each area of securities operations.

Table 4.10 The market shares of domestic securities companies (%)

	Big Four	Other integrated companies	Others		Big Four	Other integrated companies	Others
Stock transactions				**Bonds underwriting**			
1970	47.7	–	–	1970	–	–	–
1975	41.3	18.9	39.8	1975	75.6	18.9	5.5
1980	44.6	21.2	34.2	1980	72.9	21.4	5.7
1985	46.6	29.0	24.4	1985	69.2	26.3	4.5
1986	49.7	31.0	19.3	1986	68.9	27.4	3.7
1987	49.7	33.3	17.0	1987	68.5	27.7	3.8
1988	44.3	39.2	16.5	1988	65.1	30.1	4.8
1990	39.1	46.2	14.7	1990	74.1	24.5	1.4
Bonds trans. volume of bonds				**Revenue**			
1970	65.5	–	–	1970	44.8	–	–
1975	64.5	20.5	15.0	1975	49.2	17.7	33.1
1980	77.4	15.6	7.0	1980	49.1	18.3	32.6
1985	60.9	36.1	3.0	1985	52.6	27.6	19.8
1986	62.6	35.0	2.4	1986	54.4	29.1	16.5
1987	64.4	33.8	1.8	1987	50.9	30.5	18.6
1988	75.0	24.0	1.0	1988	47.3	35.7	17.0
1990	72.1	27.4	0.5	1990	45.0	43.0	12.0
Stock underwriting				**Profit before tax**			
1970	82.4	–	–	1970	53.2	–	–
1975	89.7	9.4	0.9	1975	69.5	9.6	20.9
1980	88.9	10.0	1.1	1980	73.0	5.2	21.8
1985	81.3	16.8	1.9	1985	64.2	20.9	14.9
1986	75.7	21.7	2.6	1986	62.9	23.8	13.3
1987	74.4	22.3	3.3	1987	57.4	29.1	13.5
1988	56.2	38.8	5.0	1988	54.8	31.6	13.6
1990	64.3	35.2	0.5	1990	66.1	24.6	9.3

Source: As for table 4.6

3.3   Affiliations among Securities Firms

As with manufacturing firms in Japan, the securities industry is also characterized by interfirm relationships based on equity capital and personnel exchange between larger and smaller firms. Most small and medium-sized securities companies maintain a special relationship with one of the top companies to varying degrees. According to Suto (1987), 125 of 230 small and medium-sized securities companies were explicitly

Table 4.11   Market shares of transactions in foreign securities and derivatives in fiscal year 1989 (%)

	Big Four	Other integrated companies	Others	Total (billions of yen)
Foreign securities				
Stocks	91.8	7.2	1.0	13,711
Others	84.0	16.0	0.0	437,333
Bonds with warrant				
Domestic	55.0	26.1	18.9	1,075
Foreign	80.3	19.2	0.5	27,965
Futures				
Stocks	55.3	42.3	2.4	634,761
Bonds	56.2	41.5	2.3	1,345,046
Options				
Stocks	61.0	38.0	1.0	882,575
Bonds	19.2	80.8	0.0	7,900
Number of firms	4	38	168	

Excluding transactions of foreign firms.

Source: Ministry of Finance, *Annual Report of the Securities Bureau*, 1990

affiliated with one of the Big Four in September 1978.[4] This situation has not fundamentally changed, so that we can still characterize the present structure of the securities industry as a "Big Four Regime."

This situation, however, might have begun to change with the entry of major foreign securities companies and some of the leading domestic banks into the securities market. Foreign firms were first allowed to obtain securities licenses in 1972. Although the number of foreign firms remained small for many years (as few as ten in 1984[5]), the number rapidly increased in the latter part of the 1980s. As of March 1991, there were 52 firms, of which 25 were members of the Tokyo Stock Exchange, and 60 branch offices. The share of foreign firms was about 19 percent of all securities companies and 20 percent of all member firms at the Tokyo Stock Exchange.

Although almost all foreign securities companies intended to provide a full range of securities services, they have all encountered difficulties in penetrating the retail market because of the lack of branch offices and of the information necessary to carry on retail business. As a result, the market share of foreign firms remains small in the four traditional areas of business (table 4.13). In the area of institutional investment (especially bond-related business), however, they have begun to establish a significant

Table 4.12   Characteristics of domestic securities companies in fiscal year 1989

	Big Four	*Other integrated companies*	*Others*
Number of firms	4	38	168
Scale per equity capital (billions of yen)	129	38	6
Number of branches	1,409.2	148.2	4.7
Number of employees	14,883	1,766	139
Income structure (%)			
Commissions and fees (CF)	76.0	80.8	73.1
of which: Brokerage	44.7	60.6	65.3
Underwriting	14.3	4.8	0.9
Cost structure (%)			
Operating cost (OC/CF)	52.7	77.0	77.7
Labor cost/CF	18.9	31.3	38.2
Labor cost/OC	30.2	40.6	49.2
Depreciation/OC	3.0	2.3	1.7
Net profit/total assets (%)			
1970–90 average (X)	3.97	1.60	1.33
1970–90 standard deviation (Y)	1.15	0.82	0.50
Y/X	0.29	0.51	0.38

Source: As for table 4.10

presence. They are increasingly becoming serious competitors to the Big Four, because they have advantages in providing the sophisticated services that institutional investors are requesting in the overseas and the domestic markets.

In the area of securities transactions in public bonds, moreover, banks have come to maintain a high market share in terms of both sales and trading volume. They have been able to compete with the securities companies on an equal footing (tables 4.14 and 4.15). As a result, the position of the Big Four been somewhat eroded by the penetration of foreign firms and banks.

4   THE CORPORATE BEHAVIOR OF JAPANESE SECURITIES COMPANIES

4.1   Regulation of Securities Companies

The behavior of securities companies and the market structure of the securities industry have been significantly affected by the protective regu-

Table 4.13   Status of foreign securities companies in Japan in fiscal year 1989

(1) Market share (%)		Total assets	1.39
Underwriting		Number of employees	4.36
Stocks	0.59	Commission received	5.25
Others	4.80		
Distribution		Operating cost	7.52
Stocks	2.19	Salaries and wages	8.68
Bonds	5.75		
Brokerage		Net gains from tradings	1.13
Stocks	7.06	Net profit before tax	1.55
Bonds	12.54		
Trading		(2) Number of firms	
Stocks	6.62	Exchange members	22
Bonds	6.06	Non-members	29
Foreign securities transactions		Total	51
	7.17		
Transactions in bonds with warrant		(3) Profit rate to total assets (%)	
Domestic	6.33	Before tax	1.67
Foreign	12.42	Net profit	0.41
Futures transactions			
Stocks	8.47		
Bonds	11.70		
Option transactions			
Stocks	3.09		
Bonds	6.22		

Source: Japan Securities Dealers' Association

latory attitude of the authorities, which is summarized by the following five major regulations:

(a)   article 65 of the Securities and Exchange Law which separates the banking business from the securities business except for government securities;

(b)   the licensing system for the four principal operations in the four principal areas;

(c)   the administrative guidance of the Ministry of Finance, which gives often arbitrary guidelines on the behavior of securities companies, including the establishment of new branch offices, the position of balance sheets, and the introduction of new financial products;

(d)   the fixed brokerage commission system in the securities exchanges;

(e)   the limitation on the number of member firms at the securities exchanges under the guidance of the Ministry of Finance.

Table 4.14 Over-the-counter sales of government bonds (hundreds of millions of yen; %)

	Long-term bonds			Medium-term bonds		
	1983	*1989*	*1990*	*1983*	*1989*	*1990*
Sales volume						
Banks	13,373	3,728	19,391	5,908	922	1,870
Securities companies	10,650	32,439	25,313	10,748	10,318	15,957
Others	1,590	1,069	2,147	311	481	249
Total	25,613	37,236	46,851	16,967	11,721	18,076
Shares						
Banks	52.2	10.0	41.4	34.8	7.9	10.3
Securities companies	47.8	90.0	58.6	65.2	92.1	89.7

Source: Ministry of Finance, *Annual Report of Securities Bureau*, annual issues

Table 4.15 Dealing in public bonds by type of institution (hundreds of millions of yen; %)

	1986	*1987*	*1988*	*1989*	*1990*
Total amount	24,580	34,168	50,943	40,847	35,068
Share					
Banks[a]	31.2	26.9	28.9	30.3	35.2
Securities companies	68.8	73.1	71.1	69.7	64.8

[a] Banks include other financial institutions.

Source: As for table 4.13

The objective of government regulation, which was finally established in the middle of the 1960s, has been to maintain the stability of the financial system and to protect investors by eliminating what the authorities call "excess" competition among securities companies. The authorities have not sought to promote competition, in order to achieve operational efficiency in the securities industry. As a result, significant entry and mobility barriers have been created that limit competition.

4.2 Regulations and Corporate Strategies

Under this regulatory framework, securities companies have pursued the following corporate strategies: propensity towards high value-added business; establishment and enhancement of interfirm networks; and full-service-oriented behavior of smaller firms.

4.2.1   Propensity towards high value-added business

In the period of high economic growth (1955–73), the activities of securities companies were heavily biased towards providing secondary market services, especially stock brokerage. Even the larger securities companies, which were legally qualified as lead underwriters or managing underwriters, tended to avoid the risk and cost associated with underwriting.

As mentioned in section 2, moreover, there was little primary market activity during this period. In fact, an important role in the primary market was played not by securities companies but by long-term credit banks (Sakakibara et al. 1982).

With the slow-down of the economy after the first oil shock, some notable changes took place in the securities market. On the supply side, the corporate sector began to rely more on capital market financing as well as on the overseas markets to reduce the funding cost. On the demand side, with declining real investment opportunities, business firms began to invest in securities and real estate in order to capture new profit opportunities. Integrated companies had a strong incentive to diversify their activities and to introduce new services. The ability to produce information and to bear risk became crucial in attracting corporate and institutional customers.

Despite the entry of medium-sized firms in the latter half of the 1980s, the share of the Big Four in underwriting has changed little. Especially in equity finance, business firms are generally reluctant to change their lead underwriters even in the 1990s (table 4.16). The Big Four have maintained stable relationships with their customers, and have played the role of full-service suppliers both in domestic and in overseas markets.

In contrast, retail services seemed far less attractive to the larger securities companies, when the growth prospect of corporate and institutional investment looked good in the 1980s. The larger firms thus made greater efforts to strengthen their relationship with their corporate and institutional customers in the latter half of the 1980s.

4.2.2   Establishment and enhancement of interfirm networks

Interfirm linkages in the securities industry have been observed since the 1950s between the major members of the Tokyo Stock Exchange and non-members. In the aftermath of the stock market crash of the mid-1960s, the Ministry of Finance severely restricted the establishment of new branch offices in order to reduce cut-throat sales competition. It has

Table 4.16 Changes in lead underwriters (April 1988–December 1990)

	Number of issues	Number of changes in lead underwriters
Stocks	457	21 (2)
Bonds with warrants	35	2 (1)
Convertible bonds	660	23 (1)
Straight bonds	84	71 (1)

[a]   Figures in parentheses refer only to the changes from one of the Big Four companies to other companies.

Source: The Securities and Exchange Council, *Report*, June 1991

become evident that what this policy accomplished was to give the major firms a greater incentive to strengthen their interfirm sales networks with smaller firms.

For the major firms, establishing networks with small firms was a means of increasing their marketing power without violating the restrictive government regulations. In this type of interfirm relationship, a large firm served as a kind of broker-dealer within its own group. At the same time, small firms had the benefit of maintaining stable relationships with large member firms of the Tokyo Stock Exchange, where the amount of bonds and stocks has been increasing since the 1970s. Thus, the government regulation of the regional expansion of securities companies, the limit on securities exchange membership, and the growth and concentration of securities transactions in the Tokyo market were all important factors in strengthening the ties between larger and smaller securities companies.

In the 1980s, interfirm relationships in the securities industry achieved a new dimension. Major firms were able to establish branch offices more easily because of the gradual relaxation of government regulations (figure 4.2). However, new incentives for interfirm affiliation emerged because of the new circumstances. First, the gap between the large and smaller firms widened in terms of information and technology. To survive competition, even smaller firms needed to diversify their retail services and secure sources of information on new markets and new products. The recent reductions in brokerage commission rates had also depressed the profit margins of smaller firms. Second, the large integrated firms tended to reduce their amount of the less profitable retail business, and allowed

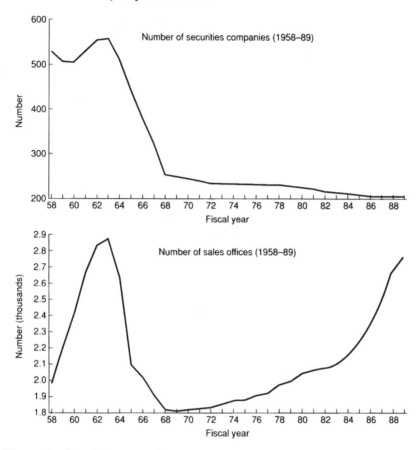

Figure 4.2   Securities companies and sales offices, 1958–89

Source: Ministry of Finance, *Shokenkyoku Nenpo* (Annual Report of the Securities Bureau), annual issues

their affiliates to take it over. For the major firms, this was necessary in order to intensify their more profitable activities and to compete more successfully with foreign firms and banks in the wholesale business. Thus, there was a new incentive to restructure interfirm networks in terms of a functional division of labor.

4.2.3   Full-line service-oriented behavior of smaller firms

The integrated securities companies, which are eligible to become lead underwriters, are in a better position to supply various types of combined services. As a result, the gap in performance and operational diversity between the integrated and other firms has also been widening. In response, small and medium-sized firms increased their equity capital through mergers or linkage with commercial banks throughout the 1980s. As a result, the number of firms qualified as integrated companies increased dramatically during the decade (table 4.9). As of March 1991, there were 42 integrated companies, of which 19 were affiliated with the Big Four and 11 are affiliated with major commercial banks.

Between 1981 and 1987, there were 13 mergers between securities companies,[6] as smaller firms sought to respond to new circumstances under the existing regulatory system. Almost all the mergers took place within the same affiliate groups; the number of integrated companies grew rapidly because of the affiliation of smaller firms with city banks that were preparing for future entry into the securities business. Although there remain legal barriers to prevent banks entering the corporate securities business, it is possible for banks to link up with existing securities companies within the limits of the Anti-monopoly Law and to raise their equity capital to the minimum level required for qualification as lead underwriters.[7] This strategy of the banks coincided with the incentive for medium-sized securities companies to extend the scope of their operations with greater capital and business opportunities.

4.3 Economies of Scale and Scope

4.3.1 Economies of scale

I have so far argued that, until the middle of the 1970s, the primary strategy of major firms was to strengthen their ability to provide brokerage services and marketing products. If this is true, the widening gap in scale between the larger and smaller firms was caused by the aggressive attempt of the larger firms to pursue economies of scale in the provision of brokerage services. This hypothesis was tested by Suto (1987), using the cross-section data of 137 securities companies for the period of 1972–7.[8] The following logarithmic Cobb–Douglas cost function was postulated for each firm.

$$\ln C = a_0 + a_1 \ln X + u \tag{4.1}$$

where C is the operating cost exclusive of tax, X is the amount of commissions and fees received, and u is a stochastic disturbance term. The hypothesis that there were economies of scale cannot be rejected if the coefficient of the log of X (a_1) is estimated to be significantly less than unity. On the basis of the results reported in table 4.17, we cannot reject the hypothesis.

In order to identify the source of scale economies, total operating

Table 4.17   The cost elasticity of exchange members with respect to commissions and fees received[a]

	Operating expenses	*Personnel costs*	*Fixed costs*	*Trading costs*
1972	0.970[b]	0.935[b]	1.158[b]	0.978
	(0.08)	(0.013)	(0.021)	(0.028)
1973	0.961[b]	0.925[b]	1.129[b]	0.985
	(0.008)	(0.014)	(0.021)	(0.027)
1974	0.969[b]	0.928[b]	1.131[b]	1.001
	(0.009)	(0.013)	(0.021)	(0.024)
1975	0.968[b]	0.925[b]	1.141[b]	0.977
	(0.009)	(0.014)	(0.018)	(0.023)
1976	0.956[b]	0.920[b]	0.115[b]	0.966
	(0.008)	(0.014)	(0.017)	(0.020)
1977	0.958[b]	0.921[b]	1.119[b]	0.967
	(0.008)	(0.013)	(0.019)	(0.020)

[a]   The number of observations is 137.
[b]   Indicates that the t-statistic is significant at the percent level; the figures in parentheses are standard errors.

expenses can be divided into labor costs, fixed equipment costs, and trading costs. Based on the estimates of the output elasticities of cost (reported in the second, third, and fourth columns of table 4.17), we find that the elasticity of labor costs was much less than unity, the elasticity of fixed costs was greater than unity, and the elasticity of trading costs was not significant. From these results, we may be able to conclude that labor costs, which accounted for more than 50 percent of operating expenses, were the major source of the economies of scale for member firms. This means that, although the larger firms spent more on computerization and office facilities, they could reduce labor costs by increasing the scale of operations.[9]

4.3.2   Economies of scope

Following the first oil shock, large securities companies gradually expanded the range of their operations in response to the diversification of investor demands. In the expanding and internationalizing marketplace of the 1980s, large integrated companies which were qualified to act as lead underwriters had a decisive advantage in providing different types of services to different types of customers in both the primary and the secondary markets. In order to see the complementarity of primary and

Table 4.18 Cost saving effect of multi-product firms

a_0	a_1	a_2	b_1	b_2	c	$\bar{R}^2$
0.748	0.670[a]	−0.015	0.0268[b]	0.512[a]	−0.373[b]	0.944
(0.434)	(0.025)	(0.015)	(0.119)	(0.196)	(0.153)	

[a] Indicates that the t-statistic is significant at the 11 percent level.
[b] Indicates that the t-statistic is significant at the 5 percent level.

Figures in parentheses are standard errors. The number of observations is 64.

secondary market services, Suto (1987) examined the hypothesis that economies of scope existed between primary market activities and secondary market activities. This was done by estimating the following translog cost function, using the panel data of the Big Four firms from 1968 to 1984:[10]

$$\ln C = a_0 + a_1 \ln Y_1 + a_2 \ln Y_2 + \tfrac{1}{2}b_1(\ln Y_1) + \tfrac{1}{2}b_2(\ln Y_2) + c\ln Y_1 Y_2 + u \tag{4.2}$$

where C is the operating cost exclusive of tax, Y_1 is the total amount of secondary market transactions, Y_2 is the total amount underwriting, a_0, a_1, a_2, b_1, b_2, and c are parameters, and u is a disturbance.

Here, Y_1 and Y_2 are proxy variables for the production of primary market activities and secondary market activities, respectively. If there were economies of scope between the two lines of activity, the following second derivative should be negative,

$$\frac{\partial^2 C}{\partial Y_1 \partial Y_2} = \frac{C}{Y_1 Y_2}\left\{\frac{\partial^2 \ln C}{\partial \ln Y_1 \partial \ln Y_2} + \frac{\partial \ln C}{\partial \ln Y_1} \cdot \frac{\partial \ln C}{\partial \ln Y_2}\right\} < 0 \tag{4.3}$$

This negativity condition follows from the complementarity of the two lines of activity.

According to the estimation results in table 4.18, that the first term in the bracket is significantly negative and the second term is insignificantly different from zero means that one cannot reject the hypothesis that economies of scope existed between primary market activities and secondary market activities for the Big Four companies. From the estimated coefficients, the total cost elasticity with respect to total production can be calculated as follows:

$$S = a_1 + a_2 + b_1 \ln Y_1 + b_2 \ln Y_2 + c(\ln Y_1 + \ln Y_2) \tag{4.4}$$

The calculated cost elasticity to total production S is yielding $S = 0.804$ with the standard derivation of 0.063. This means that, because the

Table 4.19   Composition of securities industry revenue (%)

	1965	1970	1975	1980	1985	1989
Japan						
Commission	41.9	53.5	42.5	51.8	50.7	58.1
Distribution fees	10.4	7.9	13.0	9.9	9.1	7.0
Underwriting	4.1	4.7	7.5	7.6	5.6	7.4
Trading gains	2.2	2.8	8.7	5.0	12.6	9.2
Other revenues	41.4	31.1	28.3	25.7	22.0	18.3
USA						
Commission	60.9	49.8	49.9	35.4	21.3	17.0
Underwriting	7.2	11.9	13.3	8.3	11.0	6.9
Trading, investments	8.8	15.1	15.6	23.1	28.5	21.6
Other revenues	23.1	23.2	21.2	33.2	39.2	54.5

Source: Ministry of Finance, *Annual Report of the Securities Bureau,* annual issues; Securities Industry Association, *SIA Trends,* Dec. 1988 and May 1990

estimated elasticity is significantly different from unity, there existed considerable economies of scale in the combined production.

We may thus conclude that the cost-saving effect of the joint production of different types of securities services has provided the Big Four with a significant competitive advantage. This may explain the incentive of medium-sized securities companies to qualify as integrated companies, as well as the desire of commercial banks to enter the securities business through affiliation with smaller securities companies.

This does not mean, however, that the pursuit of economies of scope by large securities companies has necessarily contributed to the improvement of their operational efficiency, although it has raised their profit rates in an oligopolistic market protected by extensive regulations.

4.4   Comparison with the US Securities Companies

A rough comparison of representative firms in the US and Japan during the past decade may be useful for understanding the characteristics of the behavior of Japanese securities companies.

A significant difference exists between Japanese and US firms in terms of operational diversification. The US firms increased the weight of more risky operations (such as underwriting and trading) in recent years, so that the share of commission in total revenue fell from 50 percent in 1975 to less than 20 percent in 1989. In contrast, Japanese firms depend more on traditional operations, so that the share of commission in total revenue was over 50 percent throughout the 1980s (table 4.19).

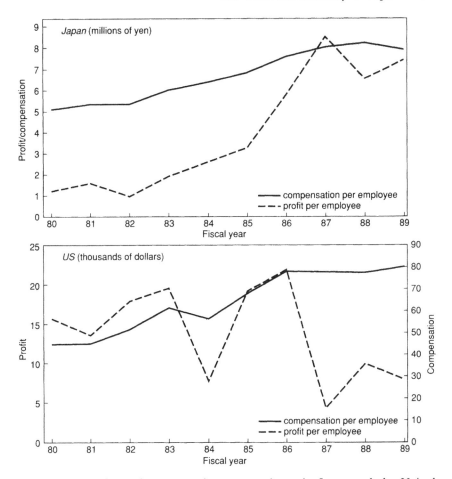

Figure 4.3 Profits and compensation per employee in Japan and the United States, 1980–9

Sources: Ministry of Finance, *Annual Report of the Securities Bureau*; Securities Industry Association, *SIA Trends*, May 1990, p. 5, chart 3

Labor costs (which includes salaries and wages, and the cost of fringe benefits) is a major expense item in both countries. Wage costs per employee increased through the 1980s similarly in both industries, while profit per employee showed divergent movements (figure 4.3). In the US, increasing wage costs depressed the profit margin, especially in the latter half of the 1980s. In Japan, net profit per employee increased faster than wage costs per employee.

The average cost (the value of total expenses divided by the value of

Table 4.20   Changes in the cost structure in Japan and the USA (%)

	A. All companies		B. Regional companies[a,b]	
	Average cost[c]	Share of labor cost[d]	Average cost	Share of labor cost
Japan				
1980	86.6	50.6	81.4	59.6
1981	79.1	47.8	87.1	56.6
1982	88.0	50.0	96.1	56.4
1983	75.8	46.5	81.6	56.4
1984	79.6	40.4	80.2	55.8
1985	68.9	42.4	76.2	53.2
1986	62.0	37.3	76.4	43.8
1987	57.0	35.7	63.5	48.4
1988	64.3	37.6	70.7	49.2
1989	62.4	37.4	72.3	39.4
USA				
1980			86.5	64.4
1981			91.6	61.4
1982			91.6	63.6
1983			89.8	64.9
1984			95.0	63.0
1985			88.7	64.8
1986			91.6	64.3
1987			102.9	62.4
1988			99.3	62.2

[a]   All securities companies other than integrated companies.
[b]   New York Stock Exchange regional members.
[c]   Average cost is total expenses divided by revenue.
[d]   Labor cost includes salaries and wages, and fringe benefit cost.

Sources: Ministry of Finance, *Annual Report of the Securities Bureau*, annual issues; Securities Dealers Association, *SIA Trends*, Dec. 1988

revenue) of Japanese firms rapidly declined after 1982, owing to the decreased share of wage costs (table 4.20). As for the US firms,[11] no trend in labor-cost saving is observable, whereas a sharp decline in the labor-cost share is observed for Japanese firms. It may be that Japanese securities companies within a more protective framework were more cost-sensitive than the US firms, with their less-regulated framework.

For Japanese firms, pursuit of internal efficiency through labor-cost saving innovations means a high profit opportunity in the current regulatory framework, which limits the range of operations and price competition. In contrast, US securities companies must diversify in order to explore new profit opportunities in a less-regulated framework. Continuous development of new fields requires additional human resources, resulting in higher labor costs.

5 CURRENT ISSUES

In the ongoing process of deregulation and internationalization in the 1990s, the securities industry is facing new challenges, including regulatory reforms, changes in the composition of investors, and internal organizational problems.

5.1 Regulatory Reforms

The Japanese regulatory system seems to have successfully achieved the initial goals of management stability and market order. Such a regulatory framework, however, gave larger securities companies an incentive to pursue aggressively scale and scope economies in the 1980s.

The securities scandals of 1991 (in which several major securities companies, including the Big Four, were found to have compensated their favored customers for trading losses) revealed an inconsistency between the old way of carrying on securities business and the new reality of the securities market. The securities firms are now being requested to change the old way of doing business. But we must remember that regulatory authorities have also lost the confidence of the general public, and that they are under pressure to change their method of supervision based on discretionary guidance. Interestingly, the securities scandals coincided with the publications of the Securities and Exchange Council and the Financial System Research Council, two advisory councils to the Minister of Finance. Although the two reports do not agree on some points, it is almost certain that commercial banks will be allowed to enter the securities business through their subsidiaries. Moreover, both reports recommended that regulations on the private placement of corporate bonds by banks be relaxed. There are also active discussions on the possibility of liberalizing fixed brokerage commissions as well as doing away with the requirements of securities companies.

5.2 Changes in the Composition of Investors

The Japanese securities market has been increasingly institutionalized. For example, the share of individual investors in stock ownership declined from 33.5 percent in 1975 to 22.6 percent in 1989, while the share of financial institutions and business corporations increased from 60.8 per-

Table 4.21   Stock ownership by type of investor (%)

	Financial institution	Business corporation	Individuals	Foreign investors	Others[a]
1975	34.5	26.3	33.5	2.6	3.1
1980	37.3	26.0	29.2	4.0	3.5
1985	40.9	24.1	25.2	5.7	4.1
1986	41.7	24.5	23.9	4.7	5.2
1987	42.2	24.9	23.6	3.6	5.7
1988	42.5	24.9	22.4	4.0	6.2
1989	42.3	24.8	22.6	3.9	6.4

[a]   Includes investment trust.

Source: Ministry of Finance, *Annual Report of Securities Bureau*, annual issues

Table 4.22   Stock trading by type of investor (%)

	Securities companies	Financial institution	Business corporation	Individuals	Foreign investors	Others[a]
1975	19.0	2.5	7.0	58.0	4.7	8.8
1980	26.0	5.3	7.3	43.6	7.4	10.4
1985	22.8	9.9	7.5	37.9	13.4	8.5
1986	24.4	15.1	10.1	30.6	11.4	8.6
1987	23.3	18.7	10.7	27.6	10.4	9.3
1988	26.3	19.9	12.3	25.1	7.5	9.9
1989	22.4	21.0	11.1	24.4	8.8	12.3

[a]   Includes investment trust.

Source: Tokyo Stock Exchange, *Statistical Monthly*, various issues

cent to 67.1 percent during the same period (table 4.21). In stock trading, too, the share of individuals declined from 58 percent to 24.4 percent during the same period, while the share of institutions and business investors increased from 9.5 percent to 32.1 percent (table 4.22).

The institutionalization of the securities market has helped the financial institutions and business corporations to accumulate financial information and funds management techniques. The narrowing gaps in information and technology between the securities companies and their customers will probably result in weakening conventional customer relationships.

In both the domestic and the international markets, competition in the wholesale business has already been increased by the entry of foreign securities companies as well as banks. As mentioned earlier, foreign firms have penetrated into the institutional investment business, while banks have assumed a significant position in the government bond trading business. If domestic banks are allowed to enter the securities business through the establishment of securities subsidiaries in a few years, large integrated securities companies may no longer be able to maintain their currently high profit margins.

Although retail services have helped to stabilize the performance of large securities companies in the past, it is known to have a higher average cost than the cost of wholesale services. It is also likely that the profit margins of retail brokerage services will be reduced by the forthcoming liberalization of the fixed commission rate system. For this reason, integrated companies may need to reduce the provision of retail services if they wish to remain competitive in the wholesale business.

In the environment of further deregulation, existing firms may have to develop new business frontiers in order to compete successfully with newcomers. As we have observed in the United States, this will require heavy investment in the development of new lines of activities, a tie-up with foreign pioneers in some key fields, or cooperation with different types of institutions. At any rate, success in this area will depend on how swiftly the government relaxes the protective regulations on the behavior of securities companies.

5.3   Problems of Internal Organization

Large integrated companies are facing several serious internal organizational problems. First, those firms which are involved in corporate issues as lead underwriters are being required to separate the finance and investment departments in order to avoid insider trading. Such organizational reform will raise the cost of providing wholesale services. Second, they are facing an organizational inconsistency between the wholesale and retail sectors because of the conflict of different interests. For example, the behavior of securities companies as underwriters of a particular corporate client could influence their behavior as agents of individual investors. The integrated companies must resolve their internal organizational problems in order to avoid the inherent inconsistency in serving different groups of customers. They must bear the heavy additional cost of internal reorganization.

6   CONCLUSION

Japan's securities industry is reaching its second turning-point since the Second World War, after the fundamental reforms of 1965. The 1965 reform strengthened government control, and oligopolistic competition ensued among the large integrated securities companies. Their provisions to pursue internal efficiency by expanding the scale and scope of activities was nothing but a rent-seeking activity.

The second turning-point was the end of the conventional strategies, of the old way of doing securities business, and of the protective regulatory framework. Japanese securities companies are now under pressure to restructure their internal organization and to change their conventional strategies aimed at growth and expansion. In the long run, ongoing reforms are expected to improve the operational efficiency of the Japanese securities market by liberalizing the securities companies from regulatory constraints and providing opportunities for potential participants. In the short run, however, a number of firms will undoubtedly suffer the pain of adjustment. The Japanese securities industry has no alternative but to accept more competition and operational diversification, because that is the only way to establish the trust and confidence of investors.

NOTES

1   According to the *International Comparative Statistics* of the Bank of Japan, the average share of equity finance in the total funds procurement of the corporate sector was 13 percent in Japan, 14 percent in the US, 11 percent in West Germany, and 15 percent in the UK, for the period 1958–62.
2   Essentially, they procured funds with working investment deposits as collateral, and conducted aggressive trading by using those funds. They gained commission by placing orders on their own accounts in the form of cross-transactions without notice to the exchanges in advance. This way of trading was called *baikai* trading and was prohibited after the stock market crisis of 1965. *Baikai* trading constituted almost one-half of total trading in the stock exchanges during the period of 1955–65, most of which was accounted for by the Big Four.
3   It was revealed in the summer of 1991 that the Big Four companies had compensated their favored customers for trading losses incurred in the stock market crash of 1990.
4   The incidence of affiliation was based on stock-holding as well as the number of managers (at least one) sent by the Big Four (see Suto 1987: table 8.2, p. 197).
5   By the end of 1985, European universal banks were able to obtain licences to establish full-service securities branches in a joint venture in which they contributed up to 50 percent of equity capital. In 1987, US and other commercial banks were also permitted to obtain licences on the same terms.
6   This figure does not include the number of mergers between *saitori* (or *nakadachi*) members of the Tokyo and Osaka Stock Exchanges.
7   The Anti-monopoly Law allows banks to hold up to 5 percent of the out-

standing stocks of securities companies. There is no legal limit on the exchange of employees between banks and securities companies or on the secondment of managers from banks to the securities companies; but the Ministry of Finance has expressed opposition to these tactics by city banks, concerned that the trend could spread to large non-bank financial institutions.

8   The data were obtained from the financial reports of the securities companies to the Japan Securities Dealers Association. The firms in the sample were all member-firms of the stock exchanges.

9   These results are consistent with those of another cross-sectional analysis by Murayama and Watanabe (1989), which estimated the economies of scale using the exponential cost functions for integrated companies only during the period 1977–87.

10 No data were available for other integrated companies. The data for the Big Four companies come from the Annual Financial Reports of the respective companies.

11 Comparable data are available only for regional firms of the New York Stock Exchange. For this reason, the comparison is made with comparable small firms in Japan.

REFERENCES

Financial System Research Council 1991: *Report.*
Government and Corporate Bonds Underwriting Association, *Koshasai Nenkan* (Annual Report), annual issues.
Ministry of Finance, *Shokenkyoku Nenpo* (Annual Report of the Securities Bureau), annual issues.
Murayama, Jun and Watanabe, Ken 1989: Wagakuni Shoken-gyo ni okeru Kibo no Keizaisei ni tuite. *Financial Review*, June, 1989, Institute of Fiscal and Monetary Policy, Ministry of Finance, 12–30.
Sakakibara, E., Feldman, R. and Harada, Y. 1982: Japanese financial system in cooperative perspective, a study prepared for the use of the Joint Economic Committee. Washington, D.C.: US Government Printing Office.
Securities and Exchange Council 1991: *Report.*
Suto, Megumi 1987: *Nihon no Shoken-gyo: Soshiki to Kyoso* (The Securities Industry in Japan: Organization and Competition). Tokyo: Toyo Keizai Shinposha.
Tokyo Stock Exchange, *Tokei Geppo* (Statistical Monthly), various issues.

5

The Regulatory Environment for Japanese Capital Markets

Hideki Kanda

1 INTRODUCTION

This chapter describes and analyzes the regulatory environment for Japanese capital markets.[1] Section 2 describes the major legal environment within which business firms raise their capital in Japanese capital markets. Section 2 focuses on the most fundamental statute, the Securities and Exchange Law, and the administrative and other customary rules under the SEL. It also briefly discusses other relevant statutes, and predicts the future of the SEL. The description in this section is illustrative rather than exhaustive. Section 3 identifies some characteristics of Japanese securities regulation in this area that might be viewed as unique to Japan, and offers an explanation as to why those characteristics exist in Japan and not in other countries. Particular attention is given to the political environment for administrative rulemaking and legislative processes. The section also examines whether these characteristics serve to enhance investors' welfare and efficient capital formation in Japan. Finally, section 4 presents concluding remarks.

2 THE LEGAL FRAMEWORK

2.1 Organizational Form

Two of the most important aspects of business planning are decisions about organizational form and about source of capital. Both decisions are influenced by the legal rules governing organizational structure, as well as the prevailing tax rules. In Japan, aside from sole proprietorship, business can be carried on in one of six organizational, or legal, forms: *kumiai* (partnership), *tokumeikumiai* (limited partnership), *gomeigaisha* (incorporated partnership), *goshigaisha* (incorporated limited partnership), *yugengaisha* (limited company) and *kabushikigaisha* (stock company). While this is not the place to describe each of these organizational forms in detail, some brief notes may be helpful.

First, of the six forms, only the first two – namely, *kumiai* and *tokumeikumiai* – enjoy single-tier income taxation, by which income tax is not imposed at the "entity" level, and individual investors report in their personal tax return their share of the profits earned by the entity. But these two forms do not offer limited liability to their investors, and are therefore not popular with large businesses in Japan. The other four are all incorporated forms (some of which provide investors with limited liability while others do not), and are subject to "double taxation." While *gomeigaisha*, *goshigaisha* and *yugengaisha* are given flexibility under the statutes as to their internal management structure and related matters, they are not suitable for raising large amounts of funds in the capital market for a variety of reasons. Consequently, in Japanese practice all major businesses take the *kabushikigaisha* form, which is similar to a business corporation in the US and a public limited company in the UK.

Various organizational rules – commonly known as corporate law or company law – are found in the Japanese Commercial Code (Law no. 48 of 1899, as amended). Thus, when a business corporation attempts to raise capital by issuing shares or bonds, it must comply with various requirements under the Commercial Code. For instance, the issuance of debt securities must be decided by the board of directors of the company. One rule that is unique to Japan and does not exist in Western countries is Article 297 of the Commercial Code, which limits the aggregate amount of outstanding bonds and debentures of *kabushikigaisha*, or a stock company, to the amount of the company's net assets, with the exception of convertible bonds, bonds with stock purchase warrant, and bonds issued outside Japan, that may be issued up to twice the amount of the issuer's net assets.

2.2 The Securities and Exchange Law

2.2.1 The structure

The Securities and Exchange Law (SEL) in Japan (Law no. 25 of 1948 as amended) was modeled on the US federal securities laws, specifically the Securities Act of 1933 and the Securities Exchange Act of 1934.[2] The SEL first provides two basic sets of rules for investor protection: mandatory disclosure and anti-fraud rules. Thus, when a firm attempts to issue "securities", as discussed later, it must file a registration statement with the Ministry of Finance (MOF),[3] which must include certain information specified under the rules promulgated by MOF. All companies whose securities are either listed at a stock exchange or traded "over the counter," and which filed a registration statement with MOF when they issued securities are subject to reporting requirements under the SEL:

reporting must be semi-annual, and their annual report must be audited by a certified public accountant.

Anti-fraud rules include prohibition of somewhat broadly defined fraudulent activities – similar to those prohibited under Section 10(b) of the US Securities Exchange Act of 1934 – and more specific activities of securities companies, such as the fraudulent solicitation of customers. Insider trading is also regulated, as is noted later. One of the important facts in this area in Japan is that there has been virtually no private litigation associated with violations of the disclosure or anti-fraud rules under the SEL.

There are at least four important differences between the legal framework of Japan and that of the United States. First, in Japan a firm must obtain a licence from the MOF to serve as a broker-dealer. The entry barrier to this intermediary service is higher in Japan than in the US, where registration rather than licensing is required to serve as a broker-dealer.[4]

Second, while the notion of "security" is broadly defined in the US, it is quite limited in Japan. The SEL, in its section 1 of article 2, defines a security as one of the following items:

(a)   government debt security;
(b)   municipal debt security;
(c)   debt security issued under a special statute by a corporation;
(d)   secured or unsecured debt security issued by a business corporation;
(e)   stock issued by a corporation organized under a special statute;
(f)   stock and warrant issued by a business corporation;
(g)   beneficial certificate under a securities investment trust or loan trust;
(h)   security or certificate issued by a foreign government or foreign corporation that has the characteristics of the security or certificate listed in the above (a)–(g); and
(i)   any other security or certificate designated by cabinet order.

Although MOF is empowered to designate any new instrument as a security under item (i), it has never exercised this power. Thus, in Japanese practice, the definition of a security is limited.

Third, the distinction between a public offering (which is subject to mandatory disclosure requirements) and a private placement (which is not) differs between the two countries. Japan adopts more formalistic criteria. The SEL defines a public offering with two basic notions: (a) an offer is made to "many and unspecific persons," and (b) an offer has uniform terms. An interpretive release promulgated by MOF declares that an offer is made to "many and unspecific persons" if the number of offerees is about 50 or more. In practice, MOF's release is "interpreted" to provide a definitive criterion of 50 or more persons.

Finally, the fourth difference between US and Japanese securities laws is that by employing the notion of a security, the SEL links its investor protection rules to Article 65 of the SEL (a rule similar to the US Glass–Steagall Act), which essentially prohibits banks (and insurance companies) from engaging in the securities business except for government and public securities.[5] This regulatory structure is known as the "one-set structure" in Japan and is the key to understanding past and future developments in the regulation of new financial instruments in Japan. If a financial product is a security, as defined by the SEL, investors enjoy the protection of the SEL, while banks are prohibited from handling such a product. Note also that article 43 of the SEL prohibits securities companies from handling a product other than a security unless they obtain special permission from MOF. If a product is not a security banks may handle it, while securities companies may not, and investors receive no protection from the SEL.

In response to the long battle between the banking and securities industries, MOF placed priority on the issue of which industry handles each new product with regard to investor protection. For example, MOF adopted a policy of allowing both banks and securities companies to handle commercial paper. The securities companies received special permission to handle commercial paper under article 43 of the SEL.[6] Meanwhile, the banking industry successfully persuaded MOF to exclude securities companies from intermediary services for residential mortgage trusts and securitized bank loans. Thus, MOF treated these instruments as non-securities, which banks may handle under the SEL.

The above approach resulted in the absence of legal protection for investors. To remedy this situation, MOF took two actions. First, it had special legislation enacted to protect investors. For example, *teitoshoken*, or a mortgage deed, is in this category. Second, by rule or administrative guidance, MOF ruled that banks (and securities companies, with respect to commercial paper) could not sell these products with a unit value of less than 100 million yen. The purpose of this limitation was to prevent the sale of these products to the general public, which needs the protection of the securities law. Commercial paper and residential mortgage trusts are in this category. Certificates of deposit are also in this category, but the "minimum unit rule" has been liberalized for this instrument.[7]

The SEL's narrow definition of "security" has been strongly criticized by commentators. As noted above, MOF took two actions on non-securities to protect investors. New legislation, however, has enormous costs; for example, hundreds of new statutes must be passed and no new financial product may be sold until corresponding legislation is enacted. The "minimum unit rule" disqualifies new financial products from potential sale to small investors, thereby hindering the development of secondary markets and raising initial financing costs. In short, there are many "non-security securities" in Japan, waiting for fundamental reform of the SEL. In this context, the Fundamental Research Committee of the Securities and Exchange Council at the Securities Bureau of MOF has been considering a complete overhaul of the SEL since 1988.[8]

2.2.2 Recent developments

The SEL has been amended frequently in the past few years. In 1988 three important amendments were made. First, the disclosure requirements were liberalized. Following the reform in the US in the early 1980s, the disclosure requirements in primary and secondary markets were integrated, and reporting companies are now entitled to issue additional new securities by filing a simplified registration statement with MOF. Also, "shelf registration" became available for certain eligible companies. Second, the regulation of insider trading was strengthened. This amendment included the introduction of new criminal sanctions and the revival of the reporting requirement for the sale or purchase of securities by insiders, which should help to enforce liability for short-swing profits.

Third, a legal framework for stock-index and other securities-related futures and options was established, and as a result such futures and options are currently traded on the Tokyo Stock Exchange and other stock exchanges.[9] In this connection, new legislation – the Financial Futures Transaction Law – was passed to introduce currency and interest-rate futures and options, and the Tokyo Financial Futures Exchange was organized for the trading of such derivatives.[10] This "dual" legal system of financial derivatives is a reflection of the battle between the banking and securities industries. Given that the commodity futures are regulated by another law, the Commodity Exchange Law, and traded on commodity exchanges, this means that there are three different statutes governing three different sets of exchanges for securities-related futures and options, currency and interest-rate futures and options, and commodity futures, respectively.

In 1990, two amendments were made with respect to corporate take-overs. First, "the 5 percent rule," which is similar to the US Securities Exchange Act of 1934 section 13(d), was introduced. Anyone who acquires 5 percent or more of the total issued shares of a public company is obliged to disclose certain information. Second, the rules on stock tender offers were liberalized, and became somewhat similar to those under the current US 1934 Act.

Also, MOF revised the rules on disclosure under the SEL, and increased disclosure is now required in three important areas. First, a public company is required to make periodic disclosure on a "segment" basis. Second, a public company is required to add to its financial statements information on the market value of the "marketable" securities it holds and that of the unsettled positions it holds with regard to futures and options transactions. Third, more detailed disclosure on certain transactions within and with respect to corporate groups, or *keiretsu*, is required now than it was before.

In 1991, as a result of the scandal in the securities industry, two amendments were made to the SEL. First, compensation by a brokerage firm to its customer for trading losses resulting from stock price declines is now explicitly prohibited, with criminal sanctions applicable to both brokerage firms and customers. Second, setting up a discretionary investment account at a brokerage firm, which was found to be the major source of such compensation schemes in the past, has also been made a criminal offence.

2.2.3 The future of the SEL

In 1992, an important bill was passed by the Diet to bring the following amendments to the SEL. First, a market surveillance committee will be established at the MOF. It is organized to be independent from other bureaux of the MOF and empowered to monitor and enforce mandatory disclosure and anti-fraud rules (including the prohibition of insider trading). It is also empowered to investigate, with search and seizure powers, any person when necessary to detect any violation of those rules.

Second, the scope of the anti-fraud rules (including the prohibition of insider trading) has been extended to cover trade in over-the-counter markets.

Another important bill amending the SEL and certain banking statutes was passed by the Diet in June 1992. The amendments are expected to go into effect in early 1993. First, the definition of security under the SEL has been amended to include the following:

(h) A promissory note issued by a corporation for funding for its business, as designated by MOF regulation;

(i) same as item (h) of the current SEL;

(j) A security or certificate issued by a foreign corporation, which represents a beneficiary trust interest or similar interest in loans by a bank or any other lending institution, as designated by MOF regulation.

Commercial paper is expected to be designated as a security under item (h) above, and securitized credit card receivables organized in the US (known as CARDS) are expected to be designated as securities under item (j) above. Of course, either of these could have been designated as securities prior to the amendment, but, as mentioned previously, no such designations were made under item (i) of the current SEL.

In addition, the catch-all provision of the current SEL, item (i), has been replaced by the following:

(k)   Any other security or certificate designated by cabinet order as necessary to ensure the public interest or investor protection, with consideration given to its transferability and other conditions.

While more narrowly drafted than the catch-all provision, this new provision is expected to be relied upon by the MOF to designate new securities. The new provision permits the MOF to have any other "paperized" (i.e., certificated) instrument designated as a security under item 11, unless the transferability of the instrument is restricted or, for instance, the instrument is governed by a different statute concerning investor protection (typically administered by a different ministry).

Section 2 of Article 2 of the SEL has been amended to expand the definition of a "deemed" security to include, not only a right which, in principle, is expected to be paperized (though it may not actually be certificated), but also a right which is not, in principle, expected to be paperized, if such right falls within one of the following three categories:

(a)   A beneficial trust interest in loans by a bank, trust company or any other financial institution or any other lending institution which provides long-term credit for housing (including land or an interest in land for housing), as designated by cabinet order;

(b)   A right in a foreign corporation that has the characteristics of a right in (a); and

(c)   Any other monetary claim designated by cabinet order as similar in transferability to a security listed in section 1, as necessary to ensure the public interest or investor protection, with consideration given to the similarity in economic characteristics to any security listed in Section 1 and other conditions.

A beneficial interest in a residential mortgage trust is expected to be designated as a security by cabinet order. In addition, the MOF will be empowered to have any right or interest designated as a security by cabinet order if the right is a monetary claim, the designation of the right as a security is necessary to ensure the public interest or investor protection and consideration is given to the transferability of the right and other conditions.

The amendments to the definition of security were shaped by compromises reached among the ministries, particularly between the MOF and the Ministry of International Trade and Industry ("MITI").

Second, the rules on private placement have also been amended. An exemption from disclosure requirements will be available when securities are issued to certain qualified institutional investors, even if the number of offerees reaches 50 or more. In addition, handling (*toriatsukai*) a private placement will be treated as a type of securities business, and banks and insurance companies will be given authorization to engage in this business.

Finally, the wall between the banking and securities industries will be lowered. For instance, a bank will be permitted to establish a subsidiary to engage in certain types of securities businesses. At the same time, fire walls will be required between a parent bank and its securities subsidiary.

3 CHARACTERISTICS OF JAPANESE SECURITIES REGULATION

3.1 The Interaction between Banking and Securities Industries

As described earlier, the political competition, or the battle, between the banking and securities industries has shaped much of the current regulatory structure in the financial services area in Japan. The rules on commercial paper and other "non-security securities" are the product of this political reality. The divided regulation between securities-related futures and options, on the one hand, and currency and interest-rate futures and options, on the other, is another product. As noted earlier, article 297 of the Commercial Code limits the amount of debt securities. Despite the strong arguments by academics and others for the repeal of this provision, the banking industry maintains that repeal should be accompanied by the repeal of another regulation: article 65 of the SEL. Thus, the domestic bond market is unlikely to be deregulated drastically unless banks are permitted to engage in securities business (at least to some extent).

3.2 The Interaction between Ministries

Political competition exists not only between the banking and securities industries but also between ministries.[11] The Ministry of International Trade and Industry (MITI) strongly opposed the proposed expansion of the definition of "security" under the SEL. MITI's concern is that, by extending the reach of the SEL, MOF would expand its jurisdiction over non-financial industries. The legislation which introduced commodity futures funds is a good example of how ministries compete for particular legislation in the financial services area.

In May 1991, new legislation was introduced in Japan to regulate commodity futures funds, known as commodity pools in the US. This law, the Law for Commodity Investment Business, has an interesting story. In 1990, when trading companies and leasing companies found that off-shore commodity futures funds were attractive for marketing to Japanese investors, these companies successfully persuaded MITI to launch a project for special legislation. MITI first contemplated legislation with the same statutory structure as the US Commodity Exchange Act, which regulates the commodity pool operator, the sponsor in this field. However, the draft prepared by MITI encountered strong opposition from MOF.

MOF rejected the statutory approach directly regulating pool operators on the grounds that the business of such operators consists of financial services. Such a business is similar to the functions of the sponsoring companies of securities investment trusts regulated by the Securities Investment Trust Law under MOF's jurisdiction, except that, in this instance, the fund invests in commodity futures instead of securities. MOF also noted that it would be expanding the definition of a "security" under the SEL. MOF further stated that units of investment funds, including commodity futures funds, should be subject to the same regulation in order to enhance investor protection. MOF argued that economic substance should control and that such funds should be regulated by the SEL, under MOF's jurisdiction. Moreover, MOF contended that when financial institutions participate in commodity futures fund business, either as a sponsor or a seller of the units, they should be subject to their home regulator, that is, to MOF.

This battle between MITI and MOF resulted in MITI's abandonment of legislation that would directly regulate the sponsor of commodity futures funds. In its place, a compromise was developed. The Law for Commodity Investment Business finally enacted was jointly sponsored by the Ministry of Agriculture, Forestry and Fisheries, MITI and MOF,[12] and the regulatory structure under this law is quite complex.[13]

3.3 Characteristics of the Japanese Legislative and Administrative Rulemaking Processes[14]

The regulatory environment for Japanese capital markets described above suggests several characteristics of the legislative and administrative rulemaking processes in Japan. While it might be universally accepted that various special-interest groups compete in most legislative and administrative rulemaking processes, the entire Japanese political environment in which private interest groups and regulators interact could be viewed as unique to Japan. As shown earlier, the treatment of "non-security securities" under the SEL might look familiar at first glance; the banking and securities industries competed, and MOF served as a mediator. The battle resulted in the classification of new financial instruments as "non-security securities" under the SEL, which enabled the banking industry to enter the market.

To ensure investor protection, MOF actively intervened either by making special legislation or by promulgating new rules or administrative guidance. MOF's action can be viewed as a function of the battle between special-interest groups. The promulgation of administrative guidelines that create the "minimum unit rule" for certain public offerings of "non-security securities" represents a victory for the securities industry, to the extent that the rule is effectively applied and enforced. Public investors suffer to the extent that "non-security securities" with small investment units are not available in the marketplace.

An important customary "rule" exists in Japan; that is, the non-existence of an "explicit" legal rule endorsing a certain activity under explicit regulatory conditions is understood to mean that such activity is prohibited in Japan. When no explicit rule exists as to whether a particular new instrument is treated as a security under the SEL or if the rules are unclear, institutions do not invent and market such instruments. Put differently, until a consensus is reached on a financial device, followed by a lengthy process for establishing an explicit rule or administrative guideline, virtually no one creates or markets such a financial instrument.

In the case of commodity futures funds, it is easy to see why MITI sought to introduce new legislation to "deregulate" the area. One common explanation is that the introduction of new means of investment in commodity futures enhances the welfare of public investors. Another explanation is found by examining the interests of trading companies and leasing companies. These companies did not want to violate the "no-rule-means-prohibition" rule. Instead, these companies persuaded their regulator, MITI, to "regulate" them. The real-estate industry did not join this chorus, simply because its regulator is the Ministry of Construction (MOC), and not MITI. MITI's plan encountered strong opposition from MOF, which apparently received support from the securities and banking industries. The result was a compromise.

The originally proposed statutory structure under which pool operators would be subject to regulation solely within the jurisdiction of MITI (and not MOF), was abandoned. But as a practical matter under the new legislation, trading companies and leasing companies could operate commodity futures funds by obtaining a seller-licence from the MITI. Financial institutions could operate such funds without a licence from MITI, but they would be subject to additional requirements promulgated by MOF. Beyond the area regulated by the new legislation, which is narrower in its scope of application than the originally proposed draft, the "no-rule-means-prohibition" rule controls. Until MOC introduces new legislation, the real-estate industry is left unregulated and subject to the "no-rule-means-prohibition" rule during the transitional period. MOC is expected to draft new legislation for property investment funds in the near future. A battle with MOF appears likely.

It is important to note that there is no litigation in this area in Japan. All relevant parties participate in the administrative rulemaking and legislative processes. Once an accord is reached, it is unlikely that it will be challenged before a court. When a dispute is resolved by introducing new legislation, it may be difficult and costly to attack such legislation judicially. Likewise, judicial challenges against administrative rulemaking are also rare. The lack of judicial challenges in this area may seem puzzling initially, but, in fact, this circumstance can be explicable.

The "special interest theory" of legislation is well-established in the United States. For instance, it has been argued that the US Glass–Steagall Act, which separates the banking and securities businesses, stemmed from the special interest of the investment banking industry, rather than from the public interest. But the exact effect which competing private interests have on the final product of legislation has not been studied in depth. It might be difficult to prove that, when legislation is the product of a battle among multiple competing private interests, a more beneficial result is achieved for the general public. The Japanese legislation on commodity futures funds, however, protects investors to the extent that it is coupled with the Japanese "no-rule-means-prohibition" rule under the SEL, though this is not the best solution.

In the United States over the past few years, federal agencies have shifted the bulk of their activities from case-by-case adjudication to general rulemaking procedures in order to develop administrative policy. While it is well known in the United States that administrative rulemaking is more vulnerable to judicial challenge than administrative adjudication, the reverse is true in Japan. Indeed, in Japan administrative adjudication has sometimes been litigated, but no one has challenged a rule that was created through a lengthy decisionmaking process in which all relevant parties participated.

The complicated and time-consuming decisionmaking process that accompanies legislation and administrative rulemaking in Japan may be viewed as a system monitoring the conduct or activities covered by legislation or administrative rulemaking. Parties with multiple interests who participate in the process serve as *ex ante* monitors, while parties who litigate legislation or administrative rules serve as *ex post* monitors. Since *ex ante* monitoring exists, it is not surprising that there are virtually no judicial challenges to legislation or administrative rules in Japan.

It is difficult to determine, as a general matter, whether *ex post* monitoring is more costly than *ex ante* monitoring. However, *ex ante* monitoring has certain advantages. First, while competing ministries and private industries seek to further their own interests, a compromise will often be reached, when a norm that enhances public interest is developed. Second, *ex ante* negotiation may mean that the cost of uncertainty is not borne by investors. Thus, in Japan investors can choose from stable alternatives. In contrast, a system that does not have *ex ante* monitoring offers more choice and more innovations, but at a greater cost.

One might ask whether there is anyone who directly represents public investors in the Japanese legislative and administrative rulemaking processes. The Japanese custom is that the decisionmaking process at the ministry level is accompanied by a lengthy discussion at an advisory council, known as *shingikai*. The advisory council is organized by the ministry, and some of its participants are selected as representatives of public investors. Although the primary purpose of the council is to accommodate the competing interests among the relevant private industries, the interests of public investors are considered, at least to some extent, through certain advisory council representatives.

Viewed in this way, the "no-rule-means-prohibition" rule makes sense in Japan. Conduct that is subject to this rule has not received the scrutiny of the *ex ante* monitoring process. Thus, if one pursues such conduct, it is likely to be monitored *ex post*, perhaps by litigation or by some other social sanction. *Ex post* monitoring may be undesirable in Japan.

The dominance of administrative rulemaking over administrative adjudication also makes sense in Japan. Less *ex ante* monitoring exists in an administrative adjudication, because the number of participants in the adjudication process is limited. Further, *ex post* litigation might be costly. Thus, the Japanese may favor general administrative rulemaking, when it is coupled with *ex ante* monitoring.

3.4   Formalism in Administrative Rulemaking

MOF's rules and guidelines under the SEL are formal. The legal norm for a particular activity or conduct consists of complex formal rules. As described earlier, in the context of differentiating between a public offering and a private placement, the term "many and unspecific persons" is interpreted to be 50 or more persons, irrespective of whether the offerees can "fend for themselves." The "minimum unit rule" for certain "non-security securities" is simply 100 million yen. Under the SEL, the determination as to whether units of an investment fund are treated as securities depends on the legal form of the fund. If the fund is organized as a corporation, the units are securities; however, if the fund is organized as a limited partnership, the units are not securities. Emphasizing legal form over economic substance often creates loopholes. The Japanese formalism therefore appears bewildering.

Since an administrative branch of government is often better equipped to gather and evaluate information in the development and implementation of a policy as compared to a judicial branch of government, one might expect that an administrative branch prefers to enforce substantive rather than formalistic rules. In Japan, the reverse is true.

In the United States, extensive studies have been conducted that analyze how an administrative branch or agency of the government chooses among multiple means in developing and implementing a policy goal. However, the studies have not focused on whether these groups prefer to enforce formalistic rules. Japan's tendency to favor formalistic rules may be better understood by focusing on the rulemaking process in Japan.

First, at the political level, a legal norm for a particular activity or conduct consists of complex formalistic rules. These rules represent the compromise that was reached during the rulemaking process. Each formalistic rule is easy to observe. The participants in the rulemaking process may clearly indicate each point in order to specify the concessions made to each participant.

Second, a legal norm with multiple formalistic rules may withstand a subsequent judicial challenge better than a substantive norm would withstand it. Judges are better equipped to make a substantive inquiry as it pertains to a particular case. Further, judges may not want to involve themselves in the hard task of dealing with a complex mixture of formalistic rules. This in turn could discourage litigation.

Third, at the theoretical level, formalistic rules might better fit *ex ante* monitoring than would substantive rules. If the legal norms or constituent rules are of a substantive nature, future activities or conduct might be difficult to identify *ex ante*. Consequently, *ex ante* monitoring may become extremely difficult and ineffective. Formalistic rules help *ex ante* monitors to identify future activities and conduct during the rulemaking process, which facilitates the development of a final legal norm.

4   CONCLUSION

The regulatory environment for Japanese capital markets is complex. For the most part, this is a reflection of the underlying political landscape in Japan, that is, the competition among ministries and private industries. It is difficult to evaluate whether public investors are victimized in this political environment. It is, however, sensible to have the ministries and private industries compete for their best interests, rather than allow public interest to control the political environment. Moreover, since this process can be viewed as an *ex ante* monitoring mechanism through legislation and administrative rulemaking, the argument can be made that this regulatory environment tends to enhance, rather than diminish, investors' welfare. The internationalization of capital markets will probably affect this distinguishing characteristic of Japanese regulation. Yet, from a theoretical perspective, future changes in the Japanese regulatory environment might not come as a surprise, if one subscribes to the notion of *ex ante* monitoring mechanisms embedded in the legislative and administrative rulemaking processes. To the extent that the *ex ante* monitoring mechanisms may be phased out, new *ex post* monitoring mechanisms may well emerge in Japan.

NOTES

1 Part of this chapter draws heavily on Kanda (1991).
2 For a general description of the SEL, see Loss, Yazawa and Banoff (1983); Yamashita (1989); Kanda (1992); Kanda and Kawachi (1992). For a comparison of the New York Stock Exchange and the Tokyo Stock Exchange, see Macey and Kanda (1989).
3 Technically, various reports must be submitted to the *Minister* of Finance. Also, a license for the securities business, for instance, must be obtained from the *Minister* of Finance.
4 The SEL originally required registration for a broker–dealer. But after the crisis in the securities industry in the early 1960s, the law was amended in 1965 and a licence is now required. A licence is given separately for each type of the four securities businesses specified under the SEL: dealing, brokerage, underwriting, and distribution (see the SEL s. 28).
5 Although the SEL s. 65 is modeled on the US Glass–Steagall Act, there are important differences between the two. For instance, under the SEL, banks (and insurance companies) are permitted to hold shares of other companies for investment purposes. The Anti-monopoly Law, however, prohibits banks from holding more than 5 percent of the outstanding shares of any company, with very narrow exceptions. For insurance companies, this limitation is 10 percent. See the Anti-monopoly Law s. 11.
6 For a detailed analysis of the introduction of the commercial paper market in both Japan and the US, see Litt, Macey, Miller, and Rubin (1990).
7 For another explanation of the minimum unit rule, see Takagi (1988: 85).
8 See Securities and Exchange Council (1991).
9 See Adachi and Kurasawa (1992).
10 See Tateno (1992).
11 For an interesting study of the Japanese political environment for certain

legislation and administrative rulemaking in the financial services area, see Horne (1985).

12 In Japan, most bills are submitted to the Diet by the Cabinet. For each bill, there is a "sponsoring" ministry or bureau of a ministry, which drafts the statute and then, once the legislation is passed, administers it. Sometimes more than one ministry jointly sponsors a bill. The SEL is "governed" by the Securities Bureau of MOF. The Financial Futures Trading Law is sponsored by the Banking Bureau of MOF. The Commodity Exchange Law is jointly governed by the Ministry of Agriculture, Forestry and Fisheries (MAFF) and MITI. MAFF has jurisdiction over agricultural commodities and MITI over non-agricultural ones. As for the Law for Commodity Investment Business, it is accurate to state that MITI and MAFF attempted to introduce new legislation. In practice, however, MAFF is unimportant in the commodity futures fund area and it did not play an important role in the enactment of the new legislation.

13 For further details of the legislation, see Kanda (1991).

14 The reference for the relevant US literature for subsections 3.3 and 3.4 is omitted. They are cited in Kanda (1991).

REFERENCES

Adachi, Tomohiko and Kurasawa, Motonari 1992: Stock futures and options markets in Japan. Chapter 12 in this volume.

Horne, James 1985: *Japan's Financial Markets: conflict and consensus in policymaking*. Sydney: George Allen & Unwin.

Japan Securities Research Institute 1992: *Capital Markets and Financial Services in Japan: regulation and practice*. Tokyo: Japanese Securities Research Institute.

Kanda, Hideki 1991: Politics, formalism, and the elusive goal of investor protection: regulation of structured investment funds in Japan. *University of Pennsylvania Journal of International Business Law*, 12, 569–88.

Kanda, Hideki 1992: Testimony before the Subcommittee on International Development, Finance, Trade and Monetary Policy of the Committee on Banking, Finance and Urban Affairs, United States House of Representatives.

Kanda, Hideki and Kawachi, Michael T. 1992: Securitisation in Japan. *Securitisation*. London: Euromoney Publishers, 63–9.

Litt, David, Macey, Jonathan, Miller, Geoffrey and Rubin, Edward 1990: Politics, bureaucracies, and financial markets: bank entry into commercial paper underwriting in the United States and Japan. *University of Pennsylvania Law Review*, 139, 369–453.

Loss, Louis, Yazawa, Makoto and Banoff, Barbara (eds) 1983: *Japanese Securities Regulation*. Tokyo: University of Tokyo Press.

Macey, Jonathan R. and Kanda, Hideki 1990: The stock exchange as a firm: the emergence of close substitutes for the New York and Tokyo Stock Exchanges. *Cornell Law Review*, 75, 1007–52.

Securities and Exchange Council 1991: How the basic system regarding capital market ought to be reformed. Document translated by Capital Markets Research Institute, Tokyo.

Takagi, Shinji 1988: Recent developments in Japan's bond and money markets. *Journal of the Japanese and International Economies*, 2, 63–91.

Tateno, Fumihiko 1992: The foreign exchange market in Japan. Chapter 14 in this volume.

Yamashita, Takeji 1989: *Japan's Securities Markets: a practitioner's guide.* Singapore: Butterworths.

Part III

The Bond Market

6

The Japanese Bond Market

Shigeru Yamamoto

1 INTRODUCTION

Driven by the remarkable development of the Japanese economy, the Japanese bond market has rapidly expanded to become one of the world's three largest international markets, along with New York and London.

The Japanese bond market currently has the following features. First, among all traded bonds such as public bonds, industrial bonds, foreign bonds, and so on, Japanese government bonds (categorized as public bonds) occupy the central position. Second, Japanese banks and securities companies jointly play a pivotal role as market intermediaries.

There is no doubt that until now the Japanese bond market has operated well as a sound place in which to raise funds. However, under the current process of liberalization and internationalization, it is becoming necessary to make a fundamental reassessment of the mechanism of the Japanese bond market, so as to make the market more responsive to the ever-changing financial environment. In this context, the framework of the Japanese bond market is currently being reviewed by the government with an eye to future reform.

This chapter is organized as follows: section 2 explains the types of bonds that are currently available in the Japanese bond market; sections 3 and 4 discuss the primary bond market and the secondary bond market, respectively. Finally, section 5 explains the issues involved in the current financial reform in Japan. Here, the major issue concerns the prospective revision of the current separation between the banking and the securities business.

2 TYPES OF BONDS IN THE JAPANESE BOND MARKET

In Japan, bonds are classified into Japanese government bonds, local government bonds, public corporation bonds, foreign bonds, corporation

Shinji Takagi provided comments on an earlier draft.

Table 6.1 Types of government bonds in Japan

Use of bond issue proceeds	*Types*	*Law authorizing the issue*
Revenue bonds (*sainyu-sai*)	Construction bonds Specially authorized bonds Refunding bonds	Fiscal Law (article 4) Government Bonds Consolidation Fund Special Account Law National Debt Consolidation Fund Special Account Law
Treasury accommodation bonds (*yuzu-sai*)	Treasury bill Food bill Foreign exchange fund bill	Fiscal Law (article 7) Foodstuff Control Special Account Law (articles 3 and 4) Foreign Exchange Fund Special Account Law (articles 4 and 18)
Deferment bonds (*kurinobe-sai*)	Government compensation bond Fiscal investment and contribution bond	

bonds and others, according to the type of issuer. Japanese government bonds, local government bonds, and public corporation bonds are collectively known as **public bonds** (*kokyo-sai*).

2.1 Public Bonds

2.1.1 Japanese government bonds (*kokusai*)

Types of Japanese government bonds

Japanese government bonds are those issued by the Japanese government. They can be classified, depending on how the proceeds are to be used, into three groups: **revenue bonds** (*sainyu-sai*) to provide revenue for the national budget; **treasury accommodation bonds** (*yuzu-sai*) to bridge the day-to-day cash flow of the Treasury; and **deferment bonds** (*kurinobe-sai*) to defer current expenditures until the bond's maturity (table 6.1).

When the term Japanese government bonds is used, it usually refers to revenue bonds. Revenue bonds are further classified as follows, depending on the law under which they are issued.[1] **Construction bonds** (*kensetsu kokusai*), also called "article 4 bonds" (*yon-jo kokusai*), are based upon article 4 of the Finance Law (*Zaisei Ho*), which in principle prohibits the issuance of Japanese government bonds, except to the extent authorized by the Diet for financing public works, fiscal investment and loans. Specially authorized bonds (*tokurei kokusai*), also called deficit financing bonds (*akaji kokusai*), are issued to finance general account expenditures such as staff wages. For issuing this kind of bond, special legislative authorization by the Diet is required. **Refunding bonds** (*karikae kokusai*) are issued under the authority of the Law Concerning the Special Account of Government Bond Consolidation Funds (*Kokusai Seiri Kikin Tokubetsu Kaikei Ho*) to finance the redemption of Japanese government bonds prior to or at maturity.

In addition to the classification described above, Japanese government bonds can also be classified into the following five groups according to maturity: super long-term coupon bonds (with a maturity of 20 years); long-term coupon bonds (with a maturity of ten years); medium-term discount bonds (with a maturity of five years); medium-term coupon bonds (with a maturity of two to four years); and short-term discount bonds (with a maturity of less than six months).

Recent developments concerning Japanese government bonds

For approximately 20 years after 1945, no new Japanese government bonds were issued to supplement government revenues. But at a time of serious economic recession in fiscal year 1965 bonds began to be issued. Initially these were construction bonds based upon the Finance Law described above. In fiscal year 1975, specially authorized bonds were issued for the first time in order to make up for the substantial reduction in tax revenues caused by the oil crisis, and the issuance of specially authorized bonds continued to increase in subsequent years. However, the prevailing opinion that a national budget heavily dependent on a large volume of national debt might bring about fiscal inflexibility, however, curtailed the issuance of new Japanese government bonds. In fact, the government decided to reduce their issuance, with the result that new issues of specially authorized bonds were terminated in the fiscal year 1990 (table 6.2).

Meanwhile, beginning in fiscal year 1985, the government began to issue short-term government bonds (discount bonds with a maturity of less than one year) as a diversified type of national debt, in order to secure the smooth redemption and refunding of previous issues. Short-term government bonds have been regarded by market participants as the core instrument in the short-term financial market, and the value issued has been increasing in recent years.

The total issue of Japanese government bonds, excluding short-term ones, had been on the 20 trillion yen level in recent years, but in fiscal

Table 6.2 Volume of new public sector bond issues (in hundreds of millions of yen)

FY:	1979	1984	1987	1988	1989	1990
Japanese government bonds						
Long-term	111,075	135,635	191,370	156,794	142,551	163,632
Treasury Bills	–	–	47,219	44,413	107,709	204,507
Others	27,850	52,519	38,422	36,016	23,920	41,359
Total	138,925	188,154	277,011	37,223	274,180	409,498
(Ref. Debt-Financing)	(63,390)	(63,714)	(25,382)	(9,565)	(4,150)	(0)
Public corporation bonds						
Government guranteed	15,186	26,060	22,311	22,573	18,208	19,083
Others	26,021	37,116	43,112	47,812	50,472	57,158
Total	41,207	63,176	65,423	70,385	68,680	76,241
Local government bonds						
Publicly offered	8,148	8,230	9,762	8,246	9,983	9,419
Others	26,850	20,014	15,758	14,473	14,625	11,188
Total	34,998	28,244	25,520	22,719	24,608	20,607
Total	215,130	279,574	367,954	330,327	367,468	506,346

Sources: Ministry of Finance; Bank of Japan; and Bond Underwriters' Association of Japan

year 1990 it reached 40 trillion yen, owing mainly to the increase in the issuance of short-term discount bonds.

2.1.2   Local government bonds (*chiho-sai*)

Types of local government bonds

Local government bonds are issued by prefectural and municipal governments as debts to be repaid over a period of two fiscal years or longer. These bonds can be issued under article 230 of the Local Autonomy Law (*Chiho Jichi Ho*), as required by the prefectural and municipal government bond programs which are prepared through consultation between the Minister of Home Affairs and the Minister of Finance.

Publicly offered local government bonds (*kobo chiho sai*) are issued through public offering. There are no legal restrictions on them. However, in order to prevent confusion in the primary market and to ensure the appropriate allocation of funds in accordance with local government bond programs, the Ministry of Home Affairs determines the eligibility criteria for issuers of publicly offered local government bonds. The criteria are based on: (a) whether the government in question has previous experience in issuing privately placed local government bonds in large quantities, and has the ability to raise sufficient non-governmental funds steadily in the future; and (b) whether the local government has sufficient standing in the market to ensure smooth public placement. At present, 16 prefectural governments and 11 cities meet the eligibility criteria to issue publicly offered local government bonds.

Privately placed local government bonds (*enko chiho-sai*) are issued by many prefectural and municipal governments (about 2,000 governments currently). These bonds are usually sold to financial institutions. In most cases, the amount of each issue is very small and such bonds have little liquidity.

Recent issues of local government bonds

The recent issues of publicly offered and privately placed bonds amounted to approximately 1 trillion yen and approximately 1.5 trillion yen respectively (table 6.2). Issuance of local government bonds has become a stable fund-raising method for local governments.

2.1.3 Public corporation bonds (*kodan/koko sai*), also called government agency bonds (*seifu kikan sai*)

Types of public corporation bonds

Public corporation bonds are issued by various public corporations and governmental enterprises under legal authorization. All bonds of this kind, except those with government guarantee, are backed by general mortgages, and thus holders of the bonds have priority over other creditors in receiving principal and interest on them.

Among bonds issued by public corporations, those guaranteed by the government as to repayment of the principal and payment of interest are called **government guaranteed bonds**. The right to issue government guaranteed bonds must be explicitly received by a public corporation according to the law. On the other hand, bonds issued by public corporations without any such guarantee by the government are **privately placed public corporation bonds**. They are often issued by taking advantage of "private" relationships between the issuer and the purchasers of the bonds (who are mainly financial institutions).

In addition, there are bonds which are underwritten by the government for the whole amount, using the funds of the Trust Fund Bureau

Special Account (*shikin unyo bu*) or Postal Life Insurance Bureau (*kanpo*) as part of the Fiscal Loans and Investment Program. These are **government underwritten bonds** (*seifu hikiuke sai*).

Recent issues of public corporation bonds

Recent issues of publicly offered and privately placed bonds amounted to approximately 2 trillion and 5 trillion yen, respectively (table 6.2). The major purchaser of privately placed bonds is the government, which buys them with the funds from postal savings and employees' pension contributions. Recently, because government funds in these accounts have been ample, the public offering of government guaranteed bonds has declined.

2.2   Corporate Bonds (*Sha-Sai*)

2.2.1   Types of corporate bond

Classification by issuer

Bonds issued by long-term credit banks and other financial institutions based upon special laws (that is, the Long-term Credit Bank Law, the Specialized Foreign Exchange Bank Law, the Central Cooperative Bank for Agriculture and Forestry Law, the Central Bank for Commercial and Industrial Cooperatives Law, and the Credit Cooperatives Law) are called **bank debentures** (*kinyu-sai*). Bank debentures may be issued without collateral. When they are issued under the provisions of the Specialized Foreign Exchange Bank Law and the Credit Cooperative Laws, the bond issue ceiling is ten times the amount of shareholders' equity plus a reserve which each issuer holds. When other types of bank debentures are issued, the bond ceiling is 30 times the amount of the shareholders' equity plus a reserve. Below these respective ceilings, the debentures may be sold on a sell-as-you-go basis, which means that the amount of each issue can be set according to the actual sales amount.

Another type of corporate bond is called an **industrial bond** (*jigyo-sai*). Among industrial bonds, those issued in large volume by electric power companies are called **electricity power bonds** (*denryoku sai*) and can thus be distinguished from other industrial bonds, which are classified as **general industrial bonds** (*ippan jigyo-sai*).

Classification by bondholders' rights

Corporate bonds are classified, according to the rights allowed to bond-holders, as **straight bonds** (*futsu sha-sai*), **convertible bonds** (*tenkan* *sha-sai*) which can be converted into equity shares of the same issuer, and **bonds with warrants** (*waranto tsuki sha-sai*) which provide bond-holders with the option to purchase the issuer's common stock in the future.

Classification by type of collateral

Corporate bonds can be classified according to type of collateral: **secured corporate bonds** (*tanpo tsuki sha-sai*) are those which are issued according to the Secured Bond Trust Law (*Tanpo Tsuki Sha-Sai Shintaku Ho*). There are 19 valid types of mortgages, including real-estate mortgages, mortgages on various types of foundations, and mortgages on the general assets of the issuing company. **Bonds with general mortgage** (*ippan tanpo tsuki sha-sai*) are those which give bondholders the right, based upon special laws, to have their bonds redeemed from the general assets of the issuer with priority over other creditors. Bonds with general mortgage which have been issued so far include electricity power bonds and the bonds issued by NTT (Nippon Telegraph and Telephone Company). **Unsecured corporate bonds** (*muhosho sha-sai*) are issued by corporations without mortgage or guarantee. Recently, these bonds have been allowed as a new type of corporate bond, and the issuance of this instrument has been increasing rapidly. The issuance of unsecured corporate bonds, however, is subject to a financial covenants clause such as a negative pledge.

2.2.2 Recent issues of corporate bonds

Publicly offered bonds

The publicly offered bonds increased steadily in issue volume until fiscal year 1989, driven by CBs and bonds with warrants (table 6.3). In the peak year of 1989, out of the total volume of publicly offered bonds (9,283.5 billion yen), straight bonds accounted for 729 billion yen, CBs for 7,639.5 billion yen, and bonds with warrants for 915 billion yen. In other words, equity-related financing accounted for 93 percent of the total. Equity-related financing had been the preferred method in Japan, as it was advantageous to issuers in the years just prior to 1989, when stock prices were rising and were expected to continue rising. For example, on the basis of fiscal year 1989 figures, the issuing cost of straight bonds was about 6 percent whereas the cost of CBs was at the 2 percent level.

Unlike their US counterparts, blue-chip corporations in Japan entertain a preference for equity-related financing in the form of CBs or

Table 6.3 Volume of new corporate and foreign bond issues (in hundreds of millions of yen)

FY:	1979	1984	1987	1988	1989	1990
Corporate Bonds						
Publicly offered						
Straight						
bonds	12,981	7,200	9,150	7,490	7,290	20,660
(Electric						
power)	(10,740)	(6,196)	(6,880)	(5,050)	(6,930)	(18,300)
Convertible						
bonds	3,535	16,115	50,550	69,945	76,395	9,110
Bonds with						
warrants	–	30	0	0	9,150	3,950
Total	16,516	23,345	59,706	77,435	92,835	33,720
Privately placed	281	502	2,484	3,330	3,579	8,561
Total	16,797	23,847	62,184	80,765	96,414	42,281
Bank debentures	117,251	196,105	329,086	335,942	356,850	469,079
Yen-denominated						
foreign bonds						
and others	3,292	12,380	6,440	7,992	10,842	13,810
Total	137,340	232,332	397,710	424,699	464,106	525,170

Sources: Ministry of Finance; Bank of Japan: Bond Underwriters' Association of Japan

bonds with warrants. Shareholding in Japan is a staid and stable affair, and an increase in CBs is not considered to spawn immediately the danger of stock cornering. Furthermore, most Japanese shareholders are quite tolerant of any dilution of value that might be caused by the conversion of CBs into shares. The latter half of fiscal year 1989, however, witnessed a sharp decline in stock prices and a bearish market. As a result, public offerings of stocks, CBs, and bonds with warrants drastically decreased in volume.

In the years ahead, it is unlikely that there will be a continuous increase in stock prices as in the years up to 1989. As the Japanese stock market becomes more international, shareholders are expected to demand higher dividends from corporations. Under these circumstances, dependence on equity-related financing may decrease and further diversification of fund-raising may be required. Consequently, issues of straight corporate bonds may increase as a funding instrument.

Privately placed bonds

The government, which formerly pursued the policy of fostering securities companies, ranked private placement as ancillary to the public offering market, and established the so-called "no-return" rule (meaning that a corporation, having issued a publicly offered bond, could not tap the private placement market). Furthermore, the amount of each issue in the private placement market was not allowed to exceed 2 billion yen. With these restrictions, most of the market participants were smaller enterprises whose stocks were not listed, and whose issuing lots remained below 1 billion yen. This is quite different from the US market where large corporations can make extensive use of private placements for large amounts of fund-raising.

The drastic changes in the environment surrounding the corporate bond market in Japan, however, induced an appraisal of private placements. As a result, so-called "large private placements" totaling 2 billion yen or more, were first introduced in July 1987. Accordingly, the "no-return" rule was abolished so that large issuers, who had previously issued bonds only through public offering, were allowed to turn to private placement.

As we saw above, the primary private placement market has gradually become more flexible, and its total volume has been steadily increasing since large private placements were introduced in 1987. Relative to public offerings, however, the size of the private placement market remains small, mainly because it is still subject to many restrictions, such as the prohibition on the sale of private placement bonds until at least two years after purchase, the establishment of a cap of 10 billion yen per issue lot, and the limitation on the annual total amount of private placement bonds.

2.3 Foreign Bonds (*Gai-Sai*)

2.3.1 Types of foreign bonds

Foreign bonds are bonds issued in the Japanese capital market by non-residents. Of these, bonds denominated in yen are called **yen-denominated foreign bonds** (the so-called "*samurai* bonds"), and those denominated in foreign currency are called **foreign currency-denominated foreign bonds** (or "*shogun* bonds"). In particular, *daimyo* bonds are the foreign-currency-denominated foreign bonds which are issued by international organizations such as the World Bank and the Asian Development Bank, the certificates of which are held by Euroclear and other international clearing houses. **Dual currency bonds** represent another financing instrument, in which the currency of issue is the yen, and the currency of redemption is a foreign currency. Yet another instrument is the **reverse dual currency bond**, with the roles of the yen and the respective foreign currency reversed from that of the dual currency bonds.

2.3.2   Recent issues of foreign bonds

In the yen-denominated foreign bond market, there was a "no-return" rule, which prohibited an issuer from tapping the yen private placement market once it had made a public bond offering. This rule was abolished in 1986, however; so an issuer can now choose either public offering or private placement at any time.

In 1970 the Asian Development Bank (ADB) became the first issuer of *samurai* bonds, and the World Bank followed in 1971. Australia became the first sovereign issuer in 1972 and Sears Roebuck the first corporate issuer in 1979. The *samurai* bonds issued so far can be categorized, according to the type of issuer, into four groups: (a) international organizations, such as the World Bank and the Asian Development Bank; (b) sovereign issuers, such as Austria, Sweden, and New Zealand; (c) governmental institutions in various foreign countries; and (d) corporate issuers. Each of the first three groups accounts for 30 percent of the total balance of *samurai* bonds. The balance itself already exceeds 10 trillion yen. Favored by the development and internationalization of the Japanese bond market, the *samurai* bond market is now establishing its position as a place for international long-term fund raising. A single A-rating is the minimum requirement for a *samurai* bond issuer: however, in the case of developing countries, this requirement has been relaxed somewhat in order to encourage capital flows to those countries.

3   THE PRIMARY MARKET

3.1   The Primary Market of Public Bonds

3.1.1   The procedures of public bond issues

Japanese government bonds

In this section, we shall explain a major manner in which Japanese government bonds are issued: the **syndicated underwriting system** (*shidan hikiuke hoshiki*). Under this system the syndicated members underwrite a certain portion by committing themselves to purchasing it if it remains unsold after offering. Almost all the financial institutions and securities companies in Japan belong to the underwriting syndicate. As of November 1991, the syndicate consists of 674 financial institutions (approximately 70 percent of the total) and 158 securities companies (approximately 30 percent). As far as foreign companies are concerned, 30 foreign banks and 34 foreign securities companies are members of the syndicate.

Until 1983 the offering of bonds to the public belonged exclusively to securities companies. However, financial institutions including banks were permitted to sell government bonds to public investors under the Securities and Exchange Law.

The syndicated underwriting system has played a pivotal role in the Japanese capital market since the massive issuance of government bonds began in 1965. At present, long-term coupon bonds and medium-term discount bonds are issued through this kind of underwriting system.

Since April 1989 long-term coupon bonds have been issued under a partial competitive bidding system (*kakaku kyoso nyusatsu hoshiki*), which is a mixture of syndicated underwriting and competitive bidding. Under this hybrid system, a certain portion of the issue is subject to competitive bidding by the syndicate and the remainder is purchased by the syndicate members on a pro rata basis. The competitive bidding portion, initially 40 percent, was increased to 60 percent in October 1990. In the competitive bidding portion, successful bidders have different prices for purchasing Japanese government bonds. However, the syndicated underwriting portion enables each participant to underwrite government bonds at the same price, which is equal to the average of the successful bid prices.

Long-term Japanese government bonds, which have a central role in the Japanese government bond market, basically depend upon the syndicated underwriting system for issuance so that they can be smoothly absorbed by investors, even under unfavourable market conditions. However, the competitive bidding system has been introduced in part to increase the transparency and effectiveness of the Japanese capital market. Medium-term discount Japanese government bonds, on the other hand, use only the syndicated underwriting system, in which the total issue amount is underwritten, based upon the pro rata rule previously agreed upon by the syndicate members.

3.1.2 The role of intermediaries in the market

Intermediaries

As described above, financial institutions and securities companies act as intermediaries in the primary market for public bonds. In the case of public corporation bonds and local government bonds, financial institutions serve as commissioned companies, handling some administrative work on behalf of issuers and also protecting the interests of bondholders (investors). Today, these intermediaries play an important role in the issuance of public bonds and in their secondary trading. Looking back over the long history of public bonds since 1945, the function of financial institutions as intermediaries has been particularly significant.

Sales of Japanese government bonds

Japanese government bonds began to be issued in large quantities in fiscal year 1965, and the volume of issues became massive after fiscal year 1975. Most of these bonds were purchased by banks and other financial institutions, who held the majority in their investment portfolios. At that time, financial institutions were expected, as stable investors, to hold these bonds until maturity, and thus the bonds actually had no liquidity. Later, the financial institutions gradually began to remove Japanese government bonds from their portfolios, feeling the strong need to improve their fund positions. Encouraged by the relaxation of the self-imposed restriction on sales of Japanese government bonds, the secondary market for Japanese government bonds began to expand in fiscal year 1977.

The beginning of bank counter sales and bank dealings

In the past, financial institutions were not allowed to sell Japanese government bonds to the public. As the massive issuance of these bonds continued, however, it became necessary to promote purchases by individuals. In this situation, financial institutions made strong representations that they should be allowed to sell Japanese government bonds to the public. Whether or not financial institutions should be allowed to sell Japanese government bonds over their counters was extensively debated as an issue concerning "a boundary between banks and securities companies."

As a result, the Banking Law (*Ginko ho*) and other relevant laws were amended in 1981, and over-the-counter sales started in April 1983 (banks concurrently began over-the-counter sales of local government bonds and government guaranteed bonds). Also, in June 1984 financial institutions authorized by the government began to deal in Japanese government bonds, government guaranteed bonds, and local government bonds. As described above, financial institutions were allowed to deal with a wide range of activities in the primary and secondary markets.

This strengthened market price-forming capabilities and made the market more solid. The expansion of the publicly offered bonds market, especially the enhancement of the primary and secondary markets for Japanese government bonds, was to be a driving force in the deregulation of interest rates and of the domestic financial and capital markets as a whole.

3.2 The Primary Market in Corporate Bonds

3.2.1 Features of the primary market in corporate bonds

The main feature of the primary corporate bond market in Japan is that its mechanism is sufficient for maintaining its soundness, and this mechanism has continued to operate well, thanks to the efforts of the market participants. As a result, Japanese corporate bonds, which have maintained a high level of safety, have won the confidence of a widening range of investors. Specifically, there have been only a dozen bond defaults in Japan since the end of the Second World War. It is generally accepted that Japanese corporations can issue corporate bonds on favorable terms and conditions in the Eurobond market and other capital markets overseas.

The primary market conference (the so-called *kisaikai*, in Japanese), in which banks and securities companies participate, historically determined important matters concerning the issuance of Japanese corporate bonds. However, its function now is to disseminate general information on corporate bonds among the participants.

In describing the mechanism of the corporate bond market, it should be emphasized that the framework is subject to constant review in response to changes in the financial environment, and that market participants are always engaged in efforts to make the market more open and efficient.

Eligibility standards and financial covenants clause

Eligibility standards are qualifications that corporations must satisfy in order to issue corporate bonds. Under the Commercial Code of Japan, any joint stock company (*Kabushiki kaisha*) is entitled to issue bonds, but the eligibility standards impose a set of requirements in order to maintain confidence in the bond market. At present, corporations intending to issue corporate bonds must satisfy rating standards. The bond ratings required as eligibility standards are subject to the type of bond and the availability of collaterals. In the past, all bonds issued in Japan were required to be secured bonds. However, unsecured bonds can now be issued, provided they can meet financial covenants, including limitations on offerings of liens to third parties (a negative pledge) and so on.

Taking into consideration the improved financial conditions of Japanese corporations and the availability of rating information, the eligibility standards for both secured bonds and unsecured bonds have gradually relaxed, and simultaneously ratings have been widely utilized. The traditional eligibility standards used double-feature tests: the rating test; and the numerical test, in which numerical items such as net worth and various financial ratios are checked. Under these standards, a bond could be issued if it passed either the rating test or the numerical test. The standards were changed in November 1990, and now only the rating standard may be used to determine eligibility.

At present, secured convertible bonds to be issued in Japan must have as a minimum a double B (BB) rating. Secured straight bonds and secured bonds with warrants may be issued with a minimum rating of a triple B (BBB). About 60 percent of all listed firms in Japan (excluding banks and securities companies) would be eligible to issue both straight and convertible bonds. The firms which cannot issue either bond are mostly those whose corporate performance in profits and dividend payouts is so poor that they have not even issued new shares.

The financial covenants have been also gradually relaxed because of improved creditworthiness. In this regard, the review of the clause in November 1990, paying attention to the balance between the funding needs of the issuers and the protection of bondholders' interests, focused on relaxing the limitation on security offered to a third party (the negative pledge) as well as the conditions in the event of default. If the use of ratings becomes an accepted practice and investors in general embrace the principle of *caveat emptor*, it will be important to further review restrictions on corporate issuers so that their business activities are not disturbed too much.

Bond issue ceilings

Bond issue ceilings under the Commercial Code also play an important role in maintaining the soundness of the corporate bond market. This rule restricts the issue of bonds beyond the value of the net assets of the company, in order to protect the bondholders' interests and to maintain the soundness of the market. The rule has been gradually relaxed (as described below), so that unsecured bonds can now be issued up to an amount equivalent to their net worth. As a result, secured bonds, convertible bonds, bonds with warrants, and corporate bonds offered in a foreign country can be issued up to an amount double the value of the net worth of an issuer, in accordance with the Temporary Law on Bond Issue Ceilings.[2]

While corporate bonds became more important as an instrument of corporate fund-raising, industries began to require a higher corporate bond issue volume. It was also recognized that few foreign countries were setting ceilings on bond issues. Taking these factors into account, the Commercial Code was amended in 1990, abolishing the former system by which the bond issue ceiling was the sum of capital and reserve or the amount of net worth, whichever was the smaller. Under the new system, only the amount of net worth is left as the standard for the statutory ceiling. At the same time, corporate bonds with warrants were added to the categories of corporate bonds (secured bonds, bonds with warrants, and foreign bonds) to which the double amount was applicable under the Temporary Law on Bond Issue Ceilings. These amendments came into effect on April 1, 1991. The amount of the net worth differs from one company to another, but it is estimated that, on average, the amended bond issue ceiling will be approximately doubled.

The commissioned company system

In Japan there exists a commissioned company system under which commissioned banks play a role in the operation of the Japanese corporate market. Commissioned companies perform several functions, based upon the Commercial Code and the Secured Bond Trust Law.

First, commissioned banks give advice as to the timing, method and amount of an issue for successful bond flotation, draw up the various related contracts and other necessary documents, prepare application forms, the roster of bondholders and bond certificates, and check the paid-up amount from the subscribers.

Second, they act as quasi-fiduciary for the protection of bondholders' rights, such as receipt of payments of redemption and interest on behalf of bondholders. A commissioned company, under the Commercial Code, performs all the necessary acts, both inside and outside a court of law, which are required to protect the interests of bondholders until the bond reaches maturity.

Third, a commissioned company ascertains whether or not a financial convenants clause has been appropriately included in the agreement at the time of issuance, and then checks whether or not the issuer observes the clause.

Finally, when secured bonds go into default, a commissioned company will obtain, preserve, and execute the collateral on behalf of bondholders, under the provisions of the trust contract agreed to by the issuer.

In practice, corporate bonds have only infrequently fallen into default during the postwar period. When it has happened that secured corporate bonds have fallen into default, in most cases commissioned companies purchased these bonds from bondholders and participated in the legal proceedings. Of course, commissioned companies have no legal obligation to purchase secured bonds. However, they have bought them voluntarily because of their desire to maintain the soundness of the corporate bond market. As far as unsecured corporate bonds are concerned, commissioned companies have difficulties in purchasing defaulted or defaulting bonds because they have to protect depositors' interests. The only possible way to purchase defaulted or defaulting unsecured corporate bonds is to change their status to that of secured corporate bonds.

At present, only ordinary and trust banks can perform as commissioned companies under the Commercial Code and the Secured Bond Trust Law.

3.2.2   Demarcation in roles of intermediaries

Article 65 of the Securities and Exchange Law separates the banking business from the securities business. For example, banks cannot underwrite corporate bonds: bond underwriting belongs exclusively to securities companies. In collaboration with a securities company acting as an underwriter, however, a bank acting as a commissioned company can perform the role of intermediary. Thereby smoothing market operations and protecting the interests of bondholders.

Before the Second World War, Japanese banks underwrote public bonds, corporate bonds and stocks. They were the main players in the primary market. The promulgation of the Securities and Exchange Law in 1948, however, separated the banking business from the securities business in general, and prohibited banks from underwriting securities, except public bonds. Underwriting corporate bonds and stocks became the work of securities companies. Unlike commercial banks in the United States, however, Japanese banks have retained partial underwriting functions. Taking advantage of their expertise gained in prewar days, Japanese banks perform well as commissioned companies in providing advice to corporate issuers and in operating in the whole bond market in collaboration with securities companies.

3.2.3   Current topics on corporate bonds

Recently, banking deregulation and the perceived need to foster international access and reciprocity have started in motion wide-ranging changes in the Japanese corporate bond market. In response to these changes, the current structure of the Japanese capital market is undergoing a drastic re-examination. The ultimate goal is to restructure the present system in order to revitalize the Japanese corporate bond market and to allow a wider range of market players, such as issuers, investors, and intermediaries, to participate more competitively in the market through diversified forms of transactions. In this process of restructuring, ratings and disclosure must be made more easily available in investment decisions in order to foster the self-accountability of investors. As improvements are made in this regard, greater restructuring in the corporate bond market may be attempted, by relaxing eligibility standards and so on. In fact, the report by the Securities and Exchange Council in December 1987, which suggested a review of the primary market in corporate bonds, has greatly stimulated reform proposals, which are outlined below.

The disclosure system

As corporate activities become increasingly global and diversified, both Japanese and foreign issuers have begun to require mobility and flexibility in fund-raising, along with simplified disclosure procedures which are currently being simplified, with the requirements shifting in emphasis from registration statements to periodic reports.

Japan's disclosure system, designed to enable investors to obtain information on the target investment in a timely and accurate way, consists of the following two kinds of report: the securities registration statement that discloses financial conditions and business affairs at the time of the issuance of securities; and annual reports (including financial statements) that are necessary to follow up the activities of the target company following issuance.

Through an amendment in the Securities and Exchange Law in 1988, a number of simplifications and revisions concerning disclosure were made. The first was to adopt a "reference system" whereby in cases where specified conditions are met, corporations are permitted to omit statements, referring instead to the pertinent annual securities report. The second was to introduce the "integrated registration system" (which is quite similar to shelf registration in the US), whereby corporations may omit registration statements *in toto*, merely by filing simple supplementary documents. The third was to shorten the time-lag between disclosure and actual issue. Finally, the fourth was to disclose business operations on a segment basis for corporations straddling more than one industrial sector.

As for periodic reports, it was decided in April 1987 to enlarge the scope of information on a consolidated basis, and to include cash flow tables, so that disclosure could appropriately reflect diversified and international industrial activities.

Ratings

The rating system has been well developed and widely used in the United States. In Japan, the Securities and Exchange Council took up this subject and proposed its early adoption in 1977. In 1984 deregulation and internationalization in the Japanese securities market accelerated soon after the so-called US–Japan Yen–Dollar Committee issued a report. As a result, in 1985 three rating agencies were established in Japan, and US rating agencies branched out into Japan.

In principle, Japanese rating criteria and symbols are the same as those in the US. Considering that the rating system plays an important role in the determination of the terms and conditions of an issue as well as in investors' decisionmaking on investment, market participants are trying to widen the circumstances in which ratings are used, for example, by introducing them into eligibility standards and so on. The number of rated bonds and convertible bonds is now increasing. In the current Japanese capital market, the rating agencies should make further efforts to increase the penetration of the rating system throughout the market.

At present, there are three rating agencies in Japan: Nippon Investors Services Inc. (NIS, established in 1985), Japan Credit Rating Agency Inc. (JCR, established in 1985), and the Japan Bond Research Institute (JBRI, established in 1985). Although NIS and JCR are mainly owned by financial institutions, their rigid by-laws ensure that they are independent of shareholders and protected from information leakage.

Bond proposals

In the past, the pricing of new corporate bonds was determined by reference to that of Japanese government bonds for the same month, and the secondary market was not well developed. However, it was thought desirable both to make bond issues flexible and to determine pricing based on individual negotiations so as to make the primary market more open and free for effective fund-raising. For this reason, the so-called bond proposal system was introduced in 1987.

The bond proposal system is a kind of competitive bidding system in which a securities company is nominated by the issuer as a lead manager among securities companies which bid on terms such as coupon rates and issuing prices. The lead manager is responsible for determining prices, taking into consideration necessary factors such as the fund-raising needs of the issuer and the actual situation of the prevailing secondary market.

Although the secondary market is still not sufficiently developed to justify full adoption of the bond proposal system, it is believed that it will function better as the secondary market develops.

The corporate bond law

The necessity to revise the Corporate Bond Law (the Commercial Code and the Secured Bond Trust Law) has been obvious for some time, in light of the change in the financial environment. In response, the Commercial Code section of the Legal System Council is currently conducting fundamental reviews, the two main themes of which represent the relaxation of bond-issue ceilings and the revision of the commissioned company system. Needless to say, the revision of the law is highly correlated with the financial reform issues, including the separation of the banking business and the securities business, which both the Financial System Research Committee and the Securities and Exchange Council are currently discussing (as described below). The Commercial Code section is, therefore, reviewing the Corporate Bond Law, directing their attention to maintaining harmony with other groups and their ongoing work in financial reform.

4 THE SECONDARY BOND MARKET

4.1 Bond Trading

Bonds change hands in the secondary market either through transactions at a securities exchange or through over-the-counter trading between a securities company (or licensed financial institution) and its client or between securities companies (or licensed financial institutions). Because a large number of bonds are traded in the market and trading lots vary, trade takes place primarily over the counter. As shown in table 6.4, over-the-counter trading accounts for over 95 percent of total secondary bond trading (in the Tokyo market) in fiscal year 1990.

The total volume of bonds traded (in the Tokyo market), propelled by the start of the massive issuance of Japanese government bonds, increased to approximately 5,000 trillion yen in fiscal year 1987. The total volume in fiscal year 1990, however, fell by 6.7 percent to around 3,400 trillion yen from the previous fiscal year, and down by as much as 26 percent from fiscal year 1985. The reduction in the trading volume since fiscal year 1988 can be attributed to a decline in short-term transactions in Japanese government bonds and other instruments, and to the reluctance of market participants to trade bonds because of the general trend towards higher interest rates.

Table 6.4   Volume of bond trading[a] (in billions of yen; percent)

FY	Over-the-counter		Exchanges		Total	
1980	281,011	97.3	7,740	2.7	288,751	100
1985	2,514,653	94.5	145,128	5.5	2,659,782	100
1986	3,490,264	93.9	227,200	6.1	3,717,464	100
1987	5,094,292	96.4	192,316	3.6	5,286,608	100
1988	4,084,666	96.3	156,331	3.7	4,240,997	100
1989	3,506,792	96.4	132,342	3.6	3,639,134	100
1990	3,285,769	96.8	108,276	3.2	3,394,045	100

[a]   Trading includes selling and buying.

Sources: Japan Association of Securities Dealers; Tokyo Stock Exchange

A review of the trading volume (in the Tokyo market) by type of bond reveals that the majority of over-the-counter trading has been in Japanese government bonds (table 6.5). The annual volume of Japanese government bonds (fiscal year 1990) reached 3,160 trillion yen, accounting for 96 percent of the total volume, as shown in table 6.6. The turnover ratio (calculated by dividing the trading volume for each type of bond by the outstanding balance of the bonds at the end of March 1991) of Japanese government bonds was much higher, at about 31 times per year, then that of any other investment, each of which had a turnover ratio of less than once a year (table 6.7). The trading volume of Japanese government bonds began to increase sharply for the following reasons: first, the outstanding balance of Japanese government bonds in the market increased substantially; second, financial institutions began to deal in Japanese government bonds one after another from June 1984.

In addition to Japanese government bonds, the bonds traded at the securities exchanges (mainly the Tokyo Stock Exchange) include convertible bonds, which accounted for about 55 percent of total bond trading in fiscal years 1988 and 1989. This was due to active short-term buying and selling by financial institutions, corporations, and individual investors, who aimed primarily at capital gains. In fiscal year 1990, however, trading of convertible bonds was approximately 35 percent of total bond trading, less than the track record of the two previous financial years, due to the sluggish stock market (table 6.5).

4.2   Over-the-counter Trading of Bonds

Participants in the over-the-counter market include securities companies and financial institutions authorized to deal in public bonds. Securities companies and financial institutions formulate a yield and price on a daily basis as a benchmark for trading. In order to ensure that each over-the-counter trade is fair and smooth, information relevant to pricing in the entire market must be disclosed quickly and impartially. For this purpose, the Japanese Association of Securities Dealers selects 20 to 30 frequently traded bonds which most appropriately reflect the market trends, and announces daily index quotes to buyers and sellers for each issue, based on reports from securities companies and financial institutions. In addition, the Association selects approximately 260 most frequently traded bonds for each type, each maturity and each yield, and makes a weekly announcement (on Thursdays) of its bid and offer price as the middle price quotation, on the basis of reports from securities companies and financial institutions.

Furthermore, from June 1986 securities companies began to make announcements of quotes with purchase commitments for the major issues of yen-denominated foreign bonds and to conduct transaction-based market-making. A similar announcement and market-making process began in September 1986 for the last two issues of government guaranteed bonds, local government bonds and industrial bonds by securities companies and financial institutions (financial institutions were not allowed to deal in industrial bonds). Then, in August 1988 the Japan Mutual Securities Company (*Nippon Sogo Shoken*), as an intermediary for traders, began announcing publicly the actual traded prices and indications of those bonds that were being most actively traded over the counter and most accurately reflected market movements among government guaranteed bonds, local government bonds, bank debentures, and so on. As for all issues floated under the proposal system, in April 1986 a lead underwriting manager began making the market for at least one month after issue through the Japan Mutual Securities Company.

4.3   Trading of Bonds on the Securities Exchanges

At present, all issues of long-term Japanese government bonds and all issues of convertible bonds are not only traded over the counter but are also listed at the exchanges. A part of the issues of government guaranteed bonds, local government bonds, and industrial bonds are also listed. Listing of industrial bonds, convertible bonds, and bonds with warrants requires the approval of the Minister of Finance, which can be obtained if the bonds satisfy certain eligibility standards set by the exchanges. However, Japanese government bonds, government guaranteed bonds, and local government bonds do not require

Table 6.5　Volume of transactions at the Tokyo Stock Exchange by type of bond[a] (in trillions of yen; percent)

FY:	1980		1985		1988		1989		1990	
Japanese government bonds	33,586	43.4	876,438	60.4	663,518	42.4	598,554	45.2	703,046	64.9
Government guaranteed bonds	6	0.0	6	0.0	6	0.0	4	0.0	5	0.0
Local government bonds	6	0.0	6	0.0	6	0.0	4	0.0	5	0.0
Bank debentures	28	0.0	28	0.0	26	0.0	24	0.0	25	0.0
Industrial bonds	1,406	1.8	528	0.0	366	0.0	268	0.0	201	0.0
Convertible bonds	42,076	54.4	572,992	39.5	898,666	57.5	724,292	54.7	379,151	35.0
Others	292	0.4	1,284	0.1	722	0.0	274	0.0	324	0.0
Total	77,398	100.0	1,451,284	100.0	1,563,310	100.0	1,323,424	100.0	1,082,756	100.0

[a]　Transactions include selling and buying.

Source:　Tokyo Stock Exchange

Table 6.6 Volume of transactions in the Tokyo over-the-counter market[a] (in millions of yen; percent)

FY:	1980		1985		1988		1989		1990	
Japanese government bonds	1,643,604	58.5	24,042,528	95.6	39,422,697	96.5	34,043,892	97.1	31,561,778	96.1
Government guaranteed bonds	117,419	4.2	298,546	1.2	375,250	0.9	175,476	0.5	165,781	0.5
Local government bonds	68,740	2.4	90,636	0.4	67,514	0.2	41,371	0.1	40,764	0.1
Bank debentures	501,872	17.9	287,570	1.1	651,107	1.6	626,517	1.8	894,487	2.7
Industrial bonds	124,148	4.4	76,268	0.3	99,216	0.2	71,800	0.2	86,107	0.3
Convertible bonds	3,277	0.1	34,586	0.1	5,512	0.0	7,727	0.0	1,967	0.0
Others	351,054	12.5	316,397	1.3	225,359	0.6	101,137	0.3	106,805	0.3
Total	2,810,114	100.0	25,146,531	100.0	40,846,655	100.0	35,067,920	100.0	32,857,689	100.0

[a] Includes selling and buying; dealings by financial institutions are also included.
Transactions include securities operations of the Bank of Japan as well as trading by Japan Mutual Securities Company.

Source: Japanese Association of Securities Dealers

Table 6.7   Turnover ratio by type of bond in the Tokyo over-the-counter market (times per year)

	Japanese government bonds	*Government guaranteed bonds*	*Local government bonds*	*Bank debentures*	*Industrial bonds*
Turnover ratio[a]	30.8	0.8	0.6	0.8	0.9

[a]   The turnover ratio is computed by dividing the trading volume for each type of bond by the outstanding balance of the bond at the end of March 1991.

Sources: Japan Association of Securities Dealers; Industrial Bank of Japan

Table 6.8   Volume of transactions in JGB futures (in trillions of yen)

FY	*1985*	*1986*	*1987*	*1988*	*1989*	*1990*
Volume	158	1,366	1,705	1,922	1,853	1,563

Sources: Tokyo Stock Exchange; Industrial Bank of Japan

the approval of the Minister of Finance to be listed at the securities exchanges.

Whether dealing on their own accounts or broking for customers, member securities companies are not allowed, outside the exchanges, to handle listed Japanese government bonds of 1–10 million yen, any listed convertible bonds, and listed bonds with warrants of less than 30 million yen.

4.4   Bond Futures and Options

The Tokyo Stock Exchange established a bond futures market in October 1985, with trading of futures on standard long-term (10-year) Japanese government bonds. The decision reflected the significant increase in the volume of trading in government bonds as well as the considerable deregulation and internationalization of the Japanese financial and capital markets prior to that time. These developments had created the need to hedge the risk associated with bond-price fluctuations. In July 1988, trading of futures on super long-term (20-year) government bonds commenced.

The bond futures market grew steadily after its establishment and trading volume in fiscal 1988 exceeded 1,900 trillion yen, including both

10-year and 20-year bonds (table 6.8). In fiscal 1989, however, the fall in the volume of spot trading in government bonds caused the volume of futures trading to decline as well.

As to other developments, over-the-counter trading in bond options began in April 1989, and short sales and lending transactions were deregulated in May 1989. In May 1990, trading of options on bond futures began on the Tokyo Stock Exchange, which has contributed to the further development of the bond market in Japan.

5 REVISION OF THE FUNDAMENTAL STRUCTURE

5.1 Changes in the Financial Environment and Financial Reforms in Other Countries

5.1.1 Change in the financial environment of the Japanese market

The changes in the financial environment of the Japanese market may be summarized as deregulation, internationalization, securitization, and an overhaul of financial engineering renovation. These changes demand a fundamental review of not only the framework of capital market operations but also the roles of intermediaries in the market.

Progress in globalization

Recently, there has been notable progress in globalization. In the past, the money and capital markets of each country were independent of one other and existed separately. Today, these markets are more closely interlinked through the development of telecommunications and data-processing systems, the emergence of new transactional techniques, and an overhaul of financial engineering. The most notable example is the on-line, real-time linkage of the various financial markets of the world. Using this innovation, both securities issuers and investors (both inside and outside Japan) can now select the most suitable capital market for issuance or investment by comparing various forms of financial instrument and the convenience provided by each capital market. As far as Japan is concerned, guidelines on Euroyen bond issues by both residents and non-residents have been gradually relaxed following the trend towards deregulation of Euroyen transactions since the report of the Japan–US Yen–Dollar Committee was published in 1984. This relaxation is aimed at encouraging borrowers or investors to make use of the

Japanese capital market, because the Euromarket is expanding its territory into the domestic market as a preferred source of finance.

Many foreign securities are currently sold to domestic investors, and various securities have begun simultaneous issuance in various markets. In addition, Japanese stocks are listed on foreign stock exchanges and there is an increase in the many derivative products backed by foreign securities. The movements of overseas markets, therefore, have a direct impact on the domestic market.

Progress in securitization

In recent years, the securitization of finance is progressing in parallel with globalization. During the course of securitization, stocks or bond issues have been more frequently used as a means of corporate finance, and direct corporate dependency upon the capital market has increased. This type of market-oriented funding, which has been particularly well developed in the Eurocurrency market and is preferred by corporations and financial institutions aiming at effectiveness, further accelerates globalization, which in turn further stimulates the progress of securitization.

On the other hand, securitization brings about the diversification of financial products which take the form of securities. In overseas markets, for instance, new financial engineering techniques have devised hybrid products with swaps and futures options. There have appeared asset-backed securities which are collateralized by such assets as mortgage loans, credit-card loans, and real estate. In the Japanese market, too, securitization products such as mortgage loan trusts are gradually appearing.

This progress in the securitization of finance has also brought about a new phenomenon called the unbundling of banking. In effect, this allows a degree of amalgamation of the banking business and the securities business. If banks sell assets by securitizing, they can achieve results similar to the underwriting and selling of corporate bonds, which are now categorized as securities business. Of course, this is only valid if the time lag between financing and investment in the banking business is ignored. This phenomenon is thus causing the demarcation between banking business and securities business to blur, as is obvious in the United States. It is quite possible that, through unbundling, the securitization of bank assets will become more popular in Japan.

Reciprocal entry of players in the capital market

The above-mentioned changes in the capital market environment have also accelerated the reciprocal entry of capital market players. As of

March 31, 1990, 34 Japanese securities companies had a total of 134 overseas subsidiaries, and 29 Japanese banks a total of 142 overseas securities business subsidiaries. The enactment in 1971 of the Foreign Securities Companies Law in Japan paved the way for the entry of foreign securities companies into the Japanese market. From 1985, there was a rush of entries due to the attractiveness of the enlarged Japanese market. As of January 31, 1991, there were 70 foreign securities companies operating in Japan. On three occasions in the past, membership of the Tokyo Stock Exchange (TSE) was offered to foreign applicants, and as of November 1990 25 foreign securities companies had membership.

5.1.2 Financial reforms abroad

The US, the UK, and other major industrialized countries are making quite drastic financial reforms in response to the changing financial environment described above.

The US Federal Reserve Board (FRB) has authorized securities subsidiaries of bank holding companies to engage in underwriting and dealing in stocks and bonds. In February 1991, the US Treasury Department proposed far-reaching financial reforms, including abolition of the Glass–Steagal Act, which stimulated the separation of banking business and securities business. Based on this proposal, Congress is now discussing a bill, the Financial Institutions Safety and Customer Choice Act 1991, which would allow both banks and securities companies to enter into each other's territory through their holding companies.

In Canada, financial reform that involves abolishing the separation of business between banks and securities companies will be completed soon.

The United Kingdom, where the Big Bang took place years ago, and other European countries are undertaking readjustment and reform in their respective financial markets in preparation for EC market integration in 1992. Most EC countries have adopted a universal banking system which permits straddling in banking business and securities business, and it is now expected that a unified licensing system under universal banking will be introduced throughout the EC countries by January 1993.

Taking the backgrounds of each individual nation into account, financial reforms are aiming for more competitiveness, effectiveness, and convenience in the markets, responding to globalization and securitization.

5.2 Adaptation to Changes in the Financial Environment

In response to the changing environment described above, there has been an acknowledged need to review the framework of the Japanese capital market, including the roles of market intermediaries and participants, with a view to diversifying financial products and services.

Under article 2 of Japan's Securities and Exchange Law, securities defined as such by the law are subject to investor protection provisions, including disclosure. Under article 65 of the law, which regulates the separation of banking business and securities business, banks are prohibited from engaging in securities business except for public bonds.[3]

However, under the current regulations that limit the range of financial products each financial institution can handle, it is difficult to take advantage of financial engineering techniques and respond to the diverse and sophisticated needs of corporate and individual investors.

It is true that, even under the current regulations, the capital and financial markets have so far contributed to the development of the national economy. However, there is now less and less distinction between the financial and the capital markets. Thus, it is most important to establish a new financial system in which complex financial products can be developed and synthetic financial services can be provided beyond the current framework for market intermediaries. This will enable the Japanese market to respond appropriately to the ongoing environmental changes.

The Japanese market has grown to become equal in size to those in New York and London. With international recognition, the Japanese market now has the responsibility of playing an important role in serving the world economy beyond its own narrow national interests. From the international standpoint as well, therefore, it is quite urgent and important to reform Japan's current financial system so as to make it more compatible with those of other major markets.

Before the Second World War, banks underwrote and sold public and corporate bonds. In many cases, corporate bonds were initially underwritten by banks, and securities companies assumed the responsibility for selling them. After the war, however, the access of banks to securities business was substantially restricted. When the prewar securities-related laws were abolished and the Securities and Exchange Law came into effect in 1947, banks were not initially denied access to securities business. When the Securities and Exchange Law was extensively amended in 1948, article 65 was introduced, restricting banks and other financial institutions from engaging in securities dealings in principle. This article, however, did not prohibit banks and other financial institutions from undertaking securities business with regard to Japanese government and other public bonds, from handling sales and purchases of securities in writing, or from selling and buying securities for investment purposes.

5.3 Financial Reform in Japan

The Securities and Exchange Council (with the Banking Bureau of the Ministry of Finance serving as its secretariat) and the Financial System Research Council (which had the Securities Bureau of the Ministry of Finance as its secretariat), both advisory bodies to the Minister of Finance, discussed the possible revision of the Japanese financial system, including the separation of banking business and securities business. These two councils issued their interim reports in June 1990. Both reports mentioned the need for new entries into the capital market, including entry by banks, with a view to making the Japanese financial and capital markets truly international and efficient, for the benefit of consumers and customers. For example, the report by the Securities and Exchange Council listed as advantages which would accrue from banks undertaking securities business: promotion of the development of instruments with both banking and securities features; encouragement of competition among intermediaries by allowing encroachment onto each other's business through their sophisticated knowledge of the market; and compatability of the Japanese market with other markets at a time when many other countries are taking similar steps.

The two councils continued their deliberations after the fall 1990 and issued their final reports in June 1991, suggesting a new framework for Japanese financial and capital markets in the future. Specifically, they argued that new entries in the securities business would encourage competition and make the market more efficient and understandable for the benefit of consumers, and both reports concluded that the existing separation between banking business and securities business should be revised. Furthermore, the reports expressed the idea that new entries would best be made by establishing separate subsidiaries for each of specified financial areas (for example, a bank would need to establish a subsidiary to carry on its securities business). In particular, the Securities and Exchange Council expressed the view that new entries should be permitted mainly into the primary market, which is currently dominated by the largest securities companies, for the purpose of encouraging more effective and appropriate competition there.

These proposals should come into effect through a revision of the securities-related laws. In preparation for making changes, the Japanese government is at present examining the issues, related to the scope of business of banks' securities subsidiaries and the range of securities (including securitization-related instruments, straight bonds, convertible bonds, bonds with warrants, and stock), that these subsidiaries would be able to handle. As stated earlier, the recent changes in the financial environment and financial reforms around the world clearly point to the elimination of barriers between banking business and securities business. In this regard, when banks establish subsidiaries, they need to be given full access to securities business (including brokerage and dealing business) as soon as possible, in order to give significant meaning to the financial system reform.[4]

The two reports also listed a few potential problems which might accompany the entry of banks into securities business, including the implications for the soundness of banks, and conflict of interest. One possible way of preventing these problems is to establish a fire wall similar to that which US banks have against affiliated securities companies. Most of the anticipated problems can be prevented, however, by promoting competition among intermediaries, by restricting the unfair use of insider information, by introducing measures supplementary to the current disclosure system, and by ensuring monitoring by the government. Although discussing ways in which these problems may be reduced is important, care is needed to ensure that excessive restrictions (such as the fire wall) do not minimize the advantages of reform, such as the increased benefits to customers and the increased efficiency of the economy as a whole.

As the Securities and Exchange Council also pointed out in its report, there is a need to revise the definition of "securities" and to amend related laws concerning private placement. In ensuring the sound development of the Japanese capital market, this step is probably as important as the revision of the financial system itself. The Japanese Securities and Exchange Law, as it stands today, has a list of specific instruments qualified as "securities." The report suggests that, by studying the definitions in the US and Europe as models, a new definition should be adopted which is extensive enough to include securitization-related instruments as an integral part of securities. At the same time, the report recommends that the framework for investor protection be streamlined. These measures are expected to encourage the development of new securitization-related instruments, to help make the Japanese capital market more solid and effective, and to foster an environment which promotes capital transactions around the world.

The report also stated that the private placement market needs to be streamlined and its functions expanded, given the increasing presence of institutional investors and the internationalization of the capital market. According to the report, these measures are desirable to make sure that issuers and investors both inside and outside Japan can make use of the Japanese market to raise and manage funds according to their needs. The Japanese private placement market is still subject to various restrictions, and its market size is much smaller than the public offering market. On the other hand, the market has become highly institutionalized in recent years, as has been demonstrated by the expansion of pension and investment trust funds. Instruments available for investment have become diversified and sophisticated due to securitization, deregulation, and technological progress, and investors can invest in overseas markets as well. Under these circumstances, investors need to become more sophisticated or otherwise able to trust professionals who can manage their assets on their behalf. At the same time, the private placement market is looked to as one that can freely introduce instruments tailor-made to the individual needs of issuers and investors. Therefore, it is of vital importance to streamline and develop the private placement market, which is composed of highly efficient and sophisticated investors with an in-depth understanding of the market.

Looking abroad, the Euromarket has few restrictions and is made up almost entirely of institutional and other professional investors. It trades in a wide variety of sophisticated financial products, as in a private placement market. In the US, private placement is also quite active: the issue volume has reached almost half the volume issued through public offering. In April 1990, a new rule concerning resale restrictions on privately placed securities, 144A, was introduced that has substantially increased the liquidity of privately placed securities. This will further encourage issues through private placement in the US. In this respect, the expansion of the market for professionals has become virtually a worldwide trend.

Increasing the flexibility of private placement and developing the entire private placement market in order to take full advantage of its inherent flexibility should be the ultimate goal in Japan as well. This is necessary to increase benefits to issuers and investors, as well as the benefits of individual investors whose assets are managed by professionals, thus promoting competition among different markets around the world.

6 CONCLUSION

Globalization requires that the Japanese bond market respond to the more complex and sophisticated needs of market participants. Taking a look abroad, we see that the major capital markets have already started to take the necessary steps to reform the current financial system, thereby affecting the surrounding financial environment.

In response to these domestic and international circumstances, wide-ranging financial reforms, including the demarcation of market intermediaries, are being considered by the Japanese government. The ultimate goal of the on-going financial reforms in Japan should be not only to provide increased convenience and competitiveness to attract borrowers and fund providers to the market, but also to strengthen Japan's reputation as a leading market, capable of contributing to the prosperity of the world economy. During the process of the financial reforms, maintaining the soundness of the market and simultaneously protecting the interests of bondholders should, of course, be taken into account.

APPENDIX

Articles 2 and 65 of the Securities and Exchange Law

[Definitions]

Article 2.   Securities referred to in this Law shall be as follows:

(1)   government securities,
(2)   municipal bonds,
(3)   debt securities issued under special enabling laws by juridical persons,
(4)   secured corporate bond or unsecured corporate debenture bonds,
(5)   equity investment certificates issued by juridical persons under special enabling laws,
(6)   share certificates (including certificates representing fractions of a share: the same shall apply to the term hereinafter) or certificates representing the right to subscribe to new shares,
(7)   beneficiary certificates of securities investment trusts or loan trusts,
(8)   securities or certificates issued by foreign countries or foreign juridical persons which are of the same nature as the securities or certificates referred to in the foregoing items, and
(9)   such other securities or certificates as may be prescribed by a Cabinet Order.

[Prohibition of securities business by financial institutions]

Article 65.

1.   No bank, trust company and such other financial institutions as may be prescribed by an Ordinance of the Ministry of Finance shall do as its business any of the acts set forth in the items of Paragraph 8 of Article 2: provided that this shall not apply to cases where any bank buys or sells securities or effects securities index futures trading, securities options trading or foreign market's securities futures

trading pursuant to a written order received from its customer for the account of such customer or where any bank, trust company and such other financial institutions as may be prescribed by a Cabinet Order buys or sells securities or effects securities index futures trading, securities options trading or foreign market's securities futures trading for the purpose of investment or pursuant to a trust agreement signed with its customers and for the account of such customers in accordance with the provisions of other laws.

2. The provisions of the main text of the preceding paragraph shall not apply to cases where any bank, trust company or such other financial institutions as may be prescribed by a Cabinet Order do any of the acts set forth in the following items with respect to securities or transactions set forth therein:

(1)· In the case of government securities, municipal bonds, bonds with respect to which the government guarantees the redemption of their principal and the payment of interest thereon, and other bonds (hereinafter in this Paragraph,, the next article and Paragraph 1 of Article 107-2 referred to as "government securities, etc."; acts referred to in the items (1) to (3), inclusive, or the same paragraph, only the buying or selling securities, and acts relating to the buying or selling of securities);

(2) In the case of transactions set forth below: acts referred to in items (1) to (3), inclusive, Paragraph 8 of Article 2;

(a) securities index futures trading and securities options trading relating to government securities, etc. (including securities index trading relating only to government securities, etc.);

(b) foreign market's securities futures trading (only government securities, etc. and securities index trading relating only to government securities, etc.);

(c) securities futures trading relating only to such securities referred to in item (8), Paragraph 1 of Article 2 which have the attributes of government securities;

(d) securities index futures trading and securities options trading relating to foreign government securities (including securities index trading of only foreign government securities);

(e) transactions similar to securities futures trading on foreign securities markets (only those relating to foreign government securities); and

(f) foreign markets securities futures trading (only those relating to foreign government securities and securities index of only foreign government securities).

NOTES

1   Although Japanese government bonds have different names depending on their legal basis, they are all identical in their economic meaning.
2   The bond issue ceiling is only a general principle. Some types of corporate bonds have special bond issue ceilings according to specific laws. For example, electricity power companies are allowed to issue bonds up to six times the net worth, and NTT (privatized in 1985) can issue bonds up to four times the net worth. Long-term credit banks can issue bank debentures up to 30 times the shareholders' equity and reserve.
3   The origin of the separation between banking business and securities business is not known in detail. It is generally believed that article 65 of the Securities and Exchange Law was introduced, without discussion, at the direction of the General Headquarters of the allied nations after the Second World War. See the appendix for the text of relevant sections of the law.
4   The report by the Financial System Research Council in 1989 referred to a multifunction subsidiary, capable of undertaking both banking and securities activities, as an exceptional arrangement for wholesale services. There are to be more discussions on this point.

REFERENCES

Annual Securities Statistics, Tokyo Stock Exchange, various issues.
Bond Review, Bond Underwriters' Association of Japan, various issues.
The Commercial Code of Japan (EHS Law Bulletin Series), ed. and trans. Fukio Nakane Eibun-Horei-Sha, Inc., Tokyo.
Economic Statistics Annual, Bank of Japan, various issues.
Economic Statistics Monthly, Bank of Japan, various issues.
Fundamental Research Committee of the Securities and Exchange Council 1990a: On restructuring the legal framework to deal with the securitisation of finance. Capital Market Research Institute, Tokyo.
Fundamental Research Committee of the Securities and Exchange Council 1990b: Restructuring Japan's capital market: toward an international market. Capital Market Research Institute, Tokyo.
Monthly Securities Report, Tokyo Stock Exchange, various issues.
Securities Business Report (*Shoken Gyo Ho*), Japan Association of Securities Dealers, various issues.
Securities and Exchange Council 1991: How the basic system regarding the capital market ought to be reformed. Capital Market Research Institute, Tokyo.
Securities and Exchange Law, July 1989, Capital Market Research Institute, Tokyo.

7

The Secondary Government Bond Market in Japan

Toshiharu Takahashi

1 INTRODUCTION

The government bond market is now the most important bond market in Japan in terms of size, trading volume, and function. In terms of size, the government bond market is by far the largest market, with an outstanding balance of 166 trillion yen (45.5 percent of the total outstanding bonds) at the end of March 1991. In terms of trading volume, the share of the government bond market is even greater. During 1990, for example, the trading volume (the sum of sales and purchases) of government bonds amounted to 2,693 trillion yen, or 78.8 percent of the total trading volume in the bond markets.[1] Finally, the government bond market has come to serve as a central market in which the term structure of interest rates is formed under the influence of the Bank of Japan's open-market operations.

In the early 1970s, the government bond market was only small. It began to expand, however, in the mid-1970s when the slowing down of the Japanese economy resulted in a widening of the public sector deficit and large-scale issues of government bonds. Between 1978 and 1986, for example, more than 10 trillion yen of government bonds were issued annually. As a result, the government bond market has expanded tremendously in last 15 years.

During this period of rapid growth, this market went through some important structural changes, including the relaxation of regulations on banks selling government bonds in 1977, the authorization for banks to deal in government and other public bonds in 1984, and the introduction of such derivative markets as the bond futures market (in 1985), the OTC option market for bonds (in 1989), and the option market for government bond futures (in 1990).

I am grateful to Shinji Takagi, Megumi Suto, and Akiyoshi Horiuchi for helpful comments and discussions. Financial support from the Japan Securities Scholarship Foundation is gratefully acknowledged.

The purpose of this chapter is to review the remarkable development of the Japanese government bond market. In so doing, it pays particular attention to the existence of benchmark issues and examines how it is related to the liquidity-creating function of the secondary market for government bonds.[2]

The remainder of the chapter is organized as follows. Section 2 reviews the rapid development of the government bond market from 1966 to 1990. Section 3 explains important organizational changes in the inter-dealer market, which led to the extremely rapid expansion of the government bond market in the 1980s. Section 4 discusses the interesting phenomena observed in the Japanese government bond market, that most trading is concentrated in single issue, called *shihyo meigara* (or benchmark issue), at a time, and that one benchmark issue is replaced by another at intervals of approximately one year. In this section, we argue that the presence of benchmark issues is closely related to the liquidity-creating function of the secondary government bond market. Finally, section 5 presents concluding remarks.

2   THE RAPID DEVELOPMENT OF THE GOVERNMENT BOND MARKET

Under its balanced budget principle, the central government issued no government bonds for revenue purposes from the middle of the 1950s until 1965, when the government began to issue seven-year fixed coupon bonds for the first time.[3] Since then, the government has continued to issue bonds up to the present time.

In characterizing the development of the government bond market, the period 1965–90 can be divided into two subperiods: from 1965 to 1974, and from 1975 to 1990. During first period strict regulations on banks limited the growth of the government bond market.[4] In contrast, the second period saw a rapid expansion of this market, owing to large-scale flotations of government bonds after 1975, as well as to the relaxation of regulations on banks.

2.1   Increase in the Outstanding Balance of Government Bonds

To begin with, let us place the Japanese government bond market in an international perspective by comparing it with the United States, the United Kingdom, and West Germany. According to figure 7.1, which shows the outstanding balance of government liabilities as a percentage of nominal GNP in each country from 1966 to 1988, Japan and West

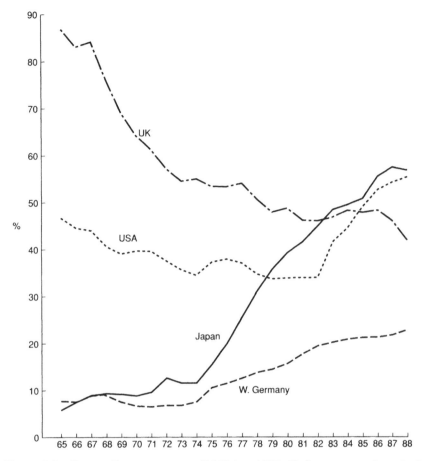

Figure 7.1 Outstanding government liabilities, 1965–88 (in percent of nominal GNP)

Source: Bank of Japan, *Kokusai Hikaku Tokei*, various issues

Germany had low debt–GNP ratios prior to 1975, while the UK and the US had high debt–GNP ratios. However, the ratios in the US and the UK gradually declined, while those in Japan and West Germany slowly increased during this period. In contrast, the debt–GNP ratio in all four countries began to rise after 1975. This tendency was particularly strong in Japan, and its debt–GNP ratio in turn exceeded West Germany in 1968, the US in 1979, and the UK in 1983. This rapid expansion of the Japanese government bond market was naturally accompanied by remarkable structural changes.

Table 7.1   Classification of bonds by type of issuer

Public bonds

Publicly offered bonds
- Government bonds
- Financing bills
- Government guaranteed bonds
- Municipal bonds
- Government affiliated corporation bonds

Privately placed bonds
- Government affiliated corporation bonds
- Municipal bonds

Corporate bonds

Publicly offered bonds
- Corporate bonds
- Convertible bonds
- Bonds with warrants

Privately placed bonds

Debentures

Foreign bonds

Next, let us review the position of the government bond market relative to all Japanese bond markets, where bonds can be classified by type of issuers as public bonds, corporate bonds, bank debentures, and foreign bonds (table 7.1).[5] According to figure 7.2, which shows the outstanding balance of each type of bond during the period 1965–90, the balance of public bonds was larger than that of any other type of bond for the period as whole. From 1966 to 1974, however, the difference was small. In fact, the outstanding balance of bank debentures was almost as large as that of public bonds. The share of public bonds began to increase at a rapid pace after 1975, and reached about 80 percent in the 1980s. Needless to say, the large-scale flotations of government bonds after 1975 were the driving force behind this development.

2.2   Policy of Pegging Government Bond Prices

Although the outstanding balance of government bonds increased from 1965 to 1974, the secondary market for government bonds did not develop sufficiently during this period because of the policy of pegging government bond prices. The Japanese government pursued this policy in order to raise funds at the regulated lower interest rates.[6]

From the beginning of the 1930s to the end of the Second World War, the Bank of Japan directly purchased government bonds, giving rise to

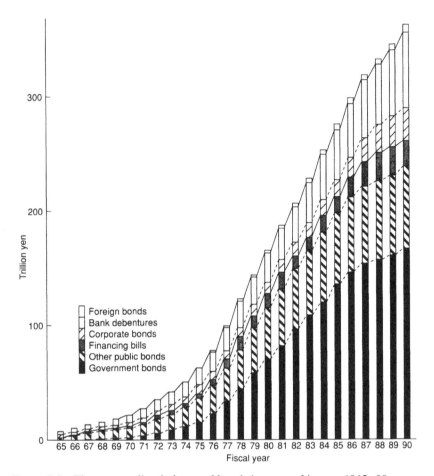

Figure 7.2 The outstanding balance of bonds by type of issuer, 1965–90

Source: Bond Underwriters' Association of Japan, *Koshasai Geppo*, various issues

the acceleration of inflation during the war. Because of this experience, article 5 of the Finance Law of 1947 was made, in principle, to prohibit the Bank of Japan from directly subscribing to government bonds. As a result, the Japanese government has issued government bonds only by "public issue" during the postwar period.

In Japan, however, the meaning of the term "public issue" has been widely understood to include public auction, fixed-rate auction, indirect public issue, and offer for sale. The most widely used method of public issue for government bonds was indirect public issue, in which a syndicate of banks and securities companies directly subscribed more than one-half of government bond issues. In the traditional operation of this system, the share of each bank was determined according to its financial power, and only about 10 percent of government bond issues were sold through securities companies to individual investors. In the case of undersubscription, the syndicate would subscribe the remainder.[7]

Moreover, the issuing rates of government bonds were determined at levels lower than their corresponding secondary market yields. This was feasible for the following reasons. First, banks were strictly prohibited from selling their government bonds freely in the secondary market. Second, there was an implicit understanding that the Bank of Japan would purchase most of the subscribed government bonds from the banks after one year. In this manner, the liquidity of government bonds was assured, despite the fact that the secondary market was not well developed.

Furthermore, the Bank of Japan determined the buying price of government bonds so as to minimize the banks' capital loss, if any, of selling government bonds. This practice was based on the following three principles. First, the buying prices were determined according to the secondary prices formed at the stock exchanges. Second, however, securities companies were obliged to buy government bonds at predetermined prices at the exchanges when there was a possibility that selling pressure might cause the prices to decline. Third, the Bank of Japan actively purchased government bonds held by securities companies with a view to providing them with the needed liquidity.

The method of public issue in which the syndicate played the major role was in fact a system of *indirect subscription of government bonds* by the Bank of Japan, because the system was based on the implicit guarantee that the subscribed bonds would be purchased by the Bank of Japan at predetermined prices after one year. While this system supported the policy of pegging the prices of government bonds and provided liquidity, it impeded the well-balanced development of a secondary government bond market in Japan.

2.3   Deregulation of Government Bond Transactions

The large-scale flotations of government bonds after 1975 necessitated measures to relax or abolish the regulations in the government bond market. Liberalization was more pronounced in the secondary market than in the primary market, although both were significantly affected.

2.3.1   Primary market

The authorities have introduced some important measures in the primary market for government bonds. For example, in addition to long-term

(10-year) fixed-coupon government bonds which have continued to occupy the central part of government bond issues, they began to issue new types of bonds in order to facilitate the absorption of government bonds in the market, including discount government bonds (January 1977), medium-term government bonds (June 1978), 15-year variable-rate government bonds (February 1983), short-term government bonds (February 1986), and 20-year fixed-coupon government bonds (October 1986).

The authorities also introduced public auctions in the public issues of medium-term government bonds, short-term government bonds, and 20-year fixed-coupon government bonds. In the case of the long-term government bonds, they introduced public auctions by syndicate of a portion of new issues in April 1989. While the structure of the primary market for government bonds has changed, however, there are still regulations remaining that need to be eased or abolished to allow the further development of the secondary market in coming years.[8]

2.3.2 Secondary market

Figure 7.3 shows trading volume of the secondary market by type of bond during the period 1966–90 (see also table 7.1). It shows that bank debentures were the most actively traded bonds between 1966 and 1978, when they were replaced by government bonds. It is noticeable that there has always been a definite tendency for secondary bond transactions to converge on a specific type of bond in each period.

The share of government bonds in total bond trading between 1979 and 1990 was much higher than that of bank debentures between 1966 and 1978. For example, the share of bank debentures was 40.6 percent in 1970 and 40.1 percent in 1975, while the share of government bonds was 58.1 percent in 1980 and 78.8 percent in 1990. The average annual growth rate of government bond transactions was 162.3 percent between 1975 and 1980, 59.5 percent between 1980 and 1985, and 9.2 percent between 1985 and 1990, indicating that the development of the government bond market conditioned that of the Japanese secondary bond market as a whole in the 1980s.

As will be discussed more fully in section 3, there is little doubt that easy monetary policy contributed to the rapid growth of the secondary government bond market in the second half of the 1980s. At the same time, we must not underestimate the importance of a series of deregulatory measures on government bond transactions, which were implemented under the conditions of large issues of government bonds after 1975. In particular, one of the two most important developments was the series of measures (begun in April 1977) to liberalize the restrictions on

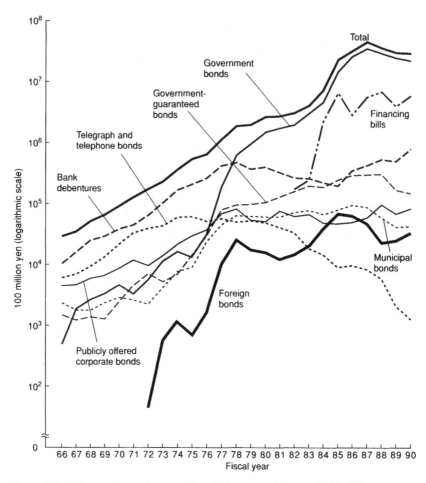

Figure 7.3   The trading volume of bonds by type of issuer, 1966–90*

*   The trading volume in the *gensaki* market (repurchase market) is included in the data.

Sources: Securities Dealers' Association, *Shoken Gyoho* (Report on the Securities Industry), various issues; and Tokyo Stock Exchange, *Tosho Tokei Geppo* (Monthly Statistics Report), various issues

the sales of subscribed government bonds by banks. With these measures, the policy of pegging government bond prices was virtually abandoned. The other important development was the series of measures (begun in June 1984) to allow banks to deal in public bonds (so-called *bank dealing*).[9] Bank dealing provided an institutional foundation for the rapid development of the interdealer market for government bonds, as is explained in the next section.

3 STRUCTURAL CHANGES AND GROWTH OF THE INTERDEALER MARKET

The secondary bond market can be divided into the interdealer market (where dealers trade bonds with one another) and the dealer–customer market (where bond dealers transact bonds with public investors). According to this classification, the so-called over-the-counter (OTC) market consists of transactions in the dealer–customer market and direct transactions between bond dealers in the interdealer market. A considerable part of the structural changes and growth of the Japanese bond markets in the 1980s concerned the interdealer market.

3.1 Structural Changes in the Interdealer Market

The interdealer market now consists of three channels of trading: direct trading, trading through bondbrokers, and trading on the stock exchanges. Before the middle of the 1970s, however, the interdealer market outside the stock exchanges was made up of four separate direct trading markets, each of which was dominated by one of the Big Four securities companies, Nomura, Nikko, Daiwa, and Yamaichi. Each market had as its members those affiliated securities companies (called *keiretsu* companies) which were licenced for bond dealing. In other words, each interdealer market was highly segmented, with one of the Big Four at the top, and with the medium and smaller companies of its *keiretsu* group forming the rest of the market.[10]

In 1973, however, the Securities Exchange Council (an advisory body to the Minister of Finance) questioned the rationality of such a segmented market structure, and recommended that the four internal bond markets be integrated in order to increase the transparency of price formation in the interdealer market for public investors. In response, securities companies (including the Big Four) jointly established a bondbroker company, called *Nihon Sogo Shoken* (the Japan Bond Trading Corporation, abbreviated in Japan as BB for Brokers' Broker) in 1973.[11] Although we shall not discuss the role which the BB has played in the integration process of the interdealer market, it is certain that it has significantly contributed to the expansion of government bond transactions between the Big Four securities companies, especially after 1977. The BB also played a catalytic role in expanding bond trading at the stock exchanges of Tokyo, Osaka, and Nagoya, which were all thus stimulated to begin block trading of government bonds in 1979.[12]

The authorization of bank dealing in government bonds was another important structural development in the interdealer market.[13] The number of banks authorized for bankdealing, which was only 34 in 1984,

Table 7.2   Trading volume in the interdealer market (IDM) (in hundreds of millions of yen; percent)[a]

Calendar year	IDM (A)	Total (B)	(A)/(B)
1977	32,650	339,637	9.61
1978	121,439	906,028	13.40
1979	132,570	890,027	14.90
1980	237,034	1,130,383	20.97
1981	313,350	1,469,824	21.32
1982	470,609	1,875,183	25.10
1983	687,295	2,494,390	27.55
1984	1,928,437	5,463,032	35.30
1985	12,922,269	17,768,307	72.73
1986	12,045,727	16,395,205	73.47
1987	24,289,837	31,280,681	77.65
1988	14,677,665	20,376,158	72.03
1989	12,371,166	16,805,519	73.61
1990	11,171,704	14,645,972	76.28

[a]   The trading volume is defined as the sum of sales and purchases. The trading volume in the repurchase market is not included in the data.

Source: Securities Dealers' Association, *Shoken Gyoho* (Report on the Securities Industry), various issues

gradually increased and reached 216 at the end of 1988, a comparable figure to the 220 securities companies. The authorization of bankdealing in public bonds implied that banks could now participate in the inter-dealer market, so that the transaction network among market participants expanded greatly within a short period. At the same time, it gradually changed the implicit *transaction rules* that prevailed under conditions of direct trading between securities companies dominated by the Big Four. This must have helped to integrate the interdealer market and to promote competition among bond dealers.

3.2   Growth of Government Bond Transactions in the Interdealer Market

Let us move on to characterize the developments of the interdealer market. Table 7.2 shows the volume of bond trading (the sum of sales and purchases) in the interdealer market as well as in the entire sec-ondary bond market from 1977 to 1990. From the table, we find that the growth rate of trading volume in the interdealer market was much higher than that in the secondary bond market as a whole. From 1977 to 1988, the average compounded rate of growth was 56.4 percent per year in the interdealer market, as compared with 36.7 percent in the secondary bond market (Takahashi 1991). This means that secondary bond transactions had a conspicuous tendency to concentrate in the interdealer market. At the end of the 1970s, the share of the interdealer market in total secondary trading was only about 10 percent, but it increased to between 70 and 80 percent in the second half of the 1980s.

Tables 7.3 and 7.4 show the volume of trading by type of bond in the BB and the stock exchanges. According to table 7.3, trading shares by type of bond in the BB changed drastically between 1973 and 1990. Until around 1976, Telegraph & Telephone coupon bonds and bank debentures were the most actively traded bonds on the BB. In 1977, however, government bonds jumped to 28.4 percent, and continued to increase in subsequent years. By 1984, most of trading in the BB had become concentrated in government bonds.

As tables 7.3 and 7.4 show, there was little difference between the BB and the stock exchanges in terms of historical changes in the trading shares of different types of bond. With the introduction of block trading of government bonds in 1979, most bond trading on the stock exchanges also began to be concentrated in government bonds. Along with the increase in trading volume, both the BB and the stock exchanges have reduced the rates of commission for different types of bond on several occasions since the end of the 1970s. In the case of government bonds, for example, the commission rate at the end of the 1980s was one-tenth of the rate in the 1970s.

The BB and the stock exchange differ in that the former is a private securities company while the latter is a membership organization consisting of many securities companies. However, their functions as *interdealer brokers* in the interdealer market are almost identical, because they both perform a similar function: searching out compatible partners among bond dealers and negotiating acceptable terms for them. Whereas direct trading was the dominant form of bond trading in the segmented inter-dealer market until the end of the 1970s, the subsequent process of market integration caused the share of direct trading to decline. For example, it decreased to 50 percent in 1982 and 30 percent in 1988.[14] The interdealer market changed structurally during the 1980s from a direct trading market to a brokered market.

4 THE LIQUIDITY-CREATING FUNCTION OF THE GOVERNMENT BOND MARKET

The development of the government bond market in the 1980s was led by the rapid expansion of the interdealer market, where most of the trading

Table 7.3　Trading volume by type of bond in the interdealer market (in hundreds of millions of yen; percent)[a]

Calendar year	Government bonds	Municipal bonds	Government guaranteed bonds	Publicly offered corporate bonds	Bank debentures	Others[b]	Total
1974	7	65	36	987	2,602	103	3,800
	(0.20)	(1.71)	(0.96)	(25.97)	(68.47)	(2.71)	(100)
1975	19	1,155	75	1,994	3,100	673	7,016
	(0.27)	(16.45)	(1.08)	(28.42)	(44.18)	(9.60)	(100)
1976	99	2,360	193	3,127	5,200	816	11,795
	(0.84)	(20.01)	(1.64)	(25.61)	(44.09)	(6.92)	(100)
1977	7,331	3,358	542	2,858	10,282	1,312	25,683
	(28.54)	(13.07)	(2.11)	(11.13)	(40.03)	(5.11)	(100)
1978	28,199	2,555	568	2,411	23,348	1,082	58,163
	(48.48)	(4.39)	(0.98)	(4.15)	(40.14)	(1.86)	(100)
1979	27,310	2,128	1,427	2,393	14,899	929	49,076
	(55.65)	(4.34)	(2.91)	(4.88)	(30.34)	(1.89)	(100)
1980	72,820	1,676	731	2,104	15,738	897	93,966
	(77.50)	(1.78)	(0.78)	(2.24)	(16.75)	(0.95)	(100)
1981	73,366	2,550	2,183	2,749	18,548	1,261	100,657
	(72.89)	(2.54)	(2.17)	(2.73)	(18.43)	(1.25)	(100)
1982	115,573	2,500	2,257	2,914	16,045	746	140,035
	(82.53)	(1.78)	(1.61)	(2.08)	(11.46)	(0.53)	(100)

1983	208,834	4,557	5,529	1,377	19,190	817	240,304
	(86.90)	(1.90)	(2.30)	(0.57)	(7.99)	(0.34)	(100)
1984	496,307	2,004	3,107	296	16,279	439	518,432
	(95.73)	(0.39)	(0.60)	(0.06)	(3.14)	(0.09)	(100)
1985	2,561,035	377	667	83	7,125	417	2,569,704
	(99.66)	(0.02)	(0.02)	(0)	(0.28)	(0.01)	(100)
1986	5,227,349	90	470	0	8,057	93	5,236,059
	(99.83)	(0)	(0.01)	(0)	(0.15)	(0)	(100)
1987	12,849,983	91	226	0	6,532	2	12,856,834
	(99.95)	(0)	(0.01)	(0)	(0.05)	(0)	(100)
1988	8,815,199	927	15,641	461	32,796	44	8,865,068
	(99.44)	(0.01)	(0.18)	(0.01)	(0.37)	(0)	(100)
1989	8,021,111	956	12,421	1,474	60,085	394	8,096,441
	(99.07)	(0.01)	(0.15)	(0.02)	(0.74)	(0)	(100)
1990	7,528,770	616	4,508	1,360	66,131	267	7,601,652
	(99.04)	(0.01)	(0.06)	(0.02)	(0.87)	(0)	(100)

a   The trading volume is defined as the sum of sales and purchases. These figures refer only to those transactions effected through the *Nihon Sogo Shoken* (BB). The numbers in parentheses are percentages of total.
b   Others include convertible bonds, yen-denominated foreign bonds, and so on.

Source: Nihon Sogo Shoken, as privately provided to the author

Table 7.4 Trading volume by type of straight bonds at the stock exchanges (in hundreds of millions of yen; percent)[a]

Calendar year	Government bonds	Block trading	Telegraph and telephone bonds	Bank debentures	Publicly offered corporate bonds	Foreign bonds	Others[b]	Total
1970	469 (9.27)		4,200 (82.96)	42 (0.83)	292 (5.78)		59 (1.17)	5,063 (100)
1971	526 (7.03)		6,577 (87.94)	38 (0.50)	282 (3.77)		57 (0.76)	7,479 (100)
1972	574 (6.32)		8,022 (88.30)	68 (0.74)	361 (3.98)		60 (0.66)	9,085 (100)
1973	971 (17.78)		3,826 (70.07)	70 (1.28)	393 (7.20)	137 (2.51)	64 (1.17)	5,461 (100)
1974	1,133 (33.50)		1,634 (48.30)	68 (2.02)	388 (11.47)	96 (2.85)	63 (1.86)	3,383 (100)
1975	1,117 (33.59)		1,543 (46.41)	74 (2.22)	378 (11.37)	163 (4.89)	51 (1.53)	3,326 (100)
1976	715 (23.06)		1,730 (55.78)	80 (2.58)	361 (11.64)	169 (5.46)	46 (1.47)	3,102 (100)
1977	1,143 (30.23)		1,862 (49.25)	80 (2.12)	349 (9.24)	301 (7.96)	46 (1.21)	3,780 (100)
1978	1,465 (34.60)		1,936 (45.73)	80 (1.88)	337 (7.96)	371 (8.75)	46 (1.08)	4,235 (100)
1979	16,854 (86.11)	14,339 (73.26)	1,937 (8.90)	80 (0.41)	338 (1.72)	318 (1.62)	46 (0.23)	19,573 (100)
1980	37,390 (93.20)	33,593 (83.73)	1,963 (4.89)	80 (0.20)	336 (0.84)	304 (0.76)	46 (0.11)	40,119 (100)

1981	58,401 (95.68)	55,080 (90.24)	1,879 (3.08)	80 (0.13)	332 (0.54)	298 (0.49)	46 (0.07)	61,035 (100)
1982	101,409 (97.53)	97,416 (93.69)	1,842 (1.77)	80 (0.08)	318 (0.31)	282 (0.27)	46 (0.04)	103,976 (100)
1983	203,142 (98.96)	198,566 (96.74)	1,424 (0.69)	80 (0.04)	319 (0.16)	255 (0.12)	46 (0.02)	205,266 (100)
1984	491,234 (99.67)	485,750 (98.55)	977 (0.20)	80 (0.02)	286 (0.06)	258 (0.05)	46 (0.01)	492,880 (100)
1985	862,233 (99.81)	856,490 (99.14)	869 (0.10)	80 (0.01)	256 (0.03)	407 (0.05)	46 (0.01)	863,891 (100)
1986	1,087,761 (99.83)	1,082,200 (99.32)	774 (0.07)	78 (0.01)	226 (0.02)	751 (0.07)	45 (0)	1,089,635 (100)
1987	1,254,044 (99.78)	1,242,638 (98.87)	695 (0.06)	77 (0.01)	220 (0.02)	1,768 (0.14)	42 (0)	1,256,845 (100)
1988	788,124 (99.83)	780,586 (98.87)	597 (0.08)	76 (0.01)	213 (0.03)	420 (0.05)	52 (0)	789,482 (100)
1989	656,234 (99.85)	653,450 (99.43)	419 (0.06)	70 (0.01)	190 (0.02)	254 (0.04)	45 (0)	657,214 (100)
1990	845,291 (99.90)	836,680 (98.89)	291 (0.03)	69 (0.01)	177 (0.02)	231 (0.03)	45 (0)	846,103 (100)

a The trading volume is defined as the sum of sales and purchases at the Tokyo, Osaka, and Nagoya Stock Exchanges. The numbers in parentheses are percentages of total.
b Others include municpal bonds and government guaranteed bonds.

Sources: Tokyo Stock Exchange, *Tosho Tokei Geppo;* Osaka Stock Exchange, *Daisho Tokei Geppo;* and Nagoya Stock Exchange, *Meisho Tokei Geppo,* various issues was concentrated in government bonds. An additional feature of the Japanese government bond market, moreover, is the phenomenon that, among many outstanding issues of government bonds, a succession of single issues, called *shihyo meigara* (or benchmark issues), has dominated the secondary trading. As it turns out, the presence of *shihyo meigara* is closely related to the liquidity-creating function of the secondary market for government bonds.

4.1   Characteristics of Benchmark Issues

Shihyo meigara in the Japanese government bond market is often said to correspond to a benchmark issue in the US government securities markets. In fact, the meaning of *shihyo* in Japanese is almost equivalent to "benchmark" in English. However, there is an important difference between them. A benchmark issue in the US is a most-recent government securities issue, whose price conveys information for those who plan to issue similar securities. In contrast, *shihyo meigara* in Japan is defined as an issue of long-term (10-year fixed-coupon) government bonds with the largest trading volume in the secondary market. Although it is similar to a benchmark issue in that it conveys a kind of compressed information concerning secondary bond market conditions, it may not necessarily be the most recent government bond issue. Despite this conceptual difference, we shall use *shihyo meigara* and benchmark issues inter-

Table 7.5   Benchmark issues of government bonds, 1979–91

Benchmark issue	Redemption date	Coupon (percent)	Tenure as a benchmark issue	Number of months
G.10	May 88	6.1	Apr. 79–Oct. 81	31
G.21	Aug. 89	7.7	Nov. 81–Jul. 82	9
G.41	Feb. 91	8.0	Aug. 82–Nov. 82	4
G.21	Aug. 89	7.7	Dec. 82–Aug. 82	9
G.53	Jan. 93	7.5	Sep. 83–Aug. 84	12
G.59	Dec. 93	7.3	Sep. 84–Apr. 85	8
G.68	Dec. 94	6.8	May 85–Dec. 85	8
G.78	Jul. 95	6.2	Jan. 86–Oct. 86	10
G.89	Jan. 96	5.1	Nov. 86–Nov. 87	13
G.105	Dec. 97	5.0	Dec. 87–Nov. 88	12
G.111	Jun. 98	4.6	Dec. 88–Nov. 89	12
G.119	Jun. 99	4.8	Dec. 89–Jan. 91	14

Sources: Tokyo Stock Exchange, *Tosho Tokei Geppo* (Monthly Statistics Report); and *Nihon Sogo Shoken*, as provided privately to the author

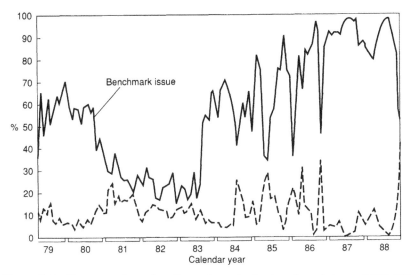

Figure 7.4 Concentration of trading volume in the benchmark issue, 1979–88*

* The solid line represents the ratio of trading volume of the benchmark issue to the volume of total trading; the dotted line represents the ratio of trading volume of the second most actively traded issue.

Sources: Tokyo Stock Exchange, *Tosho Tokei Geppo* (Monthly Statistics Report); and *Nihon Sogo Shoken*, as provided privately to the author

changeably during the rest of this chapter as long as there is no possibility of confusion.

Table 7.5 lists the benchmark issues of government bonds in the BB and the Tokyo Stock Exchange from 1979 to 1990.[15] The table indicates that one benchmark issue was successively replaced by another one, and that each issue had a certain measure of continuity, with tenure ranging from 4 to 31 months.

Figure 7.4 shows the ratio of the trading volume of the benchmark issues (the most actively traded issue) to the volume of total trading (the solid line) as well as the ratio of the second most actively traded issue (the dotted line) between 1979 and 1988. Concentrating on the solid line, we can divide the entire period into two subperiods, from April 1979 to August 1983, and from September 1983 to December 1988. After a jump in September 1983, the concentration ratio of benchmark issues remained at a high level in subsequent months, except when an old benchmark issue was replaced by a new one. When the 89th issue of government bonds (abbreviated as G.89) was the benchmark issue in 1986 and 1987, the concentration ratio was as high as 80 to 90 percent. In contrast, the

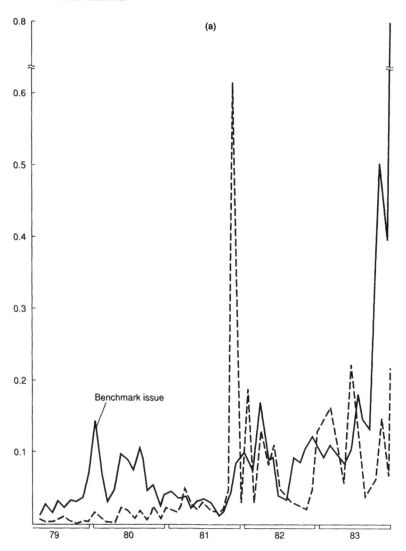

Figure 7.5 Turnover rate of benchmark issues, 1979–88*

* The solid line represents the ratio of monthly trading volume to the amount outstanding of the benchmark issue; the dotted line shows the ratio for the second most actively traded issue.

Source: as for figure 7.4

concentration ratio of the second most actively traded issue shows no observable difference across the entire sample period.

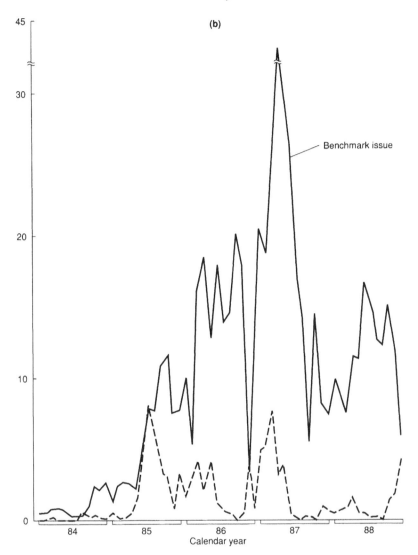

Next, let us see the turnover rate of benchmark issues (the solid line), defined as the ratio of the monthly trading volume to the amount outstanding (figures 7.5a and 7.5b). Both figures make it clear how government bonds trading in the interdealer market became concentrated in benchmark issues. While the turnover rate was between 0.01 and 0.2

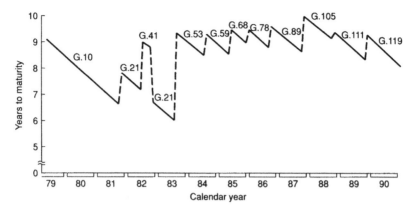

Figure 7.6   The maturities of benchmark issues, 1979–90

Source: as for figure 7.4

before September 1983, it increased rapidly in subsequent months, reaching 11.6 (for G.68) in November 1985, 20.4 (for G.78) in September 1986, and 43.6 (for G.89) in April 1987. As the turnover rate of the second most actively traded issue (the dotted line) shows no appreciable increase over this period, the rapid increase in the turnover rate since September 1983 was specific to benchmark issues.

Finally, figure 7.6 shows maturities of benchmark issues. According to the figure, the maturity ranged from six to nine years before 1984. After 1984, however, the maturity was always more than eight years, although it changed cyclically.

4.2   Functions of Benchmark Issues

The characteristics of benchmark issues pose at least two interesting questions. First, what accounts for the creation of benchmark issues in the interdealer market? Second, what is the mechanism by which one benchmark issue is successively replaced by another? We shall discuss the first question in this subsection, and the second question in the next subsection.

It is convenient to think of a trading process among bond dealers in the interdealer market as consisting of at least three steps: (a) search, (b) negotiation, and (c) settlement. Imagine a general case in which a bond dealer wants to purchase a specific issue of a government bond. In the first place, the dealer must search out a compatible seller and negotiate with him concerning the terms and conditions (for example, the price, the settlement day, the minimum unit of transaction) so as to achieve a contract acceptable to both sides. And if the dealer does not hold sufficient cash, he will have to finance the deficit fund until settlement day.

Now, suppose that there is a transaction cost in each step, so that the total transaction cost can be expressed as the sum of (a) search cost, (b) negotiation cost, and (c) settlement cost.[16] We can then consider the function of the BB as that of reducing the first two components of the transaction cost through its brokerage services. Of course, this argument also applies to the brokerage function of the stock exchanges.[17]

Even in such a brokered market, however, compatible trading partners may not be readily identifiable because there are many government bond issues with different maturities, coupon rates, and outstanding amounts. It is for this reason that there is additional room for reducing the transaction cost. For example, the transaction cost can be reduced further if the interdealer market endogenously creates certain *transaction rules* for many market participants to follow implicitly. In this sense, the use of benchmark issues can be considered as one such transaction rule.

4.2.1 Benchmark issues I

In general, a bond dealer keeps an inventory stock of various issues of bonds in order to respond quickly to the buying and selling orders of public investors. However, he cannot accurately forecast future orders, so he relies on the interdealer market to make inventory adjustments when there is an excess or shortage of desired bond issues. However, there remains a possibility that the bond dealer may not be able to find a compatible partner.

Suppose that the bond dealer happens to run short of (or hold an excess) of a particular bond issue (I_i) and desires to restore the optimum inventory stock. In this case, he may first purchase (sell) a different bond issue (I_B) in the interdealer market, just to recover the initial inventory level, and decide to wait for a compatible seller (buyer) of (I_i). When the appropriate seller (buyer) is found, he will then replace $I_B(I_i)$ with $I_i(I_B)$ so as to restore the optimum inventory position. In this example, if most of bond dealers behave the same way, trading of I_B could become active in the interdealer market, thus reducing the search and negotiation costs.

We argue that a bond issue such as I_B corresponds to the benchmark issues in the interdealer market before September 1983 (hereafter, designated *benchmark issues I*); the applicable government bond issues ranged from G.10 to G.21 (table 7.5). It is important to understand that benchmark issue I is not only individual bond issues but also represents a transaction rule that is effective within the interdealer market. It should be emphasized that benchmark issue I is not necessarily peculiar to the

Japanese government bond market. For example, the concept is similar to the use of a vehicle currency (such as the US dollar) in international transactions. Both could be considered as transaction rules that have been endogenously created among market participants as a means of reducing transaction costs.

4.2.2   Benchmark issues II

It seems that the functions of benchmark issues were expanded in the latter half of the 1980s, with an increasing number of banks being authorized to deal in government bonds and the Bank of Japan easing monetary conditions. During this period, in addition to the functions of benchmark issues I to reduce the search and negotiation costs, benchmark issues II have performed the additional function of reducing the settlement cost arising from the rapid expansion of speculative bond trading in the latter half of the 1980s.[18]

According to the Japanese practice of bond trading, all contracts whose maturity dates fall within a certain contract period can be settled on the same future day. This is why benchmark issues II can reduce the settlement cost. Suppose that, at the beginning of the contract period, a bond dealer makes a buying (selling) contract in expectation that the bond price will rise (fall), and that the expectation will be realized. In this case, the dealer can close his buying (selling) position by simultaneously making an offsetting selling (buying) contract within that period; he can obtain the capital gain without making a cash payment (taking physical delivery). If we further assume that most bond dealers implicitly agree to carry out speculative bond trading by means of a common bond issue, we can easily understand why benchmark issues II can reduce not only the search and negotiation costs but also the settlement cost.

When benchmark issues II have such a transaction cost-saving (or liquidity-creating function), its yield is expected to be lower than the yield of other government bond issues with a similar maturity and coupon rate. That is to say, benchmark issues II are expected to have a *liquidity premium*. In fact, between August 1985 and January 1986, the benchmark issue G.68 (with a coupon rate of 6.1 percent and a redemption date of December 20, 1994) had a liquidity premium over another issue, G.71 (with a coupon rate of 6.1 percent and a redemption date of January 20, 1995). Figure 7.7 shows that the simple yield of G.71 was higher than that of G.68 by between 0.1 and 0.5 percentage points.[19] The magnitude of the liquidity premium is regarded by most bond dealers as non-negligible.[20]

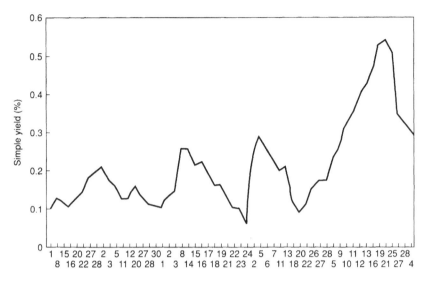

Figure 7.7 The liquidity premium of the benchmark issue, August 1, 1985 to January 4, 1986*

* The benchmark issue during this period was the government bond issue G.68; G.71 was used as the alternative bond issue to calculate the liquidity premium.

Source: *Nihon Sogo Shoken*, as provided privately to the author

4.2.3 Switching in benchmark issues II

Next, we must examine the process by which one benchmark issue II is replaced by another with a certain measure of regularity. Figure 7.8 shows how such a switch might occur. On December 26, 1985, G.78 immediately took over from benchmark issue G.68, in terms of both trading volume and yield. An examination of other cases suggests that a switch in benchmark issues II has usually completed its process within a few days. We believe that the switching process is closely related to the creation of a liquidity premium as well as to the changes in the maturity of benchmark issues.

On the one hand, it is desirable to keep the same benchmark issue II as long as possible in order to minimize transaction costs in the inter-dealer market. On the other hand, a bond dealer holding the current benchmark issue is always faced with the possibility of capital loss because sooner or later it will be replaced by a new benchmark issue and lose its liquidity premium. Alternatively, the dealer can make a capital gain if the candidate issue that he purchases in anticipation of a switch does become the next benchmark issue and obtains a liquidity premium.

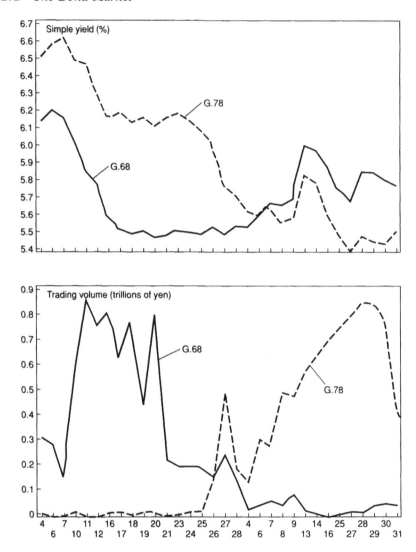

Figure 7.8 Switching of benchmark issues, December 4, 1985 to January 31, 1986

Source: as for figure 7.7

Because most bond dealers attach importance to the opportunities of capital gains and losses, their expectations alone can sever the continuity of benchmark issues II.

Another aspect of the switching process concerns the changing maturity of the benchmark issue II. As a matter of necessity, the maturity of a benchmark issue II becomes continuously shorter, resulting *ceteris paribus* in a smaller price volatility. Most bond dealers in the latter half of the 1980s, however, preferred short-term speculative bond trading; these same dealers are said to have frequently completed a round of buying and selling transactions on the same trading day. It was for this reason that many dealers preferred, other things being equal, a benchmark issue II with a longer maturity.

To summarize, benchmark issues II have two characteristics. First, they represent a transaction rule to reduce the transaction cost and create liquidity. Second, they serve as a financial instrument by which most bond dealers carry out speculative trading to obtain capital gains. A balance of these forces triggers a switching of benchmark issues II.

Finally, one last remaining question concerns who or what determines the switch. One simple answer may be that one of the Big Four securities companies determines the switch either individually or collectively. However, this answer ignores the fact that many leading banks in Japan have also entered the interdealer market since 1984, so that the market is now much larger and more competitive than it used to be. It is probably safe to say that even the Big Four securities companies do not have enough influence to determine the candidate for the next benchmark issue II, much less the timing of the switch. A more likely answer would be that the switch of benchmark issues has been endogenously determined by the implicitly cooperative behavior of bond dealers in the interdealer market.[21]

5 CONCLUDING REMARKS

In this chapter we have discussed the rapid development of the Japanese government bond market, focusing attention on the relationship between the remarkable structural changes in the secondary market and its liquidity-creating function. In this context, three developments since 1975 are noteworthy. First, most of secondary bond trading in the Japanese bond markets became concentrated in government bonds. Second, there was a remarkable development of the interdealer market in the secondary bond market. Third, trading of government bonds in the interdealer market became concentrated in benchmark issues of government bonds (*shihyo meigara*). In sum, trading in the Japanese bond markets has tended to converge on *shihyo meigara* since the end of the 1970s.

We have argued that this interesting phenomenon is closely associated with the transaction-cost-saving or liquidity-creating function of the secondary bond market. Certainly, there is little doubt that the recent deregulation of government bond transactions has contributed to the development of the government bond market in Japan. As far as the creation of benchmark issues is concerned, however, it appears that the secondary bond market, especially the interdealer market, has created transaction rules endogenously as a means of reducing transaction costs.

During the period 1966–77, the policy of pegging government bond prices was pursued, and the liquidity of government bonds was ensured by the Bank of Japan through its operations to purchase government bonds from private banks and securities companies. We can interpret this as a kind of transaction rule for liquidity creation. When the policy of pegging government bond prices was abandoned, market participants endogenously created private transaction rules to create liquidity in the form of benchmark issues of government bonds.

NOTES

1   In this chapter, figures are quoted on a fiscal year basis, unless otherwise noted. Note that March is the last month of the fiscal year.
2   For a general treatment of the Japanese government bond market, see Fabozzi (1990) and Matukawa (1990).
3   The central government did issue short-term government bills to cover temporary shortfalls of Treasury funds. In addition, local government bonds and government guaranteed bonds were also issued throughout the postwar period.
4   The banking sector consists of city banks, regional banks, long-term credit banks, trust bands, and other types of small banks. See Suzuki (1987) for an explanation of Japanese financial institutions.
5   Bank debentures are issued by three long-term credit banks, the Bank of Tokyo, the *Norin Chukin* Bank, and the *Shoko Chukin* Bank.
6   The maturity of long-term government bonds was increased from seven years to ten years in January 1972.
7   The Trust Fund Bureau (*Shikin Unyo Bu*) of the Ministry of Finance is a public financial institution that has also subscribed a portion of government bond issues.
8   We do not discuss these problems in detail. See Matukawa (1990).
9   Over-the-counter sales of government bonds by banks, authorized in 1983, served as an important step leading to the authorization of bankdealing.
10   The number of securities companies was 271 at the end of 1970 and 258 at the end of 1975. See Suto (1987) for an analysis of *keiretsu* relations between Japanese securities companies.
11   There is another bondbroker company called *Nakadachi Shoken*. In the following discussion, however, this company will be ignored because its trading volume is small relative to the trading volume of the *Nihon Sogo Shoken*.

12 The block trading of government bonds (for 10 million yen or more in par value) in the securities exchanges also follows the continuous *zaraba* trading rule of the BB.

13 For one year, there was a restriction that banks could deal only in public bonds with a maturity of less than two years.

14 Because there are no available data on the volume of direct trading, I have made a rough estimate of it by subtracting the volume of trading in the BB and the stock exchanges from the volume of trading in the entire interdealer market. See Takahashi (1991).

15 Although the data include only the BB and the Tokyo Stock Exchange because of data availability, they can be considered to represent the entire government bond market for all practical purposes.

16 Since 1980, the Bank of Japan has operated the government bond book-entry system to facilitate the delivery and custody of government bonds. This system must have contributed to a reduction in the settlement cost.

17 In government bond transactions, the securities transfer tax of 0.03 percent is levied on the transferer. In the case of securities companies, however, the reduced rate of 0.01 percent is applicable. Along with the government and local public bodies, the BB and the stock exchanges are exempt from the payment of the securities transfer tax.

18 The government securities lending market, set up in May 1989, is also expected to help reduce the settlement cost. The fact that more than half of the lending volume has been accounted for by benchmark issues gives additional support to our argument.

19 The simple yield (i) in figure 7.7 is defined as:

$$i = \{C + (F - P)/m\}/P.$$

where C is the coupon rate, F is the redemption value, m is the maturity, and P is the transaction price.

20 No significant liquidity premium was present in benchmark issues I.

21 This mechanism can be regarded as a self-organizing system to create its own rules. See Takahashi (1991).

REFERENCES

Arai, Yo 1991: *Nichibei Koshasai Shijo Hikaku* (Comparative Study of Bond Markets in the US and Japan). Tokyo: Nihon Keizai Shinbun Sha.

Argyrople, Christopher and Rutledge, Thomas C. 1990: The Japanese government bond market. In Frank J. Fabozzi (ed.), *The Japanese Bond Markets*, Chicago: Probus Publishing.

Fabozzi, Frank J. (ed.) 1990: *The Japanese Bond Markets*. Chicago: Probus Publishing.

Matukawa, Takashi (ed.) 1990: *Kokusai* (Japanese Government Bond). Tokyo: Okura Zaimu Kyokai.

Shimura, Kaichi (ed.) 1980: *Nihon Koshasai Shijo Shi* (A History of the Japanese Bond Markets). Tokyo: Koshasai Hikiuke Kyokai.

Shoken Torihiki Shingi Kai (Securities and Exchange Council) 1973: Naigai no Kinyu Josei no Henka nitomonau Koshasai Shijo no Arikata nitsuite (What should the Japanese bond markets be with changes in economic and monetary situations at home and abroad?). Tokyo.

Suto, Megumi 1987: *Nihon no Shoken Gyo* (The Securities Industry in Japan). Tokyo: Toyo Keizai Shinpo Sha.

Suzuki, Yoshio (ed.) 1987: *The Japanese Financial System*. Oxford: Clarendon Press.

Takagi, Shinji 1987: Transactions costs and the term structure of interest rates. *Journal of Money, Credit, and Banking*, 19(4), 516–27.

Takahashi, Toshiharu 1991: *Nihon no Koshasai Shijo to Kinyu Shisutemu* (The Bond Markets and the Financial System in Japan). Tokyo: Toyo Keizai Shinpo Sha.

Williamson, Oliver E. 1985: Transactions-cost economics. *Journal of Law and Economics*, 22(4), 233–61.

Part IV

The Equity Market

8

Seasoned Equity Issues in Japan

Hideki Hanaeda

1 INTRODUCTION

This chapter analyzes *seasoned* (as opposed to *initial*) equity issues in Japan, which are issues of stock occurring when common stocks of the companies concerned have previously been issued publicly.[1] Although new equity issues have been relatively insignificant as a financing method for Japanese corporations, the relative importance of new equity shares has been increasing in recent years. Moreover, there is an interesting analytical issue relating to the choice between rights offerings and public offerings. This chapter will offer and test several hypotheses to explain why new stock issues have been predominantly public offerings in Japan.

To get a grasp of the overall position of new equity issues in the financing of Japanese corporations, table 8.1 summarizes the financing patterns of large Japanese corporations during the period 1970–89. Drastic changes in the method of financing can be seen during this period. For example, the proportion of internal funds (which includes retained earnings, reserves, and depreciation) increased dramatically from 29.9 percent in 1970–4 to 64.8 percent in 1985–9. In contrast, the proportion of external sources declined significantly from 70.1 percent to 35.2 percent during the same period.

The relative increase in the proportion of internal funds mainly reflects the decrease in borrowing from 35.8 to 3.3 percent. While the main sources of funds for Japanese corporations were borrowings from banks (particularly big city banks and long-term credit banks) through the 1960s, many of them were faced with sharp declines in profits and a heavy burden of interest payments on borrowings at the time of the oil crises of 1973 and 1979. Faced with such situations, they realized the necessity of avoiding heavy dependence on borrowing and decreasing the debt–equity ratio of capital. As a result, the proportion of borrowing to total financing decreased to 20.4 percent in 1975–9, and the decline continued from then on.

In contrast, the proportion of corporate bonds increased from 4.3

Shinji Takagi provided comments on an earlier draft.

Table 8.1   Internal and external financing of Japanese corporations, 1970–89 (percent of total)

	1970–4	*1975–9*	*1980–4*	*1985–9*
Internal sources	29.9	47.0	51.6	64.8
of which:				
retained earnings	5.9	7.7	10.8	14.6
reserves	5.2	3.7	2.4	3.2
depreciation	18.8	35.6	38.4	47.0
External sources	70.1	53.0	48.4	35.2
of which:				
new equity issues	2.9	7.8	9.6	16.9
borrowing[a]	35.8	20.4	15.3	3.3
corporate bonds[b]	4.3	10.1	7.8	19.2
trade payables	15.1	7.3	7.5	−9.4
miscellaneous	12.0	7.4	8.2	5.2

[a]   Short-term and long-term borrowing plus bills discounted.
[b]   Straight bonds, convertibles, and bonds with warrants.
The number of corporations is about 620; they are all listed on the stock exchange, with capital of one billion yen or over. Financial institutions and insurance companies are not included.

Sources: Bank of Japan, *Shuyo Kigyo Keiei Bunseki* (Business Analysis of Main Enterprises in Japan), various issues

percent in 1970–4 to 19.2 percent in 1985–9. Among corporate bonds, the issue of convertible bonds and bonds with warrants became predominant in 1985–9, as shown in figure 8.1. This resulted from the considerable deregulation of the Japanese capital market in the latter half of the 1980s (Hodder and Tschoegl 1993; Hoshi, Kashyap, and Scharfstein 1990), as well as the fact that many Japanese corporations could issue equity-linked securities at very low coupon rates (about 1 or 2 percent, when the coupon rate of straight bonds was about 5 percent) because investors held high expectations that the bonds would be converted into stocks at a comfortable profit, once the underlying share price rose above the conversion price.

Finally, the proportion of new equity issues increased from 2.9 percent in 1970–4 to 16.9 percent in 1985–9, as shown in table 8.1. This was mainly a result of sharp increases in stock prices in the Tokyo stock market during 1985–9. Because of the stock market crash, however, the issue volume of new equities sharply declined in 1990 and 1991. The total amount of equity issues by listed firms is shown for each year from 1970 to 1990 in table 8.2. Here, it is also noticeable that the share of rights

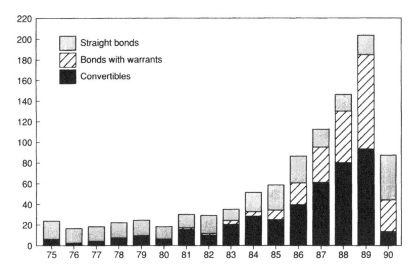

Figure 8.1   New issues of corporate bonds (in hundreds of billions of yen)*

*   Each amount includes both the domestic and the overseas issues.

Source: Bond Underwriters' Association of Japan, *Koshasai Geppo* (Bond Review), various issues

offerings fell from 79 percent in 1970 to 26.5 percent in 1990, while the share of public offerings increased from 20.3 percent to 63.4 percent during the same period.[2]

In fact, the only method used to raise additional equity capital by listed corporations in Japan was rights offerings until 1968, where the subscription price for each new share was par value. It was only in 1969 that a listed corporation used underwritten public offerings for the first time. As table 8.2 indicates, underwritten public offerings have rapidly increased in importance, so that more than 70 percent of the total amount raised by equity financing has been by public offerings since 1980.[3]

The remainder of the chapter is organized as follows. Section 2 discusses the reasons why a majority of Japanese corporations now choose public offerings. It also examines the characteristics of those corporations that use only rights offerings when most others use public offerings. Section 3 analyzes stock price behavior associated with public offerings. The analysis addresses the problem of conflict between current stockholders and new stockholders. If the offer price is greater than the true value of the issued security and the stock price drops after the issue, investors who bought the new issue realize low rates of return on their investment. This means that old stockholders gain at the expense of new

Table 8.2 Equity issues and offering methods of listed firms (in billions of yen; percent of total)

| | Total issues | Offering methods | | |
		Rights offering	Public offering	Private offering
1970	681	79.0	20.3	0.7
1971	537	76.2	15.6	8.2
1972	1,041	27.3	63.9	8.8
1973	939	36.6	60.2	3.2
1974	544	44.9	50.9	4.2
1975	1,001	77.0	22.2	0.8
1976	689	26.1	72.6	1.3
1977	923	31.5	65.4	3.1
1978	897	29.8	63.0	7.2
1979	953	27.5	66.0	6.5
1980	1,052	8.6	83.7	7.7
1981	1,926	25.6	72.5	1.9
1982	1,347	16.6	81.9	1.5
1983	772	17.5	61.1	21.4
1984	977	0.9	84.0	15.1
1985	722	25.3	70.1	4.6
1986	500	13.8	80.0	6.2
1987	1,939	22.5	71.9	5.6
1988	3,473	22.7	74.3	3.0
1989	6,659	10.9	87.6	1.5
1990	3,115	26.5	63.4	10.1

Source: *Tokyo Stock Exchange Fact Book, 1991*

stockholders. On the other hand, if the offer price is lower than the true value, new stockholders get a bargain at the expense of old stockholders, and receive capital gains when the stock price rises subsequent to new issues.

Section 4 uses the same methodology to examine the stock price behavior of firms issuing rights offerings. Here, the interesting question is whether or not stock prices associated with rights offerings have a different pattern of movement from those associated with public offerings. Section 5 analyzes whether or not stock price changes that occur after public offerings can be explained by either stock price changes occurring prior to the offering or the volume of the issue. Finally, section 6 presents concluding remarks.

2 REASONS FOR THE CHOICE OF PUBLIC OFFERINGS

2.1 Relative Cost of Public Offerings

The flotation costs, or the out-of-pocket expenses, associated with raising additional equity capital consist mainly of taxes, commission and fees, printing expenses, and mailing and communications expenses. For underwritten public offerings, commission paid to underwriters for underwriting services amounts to 3.5 to 4 percent of the money raised and equals almost 80 percent of total out-of-pocket expenses. For rights offerings, no commission needs to be paid to underwriters, and the out-of-pocket expenses are about 40 percent less than in underwritten public offerings.[4]

In underwritten public offerings, other costs are incurred in addition to

Table 8.3 The rates of discount of offering prices in public offerings (percent)

Year	Average	Maximum	Minimum
1970	12.75	22.59	3.85
1971	15.08	27.71	5.38
1972	13.52	29.27	5.38
1973	9.71	17.76	6.86
1974	9.68	15.00	4.75
1975	9.56	10.77	5.75
1976	9.54	10.12	8.16
1977	7.63	9.35	5.88
1978	6.29	7.27	3.45
1979	5.71	6.52	3.81
1980	5.43	6.02	3.53
1981	4.81	6.43	3.38
1982	4.78	5.09	3.80
1983	4.33	5.00	2.78
1984	3.40	4.00	2.74
1985	3.29	4.00	2.66
1986	3.33	3.69	2.64
1987	3.32	4.51	2.78
1988	3.27	3.84	2.83
1989	3.21	3.50	2.88

Source: Shoji Homu Kenkyukai, *Shoji Homu* (The Commercial Law Review), annual issues

the out-of-pocket expenses. In the Japanese stock market it is a common practice to discount an offer price at some percentage of the market price of each stock at the issuing date. Table 8.3 shows a recent history of average discount rates. The average rate gradually fell from 12.75 percent in 1970, but it was still 3.21 percent in 1989. This creates an additional cost for current stockholders.

Based on a comparison of the out-of-pocket and other costs, there is little doubt that rights offering is a cheaper method of raising additional equity capital than is underwritten public offering. Yet the majority of Japanese corporations now choose underwritten public offerings rather than rights offerings. The question of why many corporations would prefer underwritten public offerings has created a puzzle for corporate finance analysts.

2.2   Two Traditional Reasons for Public Offerings

At least two reasons have in the past been proposed to explain this phenomenon. First, the most common argument relates to the uncertainty of returns from real investment and the common dividend policy practice of Japanese corporations. With rights offerings, corporations can arbitrarily set the subscription price. Although the subscription price does not have to be at par, many Japanese corporations have followed the practice of setting it at par for many years. (However, this practice has gradually been changing.)

If a firm financed investment by a rights offering when the market price was higher than par value, more shares would be issued than with a public offering under the same conditions. Meanwhile, many Japanese corporations have their own target dividend per share that they intend to sustain. Given this dividend policy, a firm would be faced with higher dividend payments immediately after a rights offering, even though it usually takes a few years before it can start to pay back the initial outlay on real investment. Moreover, it is uncertain at the time of the rights offering how large a return can be obtained in the future.

Consequently, firms prefer to limit the increase of outstanding stocks by choosing public offering. In many cases, when earnings actually increase or the prospect of future earnings becomes certain, some stocks are granted gratis to the existing stockholders and more dividends are disbursed as a result of the increase in the number of outstanding stocks.

The fact that only the rights offering was used prior to 1968 has been used to support this argument. For a short period after the Second World War, the discrepancy between the market value and the par value of common stocks was small, so that managers did not have a strong incentive to issue underwritten public offerings. Hence both managers and investors considered rights offerings as the only available method of raising capital, and that practice continued for a long time.

However, the rapid increase of the stock prices of many corporations during 1969 and 1970 brought about a huge discrepancy between the market value and the par value of common stocks. At this time, managers began to have an incentive to use underwritten public offerings, even though the direct expenses of using them were higher than with rights offerings. (In this period, the Japanese government also encouraged the introduction of underwritten public offerings because of its worldwide use.)

Second, another argument to explain the choice of public offerings relates to the importance of retained earnings in the context of informational asymmetry. If total dividend payments are limited by public offering, a firm can accumulate more retained earnings after the issue. The existence of informational asymmetry between outside investors and the inside manager about the future prospects of the firm reinforces the manager's preference toward retained earnings, as is suggested by Myers and Majluf (1984). The persistent increase of the proportion of retained earnings in the total sources of financing (from 5.9 percent in 1970–4 to 14.6 percent in 1985–9), as shown in table 8.1, is consistent with this argument.

2.3   Two Additional Reasons for Public Offerings

In addition to these traditional reasons, I propose that two additional reasons exist to explain the preference of Japanese corporations for public offerings. Both of these reasons have easily testable implications. In what follows, I list these two reasons and then test their implications against recent data.

First, the choice between the use of rights offerings and public offerings is also influenced by ownership distribution. For example, a firm which does not want to disperse equity ownership, such as an owner-managed firm or a subsidiary company, would want to keep equity ownership concentrated. With public offerings, current stockholders who have majority votes of control would risk the dilution of equity ownership and face the possibility of large block purchases by hostile investors. In contrast, a manager who is not concerned about the dilution of equity ownership tends to choose public offering because of the reasons mentioned in the previous subsection.

Second, the choice of underwritten public offerings helps to establish a close and long-term relationship with an underwriter, thus allowing a firm to obtain comprehensive services from that underwriter concerning the issue of equity, straight bonds, convertible bonds, and bonds with warrants. The most important point in the financing decision of the firm is to choose an optimal mix of financing methods and to time these issues in a way that is most suitable to the firm's strategic and financial planning. The amount and timing of the issue of each security should be determined simultaneously and be consistent with long-term financial planning.

In Japan, these underwriting services are provided mainly by the Big Four securities companies: Nomura, Daiwa, Nikko and Yamaichi. These companies also provide brokerage and dealer services, as well as advisory services for firms, portfolio management, and financing. If this argument about the usefulness of having access to comprehensive services is valid, firms which seek the overall and continuing advice of underwriters should prefer underwritten public offerings. In this context, Suto (1987) argues that there are stable and persistent relationships between particular firms and securities companies.

2.4   Characteristics of Rights Offering Firms

As an indirect test of these additional hypotheses, I shall examine firms that used only rights offerings as their method of equity financing, even during the recent period when public offerings were popular. The hypotheses imply that these firms were seriously concerned about the dilution of equity ownership and that they did not need the overall advice or services to corporate finance from the underwriters.

I first examine firms that used only rights offerings as the method of equity financing between 1972 and 1988, excluding banks and other financial institutions. The sample firms include companies listed on the Tokyo and other stock exchanges. In total, 394 firms issued rights offerings during this period. Of these, 151 firms did not use public offerings at all. Though the subscription prices were equal to par value in many cases, 19 firms placed the subscription prices above par value.

In order to examine the characteristics of these 151 firms, it is useful to group them by ownership structures as follows: A, owner-managed or family-partnership firms; B, subsidiary or affiliated firms; and C, other firms. The number of firms belonging to types A, B, and C are 39, 64, and 48, respectively. The total number of A and B types is 103, meaning that about 70 percent of the 151 firms represented are of type A or B (table 8.4). According to the first hypothesis, type A and B firms should dislike the dilution of ownership caused by public offerings. The result, showing that a majority of the firms which used only rights offerings were either type A or B, is consistent with this hypothesis. In this context, Hansen and Pinkerton (1982) reported that a characteristic of many rights offering firms in the US was also that the ownership of equity was concentrated in a few stockholders.

Table 8.4 Characteristics of rights offering firms

Firm type[a,b]	*Average size*[c] (millions of yen)	Convertible bonds	Bonds with warrants	Private placement
A (39)	320,000	4	1	7
B (64)	510,000	3	5	16
C (48)	4,070,000	22	15	2
Total (151)		29	21	25

[a] A = owner-managed or family-partnership firms
    B = subsidiary or affiliated firms
    C = other firms
[b] Figures in parentheses are numbers of firms of each type.
[c] The figures are the average size of total assets in each firm type.

Moving on to the hypothesis about the usefulness of comprehensive services, table 8.4 shows the number of firms which issued convertible bonds, bonds with warrants, and private placements of equity among the 151 firms, classified by type A, B, and C, as in the preceding paragraph. The total number of these firms which issued convertible bonds and bonds with warrants are 29 and 21, respectively. Although not listed in the table, 10 firms issued both types of bonds, so that the numbers of firms issuing only convertible bonds or bonds with warrants are 19 and 11, respectively, bringing the total number of firms issuing either type of bonds to 40, or only 26 percent of 151 firms. This seems to show that rights offering firms rarely needed bond financing advice from a underwriter, thus giving support to our hypothesis.

Moreover, 25 percent of type B firms placed equity privately. Nearly entire issues of private placement were sold to the parent company or group companies. Apparently, in such situations the parent company advises its subsidiary on financial planning in a way consistent with its own, and buys the new equity from the subsidiary through private placement. As a result, type B firms have no need to depend on underwriters.

Finally, the average size of the total assets of the 151 firms is 32 billion yen for type A, 51 billion yen for type B, and 407 billion yen for type C firms. These figures suggest that type A and type B firms are relatively small. From this evidence, it might be argued that they were precluded from the use of public offerings because they did not satisfy the necessary criteria and consequently resorted to rights issues.

In the Japanese stock market, public offerings are substantially regulated by a voluntary rule called the *jishu* rule. This rule, which is an agreement made among underwriters in 1973, has restricted the number of new issues to less than 10 percent of the total outstanding equity for small firms that have equity capital of under 5 billion yen. The voluntary restriction, however, has gradually been relaxed, and in 1981 the figure was raised to 15 percent of the total outstanding equity. In special cases, moreover, an increasing number of small firms with equity capital of less than 500 million yen have been allowed to issue new equity up to 20 percent of the outstanding amount of equity. Under these more relaxed rules, we believe that even small type A and B firms should now be able to raise necessary funds by public offering.[5]

3   PUBLIC OFFERINGS AND STOCK PRICE BEHAVIOR

3.1   Two Opposing Views of Stock Price Behavior

In Japan's business community, there are two diametrically opposed opinions concerning the stock price behavior that surrounds public offerings. Some argue that it is a good bargain to buy the stock of firms which plan to issue new stocks, because underwriters cause the market stock price to rise through their selling efforts. According to this view, there is such severe competition for the lead underwriter position among the Big Four securities companies that they sometimes manipulate the market price of the stock of a firm that plans a new equity issue.

On the other hand, others argue that the stock price of the issuing firm drops after the issue, because the issuing firm sometimes manipulates its stock price in the planning stage so as to offer an artificially higher issue price, and the stock price declines to its natural level after the issue. In addition, they also mention the possibility that an increased supply of stock creates downward price pressure. In this section, we study the average stock price behavior of many public offering firms in order to examine this controversy.[6]

3.2   Procedure for a New Public Issue

Before proceeding further, it may be useful to describe briefly the practical procedure for public offerings and the discounting of the offer price in the primary stock market in Japan. The offer price is determined about one month after formal approval by the firm's board of directors and the announcement of the public offering of new stock. It is common practice to set the offer price some percentage points lower than the market price at that date.

There are about ten days between the determination of the offer price and the final offer date. During this period, the underwriter is allowed by the Securities and Exchange Law to support the market price by repurchasing stocks at that price. The final payment date is usually in the latter half of the month and the period between the final offer date and final payment is about 10 days. Table 8.3 shows the average discount rates of public offerings during the period 1970–89. As previously mentioned, the average rate has gradually fallen from 12.75 percent in 1970, but remained steady at 3.21 percent in 1989.

3.3 The Analytical Method

We employ an event study analysis to examine whether or not equity issues cause abnormal price changes in stocks around public offerings.[7] The return to security i in month t is represented by

$$R_{it} = \alpha_i + \beta_i R_{mt} + e_{it} \tag{8.1}$$

where R_{it} is the return to security i in month t adjusted for capital structure changes, R_{mt} is the return to the market portfolio in month t, and e_{it} is a stochastic disturbance on the ith security for month t.

If the expected value of e_{it} is assumed to be zero, then the expected value of the return to security i is expressed as $\alpha_i + \beta_i R_{mt}$. This is the normal return to security i. The difference between the actual return and the normal return to security i is called the excess return, EXR_{it}, which is represented by

$$EXR_{it} = R_{it} - (\alpha_i + \beta_i R_{mt}) \tag{8.2}$$

Setting $t = 0$ for the month of the public offering, $t = -1$ for the month just prior to the public offering, $t = +1$ for the month immediately following the public offering, and so on, we calculate EXR_{it} for each security for 25 months around the offering. We then calculate the average excess return of sample firms for each t and call it the average excess return, EXR_t.

$$EXR_t = \frac{1}{N} \sum_{i=1}^{N} EXR_{it} \tag{8.3}$$

The value which cumulates the average excess returns from $t = K$ to $t = L$ is called the average cumulative excess return ($CER_{K,L}$):

$$CER_{K,L} = \sum_{t=K}^{L} EXR_t \tag{8.4}$$

3.4 Data

Based on the information collected from special issues of *Shoji Homu* (The Commercial Law Review), we obtained a sample of firms which satisfied the following five criteria: (a) firms must have made public

Table 8.5   The number of sample firms

Year	Public offerings Case A	Case B	Rights offerings
1975		20	5
1976		40	2
1977	9	18	7
1978	12	29	7
1979	11	25	1
1980	26	30	12
1981	32	33	13
1982	17	20	3
1983	7	5	5
Total	114	220	55

offerings during the period 1975–83; (b) firms must have been listed on the First Section of the Tokyo Stock Exchange; (c) The number of new issues in public offering must have exceeded one million shares, in order to avoid the problem of small issue size; (d) firms must not have made another rights offering, private placement, or public offering within one year of the public offering; (e) firms must have complete data which allow the calculation of the rate of return on equity. The data on the rate of return were selected from the monthly data of the Japan Securities Research Institute, *Kabushiki Toshi Shuekiritu* (The Rate of Returns of Stock Investment).

Table 8.5 shows the number of firms which satisfied the above criteria. In the table, case A represents those firms that raised funds for fixed investment only, while case B comprises those firms that also raised funds for working capital or repayment of debt. Since the use of funds raised was not made explicit prior to 1977, all firms are included in case B for 1975 and 1976.

3.5   Empirical Results

3.5.1   Case A firms

The values of α_i and β_i in equation (8.1) must be estimated before we can obtain the excess returns in equation (8.2). I calculate these values in two ways. First, by setting $t = 0$ for the month of the public offering, we estimate the parameters α_i and β_i from the market portfolio and the rate of return data for the 36 months from $t = -48$ to $t = -13$ for each firm.

These estimates are then used to calculate the excess returns from
$t = -12$ to $t = 0$ in equation (8.2). In addition, the excess returns from
$t = +1$ to $t = +12$ are calculated by using the estimates of α_i and β_i,
which are similarly estimated by using data from $t = +13$ to $t = +48$. We
refer to these results as model 1.

Second, we estimate α_i and β_i using the market portfolio and the rate
of return data for 72 months for each firm, excluding the 25 months
around the date of the offering (that is, from $t = -48$ to $t = -13$, and
from $t = +13$ to $t = +48$). The estimates of α_i and β_i are then used to
calculate EXR_{it} in equation (8.2) for each firm for the 25 months around
the offering. The results obtained by this method are referred to as
model 2.

Table 8.6 Excess and cumulative excess returns of Case A firms in public
offerings (percent)

t	Model 1		Model 2		Model 3	
	EXR_t	$CER_{-12,t}$	EXR_t	$CER_{-12,t}$	EXR_t	$CER_{-12,t}$
−12	1.513	1.513	1.818	1.818	2.316	2.316
−11	−0.576	0.937	−0.268	1.550	0.111	2.427
−10	−0.901	0.036	−0.447	1.103	−0.171	2.256
−9	1.094	1.130	1.675	2.778	1.824	4.080
−8	0.202	1.332	0.760	3.538	0.985	5.065
−7	1.083	2.415	1.221	4.759	1.663	6.728
−6	1.063	3.478	0.650	5.409	1.067	7.795
−5	−1.755	1.723	−1.841	3.568	−1.563	6.232
−4	0.397	2.120	0.547	4.115	0.769	7.001
−3	0.082	2.202	0.157	4.272	0.610	7.611
−2	−0.485	1.717	−0.363	3.909	0.178	7.789
−1	1.003	2.720	0.879	4.788	1.282	9.071
0	1.322	4.042	1.086	5.874	1.432	10.503
+1	−1.993	2.049	−2.053	3.821	−1.704	8.799
+2	−1.129	0.920	−1.169	2.652	−0.890	7.909
+3	−1.505	−0.585	−1.514	1.138	−1.489	6.420
+4	−0.939	−1.524	−1.000	0.138	−0.713	5.707
+5	−0.139	−1.663	−0.241	−0.103	0.201	5.908
+6	−0.893	−2.556	−1.012	−1.115	−0.831	5.077
+7	1.055	−1.501	0.993	−0.122	1.368	6.445
+8	−0.873	−2.374	−0.917	−1.039	−0.727	5.718
+9	−0.956	−3.330	−1.035	−2.074	−1.511	4.207
+10	−0.377	−3.707	−0.373	−2.447	0.114	4.321
+11	0.515	−3.192	0.393	−2.054	0.421	4.742
+12	0.980	−2.212	0.818	−1.236	0.889	5.631

For both models, we then average the excess returns (EXR_t) over all firms for each month in the interval of $t = -12$ to $t = +12$ in equation (8.3). These average excess returns are then cumulated from month $t = -12$ to the event month. The results for case A (firms which raised funds for fixed investments only) are presented in table 8.6 and figure 8.2.

The results show that there is no substantial difference between model 1 and model 2. The monthly average excess returns in the year before the offering are positive, except for four months. But after the offering, all average excess returns from $t = +1$ to $t = +10$ are negative except at $t = +7$. Since the average excess returns in the months of $t = +11$ and $t = +12$ are positive, the downward tendency of the excess return seems to disappear one year after the offering. From these results, however, we cannot immediately conclude that the subscribers of the public offerings gained less than the risk-adjusted normal returns. As explained earlier in this section, we must take the discounting of the offer price into consideration.

As the final payment date is usually in the latter half of the month and the period between the final offer date and final payment is about ten days, we can assume that the announcement of the offer price, the offer, and the payment are all made at $t = 0$, and that the announcement of the public offering is made at $t = -1$. The price change between the announcement of the offer price and the final payment date is considered negligible because of the underwriter's efforts to stabilize the price. If the offer price is set equal to the market price when it is announced, the rate of return for the subscriber of the new issue at one month after the

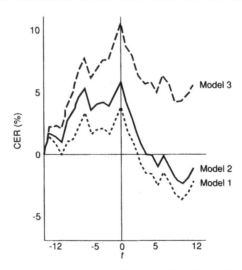

Figure 8.2   Cumulative excess returns of Case A firms in public offering

offering is given by $R_1 = ((p - p_0) \times 100)/p_0$ where p_1 is the price at $t = +1$ and p_0 is the price at $t = 0$. When the offer price is discounted below the market price, however, R_1 has to be revised according to

$$R_1^* = \frac{p_1 - (1 - \delta)p_0}{(1 - \delta)p_0} \times 100 = \frac{100\delta + R_1}{1 - \delta} \qquad (8.5)$$

where R_1^* is the rate of return with discounting, and δ is the discount rate. Likewise, the excess return also has to be revised according to

$$EXR_1^* = \frac{100\delta + EXR_1}{1 - \delta} \qquad (8.6)$$

where EXR^* is the excess return with discounting.[8]

In model 1, for example, EXR_1 is -1.993 percent, while the revised EXR_1^* equals 3.583 percent if the discount rate is set at 5.383 percent (the average of annual average discount rates from 1977 to 1983, weighted by the number of sample firms in each year). Using the revised EXR^*, the average cumulative excess return $CER_{1,12}$ from $t = +1$ to $t = +12$ is -0.678 percent in model 1 and -1.538 percent in model 2. From these results, we may conclude that the excess return over one year for the subscribers is close to zero and not unduly low, although neither did they receive excessively high returns. Rather, they received normal rewards consistent with the risk.

In order to check the sensitivity of these conclusions, we now calculate the excess rate of return for each stock by replacing equation (8.2) with the following:

$$EXR_{it} = R_{it} - R_{mt} \qquad (8.7)$$

Equation (8.7) expresses the excess rate of return of each stock as the difference between the actual rate of return and the average market rate of return, according to the market-adjusted returns model. We refer to this as model 3, the results of which are also shown in table 8.6. Although CER is relatively higher in model 3 than in model 1 or model 2, it has a similar pattern of change across different models. A more interesting result concerns the behavior of CER after the offering. The CER which was calculated by using the revised EXR^* is 0.72 percent and close to zero, as is the case for model 1 and model 2. All the models indicate that investors who subscribed to the new issues of stocks did not receive higher or lower rates of return than the risk-adjusted normal return.

3.5.2 Case B firms

Next, we perform the same analysis for the 220 firms categorized as case B in table 8.5. The results are reported in table 8.7 and figure 8.3. *CER*

Table 8.7   Excess and cumulative excess returns of Case B firms in public offerings (percent)

t	Model 1		Model 2		Model 3	
	EXR_t	$CER_{-12,t}$	EXR_t	$CER_{-12,t}$	EXR_t	$CER_{-12,t}$
−12	0.438	0.438	0.847	0.847	1.198	1.198
−11	1.249	1.687	1.760	2.607	2.530	3.728
−10	1.990	3.677	2.479	5.086	2.662	6.390
−9	0.786	4.463	1.287	6.373	1.428	7.818
−8	1.954	6.417	2.531	8.904	2.890	10.708
−7	0.334	6.751	0.947	9.851	1.249	11.957
−6	−0.027	6.724	0.589	10.440	1.078	13.035
−5	−0.553	6.171	−0.036	10.404	0.260	13.295
−4	0.271	6.442	0.716	11.120	1.097	14.392
−3	−0.240	6.202	0.251	11.371	0.696	15.088
−2	−0.702	5.500	−0.091	11.280	0.184	15.272
−1	1.848	7.348	2.321	13.601	2.789	18.061
0	1.086	8.434	1.522	15.123	2.074	20.135
+1	−0.057	8.377	−0.360	14.763	−0.056	20.079
+2	−0.649	7.728	−1.141	13.622	−0.998	19.081
+3	−0.259	7.469	−0.618	13.004	−0.440	18.641
+4	0.197	7.666	−0.278	12.726	−0.285	18.356
+5	−0.888	6.778	−1.310	11.416	−1.107	17.249
+6	0.365	7.143	0.068	11.484	−0.130	17.119
+7	−1.280	5.863	−1.634	9.850	−1.451	15.668
+8	−0.631	5.232	−0.869	8.981	−0.539	15.129
+9	−0.311	4.921	−0.583	8.398	−0.772	14.357
+10	0.096	5.017	−0.201	8.197	−0.167	14.190
+11	0.636	5.653	0.417	8.614	0.658	14.848
+12	0.533	6.186	0.148	8.762	0.479	15.327

shows a similar pattern across the three models, except for some event months. After the issue, the excess returns continue to have negative values, but this tendency seems to disappear after about one year.

Based on the discounting of the issue price, we then calculate *CER* using the revised excess returns as we did for case A. For the discount rate δ, we use the average annual discount rate from 1975 to 1983, weighted by the number of firms in each year. With the value of δ calculated at 6.701 percent, the revised *CER* was 4.93 percent in model 1, 0.795 percent in model 2, and 2.37 percent in model 3. From these results, we may conclude that the investors who subscribed to public offerings received a slightly higher excess rate of return than the rates of return found for case A.

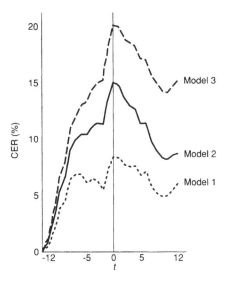

Figure 8.3 Cumulative excess returns of Case B firms in public offering

4 RIGHTS OFFERING AND STOCK PRICE BEHAVIOR

In this section we examine the stock price behavior of rights offerings firms in order to see whether or not their stock prices show a similar pattern of movement to those of public offering firms. The analytical method of the preceding section is employed, and the selection of sample firms is based on the same selection rule as in the case of public offerings. For the period 1975–83, 55 firms are selected, as shown in table 8.5. We wish to examine the rate of return to investors subscribing to rights offerings, assuming that they buy stocks just before the date of the assignment of rights (that is, at $t = 0$).

The empirical results are shown in table 8.8 and figure 8.4. In figure 8.4, the excess return at $t = -2$ is very high (4 or 5 percent) in each model. Since the determination and announcement of rights offerings are usually made two months before the offering date in Japan, $t = -2$ is the month of the announcement of the rights offering, and the stock price responded positively in that month. After the issue, the average excess return EXR_t is negative from $t = 0$ to $t = +6$, except for $t = +2$ and $t = +5$, the average cumulative excess return CER decreases for these months. After $t = +7$, however, CER increases because of a positive EXR_t.

Table 8.8   Excess and cumulative excess returns of rights offering firms (percent)

t	Model 1		Model 2		Model 3	
	EXR_t	$CER_{-12,t}$	EXR_t	$CER_{-12,t}$	EXR_t	$CER_{-12,t}$
−12	2.236	2.236	3.111	3.111	3.629	3.629
−11	−0.897	1.339	−1.221	1.890	−0.479	3.150
−10	−1.619	0.280	−1.498	0.392	−1.332	1.818
−9	−1.629	−1.909	−2.198	−1.806	−1.533	0.285
−8	−1.052	−2.961	−1.210	−3.016	−0.781	−0.496
−7	0.337	−2.624	0.312	−2.704	1.218	0.722
−6	0.865	−1.759	1.013	−1.691	1.921	2.643
−5	1.911	0.152	1.620	−0.071	2.223	4.866
−4	1.313	1.465	1.245	1.174	1.589	6.455
−3	1.331	2.796	1.275	2.449	1.820	8.275
−2	4.629	7.425	4.606	7.055	5.211	13.486
−1	−0.349	7.076	0.141	7.196	0.382	13.868
0	−0.377	6.699	−0.799	6.397	0.222	14.090
+1	−1.829	4.870	−1.636	4.761	−0.715	13.375
+2	2.128	6.998	1.882	6.643	2.190	15.565
+3	−3.754	3.244	−3.793	2.850	−2.918	12.647
+4	−0.781	2.463	−0.723	2.127	−0.419	12.228
+5	0.064	2.527	0.024	2.151	0.459	12.687
+6	−0.884	1.643	−1.217	0.934	−1.430	11.257
+7	0.763	2.406	0.481	1.415	0.282	11.539
+8	1.587	3.993	1.154	2.569	1.183	12.722
+9	2.546	6.539	1.885	4.454	2.701	15.423
+10	1.258	7.797	0.794	5.248	1.525	16.948
+11	0.946	8.743	−0.831	4.417	−0.247	16.701
+12	−0.127	8.616	−0.287	4.130	−0.060	16.641

Figure 8.4 shows that *CER* shows a similar pattern of movement in all three models. Because there is no need to consider the discounting of the offering price in the case of rights offering, the value of $CER_{1,12}$ represents the excess return for one year after the rights issue. This value is 1.917 percent in model 1, −2.267 percent in model 2, and 2.551 percent in model 3. From these results, it is possible to argue that investors either received extraordinarily high or low returns in the case of rights offering, whereas the possibility of abnormal returns could be ruled out in the case of public offerings.

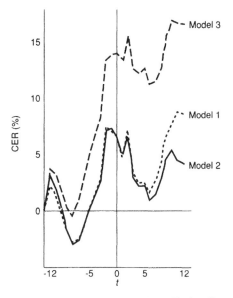

Figure 8.4 Cumulative excess returns of rights offering firms

5 EXPLAINING THE DECLINE OF STOCK PRICES AFTER PUBLIC OFFERINGS

Large stock price declines that occur after public offerings might correspond to large price increases prior to the issue, and the stock prices can simply be seen as returning to normal levels. Alternatively, large stock price declines may be caused by the liquidity effect of large issue volumes, which put downward pressure on prices. In this section, I further examine these possibilities.

For this purpose, we conduct regression analysis to examine whether or not there are relationships between the stock price change before the new issue, the volume of the issue, and the stock price change after the issue. The dependent variables are the excess return one month after the issue (EXR_1), and the cumulative excess return from $t = +1$ to $t = +3$ ($CER_{1,3}$). The explanatory variables are the cumulative excess return for the year prior to the issue ($CER_{-12,0}$) and the percentage increase in the outstanding number of stocks (ΔN). The sample is the same as that used in section 3.

A negative relationship between $CER_{-12,0}$ and the dependent variables would provide a piece of corroborating evidence of stock manipulation to increase price. A negative relationship between ΔN and the dependent variables would imply that an increase in the outstanding number of stocks caused the stock price to decline. The results corresponding to case A and model 1 are as follows, where figures in parentheses indicate t-values:

$$EXR_1 = -0.423 - 0.171\Delta N + 0.057CER_{-12,0}$$
$$(-0.21) \quad (-0.91) \quad (2.24) \qquad \bar{R} = 0.027$$

$$CER_{1,3} = -1.754 - 0.294\Delta N + 0.079CER_{-12,0}$$
$$(-0.47) \quad (-0.83) \quad (1.64) \qquad \bar{R}^2 = 0.007$$

The $\bar{R}^2$ is very low, meaning that the independent variables ΔN and $CER_{-12,0}$ explain only a small portion of the variance of the dependent variables. The coefficient of ΔN is about -0.2, indicating that a 1 percent increase in the outstanding number of stocks causes a 0.2 percent decrease in excess return after the issue, although that value is not statistically significant. In contrast, the coefficient of $CER_{-12,0}$ is positive with a relatively high t-value. Because the value of the coefficient is very small, however, an increase of 1 percent of $CER_{-12,0}$ has little influence on the excess return after the issue (that is, 0.06 percent or 0.08 percent). Although not reported here, the signs of the coefficients in models 2 and 3 are the same as in model 1, but their $\bar{R}^2$ is much smaller.[9]

Our analysis thus does not support the popular argument that unduly high stock prices are caused by the stock price manipulation prior to the issue, and that they return to their normal price after the issue. Moreover, there is little evidence that the stock price is depressed by the increase in the supply of stocks. We may thus conclude that the increase in the stock price prior to the issue seems to reflect the behavior of the issuing firm which sets the timing of the new issue when the stock price is rising in order to escape the dilution of equity capital which would otherwise be caused by a low issue price.

6 CONCLUSION

This chapter has analyzed seasoned equity issues in Japan. While the main financing method of Japanese corporations was bank borrowings through the 1960s, the relative importance of equity financing has been increasing in recent years. Though the only method used to raise additional equity capital by listed corporations in Japan was rights offerings until 1968, underwritten public offering has now become the predominant method. We proposed four reasons – two old and two new – why a majority of Japanese corporations now choose underwritten public offerings when rights offerings are clearly the cheaper method of equity issues in terms of flotation costs.

The two traditional reasons relate to the common dividend policy practice of Japanese corporations, which have their own target for the dividend per share that they intend to sustain. Given this dividend policy, a firm would prefer to limit the increase of outstanding shares by choosing public offering. The first of the newly proposed reasons relates to equity ownership: a firm which does not want to disperse equity ownership wants to keep equity ownership concentrated by choosing rights offering. The second reason is that underwritten public offerings help to establish a close and long-term relationship with an underwriter. Based on our examination of the characteristics of those corporations which used only rights offerings, we found evidence that was consistent with both these hypotheses.

We have also examined the average stock price behavior associated with both public and rights offerings. Our analysis has suggested that the investors who subscribed to new issues generally received risk-adjusted normal returns, regardless of which method of equity financing was used. We have found no evidence of a statistically significant relationship between the stock price change after public offerings and the issued volume of new stocks, or the stock price change before the issue. The observed increase in stock prices prior to the issue is likely to reflect the behavior of the issuing firm which sets the timing of the new issue when the stock price is rising.

NOTES

1 The first public equity issue made by a company is referred to as the initial public offering (IPO) or unseasoned new issue. In Japan, a company goes public by listing on a stock exchange or registering its stock with the Japan Association of Securities Dealers (JASD). Such registered stocks are traded in the over-the-counter (OTC) market. Because of the relaxation of listing and registration requirements since the mid-1980s, the number of companies making initial public offerings has increased in recent years.

2 The private placement of equity is made to important customers, suppliers, and main banks to strengthen the interfirm relationships as well as the financial position of the issuing company. See Kato and Schallheim (1991).

3 In Japan, a "firm commitment underwritten offer," in which the underwriter agrees to purchase the whole issue from the issuing company at a particular price for resale to the public, is the dominant method of public offerings. In rights offerings, an "uninsured rights offer" is a common method, in which the issuing companies protect against undersubscription by choosing a low subscription price below the market price of the stock. See Kunimura and Iihara (1985) for a discussion of underwriting agreements in the Japanese stock market.

4   These figures are based on the Yamaichi Research Institute and Yamaichi Securities Co. (1984: 198–203). In the US, similar evidence on flotation costs is reported by Smith (1977).
5   The voluntary rule requires that the issuing firms satisfy the following two conditions: (a) the dividend per share in the recent business year must be at least 10 percent of the par value; and (b) net profit per share in the recent business year must be at least 20 percent of the par value. Moreover, it is recommended that the issuing firm maintain the dividend payout ratio which was promised at the time of the new stock issue. The voluntary rule also restricts the number of new shares to a specified portion of outstanding equity, and stipulates that public offerings of any firm be at least one year apart.
6   See Hiraki (1985) for the stock price behavior associated with initial public offerings in Japan.
7   Kunimura and Severn (1990) also discuss the impact on the market stock price of public issues in the Japanese stock market (see also Asquish and Mullins, 1986; and Smith, 1986).
8   $$EXR_1^* = \frac{100\delta + R_1}{1 - \delta} - (\alpha + \beta R_{m1})$$
$$= \frac{100\delta + EXR_1}{1 - \delta} + \frac{\delta(\alpha + \beta R_{m1})}{1 - \delta}$$

As the second term on the right-hand side in the above equation has a negligibly small value, we can obtain equation (8.6) as a first-order approximation of the revised excess return (EXR_1^*) at $t = +1$.
9   The same analysis was performed, using the firms with positive $CER_{-12,0}$ as well as case B firms. However, the $\bar{R}^2$ in all cases was negligible.

REFERENCES

Asquish, Paul and Mullins, David 1986: Equity issues and offering dilutions. *Journal of Financial Economics*, 15, Jan.–Feb., 61–89.

Hansen, Robert and Pinkerton, John 1982: Direct equity financing: a resolution of a paradox. *Journal of Finance*, 37, June, 651–65.

Hiraki, Takato 1985: Pricing problems of unseasoned equity issues in Japan: an empirical test for primary and secondary market efficiency. *Japan Financial Review*, no. 4, December, 1–27.

Hodder, James and Tschoegl, Adrian 1993: Corporate finance in Japan. Chapter 3 in this volume.

Hoshi, Takeo, Kashyap, Anil and Scharfstein, David 1990: Bank monitoring and investment: evidence from the changing structure of Japanese corporate banking relationships. In Glenn Hubbard (ed.), *Asymmetric Information, Corporate Finance, and Investment*, Chicago: University of Chicago Press, 105–26.

Kato, Kiyoshi and Schallheim, James 1991: Public and private placements of seasoned equity issues in Japan. Unpublished paper, Graduate School of Business, University of Utah.

Kunimura, Michio and Iihara, Yoshio 1985: Valuation of underwriting agreements for raising capital in the Japanese capital market. *Journal of Financial and Quantitative Analysis*, 20, June, 231–41.

Kunimura, Michio and Severn, Alan 1990: The post-issue performance of new issues of Japanese stocks. In Ghon Rhee and Rosita Chang (eds), *Pacific-Basin Capital Markets Research*, Amsterdam: North-Holland, 255–63.

Marsh, Paul 1979: Equity rights issues and the efficiency of the UK stock market. *Journal of Finance*, 34, September, 839–62.

Myers, Stewart and Majluf, Nicholas 1984: Corporate financing and investment decision when firms have information that investors do not have. *Journal of Financial Economics*, 13, June, 187–221.

Scholes, Myron 1972: The market for securities: substitution versus pressure and the effects of information on share prices. *Journal of Business*, 45, April, 179–211.

Shoji Homu Kenkyukai, *Shoji Homu*, annual issues.

Smith, Clifford 1977: Alternative methods for raising capital: rights versus underwritten offerings. *Journal of Financial Economics*, 5, December, 273–307.

Smith, Clifford 1986: Investment banking and capital acquisition process. *Journal of Financial Economics*, 15, Jan.–Feb., 3–29.

Suto, Megumi 1987: *Nihon no Shokengyo*. Tokyo: Toyo Keizai Shinposha.

Yamaichi Research Institute and Yamaich Securities Co. (eds) 1984: *Shin Jidai no Kigyo Fainansu Senryaku* (Corporate Finance Strategy in the New Era). Tokyo: Toyo Keizai Shinposha.

9

The Organization and Microstructure of the Secondary Stock Market in Japan

Shinji Takagi

1 INTRODUCTION

This chapter presents a brief overview of the organization and micro-structure of the secondary stock market in Japan. It is particularly concerned with two aspects of the Japanese stock market: recent institutional changes and the intra-daily pricing of stocks. In reviewing the recent institutional developments, its focus is on the spot market, although passing references are made to the recent establishment of futures and options markets. The intra-daily pricing of stocks relates to the micro-structure of the Japanese stock market in which trading is based on competitive auction rules. The chapter presents new quantitative evidence, which may shed light on the nature of the microstructure of the Japanese stock market, to which increasing attention has been paid in the literature.[1]

The chapter is organized as follows. Section 2 describes the organization of the stock exchanges and the OTC stock market in Japan. Section 3 discusses the distribution of stock ownership and the role of securities companies in the Japanese stock market. Section 4 explains the trading rules and the pricing mechanism of the Japanese stock exchanges, the substance of which is also applicable to the OTC market. Section 5 presents descriptive statistics, and section 6 presents the preliminary results of non-parametric tests on the intra-daily movements of the prices of first section stocks at the Tokyo Stock Exchange. Finally, section 7 evaluates the microstructure of the Japanese stock market and presents concluding remarks.

The author thanks Colin McKenzie, Toshiharu Takahashi, Megumi Suto, Adrian E. Tschoegl, and Masato Hirota for useful comments, and the Suntory Foundation for financial support. However, the author alone is responsible for any remaining errors.

2 ORGANIZATION OF THE MARKET

2.1 Stock Exchanges

In Japan there are currently eight stock exchanges and an over-the-counter (OTC) market (table 9.1). Of the eight exchanges, the exchanges in Tokyo, Osaka, and Nagoya have two sections for stock trading as well as a separate section for bond trading. In addition, the Tokyo Stock Exchange has a separate section for foreign stocks and, in December 1991, the Osaka Stock Exchange began trading "country funds," which are mutual funds listed at foreign exchanges.[2]

The exchanges are membership associations whose operating revenues come from the fees charged the member firms. The Tokyo Stock

Table 9.1 Overview of the Japanese stock market (at the end of or during 1990)

	No. of member firms	No. of listed companies[a]	Trading value	Index futures	Index options
			(billions of yen)		
Exchanges					
Tokyo	124	1,752 (668)	188,683	71,775	223
Section I		1,191 (322)	176,311		
Section II		436 (346)	10,356		
Foreign		125	2,016		
Osaka	99	1,138 (218)	35,813	394,871	3,561
Section I		842 (36)			
Section II		296 (182)			
Nagoya	46	544 (97)	7,301	–	131
Section I		432 (14)	5,798		
Section II		112 (83)	1,503		
Kyoto	28	236 (1)	770	–	–
Hiroshima	20	196 (11)	261	–	–
Fukuoka	24	250 (27)	405	–	–
Niigata	18	198 (9)	334	–	–
Sapporo	18	190 (14)	286	–	–
Over-the-counter (OTC) market					
Total	–	357	6,112	–	–
Registered		342	6,041		
Managed		15	71		

[a] The numbers in parentheses refer to the number of companies whose stocks are listed only at the exchange concerned.

Sources: Ministry of Finance; and Tokyo Stock Exchange

Exchange, for example, had 124 member firms at the end of 1990, of which 25 were foreign. In addition to regular members, the exchanges in Tokyo, Osaka, and Nagoya have what are called *saitori* (*nakadachi* in Osaka): members who mediate trades between member firms (see section 4 for details). In the other exchanges (henceforth, called the "regional exchanges" for convenience), this function is performed by exchange officials.

At the Tokyo, Osaka, and Nagoya Stock Exchanges, the listing requirements of the second sections are less stringent than those of the first sections. In general, companies are initially listed on the second section and are moved to the first section only if they meet the more stringent requirements in terms of equity capital, ownership distribution, trading volume, and dividend performance. In turn, first section companies may be moved down to the second section if they cease to meet those requirements. As a rule, we can think of the second section as a market for the stocks of smaller, lesser known or newer companies. At the Tokyo Stock Exchange, for example, the volume of trading in the second section has been about 5 percent of the volume in the first section in recent years.

Recently, the three major exchanges established additional sections for trading in stock index futures and/or options.[3] In June 1987 the Osaka Stock Exchange began trading in futures contracts in a basket of 50 stocks (Osaka Stock Futures 50), in which exchange of cash for physical delivery of the underlying shares was required at final settlement for legal reasons. With the necessary legal change, however, trading in bona fide stock index futures began in September 1988, with the Tokyo Stock Exchange trading futures on the Tokyo Stock Exchange Price Index (TOPIX) and the Osaka Stock Exchange trading futures on the Nikkei Average (Nikkei-225). With the commencement of these two types of cash-settled futures, trading in Osaka Stock Futures 50 all but ceased and was eventually terminated in early 1992.

Trading in stock index options began in June 1989, when the Osaka Stock Exchange began trading in Nikkei-225 options. In October 1989 the Tokyo Stock Exchange and the Nagoya Stock Exchange followed the Osaka Stock Exchange by beginning to trade in their own stock index options, namely, TOPIX and Option-25 options, respectively. The expansion of futures trading has been so rapid that the value of trading in Nikkei-225 futures alone now exceeds the value of spot trading at all the stock exchanges in Japan combined (table 9.1). The value of trading in Nikkei-225 futures is almost six times the value of trading in TOPIX futures.

With the increasing concentration of economic activity in Tokyo as well as the improvement in telecommunication over the years, the relative importance of the Tokyo Stock Exchange in stock trading has

Table 9.2 Trading volume in Tokyo, Osaka, and other exchanges, 1960–90 (number of shares in millions; percent of total)

Year	Tokyo	Osaka	Others	Total[a]
1960	27 (62.8)	12 (28.8)	4 (8.4)	43
1965	35 (69.0)	12 (24.6)	3 (6.4)	50
1970	41 (71.9)	11 (19.9)	5 (8.2)	57
1975	52 (82.6)	9 (13.6)	2 (3.8)	63
1980	102 (85.9)	12 (10.5)	4 (3.6)	119
1985	121 (83.3)	18 (12.5)	6 (4.2)	146
1986	198 (82.9)	29 (12.2)	12 (4.9)	238
1987	264 (83.6)	37 (11.8)	15 (4.6)	315
1988	283 (86.1)	32 (9.7)	14 (4.2)	328
1989	223 (86.9)	25 (9.8)	9 (3.3)	256
1990	123 (84.4)	17 (11.8)	6 (3.8)	146

[a] Numbers may not add up to total because of rounding.

Source: Ministry of Finance

risen at the expense of the other exchanges (table 9.2). Tokyo's share in total stock trading increased by over 20 percentage points from the early 1960s to the current level of around 85 percent. In contrast, the share of the Nagoya and regional exchanges has declined from about 10 percent to around 4 percent currently.

The role of the Nagoya and regional exchanges is indicated by the small number of companies which are independently listed at each exchange (table 9.1). For example, the Kyoto Stock Exchange (KSE) has only one company whose stock is listed only at Kyoto, possibly because the KSE is located close to the larger Osaka Stock Exchange. The other regional exchanges have a somewhat greater number of companies which are independently listed, reflecting their close ties with the local economies. At the end of 1991 the Nagoya Stock Exchange had 97 independently listed companies, of which 83 companies were in the second section. These exchanges serve primarily as an exchange for a handful of local company stocks that are not listed at any other exchange.

Even the share of the Osaka Stock Exchange has declined from almost 30 percent in 1960 to around 10 percent currently. Reflecting the presence of over 200 Osaka-based companies whose stocks are listed only at Osaka, however, its share is still significant relative to the other exchanges outside of Tokyo (tables 9.1 and 9.2). Moreover, even some of the stocks that are cross-listed with the Tokyo Stock Exchange are said to be heavily traded in Osaka when the stock ownership is concentrated, or the company headquarters are located, in the Osaka area.

As an additional function, the Osaka Stock Exchange (and, to a lesser extent, the Nagoya Stock Exchange) provides a convenient facility for the timely execution of so-called *cross*-transactions, which are simultaneous submissions of large buy and sell orders at an identical price by a single securities company. With less trading and fewer participants than Tokyo, securities companies wishing to make large dealing or other cross-transactions have a better chance of success at the Osaka (or Nagoya) Stock Exchange. A fair amount of cross-trading also takes place at the regional exchanges, although the absolute volume is limited by the smaller number of listed stocks.

2.2   The OTC Market

In Japan the stock exchanges impose on member firms a requirement that listed stocks be traded only at the exchanges, except for transactions associated with takeovers and private transactions effected by non-member firms. Because of this "concentration" requirement, the OTC market in Japan has been small ever since the opening of the stock exchanges in 1949. Indeed, the role of the OTC market has been subordinate to the organized exchanges and merely consisted in providing a trading place for the stocks of companies which do not meet the listing requirements of the exchanges.

In the 1950s and at the beginning of the 1960s, however, the OTC market did play a useful role as a market for the stocks of emerging companies. During the period 1956–61, for example, the volume of trading in the OTC market amounted to as much as 10 percent of the trading volume in the Tokyo Stock Exchange, with over 300 issues traded in 1961. The establishment of second sections at the Tokyo, Osaka, and Nagoya Stock Exchanges in October 1961, however, diminished that role of the OTC market. The volume of trading in the OTC market has since accounted for less than 1 percent of total stock trading (table 9.3).

In principle, any stock that is not listed at the exchanges can be traded in the OTC market. Since 1963, however, the OTC stock market has been dominated by the trading of two types of stocks: "registered stocks" and "managed stocks." Registered stocks are those stocks which have met the registration requirements of the Japan Association of Securities Dealers (JASD). Managed stocks are those which are so designated by the JASD after they have been delisted at the exchanges.

In November 1983 the registration requirements in the OTC market were relaxed to meet the growing needs of newer and emerging companies to raise equity capital. As a result, an increasing number of companies

Table 9.3 OTC stock market in Japan, 1963–90 (number of listed stocks; number of shares traded in thousands)

	(1) Registered stocks		*(2)* Managed stocks		*(1) + (2)* Total OTC	
Year	*Number*	*Volume*	*Number*	*Volume*	*Number*	*Volume*[a]
1963	139	116	5	7	144	123 (0.21)
1964	126	29	21	33	147	62 (0.15)
1966	116	14	20	34	136	48 (0.09)
1968	110	15	22	13	132	28 (0.04)
1970	111	13	17	15	128	28 (0.05)
1972	95	39	19	59	114	98 (0.07)
1974	91	18	15	11	106	29 (0.04)
1976	87	23	8	83	95	106 (0.13)
1978	89	37	31	57	120	94 (0.08)
1980	112	41	34	182	146	223 (0.19)
1982	108	33	27	36	135	69 (0.07)
1984	118	102	23	84	141	186 (0.15)
1986	141	204	21	66	162	270 (0.11)
1987	151	181	21	171	172	352 (0.12)
1988	196	290	20	188	216	478 (0.15)
1989	263	530	16	135	279	665 (0.26)
1990	342	1,066	15	198	357	1,264 (0.87)

[a] The figures in parentheses are the percentage share of OTC trading volume in total trading volume in all exchanges.

Source: Tokyo Stock Exchange

have decided to go public by registering their stocks with the JASD. The number of registered stocks, which was as low as 87 in 1978, was 342 at the end of 1990, and is expected to continue to grow. During the same period, the volume of OTC trading as a percentage of total trading in the exchanges also increased from 0.13 percent to 0.87 percent (table 9.3). The volume of trading in the OTC market even exceeded temporarily the volume in the second section of the Tokyo Stock Exchange in May 1990.

At the time of the 1983 reform, moreover, the system of "designated dealers" was introduced to improve the liquidity of the OTC market, whereby at least two registered dealers (called TDs) are designated for each stock. The TDs are expected to be market-makers by being required to quote selling and buying prices at least once a week (twice a week after July 1985) and to respond at the quoted prices to any order involving at least 1,000 shares. In July 1984 a computerized information system was instituted in the OTC market in order to provide information on OTC stock prices.

In practice, the market-making role of TDs has been limited at best, as the TDs typically set large spreads so as to discourage any trade (Hamada, Kumagai and Nishizawa 1990). Instead of submitting orders to one of the TDs, therefore, securities companies in the OTC market generally submit all buy and sell orders to Japan OTC Securities, which in turn executes the matching of the orders.[4] It is said that over 90 percent of trading in the OTC market is conducted through the mediation of Japan OTC Securities. In this way, the OTC market in Japan resembles an organized exchange.

In October 1991, the Japan Association of Securities Dealers Automated Quotations (JASDAQ), a Japanese version of NASDAQ in the United States, was inaugurated. The idea of JASDAQ was to integrate the computer information system (which has been in place since July 1984) into the trade execution system of Japan OTC Securities. Under JASDAQ, all orders submitted by securities companies are entered on the computer-based automated trading system, and are executed expeditiously according to the auction rules based on the principles of price priority and time precedence (see section 4). In anticipation of this system, the OTC markets in Tokyo, Osaka, and Nagoya were unified into one national OTC market in August 1989.

3 CHARACTERISTICS OF THE MARKET

3.1 Distribution of Stock Ownership

In 1947 the US occupation authorities initiated the process of decentralizing corporate control and ownership by requiring that *Zaibatsu*-held stocks be sold to the public.[5] Moreover, the Antitrust Law of 1947 prohibited non-financial corporations from holding stocks of other corporations,[6] and allowed financial institutions to hold only up to 5 percent of total outstanding stocks of any non-financial corporation. The set of these and other measures (sometimes called the "democratization" of the stock market) had placed over 60 percent of total stocks in Japan in the hands of private individuals by 1950 (table 9.4).

The move to greater participation of private individuals in the equity market was partially reversed, however, with the revisions of the Antitrust Law in 1949 and 1953. The revisions lifted virtually all restrictions on the holdings of corporate stocks by non-financial corporations and raised the limit applicable to financial institutions from 5 to 10 percent of the total outstanding shares of a corporation.[7] As a result, most of the *Zaibatsu* stocks that had previously been sold to the public ended up in the portfolio of the former *Zaibatsu*-affiliated banks, and significant cross-

Table 9.4 Distribution of stock ownership by type of investor, 1945–90 (percent of total)[a]

Year	Corporations	of which: Financial institutions[b]	of which: Securities companies	Individual investors	Foreign investors
1945	46.9	(11.2)	(2.8)	53.1	–
1950	38.7	(12.6)	(11.9)	61.3	–
1960	52.3	(23.1)	(3.7)	46.3	1.4
1970	56.9	(31.0)	(1.2)	39.9	3.2
1980	66.7	(37.3)	(1.7)	29.2	4.1
1982	67.0	(38.9)	(1.8)	28.0	5.0
1984	67.7	(38.5)	(1.9)	26.3	6.0
1986	71.4	(41.7)	(2.5)	23.9	4.7
1987	72.8	(42.2)	(2.5)	23.6	3.6
1988	73.6	(42.5)	(2.5)	22.4	4.0
1989	73.5	(42.3)	(2.0)	22.6	3.9
1990	72.7	(41.6)	(1.7)	23.1	4.2

[a] Based on the number of shares owned.
[b] Includes banks and insurance companies; excludes investment trusts.

Source: Ministry of Finance

holdings of stocks among groups of affiliated companies (which are now called *keiretsu*) had become evident by 1954.

From 1950 to 1989 the percentage share of individuals in total stock ownership declined from 61.3 percent to 22.6 percent (table 9.4).[8] In contrast, the percentage share of the corporate sector rose from 38.7 percent to 73.5 percent. Within the corporate sector, 24.8 percent of total stock ownership was accounted for by non-financial corporations (not reported in the table) and 42.3 percent by banks and insurance companies. An extensive cross-holding of stocks among affiliated corporations was encouraged as a means of protection against hostile takeovers and mergers because the Antitrust Law does not allow holding companies to be formed in Japan.

Because the motive for corporate stock-holding is based on long-term relationships, the stocks held by financial institutions and other corporations are little-traded in Japan. For example, while the value of stocks held by the corporate sector was more than three times the value of stocks held by individual investors in 1989, the volume of stock trading by the corporate sector was only slightly larger than the volume of trading by individuals (tables 9.4 and 9.5). This is particularly true of stocks held by banks and non-financial corporations.

Table 9.5   Distribution of stock trading by type of investor, 1964–90 (percent of total)[a]

Year	Dealing by securities companies	Broking for investors	Corporate[b]	of which: Individual	Foreign
1964	49.3	50.7	n.a.	n.a.	n.a.
1968	34.5	65.5	n.a.	n.a.	n.a.
1972	25.5	74.5	n.a.	n.a.	n.a.
1974	19.3	80.7	14.0	62.7	4.0
1976	19.4	80.6	20.3	56.6	3.7
1978	23.1	76.9	24.3	48.4	4.2
1980	29.7	70.3	23.0	41.0	6.3
1982	31.7	68.3	18.4	40.7	9.2
1984	23.2	76.8	20.9	41.8	14.1
1986	27.6	72.4	29.1	32.7	10.6
1987	27.5	72.5	33.4	27.8	8.9
1988	27.1	72.9	37.7	26.4	6.4
1989	22.3	77.7	40.6	26.0	8.3
1990	24.3	75.7	37.0	25.1	10.2

[a]   Based on the number of shares traded by integrated securities companies in both sections of the Tokyo Stock Exchange prior to 1974, and in the first section only after 1974. The figures for 1974 are based on the value of transactions.
[b]   Includes financial institutions as well as the public sector.

Source: Tokyo Stock Exchange

The frequency of trading by the corporate sector, however, did increase by over 10 percentage points from the early 1980s to the early 1990s (table 9.5). This largely reflects the increased size and activity of professionally managed investment funds, called *tokkin* funds and fund trusts, which are placed in trust banks. Two factors contributing to this phenomenon were (a) the tax rule change made in 1983 which allowed the value of stocks held in investment funds to be different from the book value of the same stocks; and (b) the recent change in regulation which authorized investment advisory companies to manage investment funds without receiving item-by-item orders from their clients.[9] The value of stocks held in these professionally managed funds amounted to 2.7 percent of total stock holding in 1989.

3.2   Securities Companies[10]

In Japan, the market concentration requirement has meant that there are only centrally determined prices for exchange-listed stocks. Securities companies must submit all orders to the exchange and wait for the *saitori* member (or the exchange official) to find a matching order. Even in the OTC market, the dominant role of Japan OTC Securities has meant that stocks are mostly traded at a central location at uniform prices. The function of Japan OTC Securities in the OTC market is comparable to that of a *saitori* member (or an exchange official) at stock exchanges.

Because securities companies in Japan do not quote their own prices at which to execute orders at their discretion, the Japanese stock market is not generally characterized as a dealer market. Indeed, the role of securities companies as market makers in the stock market has been quite limited, particularly since the revision of the Securities and Exchange Law in 1968. For example, there is a limit on the amount of inventories securities companies are allowed to hold for dealing; and no one-way purchase of stocks on one's own account is allowed except when necessary for the smooth functioning of the market.

These limitations do not mean, however, that the securities companies in Japan do not trade on their own account. It is true that, in conducting dealing operations, exchange member companies must effect all trades through the usual auction procedures at the exchanges. However, securities companies do in fact conduct a fair amount of dealing in the Japanese stock market. At the Tokyo Stock Exchange, for example, the share of dealing transactions in total stock trading was over 24 percent in 1990 (table 9.5). It is also believed that a significant portion of so-called cross-trading represents dealing transactions of securities companies. The share of dealing, however, is now considerably smaller than what it was before the 1968 revision of the Securities and Exchange Law (for example, 49 percent of total trading at the Tokyo Stock Exchange in 1964) as well as what it would presumably be without the restrictions currently placed on dealing.

In the area of broking, securities companies in Japan still operate under a fixed commission system. In the current rate structure, which became effective in June 1990, there are ten fixed commission rates, ranging from 1.15 percent for a transaction amount of less than 1 million yen to 0.075 percent for that portion of a transactions amount exceeding 1 billion yen (financial institutions, including insurance companies, pay 80 percent, and non-member brokers pay 20 percent of the regular commission).[11] This means that the rate goes down from the maximum of 1.15 percent to 0.85 percent at 10 million yen, 0.55 percent at 50 million yen, 0.3875 percent at 100 million yen, 0.15375 percent at 1 billion yen and 0.1275 percent at 1.5 billion yen (figure 9.1). Needless to say, the average rate asymptotically approaches 0.075 percent as the amount increases further.

The current structure represents an across-the-board reduction of com-

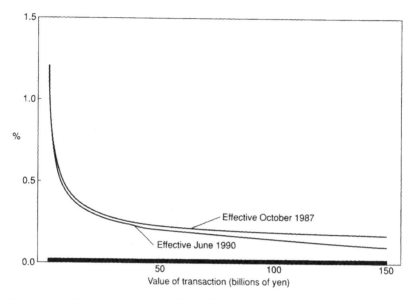

Figure 9.1   Commissions at the Tokyo Stock Exchange

mission rates from the previous structure (effective in October 1987), in which there were nine fixed rates ranging from 1.2 percent for a transaction amount of less than 1 million yen to 0.15 percent for an amount exceeding 1 billion yen. The new structure amounts to a reduction of 0.025 percent at 100 million yen, 0.0675 percent at 1 billion yen, and 0.07 percent at 1.5 billion yen (figure 9.1). Despite the recent reduction, however, the commission rates are considerably higher in Japan than in the United States for larger transactions. It is likely that brokerage commissions in Japan will be liberalized in coming years.[12]

4   MICROSTRUCTURE OF THE JAPANESE STOCK MARKET

4.1   Trading Rules[13]

The Japanese stock exchanges (as well as a large portion of the OTC market) are often described as auction markets because (a) the matching of orders is centralized; (b) the determination of prices is based on competitive auction rules; and (c) no one is required to be a market-maker. Unlike their American counterparts, the *saitori* members (the *nakadachi* members in Osaka, or exchange officials in the regional exchanges) do not take positions in any stock and do not trade on their own account. The market concentration requirement means that member firms must submit all orders in listed stocks to the exchanges.

In addition to the market concentration principle, the auction rules are based on the two other key principles of price priority and time precedence. The price priority principle is that market orders,[14] which do not specify execution price, take precedence over limit orders, which specify execution price; and that, for limit orders, sell orders with the lowest price are first matched with buy orders with the highest price. The time precedence principle means that, for two or more orders with the same price, the earlier order takes precedence over the others.

Stock trading is conducted in two sessions per day. The morning session is from 9 a.m. to 11 a.m. The afternoon session runs from 12:30 p.m. to 3 p.m. in Tokyo, Osaka, Nagoya, and Kyoto, and from 1 p.m. to 3 p.m. in the other exchanges.[15] A computerized trading system has been in operation at the Tokyo Stock Exchange since January 1982, and at the Osaka Stock Exchange since March 1991. At both exchanges, almost all listed stocks are now traded on the computerized system, leaving only the 150 most active stocks to the floor.

Two types of auction method, called *itayose* and *zaraba*, are employed to set transaction prices. The *itayose* method, which in effect is a call auction, establishes prices at the beginning of a trading session, after an interruption in trading, or at the end of a session. For each stock, the *itayose* method places all orders received during a specified period according to the price priority principle only, and sets the opening price so as to clear the market. Once the opening price is established, the *zaraba* method, which in effect is a continuous auction, sets stock prices on an on-going basis till the end of the session, when the *itayose* method may again be used to set the closing price.

4.2   Pricing Mechanism

4.2.1   *Itayose*

Suppose that, during a specified period preceding the opening of a trading session, a *saitori* member has received sell and buy orders for a given stock as indicated in table 9.6. This represents a trading book (called *ita*, which literally means "plate" or "board") of the *saitori* member. The book lists the numbers of orders by type, price, and firm (identified by A through H in this example). For instance, the table indicates that firm A has a market order to sell 6,000 shares, a market order to buy 5,000 shares, a limit order to sell 3,000 shares at 104 yen per share, a limit order to buy 6,000 shares at 104 yen, and so forth.

Table 9.6   An example of the *itayose* method (in thousands of shares)[a]

(Total)	Selling	Price (yen)	Buying	(Total)
38	5 9 8 7 6 3 B E F H A C	Market orders	9 5 2 4 7 6 3 G A E D B F C	36
10	2 3 5 B A G	104	6 4 A E	10
18	6 5 3 4 D A E C	103	5 1 7 2 F G A B	15
26	8 6 4 3 5 E D B F C	102	8 2 5 1 C A D E	16
39	7 5 6 8 4 9 E F H A D C	101	5 4 9 3 7 G F A D H	28
15	3 6 2 4 H G B E	100	3 5 8 6 4 B C E A D	26
11	7 3 1 C F A	99	5 6 3 1 D F E C	15
2	2 D	98	7 5 2 E D G	14

[a]   A, B, C, D, E, F, G, H refer to the respective member securities companies of the exchange.

This particular configuration of sell and buy orders can be translated into the set of demand and supply schedules of the type depicted in figure 9.2, where quantity is drawn along the vertical axis and price along the horizontal axis. Market orders, which do not specify a price, would simply shift up the demand and supply schedules vertically. Then the market clears when the price is 101 yen per share and 105,000 shares are exchanged.

In general, the market-clearing price may not turn out to be an integer.[16] In such a case, one of the closest integers that minimizes the amount of order imbalance is usually chosen as the opening price. Depending on whether there is an excess of sell orders or of buy orders, the balance of executable orders is allocated among the member firms that had submitted the limit orders at that price according to certain rationing rules. When two integers give the same amount of order imbalance, however, no opening price can be established. This is also true when the order imbalance is such that the demand and supply schedules do not intersect.[17]

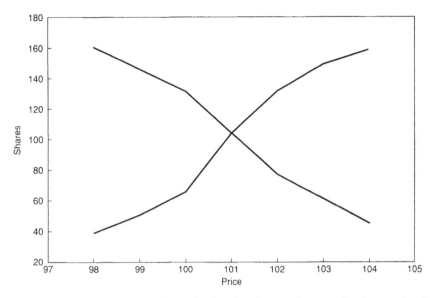

Figure 9.2 Opening price determination by *itayose* (in yen; in thousands of shares)

4.2.2 *Zaraba*

After the initial price has been established and market orders, limit sell orders of 101 yen or less, and limit buy orders of 101 yen or more have all been executed, the trading book of the *saitori* member looks like the one depicted in table 9.7. For the execution of the remaining orders under the *zaraba* method, the order of execution moves from high to low (that is, 100, 99, 98, and so on) for buy orders and from low to high (102, 103, 104, and so on) for sell orders.[18]

Figure 9.3 is a graphical representation of table 9.7. With the aid of figure 9.3, let us consider two possible movements of stock prices under the *zaraba* method.

First, suppose that a *large* (relative to existing limit orders) market order comes to the exchange. If it is an order to buy 50,000 shares, the *saitori* member would match it with (a) the limit sell orders of 26,000 shares at 102 yen, (b) the limit sell orders of 18,000 shares at 103 yen, and (c) the limit sell orders of up to 6,000 shares at 104. Thus, the transaction price moves from low to high, namely, from 102 yen to 103 yen, then to 104 yen. If the market order is an order to sell 50,000 shares, on the other hand, the *saitori* member would match (a) the limit buy orders of 26,000 shares at 100 yen, (b) the limit buy orders of 15,000 shares at 99 yen , and

Table 9.7   Beginning of a *zaraba* session (in thousands of shares)[a]

(Total)	Selling	Price (yen)	Buying	(Total)
		Market orders		
10	2 3 5 B A G	104		
18	6 5 3 4 D A E C	103		
26	8 6 4 3 5 E D B F C	102		
		101		
		100	3 5 8 6 4 B C E A D	26
		99	5 6 3 1 D F E C	15
		98	7 5 2 E D G	14

[a]   A, B, C, D, E, F, G, H refer to the respective member securities companies of the exchange.

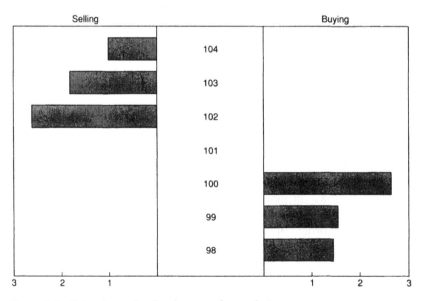

Figure 9.3   Price determination in a *zaraba* market

(c) the limit buy orders of up to 9,000 shares at 98 yen. Thus, the transaction price moves from high to low, namely, from 100 yen to 99 yen, then to 98 yen.

Second, suppose that *small* (relative to existing limit orders) market sell and market buy orders randomly come to the exchange. The *saitori* member would then match the market sell order with existing limit buy orders at 100 yen per share, and the market buy order with existing limit sell orders at 102 yen per share. This means that, as long as there remain limit buy orders at 100 yen and limit sell orders at 102 yen, the transaction price moves back and forth between 100 yen and 102 yen.

4.3 Price Movements in the *Zaraba* Market

When specialists are required to provide centralized market making as in the New York Stock Exchange, they charge a price spread as a compensation for assuming the liquidity risk (Demsetz 1968). In this type of market, therefore, the market price is bounded by the spread, and successive changes in the price tend to be negatively correlated (Roll 1984). In a *zaraba*-type continuous auction market, however, there is no centralized market-making. Thus, there is not necessarily a spread to bound the price movement and the range of price fluctuation may become wide even with no change in market fundamentals.

Indeed, there is a presumption that price movements in a *zaraba* market are not bounded by a spread and tend to be in one direction when left entirely to market forces. This unidirectional price change corresponds to the first scenario considered in the above example, where large (relative to existing limit orders) market orders come to the exchange. Another possibility which may give rise to this type of price movement is that small market orders of the same type (either sell or buy) consecutively come to the exchange. In this case, the price would move sharply in an opposite direction when a market order of the other type comes to the exchange.

The presumption of stock price volatility in the *zaraba* market is indicated by the adoption by the exchanges of two measures to prevent a short-term sharp price fluctuation: (a) the system of daily price limits, and (b) the system of special price quotations. First, the Japanese exchanges impose daily limits on the amount of price change from the previous day's closing price. Listed stocks cannot be traded at a price higher or lower than the daily limit given by the previous day's closing price. For instance, the maximum permissible amount of daily price change is 80 yen for the previous closing price of 500 yen, 100 yen for 1,000 yen, 200 yen for 1,500 yen, 300 yen 2,000 yen, and so forth.

Second, when there is a major order imbalance, the exchange posts a "special bid quote" or "special asked quote" to solicit counter orders instead of allowing the price to move too much too fast. If no counter orders are received for some time, a new special quote may be posted within the price quotation spread specified by the exchange (for example, a one-time upward or downward movement from the last price is 5 yen if the price is less than 500 yen, 10 yen if less than 1,000 yen, 20 yen if less than 1,500, and so on).

Of course, actual price behavior would depend crucially on the probability distribution of order arrivals and order size, and other patterns of price behavior are certainly possible in the *zaraba* market. Another possibility was indicated by the second scenario considered in the above example, where small market orders of either type come to the exchange at random. In this case, the market price fluctuates between the lowest selling price and the highest buying price, in a way analogous to the situation where the market price is bounded by a spread between the asking and bidding prices of a specialist-dealer. In order for us to observe this type of price behavior, two conditions must be met: (a) market orders are random and small relative to existing limit orders; and (b) a sufficient number of limit orders remain at those two prices on the book of the *saitori* member.

5   INTRA-DAILY STOCK PRICE DATA

5.1   Data Description

The best way to test the presumption of stock price volatility in a *zaraba* market is to test it against the data of actual transactions prices. Unfortunately, the Japanese stock exchanges have a long-standing policy of not disclosing intra-daily transactions data, making it impossible to obtain a large quantity of such data through electronic means. What one can obtain, however, is a running record ("ticker tape") of transactions prices as they are displayed on the computer screens of brokerage houses on a daily basis. In what will follow, a preliminary statistical analysis will be performed on a limited amount of manually obtained price data.

In particular, we use the intra-daily data of the transaction prices of six first section stocks of the Tokyo Stock Exchange recorded in the afternoon sessions of December 11 and 12, 1990. Three of the six stocks (abbreviated as NS, TE, and HT) were initially chosen on the presumption that they were actively traded, while the other three were chosen on the presumption that they were not (see table 9.8). It has turned out, however, that one stock (KE) which was chosen on the presumption of

Table 9.8 Number and volume of transactions in six first section Tokyo Stock Exchange stocks (December 11 and 12, 1990)

	Opening price (yen)	Number	Transactions Volume (shares)	Value[a] (millions of yen)
NS				
NS11	433	107	7,792,000	3,374
NS12	436	117	10,059,000	4,386
TE				
TE11	3,560	157	1,269,700	4,520
TE12	3,610	122	2,533,900	9,147
HT				
HT11	1,130	44	3,298,000	3,727
HT12	1,130	42	1,724,000	1,948
KE				
KE11	2,500	80	523,100	1,308
KE12	2,610	53	296,800	775
YS				
YS11	710	16	118,000	84
YS12	750	14	192,000	144
TS				
TS11	3,420	31	205,000	701
TS12	3,500	15	289,000	1,012

[a] Measured at the opening price.

less trading activity in terms of *trading volume* had similar characteristics to those of the three presumably active stocks (NS, TE, and HT), possibly because it was actively traded in terms of *trading frequency* (see table 9.8).

These stocks are of six major corporations from three industry groups, with two stocks (one active and the other not so active) representing each group. It should be noted that, on December 11 and 12, 1990, there was apparently no significant "news" which might have caused a change in the fundamental determinants of the stock prices. We assume, therefore, that the intra-daily price movements of these stocks on those days represented only random factors attributable to the "temporal fragmentation" of market participants in the context of the established trading rules (Garbade and Silber 1979).

Table 9.9   Basic statistics of first differences

	No. of observations	Sample mean	t-stat mean = 0	Skewness	Kurtosis
NS11	105	−0.03	−0.20	0.05	−0.96
NS12	115	0.01	0.07	0.08	−1.32
TE11	155	0.26	0.28	0.03	−1.54
TE12	120	−0.08	−0.07	0.09	2.27
HT11	42	0.00	0.00	−0.00	−1.57
HT12	40	0.00	0.00	0.00	−2.11
KE11	78	0.64	0.40	−0.31	−0.91
KE12	51	−1.18	−0.62	0.17	−0.36
YS11	14	−0.64	−0.49	0.28	0.81
YS12	12	−0.67	−0.33	−0.27	−1.72
TS11	29	1.03	0.32	−0.68	0.31
TS12	13	−7.69	−0.95	0.63	−0.34

5.2   Descriptive Statistics

First, let us review the statistical properties of price changes, excluding the first and last price changes of each session, in order to remove the influences of the *itayose* method (table 9.9). We observe that, for each of the 12 data sets (6 stocks × 2 sessions), the mean of price changes was roughly zero and never exceeded a single tick (1 yen if the price is under 1,000 yen and 10 yen if the price is more than 1,000 yen). In fact, the *t*-statistics do not reject the null hypothesis that the mean was zero in any of the data sets.

In terms of distributional characteristics, skewness indicates that the distribution of price changes was symmetric for each data set (table 9.9). Kurtosis, however, indicates that the distributional of intra-daily stock price changes was flat relative to the normal distribution. The hypothesis that the distribution was normal can be rejected for all data sets as the value of kurtosis significantly falls short of 3. The flat shape of the distribution of intra-daily price changes is in sharp contrast to the distribution of daily or weekly asset price changes which is known to be peaked and fat-tailed (for a survey of the literature, see Takagi 1989).

Finally, in terms of absolute first differences, price changes ranged between 0.3 percent and 1.0 percent (table 9.10). It is noteworthy that there is a difference in the behavior of the price change between the first four stocks (NS, TE, HT, and KE) and the last two stocks (YS and TS) when measured as a percentage of a single tick. For the first four stocks, the mean of first absolute differences was roughly equal to a single tick

Table 9.10 Basic statistics of first absolute differences

	Initial price	Sample mean (percent)	Standard deviation	Coeff. of determination
NS11	433	1.34 (0.31)	0.60	0.45
NS12	436	1.21 (0.28)	0.43	0.36
TE11	3,560	10.97 (0.31)	2.97	0.27
TE12	3,610	11.25 (0.31)	6.02	0.54
HT11	1,130	10.95 (0.97)	2.97	0.27
HT12	1,130	10.00 (0.88)	0.00	0.00
KE11	2,500	12.95 (0.52)	5.61	0.43
KE12	2,610	12.16 (0.47)	5.77	0.47
YS11	710	3.79 (0.53)	3.07	0.81
YS12	748	6.17 (0.82)	2.95	0.48
TS11	3,420	14.83 (0.43)	9.11	0.61
TS12	3,500	26.15 (0.75)	13.25	0.51

(that is, 1 yen for NS and 10 yen for the others). In contrast, the mean was considerably greater than a tick for the other two stocks; the mean (6.17 yen) was over six times the tick (1 yen) in the case of YS12. In terms of the coefficients of variation, however, there does not seem to be a noticeable relationship between trading volume and the volatility of price changes.

6 NON-PARAMETRIC TESTS OF INTRA-DAILY DATA

The difference in the behavior of price changes which was alluded to in table 9.10 becomes quite evident when the data are visually displayed. Figures 9.4–9.9 depict the intra-daily movements of stock prices for the six stocks on December 11–12, 1990. We observe that, for the four stocks which are more actively traded, there is a greater tendency for successive price changes to be negatively correlated. Particularly for HT12 in figure 9.6, the price movement appears to be bounded by a constant price spread (which itself moved once). In contrast, price changes tend to be more unidirectional and more volatile for the two stocks which are less actively traded (figures 9.8 and 9.9).

6.1 Runs Test

In order to substantiate the visual difference in price behavior between the more active and the less active stocks, we will perform some non-

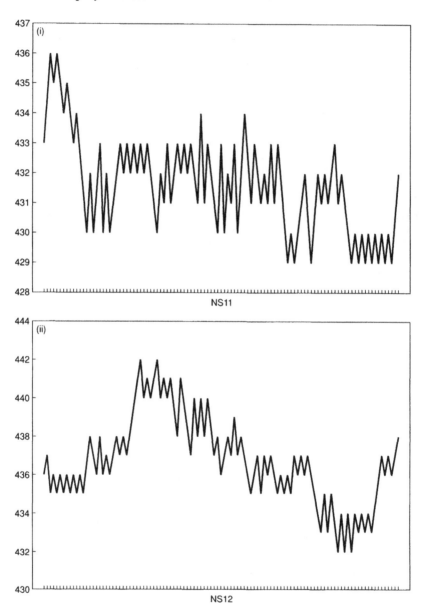

Figure 9.4   Intra-daily movements of NS stock prices
(i)   December 11, 1990
(ii)   December 12, 1990

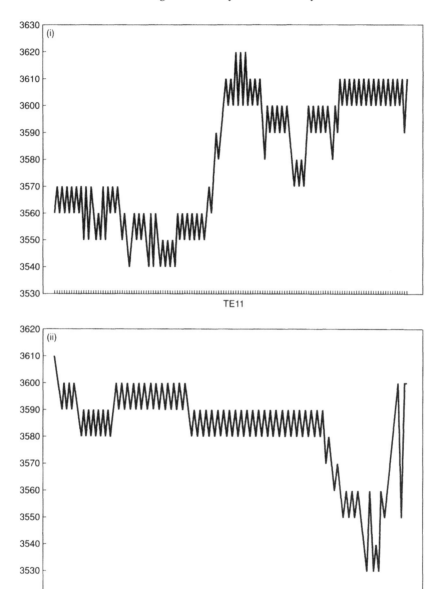

Figure 9.5 Intra-daily movements of TE stock prices
(i)   December 11, 1990
(ii) December 12, 1990

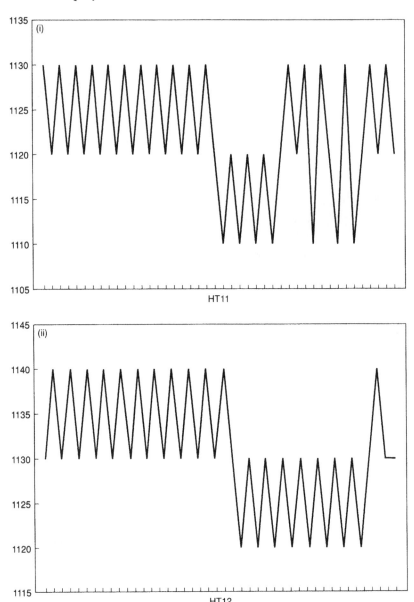

Figure 9.6 Intra-daily movements of HT stock prices
(i)   December 11, 1990
(ii)   December 12, 1990

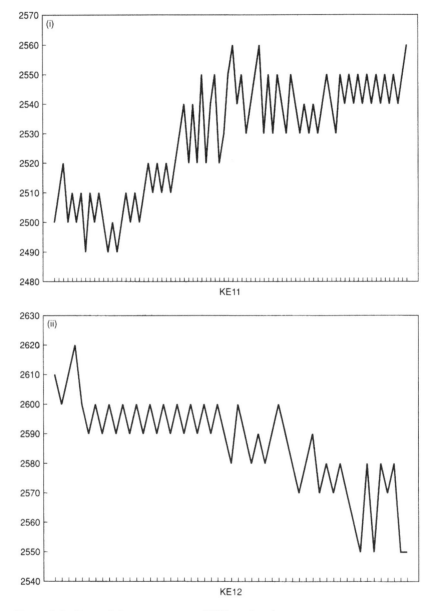

Figure 9.7 Intra-daily movements of KE stock prices
(i)   December 11, 1990
(ii)   December 12, 1990

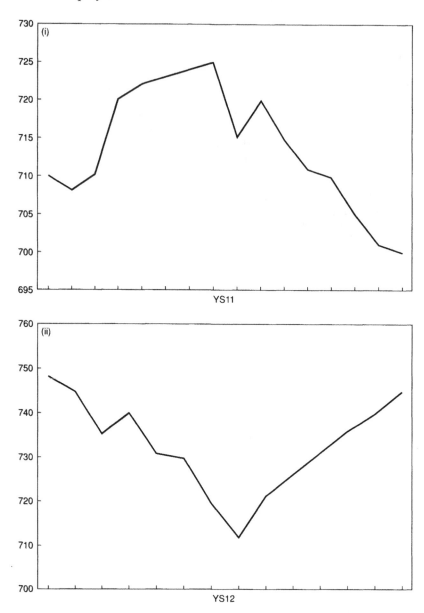

Figure 9.8 Intra-daily movements of YS stock prices
(i) December 11, 1990
(ii) December 12, 1990

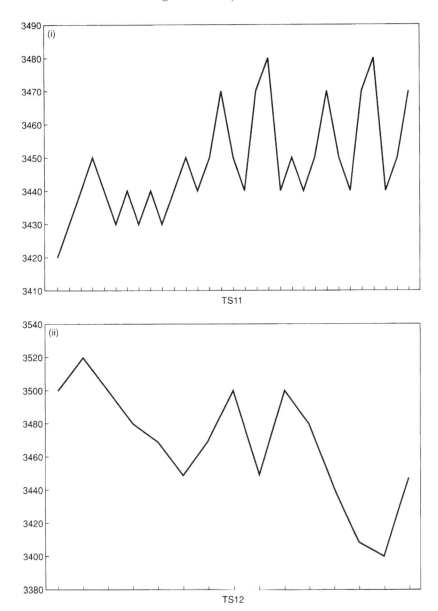

Figure 9.9   Intra-daily movements of TS stock prices
(i)   December 11, 1990
(ii)   December 12, 1990

parametric tests. First, let us perform a "runs test" of the randomness of successive price changes. A run is defined as a series of successive changes in the same direction. Suppose, for example, that we designate a rise in the stock price as A and a fall as D, and that the stock price shows the following movement during the course of a session: AAAADDDDAAAAADAA. In this example, the first four As form a run, the next three Ds form another run, and so forth. Thus, we have the total of five runs for 15 price changes. Denoting the number of runs by R, the Z-statistic is given by

$$Z = [R - E(R)]/\sqrt{V(R)}.$$

Here, $E(R)$ is the expected value of R, and $V(R)$ is the variance of R, which are given respectively by

$$E(R) = (2pq/p + q) + 1$$

and

$$V(R) = 2pq(2pq - p - q)/[(p + q)^2(p + q - 1)],$$

where p is the number of As and q is the number of Ds.

Table 9.11 reports the Z-statistic for each of the 12 data sets. In order to test the hypothesis that the price changes were random, we make use of the fact that $E(R)$ approaches the normal distribution as p and q increase in value. Thus, we reject the hypothesis when the absolute value of Z exceeds 1.96 or 2.58, depending on the chosen level of significance.

Table 9.11 Runs test of randomness[a]

	No. of observations	No. positive	No. negative	No. runs	Z
NS11	105	50	55	79	5.0*
NS12	115	57	58	83	4.6*
TE11	155	78	77	131	8.5*
TE12	120	59	61	120	8.6*
HT11	42	21	21	38	5.0*
HT12	40	20	20	38	5.5*
KE11	78	43	35	63	5.4*
KE12	51	22	29	41	4.3*
YS11	14	7	7	5	1.7
YS12	12	6	6	4	1.8
TS11	29	17	12	19	1.5
TS12	13	4	9	6	−0.4

* Indicates that the hypothesis of randomness is rejected at the 1 percent level of significance.

According to the Z-statistics, the actual number of runs (R) significantly exceeded the hypothetical number of runs one would expect if the price changes were random $E(R)$, in the case of the data sets involving the four actively traded stocks. In contrast, the hypothesis that the price changes were random could not be rejected in the case of the data sets involving the remaining two stocks whose trading volume is low.

6.2 Von Neuman Test

When we look at the serial correlations of price changes, we find a clear pattern that the coefficient of first-order serial correlation is negative and that of second-order serial correlation is positive for the four actively traded stocks. In contrast, we find little such pattern in the serial correlations of price changes for YS and TS, the two less actively traded stocks (table 9.12).

The null hypothesis that no serial correlation exists can be tested by the following Von Neuman ratio:

$$K = m^2/s^2.$$

Here
$$m^2 = \sum_{t=1}^{n-1} (p_{t+1} - p_t)^2/n - 1,$$

and
$$s^2 = \sum_{t=1}^{n} (p_t - \bar{p})^2/n,$$

Table 9.12 Serial correlations of first differences

| | Von Neuman ratio | Autocorrelation coefficients | | | | |
		Lag 1	Lag 2	Lag 3	Lag 4	Lag 5
NS11	3.18*	−0.59	0.26	−0.17	0.17	−0.25
NS12	3.12*	−0.55	0.25	−0.14	0.01	0.13
TE11	3.43*	−0.71	0.43	−0.27	0.25	−0.25
TE12	3.34*	−0.72	0.50	−0.42	0.43	−0.35
HT11	3.64*	−0.80	0.48	−0.19	0.00	0.06
HT12	3.82*	−0.88	0.75	−0.68	0.60	−0.53
KE11	3.35*	−0.66	0.28	−0.21	0.15	−0.11
KE12	3.20*	−0.62	0.29	−0.31	0.28	−0.25
YS11	2.10	0.01	0.16	0.22	...	...
YS12	1.85	0.13	0.23	0.03	...	...
TS11	2.58	−0.26	−0.49	0.26	0.13	−0.14
TS12	2.72	−0.29	−0.07	0.14	...	...

* Indicates statistically significant negative serial correlation at the 1 percent level.
... Indicates that the coefficient is not calculated.

where n is sample size, p_t is the stock price in period t, and $\bar{p}$ is the average price.

The Von Neuman ratios are calculated and reported for all the data sets in the first column of table 9.12. When the value of K exceeds some critical value, there is evidence of negative serial correlation. On the other hand, when the value of K falls short of some critical value, there is evidence of positive serial correlation.

The test statistics indicate that, for the four actively traded stocks, the coefficient of first-order serial correlation was negative and significantly different from zero. For the other stocks, there was no statistically significant serial correlation in their price changes. These results corroborate the results of the earlier runs test, that the behavior of price changes is more systematic for the more actively traded stocks than for the less actively traded stocks.

6.3   Contingency Tables

Another non-parametric test of independence is to construct contingency tables (table 9.13). Here, we have combined the two data sets (one for December 11 and the other for December 12) for each stock. For the four actively traded stocks, we find that the probability that a positive (negative) change follows a negative (positive) change is three to twelve times the probability that a positive (negative) change follows a positive (negative) change. The null hypothesis that the price changes are independent can be rejected by a chi-square test for all the four data sets.

In contrast, there is no consistent pattern for the two less actively traded stocks. In the case of YS, the probability that a positive (negative) change is followed by a positive (negative) change is two to three times larger than the probability that a positive (negative) change is followed by a negative (positive) change. The null hypothesis that the price changes were independent was also rejected. In the case of TS, the price changes seem to be completely independent.

Finally, let us calculate the conditional probabilities when two successive changes have already occurred in the same direction (table 9.14). In the case of NS, the probability (0.30) that two successive changes in the same direction are followed by a change in the same direction is only slightly higher than the probability that two successive changes are in the same direction (0.27). Similarly, the probability for TE is 0.25 (0.13 for two successive changes in the same direction), the probability for HT is zero (0.08), and the probability for KE is 0.20 (0.19).

As for the two less actively traded stocks, the probability for YS is 0.80 (0.71 for two successive changes in the same direction), and the probability for TS is 0.31 (0.43). The presumably characteristic price

Table 9.13 Contingency table (I)[a]

(1) NS

		Present change		
		+	−	Total
Previous	+	25	80	105
Change	−	80	33	113
Total		105	113	218

Test of independence: (1) = 48.1**

(2) TE

		Present change		
		+	−	Total
Previous	+	17	118	135
Change	−	119	19	138
Total		136	137	273

Test of independence: (1) = 148.0**

(3) HT

		Present change		
		+	−	Total
Previous	+	3	37	40
Change	−	37	3	40
Total		40	40	80

Test of independence: (1) = 57.8**

(4) KE

		Present change		
		+	−	Total
Previous	+	13	51	64
Change	−	52	11	63
Total		65	62	127

Test of independence: (1) = 49.2**

Table 9.13 *Continued*

(5) YS

		Present change		
		+	−	Total
Previous	+	9	3	12
Change	−	4	8	12
Total		13	11	24

Test of independence: (1) = 6.2*

(6) TS

		Present change		
		+	−	Total
Previous	+	8	12	20
Change	−	11	9	20
Total		19	21	40

Test of independence: (1) = 1.2

[a] Based on the combined data from the afternoon sessions of December 11 and 12, 1990.
** (*) Indicates that the statistic is significant at the 1 (5) percent level.

Table 9.14 Contingency table (II)[a]

Previous two consecutive changes in the same direction	Present change		
	Same direction	Opposite direction	Total
NE	17	39	56
TE	9	27	36
HT	0	6	6
KE	5	20	25
YS	12	3	15
TS	5	11	16

[a] Based on the combined data from the afternoon sessions of December 11 and 12, 1990.

movement of a *zaraba* market, namely that the prices tend to move in the same direction, seems to be more present in the less actively traded stocks.

6.4 "Experiment" of July 1991

We have found that the price behavior of the four active stocks resembled the price behavior usually associated with a specialist-dealer market, while the price behavior of the two less active stocks was more consistent with the presumed behavior of a *zaraba* market. That is to say, the successive price changes of the four active stocks were negatively correlated, with the prices bounded as if by a bid–ask spread. In contrast, the price movements of the two less active stocks tended to be more volatile and the successive price changes were more likely to be in the same direction. The question remains, however, as to the nature of the relationship between trading volume and the behavior of stock prices.

Obviously, there are two possible interpretations. One is that the behavior of price changes is somehow endogenous to trading intensity. With a greater trading intensity, trading may naturally become more continuous and the variance of the transactions price itself may become smaller (Mendelson 1982). In fact, this may be the reason why trading sessions in the Japanese stock exchanges are kept relatively short. In terms of figure 9.3, a large number of buy orders might, for example, appear at 100 yen and a large number of sell orders appear at 102 yen. As the arrival of market orders becomes more randomized, a negative serial correlation would result.

The other interpretation is that the behavior of price changes is related to the market-making activities of member firms and other market participants at the exchange. Here, the term "market-making" is used in a slightly different way, and refers to the practice of traders placing buy and sell orders simultaneously to earn a price spread. In terms of figure 9.3, a market-maker would be placing his own buy order at 100 yen and his own sell order at 102 yen. This is a form of market-making activity in the sense that it gives liquidity to the market in the context of auction rules.

In order to help discriminate between the two alternative (though not necessarily mutually exclusive) interpretations, the analysis of price data from the extraordinary month of July 1991 may be useful. In response to the revelation that the four largest securities companies had earlier been engaged in compensating their favored clients for trading losses,[19] the Ministry of Finance requested that they "voluntarily" refrain from trading for their corporate clients for four business days during the period July 10–15. As a result, trading volume sharply declined during those four days.

Table 9.15 Number and volume of transactions in three active Tokyo Stock Exchange stocks (July 11 and 12, 1991)

	Opening price (yen)	Number	Transactions Volume (shares)	Value[a] (millions of yen)
NS				
NS71	416	57	2,185,000	909
NS72	413	40	593,000	245
TE				
TE71	3,590	48	242,200	869
TE72	3,580	55	199,700	715
HT				
HT71	1,170	60	1,589,000	1,859
HT72	1,160	34	1,143,000	1,326

[a] Measured at the opening price.

Concentrating our attention on the three active stocks (NS, TE, and HT), the trading volume and frequency of NS and TE during the afternoon sessions of July 11 and 12, 1991 were considerably down from December 11 and 12, 1990, although it may be objected that the volume and frequency of NS remained high in absolute terms (tables 9.8 and 9.15). The decline in trading volume and frequency of HT, on the other hand, was not so remarkable. Thus, a rough and casual test of the competing interpretations is to see how the price behavior of TE might have changed from December 1990 to July 1991.

Figure 9.10 depicts the intra-daily price movements of TE during the afternoon sessions of July 11 and 12, 1991. Despite the decline in trading volume and frequency, we observe the same pattern of price movement to the pattern observed in December 1990. The successive price changes seem to be negatively correlated and the prices are bounded as if by a price spread. At least on this score, the price behavior of major stocks on the Tokyo Stock Exchange may well reflect the presence of market-making activities.

7 CONCLUSION

This chapter has reviewed the basic organization of the secondary stock market in Japan and analyzed the microstructure of Japanese stock exchanges. The Japanese stock exchange has frequently been character-

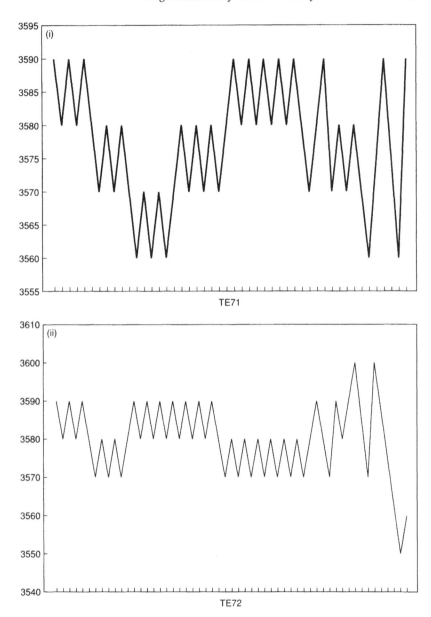

Figure 9.10   Intra-daily movements of TE stock prices
(i)   July 11, 1991
(ii)   July 12, 1991

ized as a non-dealer market because the specialist at the exchange does not provide market-making. The presumption (implicit in the rules of the exchange) has been that the price movement of stocks in such a *zaraba* market can be volatile and the successive changes are more likely to be in the same direction.

Our analysis of a limited sample of intra-daily price data has suggested that, while the price behavior of some (often less traded) stocks is consistent with the presumption of price volatility and unidirectional change, the behavior of other (often more traded) stocks is similar to the pattern of behavior observed in a specialist-dealer market, where successive price changes are negatively correlated and prices are bounded by a bid–ask spread. Because the same price behavior was observed for a major stock during the period of thin trading in July 1991, the price behavior of major stocks at the Tokyo Stock Exchange may well reflect the presence of market-making activities.

Some of the market-making activities may be provided by speculators or large institutional investors who are not exchange members. Because the trading books of *saitori* members on the Japanese exchange are open to the floor, technically anybody can become a dealer (see Macey and Kanda 1990: 1045). In order to earn a spread, anybody can thus simultaneously place sell and buy orders as limit orders at some price spread.[20] Whether market-making is provided by member firms or non-member investors, liquidity is created in the process, and the random arrival of market orders will result in a negative serial correlation of price changes.

If this interpretation is correct, the Japanese stock exchange may be better described as a market where a multiple number of dealers provide market-making at their own discretion, whereas the US stock exchange is a market where a single dealer is obligated to provide market-making. Against the background of publicly available information, Japanese dealers are free to compete with each other, while the US specialist-dealer is a monopolist who has a public function to perform, for which he is allowed to maintain information monopoly in relation to market conditions.

In the Japanese stock market, however, all dealers may decide not to provide market-making in inactively traded or particularly risky stocks. This will certainly reduce the liquidity of the market in those stocks, which should be contrasted with a likely situation in a specialist-dealer market where market-making is provided but with a large price spread. For blue-chip stocks, the *zaraba* system seems to work well: the spread is small and trading intensity is high. In this case, the choice between the Japanese exchange and the US exchange would depend on the relative size of the price spread as well as the normative question of who should claim the profits from dealing. For other stocks, however, the *zaraba* system seems to provide inadequate liquidity. In this case, the choice is between the cost of waiting in a *zaraba* market and the presumably larger price spread in a specialist-dealer market.

NOTES

1 See, for example, Amihud and Mendelson (1989); Lindsey and Schaede (1990); and Takagi (1989).
2 See Maru (1993), chapter 15 in this volume.
3 See Adachi and Kurasawa (1993), chapter 12 in this volume.
4 Japan OTC Securities was established in 1976 by a group of 187 securities companies in order to facilitate the trading of registered stocks. Its function is to mediate trades between securities companies and, for this reason, is sometimes called the brokers' broker (BB).
5 The *Zaibatsu* were large corporate groups whose shares were held by such family-owned holding companies as Sumitomo, Mitsubishi, Mitsui, and Yasuda. The US authorities regarded the *Zaibatsu* as having contributed to the war.
6 This restriction on the corporate ownership of stocks was substantially eased in 1953, as discussed below.
7 The third revision of the Antitrust Law in 1977 placed ceilings on the amount of stocks that can be held by non-financial corporations and reduced the limit applicable to financial institutions from 10 percent back to 5 percent.
8 Some argue that participation of individuals is limited by a high minimum trading unit which most Japanese corporations require for the trading of their stocks (most commonly 1,000 shares).
9 As revealed and widely publicized in 1991, these funds had been used by securities companies to compensate their favored clients for trading losses during the period of declining stock prices.
10 For an overview of the Japanese securities industry, see Suto (1993), chapter 4 in this volume.
11 In principle, each exchange can determine its own rate structure. In practice, however, the regional exchanges adopt the rate structure set by the Tokyo Stock Exchange in consultation with the Ministry of Finance.
12 Some have argued that the securities scandal of 1991, in which large securities companies were found to have compensated their favored clients for trading losses, had resulted from the fixed commission system, in which the rates facing large institutional investors were considerably higher than the actual cost of transactions facing the securities companies.
13 The microstructure of Japanese stock exchanges was first discussed in the academic literature by Takagi (1989) and Amihud and Mendelson (1989).
14 No market orders are allowed in the OTC market.
15 Prior to April 30, 1991, the afternoon session was from 1 p.m. to 3 p.m. in all eight exchanges. For certain designated stocks, the Osaka Stock Exchange begins trading at 8:50 a.m.; the Nagoya Stock Exchange ends trading at 3:10 p.m.

16 The minimum "tick" is 1 yen for stocks whose value is under 1,000 yen per share, and 10 yen for stocks whose value is more than 1,000 yen.

17 This is by no means an unusual occurrence in regional stock exchanges in Japan. Even in the first section of the Osaka Stock Exchange, there are days when opening prices fail to be established for more than 70 percent of the listed stocks.

18 Amihud and Mendelson (1989) analyzed the price discovery processes of the *itayose* and *zaraba* methods by comparing the open-to-open returns and the close-to-close returns. As they found that the open-to-open returns had a greater volatility and a more negative serial correlation than the close-to-close returns, they concluded that the *itayose* method was a more noisy price discovery process.

19 The practice of compensating clients for their trading losses, a widespread practice in Japan, was in violation of an administrative guidance of the Ministry of Finance, though it was not legally prohibited. With the revision of the Securities and Exchange Law in October 1991, however, such a practice by securities companies was made illegal.

20 In this context, the fixed commission system may be a way of increasing the cost to large institutional investors as well as to non-member firms of participating as dealers.

REFERENCES

Adachi, Tomohiko and Kurasawa, Motonari 1993: Stock futures and options markets in Japan. Chapter 12 in this volume.

Amihud, Yakov and Mendelson, Haim 1980: Dealership market: market-making with inventory. *Journal of Financial Economics*, 8, March, 31–53.

Amihud, Yakov and Mendelson, Haim 1982: Asset price behavior in a dealership market. *Financial Analysts Journal*, May/June, 50–9.

Amihud, Yakov and Mendelson, Haim 1987: Trading mechanisms and stock returns: an empirical investigation. *Journal of Finance*, 42, July, 533–55.

Amihud, Yakov and Mendelson, Haim 1989: Market microstructure and price discovery on the Tokyo Stock Exchange. *Japan and the World Economy*, 1, 341–70.

Cohen, Kalman J., Maier, Steven F., Schwartz, Robert A. and Whitcomb, David K. 1978: Limit orders, market structure, and the returns generation process. *Journal of Finance*, 33, June, 723–36.

Demsetz, Harold 1968: The cost of transacting. *Quarterly Journal of Economics*, 88, February, 33–53.

Garbade, Kenneth D. and Silber, William L. 1979: Structural organization of secondary markets: clearing frequency, dealer activity and liquidity risk. *Journal of Finance*, 34, June, 577–93.

Garman, Mark B. 1976: Market microstructure. *Journal of Financial Economics*, 3, June, 257–75.

Goldman, M. Barry and Beja, Avraham 1979: Market prices vs. equilibrium prices: returns' variance, serial correlation, and the role of the specialist. *Journal of Finance*, 34, June, 595–607.

Hamada, Yasuyuki, Kuwagai, Ko and Nishizawa, Akio 1990: *Kabushiki Tento Shijo*. Tokyo: Toyo Keizai Shinposha.

Lindsey, Richard R. and Schaede, Ulrike 1990: Specialist vs. *saitori*: market making in New York and Tokyo. Walter A. Haas School of Business, University of California, Berkeley.

Logue, Dennis E. 1975: Market-making and the assessment of market efficiency. *Journal of Finance*, 30, March, 115–23.

Macey, Jonathan and Kanda, Hideki 1990: The stock exchange as a firm: the emergence of close substitutes for the New York and Tokyo Stock Exchanges. *Cornell Law Review*, 75, July, 1007–52.

Maru, Junko 1993: The structure and performance of investment trusts in Japan. Chapter 15 in this volume.

Mendelson, Haim 1982: Market behavior in a clearing house. *Econometrica*, 50, November, 1505–24.

Ministry of Finance, *Shoken Kyoku Nenpo*, annual issues.

Niederhoffer, Victor and Osborne, M.F.M. 1966: Market making and reversal on the stock exchange. *Journal of the American Statistical Association*, 61, December, 897–916.

Roll, Richard 1984: A Simple Implicit Measure of the Effective Bid–Ask Spread in an Efficient Market. *Journal of Finance*, 39, September, 1127–39.

Silber, William L. 1975: Thinness in capital markets: the case of the Tel Aviv Stock Exchange. *Journal of Financial and Quantitative Analysis*, March, 129–42.

Smidt, Seymour 1979: Continuous versus intermittent trading. *Journal of Financial and Quantitative Analysis*, 14, November, 837–66.

Suto, Megumi 1993: The securities industry in Japan. Chapter 4 in this volume.

Takagi, Shinji 1988: On the statistical properties of floating exchange rates: a reassessment of recent experience and literature. *Bank of Japan Monetary and Economic Studies*, May, 65–95.

Takagi, Shinji 1989: The Japanese equity market: past and present. *Journal of Banking and Finance*, 13, September, 537–70.

Thomas, W.A. 1990: A dealing system for London in the 1990s: order or quote-driven? Société Universitaive Euvopéenne de Recherches Financières, Tilburg, The Netherlands, Series no. 55A.

Tokyo Stock Exchange, *Annual Securities Statistics*, annual issues. Tokyo Stock Exchange, *Fact Book*, annual issues.

Tokyo Stock Exchange, *Monthly Statistics Report*, monthly issues.

Tosho Saitori Kaiin Kyokai (Association of Saitori Members of the Tokyo Stock Exchange) 1975: *Saitori-shi*.

West, Richard R. 1970: Simulating securities markets operations: some examples, observations, and comments. *Journal of Financial and Quantitative Analysis*, 5, 115–37.

10

Stock Return Regularities on the Tokyo Stock Exchange

Kiyoshi Kato

1 INTRODUCTION

The efficient market hypothesis has interested a number of finance researchers over the last 40 years. A model that has been frequently used to test market efficiency is the capital asset pricing model. However, this one factor model has not satisfactorily explained the behavior of stock returns in both the Japanese and the US stock markets. There is considerable evidence that calendar anomalies exist in US as well as in non-US capital markets. For example, Jacobs and Levy (1988) have summarized the findings in this area and concluded that calendar effects should be of particular importance to traders.

Given the importance of stock return regularities, the objective of this chapter is to summarize the findings of such anomalies in Japanese stock returns as compared to those in US returns. In addition, the chapter will show the profitability of trading strategies based upon these anomalies. Since the Japanese stock market has become influential in the world capital market, the knowledge of stock return anomalies in Japan should be of interest to both scholars and practitioners.

This chapter is organized as follows. An overview of the Japanese stock market will be discussed in section 2. Section 3 discusses the January size effect. The intra-month effect is analyzed in section 3. Section 4 investigates the pattern of intra-day stock returns as well as the weekly patterns of daily stock returns. Section 5 discusses trading strategies based upon these anomalies. Section 6 consists of a brief summary and conclusion.

The author would like to thank the editor, Shinji Takagi, for many helpful comments. The author also gives special thanks to Julia West who provided a great deal of assistance in preparing the manuscript. This paper contains a portion of copyrighted materials which are reprinted with permission from Institutional Investor Inc.; from my paper 'Weekly patterns in Japanese stock returns', *Management Science*, 36(a) September 1990, © 1990 The Institute of Management Sciences, 290 Westminster Street, Providence RI 02903; and from the *Japanese Economic Journal*.

2 OVERVIEW OF THE JAPANESE STOCK MARKET

The stock market played a small role in the industrial development of Japan during the immediate postwar period. Japanese firms were unable to finance reconstruction from their own resources. Funds available in the capital market were insufficient for financing the strong expansion in equipment investment. In the face of an inadequate securities market at that time, the Bank of Japan lent liberally to the major commercial banks. The results was that, until recently, Japanese firms had been advancing their expansion programs by relying on debt financing, especially through banks, for most of their capital needs.

Looking at the financial market from the standpoint of fund suppliers, another interesting feature is observed. Until recently, Japanese individual investors have been relying heavily on bank savings in contrast with American counterparts who participate more actively in the stock market. Heavy reliance on bank and postal savings was due mainly to the fact that the Japanese authorities had taken a number of measures to encourage savings. The most important measure policy was tax exemption for postal savings and small savings accounts. This policy, however, was terminated in March 1988.

Internationalization of the Japanese capital market gradually progressed during the 1970s and accelerated during the 1980s. Since 1967, liberalization policies have also been instituted. Recent accumulation of household wealth has created a growing demand for new types of financial instruments in addition to bank savings, especially in the last several years. In order to meet investors' needs, the financial institutions have introduced a variety of financial instruments. As a result, the Japanese financial market has changed dramatically in the last ten years.[1]

Under the environmental restructuring mentioned above, the Japanese stock market experienced a dramatic rise in terms of both trading volume and market capitalization during the 1980s. The market value of the Japanese stock market has increased in market value over 100-fold from the beginning of 1950 to the end of 1990, although it has experienced a significant fall in value since the beginning of 1990. The summary statistics of both trading volume and market value on the world's major stock exchanges are shown in table 10.1. The transaction activities of the Tokyo Stock Exchange (TSE) are nearly as dynamic as those of the New York Stock Exchange (NYSE). This table clearly demonstrates the importance of the TSE in the world stock market.

The TSE has two sections, with the first section dominating the second section. Although it accounts for 40 percent in terms of membership, the second section is less than 10 percent of the first section, both in market

Table 10.1 Six major stock exchanges of the world (during or at end of 1989)

Stock exchange:		Tokyo	New York	Toronto	London	Frankfurt	Paris
No. of stock-listed companies	domestic	1,597	1,633	1,146	1,955	372	462
	foreign	119	87	68	604	348	223
No. of listed issues stocks	{ domestic	1,602	2,148	1,540	1,968	460	512
	{ foreign	119	98	72	766	90	238
bonds	{ domestic	1,340	2,744	} 14	2,737	5,860	2,478
	{ foreign	146	217		1,648	993	63
Total market value ($ mil.)	stocks	4,260,383	2,903,546	291,367	817,998	332,136	337,572
Trading value ($ mil.)	stocks	2,431,199	1,542,845	70,586	477,610	197,520	104,627
No. of member firms		114	535	74	409	209	44

Source: Tokyo Stock Exchange Fact Book (1991)

value and sales value. A company wishing to be listed on the TSE must go through the following process. The stock must first satisfy certain listing criteria for the second section. After being listed for at least one year on the second section, the company may move to the first section if it meets certain additional criteria. As a result of the criteria, the first section generally contains larger firms than does the second section.

Because an analysis of the firms listed on the first section should be analogous to an analysis of the firms listed on the NYSE, this chapter surveys the findings of major studies that are based on TSE's first section stocks. Generally, the data used in these studies consists of both monthly and daily returns of all common stocks listed on the first section of the TSE as well as two popular market indices in Japan, the value weighted index (TOPIX) of the Tokyo Stock Exchange and the Nikkei Stock Average (NSA). In addition, the daily returns are broken down into two periods, non-trading and trading period returns, with the latter further broken down into hourly returns for both indices.

3 THE JANUARY SIZE EFFECT

The hypothesis of capital market efficiency attracts considerable interest and critical comment among professional analysts as well as scholars. An efficient market means that no investor, on average, is able to earn abnormal returns. A significant amount of time has been spent testing this hypothesis. However, not all researchers give it their full support. A growing body of financial literature has documented anomalies that depend upon calendar time. A typical example is the January size effect, which refers to the phenomenon in which returns from small firms during January are significantly higher than those from large firms, even after adjusting for risk.

Keim (1983) provides substantial evidence of the existence of this anomalous effect in the US capital market.[2] The author notes that over half the annual size effect occurs in January, and approximately 25 percent of the annual size effect occurs during the first five trading days of January. One interesting question is whether or not the same pattern exists in Japanese stock returns.

Using the monthly stock returns, Kato and Schallheim (1985) document the June size effect as well as the January size effect from 1964 through 1980. In order to investigate these effects further, Kato (1990c) used three different returns: daily close-to-close, close-to-open, and open-to-close returns from 1974 through 1987. Five portfolios based upon stock market capitalizations are created.[3] The summary statistics are shown in table 10.2. The average market value ranges from 733 million yen for

Table 10.2   Mean return for size-related portfolios[a]

Firm size	Market value (¥ millions)	Close-to-close	Mean return Close-to-open	Open-to-close
Smallest	773	0.1492	0.1784	−0.0295
2	1,716	0.1058	0.1545	−0.0489
3	3,275	0.0859	0.1354	−0.0495
4	6,554	0.0764	0.0976	−0.0213
Largest	32,689	0.0653	0.0483	0.0168

[a] Market value for a portfolio is measured by the average, across years, of the mean market values of that size-related portfolio in each year.

the smallest portfolio to 32,687 million yen for the largest portfolio.[4] Interestingly, all close-to-open returns (overnight returns) are positive and most of the open-to-close returns are negative except in the largest portfolio.

The following regression model is used to examine the January size effect for the three different returns: close-to-close (R_{cc}), close-to-open (R_{co}) and open-to-close (R_{oc}).

$$R_i = \sum_{k=1}^{12} a_{kt}D_{kt} + u_t \qquad \text{for } i = cc, co, oc \qquad (10.1)$$

where D_{kt} are month-to-month dummy variables such that $D_{1t} = 1$ if day t occurs in January, and $D_{1t} = 0$ otherwise; $D_{2t} = 1$ if day t occurs in February, $D_{2t} = 0$ otherwise; and so on. The coefficients in equation (10.1) are the mean returns for January through December. The equality of these coefficients is examined with an F-test.

Table 10.3 presents the results of the regression analysis. Panel A displays the results regarding close-to-close returns. The average daily return in January is greater than those in the other months. That is, the average return increases as the size of the portfolios decreases. A similar pattern also exists for May, June, and July. However, a reversed size pattern is observed in March. The average return of the largest portfolio is greater than that of the smallest portfolio.

Panels B and C display the results regarding the close-to-open and open-to-close returns. The January size effect is observed for both trading and non-trading periods. The June size effect occurs mainly during the non-trading period. The March reversed size effect, on the other hand, occurs during the trading period.[5]

These size-related anomalies may be time variant. In order to examine this conjecture, Kato (1990c) divides the data into two subperiods,

Table 10.3 Average daily returns of all common stocks listed on the Tokyo Stock Exchange, classified by market capitalization, during the period January 4, 1974 through June 18, 1987

	Jan.	Feb.	Mar.	Apr.	May	Jun.	Jul.	Aug.	Sep.	Oct.	Nov.	Dec.	F
Panel A: Close-to-close return													
TOPIX[a]	0.142	0.016	0.156	0.079	-0.004	0.053	-0.012	0.096	-0.000	-0.010	0.070	0.129	3.78**
	(3.16)	(0.35)	(3.65)	(1.91)	(-0.09)	(1.32)	(-0.31)	(2.29)	(-0.01)	(-0.20)	(1.57)	(2.93)	
All firms	0.231	0.106	0.134	0.080	0.076	0.149	0.035	0.060	-0.04	0.049	0.087	0.084	11.71**
	(7.21)	(3.32)	(4.45)	(2.59)	(2.45)	(4.86)	(1.14)	(1.95)	(-0.42)	(1.56)	(2.66)	(2.59)	
Smallest	0.380	0.182	0.096	0.168	0.197	0.266	0.127	0.042	-0.009	0.075	0.157	0.106	28.9**
	(11.24)	(5.40)	(3.01)	(5.15)	(6.02)	(8.21)	(3.90)	(1.28)	(-0.26)	(2.25)	(4.54)	(3.09)	
2	0.293	0.115	0.117	0.131	0.100	0.178	0.046	0.065	-0.025	0.052	0.114	0.080	15.44**
	(8.78)	(3.45)	(3.70)	(4.06)	(3.08)	(5.56)	(1.43)	(2.02)	(-0.73)	(1.59)	(3.33)	(2.35)	
3	0.233	0.093	0.133	0.105	0.061	0.142	0.006	0.063	-0.005	0.020	0.111	0.067	10.37**
	(6.90)	(2.77)	(4.19)	(3.23)	(1.86)	(4.39)	(0.18)	(1.93)	(-0.14)	(0.60)	(3.23)	(1.95)	
4	0.178	0.076	0.145	0.099	0.041	0.128	-0.043	0.084	0.013	0.012	0.099	0.083	9.28**
	(5.49)	(2.35)	(4.73)	(3.16)	(1.30)	(4.12)	(-1.36)	(2.70)	(0.38)	(0.37)	(2.99)	(2.51)	
Largest	0.124	0.054	0.153	0.078	0.027	0.077	-0.054	0.074	0.013	0.013	0.090	0.136	6.31**
	(3.53)	(1.53)	(4.62)	(2.30)	(0.79)	(2.29)	(-1.60)	(2.18)	(0.37)	(0.36)	(2.51)	(3.81)	
Panel B: Close-to-open return													
All firms	0.181	0.118	0.157	0.126	0.116	0.154	0.091	0.086	0.050	0.091	0.089	0.106	54.06**
	(10.91)	(7.16)	(10.00)	(7.85)	(7.23)	(9.73)	(5.70)	(5.43)	(2.97)	(5.61)	(5.27)	(6.31)	
Smallest	0.278	0.194	0.184	0.179	0.191	0.253	0.170	0.114	0.100	0.128	0.171	0.173	95.08**
	(14.40)	(10.08)	(10.09)	(9.64)	(10.22)	(13.69)	(9.15)	(6.14)	(5.08)	(6.72)	(8.67)	(8.81)	
2	0.226	0.175	0.184	0.174	0.155	0.208	0.133	0.123	0.067	0.129	0.123	0.146	82.81**
	(12.66)	(9.84)	(10.91)	(10.12)	(8.94)	(12.12)	(7.73)	(7.15)	(3.68)	(7.32)	(6.75)	(8.05)	

Table 10.3 *Continued*

	Jan.	Feb.	Mar.	Apr.	May	Jun.	Jul.	Aug.	Sep.	Oct.	Nov.	Dec.	F
3	0.191	0.154	0.180	0.166	0.127	0.168	0.098	0.117	0.073	0.105	0.117	0.119	68.25**
	(11.11)	(9.00)	(11.08)	(10.00)	(7.63)	(10.17)	(5.90)	(7.03)	(4.17)	(6.22)	(6.62)	(6.78)	
4	0.143	0.105	0.149	0.136	0.100	0.134	0.039	0.073	0.043	0.063	0.094	0.084	40.96**
	(8.64)	(6.35)	(9.49)	(8.52)	(6.26)	(8.44)	(2.46)	(4.57)	(2.53)	(3.85)	(5.51)	(4.98)	
Largest	0.089	0.047	0.103	0.079	0.052	0.066	-0.011	0.031	-0.005	0.024	0.041	0.058	10.34**
	(4.79)	(2.52)	(5.86)	(4.41)	(2.88)	(3.67)	(-0.63)	(1.73)	(-0.28)	(1.32)	(2.13)	(3.08)	
Panel C: open-to-close return													
All firms	0.049	-0.013	-0.022	-0.046	-0.040	-0.006	-0.056	-0.027	-0.064	-0.043	-0.003	-0.023	2.47**
	(2.00)	(-0.52)	(-0.97)	(-1.96)	(-1.70)	(-0.26)	(-2.38)	(-1.14)	(-2.57)	(-1.77)	(-0.12)	(-0.91)	
Smallest	0.101	-0.012	-0.088	-0.012	0.006	0.013	-0.043	-0.073	-0.109	-0.053	-0.015	-0.067	6.58**
	(4.20)	(-0.51)	(-3.85)	(-0.51)	(0.25)	(0.54)	(-1.87)	(-3.13)	(-4.41)	(-2.25)	(-0.59)	(-2.72)	
2	0.067	-0.061	-0.068	-0.044	-0.055	-0.030	-0.087	-0.059	-0.092	-0.077	-0.010	-0.067	6.34**
	(2.59)	(-2.37)	(-2.80)	(-1.77)	(-2.21)	(-1.22)	(-3.52)	(-2.37)	(-3.52)	(-3.05)	(-0.39)	(-2.55)	
3	0.041	-0.061	-0.047	-0.061	-0.067	-0.026	-0.092	-0.054	-0.078	-0.086	-0.005	-0.052	5.25**
	(1.52)	(-2.28)	(-1.85)	(-2.35)	(-2.56)	(-1.02)	(-3.54)	(-2.09)	(-2.84)	(-3.23)	(-0.20)	(-1.90)	
4	0.035	-0.029	-0.004	-0.038	-0.060	-0.006	-0.082	0.011	-0.030	-0.051	0.005	-0.001	2.26**
	(1.32)	(-1.11)	(-0.16)	(-1.50)	(-2.37)	(-0.24)	(-3.26)	(0.43)	(-1.14)	(-2.00)	(0.20)	(-0.04)	
Largest	0.035	0.007	0.050	-0.001	-0.025	0.012	-0.043	0.042	0.019	-0.012	0.049	0.078	1.84*
	(1.24)	(0.24)	(1.88)	(-0.05)	(-0.92)	(0.43)	(-1.59)	(1.56)	(0.66)	(-0.42)	(1.72)	(2.73)	

[a] Daily returns of TOPIX computed during the period April 4, 1978 to June 18, 1987.

* Significant at the 5% level.
** Significant at the 1% level.

Table 10.4 Regression results for the five size-related portfolios estimating the mean rate of return for the months of January, March, and June

	Intercept	D-Jan(a1)	D-Mar(a2)	D-Jun(a3)	D(Jan)(a4)	D(Mar)(a5)	D(Jun)(a6)	F
Close-to-close	0.070	0.288	-0.010	0.118	-0.207	-0.235	-0.001	12.63**
		(5.73**)	(-0.22)	(2.47*)	(-2.97**)	(-3.57**)	(0.01)	
Close-to-open	0.123	0.083	-0.007	0.062	-0.034	-0.071	0.007	5.45**
		(2.98**)	(-0.25)	(2.33*)	(-0.88)	(-1.97*)	(0.19)	
Open-to-close	-0.053	0.205	-0.004	0.057	-0.173	-0.163	-0.006	9.08**
		(5.25**)	(-0.11)	(1.53)	(-3.19**)	(-3.18**)	(-0.12)	

t-statistics in parentheses.
* Significant at the 5% level.
** Significant at the 10% level.

Source: adapted from Kato (1990c)

1974 through 1980, and 1981 through 1987. The following regression is performed:

$$R_{St} - R_{Lt} = a_0 + a_1D_{1t} + a_2D_{3t} + a_3D_{6t}$$
$$+ a_4D_{1t}{}^*D_t + a_5D_{3t}{}^*D_t + a_6D_{6t}{}^*D_t \qquad (10.2)$$

R_s = Return for the smallest portfolio
R_L = Return for the largest portfolio
D_1 = Dummy variable for January
D_3 = Dummy variable for March
D_6 = Dummy variable for June
D_t = 0 for the pre-1981 period (1974–80)
      1 for the post-1981 period (1981–7)

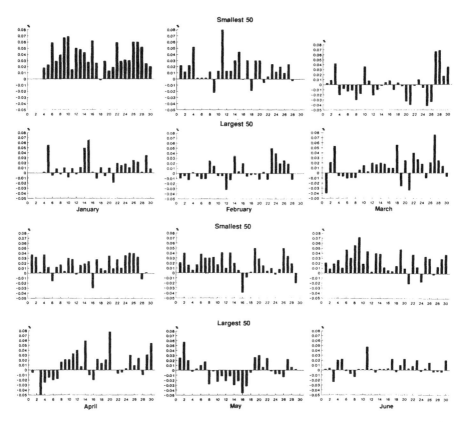

Figure 10.1 Histograms of average daily returns for each day of the month of both the 50 smallest stocks and the 50 largest stocks

Source: adapted from Kato (1990a)

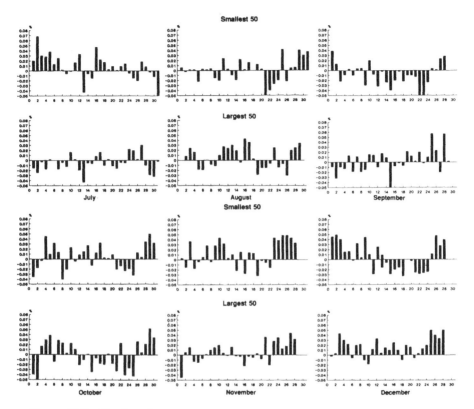

Figure 10.1 *Continued*

If the magnitude differs between these two exclusive periods, the coefficients, a_4, a_5 and a_6 should be statistically significant. If a_4 and a_6 are negative, the magnitude of the size effect decreases through time. On the other hand, if a_5 is negative, the magnitude of the reversed size effect increases through time. The results presented in table 10.4 indicate that: the magnitude of the January size effect decreases; the June size effect remains unchanged. The reversed size effect in March is more pronounced during the recent period 1981 through 1987. In fact, the reversed size effect in March is not statistically significant in the pre-1981 period.

Kato (1990a) plots the average daily return for each day of each month based upon calendar time.[6] The results are presented in figure 10.1. The upper histogram corresponds to the smallest portfolio (the 50 smallest stocks every year) and the lower histogram to the largest portfolio (the 50 largest stocks every year). In contrast with the US findings, the January size effect does not appear to be concentrated in the last day of December and the first several days of January. January returns for the smallest portfolio are consistently high. Relatively high returns are observed for the largest portfolio during the turn-of-the-year period.[7] June returns for the smallest portfolio exhibit a pattern similar to the January returns. Higher returns in March for the largest portfolio are concentrated during the last several days of the month.[8] These findings imply that investors can earn excess profits by holding small-firm stocks in January and June, and large-firm stocks during the last several day of March.

4   THE INTRA-MONTH EFFECT

The intra-month effect is the empirical regularity in which the mean daily return for stocks is positive only during the first half of each calendar month and is insignificantly different from zero during the second half. Ariel (1987) demonstrates this anomalous pattern using the US stock indices, and distinguishes this effect from the January size effect.

In order to examine whether the same phenomenon exists in the Japanese stock market, Kato (1990c) shows a histogram of the daily arithmetic mean return for the seven trading days before and after the start of each calendar month using TOPIX. The results are shown in figure 10.2. In contrast with the US findings, higher returns are concentrated in the last seven trading days to the month.

In order to investigate this effect further, Kato (1990b) replicates the procedure by dividing each month into the following three subperiods: the first ten days (F10), the following ten days (M10) and the remaining days (L10). The intra-month effect does change from month to month. In January, for example, higher returns are observed for both the first ten days and the last ten days. On the other hand, higher returns are observed for the middle ten days in August. The intra-month effect does not seem to be directly related to the January or June seasonal effects. In addition, since the *F*-statistic for the F10 group is insignificant; there appears to be no seasonal effect for the first ten days.

The intra-month effect may be related to company size. The five size-related portfolios constructed in the previous section are used to examine the relationship between the intra-month effect and the size effect. The results are presented in table 10.5. In contrast with the January seasonal effect, the size effect is most pronounced in the first ten days of the month. No size effect is observed in the last ten days of the month. Mean returns for the last ten days are consistently high across the five size-related portfolios.[9] The intra-month effect is apparently related to the size effect, although it is also time variant. For the 1950s, the mean return of the first ten days outperforms that of the last ten days. The pattern is just the opposite for the 1960s, 1970s, and 1980s.

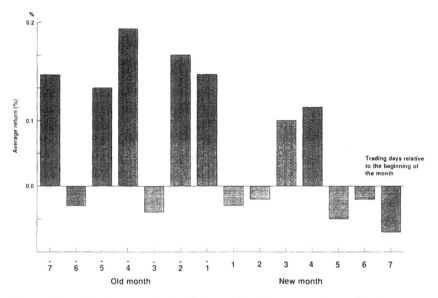

Figure 10.2 Histograms of the daily arithmetic mean returns for the seven trading days before and after the start of each calendar month from January 4, 1974 to June 18, 1987 for the TOPIX

Source: adapted from Kato (1990c)

Table 10.5 Relationship between intra-month effect and size effect

	Smallest	*2*	*3*	*4*	*Largest*	*F-statistic*
First 10 days	0.172	0.105	0.060	0.027	−0.003	69.35**
	(10.24)	(6.34)	(3.62)	(1.68)	(−0.20)	
Middle 10 days	0.111	0.072	0.053	0.055	0.059	5.44**
	(6.43)	(4.25)	(3.13)	(3.34)	(3.33)	
Last 10 days	0.162	0.137	0.140	0.143	0.136	1.05
	(9.89)	(8.55)	(8.64)	(9.21)	(8.10)	
F-statistic	81.30*	43.76*	32.53*	32.94*	25.58*	

t-statistics are in parentheses.
* Significant at the 1% level.

5 DAY-OF-THE-WEEK AND INTRA-DAY EFFECTS

Finance theory predicts that, under certain conditions, stock price follows a random walk. Cross (1973) and French (1980), however, document that the average return for Mondays is significantly negative, while the other days of the week have positive returns of varying magnitudes. The average return for Fridays is higher than that of the other days of the week. Although several studies have attempted to identify the cause of this day-of-the-week effect, none has provided a conclusive explanation of this effect.[10] Keim and Stambaugh (1984) and Keim (1987), for example, investigate the relationship between the January size effect and the day-of-the-week effect. According to their results, Friday returns are strongly related to firm size and Monday returns are consistently negative across all size portfolios for data. Connolly (1989) analyzes the robustness of the day-of-the-week effects across alternative estimation and testing procedures and concludes that the strength of the day-of-the-week effects appears to depend on the estimation and testing method.

While these studies focus on daily returns measured from the previous day's close to the current day's close, other studies employ intra-day data by breaking down daily returns into shorter periods. The results indicate that the day-of-the-week effect is time-variant.[11] Harris (1986), for example, documents that the Monday effect accrues for the first 45 minutes after the market opens.

Pettway and Tapley (1984) were the first to document the weekly pattern in the Japanese stock market using three market indices and stock data from five major Japanese firms from 1979 through 1982. They find, in contrast with the US market patterns, that Tuesday returns are the lowest and Wednesday returns are the highest. Jaffe and Westerfield (1985a, b) examine the daily stock indices for Australia, Canada, Great Britain, and Japan. Their results for Japan are similar to those of Pettway and Tapley for their longer sample period. In addition, their analysis of the structure of institutional correlations of weekly patterns indicates that the Tokyo Stock Exchange and the New York Stock Exchange did not appear to be linked during the period 1970 through 1983.[12] Measurement errors are also examined but the results do not appear to be influenced by measurement errors. Ikeda (1988) replicates several US studies using TOPIX, and obtains results similar to Pettway and Tapley's regarding the day-of-the-week effect. In addition, the weekly pattern also exists for skewness and kurtosis of the daily returns in Japan. Furthermore, according to Ikeda, the high Wednesday returns are partly the result of the settlement effect. However, low Tuesday returns are not satisfactorily explained.

These three studies utilize indices of the Tokyo Stock Exchange. Kato (1990d) examines the relationship between the day-of-the-week effect and firm size using individual stocks as well as the index. Since the size effect is concentrated in January, the results described above are also examined, with January taken separately from the rest of the year.[13] The returns are on average larger and exhibit a stronger relationship to firm size in

January than in other months. This is true for each day of the week. The weekly pattern is stronger in non-January months. As the size decreases, the weekly pattern tends to be larger. These results are consistent with the US findings. The size effect is observed for close-to-open returns in both January and non-January months. The reversal size effect during the trading period does not occur in January. One interesting observation is that negative Tuesday returns occur mainly in non-January months.[14]

The Tokyo Stock Exchange has been closed on some Saturdays since 1973.[15] This infrequent Saturday trading allows us to examine the weekend effect in greater detail. Kato (1990d) shows that large negative returns are observed on Mondays in the weeks when the previous week has closed on Friday.[16] Conversely, the Tuesday effect almost disappears in the weeks in which trading was closed on Friday. These results indicate that negative Monday and Tuesday returns in Japan may be related to Saturday trading.[17]

Kato (1990d) also examines the intra-day stock returns of TOPIX. Figure 10.3 presents the cumulative mean intra-day returns by week. One noticeable feature is the downward slope of Monday returns. In the

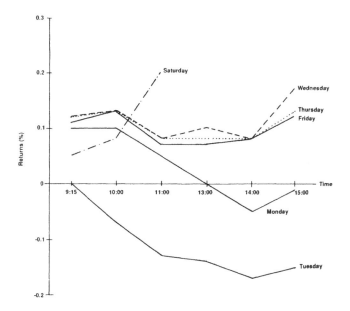

Figure 10.3 Cumulated mean intra-daily returns by week*

* The accrued return is the average rate of return experienced by the value weighted index of the Tokyo Stock Exchange; the starting points are overnight returns.

Source: adapted from Kato (1990d)

morning, Monday returns are similar to returns of Wednesday, Thursday, and Friday. However, after the morning trade is closed, Monday returns exhibit a pattern which is similar to Tuesday returns. Tuesday returns in Japan reveal a pattern comparable to Monday returns in the US.[18] In addition, the market is depressed on average from 10 to 11 a.m., except on Saturdays. The high Saturday returns from 10 to 11 a.m. are consistent with the observation that the market on average rises towards the end of a daily trading session.

Low Tuesday returns in Japan may be related to the Monday effect in the US. Since Tokyo is 14 hours ahead of New York, the Japanese weekly pattern may be analogous to the American pattern led by one day. To examine this hypothesis, correlation coefficients are computed between the Dow on the NYSE and the Nikkei Stock Average on the TSE during the period 1980 through 1987. The results appear in table 10.6. High correlation is observed between the previous day's returns ($t = -1$) of the New York Dow and the close-to-open returns ($t = 0$) of the Nikkei Stock Average.

This finding is consistent with the hypothesis that the opening price of the Tokyo market is strongly related to the previous day's New York

Table 10.6 Correlation coefficients between the Dow Jones industrial average ($t = -1$ and 0) and the Nikkei Stock Average ($t = 0$) during the period 1980 through 1987

| | | Tokyo ($t = 0$) | | |
		Close-to-open	Open-to-close	Close-to-close
New York				
($t = -1$)				
Close-to-open	r	0.3306	0.2817	0.3721
	p-value	(0.0001)	(0.0001)	(0.0001)
Open-to-close	r	0.3823	0.1091	0.2453
	p-value	(0.0001)	(0.0006)	(0.0001)
Close-to-close	r	0.5363	0.2551	0.4313
	p-value	(0.0001)	(0.0001)	(0.0001)
($t = 0$)				
Close-to-open	r	0.1556	0.0565	0.1096
	p-value	(0.0001)	(0.0138)	(0.0001)
Open-to-close	r	-0.0057	0.0591	0.0484
	P-value	(0.8031)	(0.0099)	(0.0348)
Close-to-close	r	0.0887	0.0929	0.1145
	p-value	(0.0001)	(0.0001)	(0.0001)

Source: adapted from Kato (1990d)

market performance. Lower correlation coefficients between the previous day's returns ($t = -1$) of the New York Dow and the open-to-close returns ($t = 0$) of the Nikkei Stock Average may indicate that the stock price reflects information quickly.[19,20] In order to examine this hypothesis more formally, Kato (1990d) follows Jaffe and Westerfield (1985b) and considers infrequent Saturday trading by dividing the data into two groups. The first data set consists of the weeks when the previous week has Saturday trading.[21] The second data set contains the remaining weeks.[22] The following regression is conducted for both groups.

$$R_{\mathrm{JAP},t} - R_{\mathrm{US},t-1} = \sum_{k=1}^{6} a_k D_{kt} + u_t \qquad (10.3)$$

where $R_{\mathrm{JAP},t}$ is the close-to-close return of the NSA on the Tokyo market, and $R_{\mathrm{US},t-1}$ is the previous day's close-to-close return of the New York Dow. D_{kt} is a dummy variable for the day of the week. If all coefficients equal zero, the weekly pattern of the Tokyo stock market simply reflects that of the New York stock market.

The results are striking. The F-statistic of the first data set is 0.32, which is not significant at the 10 percent level.[23] However, the F-statistic of the second data set is 3.48 which is significant at the 1 percent level. The significant F-statistic for the second data set is mainly caused by the low Monday return of the Nikkei Stock Average relative to the high Friday return of the New York Dow.[24] Considering the possibility of new information being released in Japan over the weekend, matching the Monday return of the Nikkei Stock Average to the Friday return of the New York Dow may not be appropriate.[25] In the first data set, the Monday return of the Nikkei Stock Average is automatically excluded because there is no matched day. Thus, by excluding the Monday returns from the Japanese stock returns, the hypothesis that the weekly patterns of the two markets are the same is not rejected. This finding is consistent with the conjecture that the Japanese Tuesday effect is really a reflection of the Monday effect in the US.[26] In addition, the separate Monday effect seems to exist in the Japanese daily stock returns.

The weekend effect may also be related to the intra-month effect. High Saturday returns may cause the intra-month effect.[27] The last ten days of the month (L10) are likely to contain a half-day trading on Saturday more than the first ten days of the month (F10) or the middle ten days of the month (M10).[28] As a result, the mean return of L10 should be higher than those of F10 or M10 to reflect high Saturday returns. However, the results of table 10.4 are inconsistent with this conjecture. The intra-month effect varies across the months.[29] Furthermore, the intra-month effect still exists after excluding Saturdays. Therefore, the intra-month effect cannot be a proxy of the weekend effect.

Tokunaga, Iihara, and Kato (1991) re-examine the day of the week effect allowing the change in variances and covariances over time, by using the MA (1)-GARCH (1,1) model to adjust for heteroskedasticity. Since Thursday returns are close to the average return of all days during the sample period 1950 through 1989, Tokunaga et al. introduce the following five dummy variables into the MA(1)-GARCH (1,1) model to test the day-of-the-week effect, assuming Thursday returns as a proxy of the average return.

$$R_t = \gamma_0 + \gamma_1 D_M + \gamma_2 D_T + \gamma_3 D_W + \gamma_4 D_F + \gamma_5 D_S + \varepsilon_t - \theta_1 \varepsilon_{t-1} \quad (10.4)$$

$$h_t = \alpha_0 + \alpha_1 \varepsilon_{t-1}^2 + \beta_1 h_{t-1} \quad (10.5)$$

where R_t = daily return
D_M = dummy variable for Monday
D_T = dummy variable for Tuesday
D_W = dummy variable for Wednesday
D_F = dummy variable for Friday
D_S = dummy variable for Saturday
h_t = conditional volatility
ε_t = error term which is serially uncorrelated with mean zero, but the conditional variance of ε_t equals h_t which changes through time.

If none of the coefficients of dummy variables are significant, then we can conclude that the weekend effect is a product of model misspecification. According to the results shown in table 10.7, the MA(1)-GARCH(1,1) model does not successfully capture the day of the week effect in Japan because at least one of the coefficients of dummy variables is statistically significant for any of the subsample periods.

6   THE OVER-REACTION EFFECT

DeBondt and Thaler (1985, 1987) document an "overreaction effect" of stock returns. This effect predicts that securities with abnormally high positive (negative) returns over some formation period will have abnormally high negative (positive) returns over a subsequent test period. Kato (1990b) attempts to replicate the methodologies employed by DeBondt and Thaler to investigate if the same pattern exists in the Japanese stock returns.

A series of non-overlapping six-year samples are created using the monthly rate of returns during the period 1952 through 1989. Each sample consists of a three-year formation and a three-year test period. There are 12 non-overlapping samples for this analysis. During the for-

Table 10.7 Estimation of day-of-the-week effect using MA(1)-GARCH(1,1) model

$$R_t = \gamma_0 + \gamma_1 D_{\text{Mon}} + \gamma_2 D_{\text{Tue}} + \gamma_3 D_{\text{Wed}} + \gamma_4 D_{\text{Fri}} + \gamma_5 D_{\text{Sat}} + \varepsilon_t + \theta_1 \varepsilon_{t-1}$$
$$h_t = \alpha_0 + \alpha_1 \varepsilon_{t-1}^2 + \beta_1 h_{t-1}$$

Period	γ_0	γ_1	γ_2	γ_3	γ_4	γ_5	θ_1	α_0	α_1	β_1
1950–80	0.051 (4.49)	−0.051 (−3.34)	−0.058 (−3.72)	0.060 (4.45)	0.011 (0.88)	0.060 (3.10)	−0.212 (−21.9)	0.018 (17.8)	0.179 (52.7)	0.800 (182)
1950–72	0.098 (5.76)	−0.117 (−5.24)	−0.051 (−2.18)	−0.026 (−1.29)	−0.032 (−1.64)	0.023 (0.85)	−0.199 (−14.7)	0.030 (17.5)	0.174 (26.4)	0.784 (115)
1973–89	0.012 (0.87)	0.018 (0.87)	−0.064 (−3.16)	0.137 (7.75)	0.062 (3.37)	0.092 (3.32)	−0.250 (−16.4)	0.011 (9.98)	0.188 (36.7)	0.798 (114)
1953–57	0.087 (2.46)	−0.172 (−3.75)	−0.072 (−1.58)	−0.111 (−2.84)	−0.052 (−1.33)	0.066 (1.13)	−0.341 (−12.1)	0.024 (7.58)	0.225 (11.0)	0.756 (41.8)
1958–62	0.139 (3.38)	−0.118 (−2.14)	−0.108 (−1.92)	−0.022 (−0.47)	−0.021 (−0.41)	0.026 (0.40)	−0.178 (−6.21)	0.023 (5.19)	0.136 (7.98)	0.828 (43.6)
1963–67	0.045 (1.30)	−0.130 (−2.66)	0.003 (0.07)	−0.061 (−1.26)	−0.026 (−0.58)	−0.027 (−0.53)	−0.120 (−4.44)	0.026 (4.69)	0.128 (7.94)	0.809 (32.0)
1968–72	0.126 (3.47)	0.006 (0.12)	−0.030 (−0.59)	0.002 (−0.05)	−0.038 (−0.93)	−0.038 (−0.64)	−0.102 (−2.75)	0.091 (11.9)	0.278 (13.9)	0.577 (25.5)
1973–77	0.007 (0.28)	−0.068 (−1.68)	−0.058 (−1.57)	0.138 (3.63)	0.011 (0.39)	0.035 (0.69)	−0.244 (−7.92)	0.014 (3.85)	0.159 (7.75)	0.809 (33.8)
1978–82	−0.010 (−0.50)	0.052 (1.72)	−0.060 (−2.07)	0.141 (5.72)	0.087 (3.43)	0.107 (2.66)	−0.232 (−8.21)	0.010 (6.01)	0.179 (10.4)	0.783 (39.7)
1983–87	0.083 (2.73)	0.027 (0.60)	−0.146 (−3.31)	0.116 (3.25)	0.008 (0.20)	0.101 (1.80)	−0.299 (−10.4)	0.026 (6.26)	0.309 (22.0)	0.697 (45.6)

Numbers in parentheses are *t*-statistics.

Source: adapted from Tokunaga, Iihara and Kato (1992)

Cumulative abnormal return

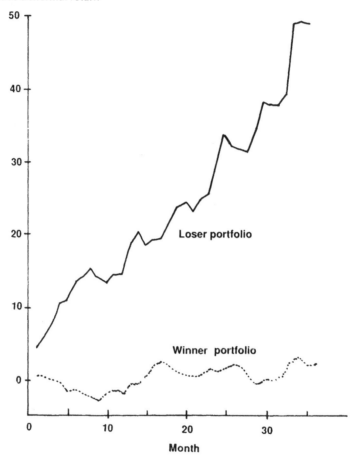

Figure 10.4 Over-reaction effect during the period 1950 to 1989

Source: adapted from Kato (1990b)

mation period, cumulative abnormal returns are cumulated for each security by subtracting the market returns given by TOPIX from the portfolio returns.[30] The loser portfolio contains 30 securities whose cumulative abnormal returns are the worst, and the winner portfolio consists of the 30 best securities. In the test periods, cumulative abnormal returns are calculated for each security and the average cumulative return of each portfolio is computed with January as the starting month. According to the results depicted in figure 10.4, a pattern similar to

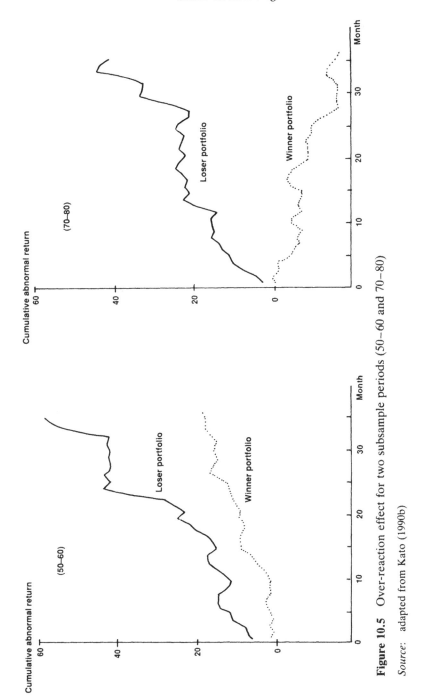

Figure 10.5   Over-reaction effect for two subsample periods (50–60 and 70–80)

Source: adapted from Kato (1990b)

that in the US is observed. One striking observation is that the loser portfolio does not exhibit the January effect.

In order to examine the stability of the overreaction effect, Kato (1990b) divides the data into two subperiods, pre-1970 and post-1970. The results are shown in figure 10.5. An interesting distinction is observed between the two periods. The overreaction effect did exist during the post-1970 period. However, only the loser portfolio exhibits overreaction during the pre-1970 period. Kato (1990c) further divides the post-1970 data into two periods, the 1970s and the 1980s. The winner portfolio earns negative abnormal returns in the test periods on average. The positive performance of the loser portfolio does not seem to be significant and is much smaller than the negative performance of the winner portfolio. During the 1980s, the overreaction effect disappeared, indicating that the effect is time variant. In addition, it is possible that some other fundamental changes occurred on the Tokyo Stock Exchange during the 1980s.[31]

7   PROFITABILITY OF TRADING STRATEGIES

Given interesting stock return regularities, investors may want to pursue the trading strategies based upon the results reported thus far in this chapter. Kato (1990c) attempts to investigate whether or not returns earned by such strategies are economically significant in the Japanese stock market for the period 1974 through 1987. Here we do not consider the overreaction effect because the effect seems to have disappeared during the 1980s.

The strategy examined includes both timing of purchases and portfolio selection. The portfolio named "largest 10-1" contains the ten largest stocks based upon market value at the end of 1974. Similarly, the portfolio named "smallest 10-1" contains the ten smallest stocks based upon market value at the end of 1974. In this strategy, an investor is required to hold his portfolio until the end of 1987. On the other hand, the portfolio named, "largest 10-2" ("smallest 10-2") contains the ten largest (smallest) stocks based upon market value at each year end. In this strategy, an investor is required to rebalance his portfolio at each year end based upon company size. Both the "smallest 10-1" and the "smallest 10-2" portfolios should be able to capture the size-related premia.

Considering the January, March, and June seasonal effects, an investor may want to rebalance his portfolio three times a year in a strategy called the anomaly fund. In this strategy an investor holds the ten smallest stocks from January to February (period 1) as well as from April to

Table 10.8 Performance of the anomaly fund

Year:	1974	1975	1976	1977	1978	1979	1980	1981	1982	1983	1984	1985	1986	1987	Mean	σ
TOPIX	−9.1	16.2	18.6	−5.2	23.0	2.0	21.8	16.3	4.0	23.0	24.9	14.9	48.0	9.1	14.8	14.4
Largest 10-1[a]	−19.4	6.7	2.7	−15.6	8.7	12.4	17.5	21.8	3.1	5.0	88.6	13.1	33.8	44.3	15.9	26.8
Smallest 10-1	−5.0	−8.4	24.9	27.2	105.5	17.2	33.9	−13.7	−5.3	56.0	41.1	72.2	17.9	38.2	26.2	35.6
Largest 10-2[b]	−19.4	3.0	13.7	−12.8	11.9	−5.1	5.3	12.3	5.1	8.6	59.7	6.3	59.5	10.0	11.3	22.6
Smallest 10-2	−5.0	−3.3	26.1	20.3	131.1	9.1	61.5	−11.0	−10.4	43.3	30.2	62.8	129.5	205.8	49.3	64.6
Anomaly fund[c]	31.0	16.8	54.7	32.3	65.2	8.6	23.2	−3.3	−6.1	41.6	39.3	81.0	278.0	82.0	53.2	70.4
Period 1	11.3	1.4	12.8	15.7	4.2	4.9	0.6	6.6	−0.8	18.3	17.6	36.1	51.5	25.8	14.7	14.8
Period 2	−1.2	0.1	0.4	−6.2	2.0	−4.3	−4.6	2.7	−7.5	2.9	16.9	−1.0	19.1	9.0	2.0	8.0
Period 3	19.1	15.1	36.6	21.9	55.4	8.2	28.4	−11.7	2.3	16.3	1.3	34.3	109.5	32.7	26.4	29.4

[a] Largest 10-1 is a portfolio including the ten largest stocks without rebalancing. Smallest 10-1 contains the ten smallest stocks without rebalancing.

[b] Largest 10-2 is a portfolio including the ten largest stocks with annual rebalancing. Smallest 10-2 contains the ten smallest stocks with annual rebalancing.

[c] Anomaly fund contains the ten smallest stocks from January to February (period 1) and from April to July (period 2), and the ten largest stocks in March (period 2). No stocks are held from August through December.

Source: adapted from Kato (1990c)

July (period 3). The same investor holds ten largest stocks in March (period 2).[32] However, no stock is purchased during any other periods.[33] Company size is evaluated by year end market value for each year.

The application of these strategies is remarkable, as can be seen in table 10.8. The "smallest 10-2", on average, earns 49.3 percent annually from 1974 through 1987. The anomaly fund beats TOPIX in 12 out of 14 years although the variabilities of annual returns for both the "smallest 10-2" and the anomaly fund are much higher than that of TOPIX.[34] The average beta for the "smallest 10-2" is 0.32, which is very small compared with the average beta of 1.12 for the "largest 10-2."[35]

Although the results here are impressive, we must be cautious about making definitive conclusions. Because the selected firms in both portfolios have a relatively small number of shares outstanding, the stock price could easily change if this strategy were pursued in a large block transaction. Thus, one of the major assumptions in finance, that of the price-taker, may not hold for these selected stocks. In fact, only three out of the hundred smallest stocks have an average daily trading volume of more than 100,000 shares.[36] Therefore, the price used in this study may not be appropriate to compute the returns of these portfolios, and there is a possibility that the profit reported is overstated. As a result, institutional investors may not gain much from this simulated strategy because the amount of money they involve would be very large. On the other hand, individual investors with a small amount of money may be able to use the results reported here in the belief that the pattern will persist into the future.[37]

8　CONCLUSIONS

This chapter has summarized the anomalous behavior of stock returns in the Japanese stock market. The size effect is mainly observed for January and June. The size reversed effect is found in March. The June size effect appears in the non-trading period. Conversely, the March effect emerges in the trading period. The January size effect decreases through time while the March effect increases through time. The intra-month effect is observed in Japan but, contrary to the US findings, higher returns are concentrated in the last several days of the month. An analysis of the relationship between this intra-month effect and the January size effect shows that the intra-month effect is partly related to the size effect, not to the day-of-the-week effect.

The weekly pattern of Japanese stock returns was also examined. Low Tuesday and high Wednesday returns are observed for the close-to-close returns. Most of the positive returns arise during the non-trading period.

Negative returns are experienced on both Mondays and Tuesdays during the trading period, especially in the last trading period of the morning. Positive returns are observed for the last trading period of the day. The Tuesday effect in Japan is related to the Monday effect in the US. The weekly pattern is related to the size effect such that the weekly pattern decreases as the size of the firm increases for close-to-close returns. The reversal size effect observed during the trading period is inconsistent with common sense, which argues that since the stocks of small firms are, on average, riskier than those of large firms, they should experience higher mean returns. An analysis of the relationship between the January effect and the weekly pattern suggests that the weekly pattern is more pronounced in non-January months, as in the US data.

The overreaction effect in the Japanese stock market was also summarized. The overreaction effect in Japan is somewhat different from that found in the US. The loser portfolio outperformed the winner portfolio until 1980. Before 1970, the winner portfolio in Japan did not lose as much as the winner portfolio in the US. The prematurity of the stock market in those days may explain the difference from the US results. During the 1980s, the overreaction effect disappeared. Our results indicate that the structure of the Tokyo market has changed drastically since 1980.[38]

The profitability of trading strategies based on these anomalies was also considered. While the trading strategy employed here may attract a certain type of investor, we cannot be sure if the past patterns will persist into the future. For one thing, the profitable strategies involved the portfolio with thinly traded stocks. The price behavior of these stocks could thus change if a large institutional investor were to implement such a strategy. Moreover, as the stock prices in the Tokyo stock market rose continuously until the beginning of 1990, the enormous profit which would have been made by these trading strategies may simply reflect the long bull market.[39]

NOTES

1 The Nomura scandal is one evidence that the business practice of a majority of Japanese financial institutions has not kept pace with the drastic change in their environment. Most of them still follow traditional management styles despite the fact that they are now operating in a totally different business environment.

2 Similar results were obtained by Reinganum (1983); Roll (1983); Givoly and Ovadia (1983); and others.

3 The five portfolios are rebalanced yearly, based upon the market value of equity for each firm at the end of the year. The stock market capitalizations

of all firms in the sample are computed by multiplying the price per share by the number of shares outstanding at year end.

4   The average market values are computed as the average across all sample years of the average market value of that size decile in each year. The number of firms included in the sample ranges from 806 to 1,069.

5   A similar analysis was conducted for the excess close-to-close returns. Since the results are not substantially different, we report only the results of the raw return analysis for the January size effect.

6   Kato (1990a) also plots the average returns for each day of these months based upon trading time. Because the results are not substantially different, only the results based on calendar time are reported.

7   There is a common belief among Japanese securities analysts regarding the behavior of stock prices at the turn of the year. Securities firms attempt to end their transactions with a good record on the last day of December. The same attitude is observed on the first day of January. If this is true, the two-day returns of the Japanese stock market at the turn of the year should be higher than the average two-day returns. Because large-firm stocks are likely to be good candidates for this artificial transaction, the high returns of the largest portfolio at the turn of the year period may thus be explained. The results here are consistent with this belief.

8   Kato (1989) examines the relationship between the March size effect and the fiscal year end of the company concerned. On average, the stock prices decline in the month following the fiscal year end. The month of the fiscal year end, on the other hand, realizes positive returns. This may be consistent with the notion that good news comes early and bad news comes later.

9   The same analysis is conducted for the excess returns computed by the market model. The results are not substantially different.

10   Gibbons and Hess (1981) propose and test the settlement hypothesis. Lakonishok and Levi (1982) add the check-clearing process to this settlement procedure. However, the results of neither study fully support the settlement hypothesis. Furthermore, Dyl and Martin (1985) provide evidence against the settlement hypothesis. Keim and Stambaugh (1984) investigate a specialist related bias by examining the stocks in the over-the-counter market and fail to find such a bias. Measurement errors are also examined by Gibbons and Hess (1981) and Keim and Stambaugh (1984).

11   Rogalski (1984) documents a non-trading weekend effect. All of the average negative returns from Friday closes to Monday closes documented in the literature take place during the non-trading period from Friday close to Monday open. Smirlock and Starks (1986) extend Rogalski's study by decomposing daily returns into six hourly return measures and extending the time periods. Their results are not consistent with Rogalski's.

12   A recent study by Hamao, Masulis and Ng (1990) reports the evidence of price volatility spillovers from the New York to the Tokyo stock market. No similar spillover effect occurs in the other direction.

13   The same analysis is conducted for three subperiods. The results are essentially the same. One striking observation in this analysis is that the weekly pattern of close-to-open returns is stronger for non-January months as

time progresses. This is especially true for the smallest portfolio. The same pattern does not exist for open-to-close returns.

14 Keim (1987) reports that negative Monday returns are observed in the US in non-January months.

15 During the sample period, the Tokyo Stock Exchange was open from Monday through Friday from 9 to 11 a.m. and from 1 to 3 p.m. The market was also open on Saturday from 9 to 11 a.m. until 1972. During the period of January 1973 through July 1983, the market was closed on the third Saturday of each month. During the period August 1983 through July 1986, the market was closed on the second Saturday of each month. Following that the market was closed on the second and third Saturday of each month until January 1989. Since February 1989, the market has been closed on all Saturdays. These changes offer an additional opportunity to examine the weekly pattern of Japanese stock returns.

16 This finding is different from the US finding by Keim and Stambaugh (1984) in which the Monday effect was observed in periods both with and without Saturday trading.

17 When we expand our sample period up to 40 years from 1950 to 1990, this Saturday effect is not clearly observed. This implies that the infrequent Saturday trading effect is not stationary. As mentioned in section 2, however, the Japanese stock market was very small during the 1950s and 1960s. The analysis of the 1970s and 1980s may thus be more interesting.

18 While Harris uses intraday returns at 15-minute intervals, Kato (1990d) employs hourly returns.

19 Kato (1990d) also divides the entire period into four subperiods. The particular time series pattern is not observed for correlation coefficients between the returns of the Nikkei Stock Average and the previous day's returns of the New York Dow.

20 Contemporaneous dependence between the New York Dow and the Nikkei Stock Average is also reported. Although most correlation coefficients are significant between New York returns ($t = 0$) and Tokyo returns ($t = 0$), the magnitude is much smaller. This result may indicate that the New York market is still the seismic center of information.

21 In this data set, the Tuesday return of the Nikkei Dow corresponds to the Monday return of the New York Dow, the Wednesday return of the Nikkei Stock Average to the Tuesday return of the New York Dow, the Thursday return of the Nikkei Stock Average to the Wednesday return of the New York Dow, the Friday return of the Nikkei Stock Average to the Thursday return of the New York Dow and the Saturday return of the Nikkei Stock Average to the Friday return of the New York Dow. The Monday return of the Nikkei Stock Average is excluded.

22 In this data set, the Monday return of the Nikkei Stock Average corresponds to the Friday return of the New York Dow in the previous weeks, the Tuesday return of the Nikkei corresponds to the Monday of the Dow, the Wednesday of the Nikkei to the Tuesday of the Dow, the Thursday returns of the Nikkei to the Wednesday of the Dow and the Friday returns of the Nikkei to the Thursday of the Dow. No daily return is excluded.

23   Kato (1990d) also runs the regression using the close-to-open returns on the Japanese index and the open-to-close returns on the US index. The results are not substantially different.

24   In order to confirm this conclusion, Kato (1990d) drops Friday returns of the New York market and Monday returns of the Tokyo market from the second data set and conducts the same regression. An insignificant F-statistic is obtained.

25   Saturday was not a day off for a relatively large number of Japanese corporations during this sample period.

26   These results are somewhat different from those of Jaffe and Westerfield (1985b) as the time period used by Kato (1990d) is more current.

27   According to Kato (1990d), Saturday returns are higher than the other days of the week, except Wednesday.

28   As discussed earlier, the Japanese stock market was closed on the second and or the third Saturdays. L10 contains the third Saturday only when the first Saturday is the seventh day of the month. On the other hand, F10 contains the second Saturday when the first Saturday is either 1st, 2nd or 3rd day of the month. M10 are likely to contain both the second and the third Saturdays.

29   Saturday returns are consistently high for all months.

30   When the market model is used to adjust for risk, the results are not substantially different. The previous 60 months are used for estimating the parameters of the market model.

31   As previously mentioned, the size-related seasonality also changed during the 1980s. There are several possible explanations for this phenomenon. One such explanation is the change in the market participants. The number of institutional investors trading in the stock market increased during the 1980s.

32   This simple strategy requires the rebalancing of portfolio three times a year.

33   An investor can purchase the risk-free assets.

34   Since the performance in period 2 is not good, this period is excluded to calculate a mean return of 47.7 percent and standard deviation of 53.2 percent. Additionally, the trading strategy which considers both weekly and monthly patterns in addition to the size effect provides better performance than the anomaly fund presented in table 10.8.

35   For US data, the beta increases as size decreases. Thus, smaller firms are viewed as having greater risk. For Japanese data, small firms have lower betas than large firms. Elton and Gruber (1988) report the same pattern. In fact, low beta stocks are likely to outperform the market in Japan.

36   Since 1,000 shares is the minimum purchase allowed for most Japanese stocks, it is commonly said that the average daily trading volume must be greater than 100,000 shares in order to avoid significant market impact.

37   We also have to consider high transaction costs in Japan. Round-trip commission costs for the smallest transactions in Japan currently is 2.3 percent of the traded value, making this strategy less attractive.

38   Institutional investors dominated the trading of the TSE during the 1980s. The major market participants in this period were quite different from those prior to 1970.

39 Surprisingly, the June size effect still existed in 1989, 1990, and 1991. The small size portfolio continuously performed well from April to July although the Tokyo stock market did not experience continuous growth during the years 1990–1.

REFERENCES

Aggarwal, R., Hiraki, T. and Rao, R.P. 1987: The nature of security returns on the TSE: P/E, size and seasonal influences. Unpublished manuscript.

Ariel, R.A. 1987: Monthly effect in stock returns. *Journal of Financial Economics*, 18, 164–74.

Banz, R.W. 1981: The relationship between return and market value of common stocks. *Journal of Financial Economics*, 9, 3–18.

Basu, S. 1983: The relationship between earnings' yield, market value and return for NYSE common stocks. *Journal of Financial Economics*, 12, 129–56.

Berges, F., McConnell, J.J. and Schlarbaum, G.G. 1983: An investigation of the turn-of-the-year effect, the small firm effect and the tax-loss-selling pressure hypothesis in Canadian stock returns. *Journal of Finance*, 39, 185–92.

Blume, M.E. and Stambaugh, R.F. 1983: Biases in computed returns: an application to the size effect. *Journal of Financial Economics*, 12, 387–404.

Brown, P., Keim, D.B., Kleidon, A.W. and Marsh, T.A. 1983: Stock return seasonalities and the tax loss selling hypothesis: analysis of the arguments and Australian evidence. *Journal of Financial Economics*, 12, 105–27.

Connolly, R.A. 1989: An examination of robustness of the weekend effect. *Journal of Financial and Quantitative Analysis*, 24, 133–69.

Corhay, A., Hawawini, G. and Mitchel, P. 1987: Seasonality in the risk-return relationship: some international evidence. *Journal of Finance*, 42, 49–68.

Cross, F. 1973: The behavior of stock prices on Fridays and Mondays. *Financial Analysts Journal*, 27, 67–9.

DeBondt, W. and Thaler, R. 1985: Does the stock market overreact? *Journal of Finance*, 40, 793–805.

DeBondt, W. and Thaler, R. 1987: Further evidence on investor overreaction and stock market seasonality. *Journal of Finance*, 42, 557–81.

Dimson, E. 1988: *Stock Market Regularities*. Cambridge: Cambridge University Press.

Dyl, E.A. and Martin, S.A. 1985: Weekend effects on stock returns: a comment. Journal of Finance, 40, 347–9.

Elton, E. and Gruber, M. 1988: A multi-index model of the Japanese stock market. *Japan and the World Economy*, 1, 21–45.

Elton, E and Gruber, M. 1989: *Japanese Financial Markets*. New York: Ballinger.

French, K.R. 1980: Stock returns and the weekend effect. *Journal of Financial Economics*, 8, 55–69.

Gibbons, M.R. and Hess, P. 1981: Day of the week effects and asset returns. *Journal of Business*, 54, 579–96.

Givoly, D. and Ovadia, A. 1983: Year-end tax-induced sales and stock market seasonality. *Journal of Finance*, 38, 171–85.

Gultekin, M. and Gultekin, N. 1983: Stock market seasonality: international evidence. *Journal of Financial Economics*, 12, 469–81.

Hamao, Y. 1988: An empirical examination of the arbitrage pricing theory using Japanese data. *Japan and the World Economy*, 11, 45–61.

Hamao, Y., Masulis, R. and Ng, V. 1990: Correlations in price changes and volatility across international stock markets. *Review of Financial Studies*, 3(2), 281–308.

Harris, L. 1986: A transaction data study of weekly and intradaily patterns in stock returns. *Journal of Financial Economics*, 16, 99–117.

Hawawini, G. 1990: Stock market anomalies and the pricing of equity on the Tokyo Stock Exchange. Unpublished manuscript.

Ikeda, M. 1988: Weekend effect and mixed normal distribution hypothesis. *Japanese Financial Review*, 8, 27–53.

Jacobs, B. and Levy, K. 1988: Calendar anomalies: abnormal returns at calendar turning points. *Financial Analysts Journal*, Nov/Dec, 28–39.

Jaffe, J. and Westerfield, R. 1985a: The weekend effect in common stock returns: the international evidence. *Journal of Finance*, 40, 433–54.

Jaffe, J. and Westerfield, R. 1985b: Patterns in Japanese common stock returns: day of the week and turn of the year effects. *Journal of Financial and Quantitative Analysis*, 20, 243–60.

Kato, K. 1989: Examining anomalous patterns in Japanese stock returns. *Nanzan Management Review*, 4(1), 27–44.

Kato, K. 1990a: Anomalies in Japanese stock returns. *Security Analysts Journal*, December, 7–20.

Kato, K. 1990b: Behavior of Japanese stock price and anomalies. *Japanese Economic Journal*, 36, 1031–44.

Kato, K. 1990c: Being a winner in the Tokyo stock market. *Journal of Portfolio Management*, Summer, 52–6.

Kato, K. 1990d: Weekly patterns in Japanese stock returns. *Management Science*, September, 1031–43.

Kato, K. and Schallheim, J. 1985: Seasonal and size anomalies in the Japanese stock market. *Journal of Financial and Quantitative Analysis*, 22, 243–60.

Kato, K., Linn, S. and Schallheim, J. 1991: Are there arbitrage opportunities in the market for American depository receipts? *Journal of International Financial Markets, Institutions and Money*, 1(1), 73–89.

Kato, K., Schwartz, S. and Ziemba, W. 1990: Day of the week effects in Japanese markets. In E. Elton and M. Gruber (eds), *The Japanese Capital Markets*, New York: Harper and Row.

Keim, D. 1983: Size-related anomalies and stock return seasonality: further empirical evidence. *Journal of Financial Economics*, 12, 13–32.

Keim, D. 1986a: The CAPM and equity return regularities. *Financial Analysts Journal*, May/June, 19–34.

Keim, D. 1986b: Dividend yields and the January effect. *Journal of Portfolio Management*, Summer, 54–60.

Keim, D. 1987: Daily returns and size-related premiums: one more time. *Journal of Portfolio Management*, Winter, 41–7.

Keim D.B. and Stambangh, R.F. 1984: A further investigation of the weekend effect in stock returns. *Journal of Finance*, 39, 819–40.

Komatsu, A. and Ziemba, W. 1989: Some tests of plausible causes for anomalous behavior in Japanese security markets. Working paper, Yamaichi Research Institute.

Lakonishok, J. and Levi, M. 1982: Weekend effects on stock returns: a note. *Journal of Finance*, 37, 883–9.

Lakonishok, J. and Smidt, S. 1989a: Are seasonal anomalies real? A ninety-year perspective. *Review of Financial Studies*, 1(4), 403–25.

Lakonishok, J. and Smidt, S. 1989b: Past price changes and current trading volume. *Journal of Portfolio Management*, Winter, 18–24.

Lo, A. and Mackinlay, C. 1990: When are contrarian profits due to stock market overreaction? *Review of Financial Studies*, 3(2), 175–205.

Nakamura, T. and Terada, N. 1984: The size effect and seasonality in Japanese stock returns. Unpublished manuscript.

Nishina, K. and Tabata, Y. 1985: Distribution of Japanese stock returns. *Osaka Economic Papers*, 135, 450–21.

Pettway, R.H. and Tapley, T.C. 1984: The Tokyo Stock Exchange: an analysis of stock market prices. *Keio Business Review*, 75–93.

Poterba, J. and Summers, H. 1988: Mean reversion in stock prices: evidence and implications. *Journal of Financial Economics*, 22, 27–59.

Reinganum, M. 1981: Empirical test of multi-factor model, the arbitrage pricing theory: some empirical results. *Journal of Finance*, 36, 313–21.

Reinganum, M. 1983: The anomalous stock market behavior of small firms in January: empirical tests for year-end tax effect. *Journal of Financial Economics*, 12, 89–104.

Reinganum, M. 1988: An anatomy of a stock market winner. *Financial Analysts Journal*, March/April, 16–28.

Reinganum, M. and Shapiro, A. 1987: Taxes and stock return seasonality: evidence from the London Stock Exchange. *Journal of Business*, 60, 281–95.

Ritter, J. and Chopra, N. 1989: Portfolio rebalancing and the turn of the year effect. *Journal of Finance*, 44, 149–66.

Rogalski, R. 1984: New findings regarding day-of-the-week returns over trading and non-trading periods: a note. *Journal of Finance*, 39, 1603–14.

Roll, R. 1981: A possible explanation of the small firm effect. *Journal of Finance*, 36, 879–88.

Roll, R. 1983: Vas ist Das? The turn-of-the-year effect and the return premia of small firms. *Journal of Portfolio Management*, 9, 18–28.

Serita, T. 1989: Conditional volatility of Japanese stock returns and risk premium. *Securities Economics*, June, 21–38 (in Japanese).

Shewert, W. 1983: Size and stock returns and other empirical regularities. *Journal of Financial Economics*, 12, 3–12.

Smirlock, M. and Starks, L. 1986: Day-of-the-week and intraday effects in stock returns. *Journal of Financial Economics*, 7, 197–210.

Stoll, H. and Whaley, R. 1983: Transaction costs and the small firm effect. *Journal of Financial Economics*, 12, 57–79.

Tinic, S. and West, R. 1984: Risk and return: January vs. the rest of the year. *Journal of Financial Economics*, 13, 561–74.

Tokunaga, T., Iihara, Y. and Kato, K. 1992: Heteroskedasticity in Japanese daily stock returns: the case for weekend effect. *Japan Finance Review*, forthcoming.

Tokyo Stock Exchange Fact Book, 1991.

Zarowin, P. 1989: Short-run market overreaction: size and seasonality effects. *Journal of Portfolio Management*, Spring, 26–9.

Ziemba, W. 1989a: Japanese security market regularities: monthly, turn of the month and year, holiday and golden week effects. Yamaichi Research Institute, mimeo.

Ziemba, W. 1989b: *Investing in Japan*, unpublished book.

Ziemba, W. 1990: Seasonality effects in Japanese futures markets. In G. Rhee and R. Chan (eds), *Pacific Basin Capital Markets*, Oxford; Amsterdam; and Tokyo. North-Holland.

11

Modeling the Behavior of Japanese Stock Indices

Adrian E. Tschoegl

> "Numbers serve to discipline rhetoric. Without them it is too easy to follow flights of fancy, to ignore the world as it is, and to remold it nearer to the heart's desire."
>
> Ralph Waldo Emerson

> "If you can look into the seeds of time, And say which grain will grow and which will not, Speak then to me."
>
> William Shakespeare, *Macbeth*, I.iii

1 INTRODUCTION

Stock market prices, and hence returns and their volatility, are subject to many influences. In the long run, stock market returns depend on the evolution of that part of the economy on which shares are a claim. This is what I mean when I say that the stock market is driven by fundamentals. However, over shorter periods, and I will deliberately leave the time-scale vague, many other, more transient factors may come into play. It is this apparent deviation of stock prices from fundamentals which has given rise to research on fads and chaos theory models and into which body of literature this paper falls.[1] In these fad or chaos approaches, stock market volatility depends on the evolution of the economic fundamentals and evolution of these non-fundamental factors.

What I have done to model the influence of economic factors on the stock market is not unique. There are many descriptions in the formal financial economics literature of similar attempts. Neither is my approach particularly sophisticated in its conception or its execution. Nevertheless, the approach appears to generate interesting results, and more importantly, further interesting questions.

Sorting out what part of present stock prices is due to economic fundamentals and what part is due to transient influences is an important

I would like to thank Shinji Takagi and Colin McKenzie for helpful comments on earlier drafts. As usual, all errors and opinions remain my own. Swiss Bank Corporation and SBCI Securities (Asia) Ltd do not necessarily endorse this research or the results.

task. It is of immense practical importance because there is money to be made from correctly separating fad from fact. It is also important to the real economy because financial markets influence the real economy through the allocation of capital.

In this chapter I shall discuss my attempts to link stock prices to economic fundamentals. I leave for another day the issue of the feedback loop, the effect of the stock market on the real economy. In section 2 I describe the approach I follow in applying econometrics to the stock market. Section 3 discusses some of the common criticisms leveled at these efforts. Section 4 evaluates the models. Section 5 uses the models to shed light on the recent evolution of the Tokyo stock index, and finally section 6 summarizes the paper.

2.   APPLYING ECONOMETRICS TO THE STOCK MARKET

2.1   The Econometric Model

There are many ways to look at the stock market, that is, to attempt this separation of the transient from the fundamental. Time series analysis, especially in its informal version, so-called technical analysis, provides one perspective using one set of tools. Structural econometric models provide another perspective using another set of tools. The experienced observer's feel for the psychology of the market and the behavior of institutions, individuals, and so on, provides a third perspective using a third set of tools. Sometimes all three approaches will agree in what they forecast for the development of the stock market over some period, but I would be surprised if they agreed more than occasionally.

The basic conceptual framework I use is a dividend discount model. The logic is as follows:

(a)   Share prices are a function of dividends.
(b)   Dividends are a function of corporate earnings.
(c)   Earnings are a function of economic factors.
(d)   Hence, share prices are a function of economic factors.

Linking share prices directly to economic factors removes a number of problems. The first is that in general Japanese companies set dividends as a percentage of a share's par value and change the percentage only rarely. Typically, they increase the effective dividend yield (dividend/current price) by gratis issues which increase the number of shares outstanding. Thus the dividend yield per share fluctuates widely and now averages less than 1 percent, even though the payout ratio averages 30 percent. The second problem is that earnings are an accounting number and subject to all manner of arbitrary conventions having to do with historical cost treatment of long-lived assets, arbitrary depreciation schedules given by tax codes, and so forth. Lastly, in the Japanese market the most accessible earnings numbers are based on parent company earnings, but shares are a claim on the consolidated company.

In order to avoid these problems, I use four key explanatory variables to drive the stock market models: industrial production, money supply, interest rates and the ¥/US$ exchange rate. Essentially, industrial production represents earnings which tend to be procyclical. The money supply inflation adjusts the real earnings for consistency with share prices which are quoted in nominal terms. The interest rate is a discount factor. The exchange rate is more of an *ad hoc* addition. International influences enter the model through the explanatory variables.

As, I discuss in section 5.2 below, international influences may also affect the discrepancy between model and market. I discuss the composition of the market indices, all four explanatory variables, and the expected sign of the coefficients in greater detail below.

2.2   About the Variables

2.2.1   The indices

The Nikkei 225 index is probably the most widely followed stock market index in Japan. It consists of a simple price-weighted arithmetic average based on the current stock price of 225 of Japan's leading companies. The NSA 225 is more widely known that the TOPIX index, and its derivative products have attracted more attention from investors.

As a price-weighted index, the NSA 225 is most heavily influenced by changes in the prices of stocks with high absolute prices. If a stock priced at ¥1,000 rises 10 percent in isolation, it would cause a 0.026 percent movement in the index. The same 10 percent movement in a stock priced at ¥4,000 would lead to a 0.182 percent rise.

The TOPIX index is a market capitalization weighted index covering all the shares listed on the Tokyo Stock Exchange's first section (TSE1). The price of each stock is multiplied by the number of shares outstanding and compared with a base value established on January 4, 1968. Volatility in stocks with a large market capitalization will have the greatest impact on the TOPIX.[2] Published every 60 seconds during market hours by the TSE, the TOPIX is the most comprehensive measure of stock price changes in Japan.

The TSE has also constructed three indices based on the market capitalization of the constituent companies: a Large, a Medium, and a

Small Capitalization Index. The Large Capitalization Index consists of the stocks of companies with 200 million or more shares listed. The Medium Capitalization Index consist of companies with 60 million or more shares but under 200 million listed. The Small Capitalization Index consists of companies with less than 60 million shares listed. The TOPIX calculates and reports its subindices six times a day.

One major drawback of all market capitalization weighted indices is that the practice of cross-holding shares seriously distorts the measurement of market capitalization. In the Japanese case, cross-holding results in an approximately 100 percent overestimation of the capitalization of the Japanese stock market. More disturbingly, cross holding can seriously distort estimates of beta and of the market price of risk.[3]

2.2.2 The explanatory variables

The first key explanatory variable is the mining and manufacturing production index for each month. Fluctuations in industrial production correlate well with fluctuations in economic growth and in corporate profits. Hence I would expect a positive coeffecient for the variable.

The long-term (the 11 years since 1980) trend for the mining and manufacturing production index is 4.1 percent growth year-on-year, almost the same as the trend for real GNP growth (4.2 percent). Moreover, mining and manufacturing production is available on a monthly basis with a one-month delay whereas GNP is only available on a quarterly basis with almost a quarter's delay. International influences enter through the effect of export demand and import competition on domestic production. Production should show a positive correlation with the index.

The second key variable is the money supply in terms of adjusted average M2 + CDs outstanding each month. I have developed an adjustment procedure to modify the nominal money supply figures to take into account the effects of deregulation.[4] Money supply growth has implications for inflation in two or three years and hence inclusion of money supply is a form of inflation adjustment to real earnings to bring them into congruence with share prices which are quoted in nominal terms. Furthermore, money supply may capture some of the gain in share prices from the effect of inflation on land values, a gain which often does not show up in earnings. I expect money supply to enter the equation with a positive coefficient.

The third key variable is the long-term prime rate. The interest rate is a discount rate for future earnings. International influences enter through interest rate parity which links interest rates and exchange rates across countries. I expect the coefficient for the interest rate variable to bear a negative coefficient.

I have found that the long-term prime rate is a more powerful explanatory factor than is the ten-year government bond yield. Part of the reason may be that the long-term prime is a more accurate representation of the interest rate environment than is the yield on the benchmark government bond.[5] Furthermore, research suggests that the NSA 225 index reacts quite strongly to changes in the long-term prime, but hardly at all to changes in the official discount rate or the short-term prime.

Using a debt interest rate means that I almost ignore the issue of estimating the risk premium for equities and including this estimated premium among the explanatory factors. The long-term prime has an element of risk premium in it as the spread between the government bond rate and five-year bank debentures, the market rate to which the long-term prime is linked, varies over time. However, one can regard the discrepancy between the market and the model estimate of the appropriate level for the market given the included factors as itself an estimate of the risk premium.

The fourth key variable is the ¥/US$ exchange rate. In the first models I developed I did not include the exchange rate, having found no statistical reason to do so. In subsequent revisions I found that the exchange rate added explanatory power. Now it may be losing importance again.

2.3 The Estimation Procedure

Each of the broad stock market indices has its own separate model. That is, I have a separate model for the NSA 225, the TOPIX, and the Large Capitalization, Medium Capitalization, and Small Capitalization Indices. The estimation technique is ordinary least squares applied to the natural logarithms of the variables, and each model uses ten years of monthly data. I deliberately use ordinary least squares (OLS) estimation techniques in preference to other, perhaps more sophisticated, techniques. Although not a robust technique in the technical (non-parametric) sense, OLS is not vulnerable to some of the problems of non-linear estimation. It is also transparent and surprisingly versatile.

The object of interest is the level of the index relative to the level given by historic correlations with the index's economic determinants, suggesting estimation in the levels, not growth rates. (The graph of actual and estimated levels from a regression in growth rates has a very unsatisfactory appearance; the estimated level basically shadows the actual level by the period over which I estimate the growth rates.) Furthermore, because the variables involved generally grow with time, estimation in the natural logarithms appears appropriate. Lastly, the coefficients of the regression have the interpretation of elasticities, that is, the gearing

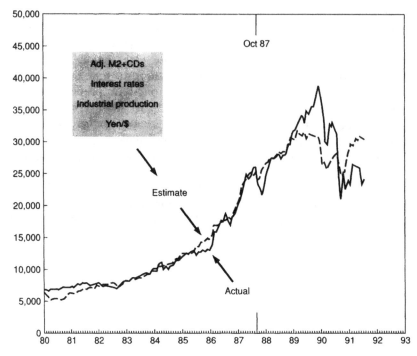

Figure 11.1   Estimate of NSA 225

(leverage) of the index with respect to a small percentage change in the explanatory variables.[6]

Because of the limitations of my graphics software, estimating in the natural logarithms does have a drawback. In the figures below where I graph the actual value and the fitted value, the discrepancy between market or actual level and the model estimate currently appears greater than the same discrepancy in the more distant past (figures 11.1–11.5). The current apparent lack of correlation between model and market is to a great degree a consequence of estimating the models in the logarithms (that is, proportions), but graphing on an absolute scale, not a logarithmic one. In the graph of the percentage error between the models and the market, one can see that the early years also saw quite large deviations (figure 11.6).

The choice of ten years of monthly data for the estimation span is arbitrary. I cannot argue that ten years is more appropriate than eight years on the one hand or twelve on the other. However, I would resist using a much longer span because the economy on which the shares are a claim is not stationary. A changing economy means changing companies.

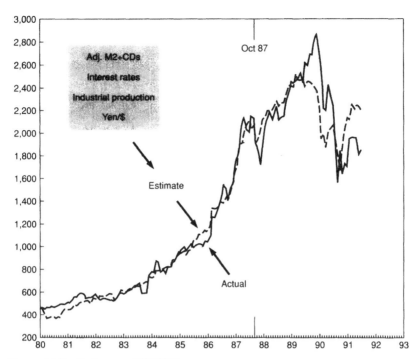

Figure 11.2 Estimate of TOPIX

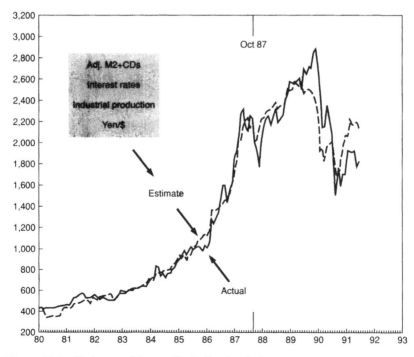

Figure 11.3 Estimate of Large Capitalization Index

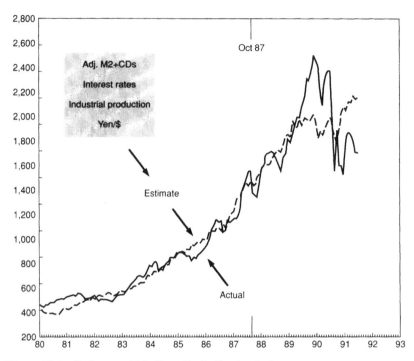

Figure 11.4 Estimate of Medium Capitalization Index

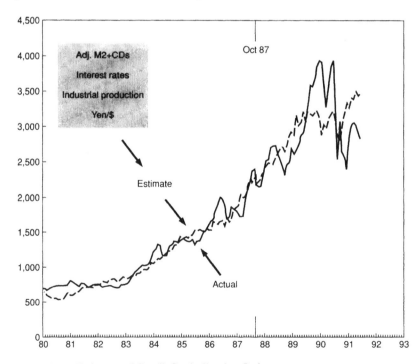

Figure 11.5 Estimate of Small Capitalization Index

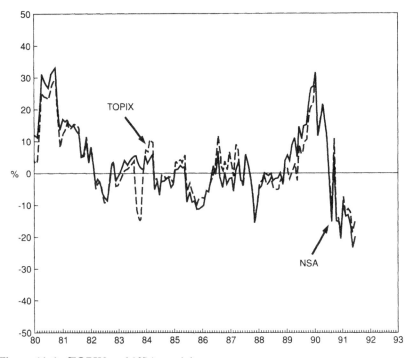

Figure 11.6 TOPIX and NSA model percentage error

Thus the index will not react in the same way to changes in interest rates today as it did 15 years ago. By the same token, a short period is too unstable. As I shall discuss below, stock markets appear to deviate from their fundamentals for as long as a year or even more, but economies usually do not change radically from year to year. Over short estimation spans aberrant periods can exercise too great an influence, biasing the results.

There are some econometric points worth mentioning before I discuss the results. The first is the issue of serial correlation. It is clear that serial correlation is high (TOPIX model: $DW = 0.51$).[7] I do not, however, adjust for first-order serial correlation. The reason is that I am trying to identify the magnitude of the discrepancy between the model and the market. Assuming that next period's discrepancy will be a function of this period's discrepancy and otherwise ignoring the magnitude is to miss a major point of the exercise. If one then wishes to estimate the expected change in the index over the next month, given the current discrepancy between the market and the model, the appropriate technique is to look at that issue directly (see section 4.1.1 below).

The second point I wish to mention is the issue of heteroskedasticity. It is clear that stock returns are not homoskedastic over time. Research into stock price returns is turning to the use of ARCH (autoregressive conditional heteroskedasticity) models.[8] In the present case, the heteroskedasticity evident in figure 11.6 is not due to a quiet times/noisy times problem but rather to my not adjusting for serial correlation in the residuals. Taking the herteroskedasticity into account would enable me to shrink the estimates of the standard errors of the coefficients. Inspection of the *t*-statistics of the models across Japanese and foreign indices suggests that generally coefficients are already significant at conventional significance levels.

The last point I wish to mention is the issue of multicollinearity. Collinearity is only likely to be a problem with respect to money supply and industrial production, both of which tend to grow monotonically over time. A collinearity problem would manifest itself as a high coefficient of determination but low *t*-statistics on the coefficients of the collinear explanatory variables. Inspection of the *t*-statistics of the models across Japanese and foreign indexes suggests that collinearity is not a problem.

2.4   What the Models Tell Us about the Indices

Table 11.1 displays the elasticities (or responsivities) of each index with respect to the explanatory variables. For example, an elasticity of −13.9 for the NSA 225 and interest rates means that, historically, a 100 basis point rise (fall) in the level of the long-term prime has been associated with a 14 percent fall (rise) in the level of the NSA 225. Similarly, a 1 percent increase in the level of the mining and manufacturing index has been associated with a 1.3 percent increase in the Small Capitalization Index.

All indices are responsive to interest rates and money supply; sensitivity to industrial production and exchange rates is more questionable. The Large Cap. Index seems relatively insensitive to industrial production and the Medium Cap. Index seems relatively insensitive to the ¥/US$ exchange rate.

The two broad indices, the NSA 225 and the TOPIX, fall between the Large and Medium Cap. Indices in terms of their coefficients. The NSA 225 appears to behave like the Large Cap. Index in everything but its responsiveness to industrial production. The TOPIX behaves even more like the Large Cap. Index except that its sensitivity to the exchange rate is more questionable.

Generally, the greatest contrast is between the Large and Small Cap. Indices. The Large Cap. Index is the most sensitive to interest rates and money supply, and the least sensitive to industrial production of the three

Table 11.1 Model of stock index behavior

Index	Interest rate (ln)	Elasticities Money supply (ln)	Industrial production (ln)	¥/US$ (ln)	R^2
NSA 225	−13.9 (−16.6)	1.3 (5.8)	0.6 (1.6)	−0.1 (−1.4)	0.97
TOPIX	−17.9 (−20.6)	1.3 (6.3)	0.4 (1.3)	−0.1 (−0.8)	0.98
Large Cap.	−20.1 (−19.8)	1.4 (6.7)	0.2 (0.7)	−0.1 (−1.6)	0.98
Medium Cap.	−8.8 (−7.5)	1.4 (5.4)	0.9 (2.4)	0.1 (1.1)	0.96
Small Cap.	−10.4 (−7.9)	1.3 (4.9)	1.3 (3.0)	0.3 (2.4)	0.96

R^2 is the coefficient of determination.
t-statistics are in parentheses.

capitalization indices. The Small Cap. Index is the least sensitive to interest rates and money supply, and the most sensitive to industrial production. The Medium Cap. Index generally falls between the Large and the Small Cap. Indices in its sensitivities to these three factors. With respect to the ¥/US$ rate, the Large Cap. Index benefited from the yen's appreciation against the US$, and the Small Cap. Index suffered. Once again, the Medium Cap. Index fell between the other two.

These results are not surprising. Large capitalization shares have long been known as asset plays, with assets being particularly sensitive to financial factors such as interest rates and excess liquidity or money supply. By contrast, Small Cap shares are often new companies with few hidden land assets and, in the case of technology companies, a great sensitivity to manufacturing growth.

For comparison purposes, table 11.2 has the regression results for the ten years to May 1989. That is, the table represents the first published version of the models. The classification of Large Caps as asset shares and Small Caps as earnings shares remains, though the elasticities with respect to the explanatory factors have changed. The sources of the changes in elasticities include the introduction of the exchange rate in the later models, the introduction of the interest rate in unlogged form in the

Table 11.2 Original (May 1989) models of stock index behavior

Index	Interest rate (ln)	Elasticities Money supply (ln)	Industrial production (ln)	R^2
NSA 225	−1.0 (−16.6)	0.8 (8.4)	1.3 (4.8)	0.98
TOPIX	−1.2 (−20.6)	1.1 (11.6)	0.9 (4.0)	0.99
Large Cap.	−1.3 (−18.6)	1.4 (12.0)	0.6 (2.1)	0.98
Medium Cap.	−0.8 (−12.0)	0.6 (5.6)	1.5 (5.3)	0.98
Small Cap.	−0.8 (−10.2)	0.4 (3.0)	2.1 (7.7)	0.97

R^2 is the coefficient of determination.
t-statistics are in parentheses.

later models versus logged form in the earlier models, and parameter drift over time.

The four variables used together account for 96–98 percent of the variation in the logarithms of the levels of the respective indexes between June 1981 and May 1991. The Large Cap. Index model is the most accurate and 95 percent of the time the model estimates should be within ±17 percent of the actual outcomes within the period of estimation. For the least accurate model, the Small Capitalization Index model, 95 percent of the time the model estimates should be within ±22 percent of the actual outcomes. I include this mention of the standard error of the regression not as a measure of the forecasting accuracy of the models (in general I do not use the models to forecast in the conventional sense) but simply as a measure of goodness of fit.

Note that I am trying to optimize fit, not maximize it; I am trying to use only economic explanatory factors and as few as possible. If I wished to maximize fit, the simplest method would be to introduce a correction for first-order serial correlation. Alternatively, a simple auto-regressive equation would have a very small standard error. In either case I would, however, lose the ability to estimate the magnitude of transient influences. What the standard errors of the regression give us is a measure of the variability of the transient influences.

2.5 International Comparisons: Japan is Not Unique

One test of this econometric approach is to replicate it on other developed markets. Below, table 11.3 presents the results for the TOPIX (Japan), S&P500 (US; figure 11.7), FT1000 (UK; figure 11.8), Commerzbank Index (Germany; figure 11.9), and the CAC (France; figure 11.10). In all cases the models use the same four key economic explanatory variables.

The first key variable is the money supply. Generally I use M2 or M3. The second key variable is long-term interest rates. Generally I use a long-term government bond rate, except in the case of Japan, for which I use the long-term prime rate. The third key variable is the industrial production index for each month. The fourth key variable is the country's exchange rate against the US$. In the case of the US, I have included both the ¥/US$ rate and the DM/US$ rate. All variables enter in the equations in their natural logarithms, except the interest rate which enters untransformed.

All five indices are responsive to the four (five) factors. These variables together account for 87–98 percent of the variation in the logarithms of the levels of the respective indices between February–May 1981 and March–April 1991.

For the most accurate model (TOPIX), 95 percent of the time the model estimates should be within ±17 percent of the actual outcomes. For the least accurate model (Commerzbank), 95 percent of the time the model estimates should be within ±31 percent of the actual outcomes. Given the models, Tokyo appears most closely to follow the fundamentals and Frankfurt to follow least closely.

Table 11.3 displays the elasticities of each index with respect to the explanatory variables. For example, an elasticity of −13.9 for the TOPIX and interest rates means that historically, a 100 basis point rise (fall) in the level of the long-term prime has been associated with a 14 percent fall (rise) in the level of the TOPIX.

Although all five markets exhibit different elasticities with respect to interest rates, money supply, industrial production, and the exchange rate, elasticities across markets are quite close to each other and reasonable in magnitude. This suggests that the models are usable representations. Differences between indices reflect differences in the mix of companies which each index represents.

Tokyo has a large number of financial institutions in its make-up and as a result the TOPIX has the greatest responsiveness to interest rates and money supply. The S&P 500 appears the least sensitive to interest rates, which is not surprising as the S&P 500 is an index of non-financial firms. The S&P 500's relatively low sensitivity to industrial production is curious, as is the asymmetric reaction to the two exchange rates.

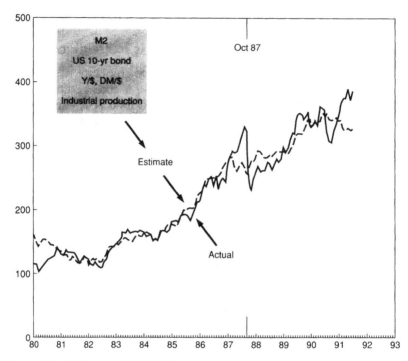

Figure 11.7 Estimate of S&P 500

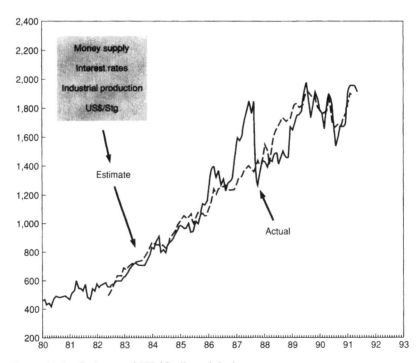

Figure 11.8 Estimate of FT (Ordinary) Index

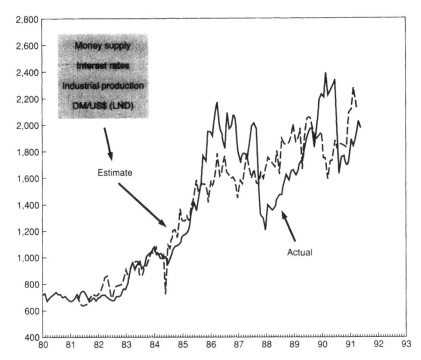

Figure 11.9 Estimate of the Commerzbank Index

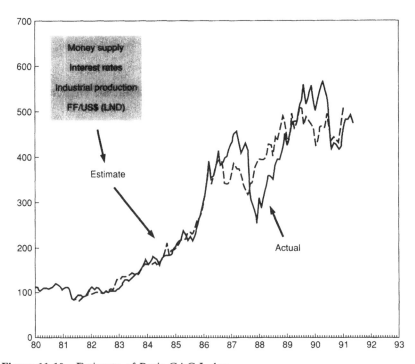

Figure 11.10 Estimate of Paris CAC Index

Table 11.3   Applying the models to other countries' market indices

			Elasticities		
Index	*Interest rate (ln)*	*Money supply (ln)*	*Industrial production (ln)*	*Exchange rate (ln)*	R^2
TOPIX	−17.9	1.3	0.4	−0.1	0.98
(Tokyo)	(−20.6)	(6.3)	(1.3)	(−0.8)	
				¥/US$	
S&P 500	−6.5	0.4	1.8	0.3 −0.3	0.96
(New York)	(−6.7)	(1.6)	(5.0)	(2.4) (−3.9)	
				¥/US$ DM/US$	
FT Ordinary	−6.2	1.0	1.3	−0.4	0.94
(London)	(−4.3)	(11.0)	(2.9)	(−4.5)	
				Lstg/US$	
Commerzbk	−13.3	0.3	3.4	0.3	0.85
(Frankfurt)	(−12.7)	(1.1)	(5.6)	(2.3)	
				DM/US$	
CAC	−11.7	0.9	2.4	−0.3	0.96
(Paris)	(−9.0)	(3.6)	(4.7)	(−3.2)	
				FFr/US$	

R^2 is the coefficient of determination.
t-statistics are in parentheses.

Yen appreciation weakens the S&P 500, but DM appreciation strengthens it. Looking at the other countries, domestic currency appreciation lifts the market in Japan and France, and weakens the market in the UK and Germany. I have no explanation, and conjecture that the reasons could include, among others, the different types of companies in each country, the markets' assessments of central bank reaction to exchange rate movements, the implications for inflation, and the relative importance of overseas earnings versus import competition.

A major implication of this evidence is that the Japanese stock market is not unique. All the factors (except the exchange rate) operate in the same way across all five markets. Furthermore, the Japanese market appears no less rational (explicable) than any of the other major markets.

3   COMMON CRITICISMS OF THE ECONOMETRIC APPROACH

As of May 1991, the models show the NSA 225 about 20 percent under-valued. Back in October 1989–January 1990 when I argued that the NSA

225 was 30–40 percent overvalued, I heard the same criticisms of the econometrics as I am hearing today:

(a) There must be a missing variable.
(b) The world has changed and historical relationships are no longer valid.
(c) The market cannot fall/rise by that much in just three months.
(d) It's just a model/theory.

3.1 The Missing Variable

Models by definition are a simplification, which means that there are always missing variables. The issues are: what is missing? how important is it? and how does it behave?

One candidate for being an important missing variable is land prices. In a cross-sectional test in some unpublished research on some 30 companies, I was able to establish a correlation between the companies' share prices and stock brokerage estimates of the companies' earnings per share and land assets per share.

The models of the Japanese market do not deal in a fully satisfactory way with the issue of land prices. I have estimated the models over a period (1/1979–2/1990) when land prices rose. I do not know what would happen if land prices were to collapse. However, the explanatory variables such as interest rates and money supply would be important variables in any equation for land prices. Nevertheless, land prices in Japan remain an important and poorly understood issue.

Perhaps the most minor of the missing factors is the rounding of prices that takes place among traders. This introduces a random error (the rounding error) into prices, an error which looms large in transaction-to-transaction comparisons but is generally trivial in year-on-year comparisons.[9] Other features of the microstructure of the market (such as commission rates, bid–ask spread rules, or whether the market has specialists or is a clearing market) also introduce volatility through their effect on the liquidity of the market.

I suspect that the key missing variable is usually market psychology or market sentiment. A more formal term might be "a time-varying risk premium," though strictly speaking the two are not the same. "Time-varying risk premium" is neutral but carries the connotation of something which follows a random walk. In that case, knowing today's risk premium tells the investor nothing about the direction in which the risk premium will change. Market psychology connotes a time-varying risk premium which is subject to an element of fad and hence is mean-reverting.

The implied process, then, is one in which market psychology or sentiment drives an index temporarily away from fundamentals. Even-

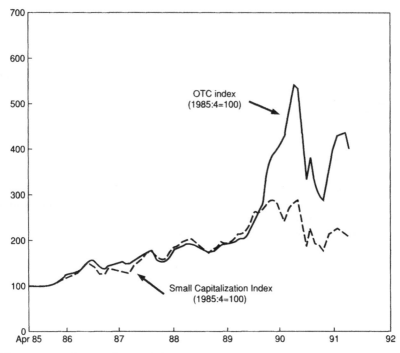

Figure 11.11   Vulnerability of OTC shares

tually, as the fad dissipates the risk premium reverts to some long-run mean and the market moves back towards the value given by the fundamentals. When sentiment is strong enough, we may call it a bubble. Sometimes the presence of a bubble may preclude model estimation. The Japanese over-the-counter (OTC) market may provide an example.

In figure 11.11, I have graphed the Over-the-counter Index and the Small Capitalization Index, both indexed in April 1984. Small Capitalization shares and OTC shares are much alike, except that Small Capitalization shares are listed on the Tokyo Stock Exchange and hence are generally more liquid than OTC shares and have more information available on them. As one can readily see, the two indices moved together until late 1989. Since then, there has been a correlation between the two series, but the structure of the relationship between them has changed dramatically. Hence, any model which worked well for the period 1984–89 would fail thereafter.

Presumably, bubbles (that is, excessive optimism or pessimism) do not last forever. Eventually, investors look around and see that they have overreacted and the index returns to its appropriate level, given the fundamentals. When investors are going to come to their senses and what will trigger the return are open questions. In the context of a "fads" model of stock market prices, then econometric models provide one way for estimating the role of psychology in the market.

3.2 The World has Changed

This argument contends that the model specification (structure) is unstable. Possible problems include time-varying parameters (multipliers) and the idea that the set of key factors itself is not constant.

Parameters do change over time. By using a rolling ten-year period I adjust somewhat for this. If I had access to more powerful software I could attempt to model the behavior of the parameters, via a Kalman filter procedure, for instance. This remains a subject for future research.

As I discuss below, the specification changes too. It is quite possible that within the last few years we have passed from a period in which the market did not treat exchange rates as fixed through a period in which the market treated exchange rates as relatively fixed and back into a period in which the market acts as if exchange rates are flexible. Nevertheless, economies rarely change dramatically over short periods. Generally, the same companies produce the same goods and services this month as they did last month. Thus sudden major changes in market prices away from the model are questionable. They may be due to sudden structural changes but when there is no outside event to suggest the possibility of such a change, such sudden changes are more likely to be due to changes in investors' sentiment.

3.3 The Market Cannot Rise/Fall by that Much

Whenever the models suggest substantial over- or undervaluation, and I suggest that the market could remove the discrepancy within three months, people have remarked that the market cannot rise (fall) by that much in that short a period. Actually, the market can move quite dramatically. Table 11.4 gives the greatest one- and two-month moves in the NSA 225 and TOPIX Indices between January 1979 and November 1990.

3.4 It's Just a Model/Theory

The statement "it's just a model (or theory)" is the least-valid criticism. All explanations are models or theories; all explanations relate something to hypothesized causal factors. Statistical models simply impose a discipline on the process.

Table 11.4   Extreme one- and two-month percentage changes in the NSA 225 and TOPIX (Jan. 1979–Nov. 1990)

	1 month	*2 months*
NSA 225		
max	20.0	21.8
min	−19.2	−32.4
TOPIX		
max	24.5	32.2
min	−20.4	−30.3

Judgement-based forecasts are subject to common cognitive biases. Forecasters have a tendency to overreact to unexpected and dramatic news events, to see illusory correlations, and to focus on a subset of the information available. What econometric models do is to force us to react to new information only in so far as it affects our variables, to apply a rule of evidence to apparent correlations (and to identify correlations not visible to the eye in two variable comparisons), and to incorporate the same set of information in each updating of our forecasts.

This brings us back to the quote from Ralph Waldo Emerson at the beginning of this chapter. Modeling may have its own limitations, but the discipline of the process serves to counteract some of the limitations of other methods.

4   USING THE MODELS TO FORECAST THE BEHAVIOR OF THE STOCK MARKET

4.1   Timing the Market

From a stockbroker's point of view, the real test of the econometric models is whether one can use them to forecast the stock market. I have performed two tests, an *ex post* or in-sample test and an *ex ante* test, both of which suggest that the models do indeed contain information about the future evolution of the indices.

4.1.1   Looking back: *ex post* or in-sample tests

Table 11.5 below presents the results of regressing the change in the index over one month on the end-of-the-month model-market discrepancy

Table 11.5 The in-sample predictive power of market-model discrepancies

| | Past market model discrepancies | | | | |
	Ln A/E (t)	Ln A/E (t − 1)	Ln A/E (t − 2)	Ln A/E (t − 3)	R^2
Ln TOPIX (t + 1) − Ln TOPIX (t)	−0.17	0.00	−0.05	0.05	0.09
	(−2.14)	(0.00)	(−0.54)	(0.62)	
Ln TOPIX (t + 1) − Ln TOPIX (t)	−0.17	−0.01			0.09
	(−2.17)	(−0.09)			

A/E represents actual divided by the estimate, or equivalently, market divided by model; *t* refers to the month; if *t* is June, then *t* − 1 is May and *t* + 1 is July.

R^2 is the coefficient of determination.
t-statistics are in parentheses.

at the end of the prior month and at the end of each of the three earlier months. The period covered is the same as that for which I have estimated the TOPIX model, and all the data for the explanatory variables is revised data. When I make the timing decision *ex ante*, the data for money supply and industrial production for the end of the month is estimated, and preliminary for the previous month.

What the regression statistics suggest is that if the model rates the market as being 10 percent over- (under)valued at the end of the month, the market will fall (rise) by 1.7 percent during the subsequent month (over and above its long-term tendency to grow by 1 percent or so per month.) This suggests that the model can add value. However, the model is optimized for its own sample period and uses data that were unavailable at the time decisions had to be made. It is therefore necessary to perform an *ex ante* test.

4.1.2 **Looking ahead:** *ex ante* **tests**

Since September 1989 I have published the results of the models each month, and advocated a cash-shares allocation for the coming month, based on the outcome of the estimation procedure, that is, on the end-of-month discrepancy between the model estimate of the fair value on the TOPIX and the actual value of the index. Table 11.6 compares the return on the timing strategy I advocated based on the TOPIX model and the return on a buy-and-hold strategy.[10]

Since September 1989 the timing model has outperformed a buy-and-hold strategy by 340 basis points of return; in the last 12 months, the outperformance is 110 basis points. This is despite the fact that, in June, being overweight in a down-market hurt performance.

Table 11.6 Comparing our timing advice with a buy-and-hold strategy, both with respect to the TOPIX index (%)

	Since Sept. 89	Last 12 months
Timing	−29.3	−21.3
TOPIX	−32.7	−22.4

When I regress the monthly returns on the timing portfolio on the monthly returns on the TOPIX index, the result is a beta of 1.13, and an alpha of 0.5 percent. This too would suggest that the timing model outperforms the buy-and-hold strategy, even on a risk-adjusted basis.

One might argue that the timing model outperformance is hardly spectacular. However, if I could guarantee to add 1 percent per annum to the value of a US$100 million portfolio for the expenditure of one afternoon of effort per month I suspect that I could come to a mutually acceptable consulting arrangement with some fund management company. What is more disturbing for the notion of efficient markets is the possibility of profit opportunities from the use of publicly available information.

4.1.3   **An *ad hoc* allocation rule**

At first, the cash-shares allocation rule I used was a subjective transformation of the end-of-the-month discrepancy between the TOPIX model and the TOPIX index. (That is, if the model showed the market 10 percent overvalued, I might advocate anywhere from 0–20 percent in cash.) Later, I came to advocate the same position in cash as given by the model-market discrepancy. (If the model showed the market 20 percent undervalued, I advocated a 120 percent shares to 20 percent cash position.)

This remains an *ad hoc* allocation rule. A more sophisticated approach would be to determine how different transformations of the discrepancy affected the riskiness of the resulting cash plus shares portfolio. Ideally, one could then pick a superior transformation, one which provided a higher return for the same risk as the market portfolio, always assuming that the models contain information. This improved allocation rule, too, remains an area for future research.

For now I maintain my rule of thumb, but base the allocation for the coming month not on the model-market discrepancy at the end of the month, but rather on the discrepancy at the end of the prior month. Examination showed that in nine out of 20 months using the penultimate month discrepancy gave a different signal than using the discrepancy in the month which had just ended; of these nine cases, using the penultimate month provided a better result in seven cases. Overall, using the penultimate month resulted in a 2.5 percent better timing performance than using the prior month. This suggests that the econometric model does a better job of identifying market direction two months ahead than one month ahead.

4.2 Longer-range Forecasts

So far I have used the models in a forecast-free way. That is, the timing I have advocated depended solely on an end-of-the-month model-market discrepancy, not on a longer-run forecast of the market level based on forecasts of the driving variables. Incorporating forecasts remains a topic for future research. In the meantime, I routinely calculate forecasts under a variety of interest rate and exchange rate alternatives, without designating any particular scenario as the most probable.

Table 11.7 presents the forecasts for June 1992 of the NSA 225 index under the assumption of 8 percent money growth year-on-year, 4 percent industrial production growth year-on-year, and a range of scenarios for interest rates and exchange rates. I chose 8 percent money growth and 4 percent industrial production because I believe that both these values represent the long-run trend growth rates for these variables.[11] Some scenarios, or combinations, for interest rates and exchange rates may be less plausible than others, or less plausible under my assumptions for money supply and industrial production than others. The results range between 38,500 and 46,100.

These scenarios enable me to turn discussion from the issue of the legitimacy of modeling and towards the implications of different expectations. How to incorporate forecasts into a timing signal, and then determine what part of total performance is due to the forecast and what part is due simply to the estimation of the discrepancy between market and model, remains an open issue.

Table 11.7 NSA 225 ('000s) at end-June 1992 under various scenarios

¥/US$	Long-term prime			
	7.2%	7.6%	7.9%	8.3%
160	42.7	41.0	39.9	38.5
150	43.4	41.7	40.6	39.1
140	44.2	42.5	41.3	39.9
130	45.1	43.4	42.2	40.7
120	46.1	44.4	43.1	41.6

5   USING THE MODELS TO ANALYZE THE DEVELOPMENT OF JAPANESE STOCK PRICES

5.1   Market Booms and Busts

Between January 1986 and December 1989, the TOPIX index rose 177 percent. At one point the apparent average price–earnings ratio (PER) on the market reached 71.4. The models suggest that much of this rise was due to the growth of the money supply. Elsewhere I have argued that the growth of the money supply was itself a consequence of Bank of Japan intervention to support the US$.[12]

Figure 11.12 shows the monthly price–earnings ratio (PER) of the Tokyo Stock Exchange (TSE) together with the ratio of the total value of foreign reserves in a given month to imports in that month. The correlation is, I would suggest, striking. Put all together, this suggests that the Japanese stock market's spectacular performance in the second

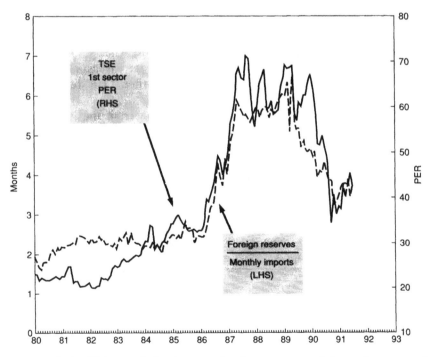

Figure 11.12   High correlation between foreign reserves and the performance of the stock market

half of the 1980s was a one-time event, linked to BOJ monetary policy, which in turn was affected by exchange rate considerations.

This further suggests that the overvaluation in Tokyo was not the result of the diffusion of the practice of indexation of investment portfolios, as some observers have suggested. The argument is that as more and more fund managers have adopted an explicit or implicit linking of their portfolios to the NSA 225, the increased demand for shares included in the NSA 225 has resulted in the NSA 225 trading at a premium to the market. The models contradict this argument.

First, the models show very similar errors for both the NSA 225 index and the TOPIX index, suggesting little difference between the behavior of the (broad market and the subsample which the NSA 225 represents, net of the differences in their composition. Second, indexation was already well diffused in the US, but the behavior of both the US and Japanese markets relative to the models (which do not incorporate any indexation factor) is so similar as to obviate the need for any such explanation.

5.1.1 The October 1987 crash

Another result of the models is that we do not need to invoke the guiding hand of Japan Inc. to explain why Japan's market did not fall further in October 1987. Table 11.8 presents the market-model discrepancy in percentages for the five international indices for September, October, and December 1987.

The models suggest that New York collapsed from a substantially overvalued position (24 percent in September) to a still overvalued 10 percent in October. New York pulled Tokyo down, but Japan's market did not collapse because Tokyo was not substantially overvalued (3

Table 11.8 Market-model discrepancies at the time of the October 1987 crash (%)

Index	Sept. 87	Oct. 87	Dec. 87
S&P 500	24	10	−10
TOPIX	3	0	−16
FT Ord.	36	−2	−2
Commerzbk	26	−2	−18
CAC	−4	−24	−4

A positive number indicates that, according to our models, the market was overvalued by that amount.

percent in September). Government intervention may have stopped over-selling, but New York was subject to as much or as little over-selling, despite limited government intervention, and by December Tokyo was more over-sold than New York.

When we look at the three European markets we see some similar situations. London appears to have been grossly overvalued (36 percent) and then to have slightly overcorrected. Paris was undervalued, over-corrected, and then rose rapidly, although it lagged its model fair value for more than a year. Frankfurt was overvalued in September, over-corrected, and then it too trailed its model fair value for almost two years.

5.1.2   The 1990–1 bear market

From its high on December 19, 1989, of 38,916, the NSA 225 index lost 18,694 points, a decline of 48 percent, by the time it reached its closing low of 20,222 on October 1, 1990. By any standards this is a large fall, and the question is, what does it mean?

The models had been suggesting for some time that the NSA 225 and TOPIX Indices were substantially overvalued. I started tracking the NSA 225 in June 1989 and at that time found the index to be about 10 percent overvalued relative to where the model suggested the market should be. The degree of overvaluation continued to grow throughout the second half of 1989, reaching about 40 percent overvaluation by the end of 1989 on a model estimated in May 1989. When I re-estimated and revised the model in February 1990, the revised model showed the maximum over-valuation (December 1989) as about 17 percent.

The market corrected in the first half of 1990. Iraq's invasion of Kuwait then threw the Japanese market into undervaluation, where it has lingered ever since. Since the invasion the market has been hit by scandals involving the major brokers and bands; scandals which may have influenced sentiment unfavorably.

5.2   International Influences

Between about mid-1985 and mid-1989, the TOPIX market-model dis-crepancies became highly correlated (0.41) with the S&P 500 market-model discrepancies. The correlation for the period from July 1985 back to January 1979 is only 0.05. The correlation for the period July 1989 to June 1991 is 0.22. For the whole period January 1979 through June 1991, the correlation is 0.07. Figure 11.13 presents the evolution of the errors (in percentage terms) of the TOPIX and S&P 500 models since January 1979.

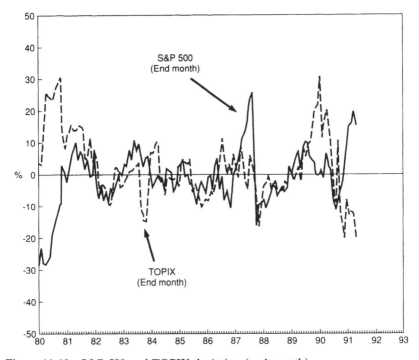

Figure 11.13 S&P 500 and TOPIX deviation (end month)

What these correlations suggest is that roughly since the Plaza Accord, the Japanese and US stockmarkets' overvaluation and undervaluation became relatively highly synchronized, but that this synchronization has now dissipated. The dissipation of the synchronization between the two markets' over- and undervaluation may reflect a waning confidence in the existence of a G-7 agreement to maintain the ¥/US$ exchange rate within a tight range.

6 CONCLUSION

In this chapter I have presented some econometric models which I have developed to link stock market indexes to economic variables. Although the models and methods I use are simple, they have produced interesting results.

First, there does seem to be a linkage between economic fundamentals and stock market indices. Furthermore, the linkages for Tokyo appear similar to those for other markets such as New York, London, Frankfurt, and Paris. Tokyo seems no less rational than these other markets.

Second, the market seems to wander back and forth about the level given by the fundamentals. In this wandering, the discrepancy between the index and the model estimate of its appropriate level does appear to contain information about the market's future direction.

I cannot rule out an overvalued market becoming more overvalued before correcting, or an undervalued one becoming more undervalued; I suspect, though, that the further the market is from the level given by the fundamentals, the more likely it is that the market will move back towards that level and the less likely it is that the market will move further away from that level. That is, my sense is that the greater the deviation between market and model, or the greater the influence of psychology relative to economic fundamentals, the less likely it is that the deviation will increase and the more likely it is that the deviation will narrow. The model cannot forecast the market's future direction with certainty. What the model does is to give a sense of the changing relative probabilities of an upward or downward move. As DeGrauwe and Vansanten (1991) put it in their discussion of a chaos model of exchange rates, near the "equilibrium" point given by fundamentals centrifugal forces dominate, and the further away from this equilibrium the exchange rate is, the more centripetal forces come to dominate.

These results suggest that exploring the linkages from the stock market to the real economy is a worthwhile endeavor. If the stock market wanders about its appropriate level and if its wandering away influences real activity, then the stock market's level may be a matter of public policy. What a government can do, if anything, to reduce deviations or to speed the rate of convergence is itself a topic for research.

NOTES

1 See the Reference list for a selection of relevant articles.
2 The TSE also publishes a similarly constructed index for its second section – TSE2 – and for subindices by industry.
3 For a detailed examination of these issues, see Fedania, Hodder, and Triantis (1990).
4 The long-term credit banks set the long-term prime rate each month at 90 basis points above the coupon rate on long-term bank five-year debentures. The banks set the coupon with reference to the previous month's market yield on such debentures. Thus the long-term prime is based on market interest rates. The benchmark government bond rate is usually quoted as a simple yield rather than a compound yield. When market interest rates deviate from the coupon rate, the simple yield may deviate quite substantially (tens of basis points) from the compound yield. Furthermore, a particular bond may remain the benchmark bond for a year or more. Thus even the

compound yield comes month-by-month to represent a shorter time to maturity. Each month's long-term prime, by contrast, represents a five-year maturity.

5 The driving variables in my adjusting and forecasting equation for the money supply are lagged values of past growth in official reserves. I have discussed this approach in brief elsewhere (see, for example, Tschoegl 1990). The link between official reserves and money supply provides a third mechanism for the introduction of international influences into the model.

6 Originally I included the long-term prime in the regression equation in the form of its logarithm. However, the interest rate is itself a logarithm. When I compared regression results, equations with the untransformed interest rate had very slightly higher R^2s and lower standard errors of the regression than equations using the logarithm of the interest rate. Now, therefore, I estimate the equations with the interest rate untransformed.

7 The statistical package I use does not provide Durbin–Watson statistics, but I use the expedient of estimating the Durbin–Watson from the serial correlation of the regression residuals.

8 See Kim, Nelson, and Startz (1988) which criticizes much of the research on mean reversion because of the problem of heteroskedasticity in asset returns. For an early discussion of some subtle effects of quiet times/noisy times on asset prices, see Ball, Torous, and Tschoegl (1985).

9 Again, see ibid.

10 By a buy-and-hold strategy I mean that the investor assumes that share prices follow a random walk (or more strictly a sub-martingale) and that he or she can do better by simply buying and holding the market index than by attempting to time the market.

11 Why I believe money supply growth currently is actually closer to 8 percent than the officially announced 2–3 percent is a separate issue which I discuss in other SBCI securities publications available on request.

12 See Tschoegl (1990).

REFERENCES

Ball, Clifford A., Torous, Walter, and Tschoegl, Adrian E. 1985: The degree of price resolution: the case of the gold market. *Journal of Futures Markets*, 5, 29–43.

DeBondt, Werner F.M. and Thaler, Richard 1987: Further evidence of investor overreaction and stockmarket seasonality. *Journal of Finance*, 42, 557–81.

DeGrauwe, Paul C. and Vansanten, Kris J.L. 1991: Speculative dynamics and chaos in the foreign exchange market. In Richard O'Brien and Sarah Hewin (eds), *Finance and the International Economy*, London: Oxford University Press.

Fedania, Mark, Hodder, James E. and Triantis, Alexander J. 1990: Cross-holding and market return measures. Madison: University of Wisconsin – Madison, June.

Jegadeesh, Narasimhan 1991: Seasonality in stock price mean reversion: evidence from the US and the UK. *Journal of Finance*, 46, 1427–44.

Kim, Myung, Nelson, Charles R. and Startz, Richard 1988: Mean reversion in stock prices? A reappraisal of the empirical evidence. Unpublished working paper, Northwestern University.

Lehman, Bruce N. 1990: Fads, martingales, and market efficiency. *Quarterly Journal of Economics*, 105, 1–28.

Poterba, James and Summers, Lawrence H. 1986: Temporary components of stock prices: evidence and implications. *Journal of Financial Economics*, 22, 27–59.

Schiller, Robert J. 1981: The use of volatility measures in assessing market efficiency. *Journal of Finance*, 36, 291–304.

Summers, Lawrence H. 1986: Does the stockmarket rationally reflect fundamental value? *Journal of Finance*, 41, 591–601.

Tschoegl, Adrian E. 1987: Noise in observed returns: the case of the London gold market. University of Michigan.

Tschoegl, Adrian E. 1990: Comment on monetary policy in Japan. In Charles A.E. Goodheart and George Sutija (eds), *Japanese Financial Growth*, London: Macmillan.

Part V

Futures, Money, and
Foreign Exchange Markets

12

Stock Futures and Options Markets in Japan

Tomohiko Adachi and Motonari Kurasawa

1 INTRODUCTION

Stock index futures began trading on the Tokyo Stock Exchange (TSE) and the Osaka Stock Exchange (OSE) in September 1988. This was followed by stock index option trading on the OSE in June 1989, and on the TSE and the Nagoya Stock Exchange (NSE) in October 1989. Government bond futures have been traded on TSE since October 1985, and government bond options over the counter since April 1989. Also, US Treasury bond futures began trading in December 1989, and US Treasury bond futures options in May 1990, both in Tokyo. In the relatively short period of time since introduction, the trading volume of futures and options has expanded to a scale comparable to that in the United States.

In this chapter, we give a brief description of the Japanese derivatives markets, and present an analysis of the effect of the introduction of stock futures and options trading on the cash stock market.

The chapter is organized as follows. Section 2 explains the three stock indices used by the three major stock exchanges of Japan. Section 3 discusses the market structure, contract specifications, trade mechanics, market size, and activities of major investor groups. Section 4 analyzes the relationship between the cash stock market and the derivatives markets, and examines the reaction of the Japanese stock market to the introduction of index futures and options. Section 5 briefly looks at some of the issues raised by the development of the derivatives markets. Finally, section 6 presents concluding remarks.

In the preparation of this chapter, we received important comments and suggestions from Shaun Conroy, formerly an options dealer at Bankers Trust Company, as well as from Shinji Takagi.

Table 12.1   Three contract indices in stock futures and options

Exchange	Index	Number of stocks included	Derivatives	Remarks
Osaka	Nikkei Average	225	Futures, options	Weighted by price
Tokyo	TOPIX	>1,100	Futures, options	Weighted by capitalization
Nagoya	Option-25	25	Options	Weighted by price

Source: the Tokyo, Osaka, and Nagoya Exchanges

Table 12.2   Correlations among three indices in 1988 (daily return)

	Nikkei	*TOPIX*	*Option-25*
Nikkei	1.0		
TOPIX	0.952	1.0	
Option-25	0.921	0.948	1.0

Source: based on data from the Tokyo Stock Exchange

Table 12.3   Volatility of three indices in 1988 (daily return)

Index	Volatility (%)
Nikkei 225	14.3
TOPIX	15.4
Option-25	18.6

Source: based on data from the Tokyo Stock Exchange

2   THREE UNDERLYING INDICES IN FUTURES AND OPTIONS

2.1   Overview of Three Indices

In Japan there are three major stock exchanges, each with an independent index on which derivative securities are contracted or written. These indices act as the underlying assets for the derivative securities, as shown in table 12.1. Two of the three indices are weighted by the price of

Table 12.4 Characteristics of three indices

	Industry weights	*Capitalization*	*Volatility*
Nikkei	High weighting for chemicals, food, textiles, and service industries.	Relatively high share of composite index for low capitalization stocks.	
TOPIX	Financial services take more than 30% share of the composite index. Electrical, chemical, general trading, and utility industries also account for a large share of the composite index.		
Option-25	High-tech, such as electric, chemical, automobile, and telecommunication industries, take the highest share of the index.	Only large capitalization stocks (more than 200 bil. yen) are included.	Highest volatility of the three.

component stocks, while the other is weighted by the capitalization of the companies.

Tables 12.2 and 12.3 show the correlations and volatilities of the three indices, based on the daily returns in 1988.[1] Table 12.4 presents the characteristics, in terms of industry weights, capitalization, and volatility, of the Nikkei Average Stock Index (Nikkei) traded on the OSE, the Tokyo Stock Price Index (TOPIX) traded on the TSE, and the Option-25 Index (Option-25) traded on the NSE.

2.2   Explanation of Individual Indices

A brief explanation of the procedure for the calculation of the individual indices is provided below (for further information, refer to the publications of the respective stock exchanges).

2.2.1   Nikkei Average Stock Index

The Nikkei Average is defined in the same manner as the Dow Jones Index in the US. It consists of 225 stocks out of more than 1,100 stocks listed on the first section of the Tokyo Stock Exchange. The formula for calculating the Nikkei Average is:

$$\text{Current Nikkei Average} = \frac{\substack{\text{Sum of current prices} \\ \text{of 225 component stocks}}}{\text{Denominator}}$$

where the denominator is the number of components on the base date, adjusted for changes in value of the components due to the subsequent activities of the individual companies. A list of such activities is given in subsection 2.3.

Although a fuller definition of the index is outside the scope of this chapter, it is important to note that the composition of the index is weighted by the prices of the component stocks. This weighting scheme sometimes results in abnormal price movements. This point will be covered in greater details in subsection 2.4.

2.2.2 Tokyo Stock Price Index

The TOPIX is weighted by the market capitalization of component stocks, which include all stocks currently listed on the first section of the TSE. The base of the index is the aggregate market value of all first-section stocks at the close of business on January 4, 1968 (the base date). The aggregate market value is calculated by (a) multiplying the number of listed shares of each component stock by its market price, and (b) summing the products so derived.

In computing the TOPIX, the aggregate market value at the base date (the base market value) is used as the denominator of the formula, and the current aggregate market value is used as the numerator. The fraction so obtained is multiplied by 100 (the index number on the base date), and is rounded to the nearest one hundredth decimal place:

$$\text{Current TOPIX} = \frac{\text{Current market value}}{\text{Base market value}} \times 100$$

Listing a new company or delisting a company from the exchange necessitates an adjustment as it changes the market value or capitalization of the index (see subsection 2.3 below).

2.2.3 Option-25 Index

When the NSE developed the Option-25 index, it decided to include only those stocks which met certain standards, such as total capitalization of over 200 billion yen, and total transactions of over one million shares during the previous three years. The index, which is weighted by price, consists of 25 component stocks, which are designed to cover 20 out of 28 industry groups.

The index is calculated as the arithmetic average of the 25 components, as follows:

$$\text{Current Option-25 Index} = \frac{\text{Sum of current prices of 25 components}}{\text{Sum of stock prices of 25 components at the base date}^2} \times 100$$

2.3 Adjustment of Indices

The following corporate activities, which affect the current market value, require an adjustment to the base market value of the index:

(a) new listing;
(b) assignment of a stock from the second section to the first section, and vice versa;
(c) delisting;
(d) rights offering;
(e) public offering;
(f) private placement;
(g) merger;
(h) exercise of a stock subscription warrant;
(i) conversion of convertible bonds or preferred stocks into common stocks.

In contrast, a corporate decision which does not change the market value of the shares requires no adjustment of the base market value. Therefore, stock splits, capitalization issues (bonus issues), and stock dividends entail no adjustment, because the new share price multiplied by the increased (or decreased) number of shares remains the same as the old share price multiplied by the old number of shares. Taking the TOPIX as an example, the formula for adjustment is given as follows:

$$\text{New base market value} = \text{Old base market value} \times \frac{\text{New market value}}{\text{Old market value}}$$

2.4 A Deeper Look at the Nikkei Average Index

Of the three indices, the Nikkei Average is the dominant index in futures and options trading. It may thus be useful to further examine the characteristics of the Nikkei Average Index.

As stated earlier, the Nikkei Average consists of 225 companies, including some relatively small capitalization stocks, which are relatively thinly traded and thus tend to show a sharper price fluctuation.

Because the composite index is weighted by price, a given percentage change in the price of a stock whose price is higher than average has a greater influence on the index than that of a lower-priced stock which may have a larger market capitalization. For example, Godo Shusei Corporation had the market capitalization of 42.1 billion yen, and the closing price of its stock was 890 yen at the end of September 1990. In contrast, Nippon Steel had the capitalization of 2,741.7 billion yen (65 times Godo Shusei), and the closing price of its stock was only 398 yen on the same day. Despite the difference in capitalization, a price change of 1 percent in Nippon Steel stock will have less than half as much impact on the Nikkei Average as a similar price change of Godo Shusei stock.

In short, the Nikkei Average can be influenced significantly by a relatively small amount of trading in high-priced stocks with small market capitalization. This creates opportunities for market manipulation by participating investors with sufficient capital and intention.

Akeda (1990) defined the "impact coefficient" (i.c.), as a measure to show the impact of trading in each component stock on the index, as follows:

$$\text{i.c.}_{(i)} = \text{share of } i\text{th stock} \times \text{price change of } i\text{th stock per daily trading unit}$$

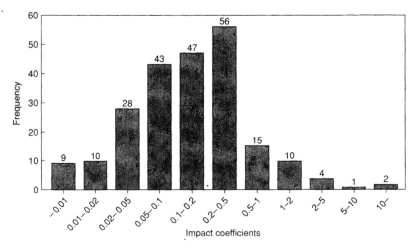

Figure 12.1   Frequency distribution of impact coefficients

Source: Akeda (1990)

Table 12.5 Thirty companies with highest average impact coefficients between July 1 and December 28, 1989 (out of 225 components of the Nikkei Average)

Code	Name of stocks	ic
8235	Matsuzakaya	11.02
3001	Katakura Industries	10.16
9601	Shochiku	5.1
2533	Godo Shusei	2.62
3302	Teikoku Sen-i	2.52
3202	Daito Woolen Spinning & Weaving	2.17
3201	Japan Wool Textile	2.06
2102	Taito	1.82
9602	Toho	1.57
9681	Tokyo Dome	1.5
5351	Shinagawa Refractory	1.41
6461	Nippon Piston Ring	1.34
8233	Takashimaya	1.31
2002	Nisshin Flour Milling	1.13
3865	Hokuetsu Paper Mills	1.08
4506	Dainippon Pharmaceutical	1.08
5901	Toyo Seikan	1.07
4201	The Nippon Synthetic Chemical Industry	0.97
5632	Mitsubishi Steel Mfg.	0.91
8511	Japan Securities Finance	0.83
5331	Noritake Co. Limited	0.82
5721	Shimura kako	0.74
5005	Tonen	0.74
8402	Mitsubishi Trust and Banking	0.65
9302	Mitsui Warehouse	0.64
4092	Nippon Chemical Industrial	0.63
5981	Tokyo Rope Mfg.	0.62
2801	Kikkoman	0.55
8236	Maruzen	0.55
7102	Nippon Sharyo Seizo	0.53

Source: Akeda (1990)

where

$$\text{price change per trading unit} = \frac{\{[(\text{high} - \text{low})/(\text{average of high and low})] \times 100\}}{\text{number of units traded on a particular day}}.$$

Figure 12.1 depicts the sample distribution of the impact coefficients of the 225 component stocks of the Nikkei Average. Table 12.5 lists the 30 stocks with highest average impact coefficients in the period between July 1, 1989 and December 28, 1989.

If we construct an equal share portfolio of these 30 stocks on February 22, 1990, we would find that the value of this portfolio dropped by 10.17 percent during the course of the following day. On the other hand, we find that the portfolio consisting of the remaining 195 stocks of the 225 Nikkei stocks dropped by only 1.49 percent. This is an example to show how the Nikkei Average is amplified by stocks with high-impact coefficients.

3   OUTLINE OF THE MARKETS IN FUTURES AND OPTIONS

3.1   Market Organization and Participants

As in the cash market, securities companies act as brokers in derivatives trading and receive orders from various types of market participants. At the same time, the dealing section of the securities companies take their own positions in both futures and options, creating liquidity in both markets.

There are no restrictions on the type of people who can participate in the derivatives market. In this sense, individual investors are not excluded from the market. However, because the "total asset requirement" that is required to open futures/options trading accounts with securities companies is relatively high (currently the minimum is 20 million yen for each account), the number of individual participants is limited, and the trading share of individuals is small.

A securities exchange receives orders for derivatives from its member firms, and these orders are then routed, executed, and reported back electronically. Once an open position is created by a member, the position is marked to the market daily, and the "variation margin," or implied lost/gained value by the price change of the day, is computed by the exchange. This value is netted out per member account and exchanged among the members. Settlement of member positions is basically effected by the daily passing of variation margins among members of an exchange, as explained above.

Investors' open positions are not marked to the market daily and the maintenance of their margin levels is kept by member securities companies. Settlement of an investor's derivatives positions is effected between the investor and the securities company by comparing the entry price with the closing-out price (or the final settlement price).

3.2 Futures Markets

Futures trading based on a basket of 50 cash stocks (with a settlement by mandatory delivery of physical stock certificates), was introduced by the OSE in June 1987. This in effect can be called stock index futures trading. The 50-stock futures contract performed the same function as today's stock index futures contract as defined by the Securities and Exchange Law. Although the market in 50-stock futures is no longer functioning, it should be credited with having played a pioneering role in stock index futures trading in Japan.

In response to the revision of the Securities and Exchange Law in 1988, the TSE began trading in TOPIX futures, and the OSE began trading in Nikkei futures on September 3 of that year.[3] Since the introduction of stock index futures trading, volume has vigorously grown each year. Today, the equivalent dollar value amount of stock index futures contracts traded on the OSE exceeds that of Standard and Poor's (S&P) 500 futures contracts traded on the Chicago Mercantile Exchange, making the OSE the largest stock index futures market in the world (table 12.6).

Nikkei futures trading accounts for over 90 percent of stock index futures trading in Japan. The value of Nikkei contracts traded in 1991 (January through October) was 458.3 trillion yen, approximately four times the amount of trading in listed stocks in the Japanese cash markets. Of this total, 57.7 percent was for the house accounts or dealer positions of securities companies, 22.6 percent was by financial institutions,[4] 6.9

Table 12.6 Index futures trading in the world (daily average in millions of US dollars)

Region	Index	Value of trading 1989	1990
North America	S&P 500	6,772	7,990
	NYSE Composite	556	569
	MMI	531	482
Pacific	Nikkei 225 (Osaka)	5,489	10,911
	Nikkei 225 (SIMEX)	423	456
	TOPIX	2,795	1,955
Europe	FT-SE 100	354	568
	CAC-40	79	360
	DAX		221

Source: Stock Index Research, Goldman Sachs, January, 1990

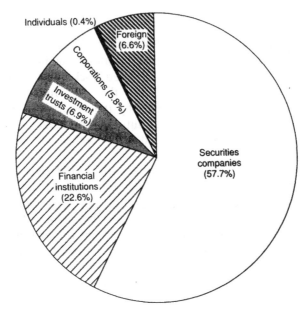

Figure 12.2   Shares of futures trading by type of investor (January–October 1991)

Source: Osaka Stock Exchange

percent by investment trusts, 5.8 percent by corporations, and 6.6 percent by foreign investors. The share of individual investors was almost zero (figure 12.2).

Participants in Japan's stock market seem to have changed their investing vehicle somewhat from cash stocks to futures, owing to the lower transaction and market impact costs, and the greater liquidity of the futures market. Over the course of market expansion, signs have emerged that the futures market is exerting impact on the cash stock market. For example, on the final trading day of stock index futures in December 1988, the actions of traders in buying futures and liquidating short positions (occasioned by arbitrage positions) led to a massive buying of cash stocks. This triggered a dramatic surge of cash stock prices, similar to "the triple witching day phenomenon" on the third Friday of the settlement month in the United States.

In order to defuse the impact of stock index futures trading (during the close-out period of contracts) on cash stock prices, the settlement date for determining futures liquidation prices was changed to the day following the final trading day from September 1989. The new system is called a special quotation (SQ). However, some observers have asserted that the liquidation of arbitrage positions from February to March 1990 caused the collapse of stock prices and led to the downward "spiral process" of both stock and futures prices through investor anxiety.

In order to dispel the apprehension of investors and to improve the transparency of the market, therefore, the TSE decided to publish the trading volume and positions of cash stocks linked to arbitrage transactions on a weekly basis. Table 12.7 shows some recent publications of arbitrage-driven cash positions as made by the TSE. It should be noted that there is almost no "sell-arb" in Japan, an arbitrage transaction that involves being short in cash stocks and long in futures.

Table 12.7 Index arbitrage transactions and positions in terms of cash stocks (September–November, 1991)

A. *Transactions through the week*		
	Sell	*Purchase*
Last day of the week	*(in billions of yen)*	
Sept. 6	54.3	31.9
Sept. 13 (SQ day)	552.9	262.2
Sept. 20	34.4	50.0
Sept. 27	11.8	124.3
Oct. 4	24.7	131.0
Oct. 11	16.6	90.3
Oct. 18	15.6	109.0
Oct. 25	24.4	123.7
Nov. 1	25.5	131.6
Nov. 8	36.6	46.3
Nov. 15	50.5	62.5

B. *Positions as of the close of the week*		
	Short	*Long*
Last day of the week	*(in billions of yen)*	
Sept. 6	2.5	931.8
Sept. 13 (SQ day)	0.0	958.4
Sept. 20	0.0	979.3
Sept. 27	0.0	1,138.7
Oct. 4	0.0	1,280.3
Oct. 11	0.0	1,324.1
Oct. 18	0.0	1,449.0
Oct. 25	0.0	1,536.5
Nov. 1	0.0	1,633.5
Nov. 8	0.0	1,582.4
Nov. 15	0.0	1,514.6

Source: Tokyo Stock Exchange

Table 12.8 Contract specifications for Nikkei futures trading (as of December 5, 1991)

Contract	Nikkei Average Futures
Trading unit	Nikkei Average Index ×1,000
Contract months	March, June, September, December*
Final trading day	The trading day immediately preceding the second Friday of each delivery month
Final settlement date	10th day of each delivery month
Method of settlement	Cash payment
Trading hours	Morning session: 9–11 a.m.
	Afternoon session: 12:30–3:10 p.m.**
Bid and asked spread	In units of 10 yen
Limit of price swing index	About 3 percent up or down from the last contract price of the preceding trading day
Margin requirements for customers	Greater of 25 percent of the contract value (of which 8 percent in cash) or 6 million yen

*   At any moment in time, trading is done for five consecutive contract months.
**   The afternoon session closes at 3 p.m. on the final trading day only.

The specifications of Nikkei futures contracts are given in table 12.8. These specifications are also applicable to the TOPIX index, with minor differences.[5]

3.3   Options Markets

The Osaka Stock Exchange introduced Nikkei Average options in June 1989, and thereby initiated option trading in Japan.[6] This was followed by the Tokyo Stock Exchange with TOPIX options trading, and by the Nagoya Stock Exchange with 25-stock index options (Option-25) trading in October 1989.[7] Trading in Nikkei Average options increased steadily and, by September 1991, its dollar volume had exceeded that of S&P 100 options trading on the Chicago Board Options Exchange (CBOE) by more than 50 percent.

Nikkei options trading, which accounted for more than 94 percent of index options trading in Japan in 1991 (January through October), was 4.49 trillion yen by premium, or 232.44 trillion yen by contract value. Of this total, 54.3 percent was traded by dealers of securities companies, 14.7 percent was by financial institutions, 3.5 percent by investment trusts, 13 percent by corporations, 4.0 percent by individuals, and 10.5 percent by foreign investors (figure 12.3).

Table 12.9 lists the specifications of Nikkei options traded on the OSE.

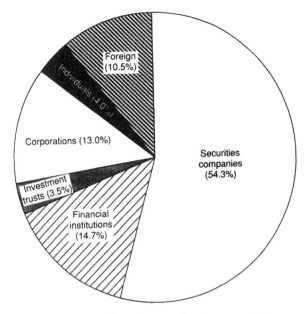

Figure 12.3 Composite share of options trading by type of investor (January–October 1991)

Source: Osaka Stock Exchange

For the most part, they are also applicable to TOPIX options on the TSE and Option-25 options on the NSE. The limits on price swings and margin and bond requirements are subject to occasional change. The right to exercise options has been limited to Thursdays only since the start of Nikkei Average options trading. The authorities claim that this is a tentative action taken for the introductory period of options trading. Finally, table 12.10 gives the exercise periods of the three traded options, as of December 5, 1991.

4 THE PERFORMANCE OF FUTURES AND OPTIONS MARKETS

4.1 The Relationship between the Cash Market and the Futures Market

We shall consider an arbitrage transaction, using a cash stock portfolio and index futures, called index arbitrage (or index arb, for short). Let us look at the following example provided by the OSE (1991):

Table 12.9 Specifications of Nikkei options trading (as of December 5, 1991)

Contract	Nikkei Average options		
Underlying asset	The Nikkei Average Stock Index		
Contract months	March, June, September, December		
Final trading day	The trading day falling on a business day immediately preceding the second Friday of each month.		
Exercise price			
(1) Intervals	500 yen		
(2) Establishment of new postitions	A total of five or six positions, two each above and below an exercise price closest to the stock index established on the day immediately preceding the starting day of the trade.		
(3) Establishment of additional positions	Two or more positions each above and below the exercise price are established on the basis of daily closing stock index.		
Trading hours	Morning session: 9–11 a.m. Afternoon session: 12:30–3:10 p.m.*		
Trading unit	1,000 times the index		
Unit of quotes	*Premium*	*Unit of quotation*	*Unit of quotation (per trading unit)*
	Less than 1,000 yen	5 yen	5,000 yen
	1,000 yen or more	10 yen	10,000 yen
Limit on price swings	A maximum of 3 percent above or below the closing Nikkei Average of the preceding session.		
Margin requirement			
(1) Minimum margin	6 million yen		
(2) The amount of margin	(premium + exercise price) × 1,000 × 0.25		
Period of exercise	Over the life of the contract.**		
Expiration of contracts	Contracts expire when the outstanding accounts for which a notification of exercise is not received before the notification deadline, or the accounts have not received any allocation.		

* The afternoon session closes at 3 p.m. on the final trading day.
** The OSE has taken the temporary action of limiting the exercise period for options to Thursdays only.

Table 12.10 Exercise periods of traded options in Japan

Option exchange	Option type	Exercise period
Nikkei Average (OSE)	Quasi-American*	Every Thursday after the first trading day
TOPIX (TSE)	American	From the first trading day to the last
Option-25 (NSE)	European	Exercisable on the expiration day only

* Options can be exercised only on a specified day of the week.

Closing prices of January 4, 1991
(1) Level of the Nikkei Average: S_{nk} = 24,069.18 (yen)
(2) Price of a futures contract with the expiration of March 1991:

$$F_{nk03} = 24,070 \text{ (yen)}$$

(3) Theoretical price of futures:

$$F_{th} = S_{nk} + S_{nk}(r - d) \times T/365 = 24,361.78,$$

where r (the short-term interest rate) = 6.8 percent d (the estimated rate of average annual dividend) = 0.46 percent, and T (the number of days to expiration) = 70.

In this example, the arbitrage profit is calculated as

$$F_{nk03} - F_{th} = 24,700 - 24,361.78 = 338.22 \text{ (yen)}[8]$$

which is 1.41 percent of the Nikkei Average (S_{nk}). We must consider, however, (a) the cost related to index arbitrage, and (b) the risk taken by the arbitragers.

Choosing January 4, 1991 as the sample day in the above example, OSE (1991) performed a simulation exercise to find the cost of index arbitrage (table 12.11). In this exercise, it is assumed that the index basket consists of all the 225 Nikkei stocks. As shown in the table, the transactions cost (txc), which is the sum of transaction commission, transaction tax, exchange tax, and consumption tax, declines for each unit of arbitrage position, as the size of the position increases.

Considering that the gross arbitrage profit is 338.22 yen in terms of index level, and the transactions cost is 317 yen for a position of 50,000 shares per component, index arbitrage is feasible only for member securities companies of the OSE and the TSE.[9] An index arbitrager must also consider the market impact cost (mic), which is estimated by institutional investors in Japan as ranging between 200 yen and 400 yen (in

Table 12.11   Cost of index arbitrage

Trading shares of each component (thousands of shares)	Value of the index basket (in millions of yen)	Futures (contract unit)	Unit transactions cost* (in yen)
1	244	10	627
10	2,438	101	461
50	12,191	507	317
100	24,382	1,013	255
200	48,764	2,026	211

*   Unit transaction cost is expressed in terms of index level.

Source: Osaka Stock Exchange (1991)

terms of index level). Given the fact that the basket includes 50,000 shares of each component stock, index arbitrage is difficult even for professional participants in the Japanese stock market.

Index arbitrage has, nevertheless, been tried by various investors; the aggregate size of the arbitrage position was over 1.6 trillion yen in November 1991. Those who are active in index arbitrage are: (a) dealing sections of securities companies, especially American firms with offices in Japan (the txc level is much lower than the simulation indicates); and (b) investors who use a stock portfolio with a smaller number of components than the 225 of the Nikkei Average. These investors while reducing their txc as well as mic, by minimizing the number of component stocks to the level of 50–100 companies in their portfolio, run the risk of tracking error.

4.2   The Relationship between the Cash Market and the Options Market

It has been pointed out by options market participants that the Nikkei Average shows an abnormal movement on options expiration days (oed), which may be related to the creation of options positions over the period preceding an expiration day. Given the particular nature of the Nikkei Average (as explained in section 2), this possibility cannot be totally ruled out. To monitor how the index moves over a period immediately preceding an oed, we conceptualize the following process.

The exercise price (K) of Nikkei Average options is set at 500 yen intervals, for example, 22,000, 22,500, and 23,000. This means that, in relation to options positions, the index moves in 500-yen price steps. Now, let us consider an option investment strategy called a "short straddle," such that short position in call options at $K = 22,500$ (yen); and short position in put options at $K = 22,500$ (yen). The pay-off pattern of the strategy on the expiration day is shown in figure 12.4. A participant who has a short straddle position wants the Nikkei Average to stay around 22,500 yen on oed, and, if feasible, attempts to hold the level at 22,500 yen.

We define the random variable d_t as the absolute difference between the closing level of the Nikkei average on day t and the potential (or existing) exercise price closest to it.[10] For example, when the closing level is 22,820 yen on day t, the closest potential exercise price is 23,000 yen, and d_t is given by

$$d_t = |22,820 - 23,000| = 180 \text{ yen}$$

Figure 12.5 shows the sample distribution of d_t, with 539 daily observations during the first 27 months (from July, 1989 to September, 1991) after the introduction of options. The statistical hypothesis that d_t is uniformly distributed cannot be rejected by the chi-squared test, suggesting that the distribution fits a uniform distribution.

The sample distribution of d_t observed on options expiration days (except on SQ days), however, is quite different (figure 12.6). In this case, the hypothesis that the distribution is uniform is rejected at the 1 percent significant level. Statistical analysis affirms that, on option

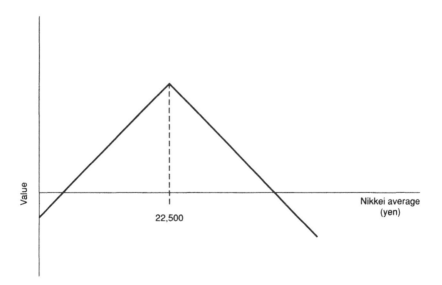

Figure 12.4 Pay-off pattern of a short straddle position on the expiration day

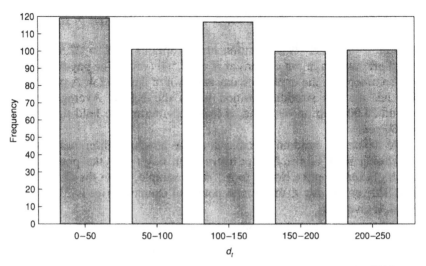

Figure 12.5 Sample distribution of d_t, July 3, 1989 to September 13, 1991*

* The variable d_t is the absolute difference between the closing price of the Nikkei Average on day t and the potential exercise price closest to it; 539 daily observations.

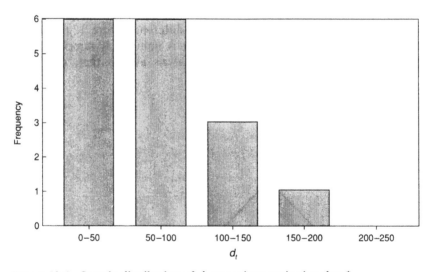

Figure 12.6 Sample distribution of d_t on options expiration days*

* The variable d_t is the absolute difference between the closing price of the Nikkei Average on day t and the potential exercise price closest to it; 16 observations.

expiration days, the index level ends closer to the exercise price than on average days.

Shown in figure 12.7 is the intra-day movement of the Nikkei Average on October 9, 1991, which was randomly selected from the set of 16

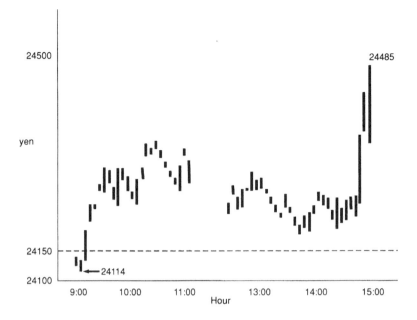

Figure 12.7   Intra-day price movement of the Nikkei Average on October 9, 1991*

* Each line represents the price movement in 5-minute intervals for the day's session.

Source: Tokyo Stock Exchange

expiration days. It is seen here that the level of the index changed dramatically in the last ten minutes of trading, unmistakably showing an abnormal price movement. Similar price movement can be observed on other expiration days. On these days, many stocks with high impact coefficients were among the 20 stocks which showed largest price movement. The index level may be influenced by these stocks to a certain extent.

4.3   The Relationship between the Futures Market and the Options Market

To see the relationship between the futures market and the options market, let us take the case of a reversal arbitrage strategy, which involves taking positions in both the futures and the options markets. The position is described as: a short position in futures; a long call position; and a short put position.

We want to see whether or not a reversal position is feasible in the

Japanese market, when the cost and risk are taken into account. The OSE (1991) simulated reversal positions by estimating the transactions cost (txc) of taking the position during the year 1991. Naturally, the transactions cost changes with the size of the position, the time to expiration, the index level, volatility, and interest rates. Irrespective of those factors, the OSE (1991) calculated the transactions cost of taking one unit of reversal over 192 days to be 74,000 yen on average, with the maximum of 126,000 yen and the minimum of 21,000 yen. These cost estimates do not include market impact cost.

On 108 out of 192 days, the arbitrage profit was positive, that is, $F - C + P > 0$, where $+F$ is a short futures position, $-C$ is a long call position, and $+P$ is a short put position. The average gross profit of the 108 observations was 164,000 yen for one unit of reversal position, and the average net profit (net of the transactions cost) was 95,000 yen. The amount of assets required for taking one unit of reversal position was approximately 10 million yen, most of which is accounted for by margin requirements. The average holding period of the position was less than one month.

Reversal arbitragers must consider the risk that their position influences the market as well as the risk that they will be exercised on the short put position. If the position takes less than 10 units at a time, market impact cost is negligible. Because the exercise rate of put options is 5 percent on average, the risk of being exercised is also relatively small. We can conclude, therefore, that arbitrage opportunities existed for reversal arbitragers in Japan throughout 1990. The reason why this arbitrage opportunity was not exploited until the arbitrage conditions disappear is not explicable.[11]

5 ISSUES RAISED BY THE DERIVATIVES MARKETS

The introduction of futures and option markets in Japan have resulted in much public discussion regarding its possible effect on the cash stock market. This public discussion has raised at least three issues.

First, it is difficult to explain rationally the existence of the large difference between the market value of the basis spread and its theoretical value, which appears as a SQ day approaches.[12] This large positive basis spread stimulates the rolling over of index arbitrage positions from one contract month to the next.[13]

Second, it can be argued that the introduction of the futures market has increased the volatility of the cash stock market. Kon-ya (1991), for example, points out that market volatility has increased since futures trading was first introduced, by referring to the evidence that, from May 1, 1945 through January 31, 1991, 20 out of 100 trading days with the sharpest recorded declines in the Nikkei were found in 1990. Moreover, 15 out of 100 trading days with the sharpest recorded gains in the Nikkei were also found in 1990. On these days, the market index showed abnormally large fluctuations. While there is no conclusive evidence to show a definitive relationship between futures trading and volatility, such a possibility continues to be a topic of serious discussion among Japanese researchers.

Third, Adachi (1991) has pointed out that index manipulation is feasible in Japan, by explicitly presenting possible procedures for such manipulation. Futures trading and a high level of index arbitrage position are essential to the success of index manipulation. When there is a large outstanding volume of index arbitrage position (that is, combinations of long cash and short futures positions), a manipulator can slightly change the level of the Nikkei Average and the futures price by placing orders,[14] and make the spread of cash index and futures price narrow enough to stimulate liquidation of the index arbitrage position.

Here, the liquidation means selling cash stocks and buying futures. If it changes the prices of both cash stocks and futures, the basis spread can be widened to its theoretical (non-arbitrage) level. If a large amount of futures are offered to the market, however, the futures price will go down (instead of up), and the basis spread remains narrower than the theoretical level, thus encouraging continued arbitrage liquidation. What the market participants observe is the downward movement of both the cash index and the futures prices. Considering the possibility that such manipulation actually took place in 1990, it can be argued that the introduction of futures trading indeed contributed to increased market volatility in the Japanese stock market.

6 CONCLUDING REMARKS

Since they were first introduced, the stock derivatives markets in Japan have expanded steadily to a size comparable to that in the United States. The phenomenal expansion of the markets can be explained by the low transactions cost as well as the high liquidity and accessibility of the markets, which have enabled the market participants to change their position and risk exposure at a lower cost than in the cash stock market. The dominant underlying asset of the stock index derivatives market is the Nikkei Average Index, which accounts for more than 90 percent of total trading.

It should be noted, however, that the Nikkei Average is not robust enough to withstand index manipulation. Any derivatives which are written or contracted on the Nikkei Average are thus subject to the risk of market malfunctioning. Any investor who intends entering the Japanese market should be well aware of this risk.

NOTES

1   Before the introduction of options trading.
2   The base date is January 4, 1988, and the stock prices used in the index are those at the TSE.
3   See Kanda (1993), chapter 5 in this volume.
4   Here, financial institutions include banks, trust banks, and life insurance companies.
5   The trading unit for TOPIX is multiplied by 10,000 instead of 1,000, and the bid and asked spread becomes one TOPIX point.
6   Index options may have been traded over the counter before June, 1989, but no data on such trading is available.
7   Options traded on any of the exchanges are only of the standardized type, in the sense that the exercise prices and expiration periods are set by each exchange.
8   The arbitrage profit per futures contract is 338.22 yen multiplied by 1,000.
9   Members of the OSE pay the transaction tax of 0.001 percent of the contract value for futures trading on their own accounts. Likewise, for the trading of cash stocks on the TSE, members of the TSE pay 0.12 percent of the trading value as transaction tax. Both of the tax rates are much lower than the average commission rate paid by the other categories of the market participants.
10   Remember that an exercise price is expressed in units of 500 yen.
11   The basis spread also tended to be larger than its theoretical level in 1990. This is a common background associated with the existence of arbitrage opportunities in both index arb and reversal. Also see section 5.
12   Brenner, Subrahmanyam, and Uno (1990) present evidence that deviations from the theoretical price are not explicable either by transaction costs or by trading restrictions from late 1988.
13   The SQ day is often used as the index arb entrance day, for on that day component stocks are often sold in volume which enables arbitragers to lower the market impact cost in constructing long positions in cash stocks.
14   As the manipulator has a budget constraint, the high i.c. stocks are presumably used to change the cash index level.

REFERENCES

Adachi, Tomohiko 1991: *Nihon no Kabuka Hendo ni Kansuru Kenkyu* (A Study of Stock Price Fluctuations in Japan). Tokyo: Japan Securities Research Institute, July.

Akeda, Yoshiaki 1990: Index baibai no tekisei kibo (Optimal scale of index trading). *Shoken Anarisuto Jaanaru*, May, 1–10.

Brenner, Menachen, Subrahmanyam, Marti G. and Uno, Jun 1990: Arbitrage opportunities in the Japanese stock and futures market. *Financial Analysts Journal*, March/April, 14–24.

Japan Securities Research Institute 1990: *Securities Market in Japan*. Tokyo: Japan Securities Research Institute.

Kanda, Hideki 1993: The regulatory environment for Japanese capital markets. Chapter 5 in this volume.

Kon-ya, Fumiko 1991: *Inbesutomento*, 44 (4). Osaka Stock Exchange.

Kurasawa, Motonari 1989: *Shoken Shiryo* (Securities Report), no. 104. Tokyo: Japan Securities Research Institute.

Osaka Stock Exchange 1991: *Nikkei 225 Sakimono Opushon Repooto* (Report on Options in Nikkei 225 Futures). Osaka: Osaka Stock Exchange, January 11.

Tokyo Stock Exchange 1988: *TOPIX Futures: Outline of Tokyo Stock Price Index Futures*. Tokyo: Tokyo Stock Exchange.

13

The Money Markets in Japan

Colin McKenzie

1 INTRODUCTION

Recently, many changes of a gradual nature have been occurring in the Japanese money markets. These changes include the establishment of new markets, the relaxing of issuing conditions relating to minimum denominations, minimum and maximum maturities, and issuing ceilings, and a relaxation of conditions restricting market participation and market making (see appendix A for details). In addition, the Bank of Japan has broadened the markets and shortened the maturity of assets in which it conducts open market operations. The Bank of Japan has also begun releasing detailed information on its open market operations.

This chapter aims to detail some of these recent changes and attempts to determine the effect of some recent deregulatory measures on the pattern of causality amongst interest rates in the interbank and open markets, and on bid–ask spreads in the *gensaki* market for certificates of deposit. It is organized as follows. Section 2 provides broad details of each money market and outlines some of the recent developments in the money markets. Section 3 examines the impact of this financial liberalization on the money market by investigating how the pattern of causality has changed amongst interest rates in the call market, the discount market, and the *gensaki* market. Section 4 examines the impact of financial liberalization on the money market by investigating how buy–sell spreads in the *gensaki* market for certificates of deposit have changed between 1985 and 1991. Section 5 provides some concluding remarks.

The author wishes to thank Shinji Takagi for his many helpful comments and useful suggestions on an earlier draft of the chapter, Hiro Toda for helpful discussions, and Tomiko Uesato for her research assistance. Finally, the financial support of the Nihon Keizai Kenkyu Shorei Zaidan (Foundation to Promote Research on the Japanese Economy) is gratefully acknowledged.

2 MARKET STRUCTURE AND RECENT LIBERALIZATION[1]

Standard Japanese practice distinguishes the money market from other markets such as the bond market and the deposit market by defining money market instruments as assets which are negotiable and have maturities at issue of one year or less.[2] Certificates of deposit are generally considered to be money market assets, but the extension of their maximum maturity from one year to two years in April 1988 requires that the standard definition be amended to assets which are issued in Japan, are negotiable, and have most maturities at issue of one year or less. As a result of the negotiability requirement, all deposits (except certificates of deposit) are excluded. The maturity requirement provides the distinction between "money" and "bonds". The distinction between the three markets, the money, bond,[3] and deposit markets, is somewhat arbitrary, since bonds are sometimes the underlying instrument in the *gensaki* (repurchase agreement) market and there is likely to be a high degree of substitutability between bonds, large denomination deposits, and some money market instruments. Further liberalization of the Japanese markets will make this distinction between the three markets even less meaningful.

In Japan, it is also usual to distinguish two groups of markets within the money markets: the interbank markets and the open money markets. The interbank markets, from which non-financial institutions are excluded, are the call, bill, and dollar call markets. The open money markets are the markets for *gensaki* (repurchase agreements), certificate of deposits (CDs), commercial paper (CP), financing bills (FBs),[4] treasury bills (TBs),[5] and yen-denominated bank acceptances (BAs). In the past, another important difference between the two groups of markets related to the implementation of monetary policy. Traditionally, the Bank of Japan has conducted lending and bill operations in the interbank markets, but now open market operations are also conducted in the *gensaki*, commercial paper, and treasury bill markets.

Table 13.1 provides details of the relative size of each market in terms of the amount outstanding in each money market. In addition, for the purpose of comparison, table 13.1 provides details on the size of the market for domestic deposit-bearing market (or market related) interest rates and the size of some "foreign" markets. A number of facts are immediately apparent from table 13.1. First, the value of transactions in the money markets has increased over thirty-fold between 1970 and 1990, a rate of growth much faster than the growth in the real economy. Second, the introduction of new markets would appear to have slowed the growth of some existing markets, particularly the *gensaki* market. This is not too surprising as the *gensaki* market was viewed as the major

Table 13.1 Outstanding amounts in the money and related markets (end of calendar year)

	1970	1975	1980	1985	1986	1987	1988	1989	1990
Interbank markets[a]	1.8	6.7	10.8	15.8	23.7	29.1	33.6	45.3	41.0
Call market	1.8	2.3	4.1	5.1	10.2	16.0	15.6	24.5	24.0
Unsecured	–	–	–	0.8	1.6	2.9	6.0	10.1	12.3
Secured	1.8	2.3	4.1	4.3	8.6	13.1	9.6	14.4	11.7
Bill market	–	4.4	5.7	14.7	13.5	13.1	18.0	20.8	17.0
Dollar call market	–	(1.3)	(11.7)	(59.2)	(98.2)	(115.3)	(112.1)	(117.1)	(110.3)
Open markets (domestic)	0.6	1.8	6.9	14.3	20.0	22.4	35.7	44.5	49.6
Gensaki (in securities)	0.6	1.8	4.5	4.6	7.1	6.9	7.4	6.3	6.6
Certificates of deposit	–	–	2.4	9.7	9.9	10.8	16.0	21.1	18.6
Domestic commercial paper	–	–	–	–	–	1.1	9.3	13.1	15.8
Financing bills	–	–	–	–	0.9	0.9	1.0	0.0	1.0
Treasury bills	–	–	–	–	2.1	2.7	2.0	4.0	7.6
Yen-denominated bank acceptances	–	–	–	0.03	:	:	:	:	:

Open markets (foreign)								
Tokyo offshore market[a]	–	–	–	(193.7)	(238.8)	(414.2)	(607.6)	(605.0)
Euroyen certificates of deposit	–	–	0.0	0.0	0.2	0.3	0.3	0.4
Deposit market[b]	–	7.7	30.0	44.8	83.5	118.7	210.8	281.0
Foreign currency deposits	–	1.1	2.4	1.8	2.0	2.1	2.1	2.2
Non-resident yen deposits	–	6.6	18.0	18.7	22.9	20.2	25.6	33.6
Money market certificates	–	–	5.1	8.0	15.1	22.8	11.2	0.2
Small denomination MMCs	–	–	–	–	–	–	19.3	53.8
Large denomination deposits	–	–	4.5	16.3	43.5	73.6	152.6	191.2

[a] Total excludes dollar call market.
[b] Only included when interest rates are market-determined or market-related.
Units: trillions of yen, except figures in brackets which are in billions of $US.
– indicates that "market not in existence."
.. indicates "an extremely small positive amount."

Sources: Suzuki (1987: 110); Ministry of Finance (International Finance Bureau), *Okurasho kokusai kin'yukyoku nenpo* (Annual Report of the International Finance Bureau, Ministry of Finance), various issues; Ministry of Finance (Securities Bureau), *Okurasho shokenkyoku nenpo* (Annual Report of the Securities Bureau, Ministry of Finance), various issues; Bank of Japan, *Economic Statistics Annual*, various issues; Bank of Japan, *Economic Statistics Monthly*, various issues; Bank of Japan, *Nihon Ginko Geppo* (The Bank of Japan Monthly Bulletin), various issues; Industrial Bank of Japan (1991: 280)

unregulated market in the 1970s when the other markets were highly regulated. Section 2.1 discusses the interbank markets and section 2.2 discusses the open markets.

2.1   Interbank Markets

Until November 1988, the major difference between the call and bill markets concerned maturity (and consequently interest rates) with the call maturities being up to three weeks and the bill maturities being for longer than a month. Now, for assets of the same maturity the principal difference is that call transactions are unsecured whereas bill transactions are secured. The dollar call market is another interbank market, but the discussion here is limited to the call and bill markets.[6]

2.1.1   **Call market**

While the minimum transaction unit in the call market is 1 million yen the customary transaction unit is 100 million yen or more. The two types of transactions in this market are secured and unsecured call money transactions where, in principle, secured call transactions require as collateral securities that are eligible for borrowing from the Bank of Japan, such as government bonds, financing bills, government guaranteed bonds, or bank debentures. The maximum maturity of secured call transactions is six days, whereas the minimum and maximum maturity of unsecured call transactions are overnight and 12 months, respectively. The relative importance of secured and unsecured transactions has changed significantly since unsecured transactions were introduced. Until July 1985, all transactions in the call market were collateralized. Since then transactions in the unsecured call market have grown at such a rate that the amount outstanding in the unsecured call market now exceeds the amount in the secured call market (see table 13.1).

One important reason for the spectacular growth of the unsecured call market is a package of "reforms" implemented by the Bank of Japan in November 1988. On the one hand, the maximum maturity of transactions in the secured call market was restricted from three weeks to six days, while the maximum maturity in the unsecured call market was extended from three weeks to six months (and in April 1989 to one year: see appendix A).

There have been important changes in the share of the major borrowers in the call market over the last ten years.[7] Whereas the share of city banks was around 70 percent in the early 1980s, it is now around 50 percent. The share of foreign banks that was less than 10 percent has risen to between 25 and 30 percent and appears to have been particularly influenced by the opening of the unsecured call market. Over the same period, the share of trust banks has also risen from 2 to 9 percent. On the lending side, the share of trust banks has risen from around 25 percent to 70 percent. The other major lenders are city banks, *shinkin* banks, agricultural organizations, and regional banks.

2.1.2 Bill market

The minimum transaction unit in the bill market is 10 million yen, but the customary transaction unit is 100 million yen or more. The minimum and maximum maturities are one and twelve months, respectively. A bill transaction essentially is discounting of bills where the seller endorses a bill over to a buyer in return for payment which deducts interest payments and other costs from the face value of the bill. The eligible bills include prime commercial and industrial bills, trade bills, prime promissory notes, and yen-denominated trade bills. The role of city banks as borrowers in the bill market has declined, with their share falling from around 90 percent in the mid-1980s to around 70 percent by 1990. After the Bank of Japan, the main lenders are the trust banks, *shinkin* banks, and agricultural institutions.

Recently, some important changes have occurred relating to the implementation of monetary policy by the Bank of Japan in the bill market. At the same time as the call market reforms discussed earlier were implemented, the Bank of Japan shifted the maturities for bill operations to short-term maturities (see Nakao and Horii 1991). From May 1989 and January 1990, open market operations were also conducted in the commercial paper and the treasury bill markets. Since December 1989, the Bank of Japan has also been publishing detailed information on its open market operations.[8]

2.2 Open Markets

2.2.1 *Gensaki*[9]

A *gensaki* transaction is essentially a repurchase agreement where there is a prior promise to repurchase or resell the same security as originally transacted after a fixed time and at a fixed price. The securities that can be the subject of a *gensaki* transaction include: government bonds, local government bonds, corporate bonds (except convertible bonds), bonds issued by foreign governments and foreign enterprises, and certificates of deposit. The maximum period for a *gensaki* transaction is one year but transactions are usually between one and three months. Although the minimum transaction unit is 10 million yen, the usual amount transacted exceeds 100 million yen. Participants in the *gensaki* market must be a corporate entity, which prevents the participation of individuals.

The largest borrowers in this market (sellers of *gensaki*) are the securities companies. Between 1980 and 1990, the role of insurance companies as lenders increased significantly, while that of city banks fell significantly. On the borrowing side, while non-financial business corporations are still the largest lenders (purchasers of *gensaki*), their share fell from the 55–70 percent range in the early 1980s to the 10–20 percent range in the late 1980s. The role of trust banks has also increased.

2.2.2 Certificates of deposit

Certificates of deposit can be issued by any financial institution permitted to accept deposits. The minimum and maximum maturities are two weeks and two years, respectively. The minimum denomination of certificate of deposits is 50 million yen. Since October 1987, there have been no ceilings on the amount of certificates of deposit that a financial institution can issue. City banks have the largest share of certificates of deposits outstanding, followed by regional banks (including member banks of the Second Association of Regional Banks), long-term credit banks and foreign banks.

2.2.3 Commercial paper[10]

As can be seen from table 13.1, the commercial paper market has proven to be extremely attractive since its establishment in November 1987. Its size has now far outstripped the *gensaki* market and is approaching the size of the market for certificates of deposit. In Japan, commercial paper is treated as an unsecured promissory note. Commercial paper enables non-financial corporations to raise funds directly from the money markets and thus avoid, to some extent, borrowing from banks. The minimum and maximum maturities of commercial paper are two weeks and nine months, respectively. Their minimum denomination is 100 million yen. Companies that can satisfy one of several issuing standards are eligible to issue commercial paper. One issuing standard relates to eligibility to issue straight bonds, another to net worth levels and ratio requirements, and yet another relates to the company's rating. In March 1990, about 530 companies were eligible to issue commercial paper, compared with the 11 companies permitted to issue straight bonds. Of the 530 companies, only 143 had exercised their rights to issue commercial paper (see Ministry of Finance 1991). There are also standards to determine whether a company is required to have backup credit line.

2.2.4 Financing bills (*seifu tanki shoken*)

Financing bills are discount bills issued to finance temporary fund shortages of the national government. They have a typical maturity of 60 days and a minimum denomination of 10 million yen. There are three types of financing bills: treasury financing bills, food financing bills, and foreign exchange financing bills. In terms of the amounts issued, foreign exchange financing bills are the most important type. As issue rates are less than the Bank of Japan's discount rate, the Bank of Japan typically takes up the whole issue. Since May 1981, the Bank of Japan has started to resell financing bills to promote the growth of a secondary market in financing bills. As can be seen in table 13.1, the amounts outstanding in the market are still rather small (see also Industrial Bank of Japan 1991: 204).

2.2.5 Treasury bills (*tanki kokusai*)

The treasury bill market was established in February 1986 with bills of six months' maturity. They currently have a minimum denomination of 10 million. Treasury bills are short-term discount government bonds issued to facilitate the refunding of government bonds. In the primary market, bidders are restricted to financial institutions, insurance companies, and securities companies. In the secondary market, corporations but not individuals are also able to participate.

2.2.6 Bankers' acceptances

The yen-denominated bankers' acceptances market was established in June 1985 and currently has a minimum denomination of 50 million yen with maturities up to one year. A bankers' acceptance is a bill of exchange that has been accepted by a foreign exchange bank but which was originally issued by an importer or an exporter to settle a trade transaction. Hence, the fund raisers are non-financial corporations. The bankers' acceptances market has proven to be a dismal failure, with the high cost of raising funds being suggested as the principal reason. The Bank of Japan rarely publishes details of the amounts outstanding in the market[11] and its published details of the interest rates in the market suggest that several months may pass without transactions being affected.

3 THE RELATIONSHIP BETWEEN INTERBANK AND OPEN MONEY MARKETS

Causality tests provide one means of summarizing the time series behaviour of interest rates and the interactions among money markets.

Recently, causality tests have been applied to Japanese data for this purpose (see Takagi 1988a,b; and de Brouwer 1991). For example, Takagi (1988b) performs causality tests in a bivariate framework using daily data on the two-month bill and two-month *gensaki* rates over the period 1978–85. He finds no consistent causality relationship between the interbank and open market rates. In another paper, Takagi (1988a) performs causality tests in a bivariate framework using daily data on the unconditional call rate and the two-month bill discount rate over the period 1981–5 and finds that there was significant feedback between the two interbank rates. Using daily data, de Brouwer (1991) performs causality tests using a system of four interest rates over the period November 1988 through December 1990, and finds that open market rates unidirectionally cause interbank market rates, a finding directly contradicting Takagi (1988b). However, de Brouwer's (1991) results regarding the feedback relationships between the call and the bill rates are consistent with Takagi's (1988a) findings. To be able to link this causality analysis with deregulatory measures, it would be necessary to observe a consistent pattern of causality before the measure and a consistent, but possibly different, pattern of causality after the measure.

Here, the causality between the unconditional call rate, the bill rate, and the bond *gensaki* rate[12] are investigated using daily data over the period 1985–91. The bill and bond *gensaki* interest rates relate to assets of the same maturity. Specific details of the data used are contained in appendix 13.B. There are a number of reasons for another investigation of these interactions. First, as previously noted, contradictory results have been reported regarding the relationships between the interbank and money market rates for different time periods in Takagi (1988b) and de Brouwer (1991). Second, while de Brouwer (1991) highlights the November 1988 reforms implemented by the Bank of Japan discussed in section 2.1 as potentially affecting the causality results, his investigation only uses data after the reforms. Hence, his results cannot inform us about the correctness of his hypothesis that the 1988 reforms significantly affected the pattern of causality. Third, as both authors note, all the interest rates appear to have a unit root, a finding supported here by the augmented Dickey–Fuller tests[13] applied to each interest rate for each calendar year (see table 13.2).

The presence of unit roots in the variables under investigation has potentially important implications for the way causality should be tested. For example, estimating models involving only differenced data will be correct only if there are no cointegrating relationships[14] among the variables (see Toda and Phillips 1991). However, there are good theoretical reasons for believing that there will be at least one cointegrating relationship among the three variables studied, the call rate, the bill rate, and the

Table 13.2 Augmented Dickey–Fuller tests

	Gensaki *rate*	Bill rate	Call rate
1985	−1.59	−1.08	−1.21
1986	−2.30	−3.37	−2.63
1987	−2.90	−1.42	−0.83
1988	−1.82	−1.84	−2.44
1989	−1.88	−1.98	−2.46
1990	−1.68	−1.63	−3.18
1991	−2.20	−3.17	−1.85

Figures in the table correspond to the *t*-statistics associated with ϕ in the regression

$$\Delta x_t = \alpha + \beta t + \phi x_{t-1} + \sum_{i=1}^{p} \gamma_i \Delta x_{t-i} + \varepsilon_t$$

where ε_t is an error. The null hypothesis being tested is H_0: $\varphi = 0$ and the alternative hypothesis is H_1: $\varphi < 0$. The 95 percent critical value is −3.44, so that a test statistic less than −3.44 is consistent with the absence of a unit root and a test statistic greater than −3.44 is consistent with a unit root. Figures in the table are based on setting $p = 6$. It should be noted that the results are robust to choices of p between 1 and 12 except for the bill rate in 1986 for $p > 7$, and the call rate in 1989 when $p \leq 2$ and in 1990 when $p \leq 3$. Except in 1986 and 1987 when there is a strong trend in the data, excluding the time trend leads to the same conclusion.

gensaki rate. Arbitrage between the bill and *gensaki* markets should ensure that interest rates on assets of similar maturity in these two markets do not differ too much. In addition, the term structure of interest rates may imply the existence of cointegrating relationships among interest rates of different maturities (see Anderson et al. 1990).

Given the presence of unit roots in each of the variables and r cointegrating relationship among the variables, Engle and Granger (1987) indicate that the following error correction model is an appropriate representation of the relationship among the three variables, denoted y_{1t}, y_{2t}, and y_{3t}:

$$\begin{bmatrix} \Delta y_{1t} \\ \Delta y_{2t} \\ \Delta y_{3t} \end{bmatrix} = \begin{bmatrix} J_{11}(L) & J_{12}(L) & J_{13}(L) \\ J_{21}(L) & J_{22}(L) & J_{23}(L) \\ J_{31}(L) & J_{32}(L) & J_{33}(L) \end{bmatrix} \begin{bmatrix} \Delta y_{1t-1} \\ \Delta y_{2t-1} \\ \Delta y_{1t-1} \end{bmatrix}$$
$$+ \begin{bmatrix} \gamma_1 \\ \gamma_2 \\ \gamma_3 \end{bmatrix} CV_{t-1} + \begin{bmatrix} \mu_1 \\ \mu_2 \\ \mu_3 \end{bmatrix} + \begin{bmatrix} u_{1t} \\ u_{2t} \\ u_{3t} \end{bmatrix}, \tag{13.1}$$

where $\Delta y_{it} = y_{it} - y_{it-1}$, $J_{ij}(L) = \sum_{k=1}^{m} J_{ij}^{k}L^{k-1}$, L is a lag polynomial, $\gamma_i = [\gamma_{i1}, \ldots, \gamma_{ir}]$ and u_{it} are disturbances. The r cointegrating relationships are defined as

$$CV_t = a_1 y_{1t} + a_2 y_{2t} + a_3 y_{3t}, \tag{13.2}$$

where CV_t is an r by 1 vector and $a_i = [a_{i1}, \ldots, a_{ir}]'$. If there are no cointegrating relationships among the variables ($r = 0$), all the γ_i should be set equal to zero so that the appropriate model is a differenced model. If there are three cointegrating relationships among the variables ($r = 3$), the appropriate model is a levels model where all the γ_i should be set equal to zero and Δy_{it} replaced by y_{it} in (13.1).

Before the number of cointegrating vectors can be determined, it is necessary to determine the number of lags appearing in (13.1), that is, the value of m. Since $r = 3$ corresponds to the most unrestricted model, the number of lags was determined by setting $r = 3$ and initially setting $m = 8$. Then a sequence of tests that test whether H_0: $J_{ij}^{m} = 0$ $\forall_{i,j}$ using a Wald test for $m = 8,7,6$, etc. was implemented until H_0 was rejected. The results for this testing procedure and the choice of m for each year are presented in table 13.3.

Given the value of m determined in table 13.3, the number of cointegrating relationships among the three variables was investigated using Johansen and Juselius' (1990) maximum eigenvalue procedure (see also Johansen 1988). The results of these tests are presented in table 13.4 and indicate that the number of cointegrating relationships existing between the variables varies considerably over time. Since r is chosen to be three in 1986 and 1987, the appropriate model is a model in levels so that standard causality tests can be applied. The test of causality from

Table 13.3   Choice of lag length

	m	Test of m − 1 vs m	Test of m vs m + 1
1985	6	17.52*	16.80
1986	2	36.83*	11.26
1987	2	17.81*	9.35
1988	7	24.98*	15.80
1989	6	20.79*	9.18
1990	3	21.14*	12.00
1991	1	53.73*	14.42

The test of k vs $k + 1$ tests whether H_0: $J_{ij}^{k} = 0$ $\forall i,j$ ($k = m - 1, m$) in (13.1) with $r = 3$ using a Wald test and is distributed as a $\chi^2_{(9)}$ under the null hypothesis. The 95 percent critical value is 16.91 and an *indicates significance at the 95 percent significance level.

Table 13.4 Tests for the number of cointegrating vectors

Null alternative	r = 2 r = 3	r = 1 r = 2	r = 0 r = 1	Value of r
1985	0.03	17.20	19.76	2
1986	7.17*	16.77*	19.97	3
1987	4.38*	11.24	27.45*	3
1988	2.67	7.41	15.17	0
1989	0.00	8.44	16.39	0
1990	2.74	10.03	17.55	0
1991	1.71	11.23	30.26*	1
95% critical value	3.76	14.07	20.97	

Figures in the table are based on the maximum eigenvalue test procedure of Johansen and Juselius (1990) for determining the number of cointegrating vectors in an error correction model. A test statistic less than the critical value is consistent with the null hypothesis. Since a model with $r = 3$ is the most general (unrestricted) model, testing begins from that model. An * indicates significance at the 95 percent level.

variable i to variable j then tests whether lagged values of variable i are significant in the equation for variable j that includes lagged values of all the variables under consideration. Since r is chosen to be zero in 1988, 1989, and 1990, the appropriate model is a differenced model so that causality tests from variable i to variable j can be conducted in (13.1) by setting $\gamma_k = 0 \ \forall k$ and testing $J_{ji}^s = 0 \ \forall s$.

When $0 < r < 3$, tests of causality become a little more complicated. Toda and Phillips (1991) discuss appropriate procedures for testing causality in these models. The test of causality from y_{3t} to y_{1t} involves testing $J_{13}^k = 0$ for $k = 1, \ldots, m$ and $\gamma_1 \alpha_3 = 0$.[15] Their procedure 3 can be summarized as:

(a) Test H_1: $J_{13}^k = 0$, $k = 1, \ldots, m$. If H_1 is rejected, the null hypothesis of no causation from y_{3t} to y_{1t} is rejected. Otherwise, proceed to (b).

(b) Test H_2: $\alpha_3 = 0$ and H_3: $\gamma_1 = 0$ separately. If either or both hypotheses are accepted, the null hypothesis of no causation from y_{3t} to y_{1t} is accepted. Otherwise, proceed to (c).

(c) If $r = 1$ reject the null hypothesis of no causality. If $r > 1$, test H_4: $\gamma_1 \alpha_3 = 0$. If this hypothesis is accepted, accept the null hypothesis of no causality. Otherwise, it is rejected.

Tables 13.5 and 13.6 provide details of the test statistics for testing the hypotheses H_1, H_2, H_3 and H_4 for causality between each of the interest

Table 13.5   Tests of H_1

Variable equation	Gensaki call	Gensaki bill	Bill call	Bill gensaki	Call gensaki	Call bill	Critical value
1985	10.38	24.45*	6.14	59.51*	7.92	4.08	12.59 (6)
1986	15.82*	37.94*	9.17*	21.38*	5.31	5.85	7.82 (3)
1987	12.34*	63.50*	1.37	1.90	12.04*	2.44	7.82 (3)
1988	8.60	8.22	3.50	5.20	11.72	6.92	14.07 (7)
1989	28.60*	11.08	24.49*	8.83	11.37	26.17*	12.59 (6)
1990	0.20	2.28	5.20	2.38	0.98	6.27	7.82 (3)
1991	0.38	8.06*	8.46*	0.18	3.48	0.02	3.84 (1)

For 1986 and 1987, the tests are conducted in a levels model. For 1988, 1989, and 1990, the tests are conducted in a differenced model. For 1985 and 1991, the tests are conducted in an error correction model. The test statistics are distributed as $\chi^2_{(j)}$ under the null hypothesis where the value of j appears in brackets. The critical values are for the 95 percent level and an * indicates significance at the 95 percent level.

Table 13.6a   Tests of H_2 and H_3

	H_2				H_3		CV
	α_C	α_B	α_G	γ_C	γ_B	γ_G	
1985	15.93*	13.99*	14.26*	17.47*	1.15	16.44*	5.99
1991	10.01*	16.58*	17.44*	12.03*	4.83*	4.92*	3.84

The test statistic for α_i tests whether the coefficient(s) associated with the interest rate in market i in the cointegrating vector(s) is zero and is distributed as $\chi^2_{(r)}$ under the null hypothesis, where r is the number of cointegrating vectors. The test statistics for γ_i tests whether the lagged cointegrating vector is a significant explanatory variable in the error correction model for the interest rate in market i, where $i = C, B, G$ refers to the call, bill and *gensaki* markets, respectively. The test statistic is distributed as $\chi^2_{(r)}$ under the null hypothesis, where r is the number of cointegrating vectors. *CV* refers to the 95 percent critical value. An * indicates significance at the 95 percent level.

Table 13.6b   Tests of H_4

	$\gamma_C\alpha_B$	$\gamma_C\alpha_G$	$\gamma_B\alpha_C$	$\gamma_B\alpha_G$	$\gamma_G\alpha_C$	$\gamma_G\alpha_B$
1985	13.13*	10.91*	0.43	1642*	0.04	245.9*

The test statistic tests whether the product of the vectors $\gamma_i\alpha_j = 0$ and is distributed as $\chi^2_{(1)}$ under the null hypothesis. The 95 percent critical value is 3.84 and an * indicates significance at the 95 percent level. The labeling of γ_i and α_j is as for table 13.6a.

Table 13.7 Summary of the pattern of causality

From to	Gensaki *call*	Gensaki *bill*	*Bill call*	*Bill gensaki*	*Call gensaki*	*Call bill*
1985	C	C	C	C	NC	NC
1986	C	C	C	C	NC	NC
1987	C	C	NC	NC	C	NC
1988	NC	NC	NC	NC	NC	NC
1989	C	NC	C	NC	NC	C
1990	NC	NC	NC	NC	NC	NC
1991	C	C	C	C	C	C

This summary is based on a reading of the results of tables 13.5 and 13.6. An entry of C indicates causality while an entry of NC indicates non-causality.

rates. Since the testing of the significance of lags in step (a) is similar to what is required for testing causality in levels and differenced models, these tests for 1986–90 are also labelled as tests of H_1 in table 13.5.

Table 13.7 provides a summary in terms of the patterns of causality or non-causality between the interest rates in the interbank and open markets implied by the results in tables 13.5 and 13.6. The results on the feedback relationship between the interbank rates and the open market rate indicate there is no consistent causality relationship. This is consistent with Takagi's (1988b) earlier finding, but contradicts de Brouwer (1991). Similarly, there is no consistent feedback pattern among the interbank rates (cf. Takagi 1988a, and de Brouwer 1991). The fact that the pattern of causality changes so much from year to year makes it difficult to attribute the change in the pattern of causality between 1988 and 1989 to the Bank of Japan's money market reforms implemented in November 1988 as de Brouwer (1991) hypothesized. To check the robustness of the result, equation (13.1) was estimated with *m* arbitrarily set equal to 8 and *r* arbitrarily set equal to 1, and the causality hypotheses were tested once again. While there were slight differences in the pattern of causality observed, the conclusion that there is no consistent pattern of causality between the interbank and open market rates, and among the interbank rates was not reversed.

4 BUY–SELL SPREADS IN THE *GENSAKI* MARKET

In the interbank markets, the call and bill markets, transactions pass through six money market brokers (*tanshi gaisha*). The commission

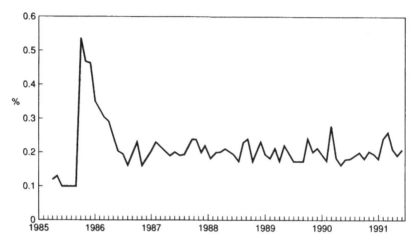

Figure 13.1   End of month bid–ask spread in the *gensaki* market for CDs, 1985–91*

*   The spreads are on transactions for less than one month.

Source: Nihon Keizai Shinbun

earned by the *tanshi* brokers, the spread between the bid and offered rates, is fixed although it has recently been reduced from 0.03125 percent to 0.015625 percent for certain transactions in the unsecured call market in April 1989 and the bill market in January 1991 (see appendix A for further details). In contrast, the bid offer spread is not fixed in open markets including the *gensaki* market (see Takagi 1988a: 80). As can be seen in figure 13.1, the bid–ask spread on CD repurchase agreements of less than one month in the *gensaki* market varies a great deal. Although not shown, bid–ask spreads on agreements relating to repurchases occurring in the next month and the month after next show similar variation. Over the period April 1985 through June 1991, the correlation coefficients calculated between spreads on transactions within the month and the next month, within the month and the month after next, and the next month and the month after next are respectively 0.96, 0.94, and 0.97. All spreads peak in November 1985. Spreads for newly issued certificates of deposit and for bank acceptances across all maturities also show a peak at the same time.[16]

The impact of financial deregulation on buy–sell spreads in the over-the-counter bond market in Tokyo has been investigated by Maru and Takahashi (1985), Bank of Japan (1986), Takagi (1987) and Mizuno (1988), using theoretical models developed by Demsetz (1968) and Stoll (1978a,b).[17] Takagi's (1987) study, for example, finds that significant reductions in buy–sell spreads occurred as a result of increased competition in the bond market due to banks being permitted to sell and deal in government bonds.

Here, an attempt is made to explain the time series behaviour of the bid–ask spread in the *gensaki* market for transactions of less than one month involving certificates of deposit using the approach outlined by Demsetz (1968) and Stoll (1978a,b). As Takagi (1988a) indicates, the Japanese applications of this approach have used the following model:

$$SPREAD = F(\underset{+}{\sigma}, \underset{-}{V}, \underset{-}{M}), \tag{13.3}$$

where *SPREAD* is the bid–ask spread, σ is a measure of the risk associated with holding the asset, V is the volume of transactions and M refers to the competitive environment in the market. The signs refer to the expected signs of the partial derivative of *SPREAD* with respect to each variable. The equations estimated in this chapter follow the earlier Japanese applications. Detailed definitions of the data used for *SPREAD*, σ and V are contained in appendix B.

In Takagi (1987), M is captured by dummy variables to take account of when banks were permitted to sell and deal in government bonds. Takagi (1987) also makes the important point that bid–ask spreads may narrow as a result of a narrowing in spreads in markets for substitute assets. This argument suggests that changes in the fixed commission in the unsecured call market in April 1989 and the bill market in January 1991 could influence the spreads in the *gensaki* market. In addition, Nakao and Horii (1991) and de Brouwer (1991) highlight the importance of the money market reforms implemented by the Bank of Japan in November 1988 as potentially strengthening the arbitrage between all sections of the money markets. As a result, dummy variables $D1$, $D2$ and $D3$ taking the values 1 from November 1988, April 1989, and January 1991 respectively, and zero elsewhere were defined.

Regression results for linear–linear and log–log approximations to (13.3) are presented in Table 13.8 using monthly data that runs from April 1985 through June 1991. The results are not particularly promising, with the risk variable being the only variable which is consistently significant. In four out of the seven equations, the transactions variable is of the right sign, but in none of the equations is it significant. This result is perhaps not too surprising when one examines the time series nature of V_t. As V_t is a strongly trending variable and the spread is not, V_t is unlikely to be a useful explanatory variable. The signs on the dummy variables are also not always consistent with our *a priori* expectations. For example, taken at face value, the results in equations (8.6) and (8.7) suggest that the reduction of commission rates in the bill market resulted

Table 13.8 Model of bid–ask spreads in the *gensaki* market (CD), April 1985–June 1991

Model	σ_t	V_t	$D1_t$	$D2_t$	$D3_t$	R^2	DW
Linear							
(8.1)	0.297	−0.308				0.29	0.908
	(2.37)*	(1.41)					
(8.2)	0.289	−0.398	−0.018	0.024	0.011	0.30	0.929
	(2.25)*	(0.83)	(0.42)	(0.63)	(0.37)		
Log–linear							
(8.3)	0.153	−0.098				0.55	0.883
	(6.73)*	(1.00)					
(8.4)	0.164	0.114				0.57	0.920
	(6.92)*	(0.66)		−0.141			
(8.5)	0.1560	−0.142		(1.49)	0.127	0.57	0.934
	(6.88)*	(1.38)			(1.33)		
(8.6)	0.176	0.158			0.208	0.60	1.056
	(7.40)*	(0.93)		−0.217	(2.09)*		
(8.7)	0.177	0.126	0.040	(2.20)*	0.210	0.60	1.064
	(7.31)*	(0.63)	(0.31)	−0.240	(2.08)*		
				(1.92)			

The linear model is of the form

$$SPREAD_t = b_0 + b_1\sigma_t + b_2V_t + b_3D1_t + b_4D2_t + b_5D3_t + \text{seasonal dummies} + e_t.$$

The log–linear model is of the form

$$\log(SPREAD_t) = b_0 + b_1\log(\sigma_t) + b_2\log(V_t) + b_3D1_t \\ + b_4D2_t + b_5D3_t + \text{seasonal dummies} + e_t.$$

Figures in brackets are the absolute value of t-statistics and * indicates a variable is significant at the 95 percent level. The transactions variable has been scaled by the factor of 10^{-6}.

in increases in the bid–ask spread! The dummies may in fact be picking up something other than the particular deregulation measure they are associated with. It is difficult on the basis of these results to say that these deregulatory measures have had a significant impact on the size of the spread in the *gensaki* market for certificates of deposit. One final point of concern is the low level of the Durbin–Watson statistics for each equation. Application of the Cochrane–Orcutt procedure did not lead to any improvement in the results in terms of the significance of the explanatory variables and so the Durbin–Watson statistics are probably indicative of model misspecification.

5 CONCLUSION

Besides discussing recent liberalization measures in the Japanese money markets, this paper has attempted to provide some empirical evidence on the patterns of causality between interbank and open money market interest rates and on the impact of this deregulation on bid–ask spreads in the *gensaki* market for certificates of deposit.

Some of the patterns of causality among the interbank interest rates and between the interbank and open market interest rates are consistent with earlier evidence and some of them are at variance with earlier evidence. Generally speaking, it is found that there is no consistent pattern of feedback relationships among the interest rates. As a result it is not possible to identify changes in the pattern of causality with particular deregulatory measures. This may be due to the step-by-step deregulatory measures, problems in the application of causality tests, or some other factor.

The model of the bid–ask spread employed is not particularly satisfactory in explaining the variation in spreads in the *gensaki* market for certificates of deposit between 1985 and 1991. The impact of three particular deregulatory measures, two associated with changing fixed bid–ask spreads in the interbank markets and one involving reform of the interbank markets on the *gensaki* market spreads, was investigated. The evidence presented does not suggest that the deregulatory measures significantly affected the size of the spread. As the number of measures detailed in appendix A indicates, structural changes in the money markets may be rather gradual in response to the step-by-step process of deregulation. This makes them rather difficult to detect empirically. It is also possible that liberalization of the money markets was for all practical purposes complete before 1985 and that recent regulatory changes have only had a marginal impact.

APPENDIX A: A CHRONOLOGY OF MAJOR LIBERALIZATION MEASURES IN THE JAPANESE MONEY MARKETS 1985–9[18]

(a) Relating to the Interbank Markets

June 1985   Introduction of 5- and 6-month instruments in the bill market.

July 1985   Unsecured call market established (overnight and 7-day maturities).

August 1985	Introduction of 2- and 3-week instruments in the secured call market.
September 1985	Introduction of 2- and 3-week instruments in the unsecured call market.
July 1987	Instruments with maturities between 2 and 6 days introduced in the unsecured call market.
November 1988	Instruments with maturities between 1 and 6 months introduced in the unsecured call market. Maturities in secured call market restricted to 6 days or less.
January 1989	The size of minimum movements for the rates in the bill, secured call and unsecured call markets reduced from 0.0625 percent to 0.03125 percent.
April 1989	Instruments with maturities between 7 and 12 months introduced in the bill and unsecured call market.
November 1990	Abolition of the quotation system for rates in the secured call market and the adoption of an offer bid system.

(b)   Relating to the Open Markets

April 1985	The minimum denomination and minimum maturity of certificates of deposit (CDs) reduced to 100 million yen and 1 month, respectively.
June 1985	Establishment of a bankers' acceptance (BA) (minimum denomination of 100 million yen and maturities between 1 and 6 months).
January 1986	Bank of Japan begins sales of financing bills (FBs) using the *gensaki* method.
February 1986	Issue of 6-month treasury bills (TBs) begins.
April 1986	Maximum maturity for CDs extended to 1 year.
December 1986	Establishment of the Japan offshore market.
April 1987	Reduction in the minimum denomination of BAs from 100 billion to 50 billion yen and extension of terms from 6 months to 1 year.
August 1987	Reduction in the minimum denomination of TBs and FBs from 100 million yen to 50 million yen.
October 1987	Introduction of a stamp duty of a fixed amount for BAs (previously a sliding scale).
November 1987	Establishment of a commercial paper (CP) market.
April 1988	Reduction in the minimum denomination of CDs to 50 million yen and permitted maturities expanded from 2 weeks to 2 years.

September 1989   Issue of 3-month TBs begins.
April 1990   Reduction in the minimum denomination of TBs and FBs from 50 million yen to 10 million yen.

(c)   Relating to Intermarket Arbitrage

March 1985   Banks permitted to issue CBs overseas.
May 1985   Securities companies authorized to lend in the inter-bank markets.
June 1985   Securities companies authorized to deal in secondary bank CDs.
November 1985   Expansion of securities companies borrowing limits in the call market.
March 1986   Bank of Japan begins open market operations using CDs involving lending directed to money market brokers.
April 1986   Securities companies authorized to deal in secondary BAs. Extension of the maturity of Euroyen CDs from 1 month to 1 year.
April 1987   Approval for banks to issue CBs domestically.
May 1987   Expansion in the instruments permitted for transactions in the yen-denominated BA market.
November 1987   Lifting of the prohibition on non-residents issuing Euroyen CPs.
December 1987   Bank of Japan begins open market operations using *gensaki* (in securities).
January 1988   Lifting of the prohibition on non-residents issuing domestic CP.
November 1988   Bank of Japan begins buying operations of bills of maturities less than 1 month.
December 1988   Revision of conditions for issuers of CP.
April 1989   Reduction in the broker's commission for both borrowers and lenders from 1/32 percent to 1/64 percent for large-denomination transactions in the unsecured call market.
May 1989   Bank of Japan begins open market operations using CP.
August 1989   Bank of Japan begins releasing forecasts and actual outcomes of fund supply and demand.
December 1989   Bank of Japan begins publishing information its lending and open market operations.
January 1990   Bank of Japan begins open market operations using TBs.
April 1990   Lifting of the prohibition on securities companies

	issuing domestic CP. Introduction of a stamp duty of a fixed amount for CP (previously a sliding scale).
July 1990	Money market brokers (*tanshi*) begin dealing in TBs. Tenders of TBs begin twice a month.
August 1990	Bank of Japan begins releasing information on reserves.
October 1990	A tendering system using a standard yield and differences in yields introduced for tenders of government bonds in open market operations.[19]
January 1991	Bank of Japan begins buying operations in bills using a tender method. Reduction in the broker's commission for both borrowers and lenders from 1/32 percent to 1/64 percent for large-denomination transactions in the bill market (transactions for one month or more and for 5 billion yen or more).

Source: Bank of Japan (1988: 54–5; 1990: 58–60; 1991a: 35–6).

APPENDIX B: DATA SOURCES

Section 3: daily interest rates in the overnight call, the bill and the bond *gensaki* market were obtained from *Kin'yu Zaisei Jijo*. Since the *gensaki* market was not open on Saturday mornings, only weekday rates were used. Until the end of November 1988, interest rates on two month bills were published in *Kin'yu Zaisei Jijo*, so that two month interest rates on bill and *gensaki* instruments were used. From December 1988, only interest rates on three-month bills were published in *Kin'yu Zaisei Jijo*, so that three-month interest rates on bill and *gensaki* instruments were used. The data set available runs from the beginning of 1985 to the end of July 1991. Because of the change in the data reported in *Kin'yu Zaisei Jijo* in 1988, the data used in the causality tests in 1988 run from January to November 1988. As a result, the number of observations available was 245 in 1985, 1986 and 1987, 225 in 1988, 250 in 1989, 247 in 1990 and 143 in 1991.

Section 4: the sample period runs from April 1985 through June 1991. The buy–sell spreads for *gensaki* transactions involving certificates of deposit are end of the month figures calculated from the buy and sell quotations for one month instruments published in the *Nihon Keizai Shinbun* since April 1985. The risk measure is calculated as the variance of the daily three-month bond *gensaki* rate over each calendar month where the daily data is obtained from *Kin'yu Zaisei Jijo*. The transactions variable, the amount of certificates of deposit outstanding at the end of each month, are taken from the Bank of Japan's *Economic Statistics Annual* and *Economic Statistics Monthly*.

NOTES

1 For earlier discussions of the structure of the Japanese money markets and recent liberalization measures, see Akiyama (1987), Bank of Japan (1988, 1990, 1991a), Bronte (1982), de Brouwer (1991), Dickson et al. (1990a,b), Feldman (1986), Fukui (1986), Kuroda (1988), McKenzie (1992), Murohara (1987), Nakao and Horii (1991), Nihon Keizai Shinbunsha (1988), Osugi (1990), Sato (1988), Sawayama (1990), Shimamura (1989), Shimasaki and Kuroyanagi (1988), Suzuki (1987), Takagi (1988a,b), Takasaki (1988), Tatsumi (1982), and Wakao (1987).

2 See, for example, Suzuki (1987: 108), Kuroda (1988: 5) and Nihon Keizai Shinbunsha (1988: 13).

3 Takahashi (1993) and Yamamoto (1993) in this volume for discussions of the government bond and bond markets, respectively.

4 More correctly, financing bills are called short-term government financing bills *(seifu tanki shoken)*.

5 More correctly, treasury bills are called short-term government bonds *(tanki kokusai)*.

6 The dollar call market is discussed in Tateno (1993) in this volume.

7 Figures on lending and borrowing shares in the call, bill, *gensaki* and certificates of deposit markets are calculated from data obtained from various issues of the Bank of Japan's *Economics Statistics Annual* and *Economics Statistics Monthly*.

8 See, for example, the information on open market operations in Bank of Japan (1991b: 92), Nakao and Horii (1991: Table 6) and Industrial Bank of Japan (1991: 281–2).

9 For more details see Dickson et al. (1990a). A Ministry of Finance directive issued in March 1976 contains fuller details on standards for *gensaki* transactions. The directive is presented in full in Industrial Bank of Japan (1991: 90–1).

10 For more details see Dickson et al. (1990b).

11 Wakao (1987: 12) and Nihon Keizai Shinbunsha (1988: 219) contain details on the outstanding balances in the yen-denominated BA market in 1985 and 1986.

12 Although the use of the *gensaki* rate as a representative open money market rate follows Takagi (1988b) and de Brouwer (1991), one potential problem with using the bond *gensaki* rate is the thinness of the market in more recent years.

13 See Dickey and Fuller (1979, 1981) for further details.

14 A variable, y_t, is said to be integrated of order one, I(1), if Δy_t is stationary (or I(0)). There exists a cointegrating relationship between two I(1) variables, x_t and y_t, if there exists an α such that the variable $x_t - \alpha y_t$ is I(0).

There is no cointegrating relationship if such an α does not exist: see Engle and Granger (1987). This definition can be easily extended to cases involving more than two variables.

15 Takagi (1988a,b) in his earlier causality tests implictly assumed that there are no cointegrating relationships so that $\gamma_1 = \gamma_2 = \gamma_3 = 0$. The results in table 13.4 for 1988, 1989, and 1990 indicate there are times when this assumption would be valid. However, in 1985, one of the years examined in both Takagi's papers, this restriction is clearly rejected.

16 Takagi (1988a: 80) argues that if the participation of non-financial institutions in the interbank markets was permitted, such a situation would not have arisen.

17 See Grossman and Miller (1988) and Cohen et al. (1979) for surveys of this literature.

18 This classification of liberalization measures follows Takagi (1988a). Takagi (1988a: 88–90) contains an earlier chronology for the money and bond markets, and McKenzie (1992) contains a more comprehensive chronology for the Japanese financial markets more generally.

19 The standard yield is, in principle, determined by returns on the Tokyo Stock Exchange at the close of trading on the previous day. The difference in yields refers to the difference between the closing yield on the bond to be sold and the standard yield.

REFERENCES

Akiyama, Akira 1987: Deregulation of financial instruments: part 1, *FAIR Fact Series: Japan's financial markets*, vol. 10. Tokyo: Foundation for Advanced Information and Research.

Anderson, Heather M., Granger, Clive W.J. and Hall, Anthony D. 1990: Treasury bill yield curves and cointegration. Working Paper in Economics and Econometrics no. 215. Canberra: Australian National University.

Bank of Japan 1986: Structural changes in the secondary market for bonds and the recent trends in yields on long-term bonds. Special Paper no. 132, Research and Statistics Department, Bank of Japan.

Bank of Japan 1988: Showa 62 nendo no kin'yu oyobi keizai doko: kozo chosei no shinten to jizokuteki seicho he no tenbo (Financial and economic trends in fiscal year 1987: the progress of structural adjustment and the prospects for lasting growth). *Chosa Geppo*, May, Research and Statistics Department, Bank of Japan, 1–55.

Bank of Japan 1990: Heisei gannen no kin'yu oyobi keizai doko: ogata keiki no genjitsu to taigai shushi chosei no shinten (Financial and economic trends in 1989: the reality of the large-scale boom and the progress of external balance adjustment). *Chosa Geppo*, May, Research and Statistics Department, Bank of Japan, 1–60.

Bank of Japan 1991a: Heisei 2 nendo no kin'yu oyobi keizai no doko: kinri no josho to sono koka hakyu (Financial and economic trends in 1990: interest rate rises and their transmission). *Nihon Ginko Geppo* (Bank of Japan Monthly Bulletin), June, Information Service Department, Bank of Japan, 1–36.

Bank of Japan 1991b: Kokunai Kin'yū Keizai Gaikan (An outline of the domestic financial economy). *Nihon Ginko Geppo* (Bank of Japan Monthly Bulletin), June, Information Service Department, Bank of Japan, 73–94.

Bronte, Stephen 1982: *Japanese Finance: markets and institutions.* London Euromoney.

Cohen, Kalman J., Maier, Steven F., Schwartz, Robert A. and Whitcomb, David K. 1979: Market makers and the market spread: a review of recent literature. *Journal of Financial and Quantitative Analysis*, 14, 813–35.

de Brouwer, G. 1991: An analysis of recent developments in the Japanese money market. University of Melbourne mimeo.

Demsetz, Harold 1968: The cost of transacting. *Quarterly Journal of Economics*, 82, 33–53.

Dickey, David A. and Fuller, Wayne A. 1979: Distribution of the estimators for autoregressive series with a unit root. *Journal of the American Statistical Association*, 74, 427–31.

Dickey, David A. and Fuller, Wayne A. 1981: Likelihood ratio statistics for autoregressive time series with a unit root. *Econometrica*, 49, 1057–72.

Dickson, Jeffrey L., Fuchida, Hiroaki and Nishizawa, Yutaka 1990a: The *gensaki* market. In Frank J. Fabozzi (ed.), *The Japanese Bond Markets: an overview and analysis*, Chicago: Probus Publishing, ch. 6.

Dickson, Jeffrey L., Fuchida, Hiroaki and Nishizawa, Yutaka 1990b: Commercial paper market. In Frank J. Fabozzi (ed.), *The Japanese Bond Markets: an overview and analysis*, Chicago: Probus Publishing, ch. 10.

Engle, Robert F. and Granger, Clive W.J. 1987: Co-integration and error correction: representation, estimation, and testing. *Econometrica*, 55, 251–76.

Feldman, Robert A. 1986: *Japanese Financial Markets: deficits, dilemmas, and deregulation.* Cambridge, Mass.: MIT Press.

Fukui, Toshihiko 1986: Recent developments of the short-term money market in Japan and changes in monetary control techniques and procedures by the Bank of Japan. Special Paper no. 130, Research and Statistics Department, Bank of Japan.

Grossman, Sanford J. and Miller, Merton H. 1988: Liquidity and market structure. *Journal of Finance*, 43, 617–37.

Industrial Bank of Japan (Securities Department) 1991: *Shoken Benran 1991–92* (Securities Compendium 1991–92). Tokyo: Industrial Bank of Japan.

Johansen, Soren 1988: Statistical analysis of cointegration vectors. *Journal of Economic Dynamics and Control*, 12, 231–54.

Johansen, Soren and Juselius, Katarina 1990: Maximum likelihood estimation and inference on cointegration – with applications to the demand for money. *Oxford Bulletin of Economics and Statistics*, 52, 169–210.

Kuroda, Akio 1988: *Nihon no kin'yu shijo: Kinyu seisaku no koka hakyu mekanizumu* (Japan's Financial Markets: the transmission mechanism of monetary policy). Tokyo: Toyo Keizai Shinposha.

Maru, Junko and Takahashi, Toshiharu 1985: Recent developments of interdealer brokerage in the Japanese secondary bond markets. *Journal of Financial and Quantitative Analysis*, 20, 193–210.

McKenzie, Colin R. 1992: Recent developments in Japan's financial markets. In Colin R. McKenzie and Michael Stutchbury (eds), *Japanese Financial Markets and the Role of the Yen*, Sydney: Allen & Unwin, ch. 2.

Ministry of Finance 1991: *Okurasho shokenkyoku nenpo heisei 2 nen* (Annual Report of the Securities Bureau, Ministry of Finance, Fiscal Year 1990). Tokyo: Ministry of Finance.

Mizuno, Keizo 1988: Fukakujitsuseika ni okeru saiken diiraa no saiteki kodo (The optimal behaviour of a securities dealer under uncertainty). *Fainansu Kenkyu*, no. 8, May, 55–67.

Murohara, Taeko 1987: Short-term money markets, part 2. *FAIR Fact Series: Japan's financial markets*, vol. 7. Tokyo: Foundation for Advanced Information and Research.

Nakao, Masaaki and Horii, Akinari 1991: The process of decision-making and implementation of monetary policy in Japan. Special Paper no. 198, Research and Statistics Department, Bank of Japan.

Nihon Keizai Shinbunsha 1988: *Tanki kin'yu shijo* (Short-term money markets). Tokyo: Nihon Keizai Shinbunsha.

Osugi, K. 1990: Japan's experience of financial deregulation since 1984 in an international perspective. BIS Economic Paper no. 26. Basle: Bank for International Settlements.

Sato, Hirokazu 1988: Deregulation of interest rates, *FAIR Fact Series: Japan's financial markets*, vol. 12. Tokyo: Foundation for Advanced Information and Research.

Sawayama, Hiroshi 1990: *Tanki kin'yu shijo: nichibeio no hikaku to waga kuni no kadai* (Short-term money markets: a comparison of Japan–America–Europe and Japan's problems). Tokyo: Toyo Keizai Shinposha.

Shimamura, Takayoshi 1989: Japan's financial system: creation and changes. *Japanese Economic Studies*, 17, 43–88.

Shimasaki, Mitsuru and Kuroyanagi, Hisaya 1988: Short-term money markets, part 1, *FAIR Fact Series: Japan's financial markets*, vol. 6. Tokyo: Foundation for Advanced Information and Research.

Stoll, Hans R. 1978a: The supply of dealer services in securities markets. *Journal of Finance*, 33, 1133–51.

Stoll, Hans R. 1978b: The pricing of security dealer services: an empirical study of NASDAQ stocks, *Journal of Finance*, 33, 1153–72.

Suzuki, Yoshio (ed.) 1987: *The Japanese Financial System*. Oxford: Clarendon Press.

Takagi, Shinji 1987: Transactions costs and the term structure of interest rates in the OTC bond market in Japan. *Journal of Money, Credit, and Banking*, 19, 515–27.

Takagi, Shinji 1988a: Recent developments in Japan's bond and money markets. *Journal of the Japanese and International Economies*, 2, 63–91.

Takagi, Shinji 1988b: Financial liberalization and the "bills-only" doctrine: a causality test of daily Japanese data, 1978–85. *Economic Studies Quarterly*, 39, 149–59.

Takahashi, Toshiharu 1993: The government bond market. Chapter 7 in this volume.

Takasaki, Masao 1988: Deregulation of financial instruments: part 2, *FAIR Fact Series: Japan's financial markets*, vol. 11. Tokyo: Foundation for Advanced Information and Research.

Tateno, Fumihiko 1993: The Tokyo foreign exchange market. Chapter 14 in this volume.

Tatsumi, Kenichi 1982: *Nihon no kin'yu-shihon shijo: kino to infure no jissho bunseki* (Japan's Money and Capital Markets: an empirical analysis of their functions and inflation). Tokyo: Toyo Keizai Shinposha.

Toda, Hiro Y. and Phillips, Peter C.B. 1991: Vector autoregression and causality: a theoretical overview and simulation study. Working Paper no. 91–07, University of Western Australia; to appear in *Econometric Reviews*.

Wakao, Akihiro 1987: Creation of the yen-denominated bankers' acceptance market, *FAIR Fact Series: Japan's financial markets*, vol. 25. Tokyo: Foundation for Advanced Information and Research.

Yamamoto, Shigeru 1993: The bond market in Japan. Chapter 6 in this volume.

14

The Foreign Exchange Market in Japan

Fumihiko Tateno

1 INTRODUCTION

This chapter presents a review of the Japanese foreign exchange market. Today, participants in foreign exchange markets are mainly connected to each other through networks of telephones and computer terminals. Unlike transactions in stocks, it is rare for an organized exchange to exist in foreign exchange transactions. It is for this reason that these transactions are increasingly concentrated in a few international financial centers, such as London, New York, and Tokyo. In Japan, almost all foreign exchange transactions are concentrated in Tokyo, with only a small market existing in Osaka and Nagoya. For all practical purposes, the Japanese foreign exchange market refers to the Tokyo foreign exchange market.

This chapter is organized as follows. Section 2 reviews the evolution of the Tokyo foreign exchange market, which has significantly changed with the development of the Japanese economy. Section 3 discusses the organization of the Tokyo foreign exchange market. In particular, the first part emphasizes the participants and market practices, while the second part highlights the characteristics of the Tokyo market in comparison to the London and New York markets.

Section 4 discusses other markets associated with the Tokyo foreign exchange market, namely, the Tokyo dollar call market, the Japan offshore market, the currency and interest rate swap markets, the market for currency options, and the Tokyo International Financial Futures Exchange. Finally, as concluding remarks, section 5 discusses the remaining issues and the future outlook for the Tokyo foreign exchange market.

Shinji Takagi and Colin McKenzie provided comments on an earlier draft.

2 THE EVOLUTION OF THE TOKYO FOREIGN EXCHANGE MARKET[1]

2.1 Early Years (1945–52)

With the end of the Second World War, Japan was placed under the administrative rule of the General Headquarters of the Allied Powers (GHQ), which in principle prohibited all its international economic transactions. As a result, foreign exchange transactions were altogether suspended in September 1945. Although a limited amount of state trade did subsequently commence through the International Trade Agency, an official exchange rate for the yen was not established for a long time.

In 1949, Joseph Dodge arrived in Japan as economic adviser to the GHQ. Dodge implemented a package of contractionary fiscal and monetary policies to arrest inflation and, on April 23, unified the exchange rate for the first time since the end of the war at the official rate of 360 yen to the dollar.

During the course of 1949, progress was made in setting up a legal system of foreign exchange control orders. In December, the GHQ transferred to the Foreign Exchange Control Committee of the Japanese government the authority to manage foreign currencies and to control foreign exchange transactions. In the same month, the Foreign Exchange and Trade Control Law came into effect for the purpose of unifying the complex body of foreign exchange control orders. This law was to remain the basic law governing the conduct of international economic transactions during the postwar period until its major revision in December 1980.

Japan's official foreign exchange reserves at that time amounted to only $200 million. Because of the scarcity of foreign exchange, the government exercised strict control of transactions related to foreign exchange and foreign trade. It was required that all foreign exchange transactions be effected through the government at the official exchange rate of 360 yen to the dollar. As a result, there was little need for a foreign exchange market.

In 1952 a foreign exchange market finally opened in Tokyo for the first time since the end of the Second World War. Foreign exchange transactions had already begun to increase in volume, as the private sector completely replaced the public sector in the conduct of international trade in 1950. On June 16, 1952, the surrender requirement for US dollars was relaxed, and foreign exchange banks were allowed to maintain a limited amount of dollars in their portfolios.

Until this time, foreign exchange banks had only been the agents of the government to collect foreign exchange from the public. With the authorization for foreign exchange banks to hold foreign exchange on their accounts, however, they began to resume their normal function as sellers and buyers of foreign exchange, contributing to the opening of the foreign exchange market in Tokyo on July 10. The market was initially organized as a place where the positions of foreign exchange banks were adjusted for US dollars only. In March 1953 the market was expanded to include transactions involving the pound sterling.

At this time, the exchange rates applicable to centralized transactions between the government and foreign exchange banks were fixed, with the selling rate of 360.03 yen to the dollar and the buying rate of 359.65 yen. The volume of trading was extremely low: $21 million was recorded for the latter half of 1952 (table 14.1).

As part of these measures, the Foreign Exchange Control Committee, which had been responsible for exchange rate policy since 1949, was abolished and its responsibilities transferred to the Ministry of Finance. On May 28, 1952, Japan's application for membership at the International Monetary Fund (IMF) was approved. Japan notified the Fund that the yen's par value would be defined in terms of 2.4685 milligrams of fine gold (or 360 yen to a dollar), and assumed the obligation to maintain the market value of the yen within one percent on either side of parity.

2.2   Formative Years (Period of Fixed Exchange Rates: 1952–67)

Although the Tokyo foreign exchange market thus reopened for trading in 1952, the range of exchange rate fluctuations remained narrow, and trading volume was extremely low for several years.

In 1959 a change was made in the official yen/dollar exchange rate applicable to centralized government transactions, whereby the rate was to be maintained within 0.5 percent on either side of the IMF parity. At the same time, the range of exchange rate fluctuations in the interbank market was widened to 3.60 yen, and the pricing of customer rates was left to the discretion of individual banks. The annual volume of foreign exchange trading in the spot market was only around $200 million (table 14.1).

In July 1960 non-residents were allowed to open yen-denominated bank accounts in Japan, and the yen was added to the list of designated currencies which could legally be used in foreign exchange transactions. With the introduction of a "yen exchange," the first step was thus taken towards establishing the convertibility of the yen.

At around the same time, Japan was entering its period of high economic growth. In June 1960, the government adopted a Foreign Trade and Foreign Exchange Liberalization Plan and began to liberalize foreign

Table 14.1 Trading volume in the Tokyo foreign exchange market, 1952–90 (in millions of US dollars)

Year	Spot	Forward[a]	Swap	Total	Annual change (%)
1952	21	–	–	21	–
1953	115	–	2	117	457.1
1954	89	–	–	89	−23.9
1955	114	11	–	125	40.4
1956	211	31	–	242	93.6
1957	234	16	–	250	3.3
1958	240	43	6	289	15.6
1959	201	116	9	326	12.8
1960	298	264	39	601	84.4
1961	441	316	83	840	39.8
1962	819	634	256	1,709	103.5
1963	1,251	959	467	2,677	56.6
1964	1,869	1,421	471	3,761	40.5
1965	2,060	1,686	770	4,516	20.1
1966	1,870	1,763	644	4,277	−5.3
1967	2,081	1,734	588	4,403	2.9
1968	2,992	2,554	671	6,217	41.2
1969	4,133	2,857	1,168	8,158	31.2
1970	4,757	4,174	2,568	11,499	41.0
1971	19,327	5,253	3,297	27,877	142.4
1972	13,027	11,241	4,872	29,140	4.5
1973	20,194	18,175	8,558	46,927	61.0
1974	18,891	24,305	16,115	59,311	26.4
1975	22,919	25,960	24,551	73,430	23.8
1976	34,972	28,616	34,924	98,512	34.2
1977	62,305	24,611	60,362	147,278	49.5
1978	117,890	34,767	128,886	281,543	91.2
1979	172,210	51,752	221,042	445,004	58.1
1980	211,844	66,782	300,593	579,219	30.9
1981	296,432	77,696	527,948	902,076	55.7
1982	365,260	63,283	785,034	1,213,577	34.5
1983	339,707	90,105	724,423	1,154,235	−4.9
1984	381,528	81,655	898,033	1,361,216	11.8
1985	462,681	4,419	968,478	1,435,578	5.5
1986	889,540	–	1,667,156	2,556,696	78.1
1987	1,354,082	–	2,421,723	3,775,805	47.7
1988	1,358,925	–	2,920,677	4,279,602	13.3
1989	1,851,382	–	3,614,309	5,465,691	27.7
1990	2,495,663	–	3,466,871	5,962,534	9.1

[a] From February 1985 forward transactions are included in swap transactions.

Source: Tokyo Foreign Exchange Market Practice Committee

trade and foreign capital transactions. In April 1964, Japan accepted the obligations of Article 8 of the IMF's Articles of Agreement, whereby it abolished the exchange restrictions on current transactions that it had maintained under the transitional arrangement approved by Article 14.

With its admittance as a member of the OECD, Japan began a series of steps to liberalize capital flows. As Japan became more open in its external orientation, the foreign exchange market in Japan also began to make a radical transition from a system characterized by extensive regulations. In April 1963 the government introduced an element of flexibility into official foreign exchange transactions by allowing the exchange rate to be freely determined in the market within 0.75 percent either side of the IMF parity of 360 yen to the dollar.

In order to maintain the predetermined margin, moreover, the system of official market intervention was established. The width of the fluctuation margin (a total of 1.50 percent), comparable to that of most major industrial countries in Europe, was introduced to strengthen the exchange-rate-based adjustment mechanism in order to correct imbalances in the balance of payments.

As a result, official transactions with the government no longer constituted the central element of foreign exchange transactions by banks, which had to reduce the risk of exchange rate fluctuations through their own foreign exchange transactions. As banks began to trade more actively on their own accounts, the trading volume of the foreign exchange market expanded rapidly. The annual volume of spot trading, for example, increased sharply from the range of $819 million (in 1962) or $1.25 billion (in 1963) to $4.76 billion in 1970 (table 14.1).

2.3   Expanding Years (Period of Transition: 1968–73)[2]

From the latter part of the 1960s, Japan began to experience chronic surpluses in the balance of payments and, by 1970, had accumulated official foreign exchange reserves of $4.4 billion. With increasing foreign criticism of Japan's trade surpluses, the possibility of yen revaluation began seriously to be discussed.

At this time, the United States was experiencing chronic deficits in its balance of payments; capital outflows from the United States as well as the excess supply of dollar assets abroad resulted in a depreciating pressure on the dollar. In 1971 the US balance of payments further deteriorated, and the deutsche mark (DM) came under speculative attack as the so-called Gnomes of Zurich began speculative purchases of marks. In May, the German authorities closed down the foreign exchange market and allowed the DM to float against other currencies. Likewise, the market exchange rate of the yen remained close to the upper limit of 357.30 yen to a dollar. As the Japanese authorities intervened to support the dollar, the balance of official foreign exchange reserves sharply increased to $7.9 billion by the end of July 1971.

Under these circumstances, US President Richard Nixon announced an economic policy package of eight measures to defend the dollar, including the suspension of the gold convertibility of the dollar and the imposition of a 10 percent import surcharge. Immediately, all European countries allowed their currencies to float; on August 28, Japan also allowed the yen to float. Thus, the Bretton Woods system of fixed exchange rates virtually collapsed after almost 30 years of existence.

After several months of discussion on possible exchange rate realignments, major industrial countries agreed, on December 18, to devalue the dollar against gold by 7.89 percent, and to make adjustments in the central rates of the other currencies against the dollar (the Smithsonian Agreement). Accordingly, the margin of exchange rate fluctuations was widened to 2.25 percent on either side of the central rate against the dollar. Although the Smithsonian System represented a return to a fixed exchange rate system, it differed from the old Bretton Woods System in that the gold convertibility of the dollar was no longer guaranteed. The yen was revalued against the dollar by 16.88 percent, namely from 360 to 308 yen per dollar.

Even under the Smithsonian System, however, disequilibria in the international balance of payments among major industrial countries remained. In 1973 international currency crises were frequent. On February 12, the United States announced a 10 percent devaluation of the dollar and, on February 14, Japan allowed the yen to float. By the end of the month, the Japanese yen, the pound sterling, and the Italian lira had moved to independent floating, while the other EC currencies had moved to a joint float. Thus, the period of generalized floating began.

During this period, the volume of spot trading in the Tokyo foreign exchange market rapidly increased: in 1973 the annual trading volume reached $20 billion (table 14.1). In April 1972 the Tokyo dollar call market was established in order to meet the need for a market in foreign currency funds and to promote the internationalization of the Tokyo money market. In May 1972, moreover, the system of central holding of foreign currencies was abolished for the first time since the end of the war, and both residents and non-residents were allowed to open foreign currency deposits at any authorized foreign exchange bank in Japan. Thus, there was progress towards making the Tokyo foreign exchange market more comparable to the other major markets in the United States and Europe.

2.4   Mature Years (Period of Flexible Exchange Rates: 1973 to the Present)[3]

For a few months after the yen began to float, the yen/dollar exchange rate remained fairly stable at around 265 yen to a dollar. With the first oil shock (which was precipitated by the Middle East crisis of October 1973) and the resulting imported inflation, however, the yen was depreciated back to the earlier range of 290–305 yen to the dollar and remained within that range until 1976 (figure 14.1).

The Japanese economy gradually began to recover from the oil shock, and Japan's current account was in surplus again. On the other hand, the US current account deteriorated and the deficit began to widen, causing confidence in the dollar to wane. The depreciation of the dollar was given further impetus by the diversification of "petrodollars" away from dollar-denominated assets once the crisis was over. The yen reached 240 yen to the dollar by the end of 1977, and continued its climb against the dollar until it fell below 200 yen in July 1978. It reached its highest point at 176.05 yen by the end of October.

The upward movement of the yen was halted when, on November 1, 1978, US President Jimmy Carter announced a package of measures to defend the dollar, and the major countries soon began coordinated foreign exchange market intervention. The United States drew on its reserve tranche at the IMF, sold special drawing rights (SDRs), issued

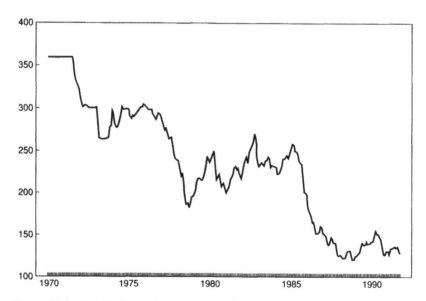

Figure 14.1   Yen/dollar exchange rates, 1970–91 (monthly averages)

"Carter bonds", expanded its swap arrangements with foreign central banks, began to intervene in the foreign exchange market on a large scale, and reduced the discount rate. Japan also joined the other industrial countries in coordinated foreign exchange market intervention. Reversing its earlier appreciating trend, the yen fell dramatically to 197.8 yen to the dollar by the end of November.

At this moment, the second oil shock was precipitated by the worsening political situation in Iran. The sharp increase in oil prices caused Japan's current account to deteriorate, and the economic performance of the Japanese economy weakened. As is often the case when oil prices increase, confidence in the yen waned and, in 1979, it began to depreciate and fell to about 250 yen to the dollar in November.

In March 1980 the Japanese and US authorities announced an increased economic policy coordination, including coordinated intervention, to arrest the sharp depreciation of the yen. In addition, the Japanese authorities announced a package of four measures to encourage capital inflows and, in terms of monetary policy, raised both the discount rate and the reserve requirement ratios. As a result, confidence in the yen gradually recovered, and it had appreciated to below 200 yen to the dollar by the end of 1980.

The appreciation of the yen, however, did not last long. From early 1981 the yen continued to depreciate, and remained at about 240 yen for some time (figure 14.1). During this period, its value remained at a depreciated level despite Japan's low inflation rate and its surplus in the current account balance. It is possible that the political instability in Europe and the Middle East as well as the debt crisis in Latin America and East Europe served to strengthen confidence in the dollar. Furthermore, the high level of US interest rates relative to those in Japan and Europe resulted in capital inflows into the United States.

US President Ronald Reagan, who had pursued a policy of rebuilding a "strong America" since taking office, now began to see a limit to the continuation of economic growth based on a strong dollar and high interest rates. Thus, the United States changed its previous policy of non-intervention in the foreign exchange market. In a meeting with the finance ministers and central bank governors of the other G-5 countries, held at Plaza Hotel on September 22, 1985, the US monetary authorities agreed to correct the imbalances in the international balance of payments by engineering a reduction in the value of the dollar. For this purpose, the G-5 countries decided to coordinate their foreign exchange market intervention as well as their macroeconomic policies.

With the determined and coordinated intervention of G-5 central banks, the dollar fell from the pre-Plaza level of 240 yen to about 150 yen within a year (figure 14.1). Although the Plaza Agreement was successful in establishing the framework of macroeconomic policy coordination among the major countries, however, it neither succeeded in the elimination of the imbalances in the international balance of payments among the major countries nor did it contribute to a noticeable improvement in the international competitiveness of the United States.

The movement of the dollar subsequent to the Plaza Agreement and the importance of policy coordination were endorsed by the joint statement of the United States and Japan in October 1986 and the meetings of the G-5 and G-7 countries in March 1987. Thus, a consensus view had now been established that the determination of exchange rates should not be left completely to market forces but should be maintained at a level consistent or compatible with the policy goal of each country. As countries have pursued policies that are directed more at maintaining certain levels of exchange rates in an environment of closer international policy coordination, the exchange rates of major currencies have been relatively stable in recent years (figure 14.1).

2.5   Legal and Institutional Developments[4]

During the period of flexible exchange rates, there were several significant legal and institutional developments. Most importantly, in December 1980 the Foreign Exchange and Foreign Trade Control Law, which strictly regulated foreign exchange transactions during the postwar period, was substantially revised for the first time in 30 years. As a result, exchange controls and foreign capital inflows were in principle liberalized.

With increasing demand from foreign countries for a further liberalization of Japan's money and capital markets, the Japan–US Yen–Dollar Committee was established in 1983 to discuss the types and the timetable of liberalization measures to be taken. The Japanese authorities thus further deregulated Euroyen transactions, lifted the restrictions on the amount of foreign exchange that could be converted into yen, and abolished the real demand rule, which had required that forward exchange contracts be associated with underlying commercial transactions.

The authorities also liberalized foreign currency transactions within Japan. As residents were allowed to borrow in foreign currencies and to open foreign currency deposits, the balance of foreign currency liabilities increased to $52.8 billion (a six-fold increase in five years) and the balance of foreign currency deposits to $21.2 billion (a three-fold increase in five years) by the end of December 1985.

Changes were also made in the area of securities transactions.[5] In the past, the Foreign Exchange Law had stipulated that advance authorization must be obtained for the acquisition of foreign currency securities by residents. Now, acquisition of foreign currency securities was almost completely liberalized; not even notification was required any longer. As a consequence, institutional investors such as life insurance companies began to diversify their investment portfolios through active purchases of foreign currency securities, especially when the foreign interest rates were higher. The balance of foreign currency securities held by domestic residents reached $59.8 billion by the end of 1985.

In 1985, moreover, market practices in the Tokyo foreign exchange market were changed to allow direct interbank trading and international broking, whereby domestic foreign exchange brokers could mediate trades with foreign markets. The Tokyo market was thus rapidly internationalized, with the result that trading volume has expanded in recent years. The annual volume of spot, forward, and swap trading, which was merely $1 billion in 1962 shortly after the market opened, accelerated to over $10 billion in 1970 and almost $100 billion in 1977. After reaching $1 trillion in 1982, the volume was almost $6 trillion in 1990 (table 14.1)

The Tokyo market has also changed qualitatively with the diversification of the currencies that are traded, and the expansion of options trading. It has matured to the point where it now ranks with the foreign exchange markets of London and New York in every sense of the word.

3   ORGANIZATION OF THE TOKYO FOREIGN EXCHANGE MARKET

3.1   Market Participants

Direct participants in the Tokyo foreign exchange market are authorized foreign exchange banks, foreign exchange brokers, and the monetary authorities. Securities companies, institutional investors such as life and accident insurance companies, trading houses, and manufacturing companies are not allowed to participate in the market directly, but must enter the market indirectly through authorized foreign exchange banks.

Because of the abolition of the real demand rule as well as the rapid growth of external capital transactions, trading volume in the customer market has continued to expand, exerting a significant influence on the determination of exchange rates in the foreign exchange market as a whole. Moreover, as the Tokyo market is closely integrated with the other markets in the same time zone (that is, Sydney, Hong Kong, and Singapore), one cannot ignore the actions of overseas banks and the monetary authorities of foreign countries operating in those markets.

3.1.1   **Authorized foreign exchange banks**

Two types of banks are authorized to conduct foreign exchange business in Japan: specialized foreign exchange banks (currently, the Bank of Tokyo only) licensed by the Minister of Finance under the authority of the Specialized Foreign Exchange Bank Act of April 1954; and financial institutions authorized by the Minister of Finance under the authority of the Foreign Exchange and Foreign Trade Control Law of January 1950. Both types are collectively called "authorized foreign exchange banks." At April 1990, there were 310 such banks, consisting of one specialized foreign exchange bank, 11 city banks, three long-term credit banks, seven trust banks, 64 regional banks, 61 member banks of the Second Association of Regional Banks, 68 *shinkin* banks, three special banks, and 92 foreign banks. Of the 92 foreign banks, 30 were American, seven French, six British, six German, and five Canadian; there were 20 Asian banks, including Korean banks. The number of authorized foreign exchange banks increased to 324 by April 1991 (table 14.2).)

Table 14.2   Authorized foreign exchange banks in Japan, 1949–91

Year	Japanese banks	Foreign banks	Total
1949	9	7	16
1950	20	8	28
1951	26	8	34
1952	29	8	37
1953	30	9	39
1954	32	9	41
1955	32	10	42
1956	32	10	42
1957	32	10	42
1958	32	10	42
1959	32	10	42
1960	44	10	54
1961	57	10	67
1962	59	10	69
1963	60	11	71
1964	64	12	76
1965	65	12	77
1966	66	12	78
1967	66	13	79
1968	69	15	84
1969	69	16	85

Table 14.2 *Continued*

Year	Japanese banks	Foreign banks	Total
1970	70	16	86
1971	70	19	89
1972	74	31	105
1973	77	38	115
1974	95	47	142
1975	101	48	149
1976	109	51	160
1977	113	58	171
1978	116	60	176
1979	119	63	182
1980	122	64	186
1981	125	69	194
1982	139	73	212
1983	144	75	219
1985/1	154	76	230
1985/12	167	78	245
1986/7	168	76	244
1987/9	184	88	272
1988/1	184	90	274
1989/2	197	92	289
1990/4	218	92	310
1991/4	227	97	324

Source: Tokyo Foreign Exchange Market Practice Committee

Many banks have entered the foreign exchange business in order to meet the needs of clients who have expanded their activities in foreign countries. With the revision of the Foreign Exchange Law and the abolition of the real demand rule, moreover, it has become easier for non-financial corporations to borrow or invest in foreign currencies, and their financial transactions have become more diversified in terms of the number of currencies. Japanese financial institutions also have a strong tendency to offer the same lines of service as their competitors, contributing to the increase in the number of foreign exchange banks in recent years (table 14.2).

When the Tokyo foreign exchange market was opened for trading, the initial number of foreign exchange banks was 16 (table 14.2). With the increasing trading volume, and particularly after the Nixon shock of 1971, a greater number of foreign banks, member banks of the Second Association of Regional Banks (after 1974), and *shinkin* banks (after 1982) have entered the market.

Authorized foreign exchange banks are the key players in the Tokyo foreign exchange market. They not only make foreign exchange transactions on their own accounts as dealers but also adjust their foreign exchange positions in response to their transactions with customers and overseas banks on a daily basis. However, not all authorized foreign exchange banks are equally active in the market. In Japan, the share of city banks, long-term credit banks, and trust banks is particularly large because they are large in size and have a wide range of customers. Resident foreign banks are mainly engaged in dealing transactions.

3.1.2 Foreign exchange brokers

In principle, any person can become a foreign exchange broker in Japan upon application to the Minister of Finance. Foreign exchange brokers match buy or sell orders which they receive from foreign exchange banks, and earn commission for this service from both sellers and buyers. In Japan, however, brokers are not allowed to trade on their own accounts and therefore cannot place orders themselves. For spot transactions, the standard rate of commission is set at 3,000 yen per 1 million US dollars. Although this standard rate is somewhat higher than those in London and New York, the Japanese rates in general are becoming more competitive with the introduction of volume discounts.

In responding to the increasing trading volume and the greater internationalization of the yen, Japanese brokers have been developing closer capital and business ties with overseas brokers. In order to facilitate communication among brokers, the Association of Tokyo Foreign Exchange Brokers was established in 1956, the name of which was changed in 1977 to the Association of Foreign Exchange and Foreign Currency Fund Brokers. As of April 1991, there were eight foreign exchange brokers in Japan.[6]

3.1.3 The Ministry of Finance and the Bank of Japan

Under a flexible exchange rate regime, rates can fluctuate sharply and cause traders to bear a greater foreign exchange risk, with undesirable consequences for a trading nation such as Japan. For this reason, the Bank of Japan occasionally intervenes in the foreign exchange market when it wishes to maintain orderly movements in the exchange rate. In this operation, the Bank of Japan acts as the agent of the Minister of Finance under the Foreign Exchange Funds Special Account of the

National Budget, established on April 1, 1951 by the Foreign Exchange Fund Special Account Law.[7]

Market intervention to peg the exchange rate began under the system of fixed exchange rates in April 1963. Since the introduction of flexible exchange rates in 1971, however, intervention has mainly taken the form of smoothing operations. In practice, the Bank of Japan can conduct market intervention either by directly entering the market through a foreign exchange broker or by requesting a foreign exchange bank to enter the market on its behalf. It appears that the latter method is more common in Japan, and that the Japanese monetary authorities generally confine their intervention operations to the spot market. The confidentiality rule associated with official intervention is in the nature of a gentleman's agreement. It is said that the Bank of Japan prefers to intervene through a foreign exchange bank because it does not want to disclose its intervention to many other banks.

In principle, official market intervention is made in the Tokyo market. In recent years, however, the increased interdependence of international markets has sometimes made it difficult for operations in Tokyo alone to influence the exchange rate in a desired direction. The Bank of Japan has thus intervened in the London and New York markets with greater frequency. In such cases, the central bank of each country intervenes on behalf of the Bank of Japan under "commissioned intervention."

3.1.4 Foreign exchange controls and regulations

As was previously mentioned, the present foreign exchange control system is based on the Foreign Exchange and Foreign Trade Control Law, which was substantially revised in December 1980. The revised Foreign Exchange Law allows in principle all foreign exchange, foreign trade, and other external transactions. The revised law classifies all external transactions into payments, capital transactions, foreign direct investment, and foreign trade, and specifies regulations for each category of external transactions. The law further specifies the functions and obligations of authorized foreign exchange banks as well as the framework of their supervision.

The government agencies which are given primary responsibility for the regulation of the respective categories of foreign transactions are: the Ministry of Finance (technically, the Minister of Finance), which is responsible for the regulation of foreign exchange rate determination, the designation of currencies to be used in external transactions, the licensing of authorized foreign exchange banks and foreign exchange brokers, and all non-trade transactions; and the Ministry of International Trade and Industry (technically, the Minister of International Trade and Industry), which is responsible for the regulation of import and export transactions as well as transactions involving the transfer of mining rights and industrial ownership. In the case of transactions involving direct foreign investmemt and imports of foreign technology, the Ministry of Finance assumes joint responsibility with the ministry in charge of the enterprise concerned. At any rate, it is within this regulatory framework that authorized foreign exchange banks conduct foreign exchange transactions in Japan.

3.2   Trading Methods and Practices

Like other major markets in the world, the Tokyo foreign exchange market does not have a trading floor, but is organized as a network of telephones with foreign exchange brokers at the center. Although the Tokyo market was once known for certain trading practices that were different from those of other markets, many have been modified to conform to the internationally accepted practices. In the past, the Tokyo market had the following trading practices:

(a)   All foreign exchange transactions had to be conducted through foreign exchange brokers. No direct dealing between foreign exchange banks was allowed.
(b)   Foreign exchange brokers were not allowed to mediate trades with resident banks in foreign countries (international broking).
(c)   Delivery for spot transactions was in principle made on the following business day.
(d)   Market trading hours were set and strictly observed.

All these practices, except the last one, have been discontinued and the Tokyo market now conforms to those of other markets.

3.2.1   The Tokyo Foreign Exchange Market Practice Committee

Trading practices in the Tokyo foreign exchange market are set by the Tokyo Foreign Exchange Market Practice Committee, established in October 1971. Its objectives are to enforce the observance by its members of international trading practices and to revise the market rules to conform more closely with those of the international market, as the liberalization of the yen and the internationalization of the market have increased trading volume and the number of market participants. The Committee was expected to contribute to the sound development and internationalization of the Tokyo market. Before it was established, there was already in existence a voluntary organization called the Dealers' Club, which was a forum for discussing various issues related to the Japanese foreign exchange market. Given the nature of its role in the market, however, member banks of the Dealers' Club agreed that the new Committee should be an independent organization.

The permanent member of the Committee is the Bank of Tokyo, which is the only specialized foreign exchange bank as well as its principal organizer. Initially, there were six additional members, including three city or long-term credit banks, one trust or regional bank, one foreign bank, and one foreign exchange broker. Now the membership had been expanded to 18, including 14 authorized foreign exchange banks (including four foreign banks), the Bank of Japan as an observer (not directly affecting the decisions of the Committee), two foreign exchange brokers, and the Association of Foreign Exchange Brokers.

3.2.2 Current market practices

Trading hours

Except for international broking, trading hours in the Tokyo foreign exchange market consist of two sessions: from 9 a.m. to 12 noon (the morning session) and the other from 1:30 p.m. to 3:30 p.m. (the afternoon session). It should be noted, however, that this rule applies only to the "official" hours in the Tokyo market, and not to overseas banks or non-bank customers. If they wish, foreign exchange banks can conduct foreign exchange business with their customers 24 hours a day.

Delivery

In 1984, the timing of delivery for spot transactions was changed from "on the following business day" to "in two business days." Prior to that time, the delivery for yen–dollar foreign exchange transactions and dollar call transactions was to be made on the following business day. Now all transactions in the Tokyo market are subject to the same international rule of requiring delivery in two business days. In cases where the delivery date of spot dollars falls on the day when the New York foreign exchange market is closed, however, delivery will be postponed until the next business day on which both markets are open.

"Firm" orders

In the past, foreign exchange banks were not obliged to fulfill the limit orders they placed with the brokers under the system of so-called "may-be" orders. This practice did not contribute to the smooth operation of the market because it made the matching of orders difficult. In April 1980 the system was consequently changed to that of so-called "firm" orders, by which foreign exchange banks are obliged to fulfill the limit orders they place with the brokers, unless the orders are explicitly designated as "under reference" (when requesting rate confirmation before concluding the trade).

Confidentiality

As foreign exchange brokers are in a position to know the conditions of transactions in the market, they should exercise considerable judgement in the use of information they obtain from their business relationships. Consequently, in February 1982 certain rules were established on the basis of fairness and international practice. Under these rules, banks are prohibited from asking brokers for the identity of buyers or sellers in third-party transactions or their transaction amount. Moreover, banks are not allowed to coerce the broker into disclosing the terms and conditions of large-lot transactions.

Liberalization of direct dealing

In February 1985, domestic banks were allowed to deal directly with each other in foreign exchange transactions without the mediation of brokers. In direct dealing it is always possible to find a partner for a transaction, even if the amount involved is large, as long as there is a relationship of mutual trust between dealers and banks. In transactions mediated by brokers, however, banks are only passive participants and may not be able to complete a trade if no partner can be found. In fact, direct dealing transactions are complementary to transactions through brokers. Prior to the liberalization of direct dealing, therefore, the Tokyo foreign exchange market was quite restrictive in its operation.

Commencement of international broking

When direct dealing was liberalized, Japanese brokers were now allowed to execute orders they receive from overseas financial institutions (international broking). To be specific, Japanese brokers maintain telephone hot-lines with foreign exchange brokers in Hong Kong, Singapore, or London with whom they maintain a business relationship. They use this telephone network to mediate trades between domestic and overseas banks. Because domestic and overseas brokers are now participating in several markets, the Tokyo foreign exchange market has been more closely integrated with the foreign markets, with the result that the depth of the market has increased.

Price quotation

The prices of all currencies traded in the Tokyo foreign exchange market are quoted in terms of domestic currency. In yen–dollar transactions, for example, the exchange rate would be quoted as US\$1 = 130 yen; in yen–mark transactions, it would be quoted as DM 1 = 80 yen. In cross-transactions which do not involve the yen, however, exchange rate quotations follow international practice. In dollar–mark transactions, for example, the exchange rate would be quoted as US\$1 = DM 1.6; and in dollar–sterling transactions, it would be quoted as Stg1 = US\$1.8.

Quotation in the customer market

In the customer market, each authorized foreign exchange bank publishes daily at about 10 a.m. the list of reference exchange rates of the yen against other currencies. At present, major Japanese banks publish the yen exchange rates in the customer market against as many as 35 currencies. For all currencies, telegraphic transfer buying and selling rates (TTB, TTS) are announced and used as the reference exchange rates throughout the day. For large-lot transactions, however, the rate prevailing at the time of the transactions is often used.

3.3   Characteristics of the Tokyo Foreign Exchange Market

As has been discussed, the Tokyo foreign exchange market has changed during the past several years and has become closer in its operations to the two major international markets of London and New York. Let us look at some of the characteristics of the Tokyo market by referring to the results of market surveys conducted in April 1989 by the Bank of Japan, the Bank of England, and the Federal Reserve Bank of New York. The survey conducted by the Bank of Japan covered all foreign exchange transactions, including direct dealings between banks, transactions in the customer market, and transactions through brokers (which are routinely reported on a daily basis) between 9 a.m. and 3:30 p.m.

3.3.1   **Currencies traded**

Despite the recent increase in the number of European currencies traded, the bulk of trading that takes place in Tokyo is of the US dollar against the yen. This may be a result of the fact that an overwhelming proportion of Japan's external current and capital transactions has been denominated in dollars. With the abolition of the real demand rule in April 1984 and other measures to liberalize capital flows, however, it is noticeable that foreign exchange transactions involving other currencies have been increasing. This reflects both increasing foreign investment and international portfolio diversification that is designed to reduce the exchange risk.

According to this survey, the volume of spot and swap transactions of the dollar against the yen constituted 72 percent of total transactions

Table 14.3 Trading activities in three major foreign exchange markets (April 1989)

	Tokyo	London	New York
Daily trading volume			
(in billions of US dollars)[a]	115.2	187.0	128.9
Currencies traded (%)			
US dollar vs			
yen	72.3	15.0	25.2
deutsche mark	9.7	22.0	32.9
pound sterling	4.3	27.0	14.6
Swiss franc	4.3	10.0	11.8
French franc	0.3	2.0	3.2
Others	3.0	15.0[b]	8.7[c]
Cross-trading	6.1[d]	9.0[e]	3.6[e]
Types of transactions (%)			
Spot	40.4	64.0	63.9
Swap	56.0	35.0	31.1
Futures and options	3.6	1.0	5.0
Market participants (%)			
Banks, of which:	67.1	85.0	82.0
direct dealing	(48.5)	(67.0)	(48.5)
through brokers	(51.5)	(33.0)	(51.5)
Customers	29.3	15.0	13.0
Others	3.6	n.a.	5.0

[a] The daily trading volumes of other major markets were $55 billion in Singapore, $49 billion in Hong Kong, $30 billion in Sidney, $77 billion (est.) in Frankfurt, $57 billion in Zurich, and $26 billion in Paris.
[b] Of which, the share of the Canadian dollar is 2 percent and the share of the ECU is 1 percent.
[c] Of which, the share of the Canadian dollar is 4 percent, the share of the Dutch guilder is 2.7 percent, and the share of the Australian dollar is also 2.7 percent.
[d] Including yen–deutsche mark and yen–Australian dollar.
[e] Including deutsche mark–pound sterling.

Source: Bank for International Settlements, *Foreign Exchange Turnover Survey 1989*, February 1990 (Basel)

during April, 1989 (table 14.3). The growth of transactions involving other currencies (28 percent) in the Tokyo market has been remarkable during the past ten years (table 14.4). Several factors are responsible.

First, the expansion of external transactions by non-financial institutions has diversified the currencies used. In addition to the traditional transactions of dollar–deutsche mark, dollar–pound sterling, and dollar–Swiss franc, there is now an increasing number of transactions involving the Canadian dollar, the Australian dollar, the French franc, and, more recently, the European Currency Unit (ECU). This reflects the growth of foreign securities investment by life insurance companies and other institutional investors, as well as the growth of foreign direct investment and foreign bond issues by Japanese corporations.

Second, after moving into the Asian market, US and European banks have aggressively promoted foreign exchange transactions involving currencies other than the yen. Moreover, Japanese banks have also begun to be more active in that market. The growth of direct dealing between banks has also increased the depth of the market.

In the past, it was said that the pricing of the exchange rates in Tokyo simply mirrored the development of other markets, particularly those of

Table 14.4 Volume of cross-trading in the Tokyo foreign exchange market (in millions of US dollars)[a]

	Pound sterling	Deutsche mark	Swiss franc	Others	Total
1978	1,137	2,723	338	310	4,508
1979	3,847	8,333	705	768	13,653
1980	12,598	23,920	2,047	1,788	40,353
1981	19,425	40,567	4,477	1,698	66,167
1982	14,579	69,810	10,168	4,097	98,654
1983	13,311	72,954	17,707	5,083	109,055
1984	18,551	122,766	38,579	5,297	185,193
1985	41,472	208,725	62,499	6,888	319,584
1986	72,134	396,539	144,194	21,740	638,607
1987	184,264	576,523	208,698	37,104	1,006,589
1988	289,651	703,895	259,303	63,300	1,316,149
1989	304,832	1,033,569	257,113	147,031	1,742,545
1990	491,800	1,149,400	199,900	335,000	2,176,100

[a] Foreign exchange transactions between the US dollar and non-yen currencies made through brokers.

Source: Tokyo Foreign Exchange Market Practice Committee

other currencies. Now there is no doubt that Tokyo makes its own pricing to a greater extent, and the rates determined there are exerting a noticeable influence on developments in the other markets. It is noteworthy that, with the greater interest of Japanese corporations in financial management, not only banks but also non-financial corporations are now participating in foreign exchange transactions involving other currencies.

It should be noted, however, that the growth of trading in other currencies is limited to spot trading. As far as the forward market is concerned, the volume of trading in other currencies is still low. In the case of some currencies, for example, banks are forced by time difference to wait for the opening of European markets before they can cover the positions created by their earlier transactions with customers.

3.3.2 Spot and forward transactions

A large share of forward (mainly swap) transactions in the total is an important characteristic of the Tokyo market: 56 percent, compared with 35 percent in London and 31 percent in New York (table 14.3). The high share of forward transactions reflects not only the importance of forward exchange contracts in real trade transactions but also the active use in Tokyo of forward swaps as a form of funds arbitrage. A swap transaction is between two different currencies over a specified period of time, and is in effect a capital transaction in the form of a foreign exchange transaction. In Japan, there is a tendency to use swap transactions in the foreign exchange market as a means of conducting funds arbitrage.

For example, a swap transaction can be combined with borrowing a foreign currency as follows: the borrowed foreign currency is sold in the spot market for yen, while at the same time a contract is made to sell yen for the foreign currency in the forward market. In fact, this is equivalent to borrowing yen funds for a specified period of time. Thus, the combination of a transaction in foreign currency funds and a foreign exchange swap transaction is really a yen funds transaction. It is expected, however, that the use of swaps as a means of conducting funds arbitrage transactions will diminish in the future as interest rates on yen-denominated deposits as well as the regulations on the yen capital markets are completely liberalized.

3.3.3 The customer market

Another characteristic is that the share of the customer market in Tokyo (29.3 percent) is also high, compared with London (15.0 percent) and New York (13.0 percent), as shown in table 14.3. This reflects the greater dependency of the Japanese economy on international trade, as well as the greater proportion of international trade that is denominated in dollar and other foreign currencies. Moreover, there has been a significant shift in recent years of capital transactions to foreign markets (for example, foreign securities investment and bond flotation in foreign markets). It is possible that the larger share of the customer market in Japan also reflects the greater share of financial assets of the non-financial public that are denominated in foreign currencies.

If its greater internationalization causes the yen to be more widely used in international transactions in the future, there is a possibility that the structure of foreign exchange transactions may also change. On the other hand, Japanese corporations have already been showing greater interest in foreign exchange transactions after the abolition of the real demand rule. It may be because most corporations were already quite familiar with foreign exchange transactions, through their exposure to international trade, that they have moved quickly into active foreign exchange transactions. Given the fact that many corporations are already setting up a system of exchange risk hedging and foreign exchange dealing, it is possible that the share of the customer market may even increase in the future.

3.3.4 New types of trading

In recent years there has emerged the active trading of new products such as currency options, currency swaps, and interest rate swaps. Many financial institutions are now competing to develop different products in combination with traditional foreign exchange and capital transactions. It is expected that the market in these products will expand as a means of risk management in the customer market.

4 OTHER RELATED MARKETS

4.1 The Tokyo Dollar Call Market

As was mentioned earlier, the Tokyo dollar call market was established in April 1972 in order to improve the efficiency of fund management by foreign exchange banks and to facilitate the balanced growth of the capital and foreign exchange markets. Prior to that time, foreign exchange banks had increasingly demanded the establishment of a market for foreign currency funds. It is believed that the countermeasures for increasing foreign exchange reserves also played a part in its establishment. There was no intention of it developing into an international money market such as the Euromarket. The participants were restricted

Table 14.5 The Tokyo dollar call market (in billions of US dollars)

	Trading volume	*Year-end balance*
1972	5.57	0.35
1973	18.84	0.71
1974	32.91	1.25
1975	41.78	1.30
1976	45.01	1.23
1977	53.67	1.35
1978	69.10	2.70
1979	125.69	4.94
1980	190.16	11.65
1981	276.20	23.83
1982	480.45	32.07
1983	638.11	43.42
1984	961.23	42.03
1985	1,039.18	56.81
1986	1,466.70	98.20
1987	1,748.91	115.26
1988	1,920.04	112.10
1989	2,358.30	117.10
1990	1,832.20	110.30

Source: Tokyo Foreign Exchange Market Committee

to those foreign exchange banks which had a comprehensive banking license (initially 41 out of 92 banks), and the maturity of transactions was limited to six months.

As additional banks began to participate, however, the dollar call market expanded rapidly along with the foreign exchange market (table 14.5). The growth of the market has been particularly rapid since 1980, when the revision of the Foreign Exchange Law allowed the entry of all foreign exchange banks and lifted the limitation on maturity. The dollar call market is where foreign exchange banks within Japan conduct unsecured borrowing or lending in the dollar or other foreign currencies. It is thus somewhat different in nature from the Euromarket where bank deposits are traded.

4.2   The Japan Offshore Market

The Japan Offshore Market (JOM) was established on December 1, 1986 in order to internationalize the yen, liberalize and internationalize

Table 14.6 The Japan Offshore Market (in billions of US dollars)

		Trading volume			Year-end
	Yen	US dollar	Others	Total	balance
1986[a]	15.78	29.49	0.46	36.73	93.7
1987	849.04	498.36	37.05	1,384.45	238.8
1988	1,808.56	1,127.36	176.56	3,112.48	414.2
1989	2,410.36	1,902.09	283.24	4,595.69	607.6
1990	3,066.50	2,228.40	398.60	5,693.50	582.6

[a] December 1986 only.

Source: Tokyo Foreign Exchange Market Practice Committee

Japanese financial markets, and thereby increase the international competitiveness of Japanese financial institutions. At the end of December 1990, after four years of operations, the market had grown to $582.6 billion (table 14.6). Because at first it was only $53 billion, it had grown by about 11 times in four years.

The number of banks with JOM accounts now exceeds 200. Almost all foreign exchange banks, including resident foreign banks, participate in the JOM market. It is separate from the domestic money market, and its size is considerable, even when compared with the IBF (International Banking Facility) in New York of $336.7 billion and the ACU (Asian Currency Unit) in Singapore of $327.0 billion at the end of November 1989; both these markets are also separate from their domestic side. In contrast, the size of the London market was $1,073.3 billion at the end of December 1989, and that of the Hong Kong market, $423.9 billion at the end of September 1989; both these markets are integrated with their domestic side. The JOM is next in size to the London market and is expected to grow further.

4.3   The Currency Swap Market

It has been only four or five years since swap transactions became widely used by Japanese corporations. The liberalization of foreign exchange regulations in June 1984 allowed Japanese corporations to combine currency swap (or forward exchange) transactions with the flotation of foreign currency bonds (that is, hedged bonds).

The proceeds from issuing foreign currency bonds can be converted into yen funds either by a forward exchange contract or by a currency swap. The choice between the two methods will depend on their relative funding terms. In the case of dollar-denominated warrant bonds with a maturity of four to five years, which are the major means of equity finance for Japanese corporations, it is more common to use forward exchange contracts because there is a relatively liquid forward market for that maturity length. On the other hand, it is more common to use currency swap transactions in the case of bonds denominated in deutsche marks or Swiss francs or dollar-denominated bonds with a longer maturity of seven to ten years.

In Japan, because currency swap transactions are regarded as a form of forward exchange transaction, resident corporations must make them with foreign exchange banks. Along with greater activity, there is an emerging interbank market in swap transactions, just as there is in foreign exchange transactions. During the Tokyo trading hours, there is active participation by resident foreign banks in the market.

4.4   The Yen-to-Yen Interest Rate Swap Market

Yen interest rate swap transactions (so-called yen-to-yen swaps) commenced between banks in the early part of 1986. Much interest in yen-to-yen swaps was initially expressed by the banking industry, because they were thought to break the traditional legal separation of long-term and short-term finance in Japan. Non-financial corporations, however, did not show much interest. The reason for this lack of interest probably reflected their lack of knowledge about interest rate swap transactions in general as well as a lack of awareness of interest rate risk itself.

The awareness of non-financial corporations began to change, however, as yen interest rates started to fluctuate sharply after 1987 and, under the new prime lending rate system, short-term corporate borrowing rates became linked with market interest rates. On the investment side, moreover, the deposit rate on large-denomination bank deposits also became a market rate. As a result, more and more non-financial corporations have started to use yen-to-yen swap transactions.

To financial institutions, interest rate swap transactions are not only important as a means of maintaining good customer relationships but are also useful as a means of asset and liability management. For example, Japanese financial institutions tend to lend long and borrow short. Because they incur risk when interest rates rise or when the yield curve is inverted, therefore, they always need to hedge that risk. Yen-to-yen swap transactions, which commenced in 1986, thus became an effective method of hedging interest rate risk. Although some initially expressed concern that interest rate swaps might lead to a breakdown in the separation of long-term and short-term finance, the market now has the participation of all types of banks, including city banks, trust banks, long-term credit banks, and regional banks.

4.5 The Market for Currency Options

4.5.1 **Expansion of the market**

Unlike the overseas markets in currency options, the market in Japan is mainly an over-the counter (OTC) market where options are traded on a tailor-made basis. Trading in currency options began for the first time in Japan in the spring of 1984, when the Bank of Tokyo introduced OTC currency options (forward contracts with options) for the yen–dollar exchange rate, as a new method for Japanese customers to hedge exchange rate risk.

Although many customers initially took an interest in this new instrument, they became reluctant to buy options because they felt that the options premia were too high. Thus, trading volume remained low for the first two years. From the point of view of banks, it was technically difficult to hedge the risk arising from their customer transactions because the OTC market was not well developed in Tokyo. This meant that banks had to trade options at their own risk, and thus contributed to the low volume of trading in the earlier period.

It was the introduction of zero-cost leveraged options in 1988 that reactivated trading in currency options in Japan. Zero-cost leveraged options represent a combined strategy of purchasing and selling options. In this type of strategy, customers can improve the exercise price (the contracted rate at maturity) by selling a larger amount of options than they buy and interweaving the receiving premia into the exercise price.

Trading in this type of option expanded rapidly when exporting companies were suffering from the appreciation of the yen. The options were attractive not only because their cost was zero but also because they were flexible enough to allow companies to design an exchange rate contract that could meet the internal exchange rate of the companies by taking an appropriate risk. Many different product combinations also emerged, all of which responded to the needs of the customers while keeping the cost of options at zero. It was also around this time that customers began to sell or buy straight options.

Along with the expansion of customer business, interbank trading of options also began to increase, and foreign exchange brokers began to mediate interbank trading in the spring of 1988. As a result, the size of the options market expanded rapidly.

At that time, resident foreign banks and US investment banks were the market-makers. Subsequently, previously cautious Japanese banks have increased their options trading as the use of currency options became more widespread as a method of hedging exchange rate risk and bank customers began to create a greater demand for currency options to be used in combination with their borrowing and investment needs. Currency options are no longer considered a new product, and are increasingly thought of as a conventional product.

In the latter half of 1990, the monthly volume of trading in the currency option market (interbank market) was estimated at $100–150 billion, including direct transactions as well as broker-mediated transactions.

4.5.2 Characteristics and form of transactions

In Japan, currency options are not listed in an organized exchange. Both the customer market and the interbank market are organized as an OTC market.

Customer transactions

Initially, most of the currency options were used as hedging tools against commercial transactions. More recently, they have sometimes been used for new products which are combinations of options and other market products.

As the most important characteristic of the customer market, a predominant share of trading is accounted for by sales of options by customers, including the sales of straight options and zero-cost options. The large share of options sales by customers reflects the fact that, although customers do recognize the insurance function of options, they are none the less reluctant to pay options premia. They are more willing to receive options premia by sales of options and, even if the options are exercised, such transactions can be used for commercial transactions.

The maturities of options are mainly from several weeks to six months, although sometimes options have been traded up to three years in conjunction with medium- to long-term loans, interest rate swaps, or currency swaps. The main currency in customer transactions is the yen against the US dollar, although some are for the exchange rates of the yen against other currencies.

Interbank transactions

In the interbank market, all transactions are in principle "transactions with delta" (except small-lot transactions), whereby options and hedging transactions are concluded with the same party at the same time. Option prices are expressed in terms of volatility. When concluding a trade, volatility is first set, and then the option premium based on the actual market exchange rate, and the hedging transaction (the amount and the exchange rate) is settled. Except in a few cases, options traded in the Tokyo market are European options which can be exercised only at the expiration date.

In the Tokyo market, moreover, most transactions are traded through brokers, especially transactions with Japanese banks. It is rarely the case that banks conduct transactions in options directly with each other on a reciprocal basis, in the way that spot or forward exchange transactions are conducted.

The maturities of options are mainly from one month to one year, although there are options with maturities of less than one month. Although medium- to long-term options of more than one year have emerged, they are rarely traded in practice. The market for long-term options is not yet well developed, compared with those in the United States or Europe. Although most interbank trading in options is in terms of the yen against the US dollar, the volume of trading in options in other currency pairs (the yen against European currencies, European currencies against the US dollar, and the Australian dollar against the yen) has gradually increased.

4.6 The Tokyo International Financial Futures Exchange

In June 1989 a financial futures exchange was established in Japan, with the listing of three financial products: short-term yen interest rate futures, short-term dollar interest rate futures, and yen–dollar currency futures (table 14.7).

The Tokyo International Financial Futures Exchange (TIFFE) was the first exchange in the world to list short-term yen interest rate futures, although the Singapore International Monetary Exchange (SIMEX) also listed them in October 1989. Along with the internationalization of the yen, the volume of transactions in short-term yen interest rate futures steadily increased: in October 1989, for example, the futures contracts in the short-term yen interest rate constituted 99 percent of the total of 887,000 futures contracts traded during the month. In contrast, trading activity in dollar interest rate futures and yen–dollar currency futures has remained extremely low. Activation of these markets may require the introduction of a common system of mutual settlement with foreign exchanges.

In March 1991 the pricing of currency futures contracts was changed to the common Japanese practice of expressing them in terms of yen per dollar. However, trading in currency futures continues to remain low, possibly because of competition from existing forward contracts, or because currency trading practices are cumbersome (see table 14.7 for the characteristics of the three futures contracts).

Table 14.7 Three futures products listed at the Tokyo International Financial Futures Exchange (as of December 1991)

	Short-term yen interest rate futures	*Short-term US dollar interest rate futures*	*US dollar/yen currency futures*
Trading unit	100 million yen	1 million dollars	50,000 dollars
Price quotation	00.01 (The number obtained by subtracting annualized percentage rates (on 90-day or 360-day basis) from 100; e.g., 95.25 means 4.75 percent.)	00.01	0.05 (yen per dollar)
Minimum tick	2,500 yen	25 US dollars	2,500 yen
Settlement procedure	Upon payment or receipt of the difference between the contract price and the price determined by the exchange.		Upon exchange of yen funds for dollar funds.
Final trading day (in general)	Two business days prior to the third Wednesday of each March, June, September, and December.		
Settlement day (in general)	The first business day following each trading day.		The third Wednesday of each March, June, September, and December.

Source: Tokyo International Financial Futures Exchange

When futures trading began, the exchange included 263 members, including banks, securities companies, life and accident insurance companies, and brokers (of the total, 96 were settlement members and the remainder were general members). Membership has increased since then. Although trading was initially conducted through a telephone network with the mediation of the exchange, it moved to a fully computerized system at the end of 1990. At present, the trading hours are from 9 a.m. to 12 noon and from 1:30 p.m. to 3:30 p.m. The exchange is considering the possibility of extending trading hours, in anticipation of the time when trading will take place 24 hours a day, linking Japan, Europe, and the United States.

5 THE REMAINING ISSUES AND THE FUTURE OUTLOOK FOR THE TOKYO FOREIGN EXCHANGE MARKET

The Tokyo foreign exchange market is continuing to grow, together with the expansion and internationalization of the Japanese economy. It now ranks in size with the London and New York markets as one of the three major foreign exchange markets in the world. The volume of trading in the Tokyo market has rapidly expanded against the background of increasing internationalization of Japanese firms and greater foreign currency investment by Japanese institutional investors. Growth has been particularly rapid since the abolition of the real demand rule in 1984 and the commencement of dollar depreciation following the Plaza Agreement in the fall of 1985.

The progress of internationalization has also led to the diversification of the currencies traded as well as to the sophistication of trading methods, as is reflected in the recent expansion of options trading. As the market has thus changed both quantitatively and qualitatively, past trading practices, which were quite restrictive in comparison with those of foreign markets, have almost entirely been revised with the initiatives of the Tokyo Foreign Exchange Market Practice Committee, established in October 1971. The Tokyo foreign exchange market has thus become similar to other major markets in terms of trading practices as well.

5.1 Trading Hours

In the area of trading practice, the only remaining issue is the restriction on trading hours, which does not exist in other markets. It is increasingly taken for granted that foreign exchange transactions take place at any time and at any place. Given the increasing use of the yen as an international currency, the trading-hour restriction in the Tokyo market, which is the principal center of yen-related foreign exchange transactions, is becoming a source of great inconvenience to market participants. For this reason, participants in the Tokyo market often continue to trade with each other through Hong Kong or Singapore during lunch hours and after 3:30 p.m.

On the other hand, there is a presumption in Japan that any market should have specific trading hours. Some argue that, in a country where foreign exchange dealers are not professionals but salaried employees of banks, the trading-hour restriction helps to prevent deterioration in working conditions. No settlement of the issue has been made, despite several discussions on the matter at the Market Practice Committee.

5.2   Risk from Foreign Exchange Transactions

Proper evaluation of the risk associated with increasingly complex foreign exchange transactions is essential, not only for the maintenance of sound management of banks and corporations, but also for the realization of stable and appropriate exchange rate levels. This is a concern common to the market participants and to the authorities.

The Foreign Exchange Control Law regulates the overnight position of foreign exchange held by individual Japanese banks. This regulation, however, concerns the overall position of foreign currencies *vis-à-vis* the yen, and not the position of each foreign currency *vis-à-vis* other cross-currencies. That is to say, the official position control exercised by the authorities represents a minimum measure. Each bank should take appropriate measures to deal with the exchange risk by making its own evaluation of that risk. This may involve determining the position of each currency or the position of each branch, the rationalization of the term structure of forward contracts, and the management of currency options trading.

In the context of 24-hour dealing, moreover, there is doubt as to the effectiveness of the regulation of the overnight balance of foreign exchange. A more relevant measure might be the maximum balance of foreign exchange that can be held by an individual bank at any time. There are many remaining issues in this area.

On the other hand, non-financial corporations are not subject to statutory regulation on the risk management of foreign exchange transactions. Many of them have only an inadequate system to evaluate these risks. Despite the increase in the number of corporations which conduct foreign exchange dealing, their foreign exchange transactions are not reported on their financial statements, nor are they even required to be mentioned in a footnote.

When we recognize that the balance of foreign exchange can be a crucial determinant of the profitability of a corporation, there is a need to disclose information on the value of foreign exchange transactions, the internal ceiling placed on the balance of foreign exchange, and the method of risk management used. Although these issues should have been discussed immediately after the real demand rule was abolished, they remain an important issue to be decided by the corporations and the authorities.

5.3   New Products

As was discussed earlier, financial liberalization, increased competition, and technical innovations based on computerization have all combined to introduce new products and new methods of trading such as currency swaps, interest rate swaps, and options trading. The market practices on these new products and trading methods have not yet become firmly established. How should we evaluate these new products and trading methods, from the point of view of promoting the desirable growth of the Tokyo market? How should we manage them, from the point of view of maintaining the soundness of banks and corporate management? How appropriate are the existing regulations? These are the types of question which are becoming important.

5.4   Telecommunication and Information Technology

Remarkable progress is being made in the Tokyo market to make use of increasingly sophisticated telecommunication technology and information hardware. Each bank has established a large dealing room equipped with a system based on Reuter or Telerate, thus responding to the needs of a new age. In order for the Tokyo market to become a truly international financial center, however, greater sophistication is necessary in its use of information and telecommunication technology. How to finance such an enormous investment is an important issue to be solved. For broking, a computer-based electronic system is under consideration. A major change may take place in the future in the way foreign exchange trading is conducted.

5.5   Training of Dealers

As the employment practice of Japanese banks is not based on job categories, situations often arise where there is a conflict between the loyalty of dealers to employer banks and their professionalism. With the internationalization of the Tokyo market, some young dealers are leaving employment in their banks. Under these conditions, we need to establish a job category called "foreign exchange dealers" and have them receive social recognition for that work. This must be done before foreign exchange dealers can be trained, and it presents an important issue for the future development of the Tokyo market.

NOTES

1   For a review of foreign exchange regulations in Japan, see also Fukao (1990).
2   For Japan's foreign exchange policy during the latter part of this period, see Komiya and Suda (1991).
3   For Japan's foreign exchange rate policy during the first part of this period, see also Komiya and Suda (1991).
4   For additional references on the issues discussed here, see Frankel (1984), Horne (1985), McKenzie (1985), and Takagi (1988).
5   For a detailed discussion on this matter, see Koo (1993) and Hodder and Tschoegl (1993), both in this volume.
6   They were the Tokyo Forex Co. Ltd, Hattori Marshall Co. Ltd, Nittan AP Co. Ltd, Yamane Tanshi Co. Ltd, Ueda Harlow Ltd, Kobayashi & Co. Ltd, Yagi Euro Corporation, and Meitan Tradition Co. Ltd.
7   See Takagi (1991) for a brief review of the system of foreign exchange intervention in Japan.

REFERENCES

Bank of Tokyo, Funds Administration Department 1990: *Gaitame Shijo Chishiki* (The foreign exchange market). Tokyo: Nihon Keizai Shinbunsha.

Frankel, Jeffrey A. 1984: The yen/dollar agreement: liberalizing Japanese capital markets, Policy Analyses in International Economics no. 9. Washington D.C.: Institute for International Economics.

Fukao, Mitsuhiro 1990: Liberalization of Japan's foreign exchange controls and structural changes in the balance of payments. *Bank of Japan Monetary and Economic Studies*, September.

Hodder, James E. and Tschoegl, Adrian E. 1993: Corporate finance in Japan. Chapter 3 in this volume.

Horne, James 1985: *Japan's Financial Markets: Conflict and Consensus in Policymaking*. Sydney: Allen & Unwin.

Komiya, Ryutaro and Suda, Miyako 1991: *Japan's Foreign Exchange Policy, 1971–82*. Sydney: Allen & Unwin.

Koo, Richard C. 1993: International capital flows and an open economy: the Japanese experience. Chapter 2 in this volume.

McKenzie, Colin R. 1985: Liberalization of the Japanese capital market and the determination of the yen/dollar rate, *Pacific Economic Papers* no. 130. Australia–Japan Research Center, Canberra.

Nihon Keizai Shinbunsha 1990: *Tsuka Opushon Senryaku* (Currency options strategy). Tokyo: Nihon Keizai Shinbunsha.

Takagi, Shinji 1988: Recent developments in Japan's bond and money markets. *Journal of the Japanese and International Economies*, 2, 63–91.

Takagi, Shinji 1991: Foreign exchange market intervention and domestic monetary control in Japan, 1973–89. *Japan and the World Economy*, 3, 147–80.

Tokyo Foreign Exchange Market Practice Committee 1990: *Tokyo Gaikoku Kawase Shijo no Tebiki* (Guidebook of the Tokyo Foreign Exchange Market). Tokyo: Tokyo Foreign Exchange Market Practice Committee.

Part VI

Investment Trusts and Securities Financing

15

The Structure and Performance of Investment Trusts in Japan

Junko Maru

1 INTRODUCTION

Investment trusts are diversified funds operated by investment companies that raise money from individuals for investment in stocks and bonds, comparable to mutual funds in the United States. Until the middle of the 1980s, investment trusts were the only active institutional investors in the Japanese securities market.

The major function of investment trusts is to reduce the transaction costs of securities investment as well as to minimize the risk of investing in risky securities through portfolio diversification. If investment trusts perform this function well, individual investors can enjoy indirect returns from investing in risky assets at a lower cost and with a lower risk.

The objective of an investment trust is to earn a rate of return which is commensurate with the risk of its portfolio. For this purpose, the fund must first determine the risk level, and then choose a portfolio which would maximize the expected return, given that risk level. An important question to be asked is whether or not investment trusts in Japan have performed well from the standpoint of maximizing the risk-adjusted returns for individual investors.

The share of investment trusts in total financial assets held by individual investors in Japan has remained small since the middle of the 1960s. It may be that individual investors are so risk averse that they do not want to hold investment trusts that contain any risk. A more likely explanation of the small share of investment trusts, however, may be related to their poor performance relative to the risk-adjusted market return.

After reviewing the structure of investment trusts in Japan, this chapter will evaluate the recent performance of Japanese investment trusts. It will then consider the problems associated with the current system of investment trusts in Japan. We argue that the reasons for the poor performance of investment trusts in Japan include high transaction costs, government regulations on fund activities, and lack of competition.

The chapter is organized as follows: section 2 considers the institutionalization of the securities market and the market share of investment trusts in Japan; section 3 discusses the system of investment trusts; and section 4 the portfolio selection of Japanese individual investors. Section 5 analyzes the performance measure of investment trusts, and section 6 presents the empirical results. Section 7 compares the performance of Japanese investment trusts with that of US mutual funds. Finally, section 8 presents concluding remarks.

2   THE INSTITUTIONALIZATION OF THE SECURITIES MARKET[1]

As in the US and some European countries, the securities market in Japan has become highly institutionalized in recent years. Figure 15.1 shows the changes in the composition of stock ownership by type of investor during the period of 1949–89. The share of individuals in total stock ownership consistently declined from almost 70 percent in 1949 to about 20 percent in the 1980s.

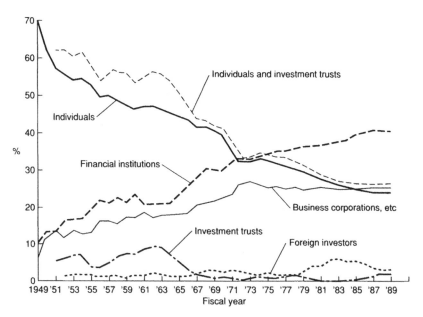

Figure 15.1   Composition of stock ownership by type of investor

Source: Securities and Exchange Council, Tokyo

On the other hand, the share of financial institutions rose continuously from 10 percent in 1949 to more than 40 percent in 1989; it rose particularly fast after the middle of the 1960s. The share of business corporations increased from the late 1960s to the early 1970s, and remained stable at around 25 percent. The institutionalization of the Japanese securities market progressed gradually during this period.

The figure also shows that the share of investment trusts in total stock ownership was as high as 10 percent in 1966 and 1967, reflecting the active participation of individual investors in the bull market. From the latter part of the 1960s, the share began to fall and reached as low as 1 percent in 1983, although it began to rise again and increased to more than 3 percent in 1989.

The institutionalization of the Japanese securities market is also evident when we look at the composition of trading volume by type of investor (table 15.1). As recently as 1978, the share of individuals in stock trading was almost 50 percent of the total. However, the share of individuals declined steadily to 25 percent in 1990. On the other hand, the share of banks, which was as low as 2.3 percent in 1978, rose to 17.1 percent in 1988. Until recently, investment trusts were the only active institutional investors in Japan, behind only the individual and foreign investors.

The institutionalization of the securities market proceeded alongside the declining share of individuals in stock ownership. This in part reflects the fact that investment in risky securities is more attractive to institu-

Table 15.1 Stock trading by type of investor, 1978–90 (%)[a]

	Dealing by securities companies	Individuals	Investment trusts	Foreigners	Banks	Others
1978	23.1	48.4	8.2	4.2	2.3	13.8
1981	30.1	39.8	4.6	9.5	3.4	12.6
1984	23.3	41.9	3.8	14.1	4.1	12.8
1985	25.0	37.7	4.2	12.0	7.9	13.2
1986	26.5	31.5	4.4	10.2	11.8	15.6
1987	27.5	27.8	4.6	8.9	15.4	15.8
1988	27.1	26.4	5.5	6.4	17.1	17.5
1989	22.3	26.1	8.8	8.3	18.4	16.4
1990	24.3	25.1	10.2	10.3	14.7	15.4

[a] Calendar years; based on the volume of transactions by integrated securities companies only.

Source: Tokyo Stock Exchange, *Annual Report*, annual issues

Table 15.2   Brokerage commission rates (effective 4 June 1990)

Value of shares traded (in yen)	Commission rate (%)
Up to 1 million	1.150[a]
Over 1 million up to 5 million	0.900
Over 5 million up to 10 million	0.700
Over 10 million up to 30 million	0.575
Over 30 million up to 50 million	0.375
Over 50 million up to 100 million	0.225
Over 100 million up to 300 million	0.200
Over 300 million up to 500 million	0.125
Over 500 million up to 1 billion	0.100
Over 1 billion	0.075

[a]   The minimum charge is 2,500 yen.

Source: Tokyo Stock Exchange, *Fact Book* (1989)

tional investors, because they enjoy the economy of scale in transaction and information costs. For example, the fixed brokerage commission rate for transactions of up to 1 million yen is 1.15 percent, while the rate for transactions of over 1 billion yen is 0.075 percent (table 15.2).[2]

Institutional investors are also better at reducing the risk of investing in stocks through portfolio diversification. If they want to minimize the risk, they can even pursue the most efficient strategy of holding the market portfolio. On the other hand, individuals with small financial assets cannot easily diversify their portfolios. Consequently, it is efficient for individuals to invest in risky securities indirectly through investment trusts.

Figure 15.2 shows the shares of investment trusts (or mutual funds) in the total financial assets of individual investors in Japan, the US, and the UK. Throughout the period 1980–90 Japan had the highest share of investment trusts. In all three countries the share of investment trusts in total individual assets rapidly increased from 1983, coinciding with the generally bullish stock markets in these countries.

As was mentioned earlier, one reason for the low level of securities holdings in personal financial assets may be related to the structure of commission rates, which imposes higher transaction costs on individual investors than on block traders such as institutional investors. This tendency towards institutionalization is becoming even more pronounced as the transactions size of institutional investors increases with the expansion of the securities market. Under these conditions, investment trusts are becoming more important as a vehicle for individual investors to earn higher returns by investing in risky assets.

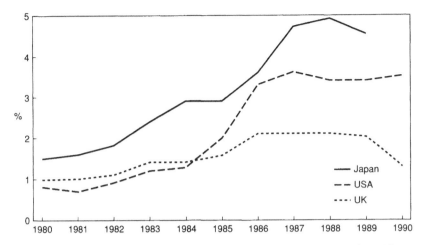

Figure 15.2 Shares of investment trusts in total individual assets, 1980–90

Source: Nomura Research Institute, *Manual of Securities Statistics* (1991)

3 THE SYSTEM OF INVESTMENT TRUSTS IN JAPAN

3.1 The Structure of Investment Trusts

While investment trusts (or mutual funds) can normally be classified into company-type and contractual-type, all investment trusts that operate in Japan are of the latter type.[4] In the company-type arrangement, investors become shareholders of companies which are established to invest in securities. Mutual funds in the United States and investment trusts in the United Kingdom are examples of company-type funds. On the other hand, contractual-type funds take the form of trust agreements between investors and trustees, who invest in securities to earn returns on behalf of the investors. Unit trusts in the United Kingdom are of the contractual type.

In Japan, the contractual-type trusts are further divided into unit-type and open-type. No new investment can be added to unit-type funds during the life of the funds, while new investment can be added to open-type funds at any time. Because of the limitation on additional investment, new unit-type funds are constantly being created. In order to facilitate the management of a series of unit-type funds which are created monthly, "family" funds are sometimes established in which a number of units are organized under a "mother" fund. Table 15.3 lists the types of investment trusts that currently operate in Japan.

Table 15.3   Types of investment trust in Japan

Unit-type
  Stock investment trusts
    Income-growth funds (e.g., family funds, unit stock-private
      bond funds, stock-convertible bond funds, and new balanced funds)
    Growth funds (e.g., capital funds)
    Income funds (e.g., convertible bond funds, bond-stock funds)
  Bond investment trusts (e.g., new government bond fund,
      jumbo, mini-jumbo, domestic and foreign bond funds,
      long-term government bond funds)

Open-type
  Stock investment trusts
    Growth funds (e.g., standard funds, international funds,
      foreign stock funds, formula funds, select funds, and index funds)
    Income growth funds (e.g., balanced funds)
    Income funds (e.g., convertible bond open funds)
  Bond investment trusts (e.g., bond investment trust, employee
      assets-building plan funds, medium-term government bond funds,
      rikin funds, and free financial funds)
  Constructive trusts (e.g., parent funds of family funds,
      parent funds of family bond funds, parent funds of convertible bond funds)

Three parties are involved in the system of investment trusts in Japan, namely investors, investment trust management companies (managers), and trust banks (trustees). First, an investment trust management company receives investment money from investors, usually through the marketing efforts of its affiliated securities companies. Then, a contract for a securities investment trust is signed between the investment trust management company as the manager and a trust bank (the trustee), which invest in securities at the instruction of the manager. This contract is made on the basis of the trust clause approved by the Minister of Finance in accordance with the Securities Investment Trust Law.

Investment trusts can be organized either as stock investment trusts or as bond investment trusts. Stock investment trusts may include both stocks and bonds, while bond investment trusts can include only bonds. Within stock investment trusts, the proportion of bonds in the portfolios varies considerably: "capital funds" actively invest in stocks, while "balanced funds" try to maintain a balance between stock and bond investment. At the end of 1991 a total of 1691 investment trusts (667 stock investment trusts and 1024 bond investment trusts) were marketed by 18 investment trust management companies.[5]

3.2 Stock Investment Trusts

Stock investment trusts consist of unit-type (established in 1951) and open-type (1952). Figure 15.3 depicts the outstanding principal of unit-type trusts, and shows that the outstanding amount rapidly rose from 1985 to 1988. In 1989, however, the amount of cancellation and redemption was equal to the amount of new issues; in 1990, when there was a significant fall in stock prices, the amount of cancellation and redemption exceeded the amount of new issues. Figure 15.4 depicts the total net asset value of unit-type trusts, and shows that, although the value rose from 1987 to 1989, it declined rapidly in 1990. Indeed, the share of stock investment trusts is sensitive to the level of stock prices.

Figure 15.5 shows that the outstanding principal of open-type trusts has risen continuously since 1984. The amount of new issues as well as the amount of cancellation have also increased since 1986. The changes in the total net asset value of open-type trusts are depicted in figure 15.6, where it is shown that the share of stocks in the total assets considerably increased in 1989.

3.3 Bond Investment Trusts

Bond investment trusts are also available in two types, namely unit-type and open-type. Open-type bond trusts, called "bond open", were launched in January 1961. In 1980 medium-term government bond funds were established mainly for small individual investors; these funds invest

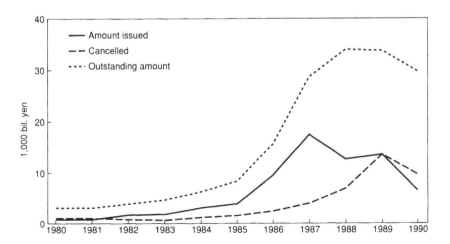

Figure 15.3 Outstanding principal of unit-type trusts

Source: The Investment Trusts Association, *Annual Report*, various issues

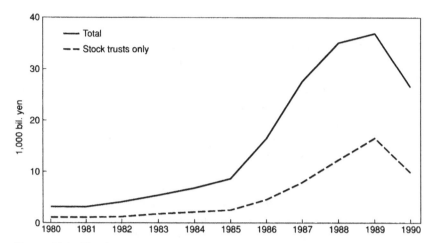

Figure 15.4   Total net asset value of unit-type trusts

Source: The Investment Trusts Association, *Annual Report*, various issues

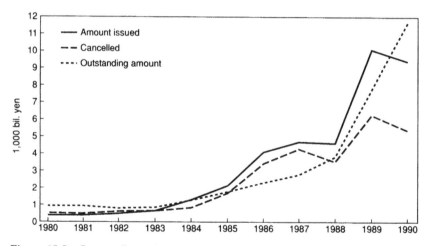

Figure 15.5   Outstanding principal of open-type trusts

Source: The Investment Trusts Association, *Annual Report*, various issues

most of their assets in interest-bearing medium-term government bonds. Interest reinvestment bond funds were then launched in 1982, and "free financial" funds in 1985. Free financial funds are designed for larger investors and were initially marketed to compete with money market certificates (MMCs) offered by banks.

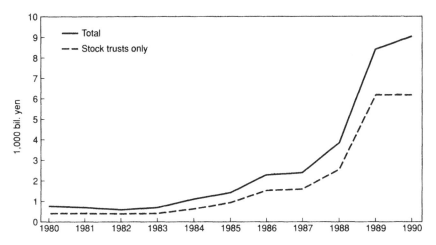

Figure 15.6   Total net asset value of open-type trusts

Source: The Investment Trusts Association, *Annual Report*, various issues

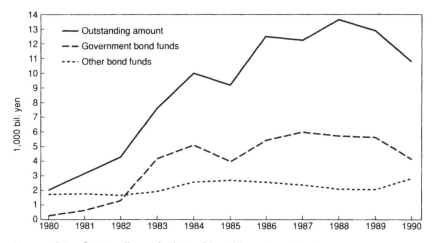

Figure 15.7   Outstanding principal of bond investment trusts

Source: The Investment Trusts Association, *Annual Report*, various issues

For unit-type bond trusts, new government bond funds, established in 1981, were followed by "jumbo" funds in 1982 and "mini-jumbo" funds in 1983. For jumbo funds, no dividend is paid and no redemption is allowed during the life of the funds; for mini-jumbo funds, redemption is allowed after three years. Domestic and foreign bond funds were established in 1984 in order to invest in foreign and domestic bonds without any restrictions. In 1986 long-term government bond funds were established.

Figure 15.7 depicts the changes in the principal of bond investment trusts, and shows that the outstanding amount increased rapidly until 1984, and rose sharply again in 1986 after a temporary fall in 1985. From 1986, the increase in the principal began to decelerate, and it declined sharply in 1990. This was particularly true of government bond funds. However, the outstanding principal of other bond funds somewhat increased in 1990.

4 THE PORTFOLIO SELECTION OF INDIVIDUAL INVESTORS

4.1 The Financial Assets and Portfolio Selection of Individual Investors

As has already been mentioned, individual investors in Japan have a high level of financial assets which have been attained by the continuously high rate of savings in an environment of rapidly growing income. Because the savings rate has remained high, the accumulation of financial assets has proceeded rapidly.

Investors select portfolios according to the degree of their risk aversion. Table 15.4 shows the portfolio composition of individual investors during the period 1960–89. The share of time deposits, which investors presumably consider riskless, varied but remained high: the share was 30 percent in 1960, 50.2 percent in 1980, and 38.1 percent in 1989. The share of demand deposits, which investors presumably hold for transactions purposes, declined over time, as the progress of computerization allowed investors to make transactions without cash. On the other hand, the shares of risky assets declined until 1980. In the 1980s, however, the shares gradually increased, reaching as much as 17.8 percent in 1989.

During this period of 30 years, the value of financial assets held by individuals increased by 36 times. This phenomenal growth partly reflects the rapid increase of stock prices during the 1980s. Investors make substitutions between various types of assets in accordance with their risk-adjusted returns. When the stock prices are increasing, investors can probably expect further price increases in the future, and as a result they make a portfolio switch from time deposits to stocks. For bonds, which are less risky than stocks, the share remained low: 1.6 percent in 1960, 4.5 percent in 1985, and 3.4 percent in 1989.

Table 15.4 Composition of personal savings, 1960–89 (all households; in percent of total)[a]

	1960	1965	1970	1975	1980	1985	1986	1987	1988	1989
Demand deposits	16.7	15.5	14.6	14.1	9.7	7.6	7.3	7.0	7.0	6.8
Time deposits	30.0	30.7	36.8	45.2	50.2	47.1	45.8	43.1	41.8	38.1
Life insurance[b]	18.3	21.8	22.5	19.6	19.7	23.3	23.0	22.4	23.8	23.8
Securities	30.4	26.5	21.1	16.7	17.1	19.6	20.9	24.8	24.5	28.6
(stocks)	(23.4)	(16.8)	(11.7)	(7.7)	(7.4)	(8.3)	(9.9)	(13.8)	(12.8)	(17.8)
(bonds)	(1.6)	(2.0)	(2.3)	(2.3)	(3.4)	(4.5)	(3.9)	(3.6)	(3.3)	(2.9)
(stock trusts)	(3.6)	(2.0)	(0.8)	(0.7)	(0.6)	(0.9)	(1.5)	(2.3)	(3.0)	(3.4)
(bond trusts)	–	(0.9)	(0.9)	(0.9)	(0.8)	(1.2)	(1.2)	(1.1)	(1.4)	(1.3)
(loan trust and money in trust)	(1.8)	(4.7)	(5.4)	(5.1)	(4.8)	(5.0)	(4.5)	(4.0)	(4.1)	(3.4)
Others	5.7	5.5	4.9	4.4	3.4	3.1	3.0	2.7	2.8	2.9

a At the end of each year.
b Includes non-life insurance for 1989 only.

Source: Management and Coordination Agency, *Family Savings Survey*, various issues

The share of investment trusts is not large relative to other financial assets. The share of stock investment trusts declined to 0.8 percent in 1980, but gradually recovered to 3.4 percent in 1989, comparable to the level in 1960. The share of bond investment trusts was generally smaller than that of stock trusts, ranging between 0.8 percent in 1980 and 1.4 percent in 1988.

4.2   Financial Assets and Stock Investment

Table 15.5 shows the composition of household savings by type of financial asset and by the amount of savings in 1989. The average amount of assets was 9.9 million yen, which was distributed among a wide range of assets. Households in lower income brackets tend to have a higher proportion of their assets in life insurance and demand deposits. Households in higher income brackets tend to have a higher proportion of their assets in time deposits and securities. For example, for income group V (with the average asset-holding of approximately 2.5 million yen) the proportion of securities was 4.5 percent; for income group IX (average asset-holding of approximately 21.7 million yen) the proportion was 30 percent.

The amount of risky assets in household portfolios naturally increases with the amount of total financial assets. This is particularly true of stock investments, the amount of which tends to increase faster than the increase of total financial assets. Thus, the ratio of risky assets to total assets rises with the increase in wealth.

The cross-sectional relationship between investment trusts and total assets is similar to the relationship between stocks or bonds, on the one hand, and total assets. We might have expected individuals in lower brackets, not those in higher brackets, to prefer investment trusts as a means of portfolio diversification because of their more stringent wealth constraint. In practice, however, the share of investment trusts increases with the value of asset holding. This may reflect the possibility that those with greater wealth are more tolerant of risk and that they have more information about the availability and characteristics of investment trusts.

5   THE MEASURE OF INVESTMENT TRUST PERFORMANCE

5.1   The Objectives of Investment Trusts

The objectives of investment trusts are to pool the resources of many individuals and to invest them in a diversified portfolio of risky securities.

Table 15.5 Composition of household savings by income group (workers' households; at end of 1989)

Income groups	Average	I	II	III	IV	V	VI	VII	VIII	IX
					(in thousands of yen)					
Annual income	6523	3932	4383	4494	5028	5423	5990	6269	6868	8378
Savings	9946	479	1239	1753	2518	3502	4458	5903	8429	21714
					(in percent of total)					
Demand deposits	7.1	31.1	20.3	16.1	14.4	11.7	11.1	10.6	9.2	5.4
Time deposits	37.1	23.6	27.8	29.8	30.1	32.5	36.6	39.1	39.4	37.1
Life insurance	27.9	41.3	48.7	49.9	47.9	48.0	42.4	37.4	34.1	22.9
Securities	23.2	1.0	0.9	0.7	4.5	4.5	5.7	6.4	11.8	30.0
(stocks)	(13.0)	(0.8)	(0.3)	(0.2)	(1.5)	(1.4)	(2.8)	(3.3)	(6.2)	(17.0)
(bonds)	(2.1)	(0.2)	(0.0)	(0.1)	(0.5)	(0.5)	(1.0)	(0.5)	(1.0)	(2.7)
(unit and open-end trusts)	(3.2)	(0.0)	(0.6)	(0.2)	(0.4)	(0.7)	(1.1)	(0.7)	(1.6)	(4.2)
(open-end bond trusts)	(1.4)	(0.0)	(0.0)	(0.2)	(0.5)	(0.3)	(0.6)	(0.7)	(1.3)	(1.6)
(loan trust and money in trust)	(3.5)	(0.0)	(0.0)	(0.0)	(1.6)	(1.6)	(0.2)	(1.2)	(1.7)	(4.5)
Others	4.7	3.1	2.3	3.5	3.1	3.3	4.2	6.5	5.4	4.5

Source: As for table 15.4

The investment trusts provide the purchasers of participation certificates with an opportunity to earn capital gains on the securities held by the respective funds. Presumably, the investment trusts attempt to maximize returns by means of professional investment analysis and by taking full advantage of scale economy in portfolio management.

5.2 Returns and Risks

Because the performance of a particular investment trust is evaluated by its risk-adjusted return, it is first necessary to estimate its risk before any evaluation can be made. If investors are risk-averse and hold a well-diversified portfolio, the relevant risk is the beta (defined below), and not the total variance of security returns.

In general, the risk of a portfolio must be estimated on the basis of a particular model of asset pricing, such as the Capital Asset Pricing Model (CAPM) or Arbitrage Pricing Theory (APT). Here, we use the CAPM to estimate the risk-adjusted return of investment trusts.

According to the CAPM, the beta of a security is defined as

$$\beta_i = \text{Cov}(R_i, R_m)/\sigma_m^2 \tag{15.1}$$

where R_i is the rate of return on security i, and R_m is the rate of return on the market portfolio, $\text{Cov}(R_i, R_m)$ is the covariance between R_i and R_m, and σ_m^2 is the variance of the rate of return of the market portfolio.

The beta is an appropriate measure of the risk of an individual security or a portfolio when all investors hold the market portfolio as the only

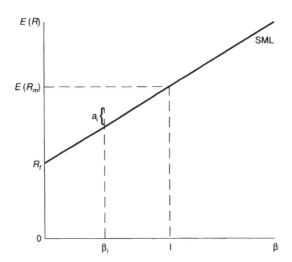

Figure 15.8 Securities market line and the excess return

risky asset. In this environment of the CAPM, there is a trade-off between expected returns on securities and their risks (β_i). The higher the
value of β becomes, the higher its expected return would also become.
This relationship is given by

$$E(R_i) = R_f + [E(R_m) - R_f]\beta_i \qquad (15.2)$$

where R_f is the riskless rate of return, and $[E(R_m) - R_f]$ is the risk
premium on the market portfolio, which is the average premium of all the
securities in the market.

Figure 15.8 shows the relationship, which is called the Securities
Market Line (SML). The excess or abnormal return on investment trust i
(a_i) is measured by the difference between the actual return, R_i, and the
expected return, $E(R_i)$, found on the SML. When a_i is positive, the
performance of investment trust i is considered "good;" when a_i is
negative, the performance is "bad."

5.3 The Data

In order to evaluate the performance of investment trusts, the SML
must first be estimated empirically. Before proceeding to this estimation,
however, let us look at the performance of the market portfolio in Japan.

Table 15.6 shows the annual rate of return of the market portfolio,
which contains all stocks listed on the first section of the Tokyo Stock
Exchange. During the past 30 years, the average rate of return was 17.7
percent with the standard deviation of 17.7 percent. On average, the rate
of return from holding stocks was considerably higher than the rate of
return on less risky assets. We note that the average rate of return
gradually increased, while the risk (standard deviation) varied considerably. For the period under investigation, the rate of return was as high as
24.7 percent, and the risk was relatively low.

Table 15.6 The performance of the market portfolio (%)[a]

Period	Average return	Standard deviation
1961–90	17.7	17.7
1961–70	14.2	13.8
1971–80	17.9	21.8
1981–90	21.0	17.9
1980–87	24.7	14.7

[a] The market portfolio includes all stocks listed in the first
section of the Tokyo Stock Exchange, with the weight of each
stock given by its market value.

Table 15.7   Mean excess returns of investment trusts in Japan

Sample period	Number of funds	JSRI[a] Simple mean	JSRI[a] Absolute mean	Simple mean without risk adjustment
			Excess returns (%)	
From 1/1980 to 12/1982	46	−2.88 (3.66)	3.79	−1.56
From 1/1981 to 12/1983	42	−2.81 (4.97)	4.32	2.86
From 1/1982 to 12/1984	39	−5.40 (3.95)	5.67	1.88
From 1/1983 to 12/1985	34	−8.61 (5.78)	8.95	0.18
From 1/1984 to 12/1986	42	−10.46 (10.54)	10.54	1.87
From 1/1985 to 12/1987	78	−5.62 (5.88)	6.16	1.14

[a]   Based on the Japan Securities Research Institute's Index. Standard deviations are in parentheses.

We now analyze the performance of investment funds based on monthly data. Table 15.7 shows six observations periods, which contain 36 months each. The returns are calculated by the end-of-month prices and the dividends paid during the month; the expected returns are assumed to be given by the average return during the period. The risks of investment trusts are estimated by regressing their rates of return on the rate of return of the market portfolio during the same period.

As the market portfolio, we use two types of portfolio: that which includes all common stocks listed on the first section of the Tokyo Stock Exchange (called MP1); and that which includes MP1 and all bonds traded in the secondary bond market (called MP2). Finally, as the riskless rate, we use the average call rate for each period.

6   THE EMPIRICAL RESULTS[6]

6.1   The Beta Risks

Figures 15.9a and 15.9b show the relationship between the average return and the beta (β), with either MP1 or MP2 as the market portfolio. The performance of the investment trusts are evaluated on the basis of whether their rates of return are above or below the SML. If the market

(a) Case 1

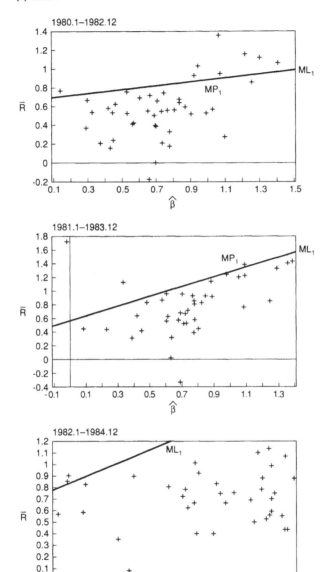

Figure 15.9 Beta risks
(a) Case 1
(b) Case 2

Source: Suto (1989)

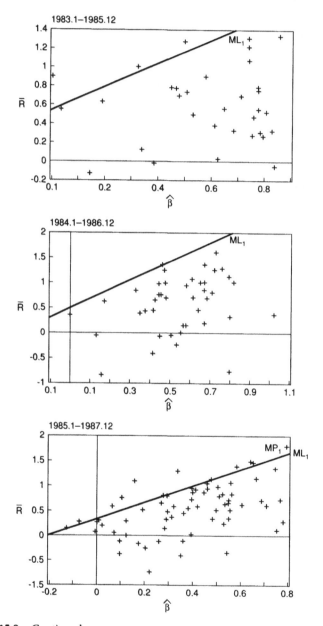

Figure 15.9　*Continued*

(b) Case 2

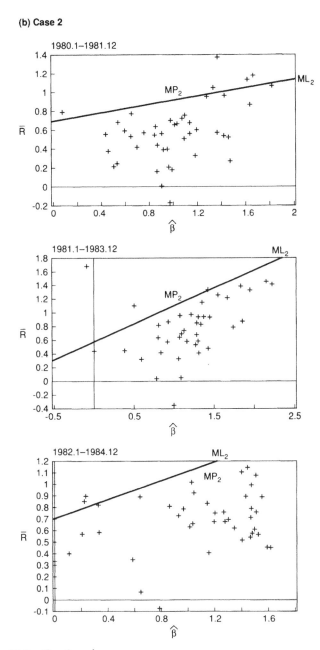

Figure 15.9 *Continued*

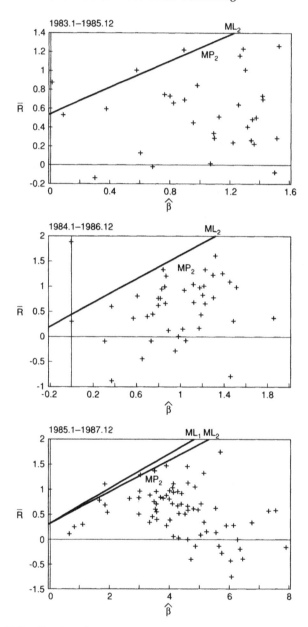

Figure 15.9   *Continued*

is efficient, in the sense that the investment trusts do not earn excess returns, the rates of return should be along the SML.

The figures show that most of the funds were below the SML, and that many were even significantly below the SML for all periods, regardless of whether MP1 or MP2 was used as the market portfolio. The inferior performance of most investment trusts may reflect large transaction costs, inefficient investment behavior, or government regulations that restrict the activities of investment trusts (to be discussed below).

6.2 The Total Risks

Figure 15.10 shows the relationship between the rate of return and the total risk (standard deviation). Given the following relationship between the total risk (the standard deviation σ) and the beta (β),

$$\beta_i = \frac{\mathrm{Cov}(R_i, R_m)}{\sigma_m^2} = \rho_{im} \frac{\sigma_i}{\sigma_m}$$

where ρ_{im} is the correlation coefficient between the return from the ith portfolio and the return from the market portfolio, complete diversification (that is, $\rho_{im} = 1$) means that β_i and σ_i have a one-to-one correspondence.

Consequently, if the relationship between $E(R_t)$ and β_i is linear, the relationship between σ_i and $E(R_t)$ is also linear. This means that, if the funds are fully diversified, the relationship between the rate of return and the total risk should be linear. For the fifth and sixth sample periods, however, the relationship between the rate of return and the total risk was not linear, indicating that the funds were not fully diversified.

7   THE RELATIVE PERFORMANCE OF JAPANESE INVESTMENT TRUSTS

7.1   Comparison with US Mutual Funds

It may be of interest to compare the performance of Japanese investment trusts, as presented in the previous section, with that of US mutual funds, as given in a recent study by Lehmann and Modest (1987).[7]

Tables 15.7 and 15.8, respectively, show the excess returns of investment trusts in Japan and of mutual funds in the US. In Japan, the average excess returns were considerably negative for all subperiods (table 15.7). The absolute values of these average excess returns were not too different from the averages of the absolute values, indicating that the excess returns were rarely positive. The average excess returns from the riskless

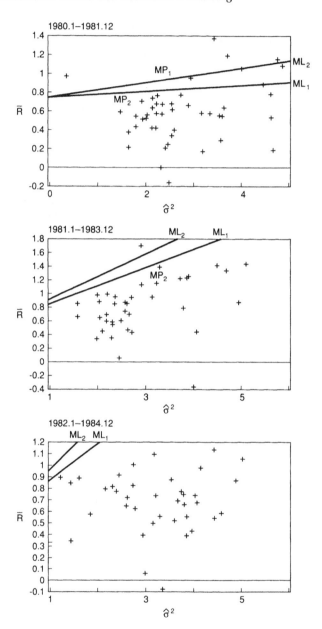

Figure 15.10   Total risks

Source: Suto (1989)

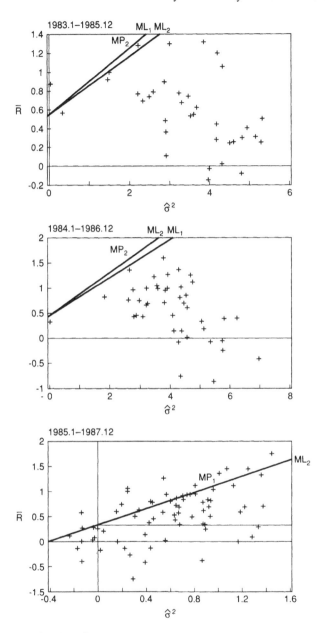

Figure 15.10 *Continued*

Table 15.8 Mean excess returns of mutual funds in the United States

Sample period	CRSP[a]		Without risk adjustment	
	Simple mean	*Absolute mean*	*Simple mean*	*Absolute mean*
From 1/1968	−1.41	3.12	6.53	6.91
to 12/1972	(4.37)		(4.07)	
From 1/1973	−0.79	3.62	1.33	3.82
to 12/1977	(4.54)		(4.83)	
From 1/1978	1.40	2.94	16.36	16.36
to 12/1982	(3.98)		(4.82)	

Excess returns (%) spans the CRSP and Without risk adjustment columns.

[a] Based on the Center for Research in Securities Prices' Index. Standard deviations are in parentheses.

Source: Lehmann and Modest (1987)

rate were positive in five subperiods, and negative in one period (1980–2) when the stock market was not very active. It does not appear, however, that these excess returns were enough to cover the risk of the funds.

The average US returns were negative for two subperiods and positive for one subperiod (table 15.8). Because the standard deviation was about 4 percent, however, the excess returns were not statistically significant for these subperiods. When we calculate the averages of the absolute values of the excess returns, we find that the rates of return of the mutual funds could be way above or way below the SML. The excess returns from the riskless rate were positive for three subperiods, and were particularly high during the period 1978–82.

7.2   The Implications of the Poor Performance

In Japan as well as in the US, it was found that the investment trusts (or mutual funds) did not, on average, "beat the market." An important reason must be the existence of transaction costs, including commission fees, information costs, investment research costs, and taxes. The liquidity risk associated with the time it takes to redeem the funds can also be included in the transaction costs. Although these are much lower than the costs faced by individuals, they are not zero, even for investment trusts.

Investment trusts (or mutual funds) frequently make transactions in securities in order to maintain an optimal portfolio. In fact, the turnover ratio of investment trusts in Japan is more than twice the market average. In order to diversify, investment trusts hold a large number of securities, although they do not hold stocks with limited liquidity. The transactions costs, therefore, are an important determinant of the profitability of investment trusts.

The difference between the actual rate of return and the SML must partially reflect these transaction costs. Although the transaction costs probably explain a substantial portion of the small negative excess returns of US mutual funds, however, one can argue that the large negative excess returns of Japanese investment trusts are too large to be explained away by the transactions costs alone.

The obligation to repurchase on investor demand is another problem associated with "open-ended" investment trusts in Japan.[8] Because of the repurchase obligation, Japanese investment trusts must hold a significant amount of liquid assets with low rates of return, or otherwise must

Table 15.9 Repurchase rates in Japan and the United States, 1968–90 (%)

	Japan *(investment trusts)*	United States *(mutual funds)*
1968	50.3	7.3
1969	71.3	7.6
1970	21.5	6.3
1971	14.9	8.6
1972	18.1	11.0
1973	21.0	12.1
1974	20.5	9.9
1975	39.5	8.7
1976	35.1	14.8
1977	30.4	13.4
1978	21.0	16.0
1979	36.4	16.2
1980	44.0	14.0
1981	50.2	13.5
1982	73.1	9.9
1983	61.1	12.9
1984	67.0	15.0
1985	108.1	13.4
1986	152.3	15.8
1987	181.7	25.6
1988	90.7	19.6
1989	80.3	16.5
1990	51.3	17.4

Source: Investment Trusts Association, *Monthly Report of Investment Trusts*, monthly issues

quickly liquidate their assets even at a capital loss. These liquidity costs and risks are reflected in the poor performance of these investment trusts.

Table 15.9 shows the ratios of repurchases to outstanding principals of investment trusts in Japan and mutual funds in the US. The ratio in Japan is much higher than the ratio in the US. The high repurchase rate in Japan may be associated with two problems. First, individual investors have a tendency to judge the performance of an investment trust on the basis of the rate of return during the immediate past. Second, the investment trust management companies earn transaction fees each time participation certificates are sold or repurchased. The companies thus have an incentive to promote the redemption of outstanding participation certificates as well as the sale of new certificates.

Government regulations on investment trusts have been relaxed in recent years to a limited extent. For example, investment trusts are now allowed to use futures and options transactions for hedging purposes.[9] However, investment trust management companies should be given greater freedom to invest in many other types of financial products.[10] In order to improve the performance of investment trusts and increase their attractiveness as investment vehicles, further deregulation as well as a further change in the investment strategy of investment trusts themselves may be necessary.

8 CONCLUSION

The most important function of investment trusts is to provide small investors with an opportunity to earn higher returns by investing in risky assets. In Japan, however, government policy has emphasized the stability of the financial system and investor protection to the detriment of this function of investment trusts. In order to ensure investor protection, the government has pursued the policy of insulating investors from investment risk. There are more controls and regulations on investment trusts in Japan than there are on mutual funds in the United States.

Many types of government rules restrict the investment strategies of investment trusts, resulting in an inefficient selection of portfolios. These restrictions have increased the transaction costs, and have prevented the investment trusts from taking optimal strategies. It was only recently that many of these restrictions began to be questioned and some liberalization measures were implemented.

Another major problem is the lack of competition among the investment trust companies.[11] Investment trusts can only be established with a license from the Ministry of Finance, so there are significant barriers to entry. Moreover, the information on the performance of individual investment trusts is not readily available to the investors. It is true that the Investment Trust Association began publishing the average (non-risk-adjusted) rates of return of investment trusts in March 1984 and that the daily *Nikkei Financial* publishes the rates of returns and the total risks. However, investment trust management companies are still prohibited from advertising their products by comparing their performance with that of the products of other companies.

As the institutionalization of the securities market proceeds, investment trusts can play an even greater role in the securities market. From this standpoint, the restrictive regulations which currently exist against investment trusts should be restructured in such a way as to contribute to the efficiency of the whole financial system.

NOTES

1 Institutionalization refers to a phenomenon in which institutional investors occupy a large share of the securities market.
2 The brokerage commission rates have been reduced several times, the latest revision being in June 1990. The rates are fixed on the basis of the estimated expenses associated with order execution plus a reasonable profit. See also Takagi (1993), chapter 9 in this volume.
3 This section relies on Japan Securities Research Institute (1991).
4 As an exception, company-type mutual funds (called "country funds") which are already listed at foreign exchanges are traded at the Osaka Stock Exchange.
5 Of this total, three were foreign companies.
6 This section relies on Suto (1989).
7 Lehmann and Modest (1987) use the weighted average return of the Center for Research in Securities Prices (CRSP) as the rate of return of the market portfolio. They also estimate the excess returns measured by the actual rates of return less the riskless rate of return.
8 All investment trusts established in Japan are "open-ended" trusts which, by definition, must be redeemed for cash on demand. There is no secondary market in which participation certificates can be traded.
9 See Adachi and Kurasawa (1993), chapter 12 in this volume.
10 In this context, the Investment Trust Law does not restrict the investment of investment trusts to "securities" as defined by the Securities and Exchange Law. See Kanda (1993), chapter 5 in this volume.
11 At the end of October 1991, 233 foreign funds were sold in Japan for an amount of over 1 trillion yen.

REFERENCES

Adachi, Tomohiko and Kurasawa, Motonari 1993: Stock futures and options markets in Japan. Chapter 12 in this volume.

Investment Trust Association, *Annual Report of Investment Trusts*, annual issues.

Investment Trust Association, *Monthly Report of Investment Trusts*, monthly issues.

Japan Securities Research Institute 1991: *Securities Market in Japan*. Tokyo.

Kanda, Hideki 1993: Regulatory environment for Japanese capital markets. Chapter 5 in this volume.

Lehmann, Bruce N. and Modest, David M. 1987: Mutual fund performance evaluation: a comparison of benchmarks and benchmark comparisons. *Journal of Finance*, 42 June, 233–66.

Maru, Junko 1989: Toshi Shintaku no Kino to Pafoomansu (The function and performance of investment trusts). Tokyo: Japan Securities Research Institute, July.

Maru, Junko 1990: *Shoken Shijo* (The securities market). Tokyo: Shinseisha.

Suto, Megumi 1989: Saikin no Toshi Shintaku Buum to Toshi Pafoomansu (The recent boom of the investment trusts and the investment performance). Tokyo: Japan Securities Research Institute, July.

Takagi, Shinji 1993: The organization and microstructure of the secondary stock market in Japan. Chapter 9 in this volume.

Yonezawa, Yasuhiro and Maru, Junko 1986: *Nihon no Shoken Shijo* (The stock market in Japan). Tokyo: Toyo Keizai Shinposha.

16
Securities Financing in Japan

Ulrike Schaede

1 INTRODUCTION

When the US occupation forces revised the Japanese securities market legislation in 1949, they introduced into the law margin transactions as known in the US. As early as 1951, however, the Japanese authorities revised the system; in 1958, they totally remodeled it. As a result, the Japanese system of margin transactions and short sales became entirely different from its model. The differences in market organization between the two countries reflect a different attitude towards the "market," "regulation," and "speculation," and the difficulty of adopting the US system of margin transactions into another country with a different historical and institutional background.

In a trade that involves margin buying, a customer buys securities with money borrowed from a third person (usually a broker). As collateral for the lender, the customer has to deposit a margin, usually some 50 percent of trading value. If the price of the securities rises subsequently, the customer sells the securities, repays the loan and takes the differential. Margin buying versus outright buying (entirely on the purchaser's own funds) entails a leverage effect, which increases both the risk and expected return of a position.

In a short sale, the customer sells securities that he does not own but which he borrowed from a third person (usually a broker); if prices drop subsequently, the customer repurchases the securities (at a lower price). With the profit he repays the stock loan and then takes the differential. Again, the leverage effect increases the position that could be taken without the stock loan; a margin serves as collateral to the lender.

Margin transactions can be based on several motivations. One is convenience: the outright sale of stocks might be impossible because the stocks themselves are not at hand at the time of the transaction. A second motivation is hedging, and a third is speculation: one assumes the risk

The author is grateful for helpful comments from staff of the Japan Securities Finance Co., D.J. Brooks, Masaharu Igarashi, Hideki Kanda, Terry Marsh, Shinji Takagi, and Adrian Tschoegl. However, all errors remain exclusively hers.

of price fluctuations for a possible profit. Often these transactions have the negative connotation of providing an undue means of "excessive speculation." While in the US economic reasoning has brought a wide acceptance of speculative behavior, in other countries speculation represents "socially unacceptable" behavior. As short sales are often labelled the quintessential speculation, they are totally or partly forbidden on some stock markets. For example, in Japan there is a different set of rules for short sales which explicitly aims at cutting speculation by securities companies.

In the US, margin transactions constitute a large part of stock transactions. On the New York Stock Exchange (NYSE), for example, purchases on less than 100 percent equity are the rule rather than the exception, while short sales have represented 2 to 8 percent of total trading volume in the postwar period. Brokers who lend money or stock to their customers for short selling finance their position either through money loans on the call market or through stock and money loans from other securities companies.

In Japan, total margin transactions account for 15 to 20 percent of trading volume. The way brokers finance their positions differs from the US due to historical reasons: while the American model had developed over the years and built on a mature call market and easy access to bank credits for the refinance of brokerage houses, there was neither a viable call market nor did brokers have stocks, let alone stocks to lend. Therefore, three specialized securities finance companies were established in Tokyo, Osaka, and Nagoya, with the explicit task of providing money to securities companies for financing margin transactions. These securities finance companies in turn refinanced themselves, especially in the early years, with government money channelled through the central bank. The market for margin transaction thus became subject to quantitative controls, and the close connections between the regulatory authorities, the stock exchanges, and the securities finance companies ensured a smooth flow of administrative guidance.

This chapter analyzes the structure and organization of margin transactions in Japan. It explicitly confines itself to an analysis of the institutional setting of margin transactions in Japan in order to lay the foundation for a more rigorous testing of the effectiveness of margin requirement policies in the future. Because major features of the current system are based on the way in which the system evolved after the Second World War, the chapter begins in section 2 with a summary of the historical background. Section 3 describes the organization and functions of the three securities finance companies. As Japan Securities Finance Co. (JSF) is the most important of these, the analysis centers on this Tokyo-based company. Section 4 examines the system for margin trades in Japan and highlights the particular aspects of interest rate regulation and "special margin stocks." Since short sales take a special position within the market, section 5 analyzes their rules and operations. Section 6 looks at changes in margin regulation as a means for guiding the stock market and finds that the Japanese authorities pursue an active margin-requirements policy mainly in order to create psychological effects. Section 7 summarizes the major findings and concludes that even in a changing market environment the Ministry of Finance will try to preserve the political and regulatory functions of the securities finance companies.

2 THE EVOLUTION OF THE POSTWAR STOCK MARKET AND MARGIN TRANSACTIONS

The prewar Tokyo Stock Exchange (TSE) traded bonds, stocks, and, primarily, futures on individual bonds and stocks. Futures transactions represented 90 percent of overall stock trading and 50 percent of total bond trading, with short sales being an integral part of trading strategies. The major, if not the only, motive for futures transactions was speculation which in fact formed the basis of the early development of Japanese stock trading. In July 1927, the *Tokabu Daiko Kabushiki-gaisha* (Eastern Stock Agency Co. Ltd) was founded in order to serve as a settlement and stock delivery institution for the Tokyo Stock Exchange; at other local stock exchanges there were similar companies that specialized in settlement business. In 1941, the Edict on Stock Price Control (*Kabushiki Kakaku Tosei-rei*) curtailed speculation and ensured that stock prices in munitions industries climbed to and stayed at high levels. In March 1943 all local exchanges were turned into branches of the central Japan Securities Exchange in Tokyo, and the Eastern Stock Agency Co. became a full exchange member. On August 10, 1945, the exchange was closed.

2.1 The Immediate Postwar Years

On September 26, 1945, the Japanese Ministry of Finance (MOF) announced the reopening of the Tokyo Stock Exchange, but the Supreme Commander for the Allied Powers (SCAP) subsequently issued a memorandum, dated back to September 25, which prohibited the reopening of exchanges without SCAP permission, and demanded a major revision of the securities legislation. Several drafts for a new securities law presented by the Japanese finance community were rejected until, in 1948, an almost literal translation of the US Securities and Exchange Act (SEA) became the new Japanese Securities and Exchange Law (SEL, *Shoken Torihiki-Ho*). Further, the Stock Exchange Law (*Shoken Torihikisho-Ho*) was also modelled on the US law, and the Tokyo Stock Exchange rule-book after the rulebook of the Pacific Stock Exchange in San Francisco.[1]

Before the stock exchanges could be reopened in May 1949, SCAP also demanded the acceptance of the "Three Rules," which were meant to curb speculation and do away with some key prewar customs:

(a)   stock exchange members must trade listed stocks exclusively on the exchange (this is equivalent to NYSE rule 390);

(b)   all transactions at the exchange must be recorded in the order/time sequence in which they are executed; and

(c)   futures transactions are prohibited.

Furthermore, equivalent to section 10 of the US SEA, section 49 of the Japanese Securities and Exchange Law stipulates that the Minister of Finance (in the US: the Federal Reserve Board) sets the maximum loan percentage (loan value), which is the complement of the minimum margin requirement, on margin transactions; in both the SEA and the SEL the percentage was set at 55 percent. However, in order to prevent excessive speculation at a time of "democratization" of the stock market associated with the dissolution of the *Zaibatsu* and also because of the depression on the stock market, SCAP had the Japanese Ministry issue an accompanying ordinance which set this rate at zero (all cash, no borrowing), thereby ruling out margin transactions for the time being (Haga 1976).[2]

Between 1945 and 1949, stocks were traded over the counter (OTC), through securities companies which organized their trading by meeting at a certain place during certain daily hours in what was called "group trading" (*shudan torihiki*). As there was no central organization to be entrusted with settlement, the Eastern Stock Agency Co. resumed its prewar business of clearing and organization of stock delivery.

The Tokyo Stock Exchange reopened on May 16, 1949 at the index of 176.15 yen, which was the last quotation at the old exchange on March 1943. The index fell 25 percent immediately, then turned highly volatile and hit its low of 85.25 in July 1950. The Dodge Plan of 1949, a strictly deflationary package based on a balanced budget, which prohibited the issue of deficit government bonds, exacerbated the capital market slump. The securities industry blamed the new stock exchange rules and requested authorization to conduct futures transactions in their prewar form. The Japanese authorities opposed this idea, however, because they did not want to invite speculative stock market behavior in its prewar dimensions, and instead decided to initiate margin transactions.[3] As a preparation for margin trading, the Law Concerning the Loan Business[4] formally legalized the establishment of the Eastern Stock Agency Co. as one of several securities finance companies; in 1949 the company changed its name to *Nihon Shoken Kinyu-gaisha* (*Nisshokin*) or the Japan Securities Finance Co. Ltd.

2.2 The Introduction of Margin Transactions

Before section 49 of the Securities and Exchange Law was put into effect in 1951, an interim system of "loan trading" was introduced in 1950. It is this system that is responsible for most of today's special features of the Japanese margin system, because it represented a mixture of prewar Japanese practices and the new US rules. Loan trading was adopted as an *ad hoc* emergency measure for the stock market: the Bank of Japan channelled 1.7 billion yen into the stock market by providing ample credit to the securities finance companies at all stock exchanges. The securities finance company would then lend money or stocks necessary to settle margin purchases or short sales as a regular-way cash transaction (four days) directly to customers, with a broker acting merely as an intermediary between the two. There were numerous regulations on the maximum loan amount, interest rates, and "approved" stocks, which were qualified to be traded on margin (only five in the beginning and 50 in 1951[5] (Haga 1976)).

One difference between margin and futures transactions is that margin transactions are part of the cash market and all transactions must be settled "regular way"; funds or stocks borrowed for the settlement come from a third party (a securities finance company). In contrast, futures transactions are not directly a part of the cash market; market participants extend loans to each other, by accepting a margin and trusting that the counterparty will not default. In 1951 the Japanese regulatory authorities argued that margin transactions were preferable to futures, because the fact that loans came from "outside" made transactions easier to control (Haga 1976). This means that the system was introduced with the explicit intention of creating a controlled market, and the ensuing revision of the law as well as additional regulation in the form of (a) ordinances with legal character (*shorei*), (b) MOF notifications without explicit legal standing (*tsutatsu*), and (c) "self-regulation" of the securities industry, a euphemism for administrative guidance, ensured that the control remain intact over the years.[6]

In May 1951 the Ministry of Finance changed the ordinance stipulating the loan percentage and raised the rate from zero to 55 percent. The first major revision of section 49 of the Securities and Exchange Law and accompanying regulations came in 1953. It was argued that strict controls of financial markets minimized the danger of excessive speculation. The stipulation which allowed the Minister of Finance to set the maximum loan amount (55 percent) was abolished, and instead, the Minister of Finance was now authorized to require the minimum margin that must be deposited (set at 30 percent in the SEL).[7] The system saw a further change in 1955, when the Securities and Exchange Law was revised to include a passage on securities finance companies which were to be licenced by the Ministry of Finance and thus came under its control. The original nine companies were consolidated into three: Japan Securities Finance (JSF, responsible for the stock exchanges in Tokyo, Fukuoka, Niigata, and Sapporo), Osaka Securities Finance (stock exchanges in Osaka, Kyoto, Hiroshima, and, until 1967, Kobe), and Chubu Securities Finance (Nagoya Stock Exchange).

3   SECURITIES FINANCE COMPANIES

The original task laid out for the securities finance companies was to be intermediaries in the margin loan process and thereby to strengthen and nurture Japan's capital market in general. In particular, these companies were to supply funds to the stock market in order to invite "speculative supply and demand," which then would smooth out price fluctuations. It seems that the idea behind this latter aspect was that the market would become more liquid. In general, a liquid market means less danger of extended price runs in one direction and large price jumps, that is, a more continuous price formation, and fewer opportunities for cornering and other manipulation.

3.1   Operations

In the beginning, the two functions of the securities finance companies were (a) to provide loans for margin transactions, and (b) to provide so-called "general loans" with securities as collateral. When the government began to deviate from the Dodge Plan by issuing deficit bonds in 1965, the securities finance companies added bond financing to the list of their activities. As securities companies became more and more independent from external funding with increasing capital strength in the 1980s, the securities finance companies again broadened their business area to include loans to corporate and individual investors. Operations are currently divided into four major groups:

(a)   Loans for margin transactions to securities companies (*taishaku torihiki*): fund loans (for buying stock on margin) or stock loans (for selling stock short) are provided to stock exchange member firms for regular-way delivery of margin transactions. These loans are settled and cleared directly through the clearing facilities of the stock exchange, and the borrower only receives notifications and receipts. The securities finance companies thus provide a backup system for margin transactions by providing flexible supply of funds and stocks, in order to secure timely execution of trades on the exchange. Outstanding margin loans by JSF totalled 627.3 billion yen in December 1990, while outstanding stock loans amounted to 223.6 billion yen.

(b) Loans collateralized by bonds, since 1960 (*kashisai*): loans on bonds as collateral are forwarded to securities companies that are in need of temporary funds to carry inventories. Also, with the increase in underwriting and distributing activities in the 1960s, securities companies experienced increasingly wider fluctuations in their cash positions, and interim financing became indispensable. Because of the lack of a brokers' loan market, interim financing had to come from securities finance companies.

Over the years, securities companies accumulated more bonds in their vaults and found different ways of financing short-term positions such as *gensaki* transactions (repurchase agreements) and borrowing from banks or the call market (to which securities companies obtained direct access in 1985). In order to remain competitive, the securities finance companies revised the collateral system for their bond loans in 1979 by devising a system in which registered bonds can be pledged as collateral.[8] Further, in response to the introduction of short sales of bonds in 1988, a bond loan market for securities companies, banks, and insurance companies was established in May 1989. In December 1990, the outstanding balance of bond financing by JSF amounted to 702 billion yen.

(c) General loans (*ippan kashitsuke*): general loans refer to (i) loans forwarded to securities companies for use as working capital, which are secured by stocks and (to a lesser extent) bonds, and (ii) loans to individuals and corporations for, among other things, purchasing and carrying securities. Fifty percent of the outstanding loan amount of 562 billion yen in February 1991 went to individuals and corporations, and the range of collateral was expanded in 1985 when customers were allowed to use securities in the custody of securities companies or trust funds as collateral. As the securities finance companies do not know the purposes of these loans, one can only speculate that they go into additional investments in the stock market or the real estate market. In effect, these general loans circumvent a broker in margin transactions, and make the securities finance companies function more like commercial or mortgage banks.

General loans for securities companies come in four varieties: (i) a "credit line loan" (*kyokudo kashitsuke*) provides the broker with an open credit line for instant short-term borrowing; (ii) normal credits (*futsu kashitsuke*) for inventory finance and advances to customers; (iii) very short-term credits (*ukewatashi tanki kashitsuke*) on a 100 percent collateral for settlement of stock transactions, where the securities finance company makes a loan to the broker and receives the repayment directly from the exchange (this credit in effect is a particular kind of stock transaction settlement conducted via the securities finance company instead of directly through the stock exchange); and (iv) special credits (*tokubetsu kashitsuke*) for longer-term working capital up to a certain credit limit and bearing a special interest rate. All of these loans can be revolving and in fact turned into medium-term positions.

(d) Custody business: custody business comprises the settlement and clearing of securities transactions, which constituted the traditional business of securities finance companies in the prewar era. After the war, custody business was expanded, under the supervision of the Bank of Japan, to expedite the payment of interest and principal on medium-term and revolving loans which use government bonds as collateral.

Of these different kinds of operations, the financing of margin transactions constituted the major part of business until the late 1970s, when securities companies turned to other sources. With the commencement of large-scale issues of government bonds in 1975, the financing of bond dealers became more important, and the 1980s saw greater efforts to attract more individuals and to expand business relationships to smaller securities companies.

In the 1950s securities companies financed up to 80 percent of their own and their customers' margin transactions through the securities finance companies, and the increase in outstanding securities finance company credit was almost proportional to the increase in margin trading volume: outstanding loans rose from 15.3 billion yen in 1958 to 106.6 billion yen in 1972; annual trading volume in margin transactions on the Tokyo Stock Exchange rose from 5 billion shares in 1958 to 51.5 billion shares in 1972, when margin transactions represented 25.63 percent of total transactions.

Figure 16.1 shows that in 1990 JSF extended loans totaling 718.8 million yen and lent 135.9 million yen-worth of stocks to member firms of the Tokyo Stock Exchange for margin purchases. The decrease in net outstanding loans in the mid-1980s can be explained by easy monetary conditions and the increased working capital and stock inventory of securities companies during these years. Conversely, the increase in net

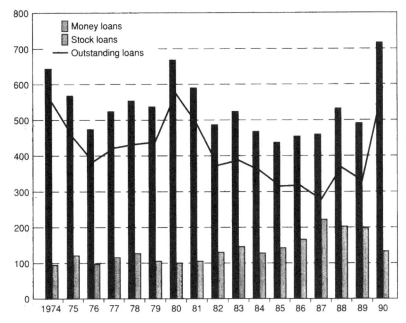

Figure 16.1 Outstanding loans for margin transactions, 1974–90

Source: *Shoken kinyu*, various issues

Table 16.1 Loans extended by Japan Securities Finance Co. (JSF) for margin transactions, 1980–90 (in billion yen)

Year	Average monthly balance of JSF money loans	Average monthly balance of margin transactions	Share of JSF loans (in %)
1980	239.0	1,449.4	16.49
1981	241.2	2,060.9	11.70
1982	184.7	1,651.8	11.18
1983	222.7	2,163.5	10.29
1984	234.7	2,511.4	9.34
1985	250.9	2,487.7	10.08
1986	328.6	4,652.1	7.06
1987	423.3	6,195.4	6.83
1988	581.2	8,616.4	6.74
1989	691.7	8,379.5	8.25
1990	943.1	5,525.5	18.04
Average	–	–	10.55

Source: *Shoken kinyu* (1991)

outstanding JSF loans in 1990 can be attributable to the stock market slump and declining profit rates of member firms after 1989. Table 16.1 confirms this movement towards a higher dependence on JSF loans in "slump" years: it shows the relationship between the average monthly yen value of margin transactions and the average monthly value of money loans forwarded by JSF between 1980 and 1990. While this ratio had been higher than 30 percent in the 1970s, it fell to as low as 6.7 percent in 1988, but again increased to 18.4 percent in 1990. The overall decrease in dependence on JSF loans to an average of 10 percent shows that the securities finance companies have lost their primary function of the direct postwar years and changed from a major to a marginal supplier of margin funds.

3.2   Refinancing

The securities finance companies finance their operations mainly through their own equity reserves and securities holdings. Another funding source is the call money market, where they use as collateral certificates issued by the stock exchange on stocks that they have lent to brokers. Because the call market was the major source of funding for the securities finance companies in 1951, and because interest rates on the call market were strictly regulated and more or less pegged to the official discount rate, interest rates in margin transactions effectively were also pegged to the discount rate. In addition to the call market, securities finance companies obtain straight interbank credit using discount bills as collateral; they also maintain lines of credit facilities with long-term credit banks, city and trust banks, as well as securities companies.

A third source of funds are direct Bank of Japan loans and loans from foundations such as the Capital Market Promotion Foundation (*Shikin-shijo Fukko Kikin*) and the Japan Joint Securities Foundation (*Nihon Kyodo Shoken Zaidan*), both of which were founded during the stock market crisis of 1965.[9] Occasionally, money also comes from the stock exchanges themselves or other security industry organizations. Since 1989, securities finance companies have also been allowed to issue commercial paper, through which 600 billion yen of working capital was raised in 1990.

3.3   Japan Securities Finance Co.

Japan Securities Finance Co. (JSF) is by far the largest and most important of the three securities finance companies: it is located in Tokyo, and it accounts for about 75 percent of all loans. As of 1990, JSF had 336 employees and a paid-up capital of 10 billion yen. Of the 6,106 shareholders, 27 percent were securities companies, 32 percent were financial institutions, 18 percent were corporations, and 23 percent were individuals. The largest single shareholders were the Tokyo Stock Exchange Members Association, with 7.5 percent; and the Industrial Bank of Japan and Nikko Securities, with 5 percent each. The president of JSF has invariably been a former Bank of Japan director, and the vice-president has customarily been a former high-ranking Ministry of Finance official. The senior managing director again is a former senior official of the Bank of Japan, while the two managing directors are typically recruited from the Industrial Bank of Japan and from JSF itself. Among the nine directors, three or four are usually the chairmen of the Big Four securities companies (Nomura, Daiwa, Nikko, Yamaichi).

JSF (1988) itself explicitly describes these close bonds: "In achieving meaningful diversification of its operations . . . JSF has maintained close contacts with the Ministry of Finance and the Bank of Japan." In addition, JSF is also directly connected with the Tokyo Stock Exchange. Apart from stockholding, the link is secured by daily close collaboration in the settling and clearing of margin transactions. In times when regulation of the market is deemed necessary, the Stock Exchange and JSF will discuss the situation; at times, before a change is initiated, securities companies are also consulted on their opinion of the market situation. A change in margin requirements is then proposed to the Ministry of Finance for appropriate response.[10]

JSF is sometimes called "the Bank of Japan of the securities industry" (Roscoe 1986). Equally justified in terms of market regulation would be a label such as "the left arm of the Ministry of Finance on the stock market," with the right arm being the president of the Tokyo Stock Exchange, who is usually a former senior Ministry of Finance official.

4 THE SYSTEM OF MARGIN TRANSACTIONS

4.1 The Regulatory Setting

The minimum initial margin rate is stipulated by the Securities and Exchange Law (30 percent or at least 300,000 yen). As there is no equivalent to the Securities and Exchange Commission in Japan, the Ministry of Finance issues additional rules in the form of ordinances. The ordinance on margin transactions prescribes current margin requirements on top of the legal minimum; changes of this ordinance are frequent. Stock exchanges set minimum maintenance margins (currently 20 percent). On top of this, securities companies have their own house rules and ask for higher minimum deposits; in 1989, for example, an initial margin of 20 to 50 million yen was required at the four leading companies. Therefore, while the legal minimum requirements are lower than in the US, the requirements change more frequently and, because they are less predictable, imply higher actual transactions costs.

In addition to the MOF ordinances, TSE business rules (*gyomu-kitei*) on margin transactions issued in 1988 (last revised in April 1990) define "approved" margin stocks which are to be announced by the exchange, based on a rather restrictive system (see subsection 4.3). Further, the "business rules" prohibit margin trading outside the exchange floor and regulate the handling of dividend payments and rights while stocks are borrowed. Securities companies cannot use stocks and funds deposited in their customers' margin accounts for proprietary trades. Moreover, the TSE "broker account regulations" (*jutaku keiyaku junsoku*) detail the exact number of stocks, maturities, and all other explicit rules for margin transactions.

Additional regulation comes in the form of credit rules set up by the securities finance companies, which can at any time require additional collateral from all or part of the securities companies on all or part of the stocks traded. They can even require the immediate repayment of loans if they see any danger of excessive margin trades, of excessive margin trading in one particular stock, of cornering or other manipulations, or if the market is severely destabilized by external or internal shocks.

Based on the system of securities finance companies, margin transactions (*shinyo-torihiki* in the broader sense) are divided into two kinds: (a) "retail" margin transactions (*shinyo-torihiki*), which refer to the creditor/debtor relationship between securities companies and their customers and which represent the system as known in the US; and (b) "wholesale" margin transactions (*taishaku torihiki*), which refer to the creditor/debtor relationship between securities companies and securities finance companies, and which are known only in Japan, being based on the existence of special refinancing institutions.

4.2   Margin Transactions

4.2.1   Retail transactions

A customer who wants to trade stocks on margin must first meet certain basic requirements in terms of capital strength, trading experience, and so on, which are checked by the broker. If cleared, the customer can then open an account at his broker by signing a "margin contract" and, as in the US, he explicitly agrees to allow the broker to lend his money and securities deposited as margin to other clients.

Margin

After placing the order, the customer must provide the initial margin of at least 300,000 yen or the amount required by the broker's "in-house" rules, by 12 noon of the business day following the day of transaction. The customer can deposit securities in lieu of cash as margin up to a certain fraction; the "cash ratio" of the margin is prescribed by the stock exchange. These securities are valued at a certain MOF-prescribed "substitute ratio" (typically 60 to 70 percent) of their market price, which for stocks is the closing price of the day before the order was placed.[11] The substitute ratio for stocks can be changed as a means of regulating the market (see subsection 6.1). If the value of the deposited margin drops below 20 percent of traded value, the broker asks for a maintenance margin (due by 12 noon on the following business day). Special requirements can be imposed on individual stocks, if there is "excessive" demand for one particular stock. For example, the record high was marked by Sumitomo Metal Mining, on which a margin deposit of 80 percent was required from 1988 to 1990.

Settlement

There are two ways of settling margin positions. First, positions are cleared by an opposite offsetting trade: the buyer sells stocks at a later point and uses the money to repay his margin, while the short seller buys stocks which he uses to repay his stock loan. Second, on rare occasions, the customer clears his obligations by physical delivery: if he bought on margin, he repays his loan in cash and takes home the actual stock; if he sold stocks short, he buys the stocks later and delivers them to the buyer and receives the actual money for his sale.

Maturities

Usually, when stock prices have moved in the desired direction, customers clear margin positions by opening opposite positions; otherwise, positions are cleared before losses become too large. As a leftover from prewar Japanese trading practices, however, Japan has maximum maturities of three or six months.[12] The customer has to choose either maximum when placing his order and, once the choice is made, he cannot change it afterwards; if the customer does not close out his position before maturity, the balance is settled on maturity by the broker, even if stock prices are adverse for the customer at the time. The official explanation for this system is "investor protection" (by curbing long-term speculation); given that speculation is rarely conducted on a long-term basis, a further motive behind adhering to the fixed maturities could be additional commission to be raised by brokers: an investor who wants to hold a position longer than maturity will, after settling the original position, fees, and commissions and reopening an identical new position, be charged roundtrip commissions.

There is a second twist to the system: the maturity day may offer ample profit opportunities if brokers, who know exactly when positions mature and how they must be cleared, can somehow predict the movement of stock prices on that day. Even though brokers are required not to make public the exact dates and positions of their customers, estimating margin settlements and their influence on the index based on an observation of weekly movements in open margin interest is relatively easy.

Rights and dividends

If dividends on stocks are paid out or rights granted during the loan period, the disbursements belong to the original stockowner. In order to avoid the situation where short sellers gain and margin buyers lose for technical reasons, the stock exchange determines the ex-dividend value or the ex-right value of the stock, which is then charged to the seller and transferred to the buyer. The payments are made through the broker, who also collects the dividend payments from the seller and transfers them to the buyer.

Fees

Brokers charge their customers a fixed fee on each open position, as prescribed by the stock exchange. For each month a position is kept, the broker charges 15 *sen* (0.15 yen)[13] per share; if shares are not traded in round lots, each share commands a fee of 100 yen, which makes trading in odd lots prohibitively expensive. The minimum charge per month and position is 100 yen, and the maximum charge is 1,000 yen.

Commissions on transactions, which must be regular-way, are regulated by the stock exchange. In 1991, there were ten rates, ranging from 1.15 percent for transactions up to 1 million yen to 0.075 percent for transactions of over 1 billion yen.

4.2.2 Wholesale transactions

The "wholesale" margin transactions follow similar rules. A stock exchange member firm calculates its daily net balance of margin buys and sales for each issue of the trading day and applies for a loan at JSF (the same mechanism applies to the other two securities finance companies). JSF

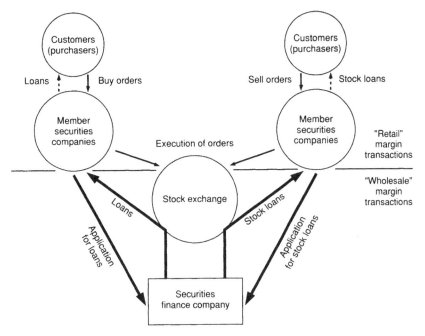

Figure 16.2 The mechanics of a securities finance loan

Source: based on *Introducing Japan Securities Finance Co., Ltd* (Tokyo, 1988)

delivers funds or equities directly to the clearing section of the stock exchange and in turn receives securities or payments from the exchange (see figure 16.2). The member is notified of its outstanding balance by the stock exchange, and the net outstanding loan of each securities company is then calculated on the basis of daily market closing prices. When a broker closes out a position financed through JSF, JSF delivers the money or equity for the reverse trade to the exchange on behalf of the securities company. The exchange in turn transfers it to the counterparty.

JSF has an aggregate "credit ceiling" which limits the total value of collateral and loans. Within this ceiling, JSF allots an individual credit line to each member firm, and if this line is exceeded, the firm must pledge additional collateral as penalty.[14]

Rates of margin requirement are the same as for retail margin transactions. The margin is marked-to-market daily and may be posted in "substitute collateral securities" in lieu of cash; substitutes must be "refilled" when they lose value, even if the margin position as a whole does not lose. The securities companies must deposit the margin by 12 noon on the day the loan is advanced. JSF can freely lend the collateral to other securities companies. If a securities company defaults on repayments or does not meet maintenance calls, JSF can liquidate the margin without warning.

The rights on the stocks are handled in the same way as with retail positions. In addition to interest, securities companies also have to pay a fee to the securities finance company, which again is 15 *sen* (0.15 yen) for each share of stock borrowed.

4.3   Margin Stocks and "Special Stocks"

The Tokyo Stock Exchange, in its business rules, specifies the stocks that are approved for margin trading (the other stock exchanges follow the same procedure, but the numbers of specified stocks differ). In principle, all 1,191 stocks of the first section of the Tokyo Stock Exchange can be traded on margin in "retail" margin trades; these stocks are referred to as "*shinyo*-issues." Through the revision of the system in December 1991, the number of *shinyo*-issues was expanded to about 150 stocks traded in the second section of the Tokyo Stock Exchange as well, subject to certain requirements. These requirements include the minimum number of shares outstanding (20 million), the distribution of stock ownership (2,000 persons or more, depending on the number of shares outstanding), and the prospects for the continued listing of the stock in the medium term. In addition, a *shinyo*-issue must also be "suitable for margin transactions, judged upon trading volume and past business records" by the Tokyo Stock Exchange in consultation with JSF. OTC stocks cannot be traded on margin.

Among the 1,300 *shinyo*-issues, there is a subset of stocks that can be borrowed from or loaned to the securities companies. These are the "wholesale" or "*taishaku*" issues which are also determined on the basis of the number of stocks outstanding (at least 40 million), the distribution of stock ownership (at least 3,200 persons), and the judgement as to whether or not they are "suitable" to be lent out by JSF. If a certain stock is picked as a margin stock and afterwards loses its eligibility, it is "delisted" as a margin stock. Following the announcement of such a "downgrading," however, the stock can still be traded on margin for one year. It is downgraded permanently only if there is no improvement in its performance during that period (Shizuka 1991).[15]

This rather complicated system of picking stocks reflects a greater difference in the nature of listed stocks between the Tokyo Stock Exchange and the NYSE. While all stocks listed at NYSE presumably possess sufficient liquidity, not all listed stocks in Tokyo are actively traded. Moreover, the liquidity of the market in Japan is reduced by the high degree of intercompany cross-holding of stocks. In order to facilitate margin transactions in Tokyo, it becomes important to pick the right stocks, although this further increases the discrepancy between more liquid and less liquid stocks.

The number of "margin stocks" has continuously increased (table 16.2). The number of loanable stocks, which can be borrowed at JSF for retail margin transactions, climbed from 466 issues in 1984 to 848 issues in December 1991. Just as not all stocks are approved for margin trading, not all stocks can be deposited as margin cash substitutes. However, the

Table 16.2   Loanable and substitute stock issues of the Japan Securities Finance Co. in the Tokyo market, 1984–91

Year/month	Loanable stocks (taishaku *issues*)	Substitute stocks
1984/7	466	805
1984/10	484	806
1984/12	493	
1985/8	523	807
1985/9		887
1985/12		978
1986/3	522	
1986/4	521	977
1986/8	551	
1986/11		1,021
1986/12	550	1,020
1987/6		1,032
1987/8	578	
1987/9	577	1,030
1988/4	576	1,029
1988/8	625	
1988/9		1,033
1989/6	624	1,032
1989/8	623	
1989/9	668	1,035
1990/3	667	1,034
1990/9	735	1,045
1990/12	734	1,044
1991/4	733	1,043
1991/12	848	1,069

Source: *Shoken kinyu* (1991/7: 45), JSF

Table 16.3 Characteristics of special stocks in Tokyo, 1990

Special stock	Highest stock price in December 1990	Lowest stock price in December 1990	Average daily trading volume in December 1990 (in 1,000 shares)	Estimated beta (1988)	PER (highest over the last 2 years)	PER (lowest over the last 2 years)
Heiwa Real Estate	1,120	970	212	1.41	162	42
Toray Industries	648	540	1,611	1.29	80	26
Asahi Chemical Industries	770	650	1,224	0.97	65	23
Nippon Oil	1,000	812	1,600	0.68	176	60
Sumitomo Electric	1,420	1,220	1,555	1.11	83	37
NEC	1,370	1,220	1,546	0.84	65	28
Matsushita Electric Industrial	1,700	1,570	1,620	0.78	47	21
Mitsubishi Heavy	735	615	7,451	1.21	82	26
Toyota Motor	1,840	1,660	1,411	0.50	28	16
Mitsui & Co.	835	637	4,749	1.36	109	39
Tokio Marine and Fire Insurance	1,410	1,220	3,245	1.92	86	38
Nippon Yusen KK	621	475	1,857	1.42	292	98
Average	–	–	–	1.124	106.2	37.7
Total	–	–	28,081	–	–	–

Source: Nikkei kabushiki toshi, 1991; Nikkei kaisha joho, 1991/III

range of substitute stocks (*daiyo meigara*) has also been broadened over the years. In December 1991, 1,069 issues traded in the first section of the Tokyo Stock Exchange could be deposited as margin in lieu of cash (table 16.2).

Between the revisions of the system in 1978 and 1991, there was a third subgroup of margin stocks, the so-called "designated" or "special issues" (*shitei meigara*). The Tokyo Stock Exchange, together with the JSF, designated 12 such special stocks, Osaka picked 20 "specials," and Nagoya 17. When traded on margin, these stocks were subject to special rules: customers could choose the maturity of either three or six months (as now possible for all margin stocks), the interest paid to the lender was twice as high as with other margin stocks, and the fees were only 60 percent of the regular fees. "Special issues" were designated mainly on the basis of trading volume, and the group represented the top blue chips of the country. Over the years, some stocks have been replaced by newcomers. Table 16.3 summarizes the average daily trading volume, the highest and lowest price quotations in December 1990, the estimated beta values as of 1988, and the highest and lowest PER values between 1988 and 1990 of the special issues traded on the Tokyo Stock Exchange in 1990.

The idea behind the "special stock" system was to pick a small number of stocks which supposedly reflected the market, and to increase the liquidity of these stocks by offering higher interest rates and lower fees. In reality, however, these stocks were traded as if they had been "articles on sale in a supermarket" (Nihon Keizai Shinbunsha 1991): not only was there increased speculation on these special issues, but there was a sharp drop in trading volume if there was a perception that the stock might be "delisted" as a special issue (or a sharp increase if someone wanted to prop it up). At the same time, likely candidates to be nominated experienced a buying spree. Table 16.4 shows that the average daily trading volume of the TSE special stocks in December 1990 was 28 million shares, which at the time represented 6.6 percent of total average daily volume. The average beta of these stocks was 1.124, while the average PER of 58.4 is very close to the average PER of 55.2 between 1989 and 1990.[16]

The Tokyo Stock Exchange and JSF had two aims with the reform of 1991, which abolished the special stock system and substantially increased the number of margin stocks: (a) to attract more individual investors, and (b) to increase the fairness of the pricing process. Both aims reflect the perception that the system had been dominated by institutional investors and that the pricing process had been influenced by various non-market factors. At the same time, the reform implemented stricter guidelines for so-called "attention issues" (*chui-meigara*), which the Tokyo Stock

Table 16.4 Interest rates and margin requirements, 1983–91 (in percent p.a.)

Effective date	"Wholesale" (taishaku) rates (and official discount rate)	"Retail" (shinyo) interest rates	Interest on collateral money[a]	Margin requirements	Substitute ratio for margin stocks
early 1983	8.00 (5.5)	8.75	4.25	50	70
1983/10/24	7.50 (5.0)	8.25	3.75		
1984/3/24				60	
1984/5/19				50	
1985/1/17				60	
1985/11/6				50 c	
1986/1/31	7.00 (4.5)	7.75	3.25		
1986/3/11	6.50 (4.0)	7.25	2.75		
1986/3/13				60	
1986/3/24					60
1986/4/22	6.00 (3.5)	6.75	2.25		
1986/7/16					50
1986/10/22					60
1986/11/4	5.50 (3.0)	6.25	1.75		
1987/2/20					50
1987/2/24	5.00 (2.5)	5.75	1.25		

Date				70 (20% in cash)	
1987/2/27				70 (20% in cash)	
1987/4/15					70
1987/7/9				70	
1987/7/22					60
1987/10/15					70
1987/10/21				50	
1988/3/17				60	
1988/6/3				70	
1989/2/23					60
1989/6/1	5.75 (3.25)	6.50	2.00		
1989/6/30				60	
1989/10/13	6.25 (3.75)	7.00	2.50		
1989/12/6					50
1989/12/26	6.75 (4.25)	7.50	3.00		
1990/1/11					60
1990/2/21				50	
1990/2/27				40	70
1990/3/22	7.75 (5.25)	8.50	4.00		
1990/8/31	8.50 (6.00)	9.25	4.75		
1990/9/6				30	
1990/10/5					80
1990/12/26	8.70	9.45	4.95		
1991/7/16	8.15 (5.5)	8.90	4.40		

[a] The interest rate paid on "special stocks" is higher by 1.75 percent.

Source: Shoken kinyu (1991/7).

Exchange identifies when they have a very large, one-sided outstanding balance which might indicate the danger of market cornering.[17] Since December 1991, the daily announcement of margin conditions especially marks "attention issues" for which three ratios are reported: (a) outstanding short sales (open short interest) to total number of listed shares; (b) open long interest to total number of listed shares, and (c) open short to open long interest.[18]

4.4   Interest Rates

Someone who borrows money (in order to buy stocks on margin) must pay interest on the loan. Conversely, someone who lends money, such as the short seller, receives interest payment. In Japan, the TSE "Business Rules Regarding Margin Trades" dictate that brokers must charge borrowing customers, and pay to lending customers, rates prescribed by the Tokyo Stock Exchange. In effect, these interest rates stipulated by the Tokyo Stock Exchange were pegged to the official discount rate until 1990.

4.4.1   **Interest on money borrowed**

Fees and interest on borrowed money are charged *per diem* and are called *hibu* (daily rates, now expressed in percent per annum). The securities finance company forwards a loan to a broker at the loan (*taishaku*) rate; until 1990, the spread between the discount rate and loan rate was set at 2.5 percent. The broker then lends the money to a customer and charges this loan rate plus a fixed percentage, set at 0.75 percent. For example, in September 1990, when the official discount rate was at 6 percent, a margin buyer had to pay 9.25 percent on his margin loan (see table 16.4). Obviously, under this fixed interest system, large brokers who do not rely on securities finance companies for financing can earn an easy spread of more than 3 percent.

As from October 1, 1990, the interest rate structure was partially deregulated. Under the new system, margin rates are adjusted weekly on the basis of the daily unsecured call rate, the one-month Euroyen rate, and the two-month bill discount rate. The simple weekly average of these three rates is adjusted by their average variance over the preceding five weeks, to yield the new benchmark rate, which is to be used in place of the discount rate. That is, the broker has to pay this base rate plus 2.5 percent to the securities finance company, and the customer has to pay this base rate plus 3.25 percent to the broker. The base rate is calculated every Monday, and if there is a change of more than 0.5 percent from the preceding week, the base rate is changed, effective from the following Tuesday.

The adoption of this complicated "base rate" system, which is partially deregulated and partially regulated, may represent a general aversion of the stock exchanges to allowing price-based competition, allegedly in order to protect individual investors and, possibly, smaller securities companies.

4.4.2 Interest on stocks borrowed

Typically, the short seller pays a fee for borrowing stocks, but at the same time receives interest on the money he deposits. Because the rate of interest to be paid to the short is fixed to the base rate minus 1.25 percent, the system in effect boosts the spread earned by brokers who internally finance their customers, from some 3 percent to 4.5 percent.

However, it is not necessarily the case that the short seller collects interest on his money. In the US, when a short seller wants to borrow a particular stock that is under high demand, he might be willing to deposit his collateral without interest if only he can get hold of the stock, that is, he deposits his money "flat." In extreme cases, he might even be willing to borrow his stock by paying a "premium." This price mechanism helps to regulate demand and supply for a particular stock.

In Japan, the demand of short sellers for a particular stock is regulated by adverse daily rates (*gyaku-hibu* or *shinakashi-ryo*). On a particular day and for a particular stock, if there are more shares borrowed than deposited at the securities finance company, the securities finance company announces a "stock squeeze" and tries to procure the net balance of demanded shares from outside lenders. It then charges a "stock lending fee" to brokers that have borrowed the stock, the amount of which is decided upon by the securities finance companies and the stock exchanges on a case-by-case basis.[19]

This system has two special features. First, the "adverse daily rate" is not charged on the excess part of stock borrowing orders only, but on all short sale positions. Because the fee can be high and stocks are usually borrowed for positions intended to be kept longer than four days (the regular-way settlement period), the price effect is considerable and likely to drive short sellers out of the market. In a situation where sell orders exceed buy orders for reasons other than short-term noise (in which case balancing out the noise would be positive), the system could erect an artificial barrier to long-term price adjustments.

Second, in addition to discretion in determining the "stock lending fee," the securities finance company may or may not charge the fee at all. The stock lending fee is partly based on how much the finance company must pay for the additional shares it borrows itself. If it can borrow these shares without paying the "adverse interest rate," it may not charge the interest rate to the brokers either. Thus, brokers have three options: (a) they accept the "stock lending fee" as well as the risk that some customers default on payments; (b) they lend the required stock out of their own inventory to the securities finance company without charging the "stock lending fee;" or else (c) they assume margin buy positions in that particular stock themselves, thereby balancing out the excess part of short sales and in effect keeping the price for the stock in question at its level. For the investor, this means uncertainty as to whether additional interest rate will be charged, that is, as to how high transactions cost will be.[20]

5 SHORT SALES

The preceding analysis of the Japanese margin transactions system in principle applies to both margin purchases and short sales. Implicit in all regulations, however, is that short sales in practice follow their own set of rules and realities. Special rules on short sales exist, because short sales are often regarded as a cause of excessive speculation.

This simple assertion that short sales are a cause of disruptive speculation, however, is subject to three qualifications. First, if short sales represent speculation, so do margin purchases, as they are both based on the expectation that prices will change considerably in the near future, either down or up. It is simply that margin purchases are considered less objectionable, because rising stock prices are considered more desirable. Second, a short sale is only one form of credit mechanism, as it is a "debt contract in goods, services, or securities instead of money" (Meeker 1932b). If buying on margin is gambling, so is buying a house on mortgage. Third, short sales have the positive effect of serving as a buffer in falling markets, because short sales must be settled by reverse purchases at some point. It could be argued that a market which does not allow for short sales is geared to climb, as it lacks a balance between upward and downward speculation; at the same time, such a market is not cushioned if a fall sets in. This point has been made for Japan in the 1980s (Roscoe 1986), and is further confirmed by the developments of the early 1990s.

The legal framework of short sales in Japan is not significantly different from the US system. Section 133(1) of the Securities and Exchange Law prohibits short sales where the seller does not own or borrow. Section 133(2) prohibits a single market participant from outbidding his own margin orders: if the price of a stock increases after one has placed a short sell order, one may not quote a higher sell order; conversely, one may not place a lower margin buy order, if prices move downwards after one has placed an initial buy order.

The MOF ordinance on short sales, however, exempts futures and options from the short sale restriction.[21] Other than in connection with derivatives arbitrage, section 1(1) of the ordinance prohibits any short sale if the seller does not have or cannot provide the securities immediately after the transaction. Section 1(2) is the uptick rule: no short sale can be conducted at a price lower than the preceding trading price (zero ticks are not mentioned); as in the US before 1938, short sales in odd lots are exempted from this rule.[22] Following a NYSE rule of 1931, each order must be marked as to whether it is "long" or "short." This regulation, however, is a dead letter in Japan, because in the early years the approved margin stocks were traded in a single price auction (*gekitaku*, stepwise abolished until 1982) at the opening and the closing of the market. This trading method allegedly made the marking of margin orders impossible (Miki 1965);[23] until today, traders have not made it a habit to mark their margin orders. This explains why the Tokyo Stock Exchange has no detailed data on the total number of short sales and reports only the balance of short interest, that is, the total of all shares sold and not yet covered as of a given date.

In principle, these regulations allow three major kinds of short sales: (a) short sales "against the box" (that is, inventory) by securities companies or corporations for hedging inventory or short-term funding; (b) short sales by customers who borrow stocks from their brokers; and (c) short sales by securities companies on proprietary accounts with stocks borrowed from institutional investors or a securities finance company. In practice, the second and the third types of short sales are highly restricted either by rules or by the mechanics of the stock market.

Short sales "against the box" by institutions are divided into "hedging sales" (*tsunagi-uri*, lit.: "connected sales") and "finance crossing" (*kinyu kurosu*). In a hedging sale, a company hedges its inventory by selling stocks short when it owns them. In a "finance cross," a company, for short-term funding, sells short stocks that it owns and at the same time buys these stocks on margin. It thus keeps the difference between the actual price and the margin requirement (usually some 70 percent) until the positions mature, usually in six months. In fact, such a transaction represents funding with stocks as collateral, and it is used mainly in periods of tight money or when access to bank credit is otherwise limited. Both of these transactions are more expensive than similar instruments such as options, futures, warrants, or straight loans. Most of the short interest on the accounts of securities companies is attributable to "hedging sales" (figure 16.3).

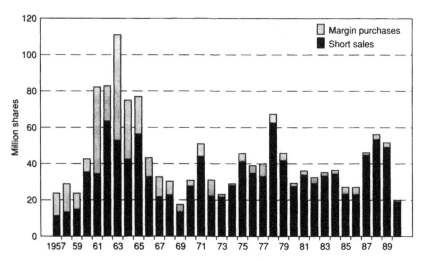

Figure 16.3   Short sales and margin purchases in proprietary accounts of securities firms*

*   Open interest at end of the year; in million shares.

Source: TSE, *Annual Securities Statistics* (1990)

As for customers' short sales conducted through brokers, there are only a few regulations. The only reason why customers should not be active shorts, other than the propensity of individual investors to bet on an upward rather than on a downward market, is that, because of the fixed interest rate structure, there is a large margin between the borrowing and the lending rate. This is confirmed by figure 16.4, which shows that a large imbalance exists between outstanding margin purchases and short sales by customers, most of whom are individuals.

Institutional investors face the same cost structure as individual investors when selling short. Moreover, they are limited by the extensive cross-holdings of stocks. Although companies and institutional investors can earn profits by lending equities they hold in their vaults, they rarely do so in Japan because their stockholding is based on some other motive. In fact, an estimated 50–60 percent of all outstanding equity is held by "friendly" companies, and in order to prove their loyalty, companies want to show that the stocks (which are not endorsed) are registered in their names. Brokers keep shares on behalf of their customers and report changes of ownership to the issuing company shortly before dividend payouts. As companies customarily pay dividends to the names on their records in March and September, stockholding records are updated in these two months also. If companies lend their stocks to other companies

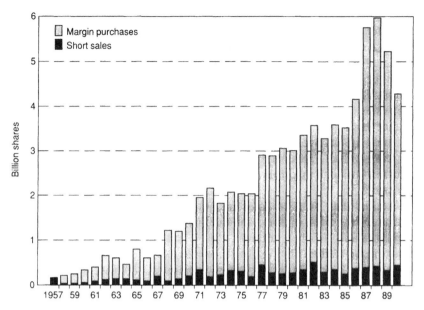

Figure 16.4 Short sales and margin purchases in the customers' account*

* Open interest at the end of the year; in billion shares.

Source: TSE, *Annual Securities Statistics* (1990)

or institutions, they make sure that the loaned stocks are returned to them by early March and September. On top of these company cross-holdings, about 30–40 percent of all stocks are held by individuals and foreigners, so that only about 10 percent of all outstanding stocks can be lent freely.

Securities companies are prohibited from selling stocks short on proprietary accounts, unless they own the stocks themselves. This rule is part of the "self-regulation" of the Association of Securities Dealers in Japan, which has become tighter over the years: while proprietary trading of securities companies was very active in the 1950s, current directives restrict most of these activities. Because the Association has a legal obligation to follow the advice of the Ministry of Finance, "self-regulation" is a form of administrative guidance. The official reason for prohibiting short sales of stocks is the fear that, if securities companies become active short sellers, it will destabilize prices. Consistently, the rule also states that for the purpose of short selling, securities companies can lend their stocks only to their own customers or, if required, to a securities finance company.

Foreign securities companies can get around this regulation by booking their transactions overseas, where they can also borrow stocks from institutional investors. As a way of circumventing MOF regulation, Japanese companies have also tried to transfer the lending business abroad. Nomura Securities and Nissay (*Nihon Seimei*), a leading life insurance company, headed this movement by establishing a joint venture in Hong Kong for the sole purpose of stock lending. When other securities companies began to work on similar arrangements, the Ministry of Finance made the five leading insurance companies "agree" (a) not to lend their stocks overseas, and (b) if at all, to lend to a securities finance company only.[24] This "agreement" ensures that almost all borrowing from institutional investors is channelled through the securities finance companies.

Detailed data on short sales are not available, although JSF publishes total monthly sales volume, and the Tokyo Stock Exchange reports the weekly balance of short interest, that is, short positions not yet covered by a reverse trade at the end of the week. Only after the October crash 1987 did the Tokyo Stock Exchange require the 72 "integrated securities companies" (which hold a licence for all four kinds of securities business: dealing, broking, underwriting, and distribution) to report the actual number of total short sales and margin purchases, as opposed to outstanding balances, for individuals and on proprietary accounts in their annual reports (table 16.5). Although the figures exclude the activities of other securities companies, they are estimated to represent as much as two-thirds of total margin volume.

Table 16.5 shows that, in general, individuals trade much more heavily on margin than securities companies do (this confirms figures 16.3 and 16.4). As opposed to the relation between the open interest of margin purchases and sales as shown in figure 16.3, however, the difference between the number of total margin purchases and short sales by individuals is rather small. This suggests that short sales tend to be conducted on a short-term basis and therefore do not appear in the open interest. At the same time, table 16.5 supports the impression created in figure 16.4: securities companies, if they trade on margin, primarily sell short.

One way of evaluating the importance of short selling is to compute the ratio of average outstanding short interest to average daily trading volume. In contrast to the US ratio of about 210 percent in the mid-1980s, the Japanese figures are significantly lower: the ratio was 104 percent in 1990, 48 percent in 1989, and 49.3 percent in 1988. Because the ratio of 150–200 percent is usually considered the upper limit of the "safe range," the authorities in Japan should be able to further relax restrictions on short sales without worrying about causing "excessive" speculation.

Table 16.5 Actual number of short sales and margin purchases reported by 72 integrated securities companies, 1988–1990 (in million shares)

Year	Individuals short sales	Individuals margin purchases	Securities companies proprietary short sales	Securities companies proprietary margin purchases	Total short selling transactions	Total margin purchase transactions
1988	26,328.9	28,044.2	3,000.1	56.4	29,329.00	28,100.60
1989	15,565.9	18,037.9	2,242.3	100.5	17,808.20	18,138.40
1990	10,660.3	12,627.6	1,025.0	57.8	11,685.30	12,685.40

Source: Tokyo Stock Exchange

6 CHANGES IN MARGIN REQUIREMENTS AND MARKET REGULATION

In the US, the Fed. has not pursued an active margin requirement policy since 1974, and even between 1933 and 1974 there had been a change, on average, about every 18 months only. In Japan, on the other hand, the political attitude of the financial authorities and the fixed interest rate structure resulted in the active use of changes in margin requirements as a policy tool. Because stock prices tend to move inversely with interest rates, in a period of low interest rates and a booming stock market low margin rates will invite margin purchases. Once the price mechanism is not functioning well in the margin loan market, it has to be replaced by quantitative controls.[25] It was for this reason that other instruments of regulation, such as the "adverse interest rate," were institutionalized.

6.1 The Mechanisms of Regulation

The Japanese authorities have three major tools to influence margin transactions: (a) a change in the minimum margin requirement; (b) a change in the discount ratio at which securities are evaluated when deposited as margin collateral; and (c) a change in the allowable proportion of "securities substitutes" in the margin (that is, the cash requirement for the margin). In addition, securities finance companies can change the terms and conditions of their loans by setting special credit ceilings for individual securities companies, requiring increased collateral, or charging an interest penalty on the excess balance. If margin transactions are concentrated on one particular stock, the stock exchanges and the securities finance companies can jointly decide to increase individual margin requirements, "apply stricter rules" on loan applications for the stock, or both. Table 16.4 shows changes in interest rates, margin requirements, and collateral substitute values between 1983 and 1991. Between March 1970 and March 1980, there were as many as 37 such changes (on average, once every three months).

In a situation where the market looks overheated and margin purchases seem "excessive," the Tokyo Stock Exchange and JSF would consult with each other on the situation and typically decide either to raise margins or to reduce the discount ratio. If they raise the margin requirement, investors must deposit more collateral relative to the total value of their position; if they reduce the discount ratio, investors need to deposit either additional securities or additional money. The constraining effects on the investor's equity ratio can be supplemented by an increase in the minimum cash deposit rate. Only rarely are these measures imposed simultaneously; rather, there seems to be a tendency to change margin requirements first and let changes in collateral conditions follow suit.

Conversely, in a situation where the market falls and is considered to need some cushioning, the Tokyo Stock Exchange and JSF could decide to lower margin requirements and increase the value of securities deposited as collateral. The intended effect is that investors need less money to assume larger positions, and thus may add "additional demand" to the market. It is these measures that attract most attention, as they are usually accompanied by a personal announcement by the Minister of Finance.

6.2   Two Examples: October 1987 and October 1990

The Tokyo Stock Exchange experienced its largest gains on October 2, 1990 (a one-day increase of 9.54 percent for TOPIX and 9.3 percent for Nikkei-225) and on October 21, 1987 (9.39 percent and 13.2 percent, respectively). Both these record increases were accompanied, if not triggered, by changes in margin requirements.

In the wake of "Black Monday," the TOPIX fell by 14.62 percent on Tuesday, October 20, 1987. It climbed 9.54 percent the following day, and Tokyo was the fastest stock exchange in the world to recover. In the afternoon of Tuesday, October 20, the Minister of Finance made an announcemcent that margin requirements were being lowered from 70 percent to 50 percent, while the collateral securities ratio was increased from 60 percent to 70 percent. At the time, margin transactions accounted for about 20 percent of total trading volume, and as the announcement coincided with the first positive news from New York, individual investors rushed back to the market and bought on margin: Next to the difference in cash flow that investors faced after the changes in margin rules, the announcement also had a psychological effect and contributed to the positive market mood.[26]

The situation was different in October 1990. In contrast to the 1987 crash, which occurred in a "boom" period, the extended slump that began in early 1990 had made many investors bearish by the 1990 crash. The so-called "Iraq shock" had exacerbated the situation, which was then topped by the "BIS shock" in September 1990, when banks had to report their balance sheets. In order to meet the BIS capital adequacy standards, the leading banks had issued large sums of subordinated debt; the tumbling bond market took the stock market with it. In the afternoon of October 1, shortly before the report deadline, the Minister of Finance announced three measures explicitly designed to rescue the stock market:

(a) a cut in futures activities, which had become the scapegoat for the falling market; (b) an increase in the ceiling of stock investments through *tokkin* funds (discretionary trust fund accounts, typically invested in the stock market) for life insurance companies; and (c) a rise in the collateral securities ratio in margin transactions.

These measures were primarily intended to break the vicious circle in attitude. Recalling the positive effect of changes in the margin system in 1987, the Ministry wanted to signal its support to the stock market by increasing the margin collateral ratio from 70 percent to 80 percent. This was a significant measure because the upper limit of this ratio is set at 70 percent in an MOF ordinance. The action had the intended effect: the market went for its record surge on October 2.

The effect, however, was only short-lived: the TOPIX lost 20.53 and the Nikkei-225 almost 571.2 points on October 4. Rather than supporting an upward trend, margin purchases decreased while the short interest increased, and most of these positions were connected to arbitrage strategies by institutional investors. The major difference from the 1987 crash was that individual investors believed in the Ministry of Finance measure only briefly, but soon retreated from the market. Propping up the market through a change in margin regulation had proved unsuccessful when the market was facing a real slump.

6.3   The Effects of Margin Regulation

In the 1930s, changes in margin requirements were picked as a means for selective credit control in the US with the primary goals of (a) preventing diversion of the nation's resources from productive commercial to speculative stock market activities (as nowadays discussed in regard to derivatives), and (b) inhibiting stock price fluctuations that stem from speculation on credit; investor protection was seen as a positive side-effect. However, changes in margin rules for these aims are now dismissed as ineffective because of the fungibility of credit and the danger of undesired distorting effects. Both of these can also be observed in Japan: on the one hand, banks and non-banks increasingly try to lure customers away from brokers by offering security credit, and on the other hand, changes in margin requirements have typically led to short-term price runs with a rather obvious lack of substance.

Research in the US on margin policies has not produced unanimous results.[27] One issue that most analyses agree upon, however, is that changes in margin requirements work by decreasing or increasing the volume of margin credit; that is, there is an indirect volume effect. However, given the low level of margin credit in the US (below 1.5

percent of the market value of NYSE listed stocks), the effect of such changes can hardly be of major importance.[28]

Further, there is evidence of the existence of an announcement effect (Largey and West 1973; Eckhardt and Rogoff 1976). Grube, Joy and Panton (1979) show that the market responds to the announcement of a change rather than to its actual implementation, and they also observe an asymmetry in response: the lowering of margin requirements has a clear, but very short-term (one day) information effect and no lag effect, while increases in requirements have no significant effect at all. Even in the absence of statistical testing, such a tendency can be observed in Japan, too.

When it comes to the effects on prices, findings get more controversial. Cohen (1966) and Largey and West (1973) show that there is no, or only a "fairly trivial," effect of changes in margin requirements on the stock price level. Also, the effects of margin requirements on volatility seem to be unclear. The most exhaustive analysis in this regard by Hsieh and Miller (1990) finds no convincing evidence that changes in margin requirements affect volatility.

In sum, the best we can say is that effects, direct or indirect, seem to be rather insignificant. Why, then, would the Japanese financial authorities pursue such an active margin policy? Assuming that there is some general truth in the research on the US market,[29] the Ministry of Finance, the Tokyo Stock Exchange, and JSF either have a different perception of the effectiveness of their policies, or they use changes in margin rules explicitly for psychological reasons, knowing that real effects are unlikely to be strong. This latter possibility is supported by the way in which margin requirement decreases are announced by the Minister of Finance himself, possibly on television, while decreases appear on page 19 of the newspaper only. This indicates that decreases in margin requirements are explicitly aimed at utilizing the positive short-term psychological announcement effect.

The mechanism works through influencing investor expectations: the signal that the Ministry of Finance is willing to support the stock market is meant to invite investors to bet on a market upswing. However, as became obvious in 1990, this effect diminishes with the severity of the slump. In the wake of the stock scandal of 1991 and the ensuing public distrust of the Ministry and its ways of market regulation, the potential influence of administrative guidance was further undermined. What remains are a restrictive margin transactions system and an increasing trend for investors to circumvent it by borrowing from banks, and for brokers by replacing a simple short sale with more complicated investment strategies.

7 SUMMARY AND CONCLUSIONS

Margin transactions account for about 20 percent of total one-way trading volume at the Tokyo Stock Exchange. They are structured in a two-tiered system, where (a) brokers execute their customers' margin orders and service their transactions (in terms of lending money or stocks and arranging dividend payment transfers and so on), and (b) brokers borrow securities needed for these transactions from a securities finance company. There are three such companies, among which the Tokyo-based Japan Securities Finance Co. is the most important. Its direct connections to the Tokyo Stock Exchange and the regulatory authorities are reflected in the composition of its board of directors which has former Bank of Japan and Ministry of Finance officials at its top and current chairmen of leading securities companies and banks at director level.

In the 1950s and 1960s, securities finance companies financed more than two-thirds of all margin transactions, which on average accounted for more than 20 percent of trading volume. By the late 1980s, outstanding margin loans by JSF had decreased to some 10 percent of all margin transactions, and its role had shifted from the major to a marginal supplier of funds. The major portion of margin transactions are on customers' accounts, mostly in the form of margin purchases by individuals, while securities companies tend to be net short sellers, if at a low volume.

Short sales are restricted by regulations which prevent securities companies from borrowing stocks for short selling on proprietary accounts, and by cross-stockholdings which restrict corporations and institutional investors from freely lending stock; the effects are compounded by a regulation that financial institutions can lend stocks to securities finance companies only. This cuts the volume of short sales significantly and relegates the securities finance companies to a dominant position in arranging stock loans to institutions.

Despite the quantitative changes, the system still bears the signs of the period of rapid growth in fixing interest rates. Rather than through the price mechanism, margin transactions are regulated through changes in margin requirements and margin securities evaluation. While an increase in margin requirements rarely hits the headlines, decreases, which are explicitly aimed at "helping the market out" in times of crisis, are announced by the Finance Minister himself and serve as a substitute for market mechanisms, such as offsetting trades for short sales, to cushion steep falls in the market.

In the process of guiding the market, JSF (like the other two securities finance companies) is merely an institution that performs the functions ascribed to it, rather than being a major player in its own right. The

Tokyo Stock Exchange, on the other hand, acts as JSF's counterpart representing "the real world" to the regulatory authority, the Ministry of Finance, which is not so much concerned about the market itself. If market movements are regarded as "excessive," the Tokyo Stock Exchange and JSF consult and then ask the Ministry of Finance for a change in margin requirements. Margin requirements policy is characteristic of Japanese stock market regulation, as it represents "institutionalized" administrative guidance where specific items are allowed, asked for, or prohibited. The system in a way reflects the necessities evoked by a regulatory structure that, for historical or systematic reasons, excludes some of the major market forces.

Recent Ministry of Finance measures indicate efforts to preserve and, possibly, expand the functions of the securities finance companies. These efforts come in two sets of measures: (a) to prohibit transactions that could undermine the viability of these companies (such as with the current system of short sales); and (b) to expand the business lines of the securities finance companies. Whenever the dependence of the market on services of the securities finance companies decreased, the companies were allowed to add newer business to their menu of activities. Further changes in this regard are expected with the revision of the Securities and Exchange Law which is planned for 1993–4; this revision will redefine the term "security" to include such instruments as commercial paper, certificates of deposits, and mortgages. If defined as "securities," these instruments could be included in the services offered by securities finance companies, in an effort to keep the regulatory mechanism intact in a changing market environment.

NOTES

1 T.H. Adams, the financial adviser to General MacArthur and a former president of the Pacific Stock Exchange, recommended that Japan copy the San Francisco rule book instead of the NYSE rule book, because the NYSE was too huge a model for "little Japan."

2 Margin requirements were raised to 100 percent (the loan ratio was 0 percent) in the US in January 1946, too, in order "to discourage speculative activity which was both a characteristic and a feeder of inflation" (Largey and West 1973: 331); the rate was lowered to 75 percent on February 1, 1947, and to 50 percent on March 30, 1949.

3 This "futures movement" gained new strength after the end of the Korean War and the subsequent slump of the Japanese economy in 1953–5. The Ministry of Finance stopped the movement by offering an unacceptable compromise: for futures trading a special licence would be issued which could also be applied for by banks and trust banks. This would have breached the

separation of the banking and the securities business in favor of banks, and the leading securities firms immediately stopped their lobbying.

4 *Kashikin-gyō tō no torishime ni kan suru hōritsu*; this law also regulates leasing companies, credit card companies, and other non-bank finance companies. Until May 1991, these institutions were supervised by MITI, not by MOF.

5 The system had one particular feature: when the total value of shares of a particular stock borrowed exceeded one-third of the amount of total loans for buying this stock, i.e., if short interest exceeded 33 percent of outstanding long (buying) interest, no shares of the stock could be borrowed. This feature was later translated into the "adverse interest" system (see subsection 4.4.2).

6 The SEL itself is very vague on the system and leaves all detailed regulations to the phrase "as stipulated elsewhere," i.e., in a ministerial ordinance. The ordinance in question is *Shōrei* No. 75, August 27, 1953, "Ministerial ordinance on trades regulated by Section 49 SEL and connected margin regulations" (*Shōkentorihikihō dai 49 jō ni kitei suru torihiki oyobi sono hoshōkin ni kan surn shōrei*); the latest revision is of 1982.

7 Given that the two are complementary and indicate the same, the new provision was a disguised way of lowering initial margin requirements. The aim was to stimulate the market and, more importantly, to stall protests because margin requirements under the new system of 1951 were higher than the 30 percent required in the interim system of loan trading.

8 This "System for Substitute Certificates for Registered Bonds as Collateral for Bond Dealer Financing" was approved by the Bank of Japan in 1979. In the collateral scheme, the Bank of Japan issues substitute certificates for registered bonds (*tōrokusai,*) which are eligible as collateral for deposit at securities finance companies. It thus became possible for securities firms to utilize their holdings of registered bonds as collateral. The system was expanded in 1982 to include medium-term bonds also.

9 In the mid-1960s, a sudden drop in stock prices almost led to the bankruptcy of the then second biggest securities firm, Yamaichi, which had to be rescued by the Bank of Japan. Emergency measures also included the foundation of Japan Joint Securities Co. (*Nihon Kyōdō Shōken*) in 1964, an institution established by market participants with the explicit task of buying stocks and stopping the free fall of stock prices. In 1965, the Japan Securities-Holding Association (*Nihon Shōken Hoyū Kumiai*) became a "stock shelving institution" with the same task. Both were financed with central bank money channelled through the securities finance companies; they still exist today.

10 An anonymous interviewee told the author: "Usually the Ministry's bureaucrats are interested not in the current market situation but in their reputation, and would therefore get involved only if there is an announcement to the public."

11 If there is no closing price for a stock, the market value of the stock is its "sentiment price" or special quote, which is determined according to TSE rules at the close, based on outstanding unmatched orders. At the TSE, up to 60 percent of the listed stocks fail to have closing prices quoted. For a detailed description of this system, see Lindsey and Schaede (1990).

12 The maturity of three months was introduced in 1972 for "designated margin stocks" only (see subsection 4.3), but was expanded to all margin stocks in the revision of the system in 1991.

13 100 *sen* is 1 yen, and 100 *ri* is 1 sen. The Japanese authorities officially kept the *per diem sen/ri* way of calculating interest rates until 1969, for stocks until 1970. *Sen* is sometimes still used in commissions. This explains why the official discount rate before 1969 had three or four digits when translated into the quotation of annual percentage terms.

14 Because it is medium- and small-sized securities firms that are the main takers, the fact that the chairmen of the Big Four sit on the board of directors of JSF may not be overly significant. Individual credit lines depend on equity capital, experience, and past trading record etc., so that some discretion is left to JSF in setting these lines. The rate of additional collateral imposed as a penalty depends on the size of the excess amount and differs in each case.

15 These rules were made when the system was revised in October 1991 so that we do not know how the system works in practice. However, one can safely assume that when a certain stock is in danger of being downgraded, supporters of the company concerned will actively trade the stock just before the end of the one-year period.

16 The PERs were higher in 1988 and 1989, and lower in 1990. The average PER for the whole market was 70.6 in 1989, and 39.8 in 1990. In this respect, the "special stocks" were indeed representative of the market portfolio. As of June 1991, however, only eight of the 12 special stocks were among the 60 most actively traded stocks of the TSE. Some of the less active stocks probably were not replaced because plans to abolish the system in 1991 were already known. Further, it can be surmised that Heiwa Real Estate remained a special issue in spite of its low trading volume because this company owns the piece of land on which the new TSE building is situated.

17 "Cornering" means purchasing a particular security on a scale large enough to give the purchaser control of the price of this security.

18 In addition, if, on a particular stock, the open short interest exceeds 10 percent of the total number of listed shares and 50 percent the open long interest, and if the number of shares borrowed for margin trade exceeds 40 percent of listed shares and 120 of percent of funds borrowed, the securities finance firm will announce the probability of limits on stock loans to brokers.

19 For example, in April 1991, adverse interest rates were imposed on a total of 30 stocks, in the range of 5 *sen* to 50 *sen per diem* and share. There is a maximum limit on the amount JSF can charge of ¥2 for stocks with a price of up to ¥1,000, plus 50 *sen* per ¥500 that the stock exceeds this price; e.g., a share of a stock which trades at ¥5,500 can cost up to ¥6.5 *per diem* in adverse rates. However, "if deemed necessary," JSF can double this amount.

20 Adverse interest rates can be charged out of the blue for other reasons, too. If an investor who is long a large position suddenly announces settlement by physical delivery, a "stock squeeze" could be announced. If adverse interest is charged, some shorts will liquidate their positions, thereby contributing to an increase in the stock price before the long has even begun to dissolve his

position. A situation could also be conceived of where big players employ this announcement strategy with the explicit aim of exploiting the adverse interest rate mechanism.

However, adverse interests can affect investors with long positions, too, because JSF can impose additional *ad hoc* rules. For example, when the scandal around Itomen and Sumitomo Bank was disclosed in April 1990, the stocks of Itomen and Fukusuke, a related firm, came under strong sell and short sell pressure. JSF immediately prohibited (a) the opening of new short positions, (b) settlement through physical delivery of long positions, and (c) offsetting sales by long investors. This meant that investors who were long Itomen or Fukusuke on margin could not dissolve their positions before maturity, until which time they could watch the prices of these stocks fall by the minute (Takato 1991).

21   The regulation concerned is *Yūka shōken no kara-uri ni kan suru kisei*, and its latest revision is of late 1988: during the first month of stock index futures trading on the Tokyo and Osada Stock Exchanges in September 1988, it became obvious that short sales were indispensable to the working of the futures market.

22   The US SEC rule had this loophole of pre-empting odd lots until 1938, when rule 435 put both round and odd lots on the same basis. There is no rule 435 in Japan, but there is a cost effect as commissions for margin trades in odd lots are significantly higher than for round lot margin trades.

23   The *gekitaku* trading method was basically a Walrasian auction, in which an auctioneer changed the bid price for the stock concerned until the market cleared; according to the Japanese brokerage houses, the marking of orders as to whether they are outright or on margin is difficult in a batch auction. In contrast, the current *zaraba* is a continuous auction where a specification of order type should be possible (see Lindsey and Schaede 1990, for details).

24   The only institutional investors who are still active in lending stocks out of London or New York are the seven trust banks. Securities firms could of course ask affiliated companies for a "favor," too. Another loophole was to borrow stocks from affiliated non-banks until these became subject to Ministry of Finance supervision in May 1991.

25   Market self-regulation based on the cost effect is further limited by the fact that the interest rate cost constitutes only a small part of total transactions costs: in the 1970s, for example, the cost of buying stocks worth ¥1 million amounted to only 2.9 percent or ¥29,000, of which ¥25,000 was for commissions, ¥4,000 for taxes and fees, and ¥2,740 for interest rate.

26   For details, see Schaede (1991).

27   For an overview, see France, 1990.

28   Data on total outstanding margin credit for Japan is not published; the ratio of total JSF loans to the market value of stocks listed on the TSE, first section, was 0.26 percent in 1990.

29   It is, of course, possible that changes in margin requirements have the desired strong effects on prices, volatility, and general market conditions in Japan, even if the rough observance does not indicate any. A more rigorous testing of these effects is left for future research.

REFERENCES

Arizawa Hiroshi (ed.) 1978: *Shoken Hyakunen-shi* (100-year history of securities). Tokyo: Nihon keizai shinbun-sha.

Cohen, Jacob 1966: Federal Reserve margin requirements and the stock market. *Journal of Financial and Quantitative Economics*, 1 (Sept.), 30–54.

Eckhardt, Walter L. and Rogoff, Donald L. 1976: 100 percent margins revisited. *Journal of Finance*, 31(3), 995–1000.

France, Virginia Grace 1990: *The Regulation of Margin Requirements: A Survey*, Faculty Working Paper No. 90–1670. College of Commerce and Business Administration, University of Illinois at Urbana-Champaign.

Grube, R. Corwin, Joy, O. Maurice and Panton, Don B. 1979: Market responses to Federal Reserve changes in the initial margin requirement. *Journal of Finance*, 34(3), 659–74.

Haga, Akira 1976: Shinyo torihiki seido no hensen (Changes in the system of margin transactions). *Shoken kenkyu*, 47, 105–62.

Hsieh, David A. and Miller, Merton H. 1990: Margin regulation and stock market volatility. *Journal of Finance*, 45(1), 3–29.

Japan Securities Finance Co. 1988: *Introducing Japan Securities Finance Co., Ltd.* Tokyo: JSF.

Japan Securities Finance Co. 1990: *Annual Report, April 1989–March 1990*. Tokyo: JSF.

Largey, James A. and West, Richard R. 1973: Margin changes and stock price behavior. *Journal of Political Economy*, 81(2), 328–39.

Lindsey, Richard R. and Schaede, Ulrike 1990: Specialist vs. *saitori*: market making in New York and Tokyo. University of California at Berkeley, IBER Working Paper 202.

Meeker, J. Edward 1932a: *The Working of the Stock Exchange*. New York: Ronald Press; reprinted in V. Carosso and R. Sobel (eds), *Wall Street and the Security Markets*, New York: Arno Press, 1975.

Meeker, J. Edward 1932b: *Short Selling*. New York: Harper & Brothers; reprinted in V. Carosso and R. Sobel (eds), *Wall Street and the Security Markets*, New York: Arno Press, 1975.

Miki, Junkichi 1965: Kara-uri seido ni tsuite (On the system of short selling). *Inbesutomento*, July 17, 54–66.

Moore, Thomas 1966: Stock market margin requirements. *Journal of Political Economy*, 74, 158–67.

New York Stock Exchange (ed.) 1990: *Fact Book 1990*. New York: NTSE.

Nihon keizai shinbun-sha (ed.) 1991: *Nikkei Kaisha Joho* (Nikkei Corporate Information, Summer 1991). Tokyo: Nihon keizai shinbon-sha.

Nihon Shoken Kinyu (Japan Securities Finance Co.)(ed.) 1980: *Nihon Shoken Kinyu Kabushikigaisha 30nen Shi* (Thirty-year history of Japan Securities Finance Co. Ltd.). Tokyo: Dai-Nihon insatsu.

Okamoto, Katsumi 1976: Shinyo-torihiki no keizaiteki kino (The economic functions of margin transactions). *Shoken Kenkyu*, 47, 163–86.

Okurasho shokenkyoku (Ministry of Finance, Securities Bureau)(ed.) 1991: *Shoken Roppo* (Securities Legislation). Tokyo: MOF.

Okurasho zaiseishitsu (Ministry of Finance)(ed.) 1991: *Showa zaisei shi, Showqa 27–49 nendo, Vol. 9/10, "Kinyu"* (Fiscal and Financial History of the Showa Period, 1952–1974, Vol. 9/10: Finance). Tokyo: Toyo keizai shinposha.

Roscoe, Bruce 1986: Not-so-invisible hand – how Japan helps keep the lid on stockmarkets. *Far Eastern Economic Review*, 20 February, 62–3.

Schaede, Ulrike 1989: *Geldpolitik in Japan 1950–1985* (Monetary Policy in Japan 1950–1985). Marburg: Marburger Japan-Reihe Bd. 1.

Schaede, Ulrike 1991: Black Monday in New York, Blue Tuesday in Tokyo: the October 1987 crash in Japan. *California Management Review*, 33(2), 39–57.

Shin Nihon Shoken chosa-sentaa (New Japan Securities Co.)(ed.) 1990: *Shoken Handobukku* (Handbook of Securities), 3rd edn. Tokyo: Toyo keizai shinpo-sha.

Shizuka, Masaki 1991: Shinyo-torihiki seido kaisei no gaiyo (Outline of the margin transactions system reform), *Shoken*, 1991. 7, 23–33.

Takagi, Shinji 1989: The Japanese equity market: past and present. *Journal of Banking and Finance*, 13, 537–70.

Takato, Koji 1991: *Kabushiki-shijo Kaizo-ron: "Kabutocho" Saisei e no Joken* (Rebuilding the Stock Market – How to Revive Kabutocho). Tokyo: Daiyamondo-sha.

Teweles, Richard J. and Bradley, Edward S. 1987: *The Stock Market*, 5th edn. New York: John Wiley.

Tokyo Stock Exchange (ed.) 1991: *Annual Securities Statistics*. Tokyo: Hosokawa.

Index

Printed and bound by CPI Group (UK) Ltd, Croydon, CR0 4YY

16/04/2025

14658821-0005